Fodor's

SCOTLAND

WELCOME TO SCOTLAND

Scotland packs spectacular landscapes, as well as rich history and tradition, into a small country. From the Lowlands to the Highlands, its lush woodlands, windswept moors, and deep lochs may take your breath away. Impressive castles, whisky distilleries, and golf courses entice, and cities such as Edinburgh and Glasgow tweak tradition with cutting-edge festivals and vibrant cultural scenes. Scotland's iconic products and customs—from tartans to bagpipes—may travel the globe, but there's nothing like experiencing them firsthand.

TOP REASONS TO GO

★ **Castles:** Stirling, Glamis, Floors, and others tell tales of a complex, turbulent past.

★ **Cool Cities:** Edinburgh's International Festival and Fringe; Glasgow's nightlife.

★ **Islands:** Skye's misty mountains, Islay's seabirds, Orkney's prehistoric remains.

★ **Whisky:** Distillery tours and tastings refine an appreciation for the national drink.

★ **Landscapes:** Crystal-clear lochs and rivers, wooded hills, wide-open moors.

★ **Golf:** The great names here include St. Andrews, Gleneagles, and Western Gailes.

13

TOP EXPERIENCES

Scotland offers terrific experiences that should be on every traveler's list. Here are Fodor's top picks for a memorable trip.

1 Prehistoric Monuments

Around Scotland, haunting structures like the Calanais Standing Stones (pictured) on the Isle of Lewis provide an intriguing glimpse into the past. Sights are scattered across the landscape, but Orkney claims a large concentration. *(Ch. 8, 10, 11)*

2 Seaside Towns

The country's jagged coastline and many islands create scenic settings for towns such as Tobermory on the Isle of Mull, with its colorfully painted houses. *(Ch. 8)*

3 Isle of Skye

With the misty Cuillin Mountains and rocky shores, Skye has few rivals among the country's islands for sheer loveliness. Links to Bonnie Prince Charlie add further allure. *(Ch. 10)*

4 Glencoe

The wild beauty of Glencoe's craggy peaks and deep valley provided the background for a tragic massacre in 1692. Today the area is popular for outdoor activities. *(Ch. 9)*

5 Whisky Tours

From Speyside to Islay (pictured), whisky distilleries offer tours and tastings of Scotland's signature drink. Their often-spectacular settings are an added bonus. *(Ch. 4, 6–11)*

6 Loch Lomond and the Trossachs

Its clear water, plus access to Edinburgh and Glasgow, make Loch Lomond a coveted retreat. The Trossachs' lakes and hills are the essence of the Highlands. *(Ch. 6)*

7 Glasgow

An urban renaissance has brought great shopping and nightlife to complement the city's rich architectural heritage and museums like the Kelvingrove (pictured). *(Ch. 3)*

8 Edinburgh

Scotland's capital charms with its Royal Mile and Old Town, and events such as the Edinburgh International Festival and the Fringe keep areas like the Grassmarket lively. *(Ch. 2)*

9 Castles

Whether in ruins or full of treasure, castles dating from the medieval period to Victorian times are among Scotland's glories. Dunnottar (pictured) overlooks the North Sea. *(Ch. 2–11)*

10 Seafood

From salmon to oysters, the superb fish and seafood from rivers, lakes, and the sea are treats to savor. Delicately smoked fish is a specialty, served hot or cold. *(Ch. 2–11)*

11 Border Abbeys

The towering ruins of the region's great medieval abbeys, such as red-sandstone Melrose (pictured), retain echoes of their past grandeur and recall Scottish history. *(Ch. 4)*

12 Jacobite Steam Train

The famous trip from Fort William to the coast at Mallaig offers spectacular views of mountains and lochs as well as a ride over the 21 arches of the Glenfinnan Viaduct. *(Ch. 9)*

13 Golf

The home of golf, Scotland claims some of the world's most challenging holes but has courses for all levels, many in beautiful settings by lakes, hills, or the ocean. *(Ch. 2–10)*

CONTENTS

CONTENTS

MAPS

ABOUT THIS GUIDE

Fodor's Recommendations

Everything in this guide is worth doing—we don't cover what isn't—but exceptional sights, hotels, and restaurants are recognized with additional accolades. Fodor'sChoice★ indicates our top recommendations. Care to nominate a new place? Visit Fodors.com/contact-us.

Trip Costs

We list prices wherever possible to help you budget well. Hotel and restaurant price categories from $ to $$$$ are noted alongside each recommendation. For hotels, we include the lowest cost of a standard double room in high season. For restaurants, we cite the average price of a main course at dinner or, if dinner isn't served, at lunch. For attractions, we always list adult admission fees; discounts are usually available for children, students, and senior citizens.

Hotels

Our local writers vet every hotel to recommend the best overnights in each price category, from budget to expensive. Unless otherwise specified, you can expect private bath, phone, and TV in your room. For expanded hotel reviews, facilities, and deals, visit Fodors.com.

Top Picks	Hotels & Restaurants
★ Fodor'sChoice	
	🏨 Hotel
Listings	🛏 Number of rooms
⊠ Address	🍴 Meal plans
⊠ Branch address	✕ Restaurant
☎ Telephone	🪑 Reservations
🖷 Fax	🕴 Dress code
⊕ Website	▭ No credit cards
✉ E-mail	$ Price
🎫 Admission fee	
⊙ Open/closed times	**Other**
Ⓜ Subway	⇨ See also
✚ Directions or Map coordinates	☞ Take note
	🏌 Golf facilities

Restaurants

Unless we state otherwise, restaurants are open for lunch and dinner daily. We mention dress code only when there's a specific requirement and reservations only when they're essential or not accepted. To make restaurant reservations, visit Fodors.com.

Credit Cards

The hotels and restaurants in this guide typically accept credit cards. If not, we'll say so.

EUGENE FODOR

Hungarian-born Eugene Fodor (1905–91) began his travel career as an interpreter on a French cruise ship. The experience inspired him to write *On the Continent* (1936), the first guidebook to receive annual updates and discuss a country's way of life as well as its sights. Fodor later joined the U.S. Army and worked for the OSS in World War II. After the war, he kept up his intelligence work while expanding his guidebook series. During the Cold War, many guides were written by fellow agents who understood the value of insider information. Today's guides continue Fodor's legacy by providing travelers with timely coverage, insider tips, and cultural context.

EXPERIENCE
SCOTLAND

SCOTLAND TODAY

Travelers arriving in Scotland were once welcomed to the "best small country in the world." It may have just 5.3 million people, but today Scotland has some big ideas about where it's headed socially, culturally, and economically. International sporting events, the lively (but ultimately defeated) 2014 referendum on whether to become an independent nation, and even First Minister Nicola Sturgeon's state visits to the United States and elsewhere continue to focus worldwide attention on Scotland.

Travel in the 21st Century

The experience of traveling in Scotland has changed markedly for the better in recent years, with wholesale improvements in standards of hospitality and food especially. Stylish modern hotels and renovated older ones satisfy the most discerning customers with the latest amenities. Around the country a culinary revolution is well under way: restaurants serve excellent food by internationally trained chefs who take advantage of Scotland's superb produce.

Today hotels and restaurants charge prices similar to those in the rest of the United Kingdom. On the other hand, most of Scotland's biggest and best museums and galleries are free. Walks through well-tended gardens, along bustling waterfronts, and in beautifully renovated neighborhoods mean that a good day out can show you everything but cost nothing at all.

In 2016 Scotland will present its first Year of Innovation, Architecture, and Design, with events celebrating the nation's contribution to architecture, engineering, renewables, fashion, textiles, science, technology, and more. Scotland's following Focus Years are 2017's Year of History, Heritage, and Archaeology and 2018's Year of Young People. All in all, it's an exciting time to travel here.

The Issue of Independence

Dominating Scotland's public life in recent years has been the relationship of Scotland with the U.K. Parliament, and the increasingly troubled state of this 300-year-old union. Through devolution, Scotland elected its first parliament in 300 years in 1999. The independence referendum of 2014 saw 55% vote No to Scotland becoming an independent country, but it has by no means resolved the matter. Indeed the referendum has reinvigorated the Scottish population in an ongoing debate about its future, and a full-blown constitutional crisis may arise in the next decade.

Why are many Scots dissatisfied with the U.K. government? In a time of budget woes, the government has been slashing public services. Many of these cuts deeply offend the Scots, who are committed to free education and free health care from the publicly owned National Health Service.

Culture

The arts continue to thrive, a sign of Scotland's creative energy. Edinburgh's arts festivals grow bigger and bigger every year, attracting visitors from around the globe. The National Theatre of Scotland has been such a resounding success that productions have made their way to Broadway. Glasgow is renowned for contemporary arts; a Glasgow artist often seems to win the Turner Prize, Britain's most prestigious art honor.

In a sign of vitality, culture is not confined only to the large cities. Far to the north, Shetland (already drawing audiences with its folk festivals) has built Mareel, a remarkable live music venue and cinema.

Dundee will be the location of the first outpost of London's Victoria and Albert Museum, due to open in 2018.

In 2013 a new mural was unveiled in Glasgow's subway system that employs the words of Scottish novelist Alasdair Gray: "Work as if you live in the early days of a better nation." Undoubtedly the artists of Scotland have taken him to heart.

Land

It's a disturbing fact that just 500 people own half the land in Scotland, many of them wealthy foreigners who have become absentee landlords. Experts say that giving residents a say on what happens to the land they live on is crucial if communities are going to thrive. New models of community ownership and management are being hard won, particularly in the Western Isles. There have been some community buyouts in which farming communities get the government's help to purchase the land where they live and work.

Still, the depopulation of rural Scotland continues. The popularity of holiday homes has meant that some villages are fully inhabited for only a few weeks each summer. Those who want to live here permanently find that low wages, a high cost of living, and a lack of affordable housing mean that they are priced out of a home surrounded by such beauty.

Wind Power

Urged by the government to help the country meet its ambitious targets for renewable energy, Scottish landowners began leasing land to the corporations behind wind farms. Scotland now has many large-scale commercial wind farms—including Europe's largest—and hundreds of smaller ones, many in community ownership. This has sparked vociferous debate. The pro-wind lobby argues in favor of emission-free energy that's better for the environment than coal or nuclear plants, while the anti-wind camp decries the environmental damage to ancient peat bogs and bird populations. At the time of writing, the new Conservative U.K. government is seeking to withdraw subsidies for renewables, and so threatening Scotland's energy targets and green energy sector.

Turbines are now being built offshore, which is another cause for dispute. Developer Donald Trump, who ignored environmental activists while building his sprawling golf estate, has had a very public fallout with government officials over the "ugly" planned offshore turbine plant that will be visible from his golf course.

Scotland, Finally Winning

When it comes to sports, the Scots have reveled in their traditional role as the underdog. But Olympic gold medal–winning cyclist Chris Hoy and tennis Grand Slam winner Andy Murray have shown that this narrative needs rewriting.

As well as regularly hosting major golf tournaments—the Ryder Cup at Gleneagles in 2014 and Open Golf at St. Andrews (2015) and Royal Troon (upcoming in 2017)—Scotland has proved itself of late as a worthy and welcoming venue for multisport international events. After the success of the Glasgow Commonwealth Games in 2014, and with a Football World Cup 2018 Qualifying Group involving a clash with the auld enemy England coming up, pride in Scottish sports is growing.

WHAT'S WHERE

1 Edinburgh and the Lothians. Scotland's captivating capital is the country's most popular city, famous for its high-perched castle, Old Town and 18th-century New Town, ultramodern Parliament building, and Georgian and Victorian architecture. Among the city's highlights are superb museums, including the newly refurbished National Museum of Scotland, and the most celebrated arts festival in the world, the International Festival. If Edinburgh's crowds are too much, escape to the Lothians and visit coastal towns, beaches, ancient chapels, and castles.

2 Glasgow. The country's largest city has evolved from prosperous Victorian hub to depressed urban center to thriving modern city with a strong artistic, architectural, and culinary reputation. Museums and galleries such as the Kelvingrove and Gallery of Modern Art (GoMA) are here, along with the Arts and Crafts architecture of Charles Rennie Mackintosh and iconic institutions such as Glasgow University. Glasgow is also the place to shop in Scotland.

3 The Borders and the Southwest. Scotland's southern gateway from England, the Borders, with its moors and gentle hills and river valleys, is rustic but historically rich. It's known for being the home of Sir Walter Scott and has impressive stately homes such as Floors Castle and ruined abbeys including Melrose. The Southwest, or Dumfries and Galloway region, is perfect for scenic drives, castles, and hiking.

4 Fife and Angus. The "kingdom" of Fife is considered the sunniest and driest part of Scotland, with sandy beaches, fishing villages, and stone cottages. St. Andrews has its world-famous golf courses, but this university town is worth a stop even for nongolfers. To the north in Angus are Glamis Castle, the legendary setting of Shakespeare's *Macbeth*, as well as the reviving riverside city of Dundee with its increasing cultural attractions.

5 The Central Highlands. Convenient to both Edinburgh and Glasgow, this area encompasses some of Scotland's most beautiful terrain, with rugged, dark landscapes broken up by lochs and fields. Not to be missed are Loch Lomond and the Trossachs, Scotland's first national park. Perth and Stirling are the main metropolitan hubs and worth a stop; Stirling Castle has epic views that stretch from coast to coast.

SCOTLAND

Atlantic

10°W

0   50 mi
0   50 km

IREL
Donegal

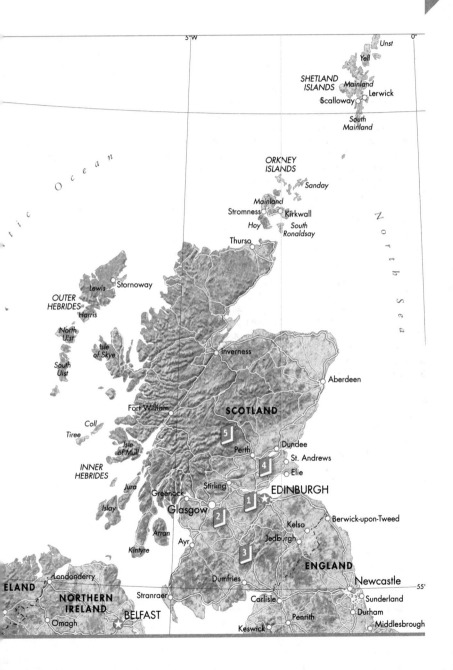

Unst

Yell

SHETLAND
ISLANDS Mainland
Scalloway   Lerwick

South
Mainland

ORKNEY
ISLANDS   Sanday

Mainland
Stromness   Kirkwall
Hoy   South
Ronaldsay

Thurso

t l a n t i c   O c e a n

N o r t h   S e a

OUTER
HEBRIDES
Lewis   Stornoway

Harris

North
Uist

Isle
of Skye

South
Uist

Inverness

Aberdeen

Fort William

SCOTLAND

Coll

Tiree

Isle
of Mull

5

Perth   Dundee

St. Andrews

4   Elie

INNER
HEBRIDES

Jura   Stirling

Greenock

Islay   Glasgow   **1**

EDINBURGH ★

2

Arran   Kelso   Berwick-upon-Tweed

Ayr   Jedburgh

Kintyre   **3**

ENGLAND

Londonderry   Dumfries   Newcastle   55°

IRELAND   Stranraer   Sunderland

NORTHERN   Carlisle   Durham
IRELAND

BELFAST   Penrith   Middlesbrough

Omagh   Keswick

5°W   0°

WHAT'S WHERE

6 Aberdeen and the Northeast. Malt-whisky buffs can use the prosperous port city of Aberdeen, known for its silvery granite buildings, as a base for exploring the region's distilleries, including those on the Malt Whisky Trail. Aberdeen also makes a good starting point for touring Royal Deeside, with its purple moors and piney hills as well as the notably rich selection of castles built over many centuries, including Balmoral.

7 Argyll and the Isles. Remote and picturesque, this less visited region of the southwestern coastline has excellent gardens, religious sites, and distilleries. To experience the region in full, catch a ferry from adorable Oban to Mull and the southern isles. If you like whisky, a trip to Islay is a must; if it's mountains you're after, try Jura; if a Christian site strikes a chord, head to Iona. The Isle of Arran is the place to see Scotland's diversity shrunk down to a more intimate size.

8 Inverness and Around the Great Glen. An awe-inspiring valley laced with rivers and streams defines this part of the country. A top spot for hikers, this Highland glen is ringed by tall mountains, including Ben Nevis, Britain's tallest mountain.

Rugged Cairngorms National Park lies to the east of this area. Glencoe and Culloden are historic sites not to miss; those who believe in Nessie, Scotland's famous monster, can follow the throngs to Loch Ness. Inverness, the capital of the Highlands, is useful as a base for exploring.

9 The Northern Highlands and the Western Isles. This rugged land is home to the lore of clans, big moody skies, and wild rolling moors. It's also the place to see one of Scotland's most picturesque castles, Eilean Donan, which you pass on the way to the beautiful, popular Isle of Skye. The stark, remote Outer Hebrides, or Western Isles, offer ruined forts and chapels. This is where you go for real peace and quiet.

10 Orkney and Shetland Islands. Remote and austere, these isles at the northern tip of Scotland require tenacity to reach but have an abundance of intriguing prehistoric sites, including standing circles, *brochs* (circular towers), and tombs, as well as wild, open landscapes. A Scandinavian heritage gives them a unique flavor. The Shetland Isles, with their barren moors and vertical cliffs, are well known for bird-watching and diving opportunities.

10°W

SCOTLAND

Atlantic

0   50 mi

0   50 km

IRELAN

Donegal

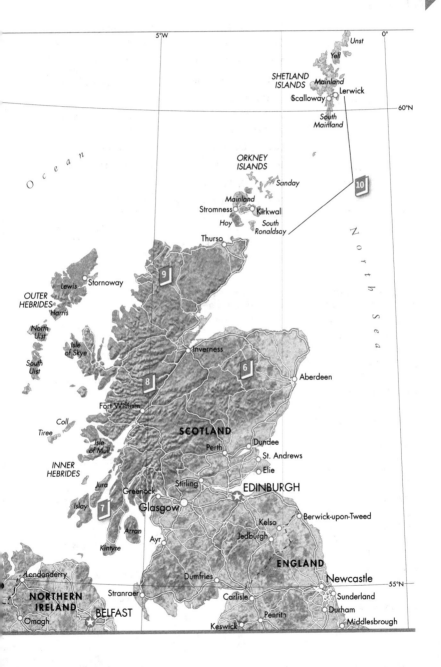

NEED TO KNOW

SCOTLAND
Edinburgh
Northern Ireland
UNITED KINGDOM
Wales
England

AT A GLANCE

Capital: Edinburgh

Population: 5,347,600

Currency: British pound

Money: ATMs common, credit cards widely accepted

Language: English

Country Code: 44

Emergencies: 999

Driving: On the left

Electricity: 230V/50 cycles; plugs have three rectangular blades

Time: Five hours ahead of New York

Documents: Up to six months with valid passport

Mobile Phones: GSM (900 and 1800 bands), UMTS (900 and 2100 bands), LTE (800, 1800, and 2600 bands)

Major Mobile Companies: O2, EE, Vodafone

WEBSITES

VisitScotland: ⊕ www.visitscotland.com

Scotland.com: ⊕ www.scotland.com

People Make Glasgow: ⊕ www.peoplemakeglasgow.com

GETTING AROUND

✈ **Air Travel:** Edinburgh and Glasgow Airports are the largest; Aberdeen and Glasgow Prestwick also get international traffic.

🚌 **Bus Travel:** Scotland's bus (short-haul) and coach (long-distance) network is extensive. Bus service is comprehensive in cities, less so in country districts. Express service links main cities and towns.

🚗 **Car Travel:** If you stick mostly to the cities, you will not need a car. For countryside jaunts, a car will make journeys faster and easier.

🚆 **Train Travel:** The extensive train service within Scotland is generally run by Abellio ScotRail.

PLAN YOUR BUDGET

	HOTEL ROOM	MEAL	ATTRACTIONS
Low Budget	£65	£15	National Museum of Scotland, free
Mid Budget	£135	£45	Edinburgh Castle, £17
High Budget	£250	£90	Opera ticket, £75

WAYS TO SAVE

Hit the local pub. Most of Scotland's local pubs serve hearty meals at reasonable prices.

Go private. Countless private apartments are available for rent for short stays in Scotland, usually offering cheaper rates than hotels as well as a full kitchen.

Explorer Pass No. 1. Scottish Citylink's 3-, 5-, and 8-day Explorer Passes offer great savings on bus travel throughout the country.

Explorer Pass No. 2. Historic Scotland also offers an Explorer Pass good for 3 or 7 days of free entry to nearly 80 top historic sights including Edinburgh and Stirling Castles.

PLAN YOUR TIME

Hassle Factor	Low. Several direct flights are available from North America, and countless connections through larger airports in England.
3 days	Explore historic Edinburgh and take a side trip to Linlithgow Palace.
1 week	Spend a couple of days in Edinburgh, then head north to the golf mecca of St. Andrews. Continue up to legendary Loch Ness and Inverness, the gateway to the Highlands. Finish with two days in Glasgow.
2 weeks	Spend three days in Edinburgh, then head north to St. Andrews and Inverness; continue to Eilean Donan Castle and the Isle of Skye. Head south to Loch Lomond and end in Glasgow.

WHEN TO GO

High Season: Peak tourist season runs from mid-May through mid-September. Crowds at main attractions can be heavy, and prices are at their highest. Summer days are very long, and temperatures can linger in the 60s, 70s, or 80s, with dry spells lasting a week or two.

Low Season: November to March marks the low season for travel. Winter sees lots of rain, some snow, and icy winds, not to mention the short days. City museums stay open year-round, but some tourist sites such as castles and historic houses close from November to Easter.

Value Season: You can get some excellent deals in spring (April to mid-May) and fall (mid-September to October); weather is cool and often rainy, but crowds are not as intense.

BIG EVENTS

January: One of the world's largest Celtic festivals is Glasgow's half-month Celtic Connections. ⊕ www.celticconnections.com

May–September: Towns all over Scotland celebrate the Highland Games, an ancient festival including music, dance, and (most important) athletic events.

August: Edinburgh Festival Fringe is the world's largest annual arts fest, with more than 3,000 shows from some 50 countries filling the Scottish capital. ⊕ www.edfringe.com

December–January: Scotland's festive version of New Year's Eve, called Hogmanay, lasts several days.

READ THIS

■ *Macbeth,* William Shakespeare. Power corrupts an early Scottish king in this Shakespeare classic.

■ *Whisky Galore,* Compton Mackenzie. A whisky-carrying cargo ship crashes off the coast during World War II.

■ *The Prime of Miss Jean Brodie,* Muriel Spark. An unconventional teacher in 1930s Edinburgh.

WATCH THIS

■ *Braveheart.* William Wallace leads a Scottish uprising against England in the 14th century.

■ *The 39 Steps.* Hitchcock's Scottish thriller is one of his finest.

■ *Trainspotting.* A look at drug-addicted Scottish youths in the 1980s.

EAT THIS

■ *Haggis*: minced offal of sheep, pig, or cow mixed with suet

■ *Scotch pie*: small, double-crusted meat pie

■ *Stovies*: stew of meat (usually beef) and vegetables

■ *Cullen skink*: thick smoked-haddock soup

■ *Clootie dumpling*: rich dessert with dried fruit

■ *Cranachan*: dessert of fresh raspberries and whipped cream, often with whisky

QUINTESSENTIAL SCOTLAND

Time for Tea

Scots are always eager to stop for a cup of tea and catch up with the local gossip. Tea is still the most popular refreshment, but the spread of café culture has introduced a new generation of coffeehouses—and not just in the cities but in the countryside. The Willow Tearooms in Glasgow and the Balmoral Hotel in Edinburgh are perhaps the most gentrified places to enjoy an afternoon pot of tea, tiny sandwiches with the crusts removed, and a slice of cake; they are well worth the stop. City coffeehouses are becoming increasingly popular; they offer a different but equally worthwhile atmosphere. But if you're looking to taste a little of what life has to offer in smaller towns and villages, there is always some local haven that can offer you tea and delicious scones, probably with homemade jam.

Pubs

Going to the pub is a pastime enjoyed by men and women of all ages and backgrounds; you can find out why when you explore a few. The no-smoking laws mean that the pub environment is fresher now. In the cities you can take your pick of every kind of pub; traditional favorites are now joined by Australian, Cuban, and chic cocktail bars. In more rural areas options may be fewer, but the quality of the experience, which may include pub quizzes or local folk bands, may be better. There isn't a pub in Scotland that doesn't sell whisky, but if you seek to sample a wee dram of the more obscure malts, ask someone to point you in the right direction. Fans of whisky will want to go beyond the pubs and head for a distillery or two for a tour and a tasting—you will find these in many areas of the country.

If you want to get a sense of contemporary Scottish culture and indulge in some of its pleasures, start by familiarizing yourself with the rituals of daily life. These are a few highlights—things you can take part in with relative ease.

Football

Listening to Scots talk about football—please don't call it soccer—gives a fine insight into the national temperament. "Win, lose, or draw, you go home to your bed just the same," sang Scottish singer Michael Marra, and the Scots will try to make you believe it's only a game. But go to a match or be in a pub when a game is on the TV, and you can see plenty of grown men (and women) having a vigorous emotional workout. Since the Rangers were relegated to the Third Division, the main league, the Scottish Premiership, has opened up a little, although Celtic still dominate. The state of the national team is debated everywhere, but although Scotland loses out in collecting trophies, the Tartan Army is consistently applauded as the most agreeable and entertaining of traveling fans.

Baked Goods

Although the treats may not perhaps be as elegant as those produced in an Italian *panificio* or a French patisserie, Scots love their bakeries. Go beyond shortbread and oatcakes and sample local favorites during your travels. From the Aberdeen buttery (a melting, salty *bap*, or roll) to the Selkirk bannock (a sweet, raisin-strewn scone, perfect when buttered and served with tea) to *Forfar bridies* (an Angus specialty, similar to a meat pasty), regional specialties are abundant. Most areas have their own interpretations of the popular Scotch pie (with beef mince, mutton, bean, and macaroni among the varieties available). There's even a Scotch Pie Championship each year. The rise of large supermarkets is putting many establishments out of business, but it's worth seeking out an independent bakery and trying the delicacies.

IF YOU LIKE

Castles

Whether a jumble of stones or a fully intact fortress, whether in private ownership or under the care of a preservation group, Scotland's castles powerfully demonstrate the country's lavish past and its once-uneasy relationship with its southern neighbor.

Caerlaverock. This triangular 13th-century fortress with red-sandstone walls in Dumfries was a last bastion in the 17th-century struggle for religious reform.

Castle Trail. Along Royal Deeside, west of Aberdeen, the Castle Trail has an eclectic group of castles all within a 100-mile radius. There's stirring Drum, stately Crathes, baronial Balmoral, memorabilia-packed Braemar, Corgarff, Kildrummy, and windswept Dunnottar.

Edinburgh Castle. This royal palace dominates the capital's history and skyline.

Eilean Donan. A ruin on the edge of several lochs in the Western Highlands, this is the most photogenic of Scottish castles and inspiration for the castle in the animated movie *Brave.*

Floors Castle. On the Duke of Roxburghe's estate outside Kelso, this castle has grand turrets, pinnacles, and cupolas.

Glamis Castle. Northeast of Dundee, Glamis Castle connects Britain's royalty from Macbeth to the late Queen Mother.

Hermitage Castle. This dark and foreboding place south of Hawick, near the English border, is where Mary, Queen of Scots, traveled to visit her lover, the Earl of Bothwell.

Stirling Castle. Beautifully restored Stirling Castle is the childhood home of Mary, Queen of Scots, and one of the finest Renaissance palaces in the United Kingdom.

Mountains and Lochs

For the snowcapped mountains and glassy lochs (lakes) for which Scotland is famous, you have to leave the south and the cities behind you—though some Lowland lakes are beautiful. Wherever you go in Scotland, nature is at your fingertips.

Ben Nevis. Looming over Fort William is dramatic Ben Nevis. No matter when you visit, you'll probably see snow on the summit.

Cairngorms National Park. The Great Glen is home to half of Scotland's highest peaks, many of them in Cairngorms National Park. This is an excellent place for hiking, skiing, and reindeer sightings.

Glen Torridon. East of Shieldaig in the Northern Highlands, Glen Torridon has the country's finest mountain scenery.

Loch Achray. This pretty loch is where you set out for the climb to Ben An, a sheer-faced mountain with fabulous views of the Trossachs.

Loch Katrine. In the heart of the Trossachs, this lake in the Central Highlands was the setting of Walter Scott's narrative poem *The Lady of the Lake.* In summer you can take the steamer SS *Sir Walter Scott.*

Loch Leven. Located in Fife, this loch is famed for its birdlife. It was also where Mary, Queen of Scots, signed the deed of abdication in her island prison.

Loch Lomond. Among Scotland's most famous lakes, Loch Lomond's shimmering shores, beautiful vistas, and plethora of water-sport options are 20 minutes from Glasgow.

Loch Maree. One of Scotland's most scenic lakes, Loch Maree is framed by Scots pines and Slioch Mountain in the Northern Highlands.

Museums

Scotland's rich history and the varied passions of its people provide a wealth of material and artifacts that fill museums and galleries across the land, from metropolitan art collections to small themed collections, many of them free.

Kelvingrove Art Gallery and Museum. Perennially popular, this grand Victorian palace in Glasgow houses Botticelli and Monet canvasses to interactive Scottish history exhibits.

McManus Galleries. Dundee's major civic collection encompasses fine and contemporary art and Dundonian life and history, and hosts world-class visiting exhibits.

National Museum of Scotland. In Edinburgh, the recently renovated Victorian grand hall is a dramatic setting for exhibits that trace the nation's history from geologic deep time to contemporary life.

Riverside Museum. Scotland's Museum of Transport and Travel, set within a striking Zaha Hadid–designed structure alongside Glasgow's River Clyde and the handsome Tall Ship at Riverside, displays a dizzying array of vehicles.

Robert Burns Birthplace Museum. This interactive museum in Alloway explores the passions and poems of the much-loved poet and complex "man o' pairts."

Scottish Fisheries Museum. Buildings facing Anstruther Harbor in Fife house an absorbing collection of exhibits that illustrate the life of Scottish fisherfolk.

Shetland Museum. A suitably sail-like tower greets visitors to Lerwick's Hay's Dock and this wonderful museum, which tells many a salty and piquant tale of Shetland's way of life down the centuries.

Whisky Tours

Whisky tours are a great way to appreciate the varied flavors of Scotland's signature drink. Many distilleries are in lovely settings, and tours explore the craft that transforms malted barley, water, and yeast. In-depth tours and special tastings are available at some places, but it's best to check ahead and reserve if needed. Here's a sampling of distilleries around the country.

Edradour. This small distillery near Pitlochry makes a fine single malt and offers an informative and fun tour.

Glenfiddich. An entertaining visitor center enhances the tour of this Dufftown distillery; it also has an art gallery.

Glenlivet. Tours at the first licensed distillery in the Highlands include not only whisky making but also the fascinating story of the founder.

Highland Park. If you make it north to Orkney, visit Scotland's northernmost distillery and try its smoky but sweet malt.

Lagavulin. Among Islay's whiskies, this one has the strongest iodine scent; the distillery offers a number of special tours.

Laphroaig. Its distinctively peaty, iodine-and-seaweed flavor has earned this Islay whisky many devoted followers.

Macallan. There's a choice of two tours at this distillery in the northeast that matures its whisky in sherry and bourbon casks.

Talisker. The single malt from the Isle of Skye's only distillery has a peaty aroma; tours are popular.

Island Havens

A remote, windswept world of white-sand beaches, forgotten castles, and crisp, clear rivers awaits you in the Scottish isles. Out of the hundreds of isles, only a handful are actually inhabited, and here ancient culture and tradition remain alive and well. Each island has its own distinct fingerprint; getting to some might be awkward and costly, but the time and expense are worth your while.

Arran. With activities ranging from golf to hiking, this island has everything you'll find on the mainland but on a smaller, more intimate scale.

Bute. One of the more affordable and accessible islands, Bute draws celebrities to its estates for lavish weddings and Glaswegians to its rocky shores for summer holidays.

Iona. This spiritual and spectacular island was the burial place of Scottish kings until the 11th century.

Islay. Near the Kintyre Peninsula, this island is where you go to watch rare birds, purchase woolen goods, and sample the smoothest malt whiskies.

Northern Isles. Orkney and Shetland, two remote island groups collectively known as the Northern Isles, have a colorful Scandinavian heritage. Both have notable prehistoric artifacts and rollicking festivals. The green pastures of Orkney are an hour from the mainland, and wind-flattened Shetland will suit those who want a more remote feel.

Skye. With hazy mountains, hidden beaches, and shady glens, the Isle of Skye is unsurpassed for sheer beauty. It also has a good selection of hotels, B&Bs, and restaurants.

Hiking

People who have hiked in Scotland often return to explore the country's memorable rural landscapes of loch-dotted glens and forested hills. From Edinburgh's Arthur's Seat to Ben Nevis, Britain's tallest peak, the country holds unsurpassed hiking possibilities, no matter what your ambitions. Keep in mind that weather conditions can and do change rapidly in the Scottish hills, even at low altitude. The best time for hiking is from May to September.

Fife Coastal Path. This seaside trail is 116 miles long but can be done in chunks. It skirts along golden beaches, rocky inlets, and picturesque fishing villages.

Glen Nevis. Home of the magnificent peak of Ben Nevis, Glen Nevis has a number of moderate hikes with footpaths leading past waterfalls, ruined crofts, and forested gorges. There are also some more challenging climbs.

The Grampians. In the northeastern part of the country, this mountain range offers walks through some of the country's most varied terrain. The eight-mile route around Loch Muick, which passes Glasallt Shiel, Queen Victoria's holiday home, is beautiful in any weather.

Southern Upland Way. The famous 212-mile coast-to-coast journey from Portpatrick to Cockburnspath is an undertaking, but it can be tackled in sections.

Trossachs National Park. In the Central Highlands, this vast area includes everything from quiet country strolls to ambitious climbs up craggy cliffs.

West Highland Way. From Milngavie to Fort William, this well-marked and well-trodden 95-mile trek follows a series of old coaching roads.

Megalithic Monuments

Scattered throughout the Scottish landscape are prehistoric standing stones, stone circles, tombs, and even stone houses that provide a tantalizing glimpse into the country's remarkable past and people. If you're interested in ancient remains, leave the mainland and head for the isles, where many of the most impressive and important sites are found.

Calanais Standing Stones. On the Isle of Lewis in the Outer Hebrides, this ancient site is reminiscent of Stonehenge. The impressive stones are believed to have been used for astronomical observations.

Jarlshof. A Bronze Age settlement dating from 2500 BC, Shetland's Jarlshof has been called the most remarkable archaeological site in the British Isles.

Machrie Moor Stone Circles. On the Isle of Arran these granite boulders and reddish-sandstone circles have a startling setting in the middle of an isolated moor.

Maeshowe. An enormous burial mound on Orkney, Maeshowe is renowned for its imposing burial chamber.

Mousa Broch. Accessible by boat on Shetland's South Mainland, this beautifully preserved fortified Iron Age stone tower is now a bird sanctuary.

Ring of Brodgar. Between Loch Harray and Loch Stennes on Orkney sits this magnificent circle made up of 36 Neolithic stones.

Skara Brae. Orkney's Neolithic village, first occupied around 3000 BC, was buried beneath the sand until its discovery in 1850. The houses are joined by covered passages, and with stone beds, fireplaces, and cupboards are intriguing remnants from the distant past.

Retail Therapy

No longer is Scotland simply the land of whisky and wool. International names from Louis Vuitton to Vivienne Westwood have all set up shop here, and top British department stores like John Lewis, Harvey Nichols, and Debenhams, as well as stylish boutiques, pepper the major cities. Rich chocolates (often with whisky fillings), marmalades, heather honeys, and the traditional petticoat-tail shortbread are easily portable gifts. So, too, are the boiled sweets (hard candies).

Aberdeen. If trying and buying malt whisky is on your itinerary, you won't find a much better spot than Aberdeen.

Central Highlands. Bristling with old bothies (farm buildings) that have been turned into small craft workshops, the villages in this region sell handmade crafts.

Dundee. Topped with a rich fruit mixture and almonds, Dundee cake is among the prize edibles on sale in the city they're named after.

Edinburgh. Jenners, Scotland's most prestigious department store, is a must-see in Edinburgh. Head toward the New Town for clusters of antiques shops.

Glasgow. Scotland's biggest city claims the best shopping in Britain, outside of London's Oxford Street. Start at Buchanan Street with Princes Gardens and Buchanan Galleries before heading to the West End for clothing boutiques and antiques shops.

Perth. A shopper's paradise, Scotland's former capital city offers a wide array of crafts, including fine china, exquisite jewelry, and freshwater pearls.

Shetland. Traditional crafts such as tartan blankets, Celtic silver, and pebble jewelry are among the big draws.

FLAVORS OF SCOTLAND

Locally Sourced, Seasonally Inspired

A new focus of culinary interest, in Scotland as elsewhere, is on local and seasonal foods. Whether restaurants are riding the green wave or just following good food sense, they are trying their best to buy from local suppliers; many proudly advertise their support. Farmers' markets, too, seem to be popping up on every other street corner.

From meats and fish to fruits and vegetables, most urban and many country restaurants are now designing their menus around seasonal foods. In winter, look for Angus beef, venison, rabbit, and pigeon on menus; in spring, summer, and fall, langoustines (small lobsters with slender claws), crab, halibut, and trout appear. The rotating array of (often organic) blackberries, brambles, raspberries, strawberries, apples, and rhubarb offers choices so fat and flavorful that the fruits themselves could make any meal memorable. When in season, asparagus and green beans are tender, but fresh enough that you can actually taste their snap. Scottish pies, puddings, and jams are also inspired by the land and time of year.

Superb Fish and Seafood

Some of the most coveted fish and seafood in the world lives in the rivers and lakes, as well as off the coasts, of Scotland. Fortunately, restaurants and markets all around the country showcase this local bounty. Treats not to miss include wild salmon, trout, haddock, mackerel, herring (often served as cold-smoked kippers), langoustines, scallops, mussels, oysters, and crabs.

Fish is prepared in a tantalizing variety of ways in Scotland, but smoked fish is the national specialty—so much so that the process of both hot and cold smoking has developed to a fine art. Scots eat smoked fish for breakfast and lunch, and as an appetizer with their evening meal. The fish is often brushed with cracked pepper and a squeeze of lemon, and accompanied by thin slices of hearty bread or oat crackers. Places like Arbroath as well as the isles of North Uist and Skye have won international praise for locally smoked haddock, salmon, and trout, which are synonymous with delicacy.

Other seafood to try includes the traditional fish-and-chips, *the* Scottish favorite not to be overlooked. The fish is either cod or haddock, battered and deep-fried until it's crispy and golden. Another classic preparation is *cullen skink,* a creamy fish stew thick with smoked haddock, potatoes, and onions. It's perfect on cold winter nights as a tasty hot appetizer. For a special treat, grilled, sautéed, or baked langoustines offer the ultimate seafood indulgence, succulent and tasty.

Tempting Baked Goods

The Scots love their cakes, biscuits, breads, and pies. There's always something sweet and most likely crumbly to indulge in, whether after a meal or with a nice cup of tea. Bakeries are the perfect places to sample fresh goodies.

Some of the local favorites range from conventional butter-based shortbreads, empire biscuits (two shortbread cookies with jam in between, glazed in white icing and topped with a bright red cherry), whisky cake, mince pies (small pies filled with brandy, stewed dried fruits, and nuts), and scones. Treacle tarts, gingerbread, butterscotch apple pie, and oatcakes (more a savory cracker than a sweet cake) with local cheese are also popular as late-morning or early-afternoon temptations.

Not to be missed are the many treats named after their place of origin: Balmoral tartlets (filled with cake crumbs, butter, cherries, and citrus peel), Abernethy biscuits (cookies with extra sugar and caraway seeds), Islay loaves (sweet bread with raisins, walnuts, and brown sugar), and Dundee cake (full of cherries, raisins, sherry, and spices). Home bakers are much celebrated, and the catering tents at Highland games are worth seeking out to sample a community's finest.

Traditional Scottish Fare
Food in Scotland is steeped in history, and a rich story lies behind many traditional dishes. Once the food of peasants, haggis—a mixture of sheep's heart, lungs, and liver cooked with onions, oats, and spices, and then boiled in a sheep's stomach—has made a big comeback in more formal Scottish restaurants. If the dish's ingredients turn you off, there's often an equally flavorful vegetarian option. You'll find "neeps and tatties" alongside haggis; the three are inseparable. Neeps are yellow turnips, potatoes are the tatties, and both are boiled and then mashed.

Black pudding is another present-day delicacy (and former peasant food) that you can find just about everywhere, from breakfast table to local fish-and-chip shop to formal dining establishment. It's made from cooked sheep's or goat's blood that congeals and is mixed with such ingredients as oats, barley, potato, bread, and meat. Black pudding can be grilled, boiled, or deep-fried. The Scottish prefer it for breakfast with fried eggs, bacon, beans, square sausages, toast, and potato scones. These fried, triangular-shape scones have the consistency of a dense pancake and are an intimate part of the Scottish breakfast, aptly called a fry-up because—apart from the beans and toast—everything else on the plate is fried. Another popular breakfast dish is porridge with salt instead of sugar, cinnamon, or honey. Sweet porridge doesn't go down well in Scotland.

Whiskies and Real Ales
"Uisge beatha," translated from Scottish Gaelic, means "water of life," and in Scotland it most certainly is. Whisky helps weave together the country's essence, capturing the aromas of earth, water, and air in a single sip.

Whiskies differ greatly between single malts and blends. This has to do with the ingredients, specialized distillation processes, and type of oak cask. Whisky is made predominantly from malted barley that, in the case of blended whiskies, can be combined with grains and cereals like wheat or corn. Malts or single malts can come only from malted barley.

The five main whisky regions in Scotland produce distinctive tastes, though there are variations even within a region: the Lowlands (lighter in taste), Speyside (sweet, with flower scents), the Highlands (fragrant, smooth, and smoky), Campbeltown (full-bodied and slightly salty), and Islay (strong peat flavor). Do sample these unique flavors; distillery tours are a good place to begin.

Real ales—naturally matured, cask-conditioned beer made from traditional ingredients—have arrived in the United Kingdom. These ales are not, at present, as popular as whisky, but are quickly making their mark on the Scottish beverage scene. Good brews to try include Arran Blonde (Arran Brewery), Dark Island (Orkney Brewery), White Wife (Shetland), Duechars (Caledonian Brewery), and Red Cuillin (Skye Brewery).

PLAYING GOLF IN SCOTLAND

There are some 550 golf courses in Scotland and only 5.3 million residents, so the country has probably the highest ratio of courses to people anywhere in the world. If you're visiting Scotland, you'll probably want to play the "famous names" sometime in your career.

So by all means play the championship courses such as the Old Course at St. Andrews, but remember they *are* championship courses. You may enjoy the game itself much more at a less challenging course. Remember, too, that everyone else wants to play the big names, so booking can be a problem at peak times in summer. Reserving three to four months ahead is not too far for the famous courses, although it's possible to get a time up to a month (or even a week) in advance if you are relaxed about your timing. If you're staying in a hotel attached to a course, get the concierge to book a tee time for you.

Happily, golf has always had a peculiar classlessness in Scotland. It's a game for everyone, and for centuries Scottish towns and cities have maintained courses for the enjoyment of their citizens. Admittedly, a few clubs have always been noted for their exclusive air, and some newer golf courses are losing touch with the game's inclusive origins, but these are exceptions to the tradition of recreation for all. Golf here is usually a democratic game, played by ordinary folk as well as the wealthy.

Tips About Playing

Golf courses are everywhere in Scotland. Most courses welcome visitors with a minimum of formalities, and some at a surprisingly low cost. Other courses are very expensive, but a lot of great golf can be played for between about £30 to £100 a round. Online booking at many courses has made arranging a golf tour easier, too.

Be aware of the topography of a course. Scotland is where the distinction between "links" and "parkland" courses was first made. Links courses are by the sea and are subject to the attendant sea breezes—some quite bracing—and mists, which can make them trickier to play. The natural topography of sand dunes and long, coarse grasses can add to the challenge. A parkland course is in a wooded area and its terrain is more obviously landscaped. A "moorland" course is found in an upland area.

Here are three pieces of advice, particularly for North Americans: (1) in Scotland the game is usually played fairly quickly, so don't dawdle if others are waiting; (2) caddy carts are hand-pulled carts for your clubs and driven golf carts are rarely available; and (3) when they say "rough," they really mean "rough."

Unless specified otherwise, hours are generally sunrise to sundown, which in June can be as late as 10 pm. Note that some courses advertise the SSS, "standard scratch score," instead of par (which may be different). This is the score a scratch golfer could achieve under perfect conditions. Rental clubs, balls, and other gear are generally available from clubhouses, except at the most basic municipal courses. Don't get caught by the dress codes enforced at many establishments: in general, untailored shorts, round-neck shirts, jeans, and sneakers are frowned upon.

The prestigious courses may ask for evidence of your golf skills by way of a handicap certificate; check in advance and carry this with you.

Costs and Courses

Many courses lower their rates before and after peak season—at the end of September, for example. It's worth asking about this. ■ TIP→ **Some areas offer regional golf passes that save you money. Check with the local tourist board.**

For a complete list of courses, contact local tourist offices or VisitScotland's official and comprehensive golf website, ⊕ *golf.visitscotland.com.* It has information about the country's golf courses, special golf trails, regional passes, special events, and tour operators, as well as on conveniently located accommodations. U.K. Golf Guide (⊕ *www.uk-golfguide.com*) has reviews by recent players. *For information about regional courses, also see individual chapters; see Tours in Travel Smart Scotland for some golf tour operators.*

Best Bets Around Scotland

If your idea of heaven is teeing off on a windswept links, then Scotland is for you. Dramatic courses, many of them set on sandy dunes alongside the ocean, are just one of the types you'll encounter. Highland courses that take you through the heather and moorland courses surrounded by craggy mountains have their own challenges.

Boat of Garten Golf Club, Inverness-shire. With the Cairn Gorm Mountain as a backdrop, this beautiful course has rugged terrain that requires even seasoned players to bring their A game. As an added bonus, a steam railway runs alongside the course.

Carnoustie Golf Links, Angus. Challenging golfers for nearly 500 years, Carnoustie is on many golfers' must-do list. The iconic Championship Course has tested many of the world's top players, while the Burnside and Buddon courses attract budding Players and Watsons.

Castle Stuart Golf Links, Inverness-shire. A more recent addition to Scotland's world-class courses offers cliff-top hazards, sprawling bunkers, and rolling fairways overlooking the Moray Firth.

Cruden Bay Golf Club, Aberdeenshire. This challenging and enjoyable links course was built by the Great North of Scotland Railway Company in 1894. Its remote location beside a set of towering dunes makes it irresistible.

Gleneagles, Perthshire. Host of the 2014 Ryder Cup championship, Gleneagles has three 18-hole courses that challenge the pros and a 9-hole course that provides a more laid-back game. It's also home to the PGA National Golf Academy.

Machrihanish Golf Club, Argyll. A dramatic location on the Mull of Kintyre and some exciting match play make these links well worth a journey.

Royal Dornoch Golf Club, Sutherland. Extending across a coastal shelf, Royal Dornoch has fast greens, pristine beaches, and mountain views. In spring yellow gorse sets the green hills ablaze.

St. Andrews Links, Fife. To approach the iconic 18th hole in the place where the game was invented remains the holy grail of golfers worldwide.

Trump Turnberry, Ayrshire. Along the windswept Ayrshire coast, Turnberry's famous Ailsa Course pits golfers against the elements and, on one hole, a stretch of ocean.

Western Gailes Golf Club, near Glasgow. This splendid links course is a final qualifying course for the British Open. Sculpted by Mother Nature, it's the country's finest natural links course.

GREAT ITINERARIES

HIGHLIGHTS OF SCOTLAND IN 10 DAYS

Scotland isn't large, but its most famous cities and most iconic landscapes take time to explore. This itinerary packs in many national icons: Edinburgh's enormous charm and Glasgow's excellent museums; a castle or two; lochs, mountains, and an island. It's a busy pace, but you'll still be able to fit in a whisky distillery visit and even a round of golf. You can do parts of this trip by public transportation, but beyond the cities, a car allows more flexibility.

Days 1 and 2: Edinburgh

The capital of Scotland is loaded with iconic sights in its Old Town and New Town. Visit Edinburgh Castle and the National Gallery of Scotland, and take tours of the National Museum of Scotland and the modern Scottish Parliament building. Walk along Old Town's Royal Mile and New Town's George Street for some fresh air and retail therapy. Later on, seek out a traditional pub with live music.

Logistics: Fly into Edinburgh Airport if you're flying via London. If you're flying directly into Glasgow from overseas, make your way from Glasgow Airport to Queen Street Station via taxi or bus. It takes an hour to travel from Glasgow to Edinburgh by car or bus, about 45 minutes to an hour by train. Explore on foot or by public transportation.

Day 3: Stirling to St. Andrews

Rent a car in Edinburgh and drive to the historic city of Stirling. Spend the day visiting Stirling Castle and the National Wallace Monument. If you're eager to tour a distillery, make time for a stop at the Famous Grouse Experience at the Glenturret Distillery in Crieff. For your

overnight stay, drive to the seaside town of St. Andrews, famous for golf.

Logistics: It's 35 miles or a one-hour drive to Stirling from Edinburgh, and 50 miles and 90 minutes from Stirling to St. Andrews. You can easily take a train or bus to these destinations.

Day 4: St. Andrews to Aviemore

Spend the morning exploring St. Andrews, known for its castle and the country's oldest university as well as its golf courses. If you've booked well in advance, play a round of golf. After lunch, drive to Aviemore. Along the way, stretch your legs at one of Scotland's notable sights, Blair Castle (just off the A9 and 10 miles north of Pitlochry). Head to Aviemore, gateway to the Cairngorm Mountains and Britain's largest national park, for two nights. The town is a center for outdoor activities and has many choices for accommodations, dining, and shopping, but you can also consider the more attractive surrounding villages and towns such as Kingussie for your stay.

Logistics: It's 120 miles from St. Andrews to Aviemore via the A9, a drive that will take 2½ hours. You can also take a train or bus.

Day 5: The Cairngorms

For anyone who enjoys outdoor pursuits or dramatic scenery, the arctic plateau of the Cairngorms is a must. Hiking, biking, and climbing are options (Glenmore Lodge is a renowned outdoor sports centre), but so is visiting attractions such as the Cairngorm Reindeer Centre and Highland Folk Museum.

Day 6: The Isle of Skye

Leave Aviemore early and head to Inverness, which has a busy center suited for a wander. Inverness Castle and the Inverness Museum and Art Gallery are

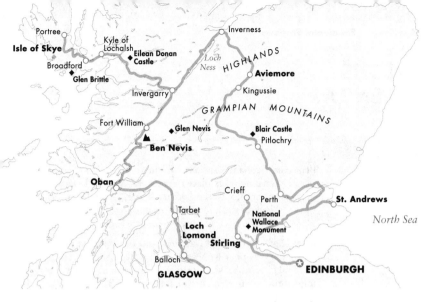

North Sea

worth seeing. The drive south to Skye is peaceful, full of raw landscapes and big, open horizons. Stop at Eilean Donan Castle on the way. Set on an island among three lochs, the castle is the stuff postcards are made of. Explore Skye; Glen Brittle is the perfect place to enjoy mountain scenery; and Armadale is a good place to go crafts shopping. End up in Portree for dinner and the night.

Logistics: It's 30 miles (a 40-minute drive) via the A9 from Aviemore to Inverness, and then it's 80 miles (a two-hour drive) from Inverness to Skye. Public transportation is possible but connections take time, so a car is best.

Day 7: Oban via Ben Nevis

Leave Skye no later than 9 am and head for Fort William. The town isn't worth stopping for, but the view of Britain's highest mountain, the 4,406-foot Ben Nevis, is. If time permits, take a hike in Glen Nevis. Continue on to Oban, a traditional Scottish resort town on the water, to overnight. Outside Oban, stop by the Scottish Sea Life Sanctuary. At night, feast on fish-and-chips in a local pub.

Logistics: It's nearly 100 miles from Skye to Oban; the drive is 3½ hours without stopping. Public transportation is challenging.

Days 8 and 9: Loch Lomond and Glasgow

Enjoy a waterfront stroll in Oban. Mid-morning, set off for Glasgow via Loch Lomond. Stop in Balloch on the loch for fresh oysters and a walk along the bonnie banks. Arrive in Glasgow in time for dinner; take in a play or concert, or just relax in a pub on the first of your two nights in this rejuvenated city. Spend the next day visiting the sights: Kelvingrove Art Gallery and Museum, Charles Rennie Mackintosh's iconic buildings, and the Riverside Museum are a few highlights.

Logistics: It's 127 miles (a three-hour drive) from Oban to Glasgow via Balloch. Traveling by train is a possibility, but you won't be able to go via Balloch. Return your rental car in Glasgow.

Day 10: Glasgow and Home

On your final day, stow your suitcases at your hotel and hit Buchanan and Sauchiehall Streets for some of Britain's best shopping. Clothes, whisky, and tartan items are good things to look for.

Logistics: It's less than 10 miles (15 minutes) by taxi to Glasgow's international airport in Paisley but more than 30 miles (40 minutes) to the international airport in Prestwick.

ON THE CALENDAR

WINTER	
Dec. 29–Jan. 2	**Hogmanay.** Scotland's ancient, still-thriving New Year's celebration, Hogmanay takes place over several days. In rural areas, neighbors "first foot" each other's houses—thereby ensuring the good luck of the household—and toast the new year with a dram. ✉ *Edinburgh* ⊕ *www.edinburghshogmanay.com.*
Jan. 25	**Burns Night.** Burns Night dinners and other events are held in memory of poet Robert Burns on his birthday, January 25. Haggis and mashed turnips, whisky, and poetry readings are familiar elements of the supper. ⊕ *www.scotland.org/whats-on/burns-night.*
Last Tues. in Jan.	**Up-Helly-Aa.** Every year, Shetlanders celebrate their Viking heritage and torch a replica Viking longship. The biggest Up-Helly-Aa is in Lerwick on the last Tuesday in January. ☎ *01595/693434* ⊕ *www.uphellyaa.org.*
Jan.	**Celtic Connections.** Glasgow's immensely popular celebration of Celtic music, Celtic Connections hosts national and international musicians during the last two weeks of January. ✉ *Glasgow* ☎ *0141/353–8000* ⊕ *www.celticconnections.com.*
SPRING	
Late Apr.–Early May	**Shetland Folk Festival.** This festival is one of the biggest folk gatherings in Scotland, and musicians from all over the world stay up for four days of fiddle frenzy. It normally falls at the beginning of May. ☎ *01595/694757* ⊕ *www.shetlandfolkfestival.com.*
Apr. 30	**Beltane Fire Festival.** This festival celebrates the rites of spring according to the traditional Celtic calendar on April 30. You can witness displays of pyrotechnics and elaborately costumed mythological creatures at Calton Hill in Edinburgh. ✉ *Edinburgh* ⊕ *www.beltane.org.*
Late May	**Orkney Folk Festival.** This annual festival brings the folkies back up to the remote Far North by the hundreds. Festivities take place over several days in late May or early June. ☎ *01856/851635* ⊕ *www.orkneyfolkfestival.com.*
SUMMER	
May–Sept.	**Highland Games.** Held annually in many Highland towns, the Highland games include athletic and cultural events like hammer throwing, caber tossing, and highland dancing.

	The fun takes place from May through September. ⊕ *www.visitscotland.com/highland-games*.
June	**Edinburgh International Film Festival.** Concentrating on the best new films from all over the world, Edinburgh International Film Festival screenings are held over two weeks in June. ✉ *Edinburgh* ☎ *0131/228–4051* ⊕ *www.edfilmfest.org.uk*.
	St. Magnus International Festival. Orkney's weeklong St. Magnus International Festival is a feast of classical and modern music each June, often showcasing new vocal or orchestral compositions. ☎ *01856/871445* ⊕ *www.stmagnusfestival.com*.
July	**Merchant City Festival.** Glasgow's transformed mercantile district–turned–cultural quarter stages nine days of pop-up performances and various artsy gatherings in late July, including comedy, dance, music, markets, fashion and design, family events, tours, heritage walks, and food and drink. ✉ *Glasgow* ☎ *0141/287–8985* ⊕ *www.merchantcityfestival.com*.
Aug.	**Edinburgh Festival Fringe.** The rowdy, unofficial counterpart to the Edinburgh International Festival, the Edinburgh Festival Fringe takes over the city during the last three weeks of August. ☎ *0131/226–0000* ⊕ *www.edfringe.com*.
	Edinburgh International Festival. The world's largest festival of the arts, the Edinburgh International Festival takes place during the last three weeks of August. ☎ *0131/473–2000* ⊕ *www.eif.co.uk*.
	Edinburgh Military Tattoo. A stirring, colorful show of marching bands and military regiments, the Edinburgh Military Tattoo takes place during the last three weeks in August. ✉ *Edinburgh* ☎ *0131/225–1188* ⊕ *www.edintattoo.co.uk*.
Early Sept.	**Braemar Royal Highland Gathering.** Kilted clansmen from all over Scotland get together for the Braemar Royal Highland Gathering on the first Saturday in September. Bagpipe bands, dancers, and athletes join in the fun and games. ☎ *013397/41098* ⊕ *www.braemargathering.org*.
FALL	
Mid-Oct.	**Royal National Mòd.** This weeklong Gaelic festival includes speech competitions and theatrical performances, in addition to piping, choir, and Highland dancing exhibitions. The location changes each year, but it's generally held in mid-October. ✉ *Inverness* ☎ *01463/709705* ⊕ *www.acgmod.org*.

		Shetland Accordion and Fiddle Festival. This festival concentrates on two of the most popular instruments of folk musicians in Scotland during five days in mid-October. ☎ *01595/693162* ⊕ *www.shetlandaccordionandfiddle.com.*
	Late Nov.–Dec.	**Glasgow Loves Christmas.** From late November through December, George Square in Glasgow is transformed into a winter wonderland: sparkling ornaments and an impressive palace facade tower over a gigantic ice rink. Festive markets and other seasonal events are part of the program, too. ✉ *Glasgow* ⊕ *www.glasgowloveschristmas.com.*

EDINBURGH AND THE LOTHIANS

Updated by
Jack Jewers

Edinburgh is to London as poetry is to prose, as Charlotte Brontë once wrote. One of the world's stateliest cities and proudest capitals, it's built—like Rome—on seven hills, making it a striking backdrop for the ancient pageant of history. In a skyline of sheer drama, Edinburgh Castle watches over the capital city, frowning down on Princes Street's glamour and glitz. But despite its rich past, the city's famous festivals, excellent museums and galleries, as well as the modern Scottish Parliament, are reminders that Edinburgh has its feet firmly in the 21st century.

Nearly everywhere in Edinburgh (the *burgh* is always pronounced *burra* in Scotland) there are spectacular buildings, whose Doric, Ionic, and Corinthian pillars add touches of neoclassical grandeur to the largely Presbyterian backdrop. Large gardens are a strong feature of central Edinburgh, while Arthur's Seat, a child-size mountain of bright green-and-yellow furze, rears 822 feet up behind the spires of the Old Town. Even as Edinburgh moves through the 21st century, its tall guardian castle remains the focal point of the city and its venerable history.

Modern Edinburgh has become a cultural capital, staging the Edinburgh International Festival and the Festival Fringe in every possible venue each August. The stunning National Museum of Scotland complements the city's wealth of galleries and artsy hangouts. Add Edinburgh's growing reputation for food and nightlife and you have one of the world's most beguiling cities.

Today the city is the second most important financial center in the United Kingdom, and regularly ranks near the top in quality-of-life surveys. In some senses showy and materialistic, Edinburgh still supports learned societies, some of which have their roots in the Scottish Enlightenment. The Royal Society of Edinburgh, for example, established in 1783 "for the advancement of learning and useful knowledge," remains an important forum for interdisciplinary activities.

Take time to explore the streets—peopled by the spirits of Mary, Queen of Scots, Sir Walter Scott, and Robert Louis Stevenson—and enjoy candlelit restaurants or a folk *ceilidh* (pronounced *kay-lee,* a traditional Gaelic dance with music), but remember that you haven't earned your porridge until you've climbed Arthur's Seat. Should you wander around a corner, say, on George Street, you might see not an endless cityscape, but blue sea and a patchwork of fields. This is the county of Fife, beyond the inlet of the North Sea called the Firth of Forth—a reminder, like the mountains to the northwest that can be glimpsed from Edinburgh's highest points, that the rest of Scotland lies within easy reach.

TOP REASONS TO GO

Kaleidoscope of culture: Edinburgh covers it all, from floor-stomping *ceilidhs* to avant-garde modern dance, from traditional painting and sculpture to cutting-edge installations, from folksy fiddlers to the latest rock bands. The city's calendar of cultural festivals, including the famous Edinburgh International Festival, is outstanding.

The Royal Mile: History plays out before your eyes in this centuries-old capital along the Royal Mile. Edinburgh Castle and the Palace of Holyroodhouse were the locations for some of the most important struggles between Scotland and England.

Awe-inspiring architecture: From the Old Town's labyrinthine medieval streets to the neoclassical orderliness of the New Town to imaginative modern developments like the Scottish Parliament, the architecture of Auld Reekie spans the ages.

Food, glorious food: Edinburgh has a burgeoning restaurant scene that attracts celebrity chefs serving up dishes from around the world. Perhaps the most exotic, however, is genuine Scottish cuisine, with its classic dishes like *cullen skink* and haggis with neeps and tatties.

Handcrafted treasures: Scotland has a strong tradition of distinctive furniture makers, silversmiths, and artists. Look to the "villages" of Edinburgh—such as Stockbridge—for exclusive designer clothing, edgy knitwear, and other high-end items.

2

GETTING ORIENTED

For all its steep roads and hidden alleyways, Edinburgh is not a difficult place to navigate. Most newcomers gravitate to two areas, the Old Town and the New Town. The former funnels down from the castle on either side of the High Street, better known as the Royal Mile. Princes Street Gardens and Waverly Station separate the oldest part of the city from the stately New Town, known for its neoclassical architecture and verdant gardens. To the north, the city sweeps down to the Firth of Forth. It is here you will find the port of Leith with its trendy pubs and fine restaurants. The southern and western neighborhoods are mainly residential, but are home to such attractions as the Edinburgh Zoo.

Old Town. The focal point of Edinburgh for centuries, the Old Town is a picturesque jumble of medieval tenements. Here are prime attractions such as Edinburgh Castle and the newer symbol of power, the Scottish Parliament. Amid the historic buildings you will find everything from buzzing nightclubs and bars to ghostly alleyways where the spirits of the past often make their presence felt.

New Town. Built in the 18th and 19th centuries to prevent the residents of overcrowded Old Town from decamping to London, the neoclassical sweep of the New Town is a masterpiece of city planning. Significant sights include the National Gallery of Scotland and Calton Hill, which offers some of the best views of the city from its summit. The city's main shopping thoroughfares, Princes Street and George Street, are also found here.

Leith. On the southern shore of the Firth of Forth, Edinburgh's port of Leith is where you'll find the former royal yacht, *Britannia*. These days it's also filled with smart bars and restaurants.

Side Trips: West Lothian and the Forth Valley, Midlothian and East Lothian. The historic houses, castles, towns, and museums in the green countryside outside Edinburgh—Midlothian, West Lothian, and East Lothian, collectively called the Lothians—can be reached quickly by bus or car, welcome day-trip escapes from the festival crush at the height of summer.

PLANNING

WHEN TO GO

Scotland's reliably variable weather means that you could visit at the height of summer and be forced to wear a scarf. Conversely, conditions can be balmy in early spring and late autumn. You may want to avoid the crowds during July and August, but you'd also miss the famed Edinburgh International Festival and other summer celebrations. May, June, and September are probably the most hassle-free months in which to visit. Short days and grim conditions make winter less appealing, but Edinburgh's New Year celebrations are justly renowned.

PLANNING YOUR TIME

One of Edinburgh's greatest virtues is its compact size, which means that it is possible to pack a fair bit into even the briefest of visits. The two main areas of interest are the Old Town and the New Town, where you'll find Edinburgh Castle, the Scottish Parliament, Princes Street Gardens, and the National Gallery of Scotland. You can cover the major attractions in one day, but to give the major sights their due, you should allow two. You can also choose between the Palace of Holyroodhouse and the important museums of Edinburgh, as well as entertaining sights such as the Real Mary King's Close, or explore the Royal Botanic Garden and Holyrood Park. Head down to leafy, village-like Stockbridge, then immerse yourself in the greenery along the Water of Leith, visiting the Gallery of Modern Art along the way.

Getting out of town is also an option for stays of more than a few days, depending on your interests: hop on a bus out to Midlothian to see the magnificent Rosslyn Chapel at Roslin (it's of interest to more than *Da Vinci Code* fans), and visit Crichton Castle, parts of which date back to the 14th century. Consider spending another half day traveling out to South Queensferry to admire the Forth rail and road bridges; then visit palatial Hopetoun House, with its wealth of portraits and fine furniture.

■ TIP→ **Don't forget that some attractions have special hours during the Edinburgh International Festival. If you want to see something special, check the hours ahead of time.**

GETTING HERE AND AROUND

AIR TRAVEL

Airlines serving Edinburgh, Scotland's busiest airport, include Air France, Aer Lingus, American, British Airways, Delta, easyJet, flybe, Iberia, Jet2, KLM, Lufthansa, Ryanair, and Virgin Atlantic.

2

American and United both fly direct to Edinburgh from New York's JFK airport. United also flies direct from Newark, and has a handful of direct flights per week from Chicago O'Hare. Otherwise your airline is likely to require a change somewhere in Europe. You could fly into Glasgow Airport, 50 miles away, or the smaller Glasgow Prestwick, another 30 miles south, but it's hard to see why you would bother.

AIRPORT Edinburgh Airport is 7 miles west of the city center. Flights bound for Edinburgh depart virtually every hour from London's Gatwick and Heathrow airports.

Airport Information Edinburgh Airport. ✉ *Glasgow Rd., Ingliston* ☎ *0844/448–8833* ⊕ *www.edinburghairport.com.*

TRANSFERS
FROM
EDINBURGH
AIRPORT
There are no rail links to the city center, so the most efficient way to do the journey on public transport is by tram; the service runs every 8 to 12 minutes and takes about half an hour. Tickets cost £5. By bus or car you can usually make it to Edinburgh in a half hour, unless you hit the morning (7:30 to 9) or evening (4 to 6) rush hours. Lothian Buses runs an Airlink express service to Waverley railway station via Haymarket that usually takes around half an hour, depending on traffic. Buses run every 10 minutes (every 30 minutes throughout the night); tickets cost £4.50 and are available from the driver or at the airport information desk. Local buses also run between Edinburgh Airport and the city center every 15 minutes or so from 9 to 5, and roughly every hour during off-peak hours; they're cheaper—just £1.50 one-way—but can take twice as long.

You can arrange for a chauffeur-driven limousine to meet your flight at Edinburgh Airport through Transvercia Chaffeur Drive, Little's, or W L Sleigh Ltd., for upwards of £50.

Taxis are readily available outside the terminal. The trip takes 20 to 30 minutes to the city center, 15 minutes longer during rush hour. The fare is roughly £25. Note that airport taxis picking up fares from the terminal are any color, not the typical black cabs.

Airport Transfer Contacts Little's. ✉ *Paisley* ☎ *0141/883–2111* ⊕ *www.littles. co.uk.* **Transvercia Chaffeur Drive.** ✉ *Leith* ☎ *0131/555–0459* ⊕ *www.transvercia. co.uk.* **W L Sleigh Ltd.** ✉ *Edinburgh* ☎ *0131/339–9607* ⊕ *sleigh.co.uk.*

BUS TRAVEL

National Express provides bus service to and from London and other major towns and cities. The main terminal, Edinburgh Bus Station, is a short walk north of Waverley Station, immediately east of St. Andrew Square. Long-distance coaches must be booked in advance online, by phone, or at the terminal. Edinburgh is approximately eight hours by bus from London.

Lothian Buses provides much of the service between Edinburgh and the Lothians and conducts day tours around and beyond the city. First runs buses out of Edinburgh into the surrounding area. Megabus offers dirt-cheap fares to selected cities if you book in advance.

Bus Contacts First. ☎ *0871/2002233* ⊕ *www.firstgroup.com.* **Lothian Buses.** ☎ *0131/554–4494* ⊕ *www.lothianbuses.com.* **Megabus.** ☎ *0900/160– 0900* ⊕ *www.megabus.com.* **National Express.** ☎ *08717/818181* ⊕ *www. nationalexpress.co.uk.*

Lothian Buses is the main operator within Edinburgh. You can buy tickets on the bus. The Day Ticket (£3.50), allowing unlimited one-day travel on the city's buses, can be purchased in advance or from the driver on any Lothian bus (exact fare is required when purchasing on a bus). The Ridacard (for which you'll need a photo) is valid on all buses for seven days (Sunday through Saturday night) and costs £17; the four-week Rider costs £51. ■TIP➡ Buses are great for cheap daytime travel, but in the evening you'll probably want to take a taxi.

Information Lothian Buses. ✉ *Waverley Bridge, Old Town* ☎ *0131/554-4494* ⊕ *www.lothianbuses.com.*

CAR TRAVEL

Driving in Edinburgh has its quirks and pitfalls, but don't be intimidated. Metered parking in the city center is scarce and expensive, and the local traffic wardens are a feisty, alert bunch. Note that illegally parked cars are routinely towed away, and getting your car back will be expensive. After 6 pm the parking situation improves considerably, and you may manage to find a space quite near your hotel, even downtown. If you park on a yellow line or in a resident's parking bay, be prepared to move your car by 8 the following morning, when the rush hour gets under way. Parking lots are clearly signposted; overnight parking is expensive and not always permitted.

TAXI TRAVEL

Taxi stands can be found throughout the downtown area. The following are the most convenient: the west end of Princes Street; South St. David Street and North St. Andrew Street (both just off St. Andrew Square); Princes Mall; Waterloo Place; and Lauriston Place. Alternatively, hail any taxi displaying an illuminated "for hire" sign.

TRAIN TRAVEL

Edinburgh's main train hub, Waverley Station, is downtown, below Waverley Bridge and around the corner from the unmistakable spire of the Scott Monument. Travel time from Edinburgh to London by train is as little as 4½ hours for the fastest service.

Edinburgh's other main station is Haymarket, about four minutes (by rail) west of Waverley. Most Glasgow and other western and northern services stop here.

Train Contacts National Rail Enquiries. ☎ *08457/484950* ⊕ *www.nationalrail. co.uk.* **ScotRail.** ☎ *0344/811-0141* ⊕ *www.scotrail.co.uk.*

TRAM TRAVEL

Absent since 1956, trams returned to the streets of Edinburgh in 2014. The 14-km (8.5-mile) stretch of track runs between Edinburgh Airport in the west to York Place in the east. Useful stops for travelers include Haymarket, Princes Street, and St. Andrew Square (for Waverley Station). Tickets are £1.50 for a single journey in the "City Zone" (which is every stop excluding the airport), or £5 to get to or from the airport. Day tickets, allowing unlimited travel, cost £4 in the City Zone and £9 including the airport.

Tram Contact Edinburgh Trams. ☎ *0131/555-6363* ⊕ *www.edinburghtrams.co.uk.*

2

POLITICAL POWER IN SCOTLAND

Three centuries after the Union of Parliaments with England in 1707, Edinburgh is once again the seat of a Scottish Parliament. A modern Parliament building, designed by Spanish architect Enric Miralles, stands adjacent to the Palace of Holyroodhouse, at the foot of the Royal Mile.

Some first-time visitors to Scotland may be surprised that the country still has a capital city at all, perhaps believing the seat of govern-ment was drained of its resources and power after the union with England—but far from it. The Union of Parliaments brought with it a set of political partnerships—such as separate legal, ecclesiastical, and educational systems—that Edinburgh assimilated and integrated with its own institutions.

In a hard-fought 2014 referendum, Scottish voters rejected full separation from the United Kingdom. However, the ensuing debate led to even further powers being transferred from London to Edinburgh, and Scotland now has significantly more control over its own affairs than at any time since 1707. The 129 Members of the Scottish Parliament (MSPs), of whom almost half are women, have extensive powers in Scotland over education, health, housing, transportation, training, economic development, the environment, and agriculture, and limited control over taxation. Foreign policy, defense, and economic policy remain under the jurisdiction of the U.K. government in London. As for the future, it seems clear that this is still a period of political discussion and change for Scotland.

TOURS
ORIENTATION TOURS

One good way to get oriented in Edinburgh is to take a bus tour. If you want to get to know the area around Edinburgh, Rabbie's Trail Burners leads small groups on several different excursions.

Edinburgh Bus Tours. The company's highly popular Mac Tours are con-ducted in vintage open-top vehicles to the city's main attractions, includ-ing Edinburgh Castle, the Royal Mile, Palace of Holyroodhouse, and museums and galleries. Buses depart from Waverley Bridge, and are hop-on/hop-off services, with tickets lasting 24 hours. ☏ *0131/220–0770* ⊕ *www.edinburghtour.com* ✉ *From £14.*

Lothian Buses. The 60-minute Majestic Tour, in an open-top bus, oper-ates with a professional guide and takes you from Waverley Bridge to the New Town, past Charlotte Square, the Royal Botanic Garden, and Newhaven Heritage Museum until it reaches the royal yacht, *Britannia*, moored at Leith. Tickets are available from ticket sellers on Waver-ley Bridge or on the buses themselves. ⊠ *Waverley Bridge, Old Town* ☏ *0131/554–4494* ⊕ *www.lothianbuses.com* ✉ *From £14.*

Rabbie's Trail Burners. Strike out farther afield on day trips run by this cheerful Edinburgh company. You can get a surprisingly long way and back in a few hours on one of their minibuses—options include Loch Ness and Glencoe, Loch Lomond National Park, Rosslyn Chapel and the borderlands, and a Highland whisky tour. Groups are kept to a guaranteed maximum of 16, giving these a less impersonal feel than some of the big enterprises. ■TIP→ **Book online for a discount.** ✉ *207 High St., Edinburgh* ☎ *0131/226–3133* ⊕ *www.rabbies.com* ▣ *From £31.*

PERSONAL GUIDES

Scottish Tourist Guides. This organization can supply guides (in 19 languages) who are fully qualified and will meet clients at any point of entry into the United Kingdom or Scotland. They can also tailor tours to your interests. ☎ *01786/451953* ⊕ *www.stga.co.uk* ▣ *From £120.*

WALKING TOURS

Cadies and Witchery Tours. Spooky tours tracing the steps of Edinburgh's ghouls, gore, and mysteries commence outside the Witchery Restaurant at 352 Castlehill. The Cadies and Witchery Tours, a member of the Scottish Tourist Guides Association, has built a reputation for combining entertainment and historical accuracy in its lively and enthusiastic Ghosts & Gore Tour and Murder & Mystery Tour, which take you through the narrow Old Town alleyways and closes. Costumed guides and other theatrical characters show up en route. ✉ *Edinburgh* ☎ *0131/225–6745* ⊕ *www.witcherytours.com* ▣ *From £9.*

Scottish Literary Pub Tours. Professional actors invoke Scottish literary characters while taking you around some of the city's most hallowed watering holes on these lively and informative tours. The experience is led by "Clart and McBrain," self-styled "bohemian and intellectual," who regale you with tales of the literary past of Edinburgh's Old and New Towns. The experience is so witty and fun that you might even forget you're learning something along the way. Tours run daily in summer, Thursday to Sunday in fall and spring, and Friday only in winter. ✉ *18–20 Grassmarket, Edinburgh* ☎ *0800/169–7410* ⊕ *www. edinburghliterarypubtour.co.uk* ▣ *£14.*

VISITOR INFORMATION

The VisitScotland Information Centre, next to Waverley Station (follow the "tic" signs in the station and throughout the city), offers an accommodations-booking service in addition to the more typical services. Complete information is also available at the information desk at the Edinburgh Airport.

Visitor Information Visit Scotland Information Centre. ✉ *3 Princes St., East End* ☎ *0131/473–3868* ⊕ *www.visitscotland.com.*

EXPLORING EDINBURGH

Edinburgh's Old Town, which bears a great measure of symbolic weight as the "heart of Scotland's capital," is a boon for lovers of atmosphere and history. In contrast, if you appreciate the unique architectural heritage of the city's Enlightenment, then the New Town's for you. If you belong to both categories, don't worry—the Old and New towns are only yards apart. Princes Street runs east–west along the north edge of the Princes Street Gardens. Explore the main thoroughfares but don't forget to get lost among the tiny *wynds* and *closes*: old medieval alleys that connect the winding streets.

Like most cities, Edinburgh incorporates small communities within its boundaries, and many of these are as rewarding to explore as Old Town and New Town. Dean Village, for instance, even though it's close to the New Town, has a character all its own. Duddingston, just southeast of Arthur's Seat, has all the feel of a country village. Then there's Corstorphine, to the west of the city center, famous for being the site of Murrayfield, Scotland's international rugby stadium. Edinburgh's port, Leith, sits on the shore of the Firth of Forth, and throbs with smart bars and restaurants.

OLD TOWN

East of Edinburgh Castle, the historic castle esplanade becomes the street known as the Royal Mile, leading from the castle down through Old Town to the Palace of Holyroodhouse. The Mile, as it's called, is actually made up of one thoroughfare that bears, in consecutive sequence, different names—Castlehill, Lawnmarket, Parliament Square, High Street, and Canongate. The streets and passages winding into their tenements, or "lands," and crammed onto the ridge in back of the Mile really *were* Edinburgh until the 18th century saw expansions to the south and north. Everybody lived here, the richer folk on the lower floors of houses, with less well-to-do families on the middle floors—the higher up, the poorer.

Time and progress (of a sort) have swept away some of the narrow closes and tall tenements of the Old Town, but enough survive for you to be able to imagine the original profile of Scotland's capital. There are many guided tours of the area, or you can walk around on your own. The latter is often a better choice in summer when tourists pack the area and large guided groups have trouble making their way through the crowds.

TOP ATTRACTIONS
Arthur's Seat. The high point of 640-acre Holyrood Park is this famously spectacular viewpoint. You'll have seen it before—the covers of countless guidebooks, brochures, and postcards have been snapped from this very spot. The "seat" in question is actually the 822-foot-high plateau of a small mountain. A ruined church—the 15th-century Chapel of St. Anthony—adds to its impossible picturesqueness. There are various starting points for the walk, but one of the most pleasant begins at the Scottish Parliament building. Follow the signposts for Volunteer's Walk; at a moderate pace the climb takes around one hour each way, and is easy so long as you're reasonably fit. However, a much faster (though far less beautiful) way to reach the summit is to drive to the small parking area at Dunsapie Loch, on Queen's Road, then follow the footpath up the hill; this walk takes about 20 minutes. ⊠ *Queen's Dr., Old Town.*

Craigmillar Castle. This handsome medieval ruin, only three miles south of the city center, is the archetypal Scottish fortress: forbidding, powerful, and laden with atmosphere. Built as a rural hideaway for the Scottish elite, the castle is best known for its association with Mary,

Queen of Scots. During her second stay here, in 1563, her courtiers (successfully) hatched a plot to murder her troublesome husband, Henry Stuart. Rumors that Mary was involved were never substantiated, though they contributed to her ultimate downfall. Today Craigmillar is one of the most impressive ruined castles in Scotland. The 15th-century tower and courtyard are in excellent condition, including a well-preserved great hall. Climb the tower for a superb view across the city. Look out for the unusually ornate defensive arrow slits, shaped like inverted keyholes. ⊠ *Craigmillar Castle Rd., South Side* ☎ *0131/661–4445* ⊕ *www.historic-scotland.gov.uk* ⊠ *£5.50* ☉ *Apr.– Sept., daily 9:30–5:30; Oct.–Mar., Mon.–Wed. and weekends 10–4. Last admission 30 mins before closing.*

FAMILY
Fodor's Choice
★

Edinburgh Castle. The crowning glory of the Scottish capital, Edinburgh Castle is popular not only because it's the symbolic heart of Scotland but also because of the views from its battlements: on a clear day the vistas—stretching to the "kingdom" of Fife—are breathtaking. You probably need at least three hours to see everything it has to offer (especially if you're a military history buff). However, an hour or so is enough for a decent wander and a look at some of the main highlights.

You enter across the **Esplanade,** the huge forecourt built in the 18th century as a parade ground. The area comes alive with color and music each August when it's used for the Military Tattoo, a festival of magnificently outfitted marching bands and regiments. Heading over the drawbridge and through the gatehouse, past the guards, you can find the rough stone walls of the **Half-Moon Battery,** where the one-o'clock gun is fired every day in an impressively anachronistic ceremony; these curving ramparts give Edinburgh Castle its distinctive appearance from miles away. Climb up through a second gateway and you come to the oldest surviving building in the complex, the tiny 11th-century **St. Margaret's Chapel,** named in honor of Saxon queen Margaret (1046–93), who had persuaded her husband, King Malcolm III (circa 1031–93), to move his court from Dunfermline to Edinburgh. Edinburgh's environs—the Lothians—were occupied by Anglian settlers with whom the queen felt more at home, or so the story goes (Dunfermline was surrounded by Celts). The **Crown Room,** a must-see, contains the "Honours of Scotland"—the crown, scepter, and sword that once graced the Scottish monarch. Upon the **Stone of Scone,** also in the Crown Room, Scottish monarchs once sat to be crowned. In the section now called **Queen Mary's Apartments,** Mary, Queen of Scots, gave birth to James VI of Scotland. The **Great Hall** displays arms and armor under an impressive vaulted, beamed ceiling. Scottish Parliament meetings were conducted here until 1840.

Military features of interest include the **Scottish National War Memorial,** the **Scottish United Services Museum,** and the famous 15th-century Belgian-made cannon *Mons Meg.* This enormous piece of artillery has been silent since 1682, when it exploded while firing a salute for the Duke of York; it now stands in an ancient hall behind the Half-Moon Battery. Contrary to what you may hear from locals, it's not *Mons Meg* but the battery's gun that goes off with a bang every weekday at 1 pm, frightening visitors and reminding Edinburghers to check their watches.

2

TIP→Avoid the queues by buying tickets online. You can pick them up from one of the automated collection points at the entrance. ⊠ *Castle Esplanade and Castlehill, Old Town* ☎ *0131/225–9846 Edinburgh Castle, 0131/226–7393 War Memorial* ⊕ *www.edinburghcastle.gov. uk* ☑ *£16.50* ⊙ *Apr.–Sept., daily 9:30–6; Oct.–Mar., daily 9:30–5; last entry 1 hr before closing.*

QUICK BITE

✕**Redcoat Café.** You can have lunch or afternoon tea with panoramic views of the city at the Redcoat Café. Cakes, sandwiches, soups, and drinks are all available at reasonable prices. Also within the castle grounds, the Tea Rooms at the top of Crown Square offer a fancier afternoon tea. ⊠ *Edinburgh Castle, Castlehill, Old Town* ☎ *0131/225–9746.*

High Kirk of St. Giles. Sometimes called St. Giles's Cathedral, this is one of the city's principal churches. However, anyone expecting a rival to Paris's Notre Dame or London's Westminster Abbey will be disappointed: St. Giles is more like a large parish church than a great European cathedral. There has been a church here since AD 854, although most of the present structure dates from either 1120 or 1829, when the church was restored.

The tower, with its stone crown towering 161 feet above the ground, was completed between 1495 and 1500. The most elaborate feature is · the **Chapel of the Order of the Thistle,** built onto the southeast corner of the church in 1911 for the exclusive use of Scotland's only chivalric order, the Most Ancient and Noble Order of the Thistle. It bears the belligerent national motto "nemo me impune lacessit" ("No one provokes me with impunity"). Inside the church stands a life-size statue of the Scot whose spirit still dominates the place—the great religious reformer and preacher John Knox, before whose zeal all of Scotland once trembled. The church lies about one-third of the way along the Royal Mile from Edinburgh Castle. ⊠ *High St., Old Town* ☎ *0131/225–9442* ⊕ *www. stgilescathedral.org.uk* ☑ *Free; suggested donation £3; photography permit £2* ⊙ *May–Sept., weekdays 9–7, Sat. 9–5, Sun. 1–5; Oct.–Apr., Mon.–Sat. 9–5, Sun. 1–5. Also for services, year-round.*

High Street. Some of Old Town's most impressive buildings and sights are on High Street, one of the five streets making up the Royal Mile. Also here are other, less obvious historic relics. Near Parliament Square, look on the west side for a **heart** set in cobbles. This marks the site of the vanished Tolbooth, the center of city life from the 15th century until the building's demolition in 1817. The ancient civic edifice housed the Scottish Parliament and was used as a prison—it also inspired Sir Walter Scott's novel *The Heart of Midlothian.*

Just outside Parliament House is the **Mercat Cross** (*mercat* means "market"), a great landmark of Old Town life. It was an old mercantile center, where in the early days executions were held, and where royal proclamations were—and are still—read. Most of the present cross is comparatively modern, dating from the time of William Ewart Gladstone (1809–98), the great Victorian prime minister and rival of Benjamin Disraeli (1804–81). Across High Street from the High Kirk of St. Giles stands the **City Chambers,** now the seat of local government.

Edinburgh's Castle Fit for a King

Archaeological investigations have established that the rock on which Edinburgh Castle stands was inhabited as far back as 1000 BC, in the latter part of the Bronze Age. There have been fortifications here since the mysterious people called the Picts first used it as a stronghold in the 3rd and 4th centuries AD. Anglian invaders from northern England dislodged the Picts in AD 452, and for the next 1,300 years the site saw countless battles and skirmishes.

In the castle you'll hear the story of how Randolph, Earl of Moray and nephew of freedom fighter Robert the Bruce, scaled the heights one dark night in 1313, surprised the English guard, and recaptured the castle for the Scots. During this battle he destroyed every one of the castle's buildings except for St. Margaret's Chapel, dating from around 1076, so that successive Stewart kings had to rebuild the castle bit by bit.

The castle has been held over time by Scots and Englishmen, Catholics and Protestants, soldiers and royalty. In the 16th century Mary, Queen of Scots, gave birth here to the future James VI of Scotland (1566–1625), who was also to rule England as James I. In 1573 it was the last fortress to support Mary's claim as the rightful Catholic queen of Britain, causing the castle to be virtually destroyed by English artillery fire.

Built by John Fergus, who adapted a design of John Adam in 1753, the chambers were originally known as the Royal Exchange and intended to be where merchants and lawyers could conduct business. Note how the building drops 11 stories to Cockburn Street on its north side.

A *tron* is a weigh beam used in public weigh houses, and the **Tron Kirk** was named after a salt tron that used to stand nearby. The kirk itself was built after 1633, when St. Giles's became an Episcopal cathedral for a brief time. In this church in 1693, a minister offered an often-quoted prayer for the local government: "Lord, hae mercy on a' [all] fools and idiots, and particularly on the Magistrates of Edinburgh." ⊠ *Between Lawnmarket and Canongate, Old Town.*

John Knox House. It's not certain that Scotland's severe religious reformer John Knox ever lived here, but there's evidence that he died here in 1572. Mementos of his life are on view inside, and the distinctive dwelling gives you a glimpse of what Old Town life was like in the 16th century. The projecting upper stories were once commonplace along the Royal Mile, darkening and further closing in the already narrow passage. Look for the initials of former owner James Mossman and his wife carved into the stonework on the marriage lintel. Mossman was goldsmith to Mary, Queen of Scots, and was hanged in 1573 for his allegiance to her. ⊠ *45 High St., Old Town* ☎ *0131/556–9579* ⊕ *www. scottishstorytellingcentre.co.uk* ⊠ *£5* ☾ *Sept.–June, Mon.–Sat. 10–6; July and Aug., Mon.–Sat. 10–6, Sun. 10–6; last admission 30 mins before closing.*

Fodor's Choice ★ **Kirk of the Greyfriars.** Greyfriars Church, built circa 1620 on the site of a medieval monastery, was where the National Covenant, declaring that the Presbyterian Church in Scotland was independent of the monarch and not Episcopalian in government, was signed in 1638. The covenant plunged Scotland into decades of civil war. Informative panels tell the story. Never mind all this, though—the real attraction here is the sprawling, hillside graveyard, surely one of the most evocative in Europe. Its old, tottering, elaborate tombstones mark the graves of some of Scotland's most respected heroes and despised villains. Some of the larger tombs are arranged in avenues; a few are closed off, but others you can wander. It's a hugely atmospheric place to explore, especially at twilight. Look out for two rare surviving *mortsafes,* iron cages erected around graves to prevent the theft of corpses for sale to medical schools, a grisly nuisance in the early 1800s. Nearby, at the corner of George IV Bridge and Candlemaker Row, stands one of the most photographed sites in Scotland: the Greyfriars Bobby statue. ⊠ *Greyfriars Pl., Old Town* ☎ *0131/225–1900* ⊕ *www.greyfriarskirk.com* ⛟ *Free* ☯ *Church: Easter–Oct., weekdays 10:30–4:30, Sat. 11–2; Nov.–Easter, Thurs. 1:30–3:30. Graveyard: daily during daylight hrs.*

FAMILY
Fodor's Choice ★ **National Museum of Scotland.** This museum traces the country's fascinating story from the oldest fossils to the most recent popular culture, making it a must-see for first-time visitors to Scotland or anyone interested in history. One of the most famous treasures is the Lewis Chessmen, 11 intricately carved 12th-century ivory chess pieces found in the 19th century on one of Scotland's Western Isles. An extensive renovation of the basement has created a dramatic, crypt-like entrance. Visitors now rise to the light-filled, birdcage wonders of the Victorian grand hall and the upper galleries in glass elevators. Highlights include the hanging hippo and sea creatures of the Wildlife Panorama, a life-size cast of a *Tyrannosaurus rex* skeleton, beautiful Viking brooches, Pictish stones, Jacobite relics, and Queen Mary's *clarsach* (harp). ■ **TIP→ Time your visit to be in the Discoveries gallery on the hour to see the magnificent Millennium clock tower come to life.** The two-story structure (which plays a Bach concerto as its chime) is filled with elaborate and fanciful animatronics, representing the highest and lowest points of the 20th century. ⊠ *Chambers St., Old Town* ☎ *0300/123–6789* ⊕ *www.nms.ac.uk* ⛟ *Free* ☯ *Daily 10–5.*

FAMILY **Our Dynamic Earth.** Using state-of-the-art technology, the 11 theme galleries at this interactive science gallery educate and entertain as they explore the wonders of the planet, from polar regions to tropical rain forests. Geological history, from the big bang to the unknown future, is also examined. Save on the ticket price by booking online. ⊠ *Holyrood Rd., Old Town* ☎ *0131/550–7800* ⊕ *www.dynamicearth.co.uk* ⛟ *£12.50* ☯ *Apr.–June, Sept., and Oct., daily 10–5:30; July and Aug., daily 10–6; Nov.–Mar., Wed.–Sun. 10–5:30; last admission 90 mins before closing.*

Fodor's Choice ★ **Palace of Holyroodhouse.** Once the haunt of Mary, Queen of Scots, and the setting for high drama—including at least one notorious murder, several major fires, and centuries of the colorful lifestyles of larger-than-life, power-hungry personalities—this is now Queen Elizabeth's official

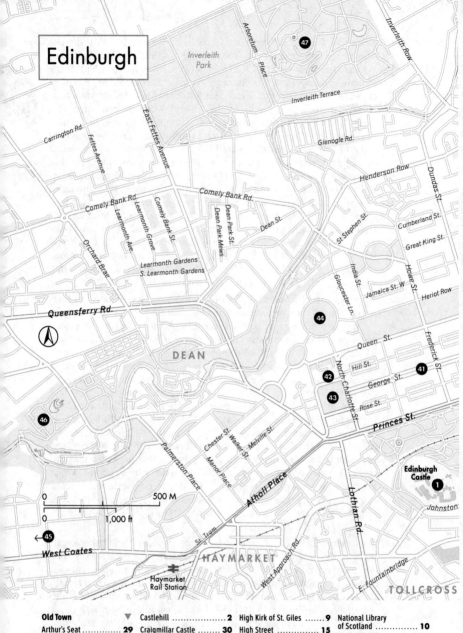

Edinburgh

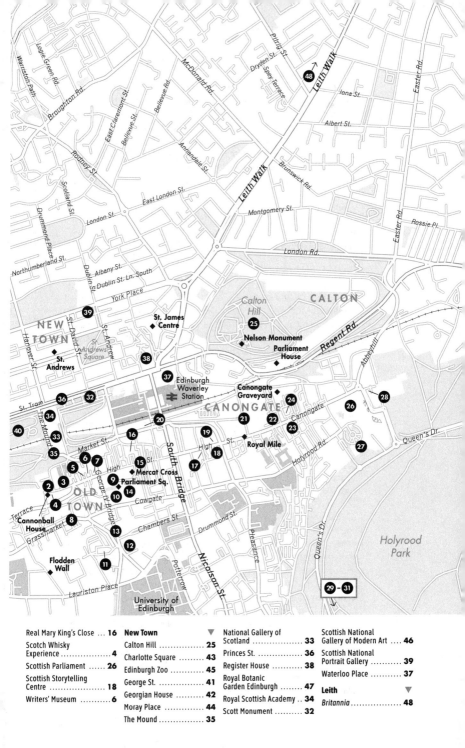

THE BUILDING OF EDINBURGH

Towering over the city, Edinburgh Castle was actually built over the plug of an ancient volcano. Many thousands of years ago, an eastward-grinding glacier encountered the tough basalt core of the volcano and swept around it, scouring steep cliffs and leaving a trail of matter. This material formed a ramp gently leading down from the rocky summit. On this *crag* and *tail* would grow the city of Edinburgh and its castle.

CASTLE, WALLED TOWN, AND HOLYROODHOUSE

By the 12th century Edinburgh had become a walled town, still perched on the hill. Its shape was becoming clearer: like a fish with its head at the castle, its backbone running down the ridge, and its ribs leading briefly off on either side. The backbone gradually became the continuous thoroughfare now known as the Royal Mile, and the ribs became the closes (alleyways), some still surviving, that were the scene of many historic incidents.

By the early 15th century, Edinburgh had become the undisputed capital of Scotland. The bitter defeat of Scotland at Flodden in 1513, when Scotland aligned itself with France against England, caused a new defensive city wall to be built. Though the castle escaped destruction, the city was burned by the English Earl of Hertford under orders from King Henry VIII (1491–1547) of England. This was during a time known as the "Rough Wooing," when Henry was trying to coerce the Scots into allowing the young Mary, Queen of Scots (1542–87), to marry his son Edward. The plan failed and Mary married Francis, the Dauphin of France.

By 1561, when Mary returned from France already widowed, the guesthouse of the Abbey of Holyrood had grown to become the Palace of Holyroodhouse, replacing Edinburgh Castle as the main royal residence. Mary's legacy to the city included the destruction of most of the earliest buildings of Edinburgh Castle; she was eventually executed by Elizabeth I.

ENLIGHTENMENT AND THE CITY

In the trying decades after the union with England in 1707, many influential Scots, both in Edinburgh and elsewhere, went through an identity crisis. Out of the 18th-century difficulties, however, grew the Scottish Enlightenment, during which educated Scots made great strides in medicine, economics, and science.

Changes came to the cityscape, too. By the mid-18th century, it had become the custom for wealthy Scottish landowners to spend the winter in the Old Town of Edinburgh, in town houses huddled between the high Castle Rock and the Royal Palace below. Cross-fertilized in coffeehouses and taverns, intellectual notions flourished among a people determined to remain Scottish despite their Parliament's having voted to dissolve itself. One result was a campaign to expand and beautify the city, to give it a look worthy of its future nickname, the Athens of the North. Thus was the New Town of Edinburgh built, with broad streets and gracious buildings creating a harmony that even today's throbbing traffic cannot obscure.

residence in Scotland. A doughty and impressive palace standing at the foot of the Royal Mile in a hilly public park, it's built around a graceful, lawned central court at the end of Canongate. When the Queen or royal family is not in residence you can take a tour. The free audio guide is excellent. There's plenty to see here, so make sure you have at least two hours to tour the palace, gardens, and the ruins of the 12th-century abbey.

Many monarchs, including Charles II, Queen Victoria, and George V, have left their mark on its rooms, but it's Mary, Queen of Scots, whose spirit looms largest. For some visitors, the most memorable room here is the little chamber in which David Rizzio (1533–66), secretary to Mary, Queen of Scots, met an unhappy end in 1566. Mary's second husband, Lord Darnley (Henry Stewart, 1545–65), burst into the queen's rooms with his henchmen, dragged Rizzio into an antechamber, and stabbed him more than 50 times; a bronze plaque marks the spot. Darnley himself was murdered the next year, which made way for the queen's marriage to her lover, the Earl of Bothwell.

The **King James Tower** is the oldest surviving section, containing the rooms of Mary, Queen of Scots, on the second floor, and Lord Darnley's rooms below. Though much has been altered, there are fine fireplaces, paneling, tapestries, and 18th- and 19th-century furnishings throughout. At the south end of the palace front, you can find the **Royal Dining Room,** and along the south side are the **Throne Room** and other drawing rooms now used for social and ceremonial occasions.

At the back of the palace is the **King's Bedchamber.** The 150-foot-long **Great Picture Gallery,** on the north side, displays the portraits of 110 Scottish monarchs. These were commissioned by Charles II, who was eager to demonstrate his Scottish ancestry—but most of the people depicted are entirely fictional, and the likenesses of several others were invented and simply given the names of real people. The **Queen's Gallery,** in a former church and school at the entrance to the palace, holds rotating exhibits from the Royal Collection. There is a separate admission charge.

Holyroodhouse has its origins in an Augustinian monastery founded by David I (1084–1153) in 1128. In the 15th and 16th centuries, Scottish royalty, preferring the comforts of the abbey to drafty Edinburgh Castle, settled into Holyroodhouse, expanding the buildings until the palace eclipsed the monastery. You can still walk around some abbey ruins, though.

After the Union of the Crowns in 1603, when the Scottish royal court packed its bags and decamped for England, the building fell into decline. It was Charles II (1630–85) who rebuilt Holyrood in the architectural style of Louis XIV (1638–1715), and this is the style you see today. Queen Victoria (1819-1901) and her grandson King George V (1865-1936) renewed interest in the palace, and the buildings were refurbished and again made suitable for royal residence. ✉ *Abbey Strand, Old Town* ☎ *0131/556–5100* ⊕ *www.royalcollection.org. uk* 🎫 *£11.60, with Queen's Gallery £16.40; with garden tour £20.20*

⊙ *Apr.–Oct., daily 9:30–6; Nov.–Mar., daily 9:30–4:30; last admission 1 hr before closing. Closed during royal visits.*

FAMILY

Fodor'sChoice

★

The Real Mary King's Close. Hidden beneath the City Chambers, this narrow, cobbled *close,* or lane, named after a former landowner, is said to be one of Edinburgh's most haunted sites. The close was sealed off in 1645 to quarantine residents who became sick when the bubonic plague swept through the city, and many victims were herded there to die. After the plague passed, the bodies were removed and buried, and the street was reopened. A few people returned, but they soon reported ghostly goings-on and departed, leaving the close empty for decades. In 1753 city authorities built the Royal Exchange (later the City Chambers) directly over the close, sealing it off and, unwittingly, ensuring it remained intact, except for the buildings' upper stories, which were destroyed. Parts of the close were still inhabited until the early 20th century, when the last sections were finally covered over. Today enthusiastic, costumed guides take you around the claustrophobic remains of the shops and houses. People still report ghostly visions and eerie sounds, especially the crying of a young girl. Over the years visitors have left small offerings for her, such as ribbons, toys, and dolls; all are neatly arranged in what has become the close's creepiest room, which many visitors find too disturbing to enter. The spookiness of the close may be its best attraction, and aside from a few harmless jump scares orchestrated by the guides, nothing here is explicit or nasty. Still, it's not for the youngest ones, and children under five are not admitted. ⊠ *Writers' Court, Old Town* ☎ *0131/225–0672* ⊕ *www.realmarykingsclose. com* ⊠ *£15* ⊙ *Apr.–July, Sept. and Oct., daily 10–9; Aug., daily 9:30–9; Nov.–Mar., weekdays 10–5, weekends 10–9.*

Scottish Parliament. Scotland's somewhat controversial Parliament building is dramatically modern, with irregular curves and angles that mirror the twisting shapes of the surrounding landscape. The structure's artistry is most apparent when you step inside, where the gentle slopes, forest's worth of oak, polished concrete and granite, and walls of glass create an understated magnificence. It's worth taking a free tour to see the main hall and debating chamber, a committee room, and other areas. Specialist tours focus on history, literature, and the building's art collection; tour reservations must be made online. Call well in advance to get a free ticket to view Parliament in action. Originally conceived by the late Catalan architect Enric Miralles, who often said the building was "growing out of the ground," the design was completed by his widow, Benedetta Tagliabue, in August 2004. ⊠ *Horse Wynd, Old Town* ☎ *0131/348–5200* ⊕ *www.scottish.parliament.uk* ⊠ *Free* ⊙ *Mon.–Sat. 10–5:30.*

Fodor'sChoice

★

Scottish Storytelling Centre. The stripped down, low-fi, traditional art of storytelling has had something of a resurgence in Britain over the last decade or so, and there are few places better than this to experience a master storyteller in full flow. Housed in a modern building that manages to blend seamlessly with the historic structures on either side, the center hosts a year-round program of storytelling, theater, music, and literary events. A café serves lunch, tea, and home-baked cakes. The center's storytellers also manage the tours of the John Knox House next

A GOOD WALK IN THE OLD TOWN

A perfect place to start your stroll through the Old Town is Edinburgh Castle. After exploring its extensive complex of buildings and admiring the view from the battlements, set off down the first part of the Royal Mile. The Camera Obscura's Outlook Tower affords more splendid views of the city. The six-story tenement known as Gladstone's Land, a survivor of 16th-century domestic life, is on the left as you head east. Near Gladstone's Land, down another close, stands the Writers' Museum, in a fine example of 17th-century urban architecture called Lady Stair's House. Farther down on the right are the Tolbooth Kirk (a *tolbooth* was a town hall or prison, and *kirk* means "church") and Upper Bow.

Turn right down George IV Bridge to reach the historic Grassmarket, where parts of the old city walls still stand. Turn left up Candlemaker Row and you can see the Kirk of the Greyfriars, and the little statue of faithful Greyfriars Bobby. On Chambers Street, at the foot of George IV Bridge, are the impressive galleries of the National Museum of Scotland.

Returning to the junction of George IV Bridge with the Royal Mile, turn right (east) down High Street to visit the old Parliament House; the High Kirk of St. Giles; the Mercat Cross; and the elegant City Chambers, bringing a flavor of the New Town's neoclassicism to the Old Town's severity. Beneath the chambers is the eerie Real Mary King's Close, a lane that was closed off in the 17th century when the bubonic plague struck the city.

A short distance down Canongate on the left is Canongate Tolbooth. The Museum of Edinburgh stands opposite, and the Canongate Kirk and Acheson House are nearby. This walk draws to a close, as it started, on a high note, at the Palace of Holyroodhouse, full of historic and architectural interest and some fine paintings, tapestries, and furnishings to admire, in Holyrood Park.

TIMING

This walk can expand greatly in length depending on how often you stop to explore different sights, so plan accordingly. You can walk the Royal Mile in an hour, take a day to stop and visit points of interest, or even spend a couple of days exploring the area.

door and wider tours of the historic Nethbrow district. ⊠ *43 High St., Old Town* ☎ *0131/556–9579* ⊕ *www.scottishstorytellingcentre.co.uk* 🎫 *Free; event prices vary* ☉ *Centre: Sept.–June, Mon.–Sat. 10–6; July and Aug., Mon.–Sat. 10–6, Sun. noon–6.*

WORTH NOTING

FAMILY **Camera Obscura and World of Illusions.** Want to view Edinburgh as Victorian travelers once did? Then head for the 17th-century Outlook Tower's camera obscura, where an optical instrument—a sort of projecting periscope—affords bird's-eye views of the whole city (on a clear day, that is) illuminated onto a concave table. The tower was significantly altered in the 1850s with the installation of the telescopic "magic lantern." Other attractions include a Magic Gallery with optical illusions, holograms, pinhole photography, and rooftop views. ✉ *Castlehill, Old Town* ☎ *0131/226–3709* ⊕ *www.camera-obscura.co.uk* 💷 *£14* ⊙ *Apr.–June, Sept., and Oct., daily 9:30–7; July–Aug., daily 9–9; Nov.– Mar., daily 10–6.*

Canongate. This section of the Royal Mile takes its name from the canons who once ran the abbey at Holyrood. Canongate—in Scots, *gate* means "street"—was originally an independent town, or *burgh,* another Scottish term used to refer to a community with trading rights granted by the monarch. Here you'll find **Canongate Kirk** and its graveyard, **Canongate Tolbooth,** and the **Museum of Edinburgh.** ✉ *Royal Mile, between High St. and Abbey Strand, Old Town.*

Canongate Kirk. This unadorned building, built in 1688, is run by the Church of Scotland and has an interesting graveyard. This is the final resting place of some notable Scots, including economist Adam Smith (1723–90), author of *The Wealth of Nations* (1776), who once lived in the nearby 17th-century Panmure House. Also buried here are Dugald Stewart (1753–1828), the leading European philosopher of his time, and the undervalued Scottish poet Robert Fergusson (1750–74). That Fergusson's grave is even marked is the result of efforts by the much more famous Robert Burns (1759–96), who commissioned an architect—by the name of Robert Burn—to design a marker. Burn also designed the Nelson Monument, the tall column on Calton Hill to the north, which you can see from the graveyard.

Against the eastern wall of the graveyard is a bronze sculpture of the head of Mrs. Agnes McLehose, the "Clarinda" of the copious correspondence in which Robert Burns engaged while confined to his lodgings with an injured leg in 1788. Burns and McLehose—a high-born, talented woman who had been abandoned by her husband—exchanged passionate letters for some six weeks that year. The missives were dispatched across town by a postal service that delivered them within the hour for one penny. The curiously literary affair ended when Burns left Edinburgh in 1788 to take up a farm tenancy and to marry Jean Armour. ✉ *153 Canongate, Old Town* ☎ *0131/556–3515* ⊕ *canongatekirk.org. uk* 💷 *Free* ⊙ *May–Sept., weekdays 10:30–4:30, Sat. 10:30–4:30, Sun. 1–4:30.*

Canongate Tolbooth and People's Story Museum. Nearly every city and town in Scotland once had a tolbooth. Originally a customhouse where tolls were gathered, a tolbooth came to mean town hall and later prison because detention cells were in the basement. The building where Canongate's town council once met now has a museum, the **People's Story Museum,** which focuses on the lives of everyday folk from the 18th century to today. Exhibits describe how Canongate once bustled with the activities of the tradespeople needed to supply life's essentials. There are also displays on the politics, health care, and leisure time (such as it was) in days of yore. Others leap forward in time to show, for example, a 1940s kitchen. ✉ *163 Canongate, Old Town* ☎ *0131/529–4057* ⊕ *www.edinburghmuseums.org.uk* 💷 *Free* ⊙ *Mon.–Sat. 10–5; also Sun. 10–5 during Edinburgh Festival.*

2

Castlehill. In the late 16th century, alleged witches were brought to what is now a street in the Royal Mile to be burned at the stake, as a bronze plaque here recalls. The cannonball embedded in the west gable of Castlehill's **Cannonball House** was, according to legend, fired from the castle during the Jacobite Rebellion of 1745, led by Charles Edward Stuart (also known as Bonnie Prince Charlie, 1720–88), the most romantic of the Stuart pretenders to the British throne. Most authorities agree on a more prosaic explanation, however; they say it was a height marker for Edinburgh's first piped water-supply system, installed in 1681. Atop the Gothic **Tolbooth Kirk,** built in 1844 for the General Assembly of the Church of Scotland, stands the tallest spire in the city, at 240 feet. The church now houses the cheery Edinburgh Festival offices and a café known as **The Hub.**

The **Upper Bow,** running from Lawnmarket to Victoria Street, was once the main route westward from the town and castle. Before Victoria Street was built in the late 19th century, the Upper Bow led down into a narrow dark thoroughfare coursing between a canyon of tenements. All traffic struggled up and down this steep slope from the Grassmarket, which joins the now-truncated West Bow at its lower end. ⊠ *East of Esplanade and west of Lawnmarket, Old Town.*

OFF THE BEATEN PATH

Duddingston Village. Tucked behind Arthur's Seat, and about an hour's walk from Princes Street via Holyrood Park, this little community, formerly of brewers and weavers, still seems like a country village. The Duddingston Kirk has a Norman doorway and a watchtower that was built to keep body snatchers out of the graveyard. The church and adjoining garden overlook Duddingston Loch, popular with bird-watchers. Pathways meander down to lochside Thomson's Tower, an octagonal tower built by William Playfair in 1825 as a curling clubhouse. Recently restored, it's home to a small museum. Moments away is Edinburgh's oldest hostelry, the Sheep Heid Inn, which serves a wide selection of beers and hearty food. For £13 you can have a go on the oldest *skittle* (bowling alley) in Scotland. To get here, take Lothian Bus 42. ⊠ *Duddingston Low Rd., Duddingston.*

Fruitmarket Gallery. This contemporary art gallery behind Waverley Station showcases cutting-edge work, mostly from Britain and the United States, and world-renowned artists like Louise Bourgeois and Turner Prize–winning artist Martin Creed. (Don't miss Creed's colorful yet subtle marbled transformation of the once-dilapidated Scotsman Steps nearby). ■ TIP➡ **Free, hour-long taster tours happen every Saturday at 2.** ⊠ *45 Market St., Old Town* ☎ *0131/225–2383* ⊕ *www.fruitmarket. co.uk* 🖾 *Free* 🕙 *Mon.–Sat. 11–6, Sun. noon–5.*

George IV Bridge. It's not immediately obvious that this is in fact a bridge, as buildings are closely packed most of the way along both sides. At the corner of the bridge stands one of the most photographed sculptures in Scotland, *Greyfriars Bobby.* This statue pays tribute to the legendary Skye terrier who kept vigil beside his master John Gray's grave in the Greyfriar's churchyard for 14 years after Gray died in 1858. The 1961 Walt Disney film *Greyfriars Bobby* tells a version of the heartrending tale that some claim to be a shaggy-dog story. ⊠ *Bank St. and Lawnmarket, Old Town.*

Gladstone's Land. This narrow, six-story tenement, next to the Assembly Hall, is a survivor from the 17th century, and the living conditions in a tenement building of the time have been re-created here. Rooms are decorated in authentic period furnishings, and the sense of how cramped life must have been, even for the moderately successful, is deftly portrayed. Typical Scottish architectural features are evident on two floors, including an arcaded ground floor (even in the city center, livestock sometimes inhabited the ground floor) and some magnificent painted ceilings. Look out for the lovely spinet in the drawing room; the ingeniously designed instrument, resembling a space-saving piano, plucks strings rather than strikes them, producing a resonantly baroque sound. ⊠ *477B Lawnmarket, Old Town* ☎ *0131/226–5856* ⊕ *www. nts.org.uk/property/gladstones-land* ⊠ *£6.50* ⊙ *Late Mar.–June and Sept.–Oct., daily 10–5; July and Aug., daily 10–6:30; last admission 30 mins before closing.*

Grassmarket. For centuries an agricultural marketplace, Grassmarket now is the site of numerous shops, bars, and restaurants, making it a hive of activity at night. Sections of the Old Town wall can be traced on the north side by a series of steps that ascend from Grassmarket to Johnston Terrace. The best-preserved section of the wall can be found by crossing to the south side and climbing the steps of the lane called the Vennel. Here the 16th-century **Flodden Wall** comes in from the east and turns south at Telfer's Wall, a 17th-century extension.

From the northeast corner of the Grassmarket, **Victoria Street,** a 19th-century addition to the Old Town, leads to the George IV Bridge. Shops here sell antiques and designer clothing. ⊠ *Grassmarket, Edinburgh* ⊕ *www.greatergrassmarket.co.uk.*

Lawnmarket. A corruption of "land market," Lawnmarket is the second of the streets that make up the Royal Mile. It was formerly the site of the produce market for the city, with a once-a-week special sale of wool and linen. Now it's home to **Gladstone's Land** and the **Writers' Museum.** At different times the Lawnmarket Courts housed James Boswell, David Hume, and Robert Burns. In nearby Brodie's Close in the 1770s lived the infamous Deacon Brodie, pillar of society by day and a murdering gang leader by night. Robert Louis Stevenson (1850–94) may well have used Brodie as the inspiration for his *Strange Case of Dr. Jekyll and Mr. Hyde.* ⊠ *Between Castlehill and High St., Old Town.*

QUICK BITE

✕ **Jolly Judge.** Several atmospheric pubs and restaurants bustle on this section of the Royal Mile. Try the friendly Jolly Judge, where firelight brightens the dark-wood beams and a mixed crowd of university professors and students sip ale and eat light lunches of soup, pasta, or baked potatoes. ⊠ *7 James Ct., Old Town* ☎ *0131/225–2669* ⊕ *www.jollyjudge.co.uk.*

FAMILY **Museum of Childhood.** Even adults tend to enjoy this cheerfully noisy museum—a cacophony of childhood memorabilia, vintage toys, antique dolls, and fairground games such as "Sweeney Todd." There are also a reconstructed schoolroom, street scene, a fancy-dress party, and a nursery. The museum claims to have been the first in the world devoted solely to the history of childhood. It's two blocks past the North Bridge–South Bridge junction on High Street. ⊠ *42 High St., Old Town* ☎ *0131/529–4142* ⊕ *www. edinburghmuseums.org.uk* 🖃 *Free* ⊗ *Mon.–Sat. 10–5, Sun. noon–5.*

Museum of Edinburgh. A must-see if you're interested in the details of Old Town life, this house dating from 1570 is home to a fascinating museum of local history, displaying Scottish pottery and Edinburgh silver and glassware, in addition to curios such as Greyfriars Bobby's dog collar. The bright yellow building, revamped after an £800,000 renovation in 2012, is also home to one of the most important artifacts in Scottish history—the National Covenant, signed by Scotland's Presbyterian leadership in 1639. This "profession of faith" was in defiance of a new, reformed liturgy imposed by King Charles I of England and ignited decades of civil war and unrest in Scotland. The museum does a good job of putting this complex history into perspective. ⊠ *142 Canongate, Old Town* ☎ *0131/529–4143* ⊕ *www.edinburghmuseums.org.uk* 🖃 *Free* ⊗ *Sept.–July, Mon.–Sat. 10–5; Aug., Mon.–Sat. 10–5, Sun. noon–5.*

> ### GRASSMARKET GALLOWS
>
> Grassmarket's history is long and gory. The **cobbled cross** at the east end marks the site of the town gallows. Among those hanged here were many 17th-century Covenanters, members of the Church of Scotland who rose up against Charles I's efforts to enforce Anglican or "English" ideologies on the Scottish people. Judges were known to issue the death sentence for these religious reformers with the words, "Let them glorify God in the Grassmarket."

National Library of Scotland. Founded in 1689, the library has a superb collection of books and manuscripts on the history and culture of Scotland and also mounts regular exhibitions. Genealogists investigating family trees come here, and amateur family sleuths will find the staff helpful in their research. ⊠ *George IV Bridge, Old Town* ☎ *0131/623–3700* ⊕ *www.nls.uk* 🖃 *Free* ⊗ *Mon., Tues., Thurs., and Fri. 9:30–8:30, Wed. 10–8:30, Sat. 9:30–1. Exhibitions weekdays 10–8, Sat. 10–5, Sun. 2–5.*

Parliament House. This was the seat of Scottish government until 1707, when the governments of Scotland and England were united, 104 years after the union of the two crowns. Partially hidden by the bulk of the High Kirk of St. Giles, it now houses the Supreme Law Courts of Scotland. Interesting exhibits are displayed under the hammer-beam roof of cavernous Parliament Hall. ⊠ *11 Parliament Sq., Old Town* ☎ *0131/225–2595* ⊕ *www.scotcourts.gov.uk* 🖃 *Free* ⊗ *Weekdays 10–4.*

Princes Street Gardens. These beautifully manicured gardens, directly overlooked by Edinburgh Castle, are just a few steps but a world away from the hyperactivity of Princes Street. The 38-acre park, which is divided by Princes Street into the East and West Gardens, was first laid out in the 1760s, on marshland created by the draining of a (long since vanished) loch. Among its flower beds are imaginative planted displays (check out the "clock" planted in commemoration of Edinburgh Zoo's centenary in 2013). There's also a children's play area and a small café. ⊠ *Princes St., Old Town* ☎ *Free* ⊘ *Apr., daily 7–7; May and Sept., daily 7–8; June–Aug., daily 7–10; Oct.–Mar., daily 7–6* Ⓜ *Princes St.*

Scotch Whisky Experience. Transforming malted barley and spring water into one of Scotland's most important exports is the subject of this popular museum. Although the process is not exactly packed with drama, the center manages an imaginative presentation that you take in while riding in low-speed barrel cars. Explore Scotland's diverse whisky regions and the flavors they impart. Sniff the various aromas and decide whether you like fruity, sweet, or smoky, and afterward experts will help you select your perfect dram. Your guide will then allow you access to a vault containing the Diageo Claive Vidiz Scotch Whisky Collection, the world's largest collection of Scotch whiskies. Premium tours (£25–£60) include such extras as a special crystal tasting glass to keep, or a full Scottish food tasting. ⊠ *354 Castlehill, Old Town* ☎ *0131/220–0441* ⊕ *www.whisky-heritage.co.uk* ☎ *£14* ⊘ *Tours daily 10:20–5.*

Writers' Museum. Down a close off Lawnmarket is the 1662 Lady Stair's House, a fine example of 17th-century urban architecture. Inside, the Writers' Museum evokes Scotland's literary past with such exhibits as the letters, possessions, and original manuscripts of Sir Walter Scott, Robert Louis Stevenson, and Robert Burns. The Stevenson collection is particularly compelling. ■ **TIP→ Free tours of the collection are offered Thursdays and Saturdays at 1 and 3.** ⊠ *Lady Stair's Close, Old Town* ☎ *0131/529–4901* ⊕ *www.edinburghmuseums.org.uk* ☎ *Free* ⊘ *Sept.– July, Mon.–Sat. 10–5; Aug., Mon.–Sat. 10–5, Sun. noon–5.*

NEW TOWN

It was not until the Scottish Enlightenment, a civilizing time of expansion in the 1700s, that the city fathers decided to break away from the Royal Mile's rocky slope and create a new Edinburgh below the castle. This was to become the New Town, with elegant squares, classical facades, wide streets, and harmonious proportions. Clearly, change had to come. At the dawn of the 18th century, Edinburgh's unsanitary conditions—primarily a result of overcrowded living quarters—were becoming notorious. The well-known Scottish fiddle tune "The Flooers (flowers) of Edinburgh" was only one of many ironic references to the capital's unpleasant environment.

To help remedy this sorry state of affairs, in 1767 James Drummond, the city's lord provost (the Scottish term for mayor), urged the town council to hold a competition to design a new district for Edinburgh. The winner was an unknown young architect named James Craig (1744–95). His plan called for a grid of three main east–west streets, balanced at either end by two grand squares. These streets survive today, though some of the buildings that line them have been altered by later development. Princes Street is the southernmost, with Queen Street to the north and George Street as the axis, punctuated by St. Andrew and Charlotte squares. A look at the map will reveal a geometric symmetry unusual in Britain. Even the Princes Street Gardens are balanced by the Queen Street Gardens, to the north. Princes Street was conceived as an exclusive residential address, with an open vista facing the castle. It has since been altered by the demands of business and shopping, but the vista remains.

The New Town was expanded several times after Craig's death and now covers an area about three times larger than Craig envisioned. Indeed, some of the most elegant facades came later and can be found by strolling north of the Queen Street Gardens.

TOP ATTRACTIONS

Georgian House. The National Trust for Scotland has furnished and decorated this house in period style to show the elegant domestic arrangements of an affluent family of the late 18th century. The hallway was designed to accommodate sedan chairs, in which 18th-century grandees were carried through the streets. ✉ *7 Charlotte Sq., New Town* ☎ *0131/226–3318* ⊕ *www.nts.org.uk/visits* ✉ *£7* ⊙ *Late Mar.–June, Sept., and Oct., daily 10–5; July and Aug., daily 10–6; Nov., daily 11–4; last admission 45 mins before closing* Ⓜ *Princes St.*

Fodor's Choice
★
National Gallery of Scotland. Opened to the public in 1859, the National Gallery presents a wide selection of paintings from the Renaissance to the postimpressionist period within a grand neoclassical building. Most famous are the old-master paintings bequeathed by the Duke of Sutherland, including Titian's *Three Ages of Man*. Many masters are here: works by Velázquez, El Greco, Rembrandt, Goya, Poussin, Turner, Degas, Monet, and Van Gogh, among others, complement a fine collection of Scottish art, including Sir Henry Raeburn's *Reverend Robert Walker Skating on Duddingston Loch* and other works by Ramsay, Raeburn, and Wilkie. The Weston Link connects the National Gallery of Scotland to the Royal Scottish Academy and includes a restaurant, bar, café, shop, and information center. ✉ *The Mound, New Town* ☎ *0131/624–6200* ⊕ *www.nationalgalleries.org* ✉ *Free* ⊙ *Fri.–Wed. 10–5, Thurs. 10–7* Ⓜ *Princes St.*

OFF THE
BEATEN
PATH
Royal Botanic Garden Edinburgh. Britain's largest rhododendron and azalea gardens are part of this 70-acre garden just north of the city center. An impressive Chinese garden has the largest collection of wild-origin Chinese plants outside China. There's a cafeteria, a visitor center with exhibits exploring biodiversity, and a fabulous gift shop selling plants, books, and gifts. Handsome 18th-century Inverleith House hosts art exhibitions. Don't miss the soaring palms in the glass-domed Temperate House and the steamy Tropical Palm House. The hilly rock garden and stream are magical on a sunny day. Daily tours (£5) take place daily from April to October, and you can book a private tour including afternoon tea (£45 for two people) at any time. Take a taxi to the garden, or ride Bus 8 from North Bridge, Bus 27 from Princes Street, or Bus 23 from Hanover Street. To make the 20-minute walk from the New Town, take Dundas Street (the continuation of Hanover Street) and turn left at the clock tower onto Inverleith Row. ✉ *23 Inverleith Row, Inverleith* ☎ *0131/552–7171* ⊕ *www.rbge.org.uk* ✉ *Free; Glasshouses £4.50* ⊙ *Nov.–Jan., daily 10–4; Feb. and Oct., daily 10–5; Mar.–Sept., daily 10–6. Last admission to Glasshouses 1 hr before closing.*

A GOOD WALK IN THE NEW TOWN

Start your walk on the Mound, the sloping street that joins the Old and New towns. Two museums immediately east of this great linking ramp, the National Gallery of Scotland and the Royal Scottish Academy, are the work of William Playfair (1789–1857), an architect whose neoclassical buildings contributed greatly to Edinburgh's title: the Athens of the North.

At the foot of the Mound is the city's most famous thoroughfare, Princes Street, the humming center of modern-day Edinburgh. Residents lament the disappearance of the dignified old shops that once lined this street; now a long sequence of chain stores has replaced them, although there is still a grand vista of the castle to the south. A block north is George Street, another row of shops, then one block farther lies Queen Street and the grand National Portrait Gallery.

The essence of the New Town spirit survives in Charlotte Square, at the west end of George Street, and especially in the beautiful Georgian House and West Register House. To explore further, choose your own route northward, down to the wide and elegant streets centering on Moray Place, a fine example of an 1820s development.

Scott Monument. What appears to be a Gothic cathedral spire chopped off and planted in the east end of the Princes Street Gardens is Scotland's tribute to one of its most famous sons, Sir Walter Scott, the author of *Ivanhoe, Waverley,* and many other novels and poems. The 200-foot-high monument, built in 1844, is centered on a marble statue of Scott and his favorite dog, Maida. It's worth taking the time to explore the immediate area, including Princes Street Gardens, one of the prettiest city parks in Britain. Here is the famous **monument to David Livingstone,** whose African meeting with H. M. Stanley is part of Scots–American history. ⊠ *Princes St., New Town* ☎ *0131/529–4068* ⊕ *www. edinburghmuseums.org.uk* 🖾 *£4* ⊙ *Apr.–Sept., daily 10–7; Oct.–Mar., daily 10–4. Last admission 30 mins before closing* Ⓜ *Princes St.*

OFF THE BEATEN PATH

Scottish National Gallery of Modern Art. This handsome former school building, close to the New Town, displays paintings and sculptures by Pablo Picasso, Georges Braque, Henri Matisse, and André Derain, among others. The gallery houses an excellent restaurant in the basement and a lavender-filled garden. Across the street in a former orphanage is the **Gallery of Modern Art Two** (formerly the Dean Gallery), which has Scots–Italian Sir Eduardo Paolozzi's intriguing re-created studio and towering sculpture *Vulcan.* Excellent temporary exhibitions (some of which are free) change out several times a year; recent highlights include Roy Lichtenstein's pop art and a retrospective on the mind-blowing pencil drawings of M.C. Escher. ⊠ *Belford Rd., Dean Village* ☎ *0131/624–6200* ⊕ *www.nationalgalleries.org* 🖾 *Free; special exhibitions £7–£10* ⊙ *Daily 10–5.*

Scottish National Portrait Gallery. A magnificent red-sandstone Gothic building dating from 1889 houses this must-see institution. Conceived as a gift to the people of Scotland, the gallery is organized under five broad themes: Reformation, Enlightenment, Empire, Modernity, and Contemporary. The refurbished complex features a photography gallery, a gallery for contemporary art, and a fancy glass elevator. The 2011 renovation saw the addition of 17 exhibition spaces. Each focuses on various aspects of Scottish history and life, including "The Visual Culture of the Jacobite Cause" and "Playing for Scotland: The Making of Modern Sport," plus excellent temporary exhibitions. ⊠ *1 Queen St., New Town* ☎ *0131/624–6200* ⊕ *www.nationalgalleries.org* 🖅 *Free* 🕙 *Fri.–Wed. 10–5, Thurs. 10–7* Ⓜ *St. Andrew Sq.*

WORTH NOTING

Calton Hill. Robert Louis Stevenson's favorite view of his beloved city was from the top of this hill. The architectural styles represented by the extraordinary collection of monuments here include mock Gothic—the Old Observatory, for example—and neoclassical. Under the latter category falls the monument by William Playfair (1789–1857) designed to honor his talented uncle, the geologist and mathematician John Playfair (1748–1819), as well as his cruciform **New Observatory.** The piece that commands the most attention, however, is the so-called **National Monument,** often referred to as "Scotland's Disgrace." Intended to mimic Athens's Parthenon, this monument to the dead of the Napoleonic Wars was started in 1822 to the specifications of a design by Playfair. But in 1830, only 12 columns later, money ran out, and the facade became a monument to high aspirations and poor fund-raising. The tallest monument on Calton Hill is the 100-foot-high **Nelson Monument,** completed in 1815 in honor of Britain's naval hero Horatio Nelson (1758–1805); you can climb its 143 steps for sweeping city views. The **Burns Monument** is the circular Corinthian temple below Regent Road. Devotees of Robert Burns may want to visit one other grave—that of Mrs. Agnes McLehose, or "Clarinda," in the Canongate Graveyard. ⊠ *Bounded by Leith St. to the west and Regent Rd. to the south, New Town* ☎ *0131/556–2716* ⊕ *www.edinburghmuseums.org.uk* 🖅 *Nelson Monument £4* 🕙 *Nelson Monument Apr.–Sept., Mon.–Sat. 10–7, Sun. noon–5; Oct.–Mar., Mon.–Sat. 10–3* Ⓜ *St. Andrew Sq.*

Charlotte Square. At the west end of George Street is the New Town's centerpiece—an 18th-century square with one of the proudest achievements of Robert Adam, Scotland's noted neoclassical architect. On the north side, Adam designed a palatial facade to unite three separate town houses of such sublime simplicity and perfect proportions that architects come from all over the world to study it. Happily, the Age of Enlightenment grace notes continue within, as the center town house is now occupied by the **Georgian House** museum. ⊠ *West end of George St., New Town* Ⓜ *Princes St.*

OFF THE BEATEN PATH

Edinburgh Zoo. Children love to visit the some 1,000 animals that live in Edinburgh Zoo, especially the star attractions: two giant pandas, Tian Tian and Yang Gaung ("Sweetie" and "Sunshine" in English). ■ TIP➡ **Free 15-minute panda-viewing sessions must be booked in advance.** The ever-popular Penguin Parade begins at 2:15 (but since penguin participation is totally voluntary, the event is unpredictable). Also a surefire hit with kids is the Koala Territory, where you can get up close to the zoo's four koalas—including Yoonarah, born in 2014, the first ever British-born koala. You can even handle some of the zoo's tamer animals from April to September. The zoo spreads over an 80-acre site on the slopes of Corstorphine Hill. Take buses 12, 26, or 31. ⊠ *Corstorphine Rd., 3 miles west of city center, Corstorphine* ☎ *0131/334–9171* ⊕ *www.edinburghzoo.org.uk* 🎫 *£17* ⊙ *Apr.–Sept., daily 9–6; Oct. and Mar., daily 9–5; Nov.–Feb., daily 9–4:30.*

George Street. With its upscale shops and handsome Georgian frontages, this is a more pleasant, less crowded street for wandering than Princes Street. The **statue of King George IV**, at the intersection of George and Hanover Streets, recalls the visit of George IV to Scotland in 1822. He was the first British monarch to do so since King Charles II, in the 17th century. By the 19th century, enough time had passed since the Jacobite uprising of 1745 for Scotland to be perceived at Westminster as being safe enough for a monarch to visit.

The ubiquitous Sir Walter Scott turns up farther down the street. It was at a grand dinner in the **Assembly Rooms,** between Hanover and Frederick Streets, that Scott acknowledged having written the Waverley novels (the name of the author had hitherto been a secret, albeit a badly kept one). You can meet Scott once again, in the form of a plaque just downhill, at 39 Castle Street, his Edinburgh address before he moved to Abbotsford, in the Borders region, where he died in 1832. ⊠ *Between Charlotte and St. Andrew Sqs., New Town* Ⓜ *Andrew Sq., Princes St.*

Moray Place. With its "pendants" of Ainslie Place and Randolph Crescent, Moray Place was laid out in 1822 by the Earl of Moray. From the start the homes were planned to be of particularly high quality, with lovely curving facades, imposing porticos, and a central secluded garden reserved for residents. ⊠ *Between Charlotte Sq. and Water of Leith, New Town.*

The Mound. This rising street originated from the need for a dry-shod crossing of the muddy quagmire left behind when Nor' Loch, the body of water below the castle, was drained (the railway now cuts through this area). Work is said to have been started by a local tailor, George Boyd, who tired of struggling through the mud en route to his Old Town shop. The building of a ramp was under way by 1781, and by the time of its completion, in 1830, "Geordie Boyd's mud brig," as it was first known, had been built up with an estimated 2 million cartloads of earth dug from the foundations of the New Town. ⊠ *From Princes St. to George IV Bridge, New Town* Ⓜ *Princes St.*

Princes Street. The south side of this well-planned street is occupied by the well-kept Princes Street Gardens, which act as a wide green moat to the castle on its rock. The north side is now one long sequence of chain stores with unappealing modern fronts apart from the handsome Victorian facade that holds Jenners department store. ⊠ *Waterloo Pl. to Lothian Rd., New Town* Ⓜ *Princes St., West End–Princes St.*

Register House. Scotland's first custom-built archives depository, Register House, designed by the great Robert Adam, was partly funded by the sale of estates forfeited by Jacobite landowners after their last rebellion in Britain (1745–46). Work on the Regency-style building, which marks the end of Princes Street, started in 1774. The statue in front

CLOSE UP

Ancestor Hunting

Are you a Cameron or a Campbell, Mackenzie or Macdonald? If so, you may be one of the more than 25 million people of Scottish descent around the world. It was the Highland clearances of the 18th and 19th centuries, in which tenant farmers were driven from their homes and replaced with sheep, that started the mass emigration to North America and Australia. Before or during a trip, you can do a little genealogical research or pursue your family tree more seriously.

VisitScotland (⊕ *www.visitscotland. com/about/ancestry*) has information about clans and surnames, books, and family-history societies. At the Register House, the ScotlandsPeople Centre (⊕ *www.scotlandspeople.gov.uk*) is the place to dip into the past or conduct in-depth genealogical research.

Willing to pay for help? Companies such as Scottish Ancestral Trail (⊕ *www.scottish-ancestral-trail. co.uk*) do the research and plan a trip around your family history. Throughout Scotland, you can check bookstores for information and visit clan museums and societies.

2

is of the first Duke of Wellington (1769–1852). The recently installed **ScotlandsPeople Centre** lets you conduct genealogical research. Access to public records and the library is £15 per day. ⊠ *2 Princes St., New Town* ☎ *0131/314–4300* ⊕ *www.nrscotland.gov.uk* 🎫 *Free* ☉ *Weekdays 9–4:30* Ⓜ *Princes St.*

QUICK
BITES

Café Royal. This high-end café serves good Scottish lagers and ales, and hearty Scottish bistro-style lunch items—sausage and mash, pies, burgers, haggis, neeps and tatties, or, the house special, a rich fish stew. The 18th-century building has bags of character, with ornate tiles, stained-glass windows and—allegedly—its own ghost. ⊠ *19 W. Register St., New Town* ☎ *0131/556–1884* ⊕ *www.caferoyaledinburgh.co.uk* Ⓜ *Princes St.*

Royal Scottish Academy. Worth visiting for a look at the imposing, neoclassic architecture, this William Playfair–designed structure hosts temporary art exhibitions. The underground Weston Link connects the museum to the National Gallery of Scotland. ⊠ *The Mound, New Town* ☎ *0131/225–6671* ⊕ *www.royalscottishacademy.org* 🎫 *Free* ☉ *Mon.– Sat. 10–5, Sun. noon–5* Ⓜ *Princes St.*

Waterloo Place. The fine neoclassical architecture on this street was designed as a piece by Archibald Elliot (d. 1823) in 1815. Waterloo Place extends over Regent Bridge, bounded by the 1815 **Regent Arch,** a simple, triumphal Corinthian-column war memorial at the center of Ionic screens bordering the bridge. ⊠ *Eastern extension of Princes St., New Town* Ⓜ *Princes St.*

CLOSE UP

Leith, Edinburgh's Seaport

On the south shore of the Firth of Forth, Leith was a separate town until it merged with the city in 1920. After World War II and up until the 1980s, the declining seaport had a reputation for poverty and crime. In recent years, however, it has been revitalized with the restoration of commercial buildings as well as the construction of new luxury housing, bringing a buzz of trendiness. All the docks have been redeveloped; the Old East and West docks are now the administrative headquarters of the Scottish Executive. Plans are afoot to make the docks a hub of renewable-energy industries.

In earlier times, Leith was the stage for many historic happenings. In 1560 Mary of Guise, the mother of Mary, Queen of Scots, ruled Scotland from Leith; her daughter landed in Leith the following year to embark on her infamous reign. A century later, Cromwell led his troops to Leith to root out Scottish royalists. An arch of the Leith Citadel reminds all of the Scots' victory. Leith also prides itself on being a "home of golf," because official rules to the game were devised in 1744 in what is today Links Park. The rolling green mounds here hide the former field and cannon sites of past battles.

LEITH

Just north of the city is Edinburgh's port, a place brimming with seafaring history and undergoing a slow revival after years of postwar neglect. It may not be as pristine as much of modern-day Edinburgh, but there are plenty of cobbled streets, dockside buildings, and bobbing boats to capture your imagination. Here along the lowest reaches of the Water of Leith (the river that flows through town), you'll find plenty of shops, pubs, and restaurants. Leith's major attraction is the former royal yacht, *Britannia*, moored outside the huge Ocean Terminal shopping mall. Reach Leith by walking down Leith Street and Leith Walk, from the east end of Princes Street (20 to 30 minutes), or take Lothian Bus 22 (Britannia Ocean Drive, Leith).

Britannia. Moored on the waterfront at Leith, Edinburgh's port north of the city center, is the former royal yacht, *Britannia*, launched in Scotland in 1953 and now retired to her home country. The royal apartments and the more functional engine room, bridge, galleys, and captain's cabin are all open to view. The land-based visitor center within the huge Ocean Terminal shopping mall has exhibits and photographs about the yacht's history. ⊠ *Ocean Terminal, Leith* ☎ *0131/555–5566* ⊕ *www. royalyachtbritannia.co.uk* 🎫 *£14* ⊘ *Apr.–Sept., daily 9:30–4:30; Oct., daily 9:30–4; Nov.–Mar., daily 10–3:30.*

HAYMARKET

West of the Old Town and south of the West End is Haymarket, a district with its own down-to-earth character and well-worn charm. It offers varied shopping and dining options that become more upmarket as you head toward the West End and Leith.

WEST END

Handsome Georgian town houses give this neighborhood a dignified feel. People head here for the small boutiques and cafés, as well as the wide range of cultural venues.

SOUTH SIDE

This residential district offers a peek at the comings and goings of regular Edinburghers. Here you'll find lots of affordable restaurants and B&Bs for cost-conscious visitors.

WHERE TO EAT

Edinburgh's eclectic restaurant scene has attracted a brigade of well-known chefs, including the award-winning trio of Martin Wishart, Tom Kitchin, and Paul Kitching. They and dozens of others have abandoned the tried-and-true recipes for more adventurous cuisine. Of course, you can always find traditional fare, which usually means the Scottish-French style that harks back to the historical "Auld Alliance" of the 13th century. The Scottish element is the preference for fresh and local foodstuffs; the French supply the sauces. In Edinburgh you can sample anything from Malaysian *rendang* (a thick, coconut-milk stew) to Kurdish kebabs, while the long-established French, Italian, Chinese, Pakistani, and Indian communities ensure that the majority of the globe's most treasured cuisines are well represented. *Use the coordinate (✠ B2) at the end of each listing to locate a site on the corresponding map.*

PRICES AND HOURS

It's possible to eat well in Edinburgh without spending a fortune. Multicourse prix-fixe options are common, and almost always less expensive than ordering à la carte. Even at restaurants in the highest price category, you can easily spend less than £30 per person. People tend to eat later in Scotland than in England—around 8 pm on average—or rather they finish eating and then drink on in leisurely Scottish fashion.

WHAT IT COSTS IN POUNDS			
	$	$$	$$$	$$$$
Restaurants	Under £15	£15–£19	£20–£25	Over £25

Restaurant prices are the average cost of a main course at dinner or, if dinner is not served, at lunch.

OLD TOWN

The most historic part of the city houses the grander restaurants that many people associate with this city. It is also home to some of Edinburgh's oldest pubs, which serve informal meals.

$$ ✕ **Angels with Bagpipes.** The name may amuse or bemuse you, but there's
MODERN BRITISH   no doubt this relaxed spot with windows overlooking the Royal Mile provides good-value, refined dining. Within the 16th-century building,

the understated decor includes a sculptural centerpiece of an angel with bagpipes copied from a carving in nearby St. Giles Cathedral. Menus are straightforward and not overlong, the service is slick, and the atmosphere is warm. Seafood and game dominate, with dishes such as salmon with salsa verde and quinoa. For the best value, opt for the seasonal lunch menu, available between noon and 6, with two courses for £155 and three for £19. [$] *Average main: £19* ✉ *343 High St., Old Town* ☎ *0131/220–1111* 🌐 *www.angelswithbagpipes.co.uk* ✥ *F4.*

$ INTERNATIONAL

🍴 **Checkpoint.** Originally run as a pop-up during the Festival Fringe, this super-cool café-bar settled down to a permanent home in 2015. The coffee is sensational, but the comfort food is as much of a draw. Go for an enormous bowl of chicken and ginger soup, or perhaps lentils with pesto and Parmesan, accompanied by fresh bread and homemade hummus. Louisiana-style po' boys are given a Scottish twist, with such combos as lobster and pork scratchings or caponata (eggplant) and Monterey jack cheese. Checkpoint turns into a bar at night, with a cocktails-and-craft-beers vibe into the small hours. [$] *Average main: £6* ✉ *3 Bristo Pl., Old Town* ☎ *0131/623–3030* ✥ *F5.*

$ ITALIAN Fodor's Choice ★

🍴 **Contini Cannonball.** The name refers to one of the most delightful quirks of Edinburgh's Old Town—the cannonball embedded in the wall outside, supposedly fired at the castle while Bonnie Prince Charlie was in residence. The atmosphere is casual and relaxed, despite the gorgeous art deco dining room, and it's all presided over by Victor and Carina Contini, whose unique brand of Italian–Scottish cuisine has been packing the crowds in for a few years now. The seasonal menus might offer up smoked ham hock with leek macaroni, or warm grouse salad with a dressing made of blackberry and *vincotto*, a sweet condiment from the Puglia region of Italy. [$] *Average main: £13* ✉ *356 Castlehill, Old Town* ☎ *0131/225–1550* 🌐 *www.contini.com/contini-cannonball* ✥ *E5.*

$ VEGETARIAN

🍴 **David Bann.** In the heart of the Old Town, this ultrahip eatery serving vegetarian and vegan favorites attracts young locals with its light, airy, modern dining room. Drinking water comes with mint and strawberries; the sizable and creative dishes include mushroom risotto and Jerusalem artichoke in puff pastry. The food is so flavorful that carnivores may forget they're eating vegetarian, especially with dishes like roast pepper risotto, and beetroot, apple, and blue cheese mousse. [$] *Average main: £12* ✉ *56–58 St. Mary's St., Old Town* ☎ *0131/556–5888* 🌐 *www.davidbann.com* ✥ *G4.*

$ BRITISH

🍴 **Doric Tavern.** Edinburgh's original gastropub offers a languid bistro environment and serves reliable Scottish favorites. The menu offers such hearty comfort food as shepherd's pie with cheesy mashed potato, and salmon fillet with lime and coriander. Try the creamy *cullen skink* soup for a filling, good-value lunchtime choice. The stripped-wood interiors upstairs have been spruced up. **TIP→ The Doric is handy for rail travelers, as it's near Waverley Station.** Sunday lunch includes a traditional roast of Border beef with all the trimmings. [$] *Average main: £14* ✉ *15–16 Market St., Old Town* ☎ *0131/225–1084* 🌐 *www.the-doric.com* ✍ *Reservations essential* ✥ *F4.*

$ MIDDLE EASTERN

🍴 **Hanam's.** Kurdish food may not be as well known as other Middle Eastern cuisines, but the *bayengaan surocrau* (marinated eggplant) and the lamb *tashreeb* (a kind of casserole) will convince you that it's among the best. There's also a great range of shish kebabs and more familiar Lebanese options. The deep-red interiors have a relaxed Middle Eastern vibe. It's possible to smoke a hookah pipe on the heated terrace, and you can bring your own alcohol. Hanam's is a stone's throw from Edinburgh Castle. [$] *Average main: £13* ✉ *3 Johnston Terr., Old Town* ☎ *0131/225–1329* 🌐 *www.hanams.com* ✣ *E5.*

$$ BRITISH

🍴 **Howie's.** The Victoria Street branch of this long-standing chain of neighborhood bistros is a reliable choice for contemporary Scottish fare, with lots of fresh local produce. Alongside the daily specials (including soup) and quality Scottish steaks and salmon creations, there are some nicely inventive vegetarian options (spaghetti with asparagus, wild mushrooms, and roast garlic, for example). Service is friendly, and the decor includes dark-wood furnishings and warm colors—it's understated and informal. The wine list is decent, if somewhat limited, and desserts include a few well-aimed curve balls such as a torte of warm chocolate and beetroot. For value, try the fixed-price lunch (£11 for two courses). There's a grander New Town branch at 29 Waterloo Place. [$] *Average main: £17* ✉ *10–14 Victoria St., Old Town* ☎ *0131/225–1721* 🌐 *www.howies.uk.com* ✣ *F3.*

$$$$ FRENCH

🍴 **La Garrigue.** Edinburgh is blessed with several excellent French bistros, and this is one of the best. Although the modern decor evokes Paris, the food has the rustic flavor of the southern Languedoc region. Fixed-price menus (£28 for two courses or £35 for three) offer regional favorites such as a starter of bouillabaisse with saffron, followed by confit of Guinea fowl with apple and grapes or rabbit stew with chickpea croquette. Try the deliciously floral verbena crème brûlée for dessert—a surprisingly light finale to a heady dining experience. [$] *Average main: £28* ✉ *31 Jeffrey St., Old Town* ☎ *0131/557–3032* 🌐 *www.lagarrigue.co.uk* ✣ *G4.*

$ BISTRO Fodor's Choice ★

🍴 **La Petite Mort.** This exceptionally fine bistro treats its seasonal, regional Scottish flavors with Continental reverence—and the crowds that pack the place to the rafters every night are testament to its success. With flavors like dukkah-spiced steak with Parmesan and red wine sauce, or sea trout with salted samphire and pea velouté, we'll entirely forgive them the indulgence of the name: La Petite Mort is French for, let's say, climax. The wine list is great, the cocktails equally so. The lively, slightly bohemian atmosphere simply adds to the wonderfully *bon viveur* vibe. Reservations are essential on weekends. [$] *Average main: £13* ✉ *32 Valleyfield St., Old Town* ☎ *0131/229–3693* 🌐 *www.lapetitemortedinburgh.co.uk* ⏲ *No lunch weekdays* ✣ *D6.*

$ CAFÉ Fodor's Choice ★

🍴 **Lovecrumbs.** Now this is a bakery with a sweet tooth—Lovecrumbs is a place that joyously, deliciously, unashamedly eschews all other forms of baked goods and focuses on what, for many of a sweet-toothed disposition, *really* matters: cake. Lovecrumbs—who can resist that name?—serves wonderful cakes of all kinds, from pistachio and chocolate to heavenly peanut butter brownies. They also make amazing tarts. Eat in with a cup of coffee, or get them to go. The opening times are rather wonderfully advertised with a caveat of "roughly," but you will know the place by the appreciative crowds at busy times. [$] *Average main:*

£4 ✉ *155 West Port, Old Town* ☎ *0131/629–0626* 🌐 *www.lovecrumbs.co.uk* ⏲ *No dinner* ✍ *Reservations not accepted* ✥ *D5.*

$$ MODERN BRITISH Fodor's Choice ★ 🍴 **Michael Neave Kitchen and Whisky Bar.** Young chef Michael Neave delivers fine food at reasonable prices in his restaurant just off the Royal Mile. Down an old close is this modern edifice with tranquil terrace. The downstairs dining area lacks much warmth, but the whisky bar upstairs sparkles. Quality Scottish produce stars in dishes influenced by Asian and European cuisines: the west coast scallops with celeriac puree, black pudding, and caviar butter makes a wonderful starter. Meaty mains match Aberdeen Angus steaks, Perthshire venison, and roasted duck breast with imaginative sauces and beautifully cooked vegetables. Seafood lovers will enjoy the sea bass with crab and crayfish. Desserts include a delicious pear tarte tatin with whisky marmalade ice cream. **■ TIP→ Two-course express lunches are a bargain at only £8.** [$] *Average main: £16* ✉ *21 Old Fishmarket Close, Old Town* ☎ *0131/226–4747* 🌐 *www.michaelneave.co.uk* ⏲ *Closed Sun. and Mon.* ✥ *F4.*

$ INDIAN 🍴 **Mother India's Café.** Despite its popularity, good Indian food is hard to find in Scotland. Not so at this humble eatery, where the emphasis is on home-style cooking. A good selection of small dishes means you can sample the myriad flavors. The lamb *karahi* (a Pakistani curry made in a wok-like pot) is particularly recommended, as are any of the fish dishes. Two-course set menus start at £22.50 per person. The split-level dining area is smart and contemporary. [$] *Average main: £13* ✉ *3–5 Infirmary St., Old Town* ☎ *0131/524–9801* 🌐 *www.motherindia.co.uk* ✥ *F5.*

$ CAFÉ 🍴 **The Hub.** For soups, sandwiches, and vegetarian-friendly options head to The Hub, housed in the grand Tolbooth Kirk. Its comfy seats, stained-glass windows, and inviting terrace create a relaxing atmosphere to refuel and hear the latest cultural chatter. [$] *Average main: £6* ✉ *Castlehill, Old Town* ☎ *0131/473–2067* 🌐 *www.thehub-edinburgh.com/cafe* ✥ *E4.*

$$$$ SEAFOOD 🍴 **Ondine.** This fabulous seafood restaurant off the Royal Mile is making waves with its expertly prepared dishes from sustainable fishing sources. A wall of windows shines bountiful amounts of sunlight on an attractive monochromatic dining room and an art deco oyster bar. Standout starters include smoked salmon with horseradish cream and salt-and-pepper-squid tempura with a tasty Vietnamese dipping sauce. Other briny delights include the juicy Shetland mussel marinière, Isle of Skye lobster Thermidor, and wild Cornish sea bass. Traditional desserts include a treacle tart with clotted cream. The wine list is strong on old-world whites. [$] *Average main: £26* ✉ *2 George IV Bridge, Old Town* ☎ *0131/226–1888* 🌐 *www.ondinerestaurant.co.uk* ⏲ *Closed Sun.* ✍ *Reservations essential* ✥ *G4.*

$$ FRENCH 🍴 **Petit Paris.** Even in typical Scottish weather it's possible to get a taste of warmer climes at this little bistro on the cobbled Grassmarket, cheerfully decorated with checked tablecloths, copper pots, and bunches of garlic. The staff is predominantly French, and the emphasis is on casual dining, local produce, and home cooking. Try the traditional French mussels in a white wine, butter, and thyme sauce, or sausage and slow-baked rabbit with Dijon-mustard sauce. The restaurant does not accept reservations during August. [$] *Average main: £15* ✉ *38–40 Grassmarket, Old Town* ☎ *0131/226–2442* 🌐 *www.petitparis-restaurant.co.uk* ✥ *F4.*

2

$ ✕**Thai Orchid.** A golden Buddha, beautiful flowers, a traditionally
THAI dressed staff, and spicy cuisine transport you to Thailand, if only for a
few hours. To start, try the *tod mun kao pod* (deep-fried corn cakes with
a sweet-and-sour peanut-and-coriander dip). Tasty main courses include
pla priew wan (monkfish poached with coconut milk) or *pedt Orchid*,
duck stir-fried with mango, chili, garlic, and red peppers. The sticky rice
with coconut milk and mango is a dessert not to be missed. The decor is
contemporary, with banquette seating and lots of natural wood. $ *Average main: £14* ⊠ *5A Johnston Terr., Old Town* ☎ *0131/225–6633*
⊕ *www.thaiorchid.uk.com* ✛ *E5.*

$ ✕**Timberyard.** There are few restaurants that feel so wonderfully fresh
BRITISH and, well, *Edinburgh* as this one. The freshest seasonal ingredients,
Fodor'sChoice mostly sourced from small local producers, go into creating delicious
★ yet unpretentious fare. You might start with a zingy mackerel with
horseradish before moving on to a plate of halibut and mussels with
peas, leeks, and broccoli or perhaps some venison with mushroom and
juniper berries. The dining room, set in a former Victorian warehouse, is
hugely atmospheric, and the crowds are always lively. $ *Average main:
£14* ⊠ *10 Lady Lawson St., Old Town* ☎ *0131/221–1222* ⊕ *www.
timberyard.co* ⊘ *Closd Sun. and Mon.* ⚞ *Reservations essential* ✛ *D5.*

$$ ✕**Wedgwood.** Rejecting the idea that fine dining should be a stuffy
MODERN BRITISH affair, owners Paul Wedgwood and Lisa Channon opened this Royal
Fodor'sChoice Mile gem. The dining space is smart but informal, and the professional
★ staff has mastered the tricky task of giving guests space to relax while
remaining attentive. But Wedgwood's food is the standout. Flavor-
ful local produce and some unusual foraged fronds enliven the taste
buds. Asian, European, and traditional Scottish influences are appar-
ent in dishes such as mackerel with sea arugula gnocchi, and beef fillet
with bone marrow fritter and brandy cream. Save space for seasonal
sweets like "very sticky" toffee pudding with butterscotch, or coco-
nut panna cotta. Consider the great two- and three-course lunch deals
(£13 and £17). $ *Average main: £19* ⊠ *267 Canongate, Old Town*
☎ *0131/558–8737* ⊕ *www.wedgwoodtherestaurant.co.uk* ⚞ *Reserva-
tions essential* ✛ *G4.*

$$$$ ✕**The Witchery.** The hundreds of "witches" who were executed on Cas-
MODERN BRITISH tlehill, just yards from where you'll be seated, are the inspiration for
this outstanding and atmospheric restaurant. The cavernous interior,
complete with flickering candlelight, is festooned with cabalistic insignia
and tarot-card characters. Gilded and painted ceilings reflect the close
links between France and Scotland, as does the menu, which includes
steak tartare, roasted quail with braised endive, shellfish bisque, and
herb-baked scallops. Two-course pre- and posttheater (5:30–6:30 and
10:30–11:30) specials let you sample the exceptional cuisine for just
£19. $ *Average main: £29* ⊠ *Castlehill, Old Town* ☎ *0131/225–5613*
⊕ *www.thewitchery.com* ⚞ *Reservations essential* ✛ *E5.*

NEW TOWN

The New Town, with its striking street plan, ambitious architecture, and professional crowd, has restaurants where you can get everything from a quick snack to a more formal dinner.

$$$ MODERN BRITISH 🍴 **Forth Floor at Harvey Nichols.** Harvey Nichols has become synonymous with chic shopping, and the department store's food hall is no slouch when it comes to style. The decor pulls off the trick of being minimalist without being too severe. Dine in the restaurant for glorious views over Princes Street Gardens and Edinburgh Castle (the alfresco terrace is delightful on a sunny day). The fixed-price menus make excellent use of local and seasonal produce, with plates such as roast duck with chard and blackberries. **TIP→ The slightly more relaxed brasserie has an excellent lunch deal—three courses plus a cocktail for £20.** Afternoon tea here is also a treat, and the Foodmarket has top-notch produce to go. [$] *Average main: £25* ✉ *Harvey Nichols, 30–34 St. Andrew Sq., New Town* ☎ *0131/524–8350* 🌐 *www.harveynichols.com* 🕓 *No dinner Sun. and Mon.* ✍ *Reservations essential* [M] *St. Andrew Sq.* ✣ *F3.*

$$$ BRASSERIE FAMILY Fodor's Choice ★ 🍴 **Galvin Brasserie de Luxe.** This Parisian-style brasserie combines handsome surroundings with first-class cuisine from London brothers Chris and Jeff Galvin. Dapper waiters glide around the cavernous dining area with a central bar and blue banquette seating. The menu stars such classic French dishes as steak tartare, duck confit, and pork cassoulet alongside Scottish staples like Loch Creran oysters, smoked salmon, and haggis. On Sunday, expect hearty, traditional options like slow-roasted beef brisket with trimmings. Desserts include the melt-in-the-mouth meringue *oeuf a la neige* (eggs in snow). The wine list is extensive, and the staff knowledgeable. **TIP→ A decent children's menu makes this a popular spot for families; kids under 11 even eat free at Sunday lunch.** [$] *Average main: £20* ✉ *Waldorf Astoria Edinburgh—The Caledonian, Princes St., New Town* ☎ *0131/222–8988* 🌐 *www.galvinrestaurants.com* [M] *West End-Princes St.* ✣ *D4.*

$ VEGETARIAN 🍴 **Henderson's.** Edinburgh's pioneering canteen-style vegetarian restaurant opened in 1962, long before it was fashionable to serve healthy, meatless creations. The salad bar has more than a dozen different offerings each day, and a massive plateful costs £8. Tasty hot options include Moroccan stew with couscous and moussaka. Live mellow music plays six nights a week, and there's an art gallery as well. Around the corner on Thistle Street is the Bistro, from the same proprietors; it serves snacks, meals, and decadent desserts such as chocolate fondue. Drop by the fabulous deli for picnic supplies, including wonderful organic bread and pastries. [$] *Average main: £9* ✉ *94 Hanover St., New Town* ☎ *0131/225–2131* 🌐 *www.hendersonsofedinburgh.co.uk* 🕓 *Closed Sun.* [M] *St. Andrew Sq.* ✣ *E3.*

$$$ BISTRO Fodor's Choice ★ 🍴 **The Honours.** Run by Martin Wishart, one of Edinburgh's true restaurant grandees, the Honours is a more relaxed (though no less pricey) alternative to his supertrendy, eponymous flagship. You could try a bowl of sweet clam-and-coconut broth, or perhaps a halibut fillet with spinach and potato—but seafood is not what this place is best known for. Meat lovers rave about the steak, from the relatively straightforward (a perfectly charbroiled sirloin or rib eye) to the unusual (Himalayan,

salt-aged rare-breed beef specially raised in Glenarm, Northern Ireland). Desserts are rich and indulgent—try the house sundae with caramelized banana, toffee, and honeycomb. $ *Average main: £25* ⊠ *58a North Castle St., New Town* ☏ *0131/220–2513* ⊕ *www.thehonours.co.uk* ⊙ *Closed Sun. and Mon.* ⌂ *Reservations essential* Ⓜ *Princes St.* ✛ *D4.*

$ | ✕ **La Favorita.** Fix a dinner date with a local, decide on pizza, and there's
ITALIAN | a good chance they'll suggest this place. La Favorita's enduring popularity rests on what it does best: simple, fresh, unpretentious Italian food, served up in a lively (if invariably slammed) dining room. The pizza and calzone are superb; try the Vesuvio, with spicy salami, chicken, and jalapeño peppers, or perhaps a gentler Genovese, with prawns and sun-dried tomatoes on a pesto base. Reservations are advisable on weekends—although if you can't get a table, they also do a roaring trade in takeout. $ *Average main: £12* ⊠ *325–331 Leith Walk, New Town* ☏ *0131/554–2430* ⊕ *www.vittoriagroup.co.uk/lafavorita* ✛ *H1.*

$$$ | ✕ **Le Café St Honoré.** Chef Neil Forbes's quintessentially Parisian-style
FRENCH | café champions sustainable local produce. From the moment you enter the beautifully lighted room, you're transported into the decadently stylish belle époque. The concise menu changes daily; you might start off with a warm salad of scallops, monkfish, chorizo, and pine nuts, followed by Perthshire venison, North Sea hake, or Scotch shepherd's pie. $ *Average main: £20* ⊠ *34 N.W. Thistle Street La., New Town* ☏ *0131/226–2211* ⊕ *www.cafesthonore.com* Ⓜ *Princes St.* ✛ *E3.*

$$$$ | ✕ **L'escargot Bleu.** Anyone still laboring under the misconception that
FRENCH | French cuisine is pretentious should pay a visit to this gem. In one of
Fodor'sChoice | the city's trendiest quarters, this friendly place would make anyone
★ | from France feel at home. The welcome is warm, the stripped wooden floors and period French posters add to a convivial atmosphere that is loud and proud, and the fixed-price menus are as authentic as a whiff of Chanel and a withering stare on the Champs-Élysées. Fixed-price menus include classic dishes such as snails in parsley butter, and beef bourguignon. Follow your nose to the French deli in the basement. ■TIP➜ **You'll struggle to find a better lunch or early evening deal in the city, with two courses for just £13.** $ *Average main: £30* ⊠ *56A Broughton St., New Town* ☏ *0131/557–1600* ⊕ *www.lescargotbleu.co.uk* ⊙ *Closed Sun.* ⌂ *Reservations essential* ✛ *F2.*

$$$$ | ✕ **Number One.** Club-like but unstuffy, this outstanding basement res-
BRITISH | taurant with a thoughtful layout perfect for intimate dining serves the
Fodor'sChoice | best of Scottish seafood and meat within the Edwardian splendor of
★ | the Balmoral Hotel. This is a place for serious special occasions; the regular three-course prix-fixe is £70, or you could choose the chef's six-course tasting menu with amuse-bouche delights, gourmet breads, and exquisite creations highlighting west coast scallops, halibut, monkfish, beef, and lamb for £78. Desserts may include a rich, bitter chocolate and orange soufflé and the lighter, candy-store-inspired hibiscus panna cotta. Service is impeccable and friendly. $ *Average main: £70* ⊠ *Balmoral Hotel, Princes St., New Town* ☏ *0131/557–6727* ⊕ *www. restaurantnumberone.com* ⊙ *No lunch* ⌂ *Reservations essential* Ⓜ *Princes St.* ✛ *F4.*

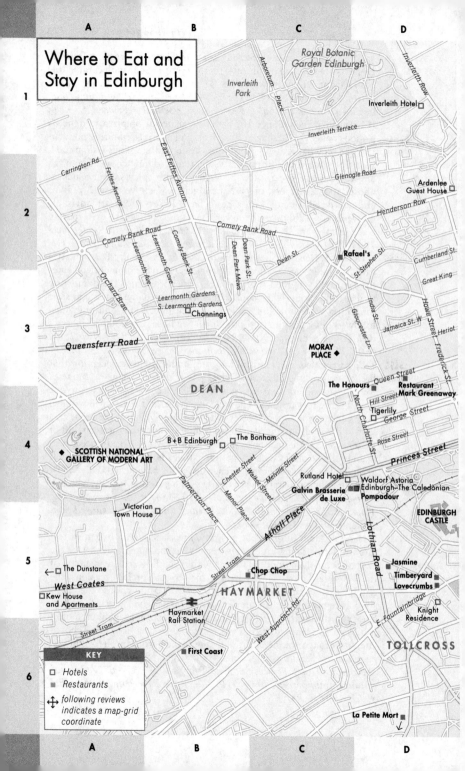

Where to Eat and Stay in Edinburgh

A B C D

1

Royal Botanic
Garden Edinburgh

Inverleith
Park

Inverleith Row

Inverleith Hotel □

Inverleith Terrace

Arboretum Place

2

Carrington Rd.

Fettes Avenue

Glenogle Road

Ardenlee
Guest House □

East Fettes Avenue

Henderson Row

Comely Bank Road

Comely Bank Road

Cumberland St.

Comely Bank St.

Dean St.

Rafael's ■

St. Stephen St.

Great King

Dean Park St.

Learmonth Ave.

Learmonth Grove

Dean Park Mews

India St.

Howe Street

Heriot

3

Orchard Brae

Learmonth Gardens

Jamaica St. W

Frederick St.

S. Learmonth Gardens

Channings □

**MORAY
PLACE** ◆

Queensferry Road

Gloucester Ln.

DEAN

The Honours ■

Queen Street

**Restaurant
Mark Greenaway** ■

Hill Street

North Charlotte St.

Tigerlily ■

4

◆ **SCOTTISH NATIONAL
GALLERY OF MODERN ART**

B + B Edinburgh □

□ The Bonham

George Street

Rose Street

Palmerston Place

Chester Street

Walker Street

Melville Street

Rutland Hotel □

□ Waldorf Astoria ⓒ
Edinburgh–The Caledonian

Princes Street

Victorian
Town House □

Manor Place

**Galvin Brasserie
de Luxe** ■

Pompadour

**EDINBURGH
CASTLE**

Atholl Place

Lothian Road

5

← □ The Dunstane

Jasmine ■

Street Tram

■ Chop Chop

Timberyard ■
Lovecrumbs ■

West Coates

Knight
Residence □

□ Kew House
and Apartments

HAYMARKET

E. Fountainbridge

Haymarket
Rail Station

West Approach Rd.

TOLLCROSS

Street Tram

First Coast ■

6

La Petite Mort ■
↓

A B C D

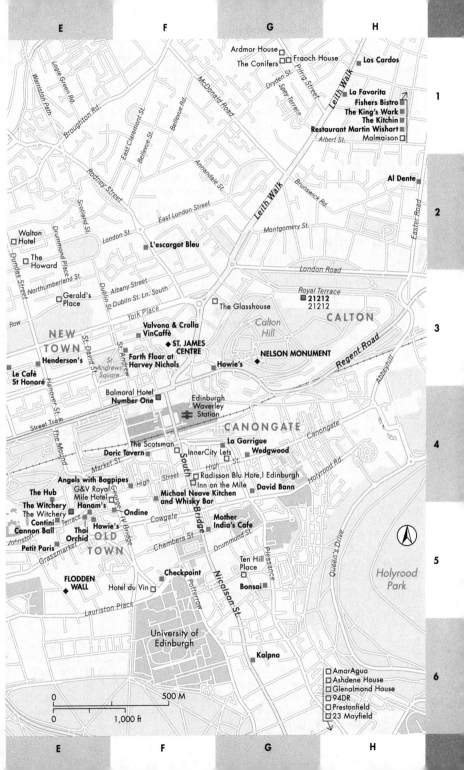

E

Loggie Green Rd.
Warriston Path
Broughton Rd.
Rodney Street
Scotland St.
East Claremont St.
Bellevue St.
Bellevue Rd.

F

McDonald Road
Annandale St.

G

Ardmor House
The Conifers
Fraoch House
Dryden St.
Pilrig Street
Spey Terrace

H

Los Cardos
Leith Walk
La Favorita
Fishers Bistro
The King's Wark
The Kitchin
Restaurant Martin Wishart
Albert St.
Malmaison

1

Al Dente

2

Leith Walk
Brunswick Rd.
East London Street
Montgomery St.
Easter Road

Walton Hotel
The Howard
Dundas Street
Drummond Place
Northumberland St.
Dublin St.
Albany Street
Dublin St. Ln. South
York Place

L'escargot Bleu

London Road

Royal Terrace
21212
21212

3

Gerald's Place
Row
NEW TOWN
Henderson's
Le Café St Honoré
Hanover St.
St. David St.
St. Andrew
Square
St Andrew
The Mound

Valvona & Crolla
VinCaffè
ST. JAMES CENTRE
Forth Floor at Harvey Nichols

The Glasshouse
Calton Hill
CALTON
NELSON MONUMENT
Regent Road
Abbeyhill

Howie's

Balmoral Hotel
Number One
Street Tram

Edinburgh Waverley Station

4

The Scotsman
Doric Tavern
Market St.
High
Angels with Bagpipes
The Hub
G&V Royal Mile Hotel
The Witchery
The Witchery
Hanam's
Contini
Cannon Ball
Thai
Orchid
Howie's
Petit Paris
OLD TOWN
Grassmarket
George IV Bridge
Terrace
Cowgate
Chambers St.
South Bridge

InnerCity Lets
St
La Garrigue
Wedgwood
Radisson Blu Hote,l Edinburgh
Inn on the Mile
Michael Neave Kitchen and Whisky Bar
Ondine
Mother India's Cafe

CANONGATE
Canongate
Holyrood Rd.
David Bann

5

FLODDEN WALL
Checkpoint
Hotel du Vin
Lauriston Place
Potterrow
Nicolson St.
Ten Hill Place
Bonsai
Drummond St.
Pleasance
Queen's Drive

Holyrood Park

6

University of Edinburgh

Kalpna

AmarAgua
Ashdene House
Glenalmond House
94DR
Prestonfield
23 Mayfield

0   500 M
0   1,000 ft

E   F   G   H

$$$$ ✕**Pompadour.** Sophisticated surroundings and sumptuous cuisine make
FRENCH FUSION this restaurant dating from 1925 one of Edinburgh's best spots for
fine dining. London chef–restaurateur brothers Jeff and Chris Galvin
impart their expertise and high standards in the classic French food and
impressive wine list. Expect exquisite dishes that let quality produce
shine: Loch Awe trout with almonds, Cumbrian chateaubriand with
shallot cream, or lemon sole with curry and raisin dressing, for example.
Desserts may include strawberry soufflé or a classic tarte tatin. The
seasonal menu offers the best value, going for £29 for two courses, or
for a splurge, look to the three-course gourmand menu (£68, with the
sommelier's wine pairings £120). $ *Average main: £32* ✉ *Waldorf Asto-
ria Edinburgh—The Caledonian, Princes St., New Town* ☎ *0131/222–
8888* ⊕ *www.thepompadourbygalvin.com* ⊘ *Closed Sun. and Mon. No
lunch* ⟁ *Reservations essential* Ⓜ *West End-Princes St.* ✛ *C4.*

$$$ ✕**Rafael's.** In a pink-hued basement room replete with eccentric trinkets,
SPANISH this quaint restaurant is clearly not in thrall to prevailing trends, and
is all the better for it. Not only does chef/proprietor/all-around-good
guy Rafael Torrubia create affordably priced fixed-price menus with
an Iberian twist, he's also likely to deliver dishes such as a sea bass and
salmon duo with pesto or a wonderfully authentic tortilla with chorizo
to your table himself. Despite his Spanish background, Torrubia's use
of ingredients such as curry in his sauces shows that as well as being a
man of the people, he is also a man of the world. $ *Average main: £24*
✉ *2 Deanhaugh St., New Town* ☎ *0131/332–1469* ⊕ *rafaels-bistro.
wikidot.com* ⊘ *Closed Sun. and Mon. No lunch* ✛ *C2.*

$$$ ✕**Restaurant Mark Greenaway.** Run by a talented chef made famous by a
MODERN BRITISH popular BBC show in 2012, this restaurant offers wonderful seasonal
Fodor's Choice dishes and indulgent desserts. Greenaway's culinary style is perfectly
★ reflected by the elegant Georgian dining room's fireplace and gleaming
brass chandeliers. For an affordable introduction to his cooking, try the
market menu (£18 and £22 for two or three courses). Go à la carte for
dishes like pan-roasted hake fillet with lobster tortellini, or duck confit
with orange and tarragon. The signature desserts include his famed
knot chocolate tart with popping candy. Ask the sommelier for a tour
of the wine cellar, in an old bank vault. $ *Average main: £24* ✉ *69 N.
Castle St., New Town* ☎ *0131/226–1155* ⊕ *www.markgreenaway.com*
⊘ *Closed Sun. and Mon.* ⟁ *Reservations essential* Ⓜ *Princes St.* ✛ *D3.*

$$$$ ✕**21212.** Paul Kitching is one of Britain's most innovative chefs, and
MODERN BRITISH the theatrical dining experience at 21212 delivers surprises galore. In a
Fodor's Choice grand Georgian house, the Michelin-starred restaurant is sumptuously
★ appointed. Belle époque decor and quirky cutlery make this a perfect
destination for couples, who should ask for a romantic alcove window
table. On display behind a large glass screen is a small army of chefs
assembling the intricate dishes—perhaps a touch overreverential, but
thankfully the knowledgeable and enthusiastic staff creates a relaxed
atmosphere in the dining room. On the fixed-price menus (which start
at £55), you can expect creative takes on old classics, such as beef and
black beans with pineapple and chilis, or deconstructed fish-and-chips.
$ *Average main: £55* ✉ *3 Royal Terr., New Town* ☎ *0131/523–1030*
⊕ *www.21212restaurant.co.uk* ⊘ *Closed Sun. and Mon.* ⟁ *Reservations essential* ✛ *G3.*

$$ ✕ **Valvona & Crolla VinCaffè.** Every Scot with a passion for food knows
ITALIAN   Valvona & Crolla, the city's first Italian delicatessen and wine merchant. This eatery of the same name may lack the old-world feel of the original on Elm Row, but the menu created by food writer and cook Mary Contini is as wonderful as you would expect. The fare is relatively simple, but the quality of the ingredients ensures that treats such as the pizza capricciosa, fried calamari, and linguine with crabmeat do nothing to tarnish the brand's reputation. Ⓢ *Average main: £16* ✉ *11 Multrees Walk, New Town* ☎ *0131/557–0088* ⊕ *www.valvonacrolla. co.uk* ⊗ *No dinner Sun.* Ⓜ *St. Andrew Sq.* ✛ *F3.*

HAYMARKET

This area has many restaurants that tend to be more affordable than those in the center of town.

$ ✕ **Chop Chop.** Authentic Chinese cuisine created by skilled chefs and
CHINESE   served in a friendly dining room makes this place especially popular. Since arriving in Edinburgh from northern China, Jian Wang has won many awards. Expect flavorful, robust creations like the trademark dumplings with spiced minced meat or vegetables, spicy squid with garlic, and lamb with cumin. The large eatery has splashes of Chinese red and is suitably relaxed. Ⓢ *Average main: £11* ✉ *248 Morrison St., Haymarket* ☎ *0131/221–1155* ⊕ *www.chop-chop.co.uk* Ⓜ *Haymarket* ✛ *B5.*

$ ✕ **First Coast.** This laid-back bistro, just a few minutes from Haymar-
BRITISH   ket Station, has won a loyal following. Hardwood floors, stone walls, soft blue hues, and seaside paintings add to the coastal theme. Savory temptations include cod fillet with lemongrass broth or pork with polenta cakes. Vegetarians have more choice than the usual one or two options; the linguine with tomato and chili is deliciously piquant. The international wine list is as varied as the daily specials. Lunch and early-evening menus offer good value—any main dish for £10 or three courses for £15.50. Ⓢ *Average main: £14* ✉ *99–101 Dalry Rd., Haymarket* ☎ *0131/313–4404* ⊕ *www.first-coast.co.uk* ⊗ *Closed Sun.* Ⓜ *Haymarket* ✛ *B6.*

WEST END

Even after business hours, the city's commercial center is the place to find a variety of international restaurants.

$ ✕ **Jasmine.** Seafood matched with just the right spices is the main attrac-
CHINESE   tion of this small, friendly Cantonese restaurant. Standout dishes at the
FAMILY   long-established place include steamed sea bass with ginger and spring onions and chicken with peanut sauce. Flickering candles add a relaxing feel to the interior, although the tables are quite closely spaced and the decor is looking a little dated. Prix-fixe lunches, starting at £9.50 for three courses, are a good value. A take-out menu is available. Ⓢ *Average main: £13* ✉ *32 Grindlay St., West End* ☎ *0131/229–5757* ⊕ *www. jasminechinese.co.uk* ✛ *D5.*

SOUTH SIDE

The presence of university professors and students means eateries that are both affordable and interesting.

$ ✕ **Bonsai.** The owners of Bonsai regularly visit Tokyo to research the
JAPANESE casual dining scene, and their expertise is setting a high standard for Japanese cuisine in Edinburgh. The succulent *gyoza* (steamed dumplings) are pliant and tasty, while the wide variety of noodle and teriyaki dishes and the classy sushi balance sweet and sour deliciously. Try the dragon *gaijin-zushi* (inside-out sushi roll with tempura prawns and avocado) or maybe just a simple plate of superfresh and tasty salmon and cucumber maki. The dining area has a bright informality, and the staff affect a casually cool air. $ *Average main: £9* ✉ *46 West Richmond St., South Side* ☎ *0131/668–3847* ⊕ *www.bonsaibarbistro.co.uk* ✢ *G5.*

$ ✕ **Kalpna.** Amid an ordinary row of shops, the facade of this vegetarian
INDIAN Indian restaurant may be unremarkable, but the food is exceptional and
Fodor's Choice a superb value. Try the *dam aloo kashmiri,* a medium-spicy potato dish
★ with a sauce made from honey, pistachios, and almonds. *Bangan mirch masala* has more of a kick, with eggplant and red chili peppers. *Thaali,* a variety of dishes served in bowls on a tray, is particularly appetizing, and a bargain at £13.95. The interior is enlivened by exotic Indian mosaics. Check out the lunchtime buffet for £8. ■**TIP→** **With lots of meatless options on the menu, veggies and vegans flock here.** $ *Average main: £9* ✉ *2–3 St. Patrick Sq., South Side* ☎ *0131/667–9890* ⊕ *www. kalpnarestaurant.com* ☽ *Closed Sun. Jan.–Mar.* ✢ *G6.*

LEITH

Seafood lovers are drawn to the old port of Leith to sample the freshest seafood and to admire the authentic seafaring feel of the docklands.

$ ✕ **Al Dente.** This friendly neighborhood favorite serves authentic Ital-
ITALIAN ian cuisine in homey surroundings. Chef Graziano Spano, from Puglia, is attuned to the freshness and flavors that typify food from the Bel Paese. Fresh pasta and local produce feature prominently. Try the Puglian favorite, *orecchiette* (little-eared pasta) with lamb ragu, or sample classic dishes from the regions of Sardinia, Liguria, Lazio, Emilia-Romagna, and Tuscany. $ *Average main: £12* ✉ *139 Easter Rd., Leith* ☎ *0131/652–1932* ⊕ *www.al-dente-restaurant.co.uk* ☽ *Closed Sun. No lunch Mon.* ⌂ *Reservations essential* ✢ *H2.*

$$ ✕ **Fishers Bistro.** Locals and visitors flock to this laid-back pub-cum-
SEAFOOD bistro down on the waterfront, and to its sister restaurant, **Fishers in the City,** at 58 Thistle Street in the New Town. The menu is much the same, but Fishers Leith has the better reputation and vibe. Bar meals are served, although for more comfort and elegance sit in the cozy, blue-walled dining room. Seafood is the specialty—have the Loch Fyne oysters and queenie scallops from Tarbert if they're on offer, or maybe the whole Aberdeen sole with wild garlic and basil if they're not. Watch for the daily specials: perhaps a seafood or vegetarian soup followed by huge North African prawns. It's wise to reserve ahead. $ *Average main: £16* ✉ *1 The Shore, Leith* ☎ *0131/554–5666* ⊕ *www. fishersbistros.co.uk* ✢ *H1.*

2

$ ╳ **The King's Wark.** Along the shoreline at Leith is a gastropub with a
BRITISH   pleasant atmosphere and quality food that continues to win plaudits. At
lunchtime, the dark-wood bar does a roaring trade in simple fare such
as gourmet burgers, fish cakes, and haggis (traditional or vegetarian),
but in the evening the kitchen ups the ante with such dishes as monkfish and crevette in a bouillabaisse broth. Old stone walls attest to the
building's 15th-century origins. Come Sunday morning to sample the
legendary breakfast menu. $ *Average main: £12* ✉ *36 The Shore, Leith*
☎ *0131/554–9260* ⊕ *www.thekingswark.com* ✛ *H1.*

$$$$ ╳ **The Kitchin.** One of Edinburgh's most perennially popular eateries,
FRENCH   Tom Kitchin's award-winning venture packs in the crowds. It's not
Fodor'sChoice   difficult to see why. Kitchin, who trained in France, runs a tight ship,
★   and his passion for using seasonal and locally sourced produce to his
own creative ends shows no sign of waning. Unfashionable ingredients
such as ox tongue, tripe, and pig's head emerge heroic after Kitchin's
alchemy, and he works his magic equally dexterously on more familiar
elements such as seafood and venison. To sample this rarified culinary
world affordably, try the three-course lunch for £26.50. $ *Average
main: £37* ✉ *78 Commercial Quay, Leith* ☎ *0131/555–1755* ⊕ *thek-
itchin.com* ⊘ *Closed Sun. and Mon.* ☖ *Reservations essential* ✛ *H1.*

$ ╳ **Los Cardos.** Offering tasty Mexican fare, Los Cardos is a superb value
MEXICAN   for those on the move in Leith. There are only a couple of tables, so
takeaway is a likely option. First decide whether you want a burrito,
quesadilla, or soft tacos, then opt for one of many fillings: marinated
steak or chicken, perhaps, or slow-cooked pork. Toppings range from
mild pico de gallo to creamy homemade guacamole with optional
grilled peppers and onions. Many locals—including *Trainspotting*
writer Irvine Welsh—have confessed their addiction to the haggis burrito. $ *Average main: £8* ✉ *281 Leith Walk, Leith* ☎ *0131/555–6619*
⊕ *www.loscardos.co.uk* ✛ *H1.*

$$$$ ╳ **Restaurant Martin Wishart.** Slightly out of town but worth every penny
FRENCH   of the taxi fare, this restaurant's well-known chef woos diners with an
Fodor'sChoice   impeccable and varied menu of beautifully presented, French-influenced
★   dishes. Poached turbot in red wine or roast grouse served with sauce
Albert typify the set menus (£75); but for the full experience, go for
one of the tasting menus (only a tasty smidgen more expensive at £80).
On weekdays, the three-course lunch is £28.50. Reservations are essen-
tial on Friday and Saturday nights. $ *Average main: £75* ✉ *54 The
Shore, Leith* ☎ *0131/553–3557* ⊕ *www.restaurantmartinwishart.co.uk*
⊘ *Closed Sun. and Mon.* ✛ *H1.*

WHERE TO STAY

From stylish boutique hotels to homey B&Bs, Edinburgh has a world-
class array of accommodations to suit every taste. Its status as one of
Britain's most attractive and fascinating cities ensures a steady influx of
visitors, but the wealth of overnight options means there's no need to
compromise on where you stay. Grand old hotels are rightly renowned
for their regal bearing and old-world charm. If your tastes are a little
more contemporary, the city's burgeoning contingent of chic-design

hotels offers an equally alluring alternative. For those on a tighter budget, the town's B&Bs are the most likely choice. If you feel B&Bs can be restrictive, keep in mind that Scots are trusting people—many proprietors provide front-door keys and few impose curfews.

Rooms are harder to find in August and September, when the Edinburgh International Festival and the Festival Fringe take place, so reserve at least three months in advance. Bed-and-breakfast accommodations may be harder to find in December, January, and February, when some proprietors close for a few weeks.

PRICES

Weekend rates in the larger hotels are always much cheaper than midweek rates, so if you want to stay in a plush hotel, come on the weekend. To save money and see how local residents live, stay in a B&B in one of the areas away from the city center, such as Pilrig to the north, Murrayfield to the west, or Sciennes to the south. Public buses can whisk you to the city center in 10 to 15 minutes. *Hotel reviews have been shortened. For full information, visit Fodors.com. Use the coordinate (✛ B2) at the end of each listing to locate a site on the corresponding map.*

WHAT IT COSTS IN POUNDS			
	$	$$	$$$	$$$$
Hotels	Under £100	£100–£160	£161–£220	Over £220

Hotel prices are the lowest cost of a standard double room in high season, including 20% V.A.T.

OLD TOWN

The narrow *pends* (alleys), cobbled streets, and steep hills of the Old Town remind you that this is a city with many layers of history. Medieval to modern, these hotels all are within a stone's throw of the action.

$$$
HOTEL
Fodor's Choice
★

🖼 **Hotel du Vin.** Leave it to one of the United Kingdom's most forward-thinking chains to convert a Victorian-era asylum into this understated luxury property that feels steeped in history and lore despite its contemporary decor and trappings, like the hip bar and restaurant. **Pros:** very unique and historical building; trendy design; lively on-site dining and drinking; great deals off-season. **Cons:** quarter-mile walk to nearest parking; bathtub-in-middle-of-bedroom affectation off-putting to some; neighborhood sometimes noisy. $ *Rooms from: £180* ✉ *11 Bristo Pl., Old Town* ☎ *0131/247–4900* ⊕ *www.hotelduvin.com* ⤳ *37 rooms, 10 suites* ¶⊙¶ *Breakfast* ✛ *F5.*

$$$$
HOTEL
Fodor's Choice
★

🖼 **G&V Royal Mile Hotel.** The daring—and to some tastes garish—delights to be found inside this übertrendy-design hotel contrast with the Gothic surroundings of the Royal Mile, but the hotel pulls it off by being simultaneously chic and welcoming. **Pros:** perfect location; in the thick of the action; as far from staid as you can get. **Cons:** a little Austin Powers in places; some find it hard to relax in such fashion-conscious surrounds. $ *Rooms from: £264* ✉ *1 George IV Bridge, Old Town* ☎ *0131/220–6666* ⊕ *www.quorvuscollection.com* ⤳ *129 rooms, 7 suites* ¶⊙¶ *Breakfast* ✛ *F5.*

2

$$ **The Inn on the Mile.** This chic and welcoming boutique inn could
B&B/INN hardly be more central—some rooms even overlook the Royal Mile.
Fodor's Choice Pros: views of the Royal Mile; lovely staff; great design. Cons: lots
★ of steps and no elevator; sometimes noisy; nearest parking at a pub-
lic lot (three-minute walk). $ *Rooms from: £130* ✉ *82 High St., Old
Town* ☎ *0131/556–9940* ⊕ *www.theinnonthemile.co.uk* ⇆ *9 rooms*
⚏ *Breakfast* ✢ *F4.*

$$ **Knight Residence.** About 10 minutes from the Grassmarket, the Knight
RENTAL is made up of 19 different apartments that offer good value and conve-
FAMILY nient locations. Pros: comfortable apartments; secure location; good for
families needing space and privacy. Cons: lack of staff won't suit everyone; better for stays of two or more nights. $ *Rooms from: £151* ✉ *12
Lauriston St., Old Town* ☎ *0131/622–8120* ⊕ *www.theknightresidence.
co.uk* ⇆ *19 apartments* ⚏ *No meals* ✢ *D5.*

$$$ **Radisson Blu Hotel, Edinburgh.** Built in the late 1980s, this city-center
HOTEL hotel was designed to blend in among the 16th-, 17th-, and 18th-
century buildings on the Royal Mile. Pros: central location; can-do
staff. Cons: expensive breakfast; pricey for what you get. $ *Rooms
from: £189* ✉ *80 High St., Royal Mile, Old Town* ☎ *0131/557–9797*
⊕ *www.radissonblu.co.uk/hotel-edinburgh* ⇆ *238 rooms, 10 suites*
⚏ *Breakfast* ✢ *F4.*

$$$$ **The Scotsman.** A magnificent turn-of-the-20th-century building, with a
HOTEL marble staircase and a fascinating history—it was once the headquarters
of the *Scotsman* newspaper—now houses this modern, luxurious hotel.
Pros: gorgeous surroundings; personalized service. Cons: no air-condi-
tioning; spa can be noisy; could do with some renovation. $ *Rooms
from: £275* ✉ *20 N. Bridge, Old Town* ☎ *0131/556–5565* ⊕ *www.
thescotsmanhotel.co.uk* ⇆ *56 rooms, 13 suites* ⚏ *Breakfast* ✢ *F4.*

$$$ **Ten Hill Place.** This stylish hotel on a quiet backstreet near the Festi-
HOTEL val Theatre is a dependable Old Town choice. Pros: well kept; close to
everything but not in the midst of the brouhaha. Cons: rooms sometimes too dark; (only semifrosted) glass doors on the bathrooms a bit
weird. $ *Rooms from: £168* ✉ *10 Hill Pl., Old Town* ☎ *0131/662–
2080* ⊕ *www.tenhillplace.com* ⇆ *78 rooms* ⚏ *Some meals* ✢ *G5.*

$$$$ **The Witchery.** This lavishly theatrical lodging promises a night to
HOTEL remember. Pros: Gothic drama and intriguing antiques; sumptuous
dining. Cons: sometimes noisy at night; decor a little cluttered; pricey.
$ *Rooms from: £325* ✉ *Castlehill, Royal Mile, Old Town* ☎ *0131/225–
5613* ⊕ *www.thewitchery.com* ⇆ *9 suites* ⚏ *Breakfast* ✢ *E5.*

NEW TOWN

Calton Hill, which offers some of the best views of the city from its
summit, is just one of the reasons to base yourself in the New Town,
filled with gorgeous 18th- and 19th-century architecture.

$$ **Ardenlee Guest House.** An exquisite Victorian-tile floor is one of many
B&B/INN original features at this dependable guesthouse tucked away from the
hustle and bustle of the city center. Pros: family-run establishment; good
value, especially for long-term stays. Cons: few amenities; uphill walk
to the city center; housekeeping sometimes slipshod. $ *Rooms from:*

£100 ⊠9 Eyre Pl., New Town ☎*0131/556–2838* ⊕*www.ardenlee. co.uk* ⟿*9 rooms, 7 with bath* ˡ◎ˡ *Breakfast* ✛ *D2.*

$$$$

HOTEL

Fodor'sChoice

★

⌂ **Balmoral Hotel.** The attention to detail in the elegant rooms—colors were picked to echo the country's heathers and moors—and the sheer élan that has re-created the Edwardian splendor of this grand, former railroad hotel make staying at the Balmoral a special introduction to Edinburgh. **Pros:** big and beautiful building; top-hatted doorman; quality bathroom goodies; top-notch spa. **Cons:** small pool; spa books up fast; restaurants sometimes very busy. Ⓢ *Rooms from: £285* ⊠*1 Princes St., New Town* ☎*0131/556–2414* ⊕*www.roccofortehotels.com/hotels-and-resorts/the-balmoral-hotel* ⟿*168 rooms, 20 suites* ˡ◎ˡ *Breakfast* Ⓜ *Princes St.* ✛ *F4.*

$$

B&B/INN

⌂ **Gerald's Place.** Although he is not a native of the city, Gerald Della-Porta is one of those B&B owners to whom Edinburgh owes so much. **Pros:** the advice and thoughtfulness of the owner; spacious rooms; lovely art. **Cons:** stairs difficult to manage; an uphill walk to the city center; no credit cards. Ⓢ *Rooms from: £140* ⊠*21B Abercromby Pl., Edinburgh* ☎*0131/558–7017* ⊕*www.geraldsplace.com* ⊟*No credit cards* ⟿*2 rooms* ˡ◎ˡ *Breakfast* Ⓜ *St. Andrew Sq.* ✛ *E3.*

$$$

HOTEL

⌂ **The Glasshouse.** Glass walls extend from the 19th-century facade of a former church, foreshadowing the daring interior of one of the city's original boutique hotels. **Pros:** near all the attractions; very modern and stylish. **Cons:** perhaps a little sterile for some; noise from the street sometimes a problem. Ⓢ *Rooms from: £190* ⊠*2 Greenside Pl., New Town* ☎*0131/525–8200* ⊕*www.theglasshousehotel.co.uk* ⟿*65 rooms, 18 suites* ˡ◎ˡ *Breakfast* ✛ *F3.*

$$$

HOTEL

⌂ **The Howard.** This hotel is in a classic New Town building, elegantly proportioned and superbly outfitted. **Pros:** small but grand building; staff's great attitude; special afternoon tea. **Cons:** decor a little tired; noisy neighborhood. Ⓢ *Rooms from: £185* ⊠*34 Great King St., New Town* ☎*0131/557–3500* ⊕*www.thehoward.com* ⟿*18 rooms, 5 suites* ˡ◎ˡ *Some meals* ✛ *E2.*

$$

B&B/INN

⌂ **Inverleith Hotel.** Across from the Royal Botanic Gardens, this renovated Victorian town house has cozy, well-lighted rooms with velour bedspreads, dark-wood furniture, and pale-gold curtains. **Pros:** quiet surroundings; knowledgeable staff; cheap parking at nearby lot (and free weekends). **Cons:** some rooms small; narrow passageways; uphill walk to the city center. Ⓢ *Rooms from: £120* ⊠*5 Inverleith Terr., New Town* ☎*0131/556–2745* ⊕*www.inverleithhotel.co.uk* ⟿*12 rooms, 2 apartments* ˡ◎ˡ *Breakfast* ✛ *D1.*

$$$$

HOTEL

⌂ **Tigerlily.** On hip George Street, this boutique hotel has everything a girl could imagine—bowls of fresh fruit, designer candles, hair straighteners—for a night away from home. **Pros:** chic yet not intimidating; laid-back but efficient staff. **Cons:** no views; sometimes noisy and very busy. Ⓢ *Rooms from: £230* ⊠*125 George St., New Town* ☎*0131/225–5005* ⊕*www.tigerlilyedinburgh.co.uk* ⟿*33 rooms* ˡ◎ˡ *Breakfast* Ⓜ *Princes St.* ✛ *D4.*

2

$$$ HOTEL Fodor'sChoice ★ 🏨 **21212.** In this handsome Royal Terrace town house, the spacious rooms are beautifully designed with an eye for detail: an enormous bed sits on a raised platform facing a stylish seating area with a flat-screen TV. **Pros:** stylish decor and service worthy of a special getaway; above one of Edinburgh's best restaurants; huge beds. **Cons:** pricey add-ons. [$] *Rooms from: £180* ✉ *3 Royal Terr., New Town* ☎ *0131/523–1030* 🌐 *www.21212restaurant.co.uk* 🛏 *4 rooms* 🍴 *No meals* ✥ *G3.*

$$$ HOTEL 🏨 **Waldorf Astoria Edinburgh—The Caledonian.** An imposing block of red sandstone beyond the west end of West Princes Street Gardens, "The Caley" has imposing Victorian decor and beautifully restored interiors. **Pros:** impeccable service; not as pricey as some other grande dame hotels; outstanding restaurants. **Cons:** Internet access extra; expensive parking (£20 per night); no "wow factor" for some. [$] *Rooms from: £191* ✉ *Princes St., New Town* ☎ *0131/222–8888* 🌐 *www.thecaledonian.waldorfastoria.com* 🛏 *241 rooms, 20 suites* 🍴 *Breakfast* [M] *West End-Princes St.* ✥ *D4.*

HAYMARKET

Close to one of the main train stations, Haymarket can make a good base for exploring the city if you're staying in one of the hotels beyond the west end of Princes Street.

$$ HOTEL 🏨 **The Dunstane.** Originally a mid-Victorian town house and now a pleasant boutique hotel, the Dunstane is a stylish and welcoming place to stay—especially if you want to keep away from the noise and bustle of the city center. **Pros:** quiet, residential area; lovely old town-house building; great staff; excellent food. **Cons:** no elevator (and stairs to climb); not near main sights. [$] *Rooms from: £130* ✉ *4 West Coates, Haymarket* ☎ *0131/337–6169* 🌐 *www.dunstane-hotel-edinburgh.co.uk* 🛏 *38 rooms* 🍴 *Breakfast* [M] *Haymarket* ✥ *A5.*

$$$ B&B/INN 🏨 **Kew House and Apartments.** With such sumptuous rooms, you might think that Kew House was a full-service hotel. **Pros:** clean as a whistle; thoughtful touches throughout; close to Water of Leith walk. **Cons:** longish walk to the city center; traffic noise on street side. [$] *Rooms from: £169* ✉ *1 Kew Terr., Haymarket* ☎ *0131/313–0700* 🌐 *www.kewhouse.com* 🛏 *6 rooms, 1 apartment* 🍴 *Breakfast* [M] *Haymarket* ✥ *A5.*

$$ B&B/INN 🏨 **Victorian Town House.** In a leafy crescent, this handsome house once belonged to a cousin of Robert Louis Stevenson, and the celebrated writer would doubtless be happy to lay his head in this good-value B&B. **Pros:** serene surroundings near Water of Leith; gracious staff. **Cons:** no parking nearby; distance from Old Town. [$] *Rooms from: £120* ✉ *14 Eglinton Terr., Haymarket* ☎ *0131/337–7088* 🌐 *www.thevictoriantownhouse.co.uk* 🛏 *3 rooms* 🍴 *Breakfast* [M] *Haymarket* ✥ *B5.*

WEST END

With easy access to some of the city's trendiest shops and cafés, the West End has lodgings that take advantage of the neighborhood's handsome Georgian-style town houses.

$$ ⚏ **B + B Edinburgh.** Standing out along an elegant and tranquil West
B&B/INN End terrace, this excellent B&B is the first Scottish outpost of super-
FAMILY trendy B+B Belgravia in London. **Pros:** fascinating building in tranquil
area; superb views; handy for river walks and central attractions. **Cons:**
no night porter; hint of previous institutional use; small bathrooms.
Ⓢ *Rooms from: £125* ✉ *3 Rothesay Terr., West End* ☎ *0131/225–5084*
⊕ *www.bb-edinburgh.com* ⌥ *27 rooms* ❍| *Breakfast* Ⓜ *West End-
Princes St.* ✛ *B4.*

$$$ ⚏ **The Bonham.** There's a clubby atmosphere throughout this hotel,
HOTEL which carries on a successful, sophisticated flirtation with modernity.
Pros: thorough yet unobtrusive service; excellent restaurant; pleasant
location. **Cons:** few common areas; can feel like a business hotel; needs
upgrading in places. Ⓢ *Rooms from: £215* ✉ *35 Drumsheugh Gardens,
West End* ☎ *0131/226–6050* ⊕ *www.thebonham.com* ⌥ *42 rooms, 6
suites* ❍| *Breakfast; Some meals* Ⓜ *West End-Princes St.* ✛ *B4.*

$$ ⚏ **Channings.** Five Edwardian terraced town houses make up this inti-
HOTEL mate, elegant hotel in an upscale West End neighborhood just minutes
from Princes Street. **Pros:** near Stockbridge shops and eateries; inventive
color schemes; good discounts available online. **Cons:** not all rooms
equally nice; breakfast could be better. Ⓢ *Rooms from: £115* ✉ *12–16 S.
Learmonth Gardens, West End* ☎ *0131/315–2226* ⊕ *www.channings.
co.uk* ⌥ *36 rooms, 5 suites* ❍| *Breakfast* ✛ *B3.*

$$ ⚏ **Rutland Hotel.** This building at the west end of Princes Street is thought
HOTEL to have been the residence of Sir Joseph Lister (1827–1912), who per-
Fodor'sChoice formed the world's first successful surgery carried out under anaesthetic,
★ but no such harsh measures are needed to guarantee a good night's sleep
at his old pad now that it's an acclaimed boutique hotel. **Pros:** friendly
staff; not pretentious; great bar and restaurant. **Cons:** decor possibly
too loud for some. Ⓢ *Rooms from: £160* ✉ *1–3 Rutland St., West End*
☎ *0131/229–3402* ⊕ *www.therutlandhotel.com* ⌥ *12 rooms, 1 apart-
ment* ❍| *Breakfast* Ⓜ *West End-Princes St.* ✛ *D4.*

SOUTH SIDE

The B&Bs and restaurants in this residential area offer good value.

$ ⚏ **AmarAgua.** Four-poster beds, a tranquil location, and bountiful
B&B/INN breakfasts set this Victorian town house B&B apart. **Pros:** quiet setting;
snug rooms; wonderful and varied breakfasts. **Cons:** far from the city
center; minimum two-night stay. Ⓢ *Rooms from: £90* ✉ *10 Kilmaurs
Terr., Newington* ☎ *0131/667–6775* ⊕ *www.amaragua.co.uk* ☾ *Closed
Jan.* ⌥ *5 rooms, 4 with bath* ❍| *Breakfast* ✛ *H6.*

$$ ⚏ **Ashdene House.** On a quiet residential street sits this Edwardian house,
B&B/INN one of the city's best value B&Bs. **Pros:** homemade breads at breakfast;
spacious rooms. **Cons:** not within walking distance of the center; not
good for families with young kids. Ⓢ *Rooms from: £110* ✉ *23 Foun-
tainhall Rd., The Grange* ☎ *0131/667–6026* ⊕ *www.ashdenehouse.com*
⌥ *5 rooms* ❍| *Breakfast* ✛ *H6.*

$$ ⚏ **Glenalmond House.** Longtime hoteliers Jimmy and Fiona Mackie are
B&B/INN well schooled in delighting guests, which makes elegant Glenalmond
House a reliable choice. **Pros:** knowledgeable owners; nice furnishings;

superb breakfasts. **Cons:** smallish bathrooms; a bit of a walk to the New Town. $ *Rooms from: £100* ✉ *25 Mayfield Gardens, South Side* ☎ *0131/668–2392* ⊕ *www.glenalmondhouse.com* ➔ *9 rooms* ⎟◎⎟ *Breakfast* ✦ *H6.*

$$ ⌂ **94DR.** Like owners Paul Lightfoot and John MacEwan—a self-
B&B/INN described "high-octane" couple—94DR reaches for the stars with its stylish decor and contemporary trappings. **Pros:** warm welcome; gay-friendly vibe; smashing breakfast. **Cons:** modern design may not please everyone; a long walk to the city center. $ *Rooms from: £160* ✉ *94 Dalkeith Rd., South Side* ☎ *0131/662–9265* ⊕ *www.94dr.com* ➔ *7 rooms* ⎟◎⎟ *Breakfast* ✦ *H6.*

$$$$ ⌂ **Prestonfield.** The cattle grazing on the hotel's 20-acre grounds let
HOTEL you know that you've entered a different world, even though you're
Fodor'sChoice five minutes by car from the Royal Mile. **Pros:** eccentric grandeur;
★ comfortable beds. **Cons:** slightly haphazard service; brooding decor can look gloomy. $ *Rooms from: £325* ✉ *Priestfield Rd., Prestonfield* ☎ *0131/225–7800* ⊕ *www.prestonfield.com* ➔ *18 rooms, 5 suites* ⎟◎⎟ *Breakfast; Some meals* ✦ *H6.*

$$ ⌂ **23 Mayfield.** A self-styled "boutique guesthouse," 23 Mayfield is a cut
B&B/INN above your average B&B: the Victorian villa features many original elements expertly complemented by dark-wood furniture, lovely artwork, and antiquarian books to create a sumptuous atmosphere. **Pros:** relaxing atmosphere; helpful yet unobtrusive service; gourmet breakfast featuring famed porridge. **Cons:** need to book well in advance. $ *Rooms from: £160* ✉ *23 Mayfield Gardens, South Side* ☎ *0131/667–5806* ⊕ *www.23mayfield.co.uk* ➔ *9 rooms* ⎟◎⎟ *Breakfast* ✦ *H6.*

LEITH

Staying here means you'll be away from the Old Town and New Town sights, but you can find some values—and good restaurants.

$$ ⌂ **Ardmor House.** This excellent guesthouse combines the original fea-
B&B/INN tures of a Victorian home with stylish contemporary furnishings. **Pros:** warm and friendly owners; decorated with great style; gay-friendly environment. **Cons:** a bit out of the way; tiny ground-floor double room. $ *Rooms from: £130* ✉ *74 Pilrig St., Leith* ☎ *0131/554–4944* ⊕ *www. ardmorhouse.com* ➔ *5 rooms* ⎟◎⎟ *Breakfast* ✦ *G1.*

$$ ⌂ **The Conifers.** This small guesthouse in a red-sandstone town house
B&B/INN north of the New Town offers simple, traditionally decorated rooms and warm hospitality. **Pros:** nice mix of old and new; many original fittings; hearty breakfasts. **Cons:** a long walk to the city center; one bathroom not en suite. $ *Rooms from: £120* ✉ *56 Pilrig St., Leith* ☎ *0131/554–5162* ⊕ *www.conifersguesthouse.com* ➔ *4 rooms, 3 with bath* ⎟◎⎟ *Breakfast* ✦ *G1.*

$$ ⌂ **Fraoch House.** This popular option manages to combine a homey
B&B/INN feel and stylish decor without leaning too far in either direction. **Pros:** a warm welcome; great DVD library; free Wi-Fi. **Cons:** uphill walk to the city center. $ *Rooms from: £115* ✉ *66 Pilrig St., Leith* ☎ *0131/554–1353* ⊕ *www.fraochhouse.com* ➔ *9 rooms* ⎟◎⎟ *Breakfast* ✦ *G1.*

$$ HOTEL [H] **Malmaison.** Once a seamen's hostel, Edinburgh's link in the pioneering boutique hotel chain draws a refined clientele. **Pros:** impressive building; elegant feel; great location; good bargains for advance booking. **Cons:** price fluctuates wildly; bar sometimes rowdy at night; a long way from the center of town. [$] *Rooms from: £115* ✉ *1 Tower Pl., Leith* ☎ *0131/468–5000* 🌐 *www.malmaison-edinburgh.com* 🛏 *100 rooms, 9 suites* 🍴 *Breakfast* ✥ *H1.*

NIGHTLIFE AND PERFORMING ARTS

PERFORMING ARTS

Those who think Edinburgh's arts scene consists of just the elegiac wail of a bagpipe and the twang of a fiddle or two will be proved wrong by the hundreds of performing-arts options. The jewel in the crown, of course, is the famed Edinburgh International Festival, which now attracts the best in music, dance, theater, painting, and sculpture from all over the globe during three weeks from mid-August to early September. The *Scotsman* and *Herald,* Scotland's leading daily newspapers, carry listings and reviews in their arts pages every day, with special editions during the festival. Tickets are generally sold in advance; in some cases they're also available from certain designated travel agents or at the door, although concerts by national orchestras often sell out long before the day of the performance.

DANCE

Festival Theatre. Scottish Ballet productions and other dance acts appear at the Festival Theatre. ✉ *13–29 Nicolson St., Old Town* ☎ *0131/529–6000* 🌐 *www.edtheatres.com.*

Royal Lyceum. Visiting contemporary dance companies perform in the Royal Lyceum. ✉ *Grindlay St., West End* ☎ *0131/248–4848* 🌐 *www.lyceum.org.uk.*

FESTIVALS

Fodor's Choice ★ **Edinburgh Festival Fringe.** While the world's largest fringe festival is going on, most of the city center becomes one huge performance area, with fire eaters, sword swallowers, unicyclists, jugglers, string quartets, jazz groups, stand-up comics, and magicians all thronging into High Street and Princes Street. Every available performance space—church halls, community centers, parks, sports fields, putting greens, and nightclubs—is utilized for every kind of event, with something for all tastes. Many events are free; others start at a couple of pounds and rise to £15 or £20. During festival time—roughly the same as the Edinburgh International Festival—it's possible to arrange your own entertainment program from morning to midnight. **■ TIP→ Just be aware if you're visiting Edinburgh specifically for the festival, hotels get booked up and bargains are virtually impossible to come by, so plan your trip as far in advance as possible.** ✉ *Edinburgh Festival Fringe Office, 180 High St., Old Town* ☎ *0131/226–0026* 🌐 *www.edfringe.com.*

CLOSE UP

Festivals in Edinburgh

Walking around Edinburgh in late July, you'll likely feel the first vibrations of the earthquake that is festival time, which shakes the city throughout August and into September. You may hear reference to an "Edinburgh Festival," but this is really an umbrella term for five separate festivals all taking place around the same time. For an overview, check out ⊕ *www. edinburghfestivals.co.uk.*

The best-known and oldest of the city's festivals is the **Edinburgh International Festival**, founded in 1947 when Europe was recovering from World War II. In recent years the festival has drawn as many as 400,000 people to Edinburgh, with more than 100 acts by world-renowned music, opera, theater, and dance performers filling all the major venues in the city.

If the Edinburgh International Festival is the parent of British festivals, then the **Edinburgh Festival Fringe** is its unruly child. The Festival Fringe started in 1947 at the same time as the International Festival, when eight companies that were not invited to perform in the latter decided to attend anyway. It's now the largest festival of its kind in the world. Its events range from the brilliant to the impossibly mundane, badly performed, and downright tacky.

Edinburgh festival time can fill almost any artistic need. Besides the International Festival and Festival Fringe, look for the **Edinburgh Jazz and Blues Festival,** the **International Book Festival,** and the **Military Tattoo.** The Edinburgh International Film Festival takes place in June.

FAMILY **Edinburgh International Book Festival.** This two-week-long event in August pulls together a heady mix of the biggest-selling and the most challenging authors from around the world and gets them talking about their work in a magnificent tent village. Workshops for would-be writers and children are hugely popular. ⊠ *Charlotte Sq. Gardens, New Town* ☎ *0131/718–5666* ⊕ *www.edbookfest.co.uk.*

Fodor'sChoice **Edinburgh International Festival.** Running from early August through early
★ September, the flagship arts event of the year attracts international performers to a celebration of music, dance, theater, and art. Programs, tickets, and reservations are available from the Hub, within the impressive Victorian-Gothic Tolbooth Kirk. Tickets for the festival go on sale in April, and many sell out within the month. However, you may still be able to purchase tickets, which range from around £4 to £60, during the festival. ⊠ *Edinburgh Festival Centre, Castlehill, Old Town* ☎ *0131/473–2000* ⊕ *www.eif.co.uk.*

Edinburgh International Film Festival. One of Europe's foremost film festivals, the Edinburgh International Film Festival is held in late June. ⊠ *Edinburgh Film Festival Office, 88 Lothian Rd., West End* ☎ *0131/228–2688* ⊕ *www.edfilmfest.org.uk.*

FAMILY **Edinburgh International Science Festival.** Held around Easter each year, the Edinburgh International Science Festival aims to make science accessible, interesting, and fun. Children's events turn science into entertainment and are especially popular. ⊠ *The Hub, Castlehill, Edinburgh* ☎ *0131/553–0320* ⊕ *www.sciencefestival.co.uk.*

Edinburgh Jazz and Blues Festival. Held in late July, the Edinburgh Jazz and Blues Festival attracts international top performers and brings local enthusiasts out of their living rooms and into the pubs and clubs to listen and play. ⊠ *89 Giles St., Leith* ☎ *0131/467–5200* ⊕ *www. edinburghjazzfestival.com.*

Edinburgh Military Tattoo. It may not be art, but the Edinburgh Military Tattoo is certainly Scottish culture. It's sometimes confused with the Edinburgh International Festival, partly because both events take place in August (though the Tattoo starts and finishes a week earlier). This celebration of martial music features bands, gymnastics, and stunt motorcycle teams on the castle esplanade. Dress warmly for late-evening performances. Even if it rains, the show most definitely goes on. ⊠ *Edinburgh Military Tattoo Office, 32 Market St., Old Town* ☎ *0131/225–1188* ⊕ *www.edintattoo.co.uk.*

Hogmanay. Other places in Scotland have raucous New Year's celebrations, but Edinburgh's multiday Hogmanay is famous throughout Europe and beyond, with something for everyone. Yes, it's still winter and cold, but joining the festivities with up to 80,000 other people can be memorable. You have to buy a ticket if you want to join the big organized street parties and concerts in the city center, but of course the festivities and general merriment are citywide. ⊠ *Princes St., Old Town* ⊕ *www.edinburghshogmanay.com* 🎟 *£25.*

FILM

Cameo. The Cameo has one large and two small auditoriums, both of which are extremely comfortable, plus a bar with late-night specials. ⊠ *38 Home St., Tollcross* ☎ *0871/902–5723* ⊕ *www.picturehouses. com/cinema/Cameo_Picturehouse.*

Fodor's Choice
★ **Filmhouse.** Generally held up to be one of the best independent cinemas in Britain, the excellent three-screen Filmhouse is an excellent venue for modern, foreign-language, offbeat, or simply less-commercial films. They also hold frequent live events and mini-festivals for the discerning cineast. The café and bar are open late on the weekend. ⊠ *88 Lothian Rd., West End* ☎ *0131/228–2688* ⊕ *www.filmhousecinema.com.*

MUSIC

Edinburgh Playhouse. This venue leans toward popular artists, comedy acts, and musicals. ⊠ *Greenside Pl., East End* ☎ *0131/524–3333* ⊕ *www.playhousetheatre.com.*

Festival Theatre. This theater hosts performances by the Scottish Ballet and the Scottish Opera. ⊠ *13–29 Nicolson St., Old Town* ☎ *0131/529–6000* ⊕ *www.edtheatres.com.*

Queen's Hall. The intimate Queen's Hall hosts small musical recitals. ⊠ *Clerk St., Old Town* ☎ *0131/668–2019* ⊕ *www.thequeenshall.net.*

Usher Hall. Edinburgh's grandest venue, Usher Hall hosts national and international performers and groups, including the Royal Scottish National Orchestra. ⊠ *Lothian Rd., West End* ☎ *0131/228–1155* ⊕ *www.usherhall.co.uk.*

THEATER

MODERN

Traverse Theatre. With its specially designed space, the Traverse Theatre has developed a solid reputation for new, stimulating plays by Scottish dramatists, plus innovative dance performances. ✉ *10 Cambridge St., West End* ☎ *0131/228–1404* ⊕ *www.traverse.co.uk.*

TRADITIONAL

Brunton Theatre. On the eastern outskirts of Edinburgh, the Brunton Theatre presents a regular program of repertory, touring, and amateur performances. ✉ *Ladywell Way, Musselburgh* ☎ *0131/665–2240* ⊕ *www.bruntontheatre.co.uk.*

Church Hill Theatre. The intimate, 335-seat Church Hill Theatre, managed by the city council, hosts high-quality productions by local amateur dramatic societies. ✉ *Morningside Rd., Morningside* ☎ *0131/220–4348* ⊕ *www.assemblyroomsedinburgh.co.uk.*

Edinburgh Playhouse. Big-ticket concerts and musicals, along with the occasional ballet and opera production, are staged at the popular Playhouse, with its enormous 3,000-seat auditorium. ✉ *Greenside Pl., East End* ☎ *0844/871–3014* ⊕ *www.playhousetheatre.com.*

Festival Theatre. This popular venue (which claims to have the largest single stage in Scotland) presents opera and ballet, as well as the occasional excellent touring play. ✉ *13–29 Nicolson St., Old Town* ☎ *0131/529–6000* ⊕ *www.edtheatres.com/festival.*

King's Theatre. Built in 1906, the art nouveau King's Theatre has a program of contemporary and traditional dramatic works. Its opulence has been augmented by vibrant murals by artist John Byrne. ✉ *2 Leven St., Tollcross* ☎ *0131/529–6000* ⊕ *www.edtheatres.com/kings.*

Royal Lyceum. Traditional plays and contemporary works, often transferred from or prior to their London West End showings, are presented here. ✉ *Grindlay St., West End* ☎ *0131/248–4848* ⊕ *www.lyceum.org.uk.*

NIGHTLIFE

The nightlife scene in Edinburgh is vibrant—whatever you're looking for, you'll most certainly find it here, and you won't have to go far. Expect old-style pubs as well as cutting-edge bars and clubs. Live music pours out of many watering holes on weekends, particularly folk, blues, and jazz. Well-known artists perform at some of the larger venues.

Edinburgh's 400-odd pubs are a study in themselves. In the eastern and northern districts of the city, you can find some grim, inhospitable-looking places that proclaim that drinking is no laughing matter. But throughout Edinburgh many pubs have deliberately traded in their old spit-and-sawdust images for atmospheric revivals of the warm, oak-paneled, leather-chaired *howffs* of a more leisurely age. Most pubs and bars are open weekdays and Saturday from 11 am to midnight, with some open until 1 or 2, and from 12:30 to midnight on Sunday.

The List and *The Skinny* carry the most up-to-date details about cultural events. *The List* is available at newsstands throughout the city, while *The Skinny* is free and can be picked up at a number of pubs, clubs, and

CLOSE UP

Hogmanay: Hello, New Year

In Scotland, New Year's Eve is called Hogmanay. Around Scotland, celebrations continue the next day with customs such as "first-footing"—visiting your neighbors with gifts that include whisky, all with the purpose of bringing good fortune. It's so important that January 2 as well as January 1 is a holiday in Scotland; the rest of the United Kingdom settles for recuperating on January 1.

WHAT TO EXPECT

Edinburgh's Hogmanay extends over several days with spectacles and performances (music, dance, and more); the yearly changing lineup includes many free events. Festivities featuring fire add a dramatic motif; buildings may open for rare night tours; a *ceilidh* offers dancing outdoors to traditional music; and family concerts and serious discussions during the day round out the agenda. At the heart of Hogmanay, though, is the evening street party on New Year's Eve, with different music stages, food and drink (and people do drink), and the heart-lifting—despite the cold—sight of glowing fireworks over Edinburgh Castle and the singing of "Auld Lang Syne," written by Scotland's own Robert Burns.

PLANNING BASICS

Besides the £25 you'll pay to get into the Princes Street celebration, expect to shell out extra for related events. For example, the big-name concert in the Princes Street Gardens will run you £30 or more. Book rooms as far ahead as possible. Obvious but essential is warmth: crazy hats and the bundled-up look are de rigueur. Check out ⊕ *www. edinburghshogmanay.com* for full details, and have a happy Hogmanay!

---

shops around town. The *Herald* and *Scotsman* newspapers are good for reviews and notices of upcoming events throughout Scotland.

OLD TOWN

BARS AND PUBS

Canons' Gait. In addition to a fine selection of local real ales and malts, the Canons' Gait has live jazz and blues performances, as well as edgy comedy shows in the cellar bar. ⊠ *232 Canongate, Old Town* ☎ *0131/556–4481.*

The Last Drop. There's plenty of atmosphere amid the nooks and crannies at the Last Drop. The name has a grim double meaning, as it was once the site of public hangings. ⊠ *74–78 Grassmarket, Old Town* ☎ *0131/225–4851* ⊕ *www.nicholsonspubs.co.uk.*

Fodor'sChoice ★ **Slighhouse.** The marriage of cocktails and geology that we've all been waiting for, Slighhouse is named (and decorated) in homage to James Hutton, the Edinburgh native who all but founded the science in 1788. How gloriously Edinburgh. The excellent cocktail menu is full of witty surprises: Thyme for Some Action blends thyme-infused pisco and blood-orange liqueur, while the brilliantly named Tincture, Tailor, Soldier, Spy mixes gin, elderflower, lavender tincture, and Cocchi Americano (a rare, sweet Italian wine). There's also a fine range of American whiskies. Food comes in the form of British and American bar classics, and brunch is served on weekends. ⊠ *54 George IV Bridge, Old Town* ☎ *0131/225–6936* ⊕ *www.slighhouse.com.*

Under the Stairs. As you might be able to guess from the name, Under the Stairs is below street level. This cozy, low-ceilinged place with quirky furniture and art exhibits serves specialty cocktails and decent bar food. ⊠ *3A Merchant St., Old Town* ☎ *0131/466–8550* ⊕ *www. underthestairs.org.*

Whiski. With 300-plus malts, this cheerful place is known for its haggis burger. Foot-stomping fiddle, bluegrass, and country music plays most nights. ⊠ *119 High St., Old Town* ☎ *0131/556–3095* ⊕ *www. whiskibar.co.uk.*

FOLK CLUBS

You can usually find folk musicians performing in pubs throughout Edinburgh, although there's been a decline in the live-music scene because of dwindling profits and the predominance of popular theme bars.

Royal Oak. With a piano in the corner, this cozy bar presents live blues and folk music most nights—usually with no cover charge. ⊠ *1 Infirmary St., Old Town* ☎ *0131/557–2976* ⊕ *www.royal-oak-folk.com.*

Whistle Binkies Pub. This friendly basement bar presents rock, blues, and folk music every night of the week, with as many as six or seven acts on Saturday nights. ⊠ *4–6 South Bridge, Old Town* ☎ *0131/557–5114* ⊕ *www.whistlebinkies.com.*

NIGHTCLUBS

Bongo Club. The bohemian Bongo Club stages indie, rockabilly, dub, and techno gigs, as well as various club and comedy nights. ⊠ *66 Cowgate, Old Town* ☎ *0131/558–8844* ⊕ *www.thebongoclub.co.uk.*

Cabaret Voltaire. The vaulted ceilings of this subterranean club reverberate with music most nights. You'll find everything from local groups to cutting-edge indie bands to trendy DJs. ⊠ *36–38 Blair St., Old Town* ☎ *0131/247–4704* ⊕ *www.thecabaretvoltaire.com.*

NEW TOWN

BARS AND PUBS

Abbotsford. A handsome Victorian-era island bar serves up an eclectic selection of craft beers and real ales at the Abbotsford. ⊠ *3 Rose St., New Town* ☎ *0131/225–5276.*

The Basement. This funky, cheerful bar has something of the 1950s jet-setter vibe—which might explain its ethnically confused, happy-go-lucky mash-up of cocktails, Mexican food, and Hawaiian-shirted bar staff. ⊠ *10A–12A Broughton St., New Town* ☎ *0131/557–0097* ⊕ *www.basement-bar-edinburgh.co.uk.*

Blue Blazer. This cozy, dark-wood bar has a top-notch selection of real ales, 50 malt whiskies, and 75 rums, all of which are enjoyed by a friendly, diverse crowd. ⊠ *2 Spittal St., West End* ☎ *0131/229–5030.*

Bramble. You could easily miss this basement bar on Queen Street—look for a spray-painted sign below a clothing-alteration shop. Friendly barmen, superb cocktails, eclectic music (DJs spin most nights), and lots of nooks and crannies in the whitewashed space make for late-night shenanigans that attract a young crowd. ⊠ *16A Queen St., New Town* ☎ *0131/226–6343* ⊕ *www.bramblebar.co.uk.*

Fodor's Choice
★ **Café Royal Circle Bar.** Famed for its atmospheric Victorian interiors— think ornate stucco, etched mirrors, tiled murals, stained glass, and leather booths—the Café Royal Circle Bar has been drawing a cast of Edinburgh characters since it opened in 1863. Regulars and new fans alike pack in for the drinks (seven real ales and more than 30 whiskies) and tasty bar food—everything from yummy sandwiches and small plates to delicious seafood platters. ⊠ *19 W. Regent St., New Town* ☎ *0131/556–1884* ⊕ *www.caferoyaledinburgh.co.uk.*

Cask and Barrel. A spacious, busy pub, the Cask and Barrel lets you sample hand-pulled ales at the horseshoe-shaped bar ringed by a collection of brewery mirrors. ⊠ *115 Broughton St., New Town* ☎ *0131/556–3132.*

Cumberland Bar. Fine ales on tap, classic pub mirrors, handsome wood trim, and a beer garden are the draws at the Cumberland Bar. ⊠ *1–3 Cumberland St., New Town* ☎ *0131/558–3134* ⊕ *www.cumberlandbar.co.uk.*

Guildford Arms. This place is worth a visit just for its interior: ornate plasterwork, elaborate cornices, and wood paneling. The bartender serves some excellent draft ales, including Orkney Dark Island. ⊠ *1 W. Register St., at east end of Princes St., New Town* ☎ *0131/556–4312* ⊕ *www.guildfordarms.com.*

FAMILY
Fodor's Choice
★ **Joseph Pearce's.** One of four Swedish-owned pubs in Edinburgh, Joseph Pearce's has a Continental feel, despite its solidly Edwardian origins. Scandinavian-themed cocktails are popular, as are meatballs and other Swedish dishes. There's a children's corner with toys to keep the small fry occupied. ⊠ *23 Elm Row, New Town* ☎ *0131/556–4140* ⊕ *www.bodabar.com/joseph-pearces.*

Fodor's Choice
★ **Juniper.** Right opposite Waverley Station, Juniper cultivates an air of glamorous fun, helped no end by its picture-worthy views of the city and the castle. The wine list is good (if a little pricey); but the wildly imaginative cocktails are what this place sells itself on. Strawberries and Steam comes in a teapot bubbling over with dry ice. Soak it up with nibbles from the modern Scottish "street food" menu—veggie haggis bon bons, anyone? ⊠ *Royal British Hotel, 20 Princes St., New Town* ☎ *0131/556–4901* ⊕ *www.juniperedinburgh.co.uk.*

Kay's Bar. Housed in a former Georgian coach house, this diminutive but friendly spot serves 50 single-malt whiskies, seven guest ales, and decent bottled beers. Check out the cute little wood-paneled library room, with its tiny fireplace and shelves full of books. ⊠ *39 Jamaica St., New Town* ☎ *0131/225–1858* ⊕ *www.kaysbar.co.uk.*

Milne's Bar. This spot is also known as "the Poets' Pub" because of its popularity with Edinburgh's literati. Pies and baked potatoes go well with seven real ales and various guest beers (meaning anything besides the house brew). Victorian advertisements and photos of old Edinburgh give the place an old-time feel. ⊠ *35 Hanover St., New Town* ☎ *0131/225–6738* ⊕ *www.taylor-walker.co.uk/pub/milnes-bar-midlothian/s1453.*

Star Bar. Well worth seeking out, the tucked-away Star Bar has a beer garden, table soccer, and—a rarity—a very good jukebox. It is also meant to be haunted—get the owners to regale you with the stories, which include a specific clause in their lease that prevents them from removing a human skull from the building. ✉ *1 Northumberland Pl., New Town* ☎ *0131/539–8070* ⊕ *www.starbar.co.uk.*

Teuchters. With more than 80 whiskies, a cozy fire, and comfy sofas, Teuchters is a fine place to relax with a dram. ✉ *26 William St., West End* ☎ *0131/225–2973* ⊕ *www.aroomin.co.uk.*

Tonic. This stylish basement bar has bouncy stools, comfy sofas, and a long list of cocktails. There's relaxing music Monday to Wednesday, live bands Thursday, and resident DJs on the weekend. ✉ *34A Castle St., New Town* ☎ *0131/225–6431* ⊕ *www.bar-tonic.co.uk.*

CEILIDHS AND SCOTTISH EVENINGS

Thistle King James Hotel. For those who feel a trip to Scotland is not complete without hearing the "Braes of Yarrow" or "Auld Robin Gray," several hotels present traditional Scottish-music evenings in the summer season. Head for the Thistle King James Hotel to see *Jamie's Scottish Evening*, an extravaganza of Scottish song, tartan, plaid, and bagpipes that takes place nightly from late March to October. It's supercheesy but reliable fun. The cost is £65, including a four-course dinner. ✉ *Thistle King James Hotel, 107 Leith St., New Town* ☎ *0871/376–9016* ⊕ *www.thistle.com.*

GAY AND LESBIAN

There's a burgeoning gay and lesbian scene in Edinburgh, and the city has many predominantly gay clubs, bars, and cafés. However, don't expect the scene to be quite as open as in London, New York, or even Glasgow. *The List* and *The Skinny* have sections that focus on gay and lesbian venues.

CC Blooms. Modern and colorful, CC Blooms plays a mix of musical styles. Open nightly, it's been a mainstay on the gay scene since the early '90s. ✉ *23–24 Greenside Pl., New Town* ☎ *0131/556–9331* ⊕ *www.ccbloomsedinburgh.com.*

Regent. With a homey vibe—dogs are welcome—the Regent is renowned for its real ales. ✉ *2 Montrose Terr., Abbeyhill* ☎ *0131/661–8198* ⊕ *www.theregentbar.co.uk.*

NIGHTCLUBS

Liquid Room. Top indie bands and an eclectic mix of club nights (techno, hip-hop, and alternative, to name a few) make the Liquid Room a superb venue. ✉ *9C Victoria St., New Town* ☎ *0131/225–2564* ⊕ *www.liquidroom.com.*

Opal Lounge. This casual but stylish nightspot with a glam VIP lounge was favored by Prince William when he was a student at St. Andrew's University. ✉ *51A George St., New Town* ☎ *0131/226–2275* ⊕ *www.opallounge.co.uk.*

SOUTH SIDE
BARS AND PUBS

Cloisters. Priding itself on the absence of music, gaming machines, and all other modern pub gimmicks, the Cloisters specializes in real ales, malt whiskies, and good food, all at reasonable prices. ⊠ *26 Brougham St., Tollcross* ☏ *0131/221–9997* ⊕ *www.cloistersbar.com.*

Leslie's Bar. Retaining its original mahogany island bar, the late-Victorian-era Leslie's is renowned for its range of traditional Scottish ales and malt whiskies. ⊠ *45 Ratcliffe Terr., South Side* ☏ *0131/667–7205* ⊕ *www.realalepubedinburgh.co.uk.*

LEITH
BARS AND PUBS

Cameo Bar. Backing onto the Water of Leith, the bright and airy Cameo Bar serves decent pub food and has big screens popular for sporting events. They're also known locally for their exceptionally good range of ciders (the European, alcoholic kind), many of which are from small producers in the United Kingdom and Ireland. ⊠ *23 Commercial St., Leith* ☏ *0131/554–9999* ⊕ *www.cameo-edinburgh.co.uk.*

Fodor's Choice
★ **The King's Wark.** A 15th-century building houses the popular King's Wark, renowned for its excellent food and good ales. Breakfasts are legendary and worth booking in advance. In warm weather you can snag a table on the sidewalk. ⊠ *36 The Shore, Leith* ☏ *0131/554–9260* ⊕ *www.thekingswark.com.*

Malt and Hops. Having opened its doors in 1749, Malt and Hops has a resident ghost. With a fine spot on the waterfront, the place serves microbrewery cask ales—with a selection good enough to be endorsed by CAMRA (the Campaign for Real Ale), a long-standing U.K. organization that champions real ale. ⊠ *45 The Shore, Leith* ☏ *0131/555–0083* ⊕ *www.barcalisa.com.*

Robbie's. This classic pub with friendly regulars is a great place for catching big sporting events while enjoying local ales. ⊠ *367 Leith Walk, Leith* ☏ *0131/554–6850.*

Wolf and Water. There's a funky, industrial vibe at this popular new bar near the Ocean Terminal in Leith. Beers and cocktails are a specialty—and in a novel twist, they also mix a range of alcoholic slushies. Decent bar food is served all night, although this place is guilty of succumbing to the no-plates school of trendy dining: you eat straight from a metal tray! ⊠ *84 Commercial St., The Shore, Leith* ☏ *0131/554–5625* ⊕ *www.wolfandwater.com.*

EAST END
COMEDY CLUBS

Stand. Throughout the year you can laugh until your sides split at the Stand, which hosts both famous names and up-and-coming acts. ⊠ *5 York Pl., East End* ☏ *0131/558–7272* ⊕ *www.thestand.co.uk.*

SHOPPING

Despite its renown as a shopping street, **Princes Street** in the New Town may disappoint some visitors with its dull modern architecture, average chain stores, and fast-food outlets. One block north of Princes Street, **Rose Street** has many smaller specialty shops; part of the street is a pedestrian zone, so it's a pleasant place to browse. The shops on **George Street** in New Town tend to be fairly upscale. London names, such as Laura Ashley and Penhaligons, are prominent, though some of the older independent stores continue to do good business.

The streets crossing George Street—Hanover, Frederick, and Castle—are also worth exploring. **Dundas Street,** the northern extension of Hanover Street, beyond Queen Street Gardens, has several antiques shops. **Thistle Street,** originally George Street's "back lane," or service area, has several boutiques and more antiques shops.

As may be expected, many shops along the **Royal Mile** in Old Town sell what may be politely or euphemistically described as tourist-ware—whiskies, tartans, and tweeds. Careful exploration, however, will reveal some worthwhile establishments. Shops here also cater to highly specialized interests and hobbies. Close to the castle end of the Royal Mile, just off George IV Bridge, is **Victoria Street,** with specialty shops grouped in a small area. Follow the tiny West Bow to **Grassmarket** for more specialty stores.

Stafford and William Streets form a small, upscale shopping area in a Georgian setting. Walk to the west end of Princes Street and then along its continuation, Shandwick Place, then turn right onto Stafford Street. William Street crosses Stafford halfway down.

North of Princes Street, on the way to the Royal Botanic Garden Edinburgh, is **Stockbridge,** an oddball shopping area of some charm, particularly on St. Stephen Street. To get here, walk north down Frederick Street and Howe Street, away from Princes Street, then turn left onto North West Circus Place.

OLD TOWN

BOOKS, PAPER, MAPS, AND GAMES

Armchair Books. Near the Grassmarket, Armchair Books is a chaotic but cheerful bookshop heaving with secondhand and antiquarian books. ⊠ 72–74 W. Port, Old Town ☎ 0131/229–5927 ⊕ www. armchairbooks.co.uk.

Carson Clark Gallery. This gallery specializes in antique maps, sea charts, and prints. ⊠ 181–183 Canongate, Old Town ☎ 0131/556–4710 ⊕ www.carsonclarkgallery.co.uk.

Main Point Books. This bibliophile's haven is stacked high with obscure first editions and bargain tomes. ⊠ 77 Bread St., Old Town ☎ 0131/228–4837 ⊕ www.mainpointbooks.co.uk.

CLOTHING BOUTIQUES

Bill Baber. One of the most imaginative of the many Scottish knitwear designers, Bill Baber's creations are a long way from the conservative pastel woolies sold at some of the large mill shops. ⊠ *66 Grassmarket, Old Town* ☎ *0131/225-3249* ⊕ *www.billbaber.com.*

Ragamuffin. Hailing from the Isle of Skye, Ragamuffin sells some of the funkiest and brightest knits produced in Scotland. ⊠ *278 Canongate, Old Town* ☎ *0131/557-6007* ⊕ *ragamuffinloves.blogspot.co.uk.*

JEWELRY

Clarksons. A family firm, Clarksons handcrafts a unique collection of jewelry, including Celtic styles. The pieces here are made with silver, gold, platinum, and precious gems, with a particular emphasis on diamonds. ⊠ *87 West Bow, Old Town* ☎ *0131/225-8141* ⊕ *clarksonsedinburgh. co.uk.*

SCOTTISH SPECIALTIES

Fodor'sChoice **Cranachan & Crowdie.** On Edinburgh's Royal Mile, this gourmet shop
★ is brimming with the finest Scottish food and drink. There's even a chocolate counter for those with a sweet tooth, as well as shortbread and oatcakes. The staff is happy to put together hampers of food for any occasion—including an impromptu picnic back in your room. They also sell tweeds, handmade candles, and other gift-worthy knick-knacks. ⊠ *263 Canongate, Old Town* ☎ *0131/556-7194* ⊕ *www. cranachanandcrowdie.com.*

Edinburgh Old Town Weaving Company. At this workshop, you can chat with the cloth and tapestry weavers as they work, then buy the products. The company can also provide information on clan histories and which tartan to wear. ⊠ *555 Castlehill, Old Town* ☎ *0131/226-1555.*

Geoffrey (Tailor) Highland Crafts. This shop can clothe you in full Highland dress, with kilts made in its own workshops. ⊠ *57–59 High St., Old Town* ☎ *0131/557-0256* ⊕ *www.geoffreykilts.co.uk.*

NEW TOWN

ANTIQUES

Fodor'sChoice **Unicorn Antiques.** This basement is crammed with fascinating antiques,
★ including artworks, ornaments, and drawerfuls of aged cutlery. ⊠ *65 Dundas St., New Town* ☎ *0131/556-7176* ⊕ *www.unicornantiques.co.uk.*

ARCADES AND SHOPPING CENTERS

St. James Centre. John Lewis, River Island, Thorntons, Wallis, and other chain stores can be found at the St. James Centre. ⊠ *Leith St., New Town* ⊕ *www.stjamesshopping.com.*

CLOTHING BOUTIQUES

Elaine's Vintage Clothing. This wee boutique on beguiling St. Stephen Street is crammed full of vintage threads for women and men. The finds span the 20th century, but most are from the '40s to the '70s. The friendly owner shares her knowledge of the many elegant and quirky outfits on her rails. ⊠ *55 St. Stephen St., New Town* ☎ *0131/225-5783.*

DEPARTMENT STORES

Harvey Nichols. Affectionately (and almost universally) known as Harvey Nicks, this high-style British chain has opened a Scottish outpost that carries the store's stylish, upscale fashion choices. ✉ *30–34 St. Andrew Sq., New Town* ☎ *0131/524–8388* ⊕ *www.harveynichols.com.*

Fodor'sChoice
★

Jenners. Traditional china and glassware are a specialty here, as are Scottish tweeds and tartans. Its famous food hall, run by Valvona & Crolla, stocks Scottish staples like shortbread, marmalade, and honey, alongside quality Continental groceries. ✉ *48 Princes St., New Town* ☎ *0344/800–3725* ⊕ *www.houseoffraser.co.uk.*

John Lewis. Part of a U.K.–wide chain, John Lewis specializes in furnishings and household goods but also stocks designer clothes. ✉ *69 St. James Centre, New Town* ☎ *0131/556–9121* ⊕ *www.johnlewis.com/our-shops/edinburgh.*

Marks & Spencer. Fairly priced, stylish clothes and accessories are on offer at Marks & Spencer. You can also buy quality food and household goods. ✉ *54 Princes St., New Town* ☎ *0131/225–2301* ⊕ *www.marksandspencer.com.*

JEWELRY

Hamilton and Inches. Established in 1866, this jeweler is worth visiting not only for its gold and silver pieces, but also for its late-Georgian interior. Designed by David Bryce in 1834, it's all columns and elaborate plasterwork. ✉ *87 George St., New Town* ☎ *0131/225–4898* ⊕ *www.hamiltonandinches.com.*

Joseph Bonnar. Tucked behind George Street, Joseph Bonnar stocks Scotland's largest collection of antique jewelry, including 19th-century agate jewels. ✉ *72 Thistle St., New Town* ☎ *0131/226–2811* ⊕ *www.josephbonnar.com.*

HOME FURNISHINGS

Hannah Zakari. Quirky handmade pieces, including embroidered cushions, are a specialty at Hannah Zakari. Also look for unusual jewelry, artwork, and accessories. ✉ *43 Candlemaker Row, New Town* ☎ *0131/516–3264* ⊕ *www.hannahzakari.co.uk.*

In House. This shop sells designer furnishings and collectibles at the forefront of modern design. ✉ *28 Howe St., New Town* ☎ *0131/225–2888* ⊕ *www.inhouse-uk.com.*

Studio One. This basement shop has a well-established and comprehensive inventory of jewelry, accessories, housewares, and more. ✉ *10 Stafford St., New Town* ☎ *0131/226–5812* ⊕ *www.studio-one.co.uk.*

OUTDOOR SPORTS GEAR

Tiso. This shop stocks outdoor clothing, boots, and jackets ideal for hiking or camping in the Highlands. There's another branch at 41 Commercial Street. ✉ *123–125 Rose St., New Town* ☎ *0131/225–9486* ⊕ *www.tiso.com.*

WEST END

CLOTHING BOUTIQUES

Concrete Wardrobe. For an eclectic mix of quirky knitwear and accessories, dive into Concrete Wardrobe. You can also find vintage furnishings. ⊠ *50a Broughton St., West End* ☎ *0131/558–7130* ⊕ *www. concretewardrobe.com.*

Herman Brown. This secondhand clothing store is where cashmere twinsets and classic luxe labels are sought and found. ⊠ *151 W. Port, West End* ☎ *0131/228–2589* ⊕ *www.hermanbrown.co.uk.*

SOUTH SIDE

ANTIQUES

Courtyard Antiques. This lovely shop stocks a mixture of high-quality antiques, toys, and militaria. ⊠ *108A Causewayside, Sciennes* ☎ *0131/662–9008.*

LEITH

ARCADES AND SHOPPING CENTERS

Ocean Terminal. The home of the former royal yacht, *Britannia*, the Ocean Terminal also houses a large collection of shops, as well as bars and restaurants. ⊠ *Ocean Dr., Leith* ⊕ *www.oceanterminal.com.*

SCOTTISH SPECIALTIES

Clan Tartan Centre. For the tartan and clan curious, there's a database containing details of all known designs, plus information on clan histories. ⊠ *70–74 Bangor Rd., Leith* ☎ *0131/553–5161.*

SPORTS AND THE OUTDOORS

FOOTBALL

Like Glasgow, Edinburgh is mad for football (soccer in the United States), and there's an intense rivalry between the city's two professional teams.

Heart of Midlothian Football Club. Better known as the Hearts, the Heart of Midlothian Football Club plays in maroon and white and is based at Tynecastle. ⊠ *Tynecastle Stadium, McLeod St., Edinburgh* ☎ *0333/0433–1874* ⊕ *www.heartsfc.co.uk.*

Hibernian Club. Known as the Hibs, the green-bedecked Hibernian Club plays its home matches at Easter Road Stadium. ⊠ *Easter Road Stadium, 12 Albion Pl., Edinburgh* ☎ *0131/661–2159* ⊕ *www.hibernianfc.co.uk.*

GOLF

The VisitScotland website has an extensive, searchable guide to Scottish courses.

Braid Hills. Known to locals and many others as Braids (no connection with famed golfer James Braid), this course is beautifully laid out over a rugged range of small hills in the southern suburbs of Edinburgh. The views to the south and the Pentland Hills and north over the city skyline toward the Firth of Forth are worth a visit in themselves. The city built this course at the turn of the 20th century after urban development forced golfers out of the city center. The 9-hole Princes Course was completed in 2003. Reservations are recommended for weekend play. ✉ *27 Braids Hill Approach, Edinburgh* ☎ *0131/447–6666 for Braids, 0131/666–2210 for Princes* ⊕ *www.edinburghleisure.co.uk/ venues/braid-hills-golf-course* ⛳ *Braids, £25 weekdays, £27 weekends; Princes, £14 weekdays, £16 weekends* ↟ *Braids: 18 holes, 5865 yards, par 71; Princes: 9 holes 2006 yards, par 31* ◔ *Daily.*

Bruntsfield Links. The British Seniors and several other championship tournaments are held at this Willie Park–designed course, three miles west of Edinburgh. The course meanders among 155 acres of mature parkland and has fine views over the Firth of Forth. Bruntsfield takes its name from one of the oldest (1761) golf links in Scotland, in the center of Edinburgh—now just a 9-hole pitch-and-putt course—where the club used to play. A strict dress code applies. ▪ **TIP ➡ Full-day tickets are available for just £20 more than the cost of a single round.** ✉ *32 Barnton Ave., Davidson's Mains, Edinburgh* ☎ *0131/336–1479* ⊕ *www. bruntsfieldlinks.co.uk* ⛳ *£75 weekdays, £80 weekends* ↟ *18 holes, 6446 yards, par 71* ◔ *Daily* ⚠ *Reservations essential.*

Duddingston Golf Club. Founded in 1895, this excellent public parkland course is two miles east of the city. The first hole is located in an idyllic deer park (watch out for four-legged spectators). Braid Burn—a stream that flows across the southern part of Edinburgh—-also runs through the course, creating a perilous hazard on many holes. Prices drop sharply in the winter months; in January and February, for instance, you can play a round for as little as £19. ✉ *Duddingston Rd. W, Duddingston* ☎ *0131/661–7688* ⊕ *www.duddingstongolfclub.co.uk* ⛳ *£23 Mar., Apr., and Oct.; £55 May–Sept.; £19 Nov.–Feb.* ↟ *18 holes, 6525 yards, par 72.*

Liberton. Built in 1920, this 82-acre public parkland course has narrow fairways and smallish greens. The 18-hole course has been well landscaped with trees and bunkers; many of the trees are still maturing, meaning that the pleasant character of the course is slowly developing over time. The club also has a treatment room, offering a wide range of holistic therapy treatments—including Reiki, Indian head massage, and deeply relaxing hot stone massages. Call ahead to book a session. ✉ *Kingston Grange, 297 Gilmerton Rd., Liberton* ☎ *0131/664–3009* ⊕ *www.libertongc.co.uk* ⛳ *£31 weekdays, £36 weekends* ↟ *18 holes, 5344 yards, par 67.*

Murrayfield. Only five minutes from the city center, this heathland-style course is kept in fine condition and commands outstanding views over Edinburgh. Another of the venerable courses that were laid out around the city during the golfing boom of the late 19th century, Murrayfield opened in 1896, and has seen several national and international champions among its fans. The club house has a handy activity and TV room where kids can be left while you play a round. Drop by on Fridays for special bistro evenings. ⊠ *43 Murrayfield Rd., Murrayfield* ☎ *0131/337–3478* ⊕ *www.murrayfieldgolfclub.co.uk* ⊠ *£40* ⚑ *18 holes, 5781 yards, par 70.*

Royal Burgess Golfing Society. Edinburgh's Victorian courses have nothing on the age of this one—Royal Burgess opened in 1735, making it one of the world's oldest golf clubs. Its members originally played on Bruntsfield Links; now they and their guests play on elegantly manicured parkland in the city's northwestern suburbs. It's a challenging course with fine, beautifully maintained greens. There's a fairly conservative dress code—no denim or T-shirts allowed, and you must wear a jacket and tie in the clubhouse. ⊠ *181 Whitehouse Rd., Barnton* ☎ *0131/339–2075* ⊕ *www.royalburgess.co.uk* ⊠ *£105* ⚑ *18 holes, 6511 yards, par 71* ☉ *Daily* ⚑ *Reservations essential.*

RUGBY

Murrayfield Stadium. Home of the Scottish Rugby Union, Murrayfield Stadium hosts matches in early spring and fall. Crowds of good-humored rugby fans from all over the world add greatly to the sense of excitement in the streets of Edinburgh. ⊠ *Roseburn Terr., Murrayfield* ☎ *0131/346–5160* ⊕ *www.scottishrugby.org.*

SIDE TRIPS: WEST LOTHIAN AND THE FORTH VALLEY

If you stand on an Edinburgh eminence—the castle ramparts, Arthur's Seat, Corstorphine Hill—you can plan a few Lothian excursions without even the aid of a map. The Lothians is the collective name given to the swath of countryside south of the Firth of Forth and surrounding Edinburgh. Many courtly and aristocratic families lived here, and the region still has the castles and mansions to prove it. The rich arrived and with them came deer parks, gardens in the French style, and Lothian's fame as a seed plot for Lowland gentility.

West Lothian comprises a good bit of Scotland's central belt. The River Forth snakes across a widening floodplain on its descent from the Highlands, and by the time it reaches the western extremities of Edinburgh, it has already passed below the mighty Forth bridges and become a broad estuary. Castles and historic houses sprout thickly on both sides of the Forth. You can explore a number of them, and the territory north of the River Forth, in a day or two, or you can just pick one excursion for a day trip from Edinburgh.

GETTING HERE AND AROUND

BUS TRAVEL First Bus and Lothian Buses link most of this area, but working out a detailed itinerary by bus isn't always easy.

CAR TRAVEL The Queensferry Road, also known as the A90, is the main thoroughfare running through this region. North of the Forth Bridge, the A985 goes to Culross, the M9 and A823 head to Dunfermiline, and the A91 passes Ochil Hills and Castle Campbell.

TRAIN TRAVEL Dalmeny, Linlithgow, and Dunfermline all have rail stations and can be reached from Edinburgh stations.

ESSENTIALS

VisitScotland has an information center about West Lothian in the town of Bo'ness, close to Blackness Castle and the House of Binns. It's open April to October. Visit West Lothian runs an information center at Burgh Halls in Linlithgow.

Visitor Information VisitScotland. ⊠ *Bo'ness Station, Union St., Bo'ness* ☎ *0845/602–3779* ⊕ *www.visitscotland.com.* **Visit West Lothian.** ⊠ *Burgh Halls, The Cross, Linlithgow* ☎ *01506/282720* ⊕ *visitwestlothian.co.uk.*

SOUTH QUEENSFERRY

7 miles west of Edinburgh.

This pleasant little waterside community, a former ferry port, is completely dominated by the Forth Bridges, dramatic structures of contrasting architecture that span the Firth of Forth at this historic crossing point. It's near a number of historic and other sights.

GETTING HERE AND AROUND

The Queensferry Road, also known as the A90, is the main artery north toward the Forth Bridge heading to Hopetoun House, the House of the Binns, and Blackness Castle.

EXPLORING

TOP ATTRACTIONS

Blackness Castle. Standing like a grounded ship on the very edge of the Forth, this curious 15th-century structure has had a varied career as a strategic fortress, state prison, powder magazine, and youth hostel. The countryside is gently green and cultivated, and open views extend across the blue Forth to the distant ramparts of the Ochil Hills. ⊠ *B903, 4 miles northeast of Linlithgow, Linlithgow* ☎ *01506/834807* ⊕ *www. historic-scotland.gov.uk/places* 🎟 *£5.75* ⊙ *Apr.–Sept., daily 9:30–5:30; Oct.–Mar., Sat.–Wed. 10–4.*

Forth Bridge. Opened in 1890 and at the time hailed as the eighth wonder of the world, at 2,765 yards long, this iconic cantilevered railroad bridge is a UNESCO World Heritage Site. The bridge expands by about another yard on a hot summer's day. Its neighbor is the 1,993-yard-long Forth Road Bridge, in operation since 1964. ⊠ *Edinburgh Rd.*

House of the Binns. The 17th-century general "Bloody Tam" Dalyell (c. 1599–1685) transformed a fortified stronghold into a gracious mansion, the House of the Binns (the name derives from *bynn,* the old Scottish word for hill). The present exterior dates from around 1810 and shows

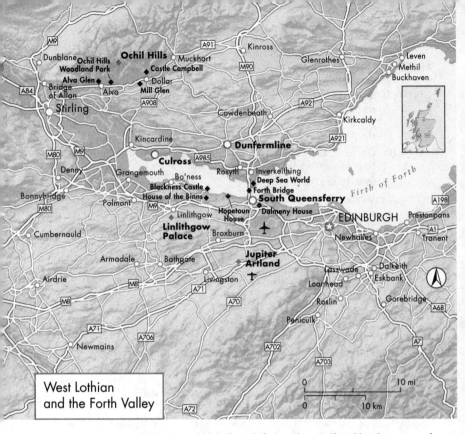

West Lothian
and the Forth Valley

a remodeling into a kind of mock fort with crenellated battlements and turrets. Inside, magnificent plaster ceilings are done in the Elizabethan style. ⊠ *Off A904, 4 miles east of Linlithgow, Linlithgow* ☎ *0844/493–2127* ⊕ *www.nts.org.uk/visits* 🎫 *£10* ⊙ *House: June–Sept., Sat.–Wed. 2–5. Estate: year-round, daily 8–7:30.*

WORTH NOTING

Dalmeny House. The first of the stately houses clustered on the western edge of Edinburgh, Dalmeny House is the home of the Earl and Countess of Rosebery. This 1815 Tudor Gothic mansion displays among its sumptuous contents the best of the family's famous collection of 18th-century French furniture. Highlights include the library, the Napoléon Room, the Vincennes and Sevres porcelain collections, and the drawing room, with its tapestries and intricately wrought French furniture. Admission is by guided tour, for two months of the year only. ⊠ *B924* ☎ *0131/331–1888* ⊕ *www.dalmeny.co.uk* 🎫 *£10* ⊙ *Tours: June–July, Sun.–Wed. 2:15 and 3:30.*

FAMILY **Deep Sea World.** The former ferry port in North Queensferry dropped almost into oblivion after the Forth Road Bridge opened, but was dragged abruptly back into the limelight by the hugely popular Deep Sea World. This sophisticated aquarium on the Firth of Forth offers a fascinating view of underwater life. Go down a clear acrylic tunnel for a diver's-eye look at more than 5,000 fish, including 250 sharks (some over 9 feet long); and visit the exhibition hall, which has an Amazon-jungle display and an audiovisual presentation on local marine life. Ichthyophobes will feel more at ease in the adjacent café and gift shop. ■ **TIP→ Save £2 (£7 on a family ticket) by booking online.** ✉ *Forthside Terr., North Queensferry* ☎ *01383/411880* 🌐 *www.deepseaworld.com* 🎟 *£13.50* 🕒 *Weekdays 10–5, weekends 10–6; last admission 1 hr before closing.*

Hopetoun House. The palatial premises of Hopetoun House, probably Scotland's grandest courtly seat and home of the Marquesses of Linlithgow, are considered to be among the Adam family's finest designs. The enormous house was started in 1699 to the original plans of Sir William Bruce (1630–1710), then enlarged between 1721 and 1754 by William Adam (1689–1748) and his sons Robert and John. There's a notable painting collection, and the house has decorative work of the highest order, plus all the trappings to keep you entertained: a nature trail, a restaurant in the former stables, farm shop, and a museum. Much of the wealth that created this sumptuous building came from the family's mining interests in the surrounding regions. The estate also specializes in clay pigeon shooting; expert-led introductory sessions can be booked for groups of at least six; prices start at £45 per person. ✉ *Off A904, 6 miles west of South Queensferry* ☎ *0131/331–2451* 🌐 *www.hopetoun.co.uk* 🎟 *£9.50; Grounds only £4.75* 🕒 *Apr.–Sept., daily 10:30–5, last admission at 4.*

WHERE TO EAT

$$ MODERN BRITISH

🍴 **The Boat House.** Scotland's natural larder is on display at this romantic restaurant on the banks of the Forth. Seafood is the star of the show, and chef Paul Steward is the man behind the imaginative yet unfussy recipes. Standouts include sea bream with an orange, ginger, and peppercorn reduction, salmon supreme with tarragon, or a choice of steaks. If you want a less formal affair, the bistro and cocktail bar next door has a friendly buzz. [$] *Average main: £19* ✉ *22 High St.* ☎ *0131/331–5429* 🌐 *www.theboathouse-sq.co.uk.*

JUPITER ARTLAND

10 miles west of Edinburgh.

For anyone drawn to interesting art and beautiful open spaces, a visit to this open-air collection of sculptures by world-renowned artists is a must.

GETTING HERE AND AROUND

To reach Jupiter Artland from Edinburgh, take the A71 toward Kilmarnock. Just after Wilkieston, turn right onto the B7015.

EXPLORING

Fodor's Choice ★

Jupiter Artland. The beautiful grounds of a Jacobean manor house have been transformed by an art-loving couple, Robert and Nicky Wilson, into a sculpture park. With the aid of a map you can explore the magical landscapes and encounter artworks by Andy Goldsworthy, Anya Gallaccio, Jim Lambie, Nathan Coley, Ian Hamilton Finlay, and Anish Kapoor, among many others. A highlight is walking around Charles

Jencks's *Cells of Life,* a series of shapely, grass-covered mounds. Run by First Bus, the 27 and X27 direct buses depart from Regent Road and Dalry Road in Haymarket. ⊠ *Bonnington House Steadings, off B7015, Wilkieston, Edinburgh* ☎ *01506/889900* ⊕ *www. jupiterartland.org* 🖃 *£8.50* ⊙ *Mid-May–June, Thurs.–Sun. 10–5; July and Aug., daily 10–5.*

LINLITHGOW PALACE

12 miles west of Edinburgh.

These lochside ruins retain impressive remnants of what was once the seat of the Stewart kings.

GETTING HERE AND AROUND

From Edinburgh, take the M9 westward to Linlithgow Palace. You can also board a train to Linlithgow Station, a short walk from the palace.

EXPLORING

Linlithgow Palace. On the edge of Linlithgow Loch stands the splendid ruin of Linlithgow Palace, the birthplace of Mary, Queen of Scots, in 1542. Burned, perhaps accidentally, by Hanoverian troops during the last Jacobite rebellion in 1746, this impressive shell stands on a site of great antiquity, though it's not certain anything survived an earlier fire in 1424. The palace gatehouse was built in the early 16th century, and the central courtyard's elaborate fountain dates from around 1535. The halls and great rooms are cold, echoing stone husks now in Historic Scotland's care. ⊠ *A706, south shore of Linlithgow Loch, Linlithgow* ☎ *01506/842896* ⊕ *www.historic-scotland.gov.uk/places* 🖃 *£5.75* ⊙ *Apr.–Sept., daily 9:30–5:30; Oct.–Mar., daily 9:30–4:30. Last admission 45 mins before closing.*

OCHIL HILLS

24 miles northwest of Edinburgh.

The scarp face of the Ochil Hills looms unmistakably. It's an old fault line that yields up hard volcanic rocks and contrasts with the quantities of softer coal immediately around the River Forth. The steep Ochils provided grazing land and water power for Scotland's second-largest textile area.

GETTING HERE AND AROUND

There are two ways to get here by car: take the A90 north of the Forth Bridge, or go via Stirling on the M9. The A91 passes Alva and the Ochil Hills.

EXPLORING

Alva Glen. There's a breathtaking gorge at Alva Glen, and walking paths (some are steep, so be prepared) that follow the gushing Alva Burn and pass many abandoned woolen mills. ⊠ *A91, Alva* ⊕ *www.alvaglen.org.uk.*

Castle Campbell. With green woods below, bracken hills above, and a view that on a clear day stretches right across the Forth Valley to the tip of Tinto Hill near Lanark, Castle Campbell is certainly the most atmospheric fortress within easy reach of Edinburgh. Formerly known as Castle Gloom, Castle Campbell stands out among Scottish castles for the sheer drama of its setting. The sturdy square of the tower house survives from the 15th century, when the site was fortified by the first Earl of Argyll. Other buildings and enclosures were subsequently added, but the sheer lack of space on this rocky eminence ensured that there would never be any drastic changes. John Knox, the fiery religious reformer, once preached here. In 1654 the castle was captured by Oliver Cromwell and garrisoned with English troops. It's now cared for by Historic Scotland and is part of the Clackmannanshire Tower Trail. To get here, follow a road off the A91 that angles sharply up the east side of the wooded defile. ⊠ *Off A91, Dollar* ☎ *01259/742408* ⊕ *www. historic-scotland.gov.uk/places* 🎫 *£5.75* ⊗ *Apr.–Sept., daily 9:30–5:30; Oct.–Mar., Mon.–Wed. and weekends 9:30–4. Last admission 30 mins before closing.*

Mill Glen. Behind Tillicoultry (pronounced tilly- *coot*-ree), Mill Glen has a giant quarry, fine waterfalls, and interesting plants, making it a good hiking option for energetic explorers. ⊠ *A91, Tillicoultry.*

Ochil Hills Woodland Park. East of Alva is the Ochil Hills Woodland Park, which provides access to lovely Silver Glen, so called because the precious metal was mined here in the 18th century. ⊠ *A91, Alva* ☎ *01259/450000* ⊕ *www.ochils.org.uk/ochils-woodland-park.*

CULROSS

17 miles northwest of Edinburgh.

The town is a fascinating open-air museum that gives you a feel for life in the 17th and 18th centuries.

GETTING HERE AND AROUND

To get here by car, head north of the Forth Bridge on the A90, then westward on the A985.

EXPLORING

Fodor'sChoice ★ **Culross.** With its Mercat Cross, cobbled streets, tolbooth, and narrow *wynds* (alleys), Culross, on the muddy shores of the Forth, is now a living museum of a 17th-century town and one of the most remarkable little towns in Scotland. It once had a thriving industry and export trade in coal and salt (the coal was used in the salt-panning process). It also had, curiously, a trade monopoly in the manufacture of baking *girdles* (griddles). As local coal became exhausted, the impetus of the Industrial Revolution passed Culross by, and other parts of the Forth Valley prospered. Culross became a backwater town, and the merchants' houses of the 17th and 18th centuries were never replaced by Victorian developments or modern architecture. In the 1930s the National Trust for Scotland started to buy up the decaying properties. With the help of other agencies, these buildings were brought to life. Today ordinary citizens live in many of the National Trust properties. A few—the Palace, Study, and Town House—are open to the public. ⊠ *Off A985, 17 miles northwest of Edinburgh* ☎ *0844/493–2189* ⊕ *www.nts.org.uk/visits* 🎫 *£10.50* ⊗ *June–Aug., daily noon–5; Apr.,*

May, and Sept., Thurs.–Mon. noon–5; Oct., Fri.–Mon. noon–4. Last admission 1 hr before closing.

DUNFERMLINE

16 miles northwest of Edinburgh.

Oft-overlooked Dunfermline was once the world center for the production of damask linen, but the town is better known today as the birthplace of millionaire industrialist and philanthropist Andrew Carnegie (1835–1919). Undoubtedly, Dunfermline's most famous son, Carnegie endowed the town with a park, library, fitness center, and, naturally, a Carnegie Hall, still the focus of culture and entertainment.

GETTING HERE AND AROUND

When you're driving, head north of the Forth Bridge on the A90, then the M90.

EXPLORING

Andrew Carnegie Birthplace Museum. Scottish-American industrialist and noted philanthropist Andrew Carnegie was born here in 1835. Don't be misled by the simple exterior of this 18th-century weaver's cottage—inside it opens into a larger hall, where documents, photographs, and artifacts relate his fascinating life story. The collection includes art from a wide range of periods, from medieval to 19th-century Arts and Crafts and art deco, and displays on the species of dinosaur named after the great man—*Diplodocus carnegii.* ⊠ *Moodie St.* ☎ *01383/724302* ⊕ *www.carnegiebirthplace.com* ⊠ *Free* ⊙ *Mar.– Nov., Mon.–Sat. 10–5, Sun. 2–5.*

Dunfermline Abbey and Palace. The complex was founded in the 11th century by Queen Margaret, the English wife of the Scottish king Malcolm III. Some Norman work can be seen in the present church, where Robert the Bruce (12744–1329) lies buried. The palace grew from the abbey guesthouse and was the birthplace of Charles I (1600–49). Dunfermline was the seat of the royal court of Scotland until the end of the 11th century, and its central role in Scottish affairs is explored by means of display panels dotted around the drafty but hallowed buildings. ⊠ *Monastery St.* ☎ *01383/739026* ⊕ *www.historic-scotland.gov.uk/ places* ⊠ *£4.50* ⊙ *Apr.–Sept., daily 9:30–5:30; Oct.–Mar., Mon.–Wed. and weekends 10–4. Last admission 30 mins before closing.*

FAMILY **Pittencrieff House Museum.** Housed in a 17th-century laird's mansion surrounded by beautiful parkland with picnic areas and resident peacocks, Pittencrieff House Museum explores the town's history. The Magic of the Glen section features a family-friendly natural-history exhibit that includes dinosaurs, fossils, and wildlife. ⊠ *Pittencrieff Park* ☎ *01383/722935* ⊕ *www.scottishmuseums.org.uk* ⊠ *Free* ⊙ *Apr.– Sept., daily 11–5; Oct.–Mar., daily 11–4.*

SIDE TRIPS: MIDLOTHIAN AND EAST LOTHIAN

Stretching east to the sea and south to the Lowlands from Edinburgh, Midlothian and East Lothian are no more than one hour from Edinburgh. In spite of the finest stone carving in Scotland at Rosslyn Chapel, associations with Sir Walter Scott, outstanding castles, and miles of rolling countryside, Midlothian, the area immediately south of Edinburgh, for years remained off the beaten path. Perhaps a little in awe of sophisticated Edinburgh to the north and the well-manicured charm of the stockbroker belt of nearby upmarket East Lothian, Midlothian was quietly preoccupied with its own workaday little towns and dormitory suburbs.

As for East Lothian, it started with the advantage of golf courses of world rank, most notably Muirfield, plus a scattering of stately homes and interesting hotels. It's an area of glowing grain fields in summer and quite a few discreetly polite "strictly private" signs at the end of driveways. Still, it has plenty of interest, including photogenic villages, active fishing harbors, and vistas of pastoral Lowland Scotland, seemingly a world away (but much less than an hour by car) from bustling Edinburgh.

GETTING HERE AND AROUND

BUS TRAVEL   City buses travel as far as Swanston and the Pentland Hills. First buses serve towns and villages throughout Midlothian and East Lothian. For details of all services, inquire at the Edinburgh Bus Station, immediately east of St. Andrew Square in Edinburgh.

CAR TRAVEL   A quick route to Rosslyn Chapel follows the A701, while the A7 heads toward Gorebridge and the National Mining Museum Scotland. The A1 passes Newhailes, Haddington, and Dunbar. Take the A198 to North Berwick, Dirleton Castle, and Tantallon Castle.

TRAIN TRAVEL   There is no train service in Midlothian. In East Lothian the towns of North Berwick, Drem, and Dunbar have train stations with regular service from Edinburgh.

NEWHAILES

5 miles east of Edinburgh.

With sumptuous interiors and relaxing grounds, this neo-Palladian villa a few miles east of Edinburgh hosted many luminaries of the Scottish Enlightenment.

GETTING HERE AND AROUND

To get here from Edinburgh take the A1 east, then transfer to the A6095. You can also get here by Lothian Bus 30 or by train to Newcraighall Station, a 20-minute walk from the villa.

EXPLORING

Newhailes. This fine late-17th-century house (with 18th-century additions), owned and run by the National Trust for Scotland, was designed by Scottish architect James Smith (circa 1645–1731) in 1686 as his own home. He later sold it to Lord Bellendon, and in 1707 it was bought by Sir David Dalrymple (c. 1665–1721), first Baronet of Hailes, who improved and extended the house, adding one of the finest rococo interiors in Scotland. The library played host to many famous figures from the Scottish Enlightenment, including inveterate Scot-basher Dr. Samuel Johnson, who dubbed the library "the most learned room in Europe." Most of the original interiors and furnishings remain intact, creating great authenticity. ✉ *Newhailes Rd., Musselburgh* ☎ *0844/493–2125* 🌐 *www.nts.org.uk/visits* 🎟 *£13* 🕒 *House: Apr.–June and Sept., Thurs.–Mon. noon–5; July and Aug., daily noon–5; Oct., weekends noon–4. Estate: daily dawn–dusk.*

ROSLIN

7 miles south of Edinburgh.

Although the town is overshadowed by its chapel, Roslin is a pleasant place to while away some time. There are some nice walks by the North River Esk.

GETTING HERE AND AROUND

By car take the A701 south. Lothian buses service also shuttle passengers from Edinburgh.

EXPLORING

Fodor's Choice ★ **Rosslyn Chapel.** This chapel has always beckoned curious visitors intrigued by the various legends surrounding its magnificent carvings, but today it pulses with tourists as never before. In the 2000s Dan Brown's bestselling novel *The Da Vinci Code* made visiting this Episcopal chapel (services continue to be held here) an imperative stop on many a traveler's itinerary. Whether you're a fan of the book or not—and of the book's theory that the chapel has a secret sign that can lead you to the Holy Grail—this is still a site of immense interest. Originally conceived by Sir William Sinclair (circa 1404–80) and dedicated to St. Matthew in 1446, the chapel is outstanding for the quality and variety of the carving inside. Covering almost every square inch of stonework are human figures, animals, and plants. The meaning of these remains subject to many theories; some depict symbols from the medieval order of the Knights Templar and from Freemasonry. The chapel's design called for a cruciform structure, but only the choir and parts of the east transept walls were completed. Free talks about the building's history are held daily. ✉ *Chapel Loan* ☎ *0131/440–2159* 🌐 *www.rosslynchapel.com* 🎟 *£9* 🕒 *Mon.–Sat. 9:30–5:30, Sun. noon–4:45.*

WHERE TO EAT

$ BRITISH 🍴 **Original Rosslyn Hotel.** Good and hearty pub lunches are available at this atmospheric inn, located on the crossroads in the center of Roslin village. Fish-and-chips, burgers, pies, hickory-smoked chicken, plus a few veggie options are crowd-pleasers. The inn is five minutes' walk from Rosslyn Chapel; just turn left until you hit Main Street, and it's easily spotted on the opposite side of the road. [$] *Average main: £9* ✉ *2–4 Main St., Roslin, Edinburgh* ☎ *0131/440–2384* 🌐 *www.theoriginalhotel.co.uk.*

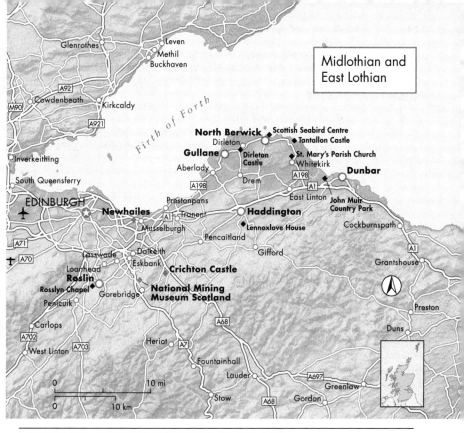

Midlothian and
East Lothian

NATIONAL MINING MUSEUM SCOTLAND

9 miles southeast of Edinburgh.

The museum provides a sobering look into the lives of coal miners and
conditions they endured down Scotland's mines.

GETTING HERE AND AROUND

To get here by car, head south on the A7 to Newtongrange. You can
also take Lothian Buses 33 or 29 or First Buses 95 or X95.

EXPLORING

National Mining Museum Scotland. In the former mining community of
Newtongrange, the National Mining Museum provides a good introduction to the history of Scotland's mining industry. With the help of
videos you can experience life deep below the ground. There are also
interactive displays and "magic helmets" that bring the tour to life
and relate the power that the mining company had over the lives of the
individual workers here, in Scotland's largest planned-mining village.
This frighteningly autocratic system survived well into the 1930s—the
company owned the houses, shops, and even the pub. The scenery is
no more attractive than you would expect, with the green Pentland
Hills hovering in the distance. ⊠ *A7, Newtongrange* ☎ *0131/663–
7519* ⊕ *nationalminingmuseum.com* 🎫 *£8.50* ☉ *Apr.–Sept., daily*

10–5; Oct.–Mar., daily 10–4; last admission 1½ hrs before closing. Guided tours daily at 11:30, 1:30, and 3.

CRICHTON CASTLE

11 miles southeast of Edinburgh.

Sitting on a terrace above the River Tyne, this 14th-century structure with a diamond-faceted façade was home to the Crichtons and later to the earls of Bothwell.

GETTING HERE AND AROUND
Heading south on the A68, take the turnoff at Pathhead.

EXPLORING
Crichton Castle. Standing amid rolling hills that are interrupted here and there by patches of woodland, Crichton was a Bothwell family castle. Mary, Queen of Scots, attended the wedding here of Bothwell's sister, Lady Janet Hepburn, to Mary's brother, Lord John Stewart. The curious arcaded range reveals diamond-faceted stonework; this particular geometric pattern is unique in Scotland and is thought to have been inspired by Renaissance styles on the Continent, particularly Italy. The oldest part of the work is the 14th-century *keep* (square tower). Note that there are no toilets at the castle. ⊠ *B6367, 7 miles southeast of Dalkeith, Pathhead* ☎ *01875/320017* ⊕ *www.historic-scotland.gov. uk/places* ⊡ *£4.75* ☉ *Apr.–Sept., daily 9:30–5:30. Last admission 45 mins before closing.*

DUNBAR

25 miles east of Edinburgh.

In the days before tour companies started offering package deals to the Mediterranean, Dunbar was a popular holiday beach resort. Now a bit faded, the town is still lovely for its spacious Georgian-style properties, characterized by the astragals, or fan-shape windows, above the doors; the symmetry of the house fronts; and the parapeted rooflines. Though not the popular seaside playground it once was, Dunbar has an attractive beach and a picturesque harbor. It's also one end of the John Muir Way, a cross-Scotland hiking trail.

GETTING HERE AND AROUND
Head east on the A1 to get to Dunbar. You can also take the train from Waverley.

EXPLORING
John Muir Country Park. Taking in the estuary of the River Tyne winding down from the Moorfoot Hills, the John Muir Country Park encompasses varied coastal scenery: rocky shoreline, golden sands, and the mixed woodlands of Tyninghame, teeming with wildlife. Dunbar-born conservationist John Muir (1838–1914), whose family moved to the United States when he was a child, helped found Yosemite and Sequoia national parks in California. ⊠ *A1087, 2 miles west of Dunbar.*

SPORTS AND THE OUTDOORS
GOLF

Dunbar Golf Club. There's a lighthouse at the 9th hole of this seaside course, first laid out in 1856. It's a good choice for experiencing a typical east-coast links. Within easy reach of Edinburgh, it has stunning views of the Firth of Forth and May Island. The club has recently started a major expansion which should add a new clubhouse and a hotel, in addition to an enlarged course. Greens fees drop by nearly half in winter. ⊠ *East Links, off A1087* ☎ *01368/862317* ⊕ *www.dunbar-golfclub. co.uk* ⛳ *£70 weekdays, £90 weekends* ⛳ *18 holes, 6597 yards, par 71* ⏰ *Fri.–Wed.* ⚑ *Reservations essential.*

HIKING

John Muir Way. Completed in 2014, this much-praised scenic hiking path stretches from Helensburgh, west of Glasgow, to Dunbar—Muir's birthplace. The 130-mile coast-to-coast route passes through some spectacular scenery (especially so at the Helensburgh end). It takes about a week to traverse completely, but the official website has maps covering all the various sections. At the Dunbar end is a small museum (*128 High St. 01368/865899*) dedicated to John Muir. ⊠ *Edinburgh* ⊕ *www. johnmuirway.org.*

NORTH BERWICK

20 miles northeast of Edinburgh.

The pleasant little seaside resort of North Berwick manages to retain a small-town personality even when it's thronged with city visitors on warm summer Sunday afternoons. Eating ice cream, the city folk stroll on the beach and in the narrow streets or gaze at the sailing craft in the small harbor. The town is near a number of castles and other sights.

GETTING HERE AND AROUND

Travel east on the A1 and A198, or take the train from Waverley.

EXPLORING

Dirleton Castle. In the center of tiny Dirleton sits the impressive looking, 12th-century Dirleton Castle, surrounded by a high outer wall. It's now a ruin but with a relatively complete outer facade, and the grounds behind the walls feature a 17th-century bowling green, set in the shade of yew trees and surrounded by a herbaceous flower border that blazes with color in high summer. The castle was occupied in 1298 by King Edward I of England as part of his campaign for the continued subjugation of the unruly Scots. ⊠ *A198, 2 miles west of North Berwick* ☎ *01620/850330* ⊕ *www.historic-scotland.gov.uk/places* 💷 *£5.50* ⏰ *Apr.–Sept., daily 9:30–5:30; Oct.–Mar., daily 10–4. Last admission 30 mins before closing.*

FAMILY **Scottish Seabird Centre.** An observation deck, exhibits, and films at the Scottish Seabird Centre provide a captivating introduction to the world of the gannets and puffins that nest on nearby Bass Rock. Live interactive cameras let you take an even closer look at the bird colonies and marine mammals at Craigleith and the Isle of May. Kids will enjoy the "tunnel of discovery," a new 3-D multimedia exhibit that simulates walking through an underwater passage, learning all about birds and sealife along the way. There are plenty of family-friendly activities, nature walks, and photography shows. ⊠ *The Harbour* ☎ *01620/890202* ⊕ *www.seabird.org* 🎫 *£9.25* ⊙ *Apr.–Aug., daily 10–6; Feb., Mar., Sept., and Oct., weekdays 10–5, weekends 10–5:30; Nov.–Jan., weekdays 10–4, weekends 10–5. Last admission 45 mins before closing.*

St. Mary's Parish Church. The unmistakable red-sandstone St. Mary's Parish Church, with its Norman tower, stands in the village of Whitekirk on a site occupied since the 6th century. It was a place of pilgrimage in medieval times because of its healing well. Behind the kirk, in a field, stands a tithe barn. Tithe barns originated with the practice of giving to the church a portion of local produce, which then required storage space. In the 15th century, the church was visited by a young Italian nobleman, Aeneas Sylvius Piccolomini, after he was shipwrecked off the East Lothian coast. Two decades later, Piccolomini became Pope Pius II. At one end of the barn stands a 16th-century tower house, which at one point in its history accommodated visiting pilgrims. The large three-story barn was added to the tower house in the 17th century. ⊠ *A198, 6 miles south of North Berwick, Whitekirk* 🎫 *Free* ⊙ *Daily 9 am–sunset.*

Tantallon Castle. Rising on a cliff beyond the flat fields east of North Berwick, Tantallon Castle is a substantial ruin defending a headland with the sea on three sides. The red sandstone is pitted and eaten by time and sea spray, with the earliest surviving stonework dating from the late 14th century. The fortress was besieged in 1529 by the cannons of King James V (1512–42). Rather inconveniently, the besieging forces ran out of gunpowder. Cannons were used again, to deadlier effect, in a later siege during the civil war in 1651. Twelve days of battering with the heavy guns of Cromwell's General Monk greatly damaged the flanking towers. Fortunately much of the curtain wall of this former Douglas stronghold, now cared for by Historic Scotland, survives. ⊠ *A198* ☎ *01620/892727* ⊕ *www.historic-scotland.gov.uk/ places* 🎫 *£5.75* ⊙ *Apr.–Sept., daily 9:30–5:30; Oct.–Mar., daily 10–4. Last admission 30 mins before closing.*

WHERE TO STAY

$$
B&B/INN

🏨 **Glebe House.** This dignified 18th-century manse sits amid its own secluded grounds, yet it's in the heart of town, a 10-minute walk east of the station. **Pros:** peaceful atmosphere; interesting antiques; sociable breakfast around a mahogany table. **Cons:** books up well in advance; too precious for some. $ *Rooms from: £140* ⊠ *Law Rd.* ☎ *01620/892608* ⊕ *www.glebehouse-nb.co.uk* 🛏 *4 rooms* ❚❘ *Breakfast.*

GULLANE

15 miles northeast of Edinburgh.

Noticeable along this coastline are the golf courses of East Lothian, laid out wherever there is available links space. Gullane is surrounded by them, and its inhabitants are typically clad in expensive golfing sweaters. Apart from golf, you can enjoy restful summer evening strolls at Gullane's beach, well within driving distance of the village.

GETTING HERE AND AROUND

From Edinburgh, drive east on the A1, then head north on the A198.

GOLF

Gullane Golf Club. Often overshadowed by Muirfield, Gullane provides an equally authentic links experience and a far more effusive welcome than its slightly snooty neighbor just along the road. The three courses here crisscross Gullane Hill and all command outstanding views of the Firth of Forth. No. 1 is the toughest, but No. 2 and No. 3 offer up equally compelling sport. Day tickets can be purchased for between £6 and £15, the cost of a single round, depending on the course. ⊠ *West Links Rd.* ☎ *01620/842255* ⊕ *www.gullanegolfclub. com* ✉ *No. 1 Course, £98; No. 2 Course, £49; No. 3 Course, £35* ⚐ *No. 1 Course: 18 holes, 6583 yards, par 71; No. 2 Course: 18 holes, 6385 yards, par 71; No. 3 Course: 18 holes, 5259 yards, par 68* ☉ *Daily* ⚑ *Reservations essential.*

Muirfield. Home of the Honourable Company of Edinburgh Golfers, the world's oldest golfing club, Muirfield has a pedigree that few other courses can match. Although this course overlooking the Firth of Forth is considered one of the world's most challenging, players also talk about it being "fair," meaning it has no hidden bunkers or sand traps. Unfortunately the club has a well-deserved reputation for being stuffy (pop star Justin Timberlake wasn't allowed in the restaurant because he wasn't wearing a jacket and tie); and, despite slow movement toward a less chauvinistic arrangement, women are still not allowed to be members (although they can play as guests). Visitors are allowed only on Tuesday and Thursday, and you must apply for a tee time well in advance. ⊠ *Duncur Rd.* ☎ *01620/842123* ⊕ *www.muirfield.org.uk* ✉ *£210 Apr.–Oct., £110 Nov.–Mar.* ⚐ *18 holes, 6601 yards, par 70.*

HADDINGTON

15 miles east of Edinburgh.

One of the best-preserved medieval street plans in the country can be explored in Haddington. Among the many buildings of architectural or historical interest is the Town House, designed by William Adam in 1748 and enlarged in 1830. A wall plaque at the Sidegate recalls the great heights of floods from the River Tyne. Beyond is the medieval Nungate footbridge, with the Church of St. Mary a little way upstream.

GETTING HERE AND AROUND

Head east on the A1, or take First Buses X6, X8, or 106.

EXPLORING

Lennoxlove House. Just to the south of Haddington stands Lennoxlove House, the grand ancestral home of the very grand dukes of Hamilton since 1947 and the Baird family before them. A turreted country house, part of it dating from the 15th century, Lennoxlove is a cheerful mix of family life and Scottish history. The beautifully decorated rooms house portraits, furniture, porcelain, and items associated with Mary, Queen of Scots, including her supposed death mask. Sporting activities from falconry to fishing take place on the stunning grounds. ⊠ *B6369* ☏ *01620/823720* ⊕ *www.lennoxlove.com* ✉ *£5* ⊗ *Tours Apr.–Sept., Wed., Thurs, and Sun. 1:30, 2:30, and 3:30.*

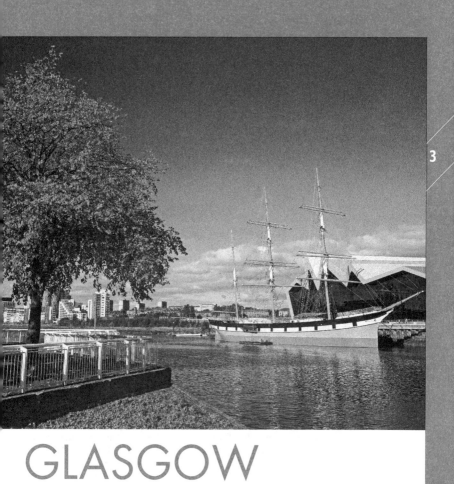

GLASGOW

Updated
by Mike
Gonzalez

Trendy stores, a booming cultural life, fascinating architecture, and stylish restaurants reinforce Glasgow's claim to being Scotland's most exciting city. After decades of decline, it has experienced an urban renaissance uniquely its own. The city's grand architecture reflects a prosperous past built on trade and shipbuilding. Today buildings by Charles Rennie Mackintosh hold pride of place along with the Zaha Hadid–designed Riverside Museum.

Glasgow (the "dear green place," as it was known) was founded some 1,500 years ago. Legend has it that the king of Strathclyde, irate about his wife's infidelity, had a ring he had given her thrown into the River Clyde. (Apparently she had passed it on to an admirer.) When the king demanded to know where the ring had gone, the distraught queen asked the advice of her confessor, St. Mungo. He suggested fishing for it—and the first salmon to emerge had the ring in its mouth. The moment is commemorated on the city's coat of arms.

The medieval city expanded when it was given a royal license to trade; the current High Street was the main thoroughfare at the time. The vast profits from American cotton and tobacco built the grand mansions of the Merchant City in the 18th century. Tobacco lords financed the building of wooden ships, and by the 19th century the River Clyde had become the center of a vibrant shipbuilding industry, fed by the city's iron and steel works. The city grew again, but its internal divisions grew at the same time. The West End harbored the elegant homes of the newly rich shipyard owners. Down by the river, areas like the infamous Gorbals, with its crowded slums, or Govan, sheltered the laborers who built the ships. They came from the Highlands, expelled to make way for sheep, or from Ireland, where the potato famines drove thousands from their homes.

During the 19th century the city's population grew from 80,000 to more than a million. The new prosperity gave Glasgow its grand neoclassical buildings, such as those built by Alexander "Greek" Thomson, as well as the adventurous visionary buildings designed by Charles Rennie Mackintosh and others who produced Glasgow's Arts and Crafts movement. The City Chambers, built in 1888, are a proud statement in marble and gold sandstone, a clear symbol of the wealthy and powerful Victorian industrialists' hopes for the future.

The decline of shipbuilding and the closure of the factories in the later 20th century led to much speculation as to what direction the city would take now. The curious thing is that, at least in part, the past gave the city its new lease on life. It was as if people looked at their city and saw Glasgow's beauty for the first time: its extraordinarily rich architectural heritage, its leafy parks, its artistic heritage, and its complex social

TOP REASONS TO GO

Design and architecture: The Victorians left a legacy of striking architecture, and Glasgow's buildings manifest the city's love of grand artistic statements—just remember to look up. The Arts and Crafts buildings by Charles Rennie Mackintosh are reason alone to visit.

Art museums: Some of Britain's best museums and art galleries are in Glasgow. The Hunterian Art Gallery and the eclectic Kelvingrove Art Gallery and Museum are definitely worth a visit, even on a sunny day.

Gorgeous parks and gardens: From Kelvingrove Park to the Botanic Gardens, Glasgow has more parks per square mile than any other city in Europe. Stop by the Botanic Gardens for outdoor theatrical productions in summer, or Bellahouston Park for the annual piping festival.

Pints and great grub: Whether you fancy a Guinness in a traditional old-man's pub like the Scotia or one of the converted churches like Òran Mór, there's a pub to fit all thirsts. Locals love their cafés and tearooms; stop by the Willow Tearoom or Where the Monkey Sleeps for cake and a rest from sightseeing.

Retail therapy: The city has become known for cutting-edge design. Look for everything from Scottish specialties to stylish fashions on the City Centre's hottest shopping streets, Ingram or Buchanan, or at the elegant Princes Square.

history. Today Glasgow is a dynamic cultural center and a commercial hub, as well as a launching pad from which to explore the rest of Scotland, which, as it turns out, is not so far away. In fact, it takes only 40 minutes to reach Loch Lomond, where the other Scotland begins.

GETTING ORIENTED

Glasgow's layout is hard to read at a single glance. The River Clyde, around which Glasgow grew up as a trading city, runs through the center of the city—literally cutting it in two. To the north, the oldest part of Glasgow, the Merchant City, stretches from High Street (the heart of the medieval city) as far as Queen Street, bounded by George Square and Argyle Street to the north and south. The Victorian city, which grew with the shipbuilding boom, reaches as far as what is now the M8 motorway and the River Clyde to the south. Crossing the M8 takes you to the West End, originally the quite wealthy area around Glasgow University. It now embraces the lovely Kelvingrove Park and the new bars and restaurants of Argyle Street, which has expanded and changed as shipbuilding gave way to riverside concerts and exhibition venues. The opposite bank of the river was the city's poorer quarter, where the workers lived, though beyond it are the park and museum around Pollok Park.

City Centre. If you're interested in how the city blossomed in the 19th century, this is where to start. Look up to see wonderful Victorian buildings expressing the confidence of a burgeoning industrial capital. George Square's City Chambers are well worth a visit before you trawl the shops along Buchanan Street, duck into one of the trendy eateries, or explore the wide variety of bars and music venues on offer.

Merchant City. In the Middle Ages, the city grew up around Glasgow Cathedral. The oldest house, Provand's Lordship, was originally the home of a bishop. As the city expanded along with the growing transatlantic trade, wealthy tobacco and cotton traders built their palatial houses here. They were laid to rest in the glorious tombs of the Necropolis, which overlooks the city. Today the area is busy with restaurants, clubs, and shops.

West End. In this quieter, slightly hillier western part of the city is Glasgow University and the more bohemian side of Glasgow. The West End's treasures include the Botanic Gardens, Kelvingrove Park, and the Kelvingrove Art Gallery and Museum. There are also plenty of well-priced restaurants and lively bars. Byres Road is at its heart, especially when it fills with weekend revelers at its bars and clubs.

The Clyde. Once a hardworking river lined with shipyards, the Clyde has been reborn as a relaxing destination that entrances visitors and locals alike. The Glasgow Science Centre and the Museum of Transport face each other across the water, while the Scottish Exhibition Centre and the new SSE Hydro are major venues for all sorts of events.

East End. What was once a neglected corner of Glasgow is being treated to a major face-lift. Glasgow Green's wonderful People's Palace draws visitors throughout the year, and on weekends the nearby Barras market is a reminder of the area's past.

South Side. Often overlooked, this less visited side of the city includes beautiful Pollok Park as well as Pollok House, with its art collection and its elegant gardens. A couple of architectural gems are here, too.

PLANNING

WHEN TO GO

The best times to visit Glasgow are spring and summer and into early fall. Although you may encounter crowds, the weather is more likely to be warm and dry. In summer the days can be long and pleasant—if the rain holds off—and festivals and outdoor events are abundant. Fall can be nice, although cold weather begins to set in after mid-September and the days grow shorter. From November to February it is cold, wet, and dark. Although thousands of people flock to Glasgow for New Year's celebrations, the winter months are relatively quiet in terms of crowds.

PLANNING YOUR TIME

You could quite easily spend five comfortable days here, although in a pinch, two would do and three would be pleasant. The best strategy for seeing the city is to start at High Street on the east side of Merchant City and work your way west. On the first day explore the city's medieval heritage, taking in Glasgow Cathedral, the Museum of Religious Life, and Provand's Lordship, as well as the Necropolis with its fascinating crumbling monuments. The gentle walk west from here to the Merchant City is also a walk through time, to 17th- and 18th-century Glasgow, and George Square, around which spread the active and crowded shopping areas. For those interested in architect Charles Rennie Mackintosh, the Mackintosh Trail connects the many buildings designed by this outstanding Glasgow designer and architect. The Mackintosh Trail Ticket (£10), which includes admission to all Mackintosh sites across Glasgow and transportation on subways or buses, is an excellent and economical way of seeing his work. Tickets can be purchased online at ⊕ *www.crmsociety.com* or at the individual sites. Another day could be well spent between the Kelvingrove Art Gallery (you can lunch here and listen to the daily concert on its magnificent organ) and the nearby Hunterian Museum and Gallery. From here it's only minutes to lively Byres Road and its shops, pubs, and cafés. Another option is to go to the South Side and seek out the House for an Art Lover and Pollok Park.

If you have a few extra days, head out to Burns country and the extraordinary Burns Birthplace Museum in Ayrshire. It's a scenic 45-minute drive from Glasgow. Most destinations on the Clyde Coast are easily accessible from Glasgow. Direct trains from Central station take you to Paisley, Irvine, Troon, and Lanark in less than an hour. These small towns need no more than a day to explore. To get a flavor of island life, take the hour-long train ride to Wemyss Bay and then the ferry to the Isle of Bute.

GETTING HERE AND AROUND
AIR TRAVEL
Airlines flying from Glasgow Airport to the rest of the United Kingdom and to Europe include Aer Lingus, Air Malta, BMI Regional, British Airways, easyJet, Flybe, Icelandair, Jet 2, and KLM. Several carriers fly from North America, including Air Canada, American Airlines, United, and Icelandair (service via Reykjavík).

Ryanair offers rock-bottom airfares between Prestwick and London's Stansted Airport. Budget-minded easyJet has similar services from Glasgow to London's Stansted and Luton airports. Loganair flies to the islands.

Air Contacts Air Canada. ☎ *0871/220–1111* ⊕ *www.aircanada.com.* **Aer Lingus.** ☎ *0333/004–5000* ⊕ *www.aerlingus.com.* **Air Malta.** ☎ *00356/2166–2211* ⊕ *www.airmalta.com.* **American Airlines.** ☎ *0207/660–2300* ⊕ *www.americanairlines.co.uk.* **BMI Regional.** ☎ *0330/337–7998* ⊕ *www.bmiregional.com.* **British Airways.** ☎ *0844/493–0747* ⊕ *www.britishairways.com.* **easyJet.** ☎ *0330/365–5000* ⊕ *www.easyjet.com.* **Flybe.** ☎ *01899/221050* ⊕ *www.flybe.com.* **Icelandair.** ☎ *0207/874–1000* ⊕ *www.icelandair.co.uk.* **Jet2.** ☎ *0800/408–1350* ⊕ *www.jet2.com.* **KLM.** ☎ *0207/660–0293* ⊕ *www.klm.com.* **Loganair.** ☎ *0371/700–2000* ⊕ *www.loganair.co.uk.* **Ryanair.** ☎ *0871/246–0000* ⊕ *www.ryanair.com.* **United.** ☎ *0845/607–6760* ⊕ *www.united.com.*

AIRPORTS Glasgow Airport (GLA) is about 7 miles west of the City Centre on the M8 to Greenock. The airport serves international and domestic flights, and most major European carriers have frequent and convenient connections to many cities on the continent; it closes overnight. There's a frequent shuttle service from London, as well as regular flights from Birmingham, Bristol, East Midlands, Leeds/Bradford, Manchester, Southampton, Isle of Man, and Jersey. There are also flights from Wales

(Cardiff) and Ireland (Belfast, Dublin, and Londonderry). Local Scottish connections can be made to Aberdeen, Barra, Benbecula, Campbeltown, Inverness, Islay, Kirkwall, Shetland (Sumburgh), Stornoway, and Tiree.

Prestwick Airport (PIK), on the Ayrshire coast about 30 miles southwest of Glasgow, is known mainly as an airport for budget airlines like Ryanair.

Airport Contacts Glasgow Airport. ✉ *Caledonia Way, Paisley* ☎ *0844/481–5555* ⊕ *www.glasgowairport.com.* **Prestwick Airport.** ✉ *A79, Prestwick* ☎ *0871/223–0700* ⊕ *www.glasgowprestwick.com.*

TRANSFERS Although there's a railway station about 2 miles from Glasgow Airport (Paisley Gilmour Street), it is not very accessible. Transport to the City Centre is either by bus or taxi and takes about 20 minutes. Metered taxis are available outside domestic arrivals, and cost around £22.

Express buses depart every 15 minutes from Glasgow Airport (outside the departures lobby) to Central and Queen Street stations and to the Buchanan Street bus station. The fare is £6.

The drive from Glasgow Airport into the City Centre is normally quite easy, even if you're used to driving on the right. The M8 motorway runs beside the airport (Junction 29) and takes you straight into the City Centre. Thereafter Glasgow's streets follow a grid pattern, at least in the City Centre.

Most companies that provide chauffeur-driven cars and tours will also do limousine airport transfers. TBR Global Chauffeuring is a worldwide organization offering chauffeur-driven transport in Glasgow and across the United Kingdom.

There's rapid half-hourly train service (hourly on Sunday) direct from Prestwick Airport's terminal to Glasgow Central. Strathclyde Passenger Transport and ScotRail offer a discount ticket that allows you to travel for half the standard fare; just show a valid airline ticket for a flight to or from Prestwick Airport. An hourly coach service makes the same trip but takes much longer than the train.

By car, the City Centre is reached via the fast M77 in about 40 minutes. Metered taxis are available at the airport. The fare to Glasgow is about £40.

Airport Transfer Contacts Little's Chauffeur Drive. ☎ *0141/883–2111* ⊕ *www.littles.co.uk.* **Strathclyde Passenger Transport Travel Centre.** ✉ *Buchanan Street Bus Station, Killermont St., City Centre* ☎ *0141/332–6811* ⊕ *www.spt.co.uk* Ⓜ *Buchanan St.* **TBR Global Chauffeuring.** ☎ *0141/280–4800* ⊕ *www.tbrglobal.com.*

BIKE TRAVEL

Glasgow has become an increasingly cycle-friendly city with networks of off-road cycle paths. In 2014 Glasgow introduced a public bike-rental scheme; ranks of blue cycles at over 30 stations around the city are available for hire. To rent a bike, provide a credit card number and a £10 deposit on the smartphone app, over the phone, or on the on-bike computer, and give them the cycle number. You'll be given the number for the combination lock and off you go. The whole process takes seconds, and it's a great way to see the city. Bikes cost £1 per 30 minutes up to 5 hours or £10 for 5–24 hours. The Glasgow Cycle Map available at all information centers provides comprehensive information on routes.

Bike Contacts Nextbike. ☎ *0208/166–9851* ⊕ *www.nextbike.co.uk.*

BUS TRAVEL

The main intercity operators are National Express and Scottish Citylink, which serve numerous towns and cities in Scotland, Wales, and England, including London and Edinburgh. Glasgow's bus station is on Buchanan Street, not far from Queen Street station.

When traveling from the City Centre to either the West End or the South Side, it's easy to use the city's integrated network of buses, subways, and trains. Service is reliable and connections are convenient from buses to trains and the subway. Many buses require exact fare, which is usually around £1.75.

Traveline Scotland provides information on schedules and fares, as does the Strathclyde Passenger Transport Travel Centre, which has an information center.

Bus Contacts Buchanan Street Bus Station. ✉ *Killermont St., City Centre* ☎ *0141/333–3708* ⊕ *www.spt.co.uk* Ⓜ *Buchanan St.* **Megabus.** ☎ *0141/352–4444* ⊕ *uk.megabus.com.* **National Express.** ☎ *0871/781–8181* ⊕ *www.nationalexpressgroup.com.* **Scottish Citylink.** ☎ *0871/266–3333* ⊕ *www.citylink.co.uk.* **Traveline Scotland.** ☎ *0871/200–2233* ⊕ *www. travelinescotland.com.*

CAR TRAVEL

If you're driving to Glasgow from England and the south of Scotland, you'll probably approach the city via the M6, M74, and A74. The City Centre is clearly marked from these roads. From Edinburgh, the M8 leads to the City Centre. From the north, the A82 from Fort William and the A82/M80 from Stirling join the M8 in the City Centre.

You don't need a car in Glasgow, and you're probably better off without one. Although most modern hotels have their own lots, parking can be trying. In the City Centre meters are expensive, running about £2.40 per hour during the day. In the West End they cost 80 pence per hour, but you often have to feed the meter until 10 pm. Don't even consider parking illegally, as fines are upward of £30. Multistory garages are open 24 hours a day at Anderston Centre, George Street, Waterloo Place, Mitchell Street, Cambridge Street, and Concert Square. Rates run between £1 and £2 per hour. More convenient are the park-and-ride operations at some subway stations (Kelvinbridge, Bridge Street, and Shields Road).

SUBWAY TRAVEL

Glasgow's small subway system—it has 15 stations—is useful for reaching all the City Centre and West End attractions. Stations are marked by a prominent letter "S." You can choose between flat fares (£1.40) and a one-day pass (£4). A £3 Smart Card will give you reduced fares. A Roundabout ticket costs £6.50 a day and covers subway and train. A Day Tripper ticket is well worth it for families, covering bus, subway, rail, and some ferries. It costs £11.50 for one adult and up to two children or £20.30 for two adults and up to four kids. Subway trains run regularly from Monday through Saturday, with more limited Sunday service. The distance between many central stops is no more than a 10-minute walk. More information is available from Strathclyde Passenger Transport Travel Centre.

TAXI TRAVEL

Taxis are a fast and cost-effective way to get around. You'll find metered taxis (usually black and of the London sedan type) at stands all over the City Centre. Most have radio dispatch. Some have also been adapted to take wheelchairs. You can hail a cab on the street if its "for hire" sign is illuminated. A typical ride from the City Centre to the West End or the South Side costs around £6.

Taxi Contact Glasgow Taxis. ☎ 0141/429–7070 ⊕ www.glasgowtaxis.co.uk.

TRAIN TRAVEL

Glasgow has two main rail stations: Central and Queen Street. Central serves Virgin trains from London's Euston station (five hours), which come via Crewe and Carlisle in England. East Coast trains run from London's Kings Cross to Glasgow's Queen Street station, which has frequent connections to Edinburgh. For details, contact National Rail.

A regular bus service links the Queen Street and Central stations (although you can easily walk if you aren't too encumbered). Queen Street is near the Buchanan Street subway station, and Central is close to St. Enoch. Taxis are available at both stations.

The Glasgow area has an extensive network of suburban railway services. Locals still call them the Blue Trains, even though most are now painted maroon and cream. For more information and a free map, contact the Strathclyde Passenger Transport Travel Centre or National.

Train Contacts National Rail. ☎ 08457/484950 ⊕ www.nationalrail.co.uk.

TOURS

You can sign on for a sightseeing tour to get a different perspective on the city and the surrounding area.

BOAT TOURS

Cruises are available on Loch Lomond and to the islands in the Firth of Clyde; contact the Greater Glasgow and Clyde Valley Tourist Board for details.

Sweeney's Cruises. This operator runs tours on Loch Lomond from Balloch, Luss, and Tarbert. ⊠ *Riverside, Balloch Rd., Balloch* ☎ *01389/752376* ⊕ *www.sweeneyscruises.com* ✉ *From £10.20.*

FAMILY **Waverley Excursions.** The paddle steamer *Waverley* is a Glasgow institution, sailing from Glasgow to the Clyde estuary (Glaswegians call it "doon the watter") and the islands of the west coast from May to October. *Waverley* is the world's last seagoing paddle steamer, retired from commercial work 40 years ago but still going strong. Her evening jazz cruises are very popular. There is a wide variety of routes; check online for timetables and prices. *Waverley* is permanently based at Lancefield

Quay, beside the science museum. ✉ *36 Lancefield Quay* ☎ *0845/130-4647* ⊕ *www.waverleyexcursions.co.uk* ✉ *From £25.*

BUS TOURS

The Greater Glasgow and Clyde Valley Tourist Board can give information about city tours and about longer tours northward to the Highlands and Islands.

City Sightseeing. Daily bus tours of Glasgow in open-topped double-decker buses are offered by City Sightseeing. It is a hop-on/hop-off service; the full tour lasts just under two hours, with an English-speaking guide aboard and a multilingual commentary. Tours begin at George Square. ✉ *153 Queen St.* ☎ *0141/204–0444* ⊕ *www. citysightseeingglasgow.co.uk* ✉ *From £13.*

Rabbie's Trail Burners. Choose from a range of well-regarded one-, two-, and three-day minibus tours with guides to Loch Lomond, Loch Ness, Stirling, and the Highlands. ☎ *0845/643–2248* ⊕ *www.rabbies.com* ✉ *From £45.*

PRIVATE GUIDES

Glasgow Taxis. Few people know the city better than taxi drivers. Glasgow Taxis will organize a guided Mackintosh tour or a Burns tour around Glasgow, including pickup and drop-off at your place of choice. These black cabs carry up to five passengers. ✉ *City Centre* ☎ *0141/429–7070* ⊕ *www.glasgowtaxis.co.uk* ✉ *From £35 per taxi.*

Little's Chauffeur Drive. Arrange personally tailored car-and-driver tours, both locally and throughout Scotland. ☎ *0141/883–2111* ⊕ *www. littles.co.uk.*

Scottish Tourist Guides Association. The association provides qualified and accredited Blue Badge Guides with specific areas of expertise and who speak a range of languages. Tours start at half a day, and driver guides are also available. All bookings should be made in advance online. ☎ *01786/451953* ⊕ *www.stga.co.uk* ✉ *From £120.*

WALKING TOURS

The Greater Glasgow and Clyde Valley Tourist Board can provide information on a whole range of self-guided walks around the city.

Glasgow Historic Walks. These walks will introduce you to the history and heritage of the city, from architectural strolls through crime sites to the local history of individuals such as St. Patrick and Mary, Queen of Scots. ☎ *No phone* ⊕ *www.glasgowhistoricwalks.com* ✉ *From £6.*

VISITOR INFORMATION

The Greater Glasgow and Clyde Valley Tourist Board provides information about different types of tours and has an accommodations-booking service, a currency-exchange office, and a money-transfer service. Books, maps, and souvenirs are also available. The tourist board has a branch at Glasgow Airport, too.

Contact Greater Glasgow and Clyde Valley Tourist Board. ✉ *10 Sauchiehall St., City Centre* ☎ *0845/225–5121* ⊕ *www.visitscotland.com/glasgow.*

EXPLORING GLASGOW

As cities go, Glasgow is contained and compact. It's set up on a grid system, so it's easy to navigate and explore, and the best way to tackle it is on foot. In the eastern part of the city, start by exploring Glasgow Cathedral and other highlights of the oldest section of the city, then wander through the rest of the Merchant City. From there you can just continue into the City Centre with its designer shops, art galleries, and eateries. From here you can either walk (it takes a good 45 minutes) or take the subway to the West End. If you walk, head up Sauchiehall Street. Once in the West End, visit the Botanic Gardens, Glasgow University, and the Kelvingrove Art Gallery and Museum. Then take a taxi to the South Side to experience Pollok House. For Glasgow's East End, walk down High Street from the cathedral to the Tron Cross; from there you can walk to the Barras market and Glasgow Green.

CITY CENTRE

Some of the city's most important historical buildings are found in the City Centre close to George Square, many of them converted to very different purposes now. Along the streets of this neighborhood you will find some of the best examples of the architectural confidence and exuberance that so characterized the burgeoning Glasgow of the turn of the 20th century. There are also plenty of shops, trendy eateries, and pubs.

GETTING HERE

Every form of public transportation can bring you here, from bus to train to subway. Head to George Square and walk from there.

TOP ATTRACTIONS

Fodor'sChoice
★
City Chambers. Dominating the east side of George Square, this exuberant expression of Victorian confidence, built by William Young in Italian Renaissance style, was opened by Queen Victoria in 1888. Among the interior's outstanding features are the entrance hall's vaulted ceiling, sustained by granite columns topped with marble, the marble-and-alabaster staircases, and Venetian mosaics. The enormous banqueting hall has murals illustrating Glasgow's history. Free guided tours lasting about an hour depart weekdays at 10:30 and 2:30; tours are very popular so pick up a ticket beforehand from the reception desk. The building is closed to visitors during civic functions. ⊠ *80 George Sq., City Centre* ☎ *0141/287–4020* ⊕ *www.glasgow.gov.uk* 🖃 *Free* ⊙ *Weekdays 9–5* Ⓜ *Buchanan St.*

George Square. The focal point of Glasgow is lined with an impressive collection of statues of worthies: Queen Victoria; Scotland's national poet, Robert Burns (1759–96); the inventor and developer of the steam engine, James Watt (1736–1819); Prime Minister William Gladstone (1809–98); and, towering above them all, Scotland's great historical novelist, Sir Walter Scott (1771–1832). The column was intended for George III (1738–1820), after whom the square is named, but when he was found to be insane toward the end of his reign, his statue was never erected. On the square's east side stands the magnificent Italian Renaissance–style **City Chambers**; the handsome **Merchants' House**

fills the corner of West George Street, crowned by a globe and a sailing ship. The fine old Post Office building, now converted into flats, occupies the northern side. There are plenty of benches in the center of the square where you can pause and contemplate. ✉ *Between St. Vincent and Argyle Sts., City Centre* Ⓜ *Buchanan St.*

Glasgow Gallery of Modern Art. One of Glasgow's boldest, most innovative galleries occupies the neoclassical former Royal Exchange building. The modern art, craft, and design collections include works by Scottish conceptual artists such as David Mach, and also paintings and sculptures from around the world, including Papua New Guinea, Ethiopia, and Mexico. Each floor of the gallery reflects one of the elements—air, fire, earth, and water—which creates some unexpected juxtapositions and also allows for various interactive exhibits. In the basement is a café and an extensive library, and a small shop is on the ground floor. The exchange building, designed by David Hamilton (1768–1843) and finished in 1829, was a meeting place for merchants and traders; later it became Stirling's Library. It incorporates the mansion built in 1780 by William Cunninghame, one of the wealthiest tobacco lords. ✉ *Queen St., City Centre* ☎ *0141/287–3050* ⊕ *galleryofmodernart.wordpress. com* ✆ *Free* ◷ *Weekdays 10–5, weekends 11–5* Ⓜ *Buchanan St.*

Fodor's Choice ★ **Glasgow School of Art.** In 2014 this emblematic Glasgow building—the most stunning example of the genius of architect Charles Rennie Mackintosh—was badly damaged in a fire that swept through its interior and destroyed its famous library. The facade still exists, to give a sense of Mackintosh's achievement, but the building will not reopen until 2018. For many Glaswegians it felt almost like a personal tragedy. Fortunately, however, there are many other Mackintosh buildings around the city that testify to his originality as artist and architect. Daily walking tours of Mackintosh's Glasgow continue to be organized from the art school shop in Stephen Holl's new Reid Building, spectacular in itself, which sits directly opposite the original School of Art. In all sorts of ways the new school is an homage to the original. A small exhibition within the new school gives a sense of the artist's work. ✉ *164 Renfrew St., City Centre* ☎ *0141/353–4526* ⊕ *www.gsa.ac.uk/tours* ✆ *Free* ◷ *Daily 10:30–5. Exhibitions Mon.–Sat. 10:30–4:30, Sat. 10–2. Tours are frequent and available all yr, times vary* Ⓜ *Cowcaddens.*

The Lighthouse. Charles Rennie Mackintosh designed these former offices of the *Glasgow Herald* newspaper in 1893, with its emblematic Mackintosh Tower. Today it serves as Scotland's **Centre for Architecture, Design and the City,** which celebrates all facets of architecture and design. Regular and changing exhibitions on its second floor address issues of urban design and sustainability. On the third floor, the **Mackintosh Interpretation Centre** is a great starting point for discovering more about this groundbreaking architect's work, illustrated in a glass wall with alcoves containing models of his buildings. From here you can climb the more than 130 steps up the tower and, once you have caught your breath, look out over Glasgow. For the less energetic there is a viewing platform on the sixth floor that can be reached by elevator. The fifth-floor Doocot Cafe is a great place to take a break from sightseeing. ✉ *11 Mitchell La., City Centre* ☎ *0141/271–5365*

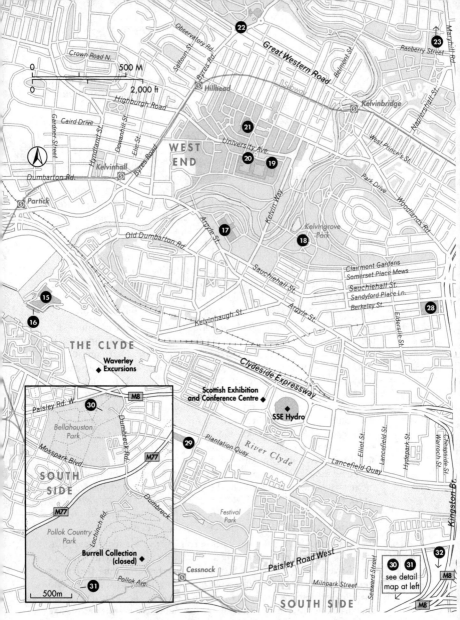

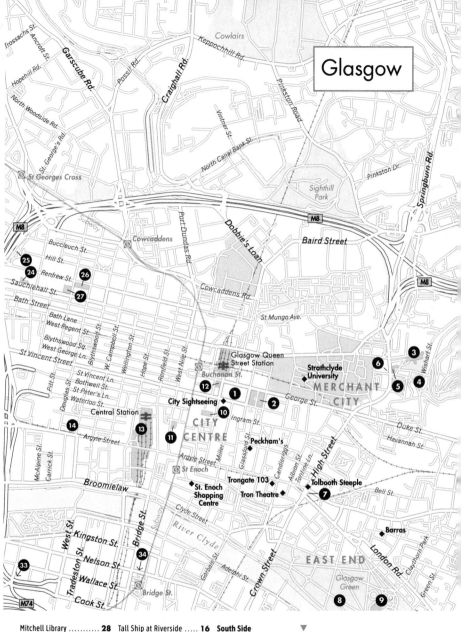

Glasgow

⊕ *www.thelighthouse.co.uk* 🔳 *Free*
⊙ *Mon–Sat. 10:30–5, Sun. noon–5*
Ⓜ *St. Enoch.*

WORTH NOTING

Central Station. The Champagne Bar in the Central Hotel is a good vantage point for watching the station concourse and its comings and goings. The railway bridge across Argyll Street behind the station is known as the Highlandman's Umbrella because immigrants from the north once gathered there to look for work in the early 20th century. ✉ *Gordon St., bounded by Gordon, Union, Argyle, Jamaica, Clyde, Oswald, and Hope Sts., City Centre* ⚓ *St. Enoch.*

MACKINTOSH TRAIL

Mackintosh Trail Ticket. If you're interested in architect Charles Rennie Mackintosh, this is an excellent and economical way of seeing his work. Tickets cost £10 and include admission to all Mackintosh sites across Glasgow, as well as transportation on subways or buses. Tickets can be purchased online or at the individual sites. ☎ *0141/946–6600* ⊕ *www.crmsociety.com* 🔳 *£10.*

Centre for Contemporary Arts (CCA). Housed in a modern building constructed around the facade of the older center, this arts center hosts a wide range of activities, including cutting-edge art exhibitions, film screenings, and educational activities for community groups. There's a small theater on the first floor and a bookshop specializing in art books. The Café Saramago sits between old and new, under a glass roof that feels a little like an open courtyard. It has very good lunch and pretheater menus. ✉ *350 Sauchiehall St., City Centre* ☎ *0141/352–4900* ⊕ *www.cca-glasgow.com* 🔳 *Free* ⊙ *Tues.–Fri. 11–6, Sat. 10–6* Ⓜ *Cowcaddens.*

Merchants' House. You will need to look up to see the golden sailing ship, a reminder of the importance of sea trade to Glasgow's prosperity, that tops this handsome 1874 Victorian building on the corner of George Square. Now home to Glasgow's chamber of commerce, the interior isn't open to the public, but the exterior is impressive. ✉ *7 West George St., City Centre* Ⓜ *Buchanan St.*

Regimental Museum of the Royal Highland Fusiliers. Exhibits of medals, badges, and uniforms relate the history of a famous, much-honored regiment and the men who served in it. ✉ *518 Sauchiehall St., City Centre* ☎ *0141/332–0961* ⊕ *www.rhf.org.uk* 🔳 *Free* ⊙ *Mon.–Thurs. 9–4, Fri. 9–3* Ⓜ *Cowcaddens.*

St. Vincent's Street Church. This 1859 church, the work of Alexander Thomson, exemplifies his Greek Revival style, replete with Ionic columns, sphinxlike heads, and rich interior color. You can see the interior by attending a service Sunday at 11 am or 6:30 pm or by appointment. ✉ *Pitt and St. Vincent Sts., City Centre* ⊕ *glasgowcityfreechurch.org* Ⓜ *Buchanan St.*

Tenement House. This ordinary first-floor apartment is anything but ordinary inside: it was occupied from 1937 to 1982 by Agnes Toward (and before that by her mother), who seems never to have thrown anything away. She was a dressmaker, and her legacy is this fascinating time capsule, painstakingly preserved with her everyday furniture and belongings. The red-sandstone building dates from 1892 and can be found in the Garnethill area north of Charing Cross station. A small museum explores the life and times of its careful occupant. ✉ *145 Buccleuch St., City Centre* ☎ *0844/493–2197* ⊕ *www.nts.org.uk* 🎫 *£6.50* ⊙ *Mar.–June, Sept., and Oct., daily 1–5; July and Aug., Mon.–Sat.11–5, Sun. 1–5 (last admission at 4:30)* Ⓜ *Cowcaddens.*

MERCHANT CITY

Near the remnants of medieval Glasgow is the Merchant City, with some of the city's most important Georgian and Victorian buildings, many of them built by prosperous tobacco merchants. Today the area is noted for its trendy eateries and for the designer stores that line Ingram Street and others. Many of Glasgow's young and upwardly mobile make their home here, in converted buildings ranging from warehouses to the old Sheriff's Court. Shopping here is expensive, but the area is worth visiting if you're seeking the youthful Glasgow style. Stick to well-lit, well-traveled areas after sunset.

GETTING HERE

Buchanan Street is the handiest subway station when you want to explore the Merchant City, as it puts you directly on George Square. You can also easily walk from Central Station or the St. Enoch subway station.

FodorsChoice
★

Glasgow Cathedral. The most complete of Scotland's cathedrals (it would have been more complete had 19th-century vandals not pulled down its two rugged towers), this is an unusual double church, one above the other, dedicated to Glasgow's patron saint, St. Mungo. Consecrated in 1136 and completed about 300 years later, it was spared the ravages of the Reformation—which destroyed so many of Scotland's medieval churches—mainly because Glasgow's trade guilds defended it. A late-medieval open-timber roof in the nave and lovely 20th-century stained glass are notable features.

In the lower church is the splendid crypt of St. Mungo, who was originally known as St. Kentigern (*kentigern* means "chief word"), but who was nicknamed St. Mungo (meaning "dear one") by his early followers. The site of the tomb has been revered since the 6th century, when St. Mungo founded a church here. Mungo features prominently in local legends; one such legend is about a pet bird that he nursed back to life, and another tells of a bush or tree, the branches of which he used to miraculously relight a fire. The bird, the tree, and the salmon with a ring in its mouth (from another story) are all found on the city's coat of arms, together with a bell that Mungo brought from Rome. ✉ *Cathedral St., Merchant City* ☎ *0141/552–6891* ⊕ *www.glasgow-cathedral. com* 🎫 *Free* ⊙ *Apr.–Sept., Mon.–Sat. 9:30–5:30, Sun. 1–5; Oct.–Mar., Mon.–Sat. 9:30–4:30, Sun. 1–4:30* Ⓜ *Buchanan St.*

FodorsChoice
★

Necropolis. A burial ground since the beginning of recorded history, the large Necropolis, modeled on the famous Père-Lachaise Cemetery in Paris, contains some extraordinarily elaborate Victorian tombs. A great place to take it all in is from the monument of John Knox (1514–72), the leader of Scotland's Reformation, which stands at the top of the hill at the heart of the Necropolis. Around it are grand tombs that resemble classical palaces, Egyptian tombs, or even the Chapel of the Templars in Jerusalem. You'll also find a smattering of urns and broken columns, a Roman symbol of a great life cut short. The Necropolis was designed as a place for meditation, which is why it is much more than just a graveyard. The main gates are behind the St. Mungo Museum of Religious Life and Art. Call ahead for free guided tours. ⊠ *70 Cathedral Sq., Merchant City* ☎ *0141/287–5064* ⊕ *glasgownecropolis.org* 🗺 *Free* ⊗ *Daily 7–dusk* Ⓜ *Buchanan St.*

Provand's Lordship. Glasgow's oldest house, one of only four medieval buildings surviving in the city, was built in 1471 by Bishop Andrew Muirhead. Before it was rescued by the Glasgow City Council, this building had been a pub, a sweetshop, and a soft drinks factory. It is now a museum that shows the house as it might have looked when it was occupied by officers of the church. The furniture is 17th century. The top floor is a gallery with prints and paintings depicting the characters who might have lived in the surrounding streets. The St. Nicholas Garden behind the house is a medicinal herb garden, and the cloisters house rather disturbing carved stone heads. ⊠ *3 Castle St., Merchant City* ☎ *0141/276–1625* ⊕ *www.glasgow.org.uk* 🗺 *Free* ⊗ *Tues.– Thurs. and Sat. 10–5, Fri. and Sun. 11–5* Ⓜ *Buchanan St.*

St. Mungo Museum of Religious Life and Art. An outstanding collection of artifacts, including Celtic crosses and statuettes of Hindu gods, reflects the many religious groups that have settled throughout the centuries in Glasgow and the west of Scotland. A Zen garden creates a peaceful setting for rest and contemplation, and elsewhere stained-glass windows include a depiction of St. Mungo himself. Pause to look at the beautiful Chilkat Blanketwoven, made from cedar bark and wool by the Tlingit people of North America. ⊠ *2 Castle St., Merchant City* ☎ *0141/276– 1625* ⊕ *glasgowlife.org.uk/museums* 🗺 *Free* ⊗ *Tues.–Thurs. and Sat. 10–5, Fri. and Sun. 11–5* Ⓜ *Buchanan St.*

WEST END

Glasgow University dominates the West End, creating a vibrant neighborhood. Founded in 1451, the university is the third oldest in Scotland, after St. Andrews and Aberdeen. (It's at least 130 years ahead of the University of Edinburgh.) The industrialists and merchants who built their grand homes on Great Western Road and the adjacent streets endowed museums and art galleries and commissioned artists to decorate and design their homes, as a stroll around the area will quickly reveal. In summer the beautiful Botanic Gardens, with the iconic glasshouse that is the Kibble Palace, becomes a stage for new and unusual versions of Shakespeare's plays. A good way to save money is to picnic in the park (weather permitting, of course). You can buy sandwiches, salads, and other portable items at shops on Byres Road.

GETTING HERE

The best way to get to the West End from the City Centre is by subway; get off at the Hillhead station. A taxi is another option.

TOP ATTRACTIONS

FAMILY

Fodor's Choice

★

Botanic Gardens. When the sun shines, the Botanics (as they're known to locals) quickly fill up with people enjoying the extensive lawns, beautiful flower displays, and herb garden. At the heart of the gardens is the spectacular circular greenhouse, the **Kibble Palace**, a favorite haunt of Glaswegian families. Originally built in 1873, it was the conservatory of a Victorian eccentric named John Kibble. Its domed, interlinked greenhouses contain tree ferns, palm trees, and the Tropicarium, where you can experience the lushness of a rain forest and briefly forget the weather outside. Another greenhouse holds a world-famous collection of orchids. In July the park becomes a stage for presentations of Shakespeare's plays. ⊠ *730 Great Western Rd., West End* ☎ *0141/276–1614* ⊕ *www.glasgowbotanicgardens.com* ⛄ *Free* ⏱ *Gardens daily 7–dusk; Kibble Palace Mar.–mid-Oct., daily 10–6; mid-Oct.–Feb., daily 10–4:15* Ⓜ *Hillhead.*

Glasgow University. Gorgeous grounds and great views of the city are among the many reasons to visit this university. The Gilbert Scott Building, the university's main edifice, was built more than a century ago and is a lovely example of the Gothic Revival style. **Glasgow University Visitor Centre,** near the main gate on University Avenue, has exhibits on the university, a small coffee bar, and a gift shop; it's the starting point for one-hour guided walking tours of the campus (Thursday–Sunday at 2). A self-guided tour starts at the visitor center and takes in the east and west quadrangles, the cloisters, Professor's Square, Pearce Lodge, and the not-to-be-missed University Chapel. ⊠ *University Ave., West End* ☎ *0141/330–5511* ⊕ *www.glasgow.ac.uk* ⛄ *Tour £10* Ⓜ *Hillhead.*

Hunterian Art Gallery. Opposite Glasgow University's main gate, this gallery houses William Hunter's (1718–83) collection of paintings. You'll also find prints, drawings, and sculptures by Tintoretto, Rembrandt, and Auguste Rodin, as well as a major collection of paintings by James McNeill Whistler, who had a great affection for the city that bought one of his earliest paintings. Also in the gallery is a replica of **Charles Rennie Mackintosh's town house,** which once stood nearby and where Mackintosh and his artist wife Margaret lived between 1906 and 1914. The rooms, faithfully rebuilt here, contain Mackintosh's distinctive art nouveau chairs, tables, beds, and cupboards, and the walls are decorated in the equally distinctive style devised by him and his wife. Free guided tours are available. ⊠ *Hillhead St., West End* ☎ *0141/330–4221* ⊕ *www.gla.ac.uk/hunterian* ⛄ *Free* ⏱ *Tues.–Sat. 10–5, Sun. 11–4* Ⓜ *Hillhead.*

Hunterian Museum. Set within Glasgow University, this museum dating from 1807 showcases part of the collections of William Hunter, an 18th-century Glasgow doctor who assembled a staggering quantity of valuable material. Look for Hunter's hoards of coins, manuscripts, scientific instruments, and archaeological artifacts in a striking Gothic building. A permanent exhibit chronicles the building of the Antonine Wall, the Romans' northernmost defense. ⊠ *University Ave., West End* ☎ *0141/330–4221* ⊕ *www.gla.ac.uk/hunterian* ⛄ *Free* ⏱ *Mon.–Sat. 9:30–5* Ⓜ *Hillhead.*

FAMILY **Kelvingrove Art Gallery and Museum.** Worthy of its world-class reputation,
Fodor's Choice the Kelvingrove Art Gallery and Museum attracts local families as well
★ as international visitors. This combination of cathedral and castle was
designed in the Renaissance style and built between 1891 and 1901.
The stunning red-sandstone edifice is an appropriate home for works by
Botticelli, Rembrandt, Monet, and others. The Glasgow Room houses
extraordinary works by local artists. Whether the subject is Scottish
culture, design, or storytelling, every wall and room begs you to look
deeper; labels are thought-provoking and sometimes witty. You could
spend a weekend here, but in a pinch three hours would do one level justice—there are three. Leave time to visit the gift shop and the attractive
basement restaurant. Daily free recitals on the massive organ (usually
at 1) are well worth the trip. ⊠ *Argyle St., West End* ☎ *0141/276–9599*
⊕ *www.glasgowlife.org.uk* ✉ *Free (though individual exhibitions in the
gallery may require admission)* ⊘ *Mon.–Thurs. and Sat. 10–5, Fri. and
Sun. 11–5* Ⓜ *Kelvinhall.*

FAMILY **Kelvingrove Park.** A peaceful retreat, the park was purchased by the city
in 1852 and takes its name from the River Kelvin, which flows through
it. Among the numerous statues of prominent Glaswegians is one of
Lord Kelvin (1824–1907), the Scottish mathematician and physicist
who pioneered a great deal of work in electricity. The shady park has a
massive fountain commemorating a lord provost of Glasgow from the
1870s, a duck pond, two playgrounds, and a skateboard park. The An
Clachan café beside the children's play area is an excellent daytime eatery and a boon to parents looking for a refuge. The park also contains
the Kelvingrove Art Gallery, originally built for a 1901 exhibition. The
public bowling greens were renovated for the Commonwealth Games
and are free, as are the tennis courts ⊠ *Bounded by Sauchiehall St.,
Woodlands Rd., and Kelvin Way, West End* ⊕ *www.glasgowlife.org.
uk* Ⓜ *Kelvinhall.*

Mitchell Library. The largest public reference library in Europe houses
more than a million volumes, including what's claimed to be the world's
largest collection about Robert Burns. A bust in the entrance hall commemorates the library's founder, Stephen Mitchell, who died in 1874.
Minerva, goddess of wisdom, looks down from the library's dome,
encouraging the library's users and frowning at the drivers thunder-
ing along the nearby motorway. The western facade, with its sculpted
figures of Mozart, Beethoven, Michelangelo, and other artistic figures,
is particularly beautiful. The on-site café is a good place to relax. The
Aye Write Literature Festival takes place here every March, as do many
other events celebrating Glasgow's history. ⊠ *North St., West End*
☎ *0141/287–2999* ⊕ *www.mitchelllibrary.org* ✉ *Free* ⊘ *Mon.–Thurs.
9–8, Fri. and Sat. 9–5* Ⓜ *St. George's Cross.*

WORTH NOTING

OFF THE **Queen's Cross Church.** The only church Mackintosh designed houses the
BEATEN Charles Rennie Mackintosh Society Headquarters and is the ideal place
PATH to learn more about the famous Glasgow-born architect and designer.
Although one of the leading lights in the art nouveau movement, Mack-
intosh died in relative obscurity in 1928. The church has beautiful
stained-glass windows and a light-enhancing, carved-wood interior. The

CLOSE UP

Charles Rennie Mackintosh

Not so long ago, the furniture of innovative Glasgow-born architect Charles Rennie Mackintosh (1868–1928) was broken up for firewood. Today art books are devoted to his distinctive, astonishingly elegant Arts and Crafts- and art nouveau-influenced interiors, and artisans around the world look to his theory that "decoration should not be constructed, rather construction should be decorated" as holy law. Mackintosh's stripped-down designs ushered in the modern age with their deceptively stark style.

AN ARCHITECT'S CAREER

Mackintosh trained in architecture at the Glasgow School of Art and was apprenticed to the Glasgow firm of John Hutchison at the age of 16. Early influences on his work included the Pre-Raphaelites, James McNeill Whistler (1834–1903), Aubrey Beardsley (1872–98), and Japanese art. But by the 1890s a distinct Glasgow style developed.

The building for the *Glasgow Herald* newspaper, which he designed in 1893, and which is now the Lighthouse Centre for Architecture, Design and the City, was soon followed by other major Glasgow buildings: Queen Margaret's Medical College; the Martyrs Public School; tearooms including the Willow Tearoom; the Hill House, in Helensburgh, now owned by the National Trust for Scotland; and Queen's Cross Church, completed in 1899 and now the headquarters of the Charles Rennie Mackintosh Society. In 1897 Mackintosh began work on a new home for the Glasgow School of Art, recognized as one of his major achievements.

Mackintosh married Margaret Macdonald in 1900, and in later years her decorative work enhanced the buildings' interiors. In 1904 he became a partner in Honeyman and Keppie and designed Scotland Street School, now the Scotland Street School Museum, in the same year. Until 1913, when he left Honeyman and Keppie and moved to England, Mackintosh's projects included buildings over much of Scotland. He preferred to include interiors as part of his overall design.

Commissions in England after 1913 included design challenges not confined to buildings, such as fabrics, furniture, and even bookbindings. Mackintosh died in London in 1928.

After 1904 architectural taste had turned against Mackintosh's style; his work was seen as strange. Mackintosh could not conform to the times; he lost commissions, drank heavily, and ended up poor and sick. His reputation revived only in the 1950s with the publication of his monographs, and has continued to grow over time.

HOW TO SEE HIS WORK

Glasgow is the best place in the world to admire Mackintosh's work: in addition to the buildings mentioned above, most of which can be visited, the Hunterian Art Gallery contains magnificent reconstructions of the principal rooms at 78 Southpark Avenue, Mackintosh's Glasgow home, and original drawings, documents, and records, plus the re-creation of a room at 78 Derngate, Northampton. The Kelvingrove Art Gallery and Museum also has displays of his creations in several galleries.

A Mackintosh Trail Ticket, purchased online or at various sites, is a good deal if you're visiting multiple sites: see ⊕ *www.crmsociety.com*.

3

center's library and shop provide further insight into Glasgow's other Mackintosh-designed buildings, which include Scotland Street School, the Martyrs Public School, and the Glasgow School of Art. The church sits near the junction of Garscube Road and Maryhill Road. A taxi is probably the best way to get here, but you can also take a bus toward Queen's Cross from stops along Hope Street or walk up Maryhill Road from the St. George's Cross subway station. ⊠ *870 Garscube Rd., West End* ☎ *0141/946–6600* ⊕ *www.crmsociety.com* ⊠ *£4, free Wed. after 1* ⊙ *Apr.–Oct., weekdays 10–5; Nov.–Mar., Mon., Wed., and Fri. 10–4* Ⓜ *St. George's Cross.*

THE CLYDE

The River Clyde has long been the city's main artery, first as a trading route and later as the place where massive shipyards built everything from warships to ocean liners. The cranes can still be seen today, although the former industrial area has been transformed into a desirable destination for locals and visitors alike. The Riverside Museum commemorates the great days of shipbuilding, while the Scottish Exhibition Centre and the Glasgow Science Centre, facing one another across the river, proclaim new times.

GETTING HERE

From the Partick subway station it's a 10-minute walk to the Riverside Museum. From that museum it's a short stroll along the river (and across a bridge) to the Glasgow Science Centre.

> ### GLASGOW'S UNDERGROUND
>
> Glasgow is the only city in Scotland with a subway. The system was built at the end of the 19th century and takes the simple form of two circular routes, one going clockwise and the other counterclockwise. All trains eventually bring you back to where you started, and the complete circle takes 24 minutes. The tunnels are small, and so are the trains. This, together with the affection in which the system is held and the bright-orange paint of the trains, gave the system its nickname, the "Clockwork Orange." If you get off at Hillhead, stop to admire Alasdair Gray's wonderful mural celebrating the city's West End.

FAMILY **Glasgow Science Centre.** On the banks of the Clyde, its space-age home has a whole wall of glass looking out on to the river. The *Body Works* exhibition explores every aspect of our physical selves—try and reconstruct a brain. There are daily events and science shows, a lovely play area for under-sevens, a planetarium, an IMAX theater, and the spectacular Glasgow Tower, 400 feet high, from which to survey the whole city from the river to the surrounding hills. Always enquire whether the tower is open—even moderate winds will close it down. ■ TIP➜ **Admission is expensive, but the tower and planetarium cost less if you buy all the tickets at the same time.** ⊠ *50 Pacific Quay, Clyde* ✦ *Across the footbridge by the Scottish Exhibition Centre* ☎ *0141/420–5000* ⊕ *www. glasgowsciencecentre.org* ⊠ *£10.59, planetarium extra £2.50, tower extra £3.50; tower only £6.50* ⊙ *Apr.–Oct., daily 10–5; Nov.–Mar., Wed.–Fri. 10–3, weekends 10–5* Ⓜ *Cessnock.*

FAMILY **Riverside Museum: Scotland's Museum of Transport and Travel.** Designed by
Fodor's Choice Zaha Hadid to celebrate the area's industrial heritage, this huge metal
★ structure with curving walls echoes the covered yards where ships were
built on the Clyde. Glasgow's shipbuilding history is remembered with
a world-famous collection of ship models. Locomotives built at the
nearby St. Rollox yards are also on display, as are cars from every age
and many countries. You can wander down Main Street, circa 1930,
without leaving the building: the pawnbroker, funeral parlor, and Italian restaurant are all frozen in time. Relax with a coffee in the café,
wander out onto the expansive riverside walk, or board the Tall Ship
that is moored permanently behind the museum. Bus 100 from George
Square brings you here, or you can walk from the Partick subway station in 10 minutes. ✉ *100 Poundhouse Pl., Clyde* ☎ *0141/287–2720*
⊕ *www.glasgowlife.org.uk/museums/riverside* 🎟 *Free* ☉ *Mon.–Thurs.
and Sat. 10–5, Fri. and Sun. 11–5* Ⓜ *Partick.*

FAMILY **Tall Ship at Riverside.** Built in 1896, this fine tall sailing ship now sits on
the River Clyde immediately behind the Riverside Museum. The *Glenlee*
once belonged to the Spanish Navy (under a different name), but carried cargo all over the world in her day. She returned to Glasgow and
the River Clyde in 1993, and now forms part of the museum. You can
wander throughout this surprisingly large cargo ship with or without an
audio guide, peer into cabins and holds, and stand on the forecastle as
you gaze down the river. Bus 100 from George Square brings you here,
or you can walk from the Partick subway station in 10 minutes. ✉ *150
Pointhouse Pl., Clyde* ⊕ *Behind the Riverside Museum* ☎ *0141/357–
3699* ⊕ *www.thetallship.com* 🎟 *Free* ☉ *Mar.–Oct., daily 10–5, last
admission 4:15; Nov.–Feb., daily 10–4, last admission 3:15* Ⓜ *Partick.*

EAST END

Glasgow Green has always been the heart of Glasgow's East End, a
formerly down-at-heel neighborhood that has seen many changes over
the past several years. One of the top attractions is the People's Palace,
which tells the story of daily life in the city. On Sunday head to the
nearby Barras market to hunt for bargains.

GETTING HERE

To get to the East End, take the subway to the St. Enoch station and
walk along Argyle Street to the Tron Cross. From there, London Road
takes you to Glasgow Green.

Glasgow Cross. This crossroads was the center of the medieval city. The
Mercat Cross (*mercat* means "market"), topped by a unicorn, marks the
spot where merchants met, where the market was held, and where crim-
inals were executed. Here, too, was the *tron,* or weigh beam, installed
in 1491 and used by merchants to check weights. The Tolbooth Steeple
dates from 1626 and served as the civic center and the place where
travelers paid tolls. ✉ *Intersection of Saltmarket, Trongate, Gallowgate,
and London Rds., East End* Ⓜ *St. Enoch.*

FAMILY **Glasgow Green.** Glasgow's oldest park, on the north side of the River
Clyde, has a long history as a favorite spot for public recreation and
political demonstrations. Note the Nelson Column, erected long before

London's; the McLennan Arch, originally part of the facade of the old Assembly Halls in Ingram Street; and the Templeton Business Centre, a former carpet factory built in the late 19th century in the style of the Doge's Palace in Venice. Don't miss the **People's Palace** and the Doulton Fountain that faces it. ⊠ *North side of River Clyde between Green St. and Saltmarket St., East End.*

FAMILY **Hampden Park.** A mecca for soccer enthusiasts, who come from far and near to tread the famous turf, the home field for the country's national team was the largest stadium in the world when it was built in 1903. There are stadium tours on nonmatch days at 11, 12:30, 2, and 3. You can then visit the Scottish Football Museum, which traces the history of the game; the museum may close on game days. ⊠ *Letherby Dr., East End* ✛ *Nearest rail stations are Mount Florida and Kings Park. Buses from City Centre* ☎ *0141/620–4000* ⊕ *www.hampdenpark. co.uk* ✉ *Stadium tour £8, museum entrance £8, combined ticket £12* ⊙ *Mon.–Sat. 10–5, Sun. 11–5.*

FAMILY **People's Palace.** An impressive Victorian red-sandstone building dating from 1894 houses an intriguing museum dedicated to the city's social history. Included among the exhibits is one devoted to the ordinary folk of Glasgow, called the "People's Story." Also on display are the writing desk of John McLean (1879–1923), the "Red Clydeside" political activist who came to Lenin's notice, and the famous banana boots worn on stage by Glasgow-born comedian Billy Connolly. On the top floor a sequence of fine murals by Glasgow artist Ken Currie tells the story of the city's working-class citizens. Behind the museum are the restored Winter Gardens and a popular café. The museum is well used by locals, for whom a visit is often a nostalgic journey into their own past. To get here from the St. Enoch subway station, walk along Argyle Street past Glasgow Cross. ⊠ *Glasgow Green, Monteith Row, East End* ☎ *0141/276–0788* ⊕ *www.glasgowlife.org.uk* ✉ *Free* ⊙ *Tues.–Thurs. and Sat. 10–5, Fri. and Sun. 11–5* Ⓜ *St. Enoch.*

SOUTH SIDE

Just southwest of the City Centre in the South Side are two of Glasgow's dear green spaces—Bellahouston Park and Pollok Country Park—which have important art collections: Charles Rennie Mackintosh's House for an Art Lover in Bellahouston, and Pollok House in Pollok Country Park. A respite from the buzz of the city can also be found in the parks, where you can have a picnic or ramble through greenery and gardens. The famous Burrell Collection is also in the area, but the museum will be closed from October 2016 until 2019 for a substantial renovation.

GETTING HERE
Both parks are off Pollokshaws Road, about 3 miles southwest of City Centre. You can take a taxi or car, city bus, or a train from Glasgow Central station to Pollokshaws West station or Dumbreck.

House for an Art Lover. Within Bellahouston Park is a "new" Mackintosh house, based on a competition entry Charles Rennie Mackintosh submitted to a German magazine in 1901. The house was never built in his lifetime, but took shape between 1989 and 1996. The building houses the Glasgow School of Art's postgraduate study center, and exhibits designs for the various rooms and decorative pieces by Mackintosh and his wife, Margaret. The main lounge is spectacular. There's also a café and shop filled with art. Buses 9, 53, and 54 from Union Street will get you here. Call ahead, as opening times can vary. ⊠ *Bellahouston Park, 10 Dumbreck Rd., South Side* ☏ *0141/353–4770* ⊕ *www. houseforanartlover.co.uk* 🖃 *£4.50* ⊗ *Apr.–Sept., Mon.–Wed. 10–4, Thurs.–Sun. 10–1; Oct.–Mar., weekends 10–1* Ⓜ *Ibrox.*

OFF THE BEATEN PATH

Holmwood House. This large mansion was designed by Alexander "Greek" Thomson, Glasgow's second most famous and most active architect (after Mackintosh), for the wealthy owner of a paper mill. Its classical Greek architecture and stunningly ornamented wood and marble are among his finest, and have been lovingly restored by the National Trust for Scotland. You can witness the ongoing renovation process one or two days a week; call to check for times. The house is half hidden behind a residential street in the Cathcart area. ⊠ *61–63 Netherlee Rd., South Side* ✛ *Train from Glasgow Central to Cathcart* ☏ *0141/571–0184* ⊕ *www.nts.org.uk* 🖃 *£6.50* ⊗ *Apr.–Oct., Thurs.– Mon. noon–5; last admission at 4:30.*

Pollok House. This classic Georgian house, dating from the mid-1700s, sits amid landscaped gardens and avenues of trees that are now part of Pollok Country Park. It still has the tranquil air of a wealthy but unpretentious country house. The Stirling Maxwell Collection housed here includes paintings by Blake and a strong grouping of Spanish works by El Greco, Murillo, and Goya. Lovely examples of 18th- and early-19th-century furniture, silver, glass, and porcelain are also on display. The house has beautiful gardens that overlook the White Cart River. The downstairs servants' quarters include the kitchen, still hung with the cooking implements of its times, which is now a café-restaurant. Eat in the small, pleasant garden if the weather allows. You can take Buses 45, 47, or 57 to the gate of Pollok County Park. ⊠ *Pollok County Park, 2060 Pollokshaws Rd., South Side* ✛ *Closest train station: Pollokshaws West, from Central station. Or you can take Bus 45, 47, or 57 to the gate of Pollok County Park* ☏ *0844/616–6410* ⊕ *www.nts.org.uk* 🖃 *Apr.–Oct. £6.50, Nov.–Mar. free* ⊗ *Daily 10–5; last admission 4:30.*

OFF THE BEATEN PATH

Scotland Street School Museum. A former school designed by Charles Rennie Mackintosh, this building houses a fascinating museum of education. Classrooms re-create school life in Scotland during Victorian times and World War II, and a cookery room recounts a time when education for Scottish girls consisted of little more than learning how to become a housewife. There's also an exhibition space and a café. The building sits opposite Shields Road underground station. ⊠ *225 Scotland St., South Side* ☏ *0141/287–0500* ⊕ *www.glasgowlife.org.uk/museums/ scotland-street* 🖃 *Free* ⊗ *Tues.–Thurs. and Sat. 10–5, Fri. and Sun. 11–5* Ⓜ *Shields Rd.*

WHERE TO EAT

In the past few years, Glasgow's restaurant culture has blossomed and grown both in range and in quality. Some of Britain's best chefs (Jamie Oliver, Nick Nairn, Antonio Carluccio) have opened restaurants in the city in recent years. It has absorbed the newest fashions in food, while still offering the best that Scotland has to offer: grass-fed beef, free-range chicken, wild seafood, venison, duck, and goose, not to mention superb fruits and vegetables. The growing emphasis on organic food is reflected on menus that increasingly provide detailed information about the source of their ingredients. The explosion of coffee shops around the city offer artisanal macchiatos and mochas.

You can eat your way around the world in Glasgow. A new generation of Italian restaurants serves updated versions of classic Italian dishes. Chinese, Indian, and Pakistani foods, longtime favorites, are now more varied and sophisticated, and, most recently, Thai and Japanese restaurants have become popular. Spanish-style tapas are now quite common, and the "small plate" craze has extended to every kind of restaurant. Seafood restaurants have moved well beyond the fish-and-chips wrapped in newspaper that were always a Glasgow staple, as langoustines, scallops, and monkfish appear on menus with ever more unusual accompaniments. And Glasgow has an especially good reputation for its vegan and vegetarian restaurants.

Smoking isn't allowed in any enclosed space in Scotland, but more restaurants have placed tables outside under awnings during the warmer summer months, some of which permit smoking. *Use the coordinate (✛ B2) at the end of each listing to locate a site on the corresponding map.*

PRICES

Eating in Glasgow can be casual or lavish. For inexpensive dining, consider the benefit of lunch or pretheater set menus. Beer and spirits cost much the same as they would in a bar, but wine is relatively expensive in restaurants. Increasing numbers of pubs offer food, but their kitchens usually close early. ■ TIP➔ **Some restaurants allow you to bring your own bottle of wine, charging just a small corkage fee. It's worth the effort.** *Prices in the reviews are the average cost of a main course at dinner or, if dinner is not served, at lunch.*

WHAT IT COSTS IN POUNDS			
$	$$	$$$	$$$$
Restaurants Under £15	£15–£19	£20–£25	Over £25

Restaurant prices are the average cost of a main course at dinner or, if dinner is not served, at lunch.

CITY CENTRE

The City Centre has restaurants catering to the 9-to-5 crowd, meaning there are a lot of fine-dining establishments as well as good restaurants catching people as they leave work, drawing them in with pretheater menus. The choice of eateries is extensive.

$ BRITISH 🍴 **The Butterfly and the Pig.** Down an innocuous-looking flight of stairs, this intimate restaurant is the type of place the locals love: flickering candles, mix-and-match crockery, and food that is inventive, inexpensive, and original. The menu reads like a comedic narrative, with descriptions like "traditional fish-and-chips, battered to death" served with "beans today, as the peas don't want to cook." Worth trying are dishes such as hearty portobello-mushroom burgers with extra-thick potato chips or black pudding with bacon, Parmesan cheese, and apples, but essentially the menu offers twists on the familiar and the reliable. The chef uses only local ingredients, so the menu changes daily. A tea shop upstairs serves wonderful cakes and old-fashioned high tea. [$] *Average main: £14* ✉ *153 Bath St., City Centre* ☎ *0141/221–7711* 🌐 *www.thebutterflyandthepig.com* [M] *Buchanan St.* ✥ *F4.*

$ ITALIAN 🍴 **Carluccio's.** Part of a well-established chain set up by the first successful Italian TV chef, Antonio Carluccio, this eatery emphasizes authenticity, which shows most clearly in the pasta dishes. No matter what you order, from fish soup to beef stew, you can watch it being prepared in the open kitchen. There's a well-stocked deli if you want to take these flavors home with you. The restaurant is bright, busy, and perhaps even a little crowded, and there is a healthy buzz of conversation partly absorbed by the high ceiling. The staff is efficient and friendly. The fixed price menu (£10.99 for two courses, £14.49 for three) is an excellent value, and the Italian wine selection is reasonably priced. [$] *Average main: £13* ✉ *W. Nile St., City Centre* ☎ *0141/248–1166* 🌐 *www.carluccios.com* [M] *Buchanan St.* ✥ *F5.*

$ THAI Fodor's Choice ★ 🍴 **Chaophraya.** This is dining at its most sumptuous and elegant. The delicate flavors of Thai cooking are at their finest here in the chef's wonderful signature Massaman lamb (and beef) curry, flavorsome Fisherman's Soup, and fusion dishes like scallops with black pudding. And the setting lives up to the quality of the menu: in the grand surroundings of what was the Glasgow Conservatoire, golden Buddhas now sit comfortably beside busts of great composers. The great hall with its chandeliers and balconies offers dining as theater; or you can book the tiny two-person table on a balcony looking down for an intimate experience. [$] *Average main: £11* ✉ *The Town House, Nelson Mandela Pl., City Centre* ☎ *0141/332–0041* 🌐 *www.chaophraya.co.uk* ✍ *Reservations essential* [M] *Buchanan St.* ✥ *F4.*

$ SOUTH AMERICAN 🍴 **Las Iguanas.** The bright interior of this fairly new restaurant echoes the Latin American–themed menu in its colors and decoration. The menu has the familiar Spanish and Mexican classics like tapas and burritos, but Brazilian dishes, too—and the cocktail list covers everything from tequila to a pisco sour. There are big and attractive menus for vegans and vegetarians and a separate gluten-free one, too. The service is especially attentive and lively. It's crowded on weekends, so book if you can. [$] *Average main: £14* ✉ *15–20 W. Nile St., City*

Centre ☎ *0141/248–5705* 🌐 *www.iguanas.co.uk* ✍ *Reservations essential* [M] *Buchanan St.* ⊕ *F5.*

$$ CANTONESE FAMILY 🍴 **Loon Fung.** The pleasant, enthusiastic staff at this popular Cantonese eatery guides you to all the best dishes, including barbecued duck, deep-fried wontons with prawns, and more-challenging dishes like pork with jellyfish or king prawn with salted egg, all specialties that have been served here over the past 40 years. A newer emphasis on seafood has enlivened the expansive menu. On most days you will find local Chinese families seated at the huge round tables enjoying the dim sum for which the restaurant is rightly famous. This isn't the place to come for quiet intimacy—the restaurant is enormous—but it's perfect for good food in a lively atmosphere. [$] *Average main: £15* ✉ *417–419 Sauchiehall St., City Centre* ☎ *0141/332–1240* 🌐 *www.loonfungglasgow.co.uk* ✍ *Reservations essential* [M] *Cowcaddens* ⊕ *E4.*

$$ SEAFOOD Fodor's Choice ★ 🍴 **Mussel Inn.** West-coast shellfish farmers own this restaurant and feed their customers incredibly succulent oysters, scallops, and mussels. The pots of mussels, steamed to order and served with any of a number of sauces, are revelatory. The surroundings are simple but stylish, with cool ceramic tiles, wood floors, and plenty of sleek wooden furniture. Another plus is the staff, which is helpful and unpretentious. This is where locals take their favorite out-of-towners. The £7.95 "lunchtime quickie" includes a bowl of mussels and either salad or fries. A pretheater meal is £10.95 for two courses, £13.95 for three. Scallops, prawns, and oysters dominate the à la carte menu and come together in a wonderful seafood pasta. [$] *Average main: £16* ✉ *157 Hope St., City Centre* ☎ *0843/289–2283* 🌐 *www.mussel-inn.com* [M] *Buchanan St.* ⊕ *F4.*

$$ ASIAN Fodor's Choice ★ 🍴 **Opium.** This eatery has completely rethought Asian cuisine, taking Chinese, Malaysian, and Thai cooking in new directions. Sauces are fragrant and spicy, but never overpowering. The specialty of the house is dim sum, prepared by a chef who knows his dumplings. The wontons are fresh and crisp, with delicious combinations of crab, shrimp, and chicken peeking through the almost transparent pastry. But leave room for the main dishes, especially the tiger prawns and scallops in a sauce made from dried shrimp and fish. Familiar dishes like beef in black bean sauce are astonishingly delicate and aromatic. The vegetarian menu is adventurous, too. There are also captivating cocktails. [$] *Average main: £17* ✉ *191 Hope St., City Centre* ☎ *0141/332–6668* 🌐 *www.opiumrestaurant.co.uk* [M] *Buchanan St.* ⊕ *F4.*

$$$ MODERN BRITISH Fodor's Choice ★ 🍴 **Rogano.** You can eat very well downstairs in the less expensive Cafe Rogano, where the brasserie-style food is more modern and imaginative, and the tables a little more crowded. The gorgeous bar serves wonderful cocktails along with elegant sandwiches and a lovely fish soup. You can even sit on the terrace, obligingly warmed by open-air heaters throughout the winter. Few people know that between 3 and 6 you get a free starter or dessert with a main dish. [$] *Average main: £22* ✉ *11 Exchange Pl., City Centre* ☎ *0141/248–4055* 🌐 *www.roganoglasgow.com* ✍ *Reservations essential* [M] *Buchanan St.* ⊕ *F5.*

$ VEGETARIAN 🍴 **Stereo.** Down a quiet lane near Central station, this ultracool eatery dishes up a fantastic range of vegan food, from paella to gnocchi to a colorful platter with hummus, red-pepper pâté, and home-baked flat bread. Roasted sweet-potato chips are the perfect side dish. The decor is homey and relaxed, and there always seems to be someone nearby reading or writing. Paintings, posters, and announcements of upcoming concerts in the space downstairs line the walls. The music is excellent, but never so loud as to disturb the serious business of eating. The kitchen closes at 9, and service is laid-back but very friendly. [$] *Average main: £10* ✉ *20–28 Renfield La., City Centre* ☎ *0141/222-2254* 🌐 *www.stereocafebar.com* ✍ *Reservations not accepted* [M] *Buchanan St.* ✥ *F5.*

$$$ SEAFOOD 🍴 **Two Fat Ladies.** One branch of the restaurant chain that raised the standard of fish cookery in Glasgow some years ago, Two Fat Ladies is named after two famous TV cooks (or alternatively after the bingo call for number 88, the number of the first eatery in Dumbarton Road in the West End). The Blythswood Street branch is airier and more central than the others. The menu is predominantly fish, from the halibut with walnut-and-thyme crust to the lemon sole with samphire. But if fish doesn't rock your boat, then the beef fillet with cherry jus is also delicious. [$] *Average main: £20* ✉ *118A Blythswood St., City Centre* ✥ *Just off Blythswood Sq.* ☎ *0141/847-0088* 🌐 *www.twofatladiesrestaurant.com* 🕒 *No lunch Sun.* ✍ *Reservations essential* [M] *Cowcaddens* ✥ *E4.*

$ CAFÉ 🍴 **Where the Monkey Sleeps.** This quirky basement café serves huge sandwiches with amusing names—the "Wytchfinder" has chorizo sausage and cheese, while the "Serious Operation" contains practically everything on the menu. All sandwiches are made to order, so be patient—it's worth the wait. Enjoy your choice with one of the wonderful smoothies. The café consists of a series of small rooms with brightly colored sofas, and the music is muted just enough to encourage intimate conversation. The place is just around the corner from Blythswood Square. [$] *Average main: £6* ✉ *182 W. Regent St., City Centre* ☎ *0141/226-3406* 🌐 *www.monkeysleeps.com* 🕒 *Closed weekends. No dinner* [M] *Cowcaddens* ✥ *E4.*

$ BRITISH 🍴 **Willow Tearooms.** Very Scottish breakfasts, lunches, and an array of cakes and scones baked in-house are served in a tearoom that was once part of a department store designed by Charles Rennie Mackintosh. At the back of a Mackintosh-theme jewelry and gift shop, it retains the designer's trademark furnishings, including high-backed chairs with elegant lines and subtle curves. Don't pass up the St. Andrew's Platter, a selection of trout, salmon, and prawns. [$] *Average main: £10* ✉ *217 Sauchiehall St., City Centre* ☎ *0141/332-0521* 🌐 *www.willowtearooms.co.uk* 🕒 *No dinner* [M] *Cowcaddens* ✥ *F4.*

MERCHANT CITY

Despite covering a relatively small area, the Merchant City has a wide variety of restaurants. The selection of cafés and restaurants includes many budget-friendly options that cater to the working population.

$$ SPANISH 🍴 **Arta.** The narrow entrance doesn't prepare you for this huge spacious venue—restaurant, bar, dance club—nor for its extravagant decor. The interior is like an enormous hacienda somewhere in southern Spain, and the menu is made to match. There's an elaborate tapas menu, accentuated by resident musicians and salsa dancing. Paellas

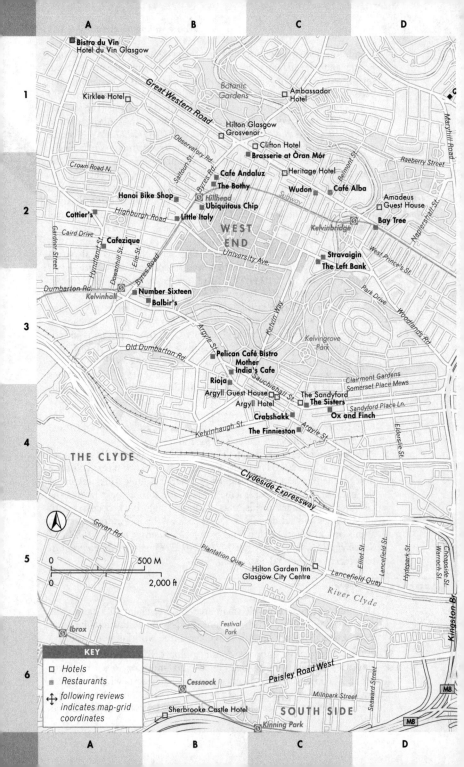

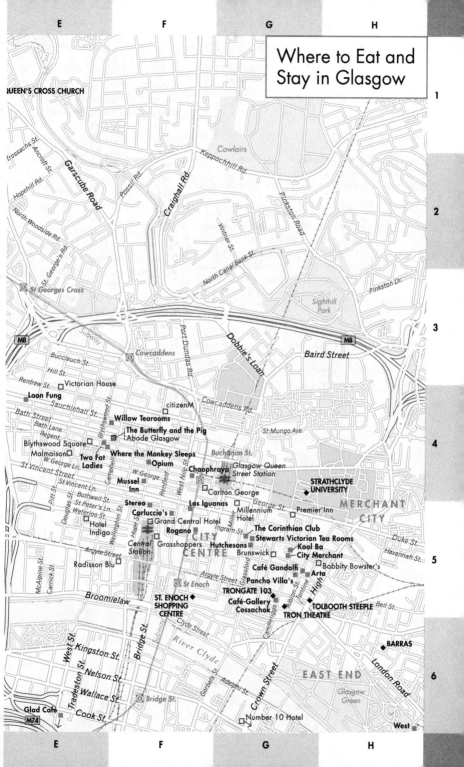

Where to Eat and Stay in Glasgow

QUEEN'S CROSS CHURCH

Cowlairs

Keppochhill Rd.

Garscube Road

Craighall Rd.

Passil Rd.

Trossachs St.
Ancroft St.
Hopehill Rd.
North Woodside Rd.
St George's Rd.

Winther St.

Pinkston Road

St Georges Cross

North Canal Bank St.

Sighthill Park

Pinkston Dr.

M8

Cowcaddens

Port Dundas Rd.

Dobbie's Loan

Baird Street

M8

Buccleuch St.
Hill St.
Renfrew St. Victorian House
Bath Street
Bath Lane
Regent
Loon Fung
Sauchiehall St.
Blythswood St.
citizenM

Willow Tearooms
The Butterfly and the Pig
Abode Glasgow
Blythswood Square
Malmaison
W. George Ln.
Two Fat Ladies
Where the Monkey Sleeps
Opium
St Vincent Street
W. George
St Vincent Ln.
Campbell
Mussel Inn
Stereo
Carluccio's
Bothwell St.
St Peter's Ln.
Waterloo St.
Pitt St.
Douglas St.
Hope St.
Renfield St.
West Nile St.

Cowcaddens Rd.

St Mungo Ave.

Buchanan St.

Chaophraya
Glasgow Queen Street Station
Carlton George
Las Iguanas
Millennium Hotel
George St.
Miller St.

STRATHCLYDE UNIVERSITY

MERCHANT CITY

Premier Inn

Duke St.

Hotel Indigo
Grand Central Hotel
Rogano
Central Station
Grasshoppers
CITY CENTRE
Argyle Street
Radisson Blu

Ingram St.
Hutchesons
Brunswick
Glassford St.
Candleriggs

The Corinthian Club
Stewarts Victorian Tea Rooms
Kool Ba
City Merchant
Babbity Bowster's
Havannah St.

McAlpine St.
Carrick St.

St Enoch

Café Gandolfi
Pancho Villa's
TRONGATE 103
Café-Gallery
Cossachok

Arta
Albion St.
Turnbull St.
High

ST. ENOCH SHOPPING CENTRE
Broomielaw
Bridge St.
Clyde Street

TOLBOOTH STEEPLE
TRON THEATRE
Bell St.

River Clyde

West St.
Kingston St.
Tradeston St.
Nelson St.
Wallace St.
Bridge St.
Gorbals St.
Crown Street
Adelphi St.

EAST END

BARRAS
London Road

Glasgow Green

Glad Café
M74
Cook St.

Bridge St.

Number 10 Hotel

West

E F G H

1 2 3 4 5 6

(with the usual meat and seafood, though there's also a vegetarian version) are substantial and delicious. $ *Average main: £16* ✉ *13–19 Wallis St., Merchant City* ☎ *0845/166–6018* ⊕ *www.arta.co.uk* ⊙ *Closed Sun.–Wed. No lunch* Ⓜ *Buchanan St.* ✛ *G5.*

$
EASTERN
EUROPEAN
✕ **Café-Gallery Cossachok.** At this spacious and quirky restaurant, the Russian owner pays homage to her homeland (and other Eastern European countries) in a menu that includes blintzes, beef Stroganoff, and a Moldavian vegetable stew called *gouvetch*. There is, of course, a variety of chilled vodkas from which to choose. The colorful shawls stretched across the ceiling, the hand-carved furniture, and the jewelry on display add to the festive atmosphere. On Sunday night there's live music, from tango to jazz. $ *Average main: £12* ✉ *10 King St., Merchant City* ☎ *0141/553–0733* ⊙ *Closed Mon.* Ⓜ *St. Enoch* ✛ *G5.*

$$
MODERN BRITISH
✕ **Café Gandolfi.** Occupying what was once the tea market, this trendy café draws the style-conscious crowd and can justly claim to have launched the dining renaissance of the Merchant City. Wooden tables and chairs crafted by Scottish artist Tim Stead are so fluidly shaped it's hard to believe they're inanimate. The café opens early for breakfast, serving croissants, eggs *en cocotte* (casserole-style), and strong espresso. The menu is varied and constantly changing, but don't miss the monkfish and prawn tagine, the venison with gratin dauphinoise, or resident dishes like smoked haddie and Stornaway black pudding. The bar on the second floor is more intimate, much less busy, and lets you order from the same menu—but that should remain a well-kept secret. $ *Average main: £15* ✉ *64 Albion St., Merchant City* ☎ *0141/552–6813* ⊕ *www.cafegandolfi.com* Ⓜ *Buchanan St.* ✛ *G5.*

$$
MODERN BRITISH
✕ **City Merchant.** If you have a penchant for fresh and flavorful cuisine, head to this welcoming spot with simple but traditional furnishings, including white tablecloths, dark wood, soft lighting, and tartan carpets. The secret is the kitchen's use of only local ingredients and its emphasis on Scottish cuisine. You can sample the tasty cuts of venison and beef (including a fillet with haggis mousse), but seafood remains the star attraction: the mussels and oysters from Loch Etive are wondrous. An outstanding starter is the trio of whisky-smoked salmon, mackerel pâté, and crispy oyster (oyster fried in tempura batter), or try the sea bass with fennel puree, olives, and chorizo. There's a relatively inexpensive selection of wines and a wonderful cheese board that's served, as the locals like it, with oatcakes, celery, and quince.

TAKE TIME FOR TEA

In the Victorian tradition, while men went to pubs, Glasgow women's social interaction would take place in the city's many tearooms and cafés. Today *everyone* goes to the café. Glaswegians have succumbed to the worldwide love for Italian-style, espresso-based coffees, but they'll never give up the comfort of a nice cup of tea, so you'll find both at most tearooms, along with scones, Scottish pancakes, and other pastries. The Glasgow tradition of high tea with fish-and-chips, cakes, and tea has been supplanted now by afternoon tea, a more genteel affair with sandwiches and cakes on a traditional cake stand.

■ **TIP→ The two-course lunch special is a bargain at £9.95.** [$] *Average main: £19* ✉ *97–99 Candleriggs St., Merchant City* ☎ *0141/553–1577* 🌐 *www.citymerchant.co.uk* ⏲ *No lunch Sun.* [M] *Buchanan St.* ✣ *G5.*

$$ MODERN BRITISH 🍴 **Corinthian Club.** Inside what was once the mansion of tobacco merchant George Buchanan, the Corinthian Club includes a restaurant, two bars, a nightclub, and a casino. In the ostentatiously elegant main restaurant, the Brasserie, you can dine, take afternoon tea, or sip a cocktail under a 26-foot-high glass dome as classical statues stare in your direction. The menu offers a good selection of seafood and steaks, and a market menu changes daily. ■ **TIP→ Food is served here until 1 am Sunday to Thursday and until 3 am Friday and Saturday.** The basement, once a criminal court, now houses a casino, to which you gain access, appropriately enough, through a Prohibition-era bar. [$] *Average main: £16* ✉ *191 Ingram St., Merchant City* ☎ *0141/552–1101* 🌐 *www.thecorinthianclub.co.uk* ✍ *Reservations essential* [M] *Buchanan St.* ✣ *G5.*

$$$ ECLECTIC 🍴 **Hutchesons.** Housed in one of the most iconic buildings in the Merchant City, the 17th-century Hutchesons Hospital, this elegant restaurant and bar is the latest addition to Glasgow's dining map. Downstairs is divided between the bar area and the café section, its dark-wood decor recalling earlier times; upstairs the dining room has tall windows and beautifully decorated ceilings that have been lovingly restored. The lunch/pretheater menu is limited but well presented and tasteful, while the main restaurant menu emphasizes fresh seafood like the shellfish platter of oysters, prawns, dressed mini-crab, winkles, whelks, and mussels. Main dishes, especially the roast monkfish tail with caper butter, are appropriately luxurious. The bar serves breakfast and lunch. [$] *Average main: £22* ✉ *158 Ingram St., Merchant City* ☎ *0141/552–4050* 🌐 *www.hutchesonsglasgow.com* [M] *Buchanan St.* ✣ *G5.*

$$ ECLECTIC 🍴 **Kool Ba.** This atmospheric haven serves an intriguing mix of Indian and Persian fare. It's all about healthy, flavorful cooking: chicken *tikka masala* in a yogurt sauce or lamb korma with coconut cream and fruit or the Persian *shashlik* are good picks. Accompany your meal with bowls of basmati saffron rice and fluffy naan bread. Thick wooden tables, Persian tapestries, and soft candlelight make you feel at home in the comfortable dining room. This popular place continues to win award after award; reserve ahead on Friday and Saturday. [$] *Average main: £15* ✉ *109–113 Candleriggs, Merchant City* ☎ *0141/552–2777* 🌐 *www.koolba.com* ✍ *Reservations essential* [M] *Buchanan St.* ✣ *G5.*

$ MEXICAN FAMILY 🍴 **Pancho Villa's.** Images of Pancho Villa and Emiliano Zapata are everywhere in this festive and authentic Mexican eatery, whose pink, yellow, and blue walls are decorated with colorful papier-mâché masks. Locals can't get enough of the cocktails or the food, which includes all the old favorites—enchiladas, burritos, tacos, and fajitas—as well as some new dishes. Try the flour tortillas filled with marinated lamb, or the chipotle chicken in a dark, spicy sauce. If what you crave is a margarita, look no further. [$] *Average main: £10* ✉ *26 Bell St., Merchant City* ☎ *0141/552–7737* 🌐 *www.panchovillas.co.uk* [M] *Buchanan St.* ✣ *G5.*

$ CAFÉ 🍴 **Stewarts Victorian Tea Rooms.** Afternoon tea, complete with cakes and tiny sandwiches served on a three-tier stand, has become popular in Glasgow. In this City Centre tearoom, decorated with the obligatory large potted plants and floral teapots, you can enjoy afternoon tea, consisting of dainty sandwiches and cakes, or high tea, an old-time ritual that includes more substantial fare along with scones and tea. [$] *Average main: £14* ✉ *89 Glassford St., Merchant City* ☎ *0141/552–0646* ⏲ *No dinner* [M] *Buchanan St.* ✣ *G5.*

WEST END

Because of Glasgow University, the eateries in this area were once just the domain of students and professors. In recent years, this elegant residential area has also attracted fine restaurants that appeal to a wide range of visitors.

$ INDIAN 🍴 **Balbir's.** Don't let the tinted windows discourage you: this place is a temple for pure, healthy Indian food that's impressive in taste and presentation. Twinkling chandeliers, immaculate white tablecloths, and perfectly polished silverware set the stage. All food is prepared with cholesterol-free canola oil; no artificial colors or additives are used. Try the chicken *tikka chasni* (with mango chutney, lemon juice, and mint), lamb korma, or the traditional celebration dish of Goanese fish curry. There are taster menus at £18.95 if you have difficulty choosing from the large menu. [$] *Average main: £13* ✉ *7 Church St., West End* ☎ *0141/339–7711* 🌐 *www.balbirsrestaurants.co.uk* ⏲ *No lunch* [M] *Kelvinhall* ✣ *B3.*

$ MIDDLE EASTERN 🍴 **Bay Tree.** This small café in the university area serves wonderful Middle Eastern food—mostly vegetarian dishes, but there are a few lamb and chicken creations as well. Egyptian *phool* (broad beans dressed with spices and herbs), Turkish *mulukia* (fried eggplant with a tomato-and-herb sauce), and *kurma* (stew with spinach, herbs, and beans) are among its delights. Two-course lunch and pretheater menus are £7.95, and both standard egg and Arabian breakfasts are served. ■ **TIP→ You can also bring your own wine; there is a good wine store just a few doors away, and there is no corkage charge.** [$] *Average main: £11* ✉ *403 Great Western Rd., West End* ☎ *0141/334–5898* 🌐 *www.thebaytreewestend.co.uk* [M] *Kelvinbridge* ✣ *D2.*

$$$ ECLECTIC Fodor's Choice ★ 🍴 **Bistro du Vin.** Stylish blue-and-green tartan carpets beckon you into one of the city's most elegant eateries, where service is impeccable and all the food is locally sourced. Romantic fires in the background, crystal chandeliers overhead, and stained-glass murals make it the perfect place for cold, wet days. From the menu of French and Scottish fare, try the venison or the halibut with risotto nero, artichokes, and crispy kale. The starters are seductive, and the sticky toffee pudding, a Scottish staple, is a tempting dessert. There is prix-fixe menu at £21.95 or £26.95 for two or three courses, respectively. [$] *Average main: £24* ✉ *Hotel du Vin, 1 Devonshire Gardens, West End* ☎ *0141/339–2001* 🌐 *www.hotelduvin.com* ✍ *Reservations essential* [M] *Hillhead* ✣ *A1.*

$$ BRITISH 🍴 **The Bothy.** Set back from Byres Road, and only a few yards from the subway station, The Bothy occupies a separate house in a lane. It seems to grow as you enter, and everywhere you look are reminders of the restaurant's Scottish theme, from the thistles on the wallpaper to the dark-wood furniture. The inventively Scottish menu includes

well-made *cullen skink* (a thick soup of smoked haddock, potatoes, and onions) and scallops and black pudding starters. The steak-and-mushroom pie and the chicken stuffed with Stornaway black pudding continue the theme. $ *Average main: £15* ⊠ *11 Ruthven La., West End* ☎ *0141/330–4040* ⊕ *www.bothyglasgow.co.uk* Ⓜ *Hillhead* ⊕ *B2.*

$$ ✕ **Brasserie at Òran Mór.** This is the more formal eatery (the other being
BRITISH the bistro-style Conservatory) within this handsome former church. There's lots of elegantly curved wood and high-backed bench seating, as well as some Alasdair Gray murals to savor. The food is equally well crafted, and you can expect contemporary treats using monkfish and Gressingham duck. The Brasserie becomes a cocktail and champagne bar Friday and Saturday from 11 pm to 3 am. $ *Average main: £16* ⊠ *731–735 Great Western Rd., West End* ☎ *0141/357–6226* ⊕ *www. oran-mor.co.uk* ⊗ *Closed Mon. No lunch Tues. and Wed.* ⌲ *Reservations essential* Ⓜ *Hillhead* ⊕ *B2.*

$ ✕ **Café Alba.** This small café is famous for its wonderful cakes and great
CAFÉ coffee. The tasty lunch options—soups, sandwiches, and quiches—are all made on the premises. There's a comfortable upstairs dining room and free Wi-Fi connections, so feel free to linger. $ *Average main: £8* ⊠ *481 Great Western Rd., West End* ☎ *0141/237–7902* ⊕ *www. albacafe.wordpress.com* ⊗ *Closed Sun. and Mon. No dinner* Ⓜ *Kelvinbridge* ⊕ *C2.*

$$ ✕ **Cafe Andaluz.** With its Spanish flair, this beautifully designed base-
TAPAS ment eatery is always busy and lively. The first tapas place to make an impact in Glasgow, its has been followed by others (and has opened a second location of its own in the City Centre) but remains one of the most successful. This is an ideal way to dine with friends: sharing the dishes as they arrive and as you down some good Spanish wine. (Rioja is always a reliable choice.) Booking ahead is strongly advised. $ *Average main: £15* ⊠ *2 Cresswell La., West End* ☎ *0141/339–1111* ⊕ *www. cafeandaluz.com* ⌲ *Reservations essential* Ⓜ *Hillhead* ⊕ *B2.*

$$ ✕ **Cafezique.** Small but inviting, this West End magnet has a vibrant,
BRITISH changing breakfast, lunch, and dinner menu that is always fresh and exciting. The dinner menu is divided into "wee things," "big things," and "sweet things." Try the Shetland mussels as your wee thing (if they're in season); the sausage, fennel, and white bean stew as your big thing; and the pistachio and rosewater meringue as your sweet thing. The excellent breakfasts are available all day until 5; you'll have to battle for a table on Sunday. The bakery two doors away is seductive, too, and serves coffee, sandwiches, and glorious cakes. $ *Average main: £15* ⊠ *66 Hyndland St., West End* ☎ *0141/339–7180* ⊕ *www.delizique. com* ⌲ *Reservations essential* Ⓜ *Hillhead* ⊕ *A2.*

$$ ✕ **Cottier's.** A converted Victorian church decorated by Glasgow artist
MODERN BRITISH Daniel Cottier is the unusual setting for this bar and restaurant. The restaurant has a small but interesting menu, including duck egg with mushrooms and truffle potato cream as a starter, and a main of turbot with calamari and prawns. Red walls and beamed ceilings warm up the cavernous downstairs bar, where the down-to-earth menu features chorizo and black pudding stew and, of course, fish-and-chips. The pretheater menu is £15 or £18.50 for two or three courses, respectively.

[$] *Average main: £15* ✉ *93 Hyndland St., West End* ☎ *0141/357–5825* 🌐 *www.cottiers.com* [M] *Hillhead* ✣ *A2.*

$ SEAFOOD Fodor's Choice ★ 🍴 **Crabshakk.** This place is anything but a shack. The intimate dining room has heavy wooden tables and chairs and a bar so shiny and inviting that it seems to almost insist you have a drink. The lamps are like half-moons, and the ceiling is elegantly ornate. The food comes from the sea—oysters, lobster, and squid—and you can have your choice served iced, grilled, roasted, or battered. The fish varies daily according to the day's catch, and only local and sustainably sourced Scottish seafood is featured. The fish sandwich and crab cakes are favorites on the lunch menu. In the evening, mussels and scallops draw the eye. The buzz of conversation and the perfectly modulated music create the right atmosphere. [$] *Average main: £12* ✉ *1114 Argyle St., West End* ☎ *0141/334–6127* 🌐 *www.crabshakk.com* ⏲ *Closed Mon.* ✍ *Reservations essential* [M] *Kelvin Hall* ✣ *C4.*

$$ SEAFOOD 🍴 **The Finnieston.** This lively and comfortable bar-restaurant is one of the family of new high-quality fish restaurants that have slowly transformed the Finnieston area from a run-down into a distinctly fashionable district. The menu allows the diner to choose the fish and how it is prepared, the sauce, and salad or vegetable sides. The heart of the restaurant are wooden booths separate from the bar, but you can also eat in the bar, which has an enormous menu of fine cocktails, including a martini list and 15 variants on gin and tonic. On Lobster Tuesday, half a lobster and a glass of champagne are £15. [$] *Average main: £16* ✉ *1125 Argyle St., West End* ☎ *0141/222–2884* 🌐 *www.thefinniestonbar.com* ✍ *Reservations essential* [M] *Kelvin Hall* ✣ *C4.*

$ VIETNAMESE 🍴 **Hanoi Bike Shop.** Glasgow's first Vietnamese canteen offers a different style of dining, which is apparent from the moment you walk through the door. There are no starters or mains as such—couples are advised to share three dishes. It could be roast pigeon with bok choy, hot-and-sour fish soup, or rice noodles in a savory broth. The setting is rustic, the tables are low, and the seating, mostly stools, take a little getting used to, but it's also part of the experience. [$] *Average main: £14* ✉ *8 Ruthven La., West End* ☎ *0141/334–7165* 🌐 *www.thehanoibikeshop.co.uk* [M] *Hillhead* ✣ *B2.*

$$ ECLECTIC FAMILY 🍴 **The Left Bank.** Close to Glasgow University, this popular hangout attracts a more mature student crowd. It's an airy spot with high ceilings, leather sofas, and wood floors, and the specialty is good, eclectic food at reasonable prices. Breakfast is your best bet, with thick-sliced French toast, or eggs served on an English muffin with spinach and smoked salmon. Tapas-style plates are an option at lunch: try roasted eggplant and wild-garlic hummus with whole grain flat bread. Among the main dishes, the mussels with Vietnamese sweet-and-sour broth stand out. The evening menu includes black- and-white sesame salmon and garlic masala fish. It is a relaxed, unhurried place, whose casual air belies its excellent cooking. [$] *Average main: £15* ✉ *33–35 Gibson St., West End* ☎ *0141/339–5969* 🌐 *www.theleftbank.co.uk* [M] *Kelvinbridge* ✣ *C2.*

$ ITALIAN FAMILY 🍴 **Little Italy.** This busy, noisy, and extremely friendly Italian café sits in the heart of the West End. You can perch on a stool by the window with a cappuccino while watching the world go by, or grab a seat at one of the crowded tables and enjoy an excellent pasta or one of the pizzas, probably the best around. Create your own combination from the many topping options and wait while it's made, or skip the main dishes and move straight to the tiramisu. [$] *Average main: £7* ✉ *205 Byres Rd., West End* ☎ *0141/339–6287* 🌐 *littleitalyglasgow.com* [M] *Hillhead* ⊕ *B2.*

$$ INDIAN 🍴 **Mother India's Cafe.** Overlooking the Kelvingrove Art Gallery and Museum, this quaint, casual eatery has a spectacular view as well as an impressive menu. It's usually quite crowded, so don't expect much intimacy. The food is served tapas-style in small dishes—the idea is that you get to try lots of different flavors. Chili-flavored king prawns, chicken cooked with lime, and *aloo saag dosa* (potato and spinach stuffed in a rice-and-lentil pancake) are all rich in flavor and presentation. The popular café doesn't accept reservations, so be prepared for a (fast-moving) line. It's worth bringing your own wine; there's a small corkage charge. [$] *Average main: £15* ✉ *1355 Argyle St., West End* ☎ *0141/339–9145* 🌐 *www.motherindiaglasgow.co.uk* ✍ *Reservations not accepted* [M] *Kelvin Hall* ⊕ *B3.*

$$ BRITISH Fodor's Choice ★ 🍴 **Number Sixteen.** This tiny, intimate restaurant serves only the freshest ingredients, superbly prepared. Halibut is served with choucroute and a passion fruit dressing—a typically unpredictable meeting of flavors. The pork belly with black pudding and piccalilli is tantalizing, and desserts are equally seductive. The menu is constantly changing. There's room (just) for 40 diners; the result is cozy but curiously it doesn't feel cramped. Book ahead, particularly on weekends. [$] *Average main: £17* ✉ *16 Byres Rd., West End* ☎ *0141/339–2544* 🌐 *www.number16.co.uk* ✍ *Reservations essential* [M] *Kelvin Hall* ⊕ *A3.*

$$$ ECLECTIC Fodor's Choice ★ 🍴 **Ox and Finch.** This fairly new but already immensely popular restaurant shines at every level—service, presentation, and taste. The menu is a variation fairly new to Glasgow on the small-plates theme. The diner chooses perhaps two or three plates—larger than tapas and beautifully presented—from meat, fish, cold starters, and vegetable lists which then arrive as they are ready. The chef combines colors and tastes in often surprising ways—coley (similar to cod) with chorizo and chicory, lamb shoulder with anchovy and salsa verde, confit duck with Thai yellow curry and rice. The desserts continue the theme with a signature lemon-and-Earl Grey baked Alaska, for example. The service is relaxed, friendly, and informative. [$] *Average main: £20* ✉ *920 Sauchiehall St., West End* ☎ *0141/339–8627* 🌐 *www.oxandfinch.com* ✍ *Reservations essential* [M] *Kelvin Hall* ⊕ *C4.*

$$ ECLECTIC 🍴 **Pelican Café Bistro.** The hum of conversation and a glimpse of the busy kitchen through the open hatch give this restaurant a relaxed vibe. A horseshoe-shape bar in dark wood contrasts with the cream-color walls displaying local art. The food is adventurous and resolutely fresh, with the source of the ingredients carefully listed on the menu. The dishes vary with the seasons and the conditions on the high seas, but you might find delicious sea bream with saffron-herb mash, or monkfish tails with a delicate pea risotto. There are always unusual and exciting options for vegetarians and vegans. The owner has a passion for wine, which shows in the huge wine list. [$] *Average main: £17* ✉ *1377 Argyle St.,*

West End ☎ *0844/573–0670* ⊕ *www.thepelicancafe.co.uk* ⊛ *Reservations essential* Ⓜ *Kelvin Hall* ✛ *B6.*

$

SPANISH

✕ **Rioja.** No tapas restaurant is more authentic than Rioja, part of the emerging dining scene in the Finnieston area. The *fideuà* (paella with vermicelli instead of rice), *carrillera* (pigs' cheeks), and *vieira* (scallop) with lettuce soup, together with the large and inexpensive wine list, meld with the muted interior to feel more Spanish than most. The virtue of tapas is they are served all day, and Rioja is relaxed, informal, and open later than most eateries. Ⓢ *Average main: £10* ✉ *1116 Argyle St., West End* ☎ *0141/334–0761* ⊕ *www.riojafinnieston.co.uk* Ⓜ *Kelvin Hall* ✛ *B3.*

$$$

BRITISH

✕ **The Sisters.** Walk up the smooth sandstone steps to this restaurant, which aims to inspire both your palate and your heart. The menu is locally sourced and always changing: a typical dish is Carluke ham with buttered savoy cabbage and colcannon mash. The source of everything on the menu is identified—and Scottish—but no matter what you choose, it will be served in generous portions. The homegrown Arran gooseberry fool is the ultimate Scottish dessert. Douglas Gray tartan pads the pristine room, and polished floorboards reflect the natural light shining in from the long windows around the unusual oval-shape room. Ⓢ *Average main: £20* ✉ *36 Kelvingrove St., West End* ☎ *0141/564–1157* ⊕ *www.thesisters.co.uk* Ⓜ *Kelvin Hall* ✛ *C4.*

$

ECLECTIC

Fodor's Choice

★

✕ **Stravaigin.** Despite its popularity and having doubled in size, the café-bar at Stravaigin has maintained the highest quality of cooking for many years. The dishes are adventurous and creative, often combining Oriental and local flavors and unusual marriages of ingredients, like the mussels in a Keralan coconut, tamarind, and curry leaf sauce, or ginger and soy hake fillet. Yet its haggis and neeps (turnips), the national dish, is famed. A wide variety of wines is available, including some uncommon ones. The downstairs restaurant serves the same menu, but the environment is quieter, and a little more sedate, though you can still hear the constant buzz of conversation above you. Ⓢ *Average main: £13* ✉ *28 Gibson St., West End* ☎ *0141/334–2665* ⊕ *www.stravaigin. com* Ⓜ *Kelvinbridge* ✛ *C2.*

$$$

MODERN BRITISH

Fodor's Choice

★

✕ **Ubiquitous Chip.** Occupying a converted stable behind the Hillhead subway station in busy Ashton Lane, this restaurant is an institution among Glasgow's media and theater communities, who most days can be found in the busy upstairs bar. The main restaurant has a large cobbled courtyard with a glass roof, offering alfresco dining without the risk of rain. The creative menu includes breast of guinea fowl with porcini gnocchi and an onion velouté or haunch of roe with roast squash. The more informal brasserie, upstairs beside the bar, serves less expensive dishes like haggis with neeps and tatties. There's an excellent lunch and pretheater menu for £15.95 for two courses and £19.95 for three. Ⓢ *Average main: £24* ✉ *12 Ashton La., West End* ☎ *0141/334–5007* ⊕ *www.ubiquitouschip.co.uk* ⊛ *Reservations essential* Ⓜ *Hillhead* ✛ *B2.*

$

JAPANESE

✕ **Wudon.** This pleasant and relaxed Japanese restaurant offers beautifully prepared food presented with great charm by the staff. Whether your taste is for hearty broths, just-made sushi, or savory rice and noodle dishes, the chef will combine the elements to your taste. The big broth noodle dishes are appetizing and substantial, as are the varied salad bowls. Vegetarians are well served here. The lunchtime bento boxes (£6.50) served between noon and 5, are a particularly good value with miso soup, rice, meat or fish or vegetables, and a piece of fresh fruit. Asian beers and a range of drinks are available, too. [$] *Average main: £9* ✉ *535 Great Western Rd., West End* ☎ *0141/357–3039* 🌐 *www.wudon-noodlebar.co.uk* [M] *Kelvinbridge* ✥ *C2.*

EAST END

The East End is not well furnished with notable places to eat. An exception is West, housed in the Templeton's Carpet Factory opposite the People's Palace.

$ GERMAN 🍴 **West.** This microbrewery serves beer brewed "according to German purity laws of 1516"—in other words, no additives to muddy the flavor. The German theme is continued with the convivial dining space dotted with large wooden tables and the food, which includes wursts, Wiener schnitzel, and goulash. A more limited bar menu is served in the very popular beer garden. West is in the famous Templeton Carpet Factory on Glasgow Green, built to resemble the Doge's Palace in Venice. You can tour the brewery Friday through Sunday with four tasters as part of the price (£11.95). A second branch has now opened on Woodlands Road in Glasgow's West End. [$] *Average main: £12* ✉ *Templeton Bldg., Templeton St., East End* ☎ *0141/550–0135* 🌐 *www.westbeer.com* [M] *St. Enoch* ✥ *H6.*

SOUTH SIDE

A number of places on the South Side are worth a stop if you're in the area.

$ CAFÉ FAMILY 🍴 **Glad Cafe.** This excellent café serves delicious homemade cakes and coffee, and the breakfast and lunch options are always worth a look. The menu changes daily according to what's available, but there is always a soup, a pâté, a pasta, a fish dish, a burger, a vegetarian option, and one of their fabulous cakes. This is a comfortable and relaxing place to be; no one seems to be in a hurry. The café holds regular cultural events, too; the calendar includes music, film, and theater. The small entrance belies the spacious premises within. To reach the café, which sits opposite Langside Halls on Pollokshaws Road, take any bus from Union Street in the City Centre to Shawlands. [$] *Average main: £9* ✉ *1006A Pollokshaws Rd., South Side* ☎ *0141/636–6119* 🌐 *www.thegladcafe.co.uk* ⏲ *No dinner* ✥ *E6.*

WHERE TO STAY

Glasgow's City Centre never sleeps, so downtown hotels will be noisier than those in the leafy and genteel West End. Downtown hotels are within walking distance of all the main sights, while West End lodgings are more convenient for museums and art galleries. Over the past few years the hotel scene has become noticeably more stylish, with new hotels opening, including Blythswood Square and Grand Central.

Although big hotels are spread out all around the city, B&Bs are definitely a more popular, personal, and cheaper option. For country-house luxury you should look beyond the city—try Mar Hall, near Paisley. Regardless of the neighborhood, hotels are about the same in price. Some B&Bs as well as the smaller properties may also offer discounts for longer stays. Make your reservations in advance, especially when there's a big concert, sporting event, or holiday (New Year's Eve is popular). Glasgow is busiest in summer, but it can fill up when something special is going on. If you arrive in town without a place to stay, contact the Glasgow Tourist Board.

PRICES AND MONEY-SAVING OPTIONS

It is always worthwhile to inquire about special deals or rates, especially if you book online and in advance. Another money-saving option is to rent an apartment. B&Bs are the best-priced short-term lodging option, and you're sure to get breakfast.

Most smaller hotels and all guesthouses include breakfast in the room rate. Larger hotels usually charge extra for breakfast. Also note that the most expensive hotels often exclude V.A.T. (Value Added Tax, the sales tax) in the initial price quote but budget places include it. *Hotel reviews have been shortened. For full information, visit Fodors.com. Use the coordinate (✛ B2) at the end of each listing to locate a site on the corresponding map.*

WHAT IT COSTS IN POUNDS			
$	$$	$$$	$$$$
Hotels	Under £100	£100–£160	£161–£220	Over £220

Hotel prices are the lowest cost of a standard double room in high season, including 20% V.A.T.

CITY CENTRE

Here you'll be close to everything—the main sights, shops, theaters, restaurants, and bars—the pulse of the city. You don't have to worry about transportation in the center of town, but it can get noisy on weekend nights.

$$
HOTEL   **Abode Glasgow.** This stylish modern hotel in an Edwardian building was once the home of a prime minister, and it retains architectural features like the wrought-iron elevator and walls lined with 2,000 gold-leaf lions. **Pros:** stylish rooms; great location. **Cons:** limited public areas; some front rooms noisy; pricey parking. $ *Rooms from: £150* ✉ *129 Bath St., City Centre* ☎ *0141/221–6789,* ⊕ *www.abodeglasgow.co.uk* ⬐ *59 rooms, 1 suite* ⦿| *Breakfast* Ⓜ *Buchanan St.* ✛ *F4.*

$$
HOTEL
Fodor's Choice
★   **Blythswood Square.** History and luxury come together at this smart conversion of the former headquarters of the Royal Automobile Club of Scotland, which occupies a classical building on peaceful Blythswood Square. **Pros:** airy and luxurious; glorious bathrooms; lovely common

areas that retain the original gold-topped columns. **Cons:** room lighting may be too dim for some; some street noise. $ *Rooms from: £150* ⊠ *11 Blythswood Sq., City Centre* ☏ *0141/248–8888* ⊕ *www. blythswoodsquare.com* ↩ *100 rooms, 6 suites* ☽ *Breakfast* Ⓜ *Cowcaddens* ✛ *E4.*

$$ ⌕ **Carlton George.** A narrow revolving doorway, a step back from busy HOTEL West George Street, creates the illusion of a secret passageway leading into this lavish boutique hotel. **Pros:** near City Centre attractions; discounted parking nearby. **Cons:** entrance very small and often crowded; area sometimes noisy at night. $ *Rooms from: £120* ⊠ *44 W. George St., City Centre* ☏ *0141/353–6373* ⊕ *www.carlton.nl/george* ↩ *64 rooms* ☽ *Breakfast* Ⓜ *Buchanan St.* ✛ *F4.*

$ ⌕ **citizenM.** There's no lobby at the futuristic citizenM—no reception HOTEL area at all, because you can only book online—but there are chic "living **Fodor's Choice** rooms" with ultramodern furnishings where guests congregate. **Pros:** ★ wonderful design; all the creature comforts; central location. **Cons:** not for the claustrophobic. $ *Rooms from: £90* ⊠ *60 Renfrew St., corner of Hope St., City Centre* ☏ *01782/488–3490* ⊕ *www.citizenm.com/ glasgow* ↩ *198 rooms* ☽ *No meals* Ⓜ *Buchanan St.* ✛ *F4.*

$$$ ⌕ **Grand Central Hotel.** This hotel certainly deserves its name, as everyHOTEL thing about it, from the magnificent marble-floor champagne bar to the **Fodor's Choice** ballroom fully restored to its original glory, is grand. **Pros:** a real air ★ of luxury; generally spacious rooms; great champagne bar for lingering. **Cons:** some noise from street; parking a couple of blocks away; some small rooms. $ *Rooms from: £165* ⊠ *99 Gordon St., City Centre* ☏ *0141/240–3700* ⊕ *www.principal-hayley.com/grandcentralhotel* ↩ *230 rooms, 3 suites* ☽ *Breakfast* Ⓜ *Buchanan St.* ✛ *F5.*

$$ ⌕ **Grasshoppers.** Not visible from the street, this hotel occupies the sixth HOTEL floor above Central station; guest rooms are on the small side but have expansive windows overlooking the glass roof of the station on one side and across the rooftops of Glasgow on the other. **Pros:** bright and clean; quiet atmosphere; central location. **Cons:** no lobby; rooms are quite small. $ *Rooms from: £110* ⊠ *87 Union St., City Centre* ✛ *Door on Union St. marked "Caledonian Chambers" leads to elevator* ☏ *0141/222–2666* ⊕ *www.grasshoppersglasgow.com* ↩ *30 rooms* ☽ *Breakfast* Ⓜ *St. Enoch* ✛ *F5.*

$$ ⌕ **Hotel Indigo.** In the center of the city, the fashionable Indigo is awash HOTEL with bold colors and modern designs that emphasize comfort and calm. **Pros:** well-designed rooms; subdued colors and lighting; no conference rooms. **Cons:** narrow corridors; only showers in the rooms. $ *Rooms from: £112* ⊠ *75 Waterloo St., City Centre* ☏ *0141/226–7700* ⊕ *www. hotelindigoglasgow.com* ↩ *94 rooms* ☽ *No meals* Ⓜ *St. Enoch* ✛ *E5.*

$$ ⌕ **Malmaison.** Housed in a converted church, this modern boutique HOTEL hotel prides itself on personal service and outstanding amenities like **Fodor's Choice** plasma televisions and high-end stereo systems. **Pros:** stunning lobby; ★ attention to detail; five-minute walk to Sauchiehall Street. **Cons:** bland views; dark hallways; no on-site parking. $ *Rooms from: £135* ⊠ *278 W. George St., City Centre* ☏ *0141/572–1000* ⊕ *www.malmaison.com* ↩ *64 rooms, 8 suites* ☽ *Breakfast* Ⓜ *Cowcaddens* ✛ *E4.*

$$ ⌷ **Millennium Hotel.** This huge hotel, which occupies almost a whole side
HOTEL of George Square and stretches above the rail station next door, has
restrained and comfortable rooms with ample bathrooms. **Pros:** couldn't
be more central; ample comfortable public areas. **Cons:** very long cor-
ridors; views of the square only from some (more expensive) rooms.
ⓢ *Rooms from: £130* ⌧ *40 George Sq., City Centre* ☎ *0141/332–6711*
⊕ *www.millenniumhotels.co.uk* ⤳ *116 rooms* ⦿ *Breakfast* Ⓜ *Bu-
chanan St.* ✛ *G5.*

$ ⌷ **Premier Inn.** It would be easy to miss the big City Centre branch of this
HOTEL budget hotel chain, since its entrance on Renfield Street is quite small,
but it's worth seeking out for its winning location just around the cor-
ner from the pedestrian precinct in Sauchiehall Street and uniform but
comfortable and clean rooms with ample bathrooms, TV, and Wi-Fi.
Pros: great location; bargain rates; modern rooms. **Cons:** some front
rooms a bit noisy; entrance easily missed at street level; no parking
facilities. ⓢ *Rooms from: £70* ⌧ *Buchanan Galleries, 141 W. Nile St.,
City Centre* ☎ *0871/527–9360* ⊕ *www.premierinn.com* ⤳ *220 rooms*
⦿ *No meals* Ⓜ *Buchanan St.* ✛ *G5.*

$$ ⌷ **Radisson Blu.** You can't miss this eye-catching edifice behind Cen-
HOTEL tral station: its glass facade makes the interior, particularly the lounge,
seem as though it were part of the street. **Pros:** kilted doorman; impeccable service; free Wi-Fi and other amenities. **Cons:** neighborhood can
get noisy; most rooms have poor views; no on-site parking. ⓢ *Rooms
from: £150* ⌧ *301 Argyle St., City Centre* ☎ *0141/204–3333* ⊕ *www.
radissonblu.co.uk/hotel-glasgow* ⤳ *247 rooms, 3 suites* ⦿ *Breakfast*
Ⓜ *St. Enoch* ✛ *F5.*

$ ⌷ **Victorian House.** Compared with the bright-yellow entrance hall, the
B&B/INN rooms in this hotel are rather plain, but its location—on a quiet residential street only a block from the Charles Rennie Mackintosh–designed
Glasgow School of Art—is prime, and the rates are reasonable. **Pros:**
appealing and central location; basement rooms very spacious. **Cons:**
perhaps a little expensive for what it offers; no elevator; on-street parking sometimes difficult to find. ⓢ *Rooms from: £85* ⌧ *212 Renfrew St.,
City Centre* ☎ *0141/332–0129* ⊕ *www.thevictorian.co.uk* ⤳ *60 rooms*
⦿ *Breakfast* Ⓜ *Cowcaddens* ✛ *E3.*

MERCHANT CITY

The hotels in the Merchant City are best for those who plan to spend
most of their time out and about. In general, this busy area is not the
place to come if you want peace and quiet.

$ ⌷ **Babbity Bowster's.** This welcoming old merchant's house in the heart
B&B/INN of the Merchant City is essentially a pub with rooms, with simple, no-
frills accommodation on its second floor. **Pros:** couldn't be more central; good food; great atmosphere. **Cons:** a bit noisy; finding parking
can be difficult; no elevator. ⓢ *Rooms from: £65* ⌧ *16–18 Blackfriars
St., Merchant City* ☎ *0141/552–5055* ⊕ *www.babbitybowster.com* ⤳ *6
rooms* ⦿ *Breakfast* Ⓜ *Buchanan St.* ✛ *G5.*

$ ⌷ **Brunswick.** This modest but comfortable six-story hotel sits at the
HOTEL heart of Glasgow's nightlife, in a prime location in the center of the

Merchant City in an area mostly closed to cars. **Pros:** excellent value; lively downstairs café; very central. **Cons:** area can be noisy on weekends; some rooms are very small; rooms at the back have unappealing views over neighboring roofs. $ *Rooms from: £65* ✉ *106–108 Brunswick St., Merchant City* ☎ *0141/552–0001* ⊕ *www.brunswickhotel. co.uk* ↩ *18 rooms, 1 suite* ◉| *No meals* Ⓜ *Buchanan St.* ✛ *G5.*

WEST END

Many lodgings are on quieter Great Western Road, set apart from busy Byres Road. There are a number of hotels on the other side of Kelvingrove Park in a lively area.

$ 🔲 **Amadeus Guest House.** This adorable Victorian town house has comfortably furnished rooms that are flooded with plenty of natural light.
B&B/INN **Pros:** near West End attractions; two-minute walk from subway; kids under six free. **Cons:** some rooms small; finding parking sometimes difficult. $ *Rooms from: £80* ✉ *411 N. Woodside Rd., West End* ☎ *0141/339–8257* ⊕ *www.amadeusguesthouse.co.uk* ↩ *9 rooms* ◉| *Breakfast* Ⓜ *Kelvinbridge* ✛ *D2.*

$ 🔲 **Ambassador Hotel.** Opposite the West End's peaceful Botanic Gardens
HOTEL and within minutes of busy Byres Road, the Ambassador is part of a
FAMILY terrace of elegant town houses on the banks of the River Kelvin. **Pros:** views of Botanic Gardens; great for families with kids; five-minute walk to public transportation and West End amenities. **Cons:** no elevator; on-street parking difficult after 6 pm. $ *Rooms from: £94* ✉ *7 Kelvin Dr., West End* ☎ *0141/946–1018* ⊕ *www.ambassador-hotel.net* ↩ *26 rooms* ◉| *Breakfast* Ⓜ *Hillhead* ✛ *C1.*

$ 🔲 **Argyll Guest House.** In this budget-minded annex to the Argyll Hotel,
B&B/INN across the road on Sauchiehall Street, the rooms are plainly furnished but scrupulously clean. **Pros:** close to Kelvingrove Park; near public transportation; bargain prices. **Cons:** front rooms noisy on weekends; no elevator. $ *Rooms from: £60* ✉ *966–970 Sauchiehall St., West End* ☎ *0141/357–5155* ⊕ *www.argyllhotelglasgow.co.uk* ↩ *20 rooms* ◉| *Breakfast* Ⓜ *Kelvin Hall* ✛ *C4.*

$ 🔲 **Argyll Hotel.** The tartan in the reception area reflects the clan theme
HOTEL throughout the hotel; each room is named after a clan, but each is also very different from the next. **Pros:** centrally located; comfortable rooms; reasonable prices. **Cons:** street a little noisy; metered parking on the street. $ *Rooms from: £80* ✉ *973 Sauchiehall St., West End* ☎ *0141/337–3313* ⊕ *www.argyllhotelglasgow.co.uk* ↩ *38 rooms* ◉| *Breakfast* Ⓜ *Kelvin Hall* ✛ *C4.*

$ 🔲 **Clifton Hotel.** Occupying two of the grand houses along a terrace above
HOTEL Great Western Road, this popular hotel offers wallet-friendly rates and simply furnished rooms done up in cheerful shades. **Pros:** conveniently located; attentive staff; good budget option. **Cons:** some rooms overlook the parking lot; no elevator. $ *Rooms from: £70* ✉ *26–27 Buckingham Terr., West End* ☎ *0141/334–8080* ⊕ *www.cliftonhotelglasgow. co.uk* ↩ *26 rooms* ◉| *Breakfast* Ⓜ *Hillhead* ✛ *C1.*

$ 🔲 **Heritage Hotel.** This small, unpretentious, but well-established hotel
HOTEL in a very central West End location has cozy but recently refurbished

rooms at very reasonable rates. **Pros:** very good location; friendly and agreeable staff; very reasonable rates. **Cons:** rooms quite small. [$] *Rooms from: £60* ✉ *4/5 Albert Terr., West End* ✣ *Entrance by Hillhead St.* ☎ *0141/339–6955* 🌐 *www.theheritagehotel.net* 🛏 *27 rooms* 🍴 *Breakfast* [M] *Hillhead* ✣ *C2.*

$$ HOTEL 🏨 **Hilton Glasgow Grosvenor.** Behind a row of grand terrace houses, this modern hotel overlooks the Botanic Gardens. **Pros:** close to Byres Road; some rooms have good views; tasty eatery. **Cons:** rooms at the back overlook a parking lot; a rather institutional feel. [$] *Rooms from: £109* ✉ *1–9 Grosvenor Terr., West End* ☎ *0141/339–8811* 🌐 *www.hilton.com/glasgowgrosvenor* 🛏 *96 rooms* 🍴 *Breakfast* [M] *Hillhead* ✣ *B1.*

$$$ HOTEL Fodor's Choice ★ 🏨 **Hotel du Vin Glasgow.** Once the legendary One Devonshire Gardens, frequented by such celebrities as Luciano Pavarotti and Elizabeth Taylor, the Hotel du Vin Glasgow is still a destination for those in search of luxury. **Pros:** stunning Scottish rooms; doting service; complimentary whisky on arrival. **Cons:** no elevator; on-street parking can be difficult after 6 pm. [$] *Rooms from: £175* ✉ *1 Devonshire Gardens, West End* ☎ *0844/736–4256* 🌐 *www.hotelduvin.com/locations/glasgow/* 🛏 *41 rooms, 8 suites* 🍴 *Breakfast* [M] *Hillhead* ✣ *A1.*

$ B&B/INN 🏨 **Kirklee Hotel.** This West End B&B occupies a cozy Edwardian town house with dark paneling and tartan carpets in the public areas; guest rooms are bright, comfortable, and simply decorated. **Pros:** friendly service; quiet street; close to West End attractions. **Cons:** challenging on-street parking; 10-minute walk from Hillhead subway. [$] *Rooms from: £85* ✉ *11 Kensington Gate, West End* ☎ *0141/334–5555* 🌐 *kirkleehotel.co.uk* 🛏 *9 rooms* 🍴 *Breakfast* [M] *Hillhead* ✣ *A1.*

$ HOTEL 🏨 **The Sandyford.** The Victorian exterior of this hotel anticipates the colorful decor you'll find inside, where the large windows in the reception area let in lots of light. **Pros:** extremely well located; minutes from several good eateries; very competitive prices. **Cons:** front rooms can get late-night noise; no elevator. [$] *Rooms from: £75* ✉ *904 Sauchiehall St., West End* ☎ *0141/334–0000* 🌐 *www.sandyfordhotelglasgow.com* 🛏 *55 rooms* 🍴 *Breakfast* [M] *Kelvin Hall* ✣ *C4.*

THE CLYDE

Besides a handful of interesting museums and a cluster of busy bars and restaurants, this up-and-coming area also has a few well-regarded lodgings.

$$ HOTEL 🏨 **Hilton Garden Inn Glasgow City Centre.** Overlooking the Clyde, this hotel is a short walk along the water from the Riverside Museum and the Glasgow Science Centre. **Pros:** beside the Hydro!; lovely terrace; some great views. **Cons:** isolated from the rest of the city. [$] *Rooms from: £113* ✉ *Finnieston Quay, Clyde* ☎ *0141/240–1002* 🌐 *www.hilton.com* 🛏 *164 rooms* 🍴 *Breakfast* ✣ *C5.*

SOUTH SIDE

This residential area near the center of the city has some lovely parks; there's not much to do at night, though.

$$ HOTEL **Number 10 Hotel.** In one of the grand houses overlooking Queens Park, this elegant hotel's guest rooms are quite large and are decorated in pleasantly muted colors. **Pros:** nice setting; ample parking; close to Hampden Park. **Cons:** can be crowded with wedding parties on weekends. [$] *Rooms from: £105* ✉ *10–16 Queens Dr., South Side* ☎ *0141/424–0160* 🌐 *www.10hotel.co.uk* 🛏 *26 rooms* 🍴 *No meals* ✣ *G6.*

$$ HOTEL **Sherbrooke Castle Hotel.** Set high above the road, the Sherbrooke is one the grand homes built by the newly prosperous industrialists of the 19th century. **Pros:** relaxed atmosphere; top-notch service; large bathrooms. **Cons:** some rooms are small; weekend functions can get very loud; no elevator. [$] *Rooms from: £150* ✉ *11 Sherbrooke Ave., South Side* ☎ *0141/427–4227* 🌐 *www.sherbrooke.co.uk* 🛏 *14 rooms* 🍴 *Breakfast* ✣ *B6.*

NIGHTLIFE AND PERFORMING ARTS

Glasgow's music scene is vibrant and creative, and many successful pop artists began their careers in its pubs and clubs. Celtic Connections is probably one of the world's most important festivals of its kind, and the city's summer jazz festival has attracted some of the world's finest players.

When it comes to nightlife, the City Centre and the West End are alive with pubs and clubs offering an eclectic mix of everything from bagpipes to salsa to punk. The biweekly magazine *List,* available at newsstands and many cafés and arts centers, is an indispensable guide to Glasgow's bars and clubs.

PERFORMING ARTS

Because the Royal Scottish Conservatoire is in Glasgow, there is always a pool of impressive young talent that's pressing the city's artistic boundaries in theater, music, and film. The city has a well-deserved reputation for its theater, with everything from cutting-edge plays to over-the-top pantomimes. The Citizens Theatre is one of Europe's leading companies, and the Kings and the Theatre Royal play host to touring productions.

Scottish Music Centre. As well as a library, the Scottish Music Centre serves as the main ticket office for all music events at venues like the Royal Concert Hall and for annual events like the Glasgow Jazz Festival. ✉ *Candleriggs, City Centre* ☎ *0141/353–8000* 🌐 *www.scottishmusiccentre.com* [M] *Buchanan St.*

ARTS CENTERS

FAMILY **Tramway.** South of the City Centre, this innovative arts center is well worth seeking out. It hosts regular exhibitions in its two galleries, and plays—often of a very experimental nature—in its flexible theater space. It has a café and a more formal restaurant on the first floor. Don't miss the Hidden Garden, which has transformed an empty lot behind the

3

building into a sculpture park. This is a great place to go with kids. ✉ *25 Albert Dr., South Side* ☎ *0845/276–0950* ⊕ *www.tramway.org.*

Trongate 103. This vibrant contemporary arts center, housed in a converted Edwardian warehouse, is home base for diverse groups producing film, photography, paintings, and prints. It contains the Russian Cultural Centre and the Sharmanka Kinetic Theatre, as well as the Glasgow Print Studio, a well-established outlet for Glasgow artists; Street Level Photoworks, which aims at making photography more accessible; and the Transmission Gallery, a key exhibition space supporting nonconceptual art in the city. ✉ *103 Trongate, Merchant City* ☎ *0141/276–8380* Ⓜ *St. Enoch.*

CONCERTS

City Halls. One of the top music venues in the City Centre, the stone-fronted City Halls hosts orchestral, jazz, and folk concerts. ✉ *Candleriggs, City Centre* ☎ *0141/353–8000* ⊕ *www.glasgowconcerthalls. com* Ⓜ *Buchanan St.*

Glasgow Royal Concert Hall. The 2,500-seat Glasgow Royal Concert Hall is the venue for a wide range of concerts, from classical to pop. It also hosts the very popular late-night club during the annual Celtic Connections festival. ✉ *2 Sauchiehall St., City Centre* ☎ *0141/353–8000* ⊕ *www.glasgowconcerthalls.com* Ⓜ *Buchanan St.*

O2 ABC. One of the city's major music venues, O2 ABC is housed inside what was once a cinema. It's the city's main showcase for well-known pop and rock bands. ✉ *300 Sauchiehall St., City Centre* ☎ *0141/332–2232* ⊕ *www.o2abcglasgow.co.uk* Ⓜ *Bridge St.*

Old Fruitmarket. A wonderful venue for almost every type of music, this was once the city's fruit and vegetable market. The first-floor balcony, with its intricate iron railings, still carries some of the original merchants' names. It's adjacent to City Halls. ✉ *Candleriggs, Merchant City* ☎ *0141/353–8000* ⊕ *www.glasgowconcerthalls.com* Ⓜ *Buchanan St.*

Royal Scottish Conservatoire. An important venue for music and drama, the Royal Scottish Conservatoire hosts regular concerts by well-known performers, as well as by its own students. The lunchtime concert series is popular. ✉ *100 Renfrew St., City Centre* ☎ *0141/332–4101* ⊕ *www. rcs.ac.uk* Ⓜ *Cowcaddens.*

Scottish Exhibition and Conference Centre. Known locally as the Armadillo for its distinctive design, the Scottish Exhibition and Conference Centre hosts large-scale pop concerts and other events. ✉ *Exhibition Way, The Clyde* ♦ *Train to Exhibition Centre station from Glasgow Central Low Level station* ☎ *0141/248–3000* ⊕ *www.secc.co.uk.*

SSE Hydro. This dramatic addition to the banks of the Clyde is a 12,000-seat arena under a silver dome. Built for the 2014 Commonwealth Games, it has proved enormously popular as a music and event venue, even attracting the annual Mercury Music Awards out of London for the first time. ✉ *SECC Exhibition Way, The Clyde* ♦ *By rail to Exhibition Centre then walk over the bridge* ☎ *0844/395–4000* ⊕ *www. thessehydro.com.*

St. Andrew's in the Square. A beautifully restored 18th-century church close to Glasgow Cross, the glorious St. Andrew's in the Square is a popular arts venue. Drop by to see fiddle players on Monday evening or take traditional Scottish dance classes on Wednesday night. Concerts are held here from time to time. The downstairs Cafe Source serves a good range of Scottish food for lunch or dinner. ⊠ *1 St. Andrew's in the Square, East End* ☎ *0141/559–5902* ⊕ *www.standrewsinthesquare. com* Ⓜ *St. Enoch.*

DANCE AND OPERA
Theatre Royal. Glasgow is home to the Scottish Opera and Scottish Ballet, both of which perform at the Theatre Royal. Visiting dance and theater companies from many countries appear here as well. ⊠ *282 Hope St., City Centre* ☎ *0141/332–9000* Ⓜ *Cowcaddens.*

FESTIVALS
Aye Write. This highly successful literary festival brings together writers from Scotland and the world to discuss their work and exchange ideas. It is held in the Mitchell Library over one week in spring. ⊠ *Mitchell Library, North St., West End* ☎ *0141/287–2999* ⊕ *www.ayewrite.com* Ⓜ *St. George's Cross.*

Fodor'sChoice ★ **Celtic Connections.** This ever-expanding music festival is held in the second half of January in a number of venues across the city. Musicians from Scotland, Ireland, and other countries celebrate Celtic music, both traditional and contemporary. There are a series of hands-on workshops and a popular late-night club at the Royal Concert Hall. ☎ *0141/353–8000* ⊕ *www.celticconnections.com.*

Glasgay! Held between November and December, Glasgay! has been the United Kingdom's largest arts festival focusing on LGBT culture. The international lineup is impressive. The festival took a break in 2015, so check online for updates. ⊠ *Glasgow* ☎ *0141/552–7575* ⊕ *www. outspokenarts.org.*

Glasgow Jazz Festival. In late June and early July, Glasgow hosts jazz musicians from around the world in venues throughout the city, though mainly in the City Centre. ⊠ *81 High St., City Centre* ☎ *0141/552–3552* ⊕ *www.jazzfest.co.uk* Ⓜ *Buchanan St.*

FILM
Center for Contemporary Arts. The center screens classic, independent, and children's films and mounts major art exhibitions and other arts events. It also has a restaurant, the Saramago, which serves vegan dishes; an upstairs bar; and a very good small independent bookshop. ⊠ *350 Sauchiehall St., City Centre* ☎ *0141/352–4900* ⊕ *www.cca-glasgow. com* Ⓜ *Cowcaddens.*

Cineworld Glasgow. An 18-screen facility, this is Glasgow's busiest movie complex. A glass-walled elevator whisks you to the top of the 170-foot-tall building, which is also the world's tallest cinema. ■TIP→ **Book your tickets online and collect them from machines at the venue to avoid the often very long queues.** ⊠ *7 Renfrew St., City Centre* ☎ *0871/200–2000* ⊕ *www.cineworld.co.uk/cinemas/28* Ⓜ *Cowcaddens.*

Fodor's Choice **Glasgow Film Theatre.** An independent operation, the three-screen
★ Glasgow Film Theatre hosts the best new releases, documentaries, and
classic films. It has several programs for young people and hosts the
annual Glasgow Film Festival. ⊠ *12 Rose St., City Centre* ☎ *0141/332–
6535* ⊕ *www.glasgowfilm.org* Ⓜ *Cowcaddens.*

Grosvenor. This popular, compact cinema has two screens and extremely
comfortable leather seats (some of them big enough for two). It's part of
a small complex, immediately behind the subway station, that includes
two street-level bars and a spacious upstairs café and bar. ⊠ *Ashton La.,
West End* ☎ *0845/339–8444* ⊕ *www.grosvenorcafe.co.uk* Ⓜ *Hillhead.*

THEATER

Ticketmaster. Tickets for theatrical performances can be purchased at theater box offices or online through Ticketmaster. ⊕ *www.ticketmaster.co.uk.*

Fodor's Choice **Citizens' Theatre.** Some of the most exciting theatrical performances take
★ place at the internationally renowned Citizens' Theatre, where produc-
tions are often of hair-raising originality. The more-experimental work
is presented in the smaller studio theater. The program is varied and
the theater has always had a strong commitment to working with the
community. Tickets for most performances are £15. Behind the theater's
striking contemporary glass facade is a glorious red-and-gold Victorian-era auditorium. ⊠ *119 Gorbals St., East End* ☎ *0141/429–0022*
⊕ *www.citz.co.uk* Ⓜ *West Street.*

Cottier's Arts Theatre. Contemporary works are staged at this theater, housed in a converted church. ⊠ *93 Hyndland St., West End*
☎ *0141/357–5825* ⊕ *www.cottiers.com* Ⓜ *Hillhead.*

King's Theatre. Dramas, variety shows, and musicals are staged at
the King's Theatre. ⊠ *297 Bath St., City Centre* ☎ *0141/240–1111*
Ⓜ *Cowcaddens.*

FAMILY **Pavilion Theatre.** This traditional variety theater hosts family-friendly
entertainment, some plays, the occasional hypnotist, and concerts,
most with a strong Glasgow flavor. ⊠ *121 Renfield St., City Centre*
☎ *0141/332–1846* ⊕ *www.paviliontheatre.co.uk* Ⓜ *Cowcaddens.*

Fodor's Choice **A Play, a Pie, and a Pint.** In a former church, Glasgow's hugely success-
★ ful lunchtime theater series called "A Play, a Pie, and a Pint" (and you
do get all three) showcases new writing from Scotland and elsewhere;
it has presented more than 250 works. Performances sell out quickly,
particularly late in the week, so book well in advance. Doors open at
12:15 and shows begin at 1 Monday through Saturday. ⊠ *Òran Mór,
731 Great Western Rd., Byres Rd. and Great Western Rd., West End*
☎ *0141/357–6200* ⊕ *www.playpiepint.com* Ⓜ *Hillhead.*

FAMILY **Sharmanka Kinetic Theatre.** A unique spectacle, Sharmanka Kinetic The-
Fodor's Choice atre is the brainchild of Eduard Bersudsky, who came to Glasgow
★ from Russia in 1989 to continue making the mechanical sculptures
that are his stock in trade. They are witty and sometimes disturbing,
perhaps because they are constructed from scrap materials. They move
in a kind of ballet to haunting, specially composed music punctuated
by a light show. ■ TIP→ **Kids under 15 get in free when accompanied by**

an adult. ✉ *103 Trongate, Merchant City* ☎ *0141/552–7080* ⊕ *www. sharmanka.com* Ⓜ *St. Enoch.*

Tron Theatre. Come here for contemporary theater from Scotland and around the world. ✉ *63 Trongate, Merchant City* ☎ *0141/552–4267* ⊕ *www.tron.co.uk* Ⓜ *St. Enoch.*

NIGHTLIFE

Glasgow's busy nightlife scene is impressive and varied. Bars and pubs often close at midnight on weekends, but nightclubs often stay open until 3 or 4 am. Traditional *ceilidh* (a mix of country dancing, music, and song; pronounced *kay-lee*) is not as popular with locals as it used to be (except at weddings), but you can still find it at many more tourist-oriented establishments.

Glasgow's pubs were once hangouts for serious drinkers who demanded few comforts. Times have changed, and many of these gritty establishments have been transformed into trendy cocktail bars or cavernous spaces with multiple video monitors, though a few traditional bars do survive. Bars and pubs vary according to location; many of those in the City Centre cater to business types, although some still draw a more traditional clientele.

> ### WHAT TO ORDER
>
> First-timers to Glasgow should order "a pint," meaning a pint of beer or lager. Bottled beers are increasingly popular though usually more expensive than draft. Most pubs now have a wide selection of world beers, too. Cocktails, which were once hard to find in Glasgow, are now available in many bars. Wine is also often on the pub menu, though with some exceptions it is not usually a very reliable option.

As elsewhere in Britain, electronic music—from house to techno to drum and bass—is par for the course in Glasgow's dance clubs. Much of the scene revolves around the City Centre, as a late-night walk down Sauchiehall Street on Friday or Saturday will reveal.

CITY CENTRE
BARS AND PUBS

Baby Grand. One of Glasgow's best-kept secrets, this intimate piano bar is hidden behind the King's Theatre. It serves good food all day, and it somehow manages to be crowded but never overcrowded, even at the busiest times. The pretheater menu is a good value, and tapas are available on weekends. ✉ *3 Elmbank Gardens, City Centre* ☎ *0141/248–4942* ⊕ *www.babygrandglasgow.com* Ⓜ *Cowcaddens.*

Black Sparrow. A cool Charles Bukowski–theme bar named after the American writer's publishing company, the Black Sparrow serves potent cocktails and sophisticated bar food. There's also a great outdoor beer garden. ✉ *241 North St., City Centre* ☎ *0141/221–5530* ⊕ *www. theblacksparrow.co.uk* Ⓜ *St. George's Cross.*

Bloc. Step behind a curious version of the Iron Curtain where Tex-Mex diner food mixes with an eclectic musical mash of DJs and live rock and folk bands. ⊠ *117 Bath St., City Centre* ☎ *0141/574–6066* ⊕ *www. bloc.ru/barbloc.html* Ⓜ *Cowcaddens.*

King Tut's Wah Wah Hut. An intimate venue showcasing up-and-coming independent bands since 1990, King Tut's Wah Wah Hut claims to have been the venue that discovered the U.K. pop band Oasis. Indeed, the list of those who have played here reads like a catalog of indie music's last 25 years. It's a favorite with students and hosts live music most nights, but the cozy and traditional pub setting draws people of all ages, and the refurbished bar is a pleasant and comfortable place for a drink or a meal. ⊠ *227A St. Vincent St., City Centre* ☎ *0141/221–5279* ⊕ *www. kingtuts.co.uk* Ⓜ *Cowcaddens.*

La Cheetah. A tiny club in the basement of Max's Bar, La Cheetah is popular precisely because it's small and intimate. It plays a variety of dance music with some surprising well-known guests who just like the atmosphere. ⊠ *73 Queen St., City Centre* ☎ *0141/221–1379* ⊕ *www. maxsbar.co.uk* Ⓜ *Buchanan St.*

Moskito. For a splash of Mediterranean style, head to Moskito. Amid the cool, aquatic hues you can watch people dancing to laid-back tunes Thursday to Sunday nights. ⊠ *200 Bath St., City Centre* ☎ *0141/331– 1777* ⊕ *www.moskitoglasgow.com* Ⓜ *Buchanan St.*

Fodor's Choice ★ **Sloans.** One of Glasgow's oldest and most beautiful pubs, the wood-paneled Sloans is always lively and welcoming and serves traditional pub food like fish-and-chips throughout the day. The upstairs ballroom is a magnificent mirrored affair, and on the floor above there's a dance floor with a ceilidh—traditional music and dancing—every Friday night. They have a good selection of beers and spirits, and the outdoor area is always lively when the weather cooperates. ⊠ *108 Argyle St., City Centre* ☎ *0141/221–8886* ⊕ *www.sloansglasgow.com* Ⓜ *St. Enoch.*

CLUBS
Stereo. The small downstairs music venue gets crowded quickly when bands play Sunday to Thursday night, but that only adds to the electric atmosphere at Stereo. There's also a hopping nightclub where DJs spin on Friday and Saturday nights until the wee hours of the morning. Upstairs, a café-bar serves tasty vegan food and organic drinks. ⊠ *20– 28 Renfield La., City Centre* ☎ *0141/222–2254* ⊕ *www.stereocafebar. com* Ⓜ *Buchanan St.*

Sub Club. This atmospheric underground venue has staged cutting-edge music events since its jazz club days in the '50s. Legendary favorites like Saturday's SubCulture (House) and Sunday's Optimo (a truly eclectic mix for musical hedonists) pack in friendly and sweaty crowds. ⊠ *22 Jamaica St., City Centre* ☎ *0141/248–4600* ⊕ *www.subclub.co.uk* Ⓜ *St. Enoch.*

MERCHANT CITY
BARS AND PUBS
Babbity Bowster's. A busy, friendly spot, Babbity Bowster's serves real ales and excellent, mainly Scottish food, prepared for more than a decade now by a French chef who adds his own very special touch. The atmosphere is lively and very friendly; there is an outdoor terrace in summer and a fireplace in winter. If you like traditional music, make a point

of coming on Saturday and Wednesday afternoon. ⊠ *16–18 Blackfriars St., Merchant City* ☎ *0141/552–5055* ⊕ *www.babbitybowster.com* Ⓜ *Buchanan St.*

Boteco do Brasil. Glasgow's only Brazilian bar/restaurant/club has salsa nights Wednesdays and Latin music to dance to weekends until 3 am. ⊠ *62 Trongate, Merchant City* ☎ *0141/548–1330* ⊕ *www.botecodobrasil.com* Ⓜ *Buchanan St.*

Fodor'sChoice ★ **Scotia Bar.** This bar serves up a taste of an authentic Glasgow pub, with traditional folk music regularly thrown in. ⊠ *112 Stockwell St., Merchant City* ☎ *0141/552–8681* ⊕ *www.scotiabar.net* Ⓜ *St. Enoch.*

CLUBS

Polo Lounge. Oozing with Edwardian style, the Polo Lounge is Glasgow's largest gay club. Upstairs is a bar that resembles an old-fashioned gentlemen's club. On the two dance floors downstairs, the DJs spin something for everyone. ⊠ *84 Wilson St., Merchant City* ☎ *0141/553–1221* ⊕ *www.pologlasgow.co.uk* Ⓜ *Buchanan St.*

WEST END
BARS AND PUBS

78. Enjoy cozy sofas, a real coal fire, and tasty vegan food throughout the day. There's live music every night, with jazz on Sunday. ⊠ *10–14 Kelvinhaugh St., West End* ☎ *0141/576–5018* ⊕ *www.the78cafebar.com* Ⓜ *Kelvinhall.*

Ben Nevis. This eccentric pub is full of Highland artifacts. There are more than 180 whiskies from which to choose and traditional live music on Wednesday, Thursday, and Sunday. ⊠ *1147 Argyle St., West End* ☎ *0141/576–5204* ⊕ *www.thebennevis.co.uk* Ⓜ *Kelvinhall.*

Dram. With mismatched furnishings and the odd stag's head on the wall, Dram's four large rooms are decorated in a style that can only be described as "ultra eclectic." There's a wide range of beers, but the place takes special pride in the 75 whiskies. On Thursday and Sunday, musicians gather in an informal jam session. Food is served every night until 9. ⊠ *232–246 Woodlands Rd., West End* ☎ *0141/332–1622* Ⓜ *Kelvinbridge.*

Òran Mór. At the top of Byres Road, Òran Mór is in a massive church that still has its beautiful stained-glass windows as well as an upper hall, once the nave of the church, gloriously decorated by Glasgow artist Alasdair Gray. In the basement, the hugely successful lunchtime theater series A Play, a Pie, and a Pint plays to capacity crowds. It also houses a busy bistro, a brasserie, and an evening music venue, as well as a late-night club. The bar fills with different crowds at different times of day, but its late license means that it tends to be very full on Friday and Saturday nights. The small beer garden fills up quickly in good weather. ⊠ *731 Great Western Rd., West End* ☎ *0141/357–6200* ⊕ *www.oran-mor.co.uk* Ⓜ *Hillhead.*

Rio Cafe. With the feel of a 1950s diner, the laid-back Rio Cafe is all things to all people. Drop by in the evening to listen to musicians, DJs, and poets (or even play poker on some nights). During the day there are economical breakfasts and lunches. ✉ *27 Hyndland St., West End* ☎ *0141/334–9909* ⊕ *www.theriocafe.com* Ⓜ *Kelvinhall.*

Tennents. A spacious corner bar, Tennents prides itself on its comprehensive selection of beers. You can expect lively conversation, as there's a refreshing lack of loud music. ✉ *191 Byres Rd., West End* ☎ *0141/341– 1021* ⊕ *www.thetennentsbarglasgow.co.uk* Ⓜ *Hillhead.*

COMEDY CLUBS

Stand Comedy Club. In the basement of a former school, the Stand Comedy Club has live shows every night of the week and is most popular on Thursday and Friday. Prices vary according to who is appearing, and the doors open at 7:30. ✉ *333 Woodlands Rd., at Park Rd., West End* ☎ *0141/212–3389* ⊕ *www.thestand.co.uk* Ⓜ *Kelvingrove.*

SHOPPING

You'll find the mark of the fashion industry on the City Centre's hottest shopping streets. In the Merchant City, Ingram Street is lined on either side by high-fashion and designer outlets like Cruise and Agent Provocateur. Buchanan Street, in the City Centre, is home to many chains geared toward younger people, including Diesel, Monsoon, and USC, and malls like the elegant Princes Square and Buchanan Galleries. The adjacent Argyle Street Arcade is filled with jewelry stores. Antiques tend be found on and around West Regent Street in the City Centre.

The West End has a number of small shops selling crafts, vintage clothing, and trendier fashions—punctuated by innumerable cafés and restaurants. The university dominates the area around West End, and many shops cater to students. The easiest way to get here is by taking the subway to Hillhead.

CITY CENTRE

ANTIQUES AND FINE ART

Compass Gallery. The gallery is something of an institution, having opened in 1969 to provide space for young and unknown artists. It shares space with Cyril Gerber Fine Arts, which specializes in British paintings from 1880 to the present. ✉ *178 W. Regent St., City Centre* ☎ *0141/221–3095* ⊕ *www.compassgallery.co.uk* Ⓜ *Cowcaddens.*

ARCADES AND SHOPPING CENTERS

Argyll Arcade. An interesting diversion off Argyle Street is the covered Argyll Arcade, the region's largest collection of jewelers under one roof. The L-shape edifice, built in 1904, houses several locally based jewelers and a few shops specializing in antique jewelry. ✉ *Buchanan St., City Centre* ⊕ *www.argyll-arcade.com* Ⓜ *St. Enoch.*

Buchanan Galleries. Next to the Glasgow Royal Concert Hall, Buchanan Galleries is packed with high-quality shops. Its top attraction is the John Lewis department store. ✉ *220 Buchanan St., City Centre* ☎ *0141/333– 9898* ⊕ *www.buchanangalleries.co.uk* Ⓜ *Buchanan St.*

Fodor's Choice **Princes Square.** The city's best shopping center is the art nouveau Princes
★ Square, a lovely space filled with high-quality shops and pleasant cafés
and restaurants. A stunning glass dome was fitted over the original
building, which dates back to 1841. ⊠ *48 Buchanan St., City Centre*
☎ *0141/221–0324* ⊕ *www.princessquare.co.uk* Ⓜ *St. Enoch.*

St. Enoch's Shopping Centre. Eye-catching if not especially pleasing, this
modern glass building resembles an overgrown greenhouse. It houses
various stores, including the huge Hamley's toy store. ⊠ *55 St. Enoch
Sq., City Centre* ☎ *0141/204–3900* ⊕ *www.st-enoch.com* Ⓜ *St. Enoch.*

BOOKS, PAPER, AND MUSIC
Art Store. Selling cards, books, and games, the Art Store has a wonderful array of all things connected with art—paper, paints, pens—as well
as craft items like beads for stringing. ⊠ *94 Queen St., City Centre*
☎ *0141/221–1101* ⊕ *www.artstore.co.uk* Ⓜ *Buchanan St.*

Monorail Music. For the latest on the city's ever-thriving music scene try
Monorail Music, inside a café-bar called Mono. The shop specializes
in indie music and has a large collection of vinyl with everything from
rock to jazz. ⊠ *12 Kings Ct., Merchant City* ☎ *0141/552–9458* ⊕ *www.
monorailmusic.com* Ⓜ *St. Enoch.*

Paperchase. For everything that stationery has to offer—cards, note-
books, books—Paperchase is the place. And there's a café where you can
decide which notebook you want to buy. ⊠ *185–221 Buchanan St., City
Centre* ☎ *0141/353–3491* ⊕ *www.paperchase.co.uk* Ⓜ *Buchanan St.*

Waterstones. In an age of online sales, bookstores seem to be becoming
scarcer. Waterstones remains as the city's main bookshop, and it has
an excellent selection on its four floors. There's also a good basement
café. ⊠ *153-57 Sauchiehall St., City Centre* ☎ *0141/248–4814* ⊕ *www.
waterstones.com* Ⓜ *Buchanan St.*

CLOTHING
Mr. Ben. A funky selection of vintage clothing is what you'll find at Mr.
Ben. ⊠ *6 King's Ct., City Centre* ☎ *0141/553–1936* ⊕ *mrbenretrocloth-
ing.com* Ⓜ *St. Enoch.*

Primark. Invariably crowded, Primark is a huge store where everything is
sold at marked-down prices. It caters to every generation. ⊠ *56 Argyle
St., City Centre* ☎ *0141/229–1343* ⊕ *www.primark.co.uk* Ⓜ *St. Enoch.*

Zara. This hugely successful Spanish-owned chain offers high contemporary fashion at affordable prices. ⊠ *10–16 Buchanan St., City Centre*
☎ *0141/227–4770* ⊕ *www.zara.com* Ⓜ *St. Enoch.*

DEPARTMENT STORES
Debenham's. One of Glasgow's principal department stores, Debenham's
has fine china and crystal as well as women's and men's clothing. ⊠ *97
Argyle St., City Centre* ☎ *0844/561–6161* ⊕ *www.debenhams.com*
Ⓜ *St. Enoch.*

Fodor's Choice **House of Fraser.** A Glasgow institution, the House of Fraser stocks wares
★ that reflect the city's material aspirations, including European designer
clothing. There are also home-produced articles, such as tweeds,
tartans, glass, and ceramics. The magnificent interior, set off by the
grand staircase rising to various floors and balconies, is itself worth a

visit. ✉ *21–45 Buchanan St., City Centre* ☎ *0141/221–3880* ⊕ *www. houseoffraser.co.uk* Ⓜ *St. Enoch.*

John Lewis. This shop is a favorite for its stylish mix of clothing, household items, electronics, and practically everything else. John Lewis claims to have "never been knowingly undersold" and prides itself on its customer service. It has a very elegant second-floor balcony café. ✉ *Buchanan Galleries, 220 Buchanan St., City Centre* ☎ *0141/353– 6677* ⊕ *www.johnlewis.com/glasgow* Ⓜ *Buchanan St.*

Marks & Spencer. With sturdy, practical clothing and accessories at moderate prices, Marks & Spencer also offers gourmet foods and household goods. There's a second location at 172 Sauchiehall Street. ✉ *2–12 Argyle St., City Centre* ☎ *0141/552–4546* ⊕ *www.marksandspencer. com* Ⓜ *St. Enoch.*

HOME FURNISHINGS AND TEXTILES

Linens Fine. This shop carries wonderful embroidered and embellished bed linens and other textiles. ✉ *Princes Sq., Unit 6, City Centre* ☎ *0141/248–7082* Ⓜ *St. Enoch.*

Time and Tide. Loosely described as a household goods store, Time and Tide is actually an eclectic mix of lamps and candleholders and cushions and things you never realized you needed until you see them. ✉ *398 Byres Rd., West End* ☎ *0141/357-4548* ⊕ *www.timeandtidestores. co.uk* Ⓜ *Hillhead.*

SCOTTISH SPECIALTIES

Hector Russell Kiltmakers. This shop specializes in Highland outfits, wool and cashmere clothing, and women's fashions. ✉ *110 Buchanan St., City Centre* ☎ *0141/221–0217* ⊕ *www.hector-russell.com* Ⓜ *Buchanan St.*

MacDonald MacKay Ltd. The well-regarded MacDonald MacKay Ltd. makes, sells, and exports Highland dress and accessories. ✉ *161 Hope St., City Centre* ☎ *0141/204–3930* Ⓜ *Buchanan St.*

SHOPPING DISTRICTS

Argyle Street. On the often-crowded pedestrian area of Argyle Street you'll find chain stores like Debenham's and some of the more popular and less expensive chains like Gap, Next, and Schuh as well as Primark and H&M. ✉ *City Centre* Ⓜ *St. Enoch.*

Buchanan Street. This pedestrian-only street has become increasingly upmarket, with Monsoon, Topshop, Burberry, Jaeger, Pretty Green, and All Saints as well as House of Fraser and other chain stores along its length. Always crowded with shoppers, it has also become a mecca for the growing community of buskers in Glasgow's streets, playing every kind of music. ✉ *City Centre* Ⓜ *Buchanan St.*

SPORTS GEAR

Tiso Glasgow Outdoor Experience. You'll find good-quality outerwear at Tiso Glasgow Outdoor Experience, handy if you're planning some Highland walks. ✉ *129 Buchanan St., City Centre* ☎ *0141/248–4877* ⊕ *www.tiso.com* Ⓜ *Buchanan St.*

MERCHANT CITY

Many of Glasgow's young and upwardly mobile types make their home in Merchant City. Shopping here is expensive, but the area is worth visiting if you're seeking the youthful Glasgow style.

ANTIQUES AND FINE ART

Fodor's Choice **Glasgow Print Studio.** Essentially an artists' cooperative, the Glasgow
★ Print Studio's facilities launched a generation of outstanding painters, printers, and designers. The work of members past and present can be seen (and bought) at the Print Studio Gallery on King Street. ✉ *103 Trongate, Merchant City* ☎ *0141/552–0704* ⊕ *www.gpsart.co.uk* Ⓜ *St. Enoch.*

CLOTHING

Agent Provocateur. One of the success stories of British retailing is this brand of erotic lingerie. It joins the Merchant City's fashion center on Ingram Street, where it has continued its success. ✉ *213 Ingram St., Merchant City* ☎ *0141/221–2538* ⊕ *www.agentprovocateur.com* Ⓜ *Buchanan St.*

Cruise. As one of the very first haute couture stores in central Glasgow, Cruise can claim to have launched a new commercial era in the city. It now has two stores in the Merchant City, where its high-fashion clothes and accessories for men and women are beautifully and characteristically displayed to those who can stretch their budgets to its levels. ✉ *180 Ingram St., Merchant City* ☎ *0141/332–5797* ⊕ *www.cruisefashion. com* Ⓜ *Buchanan St.*

Jigsaw. You'll find a wide and ever-changing range of fashion items at Jigsaw, well tailored and glamorous but at accessible prices. A U.K.–based chain, its Glasgow store is especially dramatic, occupying one of the tobacco lord's mansions on Ingram Street. ✉ *177 Ingram St., Merchant City* ☎ *0141/552–7639* ⊕ *www.jigsaw-uk.co.uk* Ⓜ *Buchanan St.*

JEWELRY

Orro. The beautiful and contemporary jewelry here uses modern designs and new materials in unexpected ways. The shop has a gallery feel, and you can browse uninterrupted. ✉ *12 Wilson St., Merchant City* ☎ *0141/552–7888* ⊕ *www.orro.co.uk* Ⓜ *Buchanan St.*

TOYS

Sentry Box. This small, lovely traditional toy shop for children is a kind of Aladdin's Cave for small people. ✉ *175 Great George St., West End* ☎ *0141/334–6070* ⊕ *www.sentryboxtoys.co.uk* Ⓜ *Hillhead.*

WEST END

BOOKS, PAPER, AND MUSIC

Caledonia Books. This well-organized and well-stocked secondhand bookstore fills the gap left by the departure of other bookstores. The owners are knowledgeable and willing to search for even the most obscure volumes. ✉ *483 Great Western Rd., West End* ☎ *0141/334–9663* ⊕ *www.caledoniabooks.co.uk* Ⓜ *Kelvinbridge.*

Fopp. This funky shop is an extravaganza of music, books, and DVDs. It's a small space, but the selection is huge. The prices are a lot more reasonable than those at most chain stores. ✉ *358 Byres Rd., West End* ☎ *0141/222–2128* ⊕ *www.foppreturns.com* Ⓜ *Hillhead.*

Papyrus. Here you'll find designer cards as well as a selection of books and a trendy kitchen shop in the basement. There's a second location in the City Centre on Sauchiehall Street. ✉ *374 Byres Rd., West End* ☎ *0141/334–6514* ⊕ *papyrusgifts.co.uk* Ⓜ *Hillhead.*

CLOTHING

Charles Clinkard. This traditional shoe store—a rare thing these days—has an impressive range of shoes, often unusual lines, principally for women but for men, too. There are also regular bargains here, and the staff knows their shoes! ✉ *149 Byres Rd., West End* ☎ *0845/017–9077* ⊕ *www.charlesclinkard.co.uk* Ⓜ *Hillhead.*

Pink Poodle. This stylish fashion boutique is mainly for younger dressers, and sells some lovely and often quirky accessories as well as dresses, tops, and trousers. ✉ *181–183 Byres Rd., West End* ☎ *0141/357–3344* ⊕ *www.lovelaboutique.com* Ⓜ *Hillhead.*

Strawberry Fields. Designer clothing for children is the speciality of Strawberry Fields. ✉ *517 Great Western Rd., West End* ☎ *0141/339–1121* Ⓜ *Kelvinbridge.*

FOOD

Demijohn. Specializing in infused wines, spirits, oils, and vinegars, Demijohn calls itself a "liquid deli." ✉ *382 Byres Rd., West End* ☎ *0141/337–3600* ⊕ *www.demijohn.co.uk* Ⓜ *Hillhead.*

Iain Mellis Cheesemonger. This shop has a superb, seemingly endless selection of fine Scottish cheeses, in addition to others from England and across Europe, as well as bread and olives. ✉ *492 Great Western Rd., West End* ☎ *0141/339–8998* ⊕ *www.mellischeese.net* Ⓜ *Kelvinbridge.*

HOME FURNISHINGS AND TEXTILES

Nancy Smillie. Local to the floorboards, Nancy Smillie is a one-of-a-kind boutique that sells unique glassware, jewelry, and furnishings. It also runs a jewelry boutique at 425 Great Western Road. ✉ *53 Cresswell St., West End* ☎ *0141/334–0055* ⊕ *www.nancysmillieshop.com* Ⓜ *Hillhead.*

SOUTH SIDE

ARCADES AND SHOPPING CENTERS

Silverburn. One of Europe's largest shopping malls, Silverburn is a good option on a rainy day. The interior feels like a village with streams, waterfalls, and restaurants galore, plus everything from small boutiques to retail giants like Marks & Spencer. Direct buses from Buchanan Street Station leave every 20 minutes. ✉ *Barrhead Rd., South Side* ☎ *0141/880–3200* ⊕ *www.shopsilverburn.com.*

EAST END

Fodor's Choice
★ **Barras.** Scotland's largest indoor market—named for the barrows, or pushcarts, formerly used by the stallholders—prides itself on selling everything "from a needle to an anchor" and is a must-see for anyone addicted to searching through piles of junk for bargains. The century-old institution, open weekends, consists of nine markets. The atmosphere is always good-humored, and you can find just about anything here, in any condition, from dusty model railroads to antique jewelry. Haggling is compulsory. You can reach the Barras by walking along Argyle Street from the St. Enoch subway station. The Barrowland ballroom, which forms part of the market, was once where Glaswegians went to dance; today it is a venue for concerts of every kind. ■ TIP→ **Across the road is one of Glasgow's oldest pubs, the Saracen's Head; enter with caution—ghosts are said to abound.** ⊠ *Gallowgate, East End.*

SPORTS AND THE OUTDOORS

You can't go far these days without seeing a runner or cyclist; because of the city's numerous parks, there is plenty of space. Rarely is the weather conducive to outdoor exercise; it rains a lot in Glasgow, but don't let that stop you. It doesn't deter the locals who play soccer, tennis, hike, bike, run, swim, and walk in the rain.

BICYCLING

Sir Chris Hoy Velodrome. Built for the 2014 Commonwealth Games and named after Scotland's most successful competitive cyclist, this magnificent cycle track is open to the public at drop-in sessions at certain times, though these may vary. Consult the website for current information. ⊠ *Emirates Arena, 1000 London Rd., East End* ☎ *0141/287–7000* ⊕ *www.emiratesarena.co.uk.*

FOOTBALL (SOCCER)

The city has been sports mad, especially for football (soccer), for more than 100 years. The historic rivalry between its two main football clubs, the Rangers and Celtic, is legendary. Partick Thistle is a less contentious alternative for football fans. Matches are held usually on Saturday or Sunday in winter. Admission prices start at about £20. Don't go looking for a family-day-out atmosphere; football remains a fiercely contested game attended mainly by males, though the stadiums at Ibrox and Celtic Park are fast becoming family-friendly.

Celtic. This famous football club wears white-and-green stripes and plays in the east at Celtic Park, or Perkhead as it is know locally. There are daily stadium tours (£10), which must be booked ahead, and the Celtic Museum is also in the stadium. ⊠ *Celtic Park, 18 Kerrydale St., East End* ☎ *0871/226–1888* ⊕ *www.celticfc.net.*

Partick Thistle. Soccer in Glasgow isn't just blue or green, nor is it dominated by international players and big money. Partick Thistle Football Club, known as the Jags, wears red and yellow, and its home field is

Firhill Park. ⊠ *80 Firhill Rd., West End* ☎ *0141/579–1971* ⊕ *www.ptfc. co.uk* Ⓜ *St. George's Cross.*

Rangers. The Rangers wear blue and play at Ibrox, on the south side of the Clyde. Stadium tours on Friday, Saturday, and Sunday cost £8, and booking ahead is essential. ⊠ *150 Edmiston Dr., South Side* ☎ *0871/702–1972* ⊕ *www.rangers.co.uk* Ⓜ *Ibrox.*

GOLF

Several municipal courses are operated within Glasgow proper by the local authorities. Bookings are relatively inexpensive and should be made directly to the course 24 hours in advance to ensure prime tee times (courses open at 7 am). A comprehensive list of contacts, facilities, and green fees of the 30 or so other courses near the city is available from the tourist board.

Douglas Park Golf Club. A charming parkland course at Milngavie, on the western outskirts of Glasgow, this attractive and varied course is set among lush rhododendron bushes and birch and pine trees. Each hole is highly individual, and though shorter than many courses it tests the careful accurate golfer rather than the big swing. The Campsie Fells form a pleasant backdrop. ⊠ *Milngavie Rd., Hillfoot, Bearsden* ☎ *0141/942–0985* ⊕ *www.douglasparkgolfclub.co.uk* ⌚ *Apr.–Oct., £30 weekdays, £40 weekends; Nov.–Mar., £15 weekdays, £20 weekends* ⅃ *18 holes, 5962 yards, par 69.*

Gailes Links. The Glasgow Golf Club originally played on Glasgow Green in the heart of the city, but as the pressure for space grew, the club moved north to the leafy suburb of Bearsden, on the road to Loch Lomond. Killermont, the club's home course, is not open to visitors, but you can play the club's other course at Gailes, near Irvine on the Firth of Clyde. The Glasgow Club's Tennant Cup, in June, is the oldest open amateur tournament in the world. ⊠ *Gailes Rd., Irvine* ☎ *0141/942–2011* ⊕ *www.glasgowgailes-golf.com* ⌚ *£95, £60 after 1:30 pm* ⅃ *18 holes, 6535 yards, par 72.*

Lethamhill. The fairways of this city-owned course overlook Hogganfield Loch, in the southeast of Glasgow. It is a parkland course, with trees in some awkward places (around holes for example) and some steep tees, which means it isn't always wise to look for maximum length or to underestimate this public course. To get here, take the M8 north to Junction 12, and drive up the A80 about a quarter mile. ⊠ *1240 Cumbernauld Rd., North City* ☎ *0141/276–0810* ⊕ *www.glasgowlife.org. uk* ⌚ *£6.50 in winter, £7.85 in summer* ⅃ *18 holes, 5836 yards, par 70.*

Littlehill. One of Scotland's public municipal courses, Littlehill is well used by Glaswegians, especially those learning to play. A fairly flat course with level fairways—many of them tree-lined—and well-kept greens, it has the added advantage of being cheap to play. Some of Scotland's finest players began here. It's about 4 miles north of the City Centre. ⊠ *Auchinairn Rd., North City* ☎ *0141/276–0704* ⊕ *www. glasgowlife.org.uk* ⌚ *£10 weekdays, £11.50 weekends* ⅃ *18 holes, 6240 yards, par 70.*

SPORTS ARENA

Emirates Arena. Built to host a number of events during the Commonwealth Games of 2014, the arena continues to present sporting events but also contains a gym and spa that are open to the public. It has transformed an East End area that was neglected and abandoned. ✉ *1000 London Rd., East End* ☎ *0141/287–7000* ⊕ *www.emiratesarena.co.uk.*

SIDE TRIPS: AYRSHIRE, CLYDE COAST, AND ROBERT BURNS COUNTRY

The jigsaw puzzle of firths and straits and interlocking islands that you see as you fly into Glasgow Airport harbors numerous tempting one-day excursion destinations. You can travel south to visit the fertile farmlands of Ayrshire—Robert Burns country—or west to the Firth of Clyde, or southeast to the Clyde Valley, all by car or by public transportation. Besides the Burns sites, key treasures in this area include the Marquess of Bute's Mount Stuart House on the Isle of Bute, and Culzean Castle, as famous for its Robert Adam (1728–92) design as it is for its spectacular seaside setting and grounds.

For many people a highlight of this region is Robert Burns country, a 40-minute drive from Glasgow. The poet was born in Alloway, beside Ayr, and the towns and villages where he lived and loved make for an interesting day out. English children learn that Burns (1759–96) is a good minor poet. But Scottish children know that he's Shakespeare, Dante, Rabelais, Mozart, and Karl Marx rolled into one. As time goes by, it seems that the Scots have it more nearly right. As poet and humanist, Burns increases in stature. When you plunge into Burns country, don't forget that he's held in extreme reverence by Scots of all backgrounds. They may argue about Sir Walter Scott and Bonnie Prince Charlie, but there's no disputing the merits of the author of "Auld Lang Syne" and "A man's a man for a' that."

On your way here you travel beside the estuary and firth of the great River Clyde and will be able to look across to Dumbarton and its Rock, a nostalgic farewell point for emigrants leaving Glasgow. The river is surprisingly narrow here, considering that the *Queen Elizabeth II* and other great ocean liners sailed these waters from the place of their birth.

GETTING HERE AND AROUND

From Glasgow you can take the bus or train (from Glasgow Central station) to Ayr for the Burns Heritage Trail; and Troon, Prestwick, and Ayr to play golf. Bus companies also operate one-day guided excursions; for details, contact the tourist information center in Glasgow or the Strathclyde Passenger Transport Travel Centre. Traveline Scotland has helpful information.

If you're driving from Glasgow, there are two main routes to Ayr. The quickest is to take the M77 to the A77, which takes you all the way to Ayr. Alloway is well signposted when you get to Ayr. The alternative and much slower route is the coast road; take the M8 to Greenock and continue down the coast on the A78 until you meet the A77 and continue on into Burns Country.

PAISLEY

7 miles south of Glasgow.

The industrial prosperity of Paisley came from textiles and, in particular, from the woolen paisley shawl. The internationally recognized paisley pattern is based on the shape of a palm shoot, an ancient Babylonian fertility symbol brought from Kashmir. Today you can explore this history at several attractions.

GETTING HERE AND AROUND

Paisley-bound buses depart from the Buchanan Street bus station in Glasgow. Trains to Paisley's Gilour Street depart daily every 5 to 10 minutes from Glasgow Central Station. If you're driving, take the M8 westbound and turn off at Junction 27, which is clearly signposted to Paisley.

ESSENTIALS

Visitor Information Paisley Visitor Information Centre. ⊠ *9A Gilmour St.* ☎ *0141/889–0711* ⊕ *www.visitscotland.com.*

EXPLORING

Paisley Abbey. Paisley's 12th-century abbey dominates the town center. Founded as a Cluniac monastery and almost completely destroyed by the English in 1307, the abbey was not totally restored until the early 20th century. It's associated with Walter Fitzallan, the high steward of Scotland, who gave his name to the Stewart monarchs of Scotland (Stewart is a corruption of "steward"). Outstanding features include the vaulted stone roof and stained glass of the choir. ⊠ *13 High St.* ☎ *0141/889–7654* ⊕ *www.paisleyabbey.org.uk* ⊠ *Free* ☉ *Mon.–Sat. 10–3:30, Sun. services at 11, 12:15, and 6:30.*

Paisley Museum. The full story of the pattern and of the innovative weaving techniques introduced in Paisley is told in the Paisley Museum, which has a world-famous shawl collection. ⊠ *High St.* ☎ *0141/887–1010* ⊕ *www.renfrewshireleisure.com/paisleymuseum* ⊠ *Free* ☉ *Tues.–Sat. 10–5, Sun. 2–5.*

Sma' Shot Cottages. To get an idea of the life led by textile industry workers, visit the Sma' Shot Cottages. These re-creations of mill workers' houses contain displays of linen, lace, and paisley shawls. Two typical cottages, built 150 years apart, are open to visitors. ⊠ *11–17 George Pl.* ☎ *0141/889–1708* ⊕ *www.smashot.co.uk* ⊠ *Free* ☉ *Apr.–Sept., Wed. and Sat. noon–4; Oct.–Mar. by appointment.*

OFF THE BEATEN PATH

Great Cumbrae. A favorite day trip for Glaswegians is an outing to the little island of Great Cumbrae (pronounced *kum-ree*). Take the train to Largs and then the ferry across to Millport, and hire a cycle for a pleasant ride around the island. It's about 12 miles around and quite gentle. ⊕ *www.millport.org.*

Ayrshire and the Clyde Coast

Furnace
Strachur
Arrochar
A83
Minard
Garelochhead
A82
Drymen
A886
Clachan of Glendaruel
A815
Helensburgh
Balloch
Blanefield
Dunoon
Gourock
A814
Greenock
River Clyde
Dumbarton
Colintraive
Port Glasgow
Langbank
A78
A886
Innellan
Inverkip
Port Bannatyne
Wemyss Bay
Skelmorlie
Glasgow
Rothesay
A78
Linwood
Paisley
Ascog
Isle of Bute
A844
Mount Stuart
Largs
Lochwinnoch
A737
Johnstone
Barrhead
A736
M77
Kingarth
Great Cumbrae Island
Kilbirnie
Beith
Lugton
A726
Sound of Bute
Millport
Dalry
A736
Dunlop
M77
A735
Stewarton
A841
West Kilbride
A78
Kilwinning
Fenwick
Corrie
Ardrossan
Saltcoats
Irvine
Kilmarnock
A71
A71
South Corriegills
Ferry
Firth of Clyde
Irvine Bay
A78
A77
Galston
B880
Brodick
A841
Troon
A719
A76
Tarbolton
Catrine
Lamlash
Prestwick
Isle of Arran
Whiting Bay
Ayr Bay
Auchinleck
ISLE OF ARRAN
Ayr
Dumfries House
Alloway
Coylton
A70
Coalhall
Cumnock
A76
TO FERRY TO BELFAST
Culzean Castle and Country Park
A719
Dalrymple
A77
Maidens
A719
Maybole
A713
Dalmellington
Turnberry
Straiton

0   10 mi
0   10 km

WHERE TO STAY

$ HOTEL 🏨 **Glynhill Hotel.** This mansion combines old-fashioned living with modern convenience; stylish and bright contemporary furnishings make the bedrooms cheerful and comfortable. **Pros:** elegant rooms; nice pool and sauna; close to transportation. **Cons:** airport noise; lacks atmosphere. [$] *Rooms from: £95* ✉ *169 Paisley Rd., Renfrew* ☎ *0141/886–5555* 🌐 *www.glynhill.com* 🛏 *145 rooms* 🍴 *Breakfast.*

$$$$ HOTEL 🏨 **Mar Hall.** This imposing baronial house sits amid formal gardens and overlooks the River Clyde and verdant woodlands. **Pros:** spacious rooms; fantastic pool; wonderful setting. **Cons:** quite remote; an expensive treat. [$] *Rooms from: £245* ✉ *Earl of Mar Estate, Mar Hall Dr., Bishopton* ☎ *0141/812–9999* 🌐 *www.marhall.com* 🛏 *53 rooms* 🍴 *Breakfast.*

ISLE OF BUTE

42 miles west of Glasgow.

The Isle of Bute affords a host of relaxing walks and scenic vistas. Mount Stuart, a stately home, is a popular attraction. Like the nearby Isle of Arran (⇨ *see Chapter 8*), the Isle of Bute was a Victorian holiday favorite convenient for Glaswegians.

Rothesay, a faded but appealing resort, is the main town, and some of its ornate Victorian architecture is striking. In the old Victorian village of Wemyss Bay there's ferry service to the island. The many handsome buildings, especially the station, are a reminder of the grandeur and style of a century ago.

GETTING HERE AND AROUND

Take the train from Glasgow Central Station to Wemyss Bay, where you can hop aboard the ferry to Rothesay. If you're driving, take the A8/A78 coast road and park at the ferry terminal.

ESSENTIALS

Visitor Information **Isle of Bute Discovery Centre.** ✉ *The Winter Garden, Victoria St., Rothesay* ☎ *08452/255121.*

EXPLORING

Mount Stuart. Bute's biggest draw is spectacular Mount Stuart, ancestral home of the marquesses of Bute. The massive Victorian Gothic palace, built in red sandstone, has ornate interiors, including the eccentric Horoscope Room and the Marble Hall, with stained glass, arcaded galleries, and magnificent tapestries woven in Edinburgh in the early 20th century. The paintings and furniture throughout the house are equally outstanding. You can also appreciate the lovely gardens and grounds. ✉ *Off A844, Rothesay* ☎ *01700/503877* 🌐 *www.mountstuart.com* 🎟 *Gardens £5.50; house and gardens £11.50* ⏲ *Gardens Mar.–Oct., daily 10–6; house Mar.–Oct., Mon., Tues., and Thurs. 11–4 (guided tours every hr), Wed., Fri., and weekends noon–4.*

Rothesay. A faded but appealing resort, Rothesay is the main town on the Isle of Bute. Some of the ornate Victorian architecture is striking.

WHERE TO STAY

$ B&B/INN **Munro's Bed and Breakfast.** Surrounded by colorful gardens, this small B&B in a peaceful residential area has a home-away-from-home feel. **Pros:** beautiful location; nicely remodeled; environmentally aware. **Cons:** hilltop location is a steep climb; no restaurant; sea-view rooms cost extra. [$] *Rooms from: £85* ✉ *Ardmory Rd., Ardbeg* ☎ *01700/502346* 🌐 *www.visitmunros.co.uk* 🛏 *6 rooms* 🍴 *Breakfast.*

IRVINE

24 miles south of Glasgow.

Beyond Irvine's cobbled streets and grand Victorian buildings, look for a peaceful crescent-shape harbor and fishermen's cottages huddled in solidarity against the Atlantic winds. The Scottish Maritime Museum pays homage to the town's seafaring past. Scotland's national poet, Robert Burns, lived here in 1781.

GETTING HERE AND AROUND

By car, take the M8 from Glasgow, then the A726 and the A736 to Irvine. By rail, it's a 40-minute journey from Glasgow Central Station.

ESSENTIALS

Visitor Information **Irvine Tourist Information Centre.** ✉ *New St.* ☎ *01294/313886.*

EXPLORING

Denny Tank. The size of a football field, this tank was where ship designs were tested. You can see how in demonstrations that are offered throughout the day—a must for anyone following the history of shipbuilding on the Clyde. Denny Tank is part of Irvine's Scottish Maritime Museum. ✉ *Castle St., Dumbarton* ☎ *01294/278283* 🌐 *www.scottishmaritimemuseum.org* 🎫 *£3.50* 🕒 *Mon.–Sat. 10–4.*

FAMILY **Scottish Maritime Museum.** On the waterfront in the coastal town of Irvine, this museum brings together ships and boats—both models and the real thing—to tell the tale of Scotland's maritime history, as well as chronicle the lives of its boatbuilders, fishermen, and sailors. The atmospheric Linthouse Engine Building, part of a former shipyard, hosts most of the displays. The museum also includes a shipyard worker's tenement home that you can explore and the Denny Tank. **TIP→ Children are admitted free.** ✉ *6 Gottries Rd.* ☎ *01294/278283* 🌐 *www.scottishmaritimemuseum.org* 🎫 *£7.50* 🕒 *Daily 10–5.*

Vennel Art Gallery. The gallery occupies the 18th-century cottage where poet Robert Burns lived and the shed where he learned to heckle—or dress—flax (the raw material for linen). Both buildings have on display paintings, photographs, and sculpture by mainly Scottish artists. ✉ *10 Glasgow Vennel* ☎ *01294/275059* 🎫 *Free* 🕒 *Thurs.–Sat. 10–1 and 2–5.*

GOLF

Fodor's Choice ★ **Western Gailes Golf Club.** Known as the finest natural links course in Scotland, Western Gailes is entirely nature-made, and the greens are kept in truly magnificent condition. This is the final qualifying course when the British Open is held at Royal Troon or Turnberry. Tom

Watson lists the par-5 6th hole as one of his favorites. Visitors can play Monday, Wednesday, Friday, and weekend afternoons. ✉ *Gailes Rd.* ☎ *01294/311649* 🌐 *www.westerngailes.com* 💳 *£135 Apr.–Sept., contact club Oct.–Mar.* ⛳ *18 holes, 6640 yards, par 71.*

TROON

4 miles south of Irvine, 30 miles south of Glasgow, 6 miles north of Ayr.

The small coastal town of Troon is famous for its outstanding golf course, Royal Troon. You can easily see that golf is popular here and in this area: at times the whole 60-mile-long Ayrshire coast seems one endless course. The town's several miles of sandy beaches provide other diversions. It's easy to get to Troon by train or bus from both Glasgow and Ayr.

GETTING HERE AND AROUND

From Glasgow Central Station, board an Ayr-bound train and get off at Troon. By car, take the M77/A77 toward Prestwick Airport and follow the signs to Troon.

WHERE TO EAT AND STAY

$$ SEAFOOD Fodor's Choice ★

🍴 **MacCallums Oyster Bar.** Located in Troon Harbor, this outstanding seafood restaurant's menu varies with the day's catch, but you can usually count on lobster in garlic butter, seared scallops, or grilled langoustines that taste of the sea. The fish pie is justly famous, and excellent light white wines match the fresh food. Wooden tables and other simple furnishings add a rustic touch. For a more modest price, or if you prefer to watch the fishing boats in the harbor, try the adjacent Wee Hurrie, possibly one of Scotland's best fish-and-chips shops, serving monkfish and oysters as well as the usual fare. Finding McCallums is a bit of an adventure, but it's worth the trek. Check before you go, as the restaurant almost closed despite its popularity. [$] *Average main: £17* ✉ *Harbour Rd.* ☎ *01292/319339* 🌐 *www.maccallumsoftroon.co.uk* 🕒 *Closed Mon. No dinner Sun.*

$$ HOTEL

🏨 **Piersland House Hotel.** A late-Victorian mansion on the southern edge of town, formerly the home of a whisky magnate, is now a country-house hotel. **Pros:** gorgeous gardens and grounds; close to golf courses; near Prestwick Airport. **Cons:** helps to have a car to get around; can get crowded with private functions. [$] *Rooms from: £130* ✉ *15 Craigend Rd.* ☎ *01292/314747* 🌐 *www.piersland.co.uk* 🛏 *37 rooms* 🍽 *Breakfast.*

SHOPPING

Regalia Fashion Salon. Many Glaswegians frequent Regalia Fashion Salon for its unusual collection of designer clothing for women. ✉ *46-48 Church St.* ☎ *01292/312162.*

Tantalus Antiques. For a fascinating look at local antiquities, visit Tantalus Antiques, which also specializes in repairing antique furniture. ✉ *79 Temple Hill* ☎ *01292/315999.*

GOLF

Royal Troon Golf Club. Of the two courses at Royal Troon, it's the Old or Championship Course—a traditional links course with superb sea views frequently used for the British Open—that is renowned among golfers. The second, Portland, shares the challenges of strong sea breezes and the gorse beside the fairways. Advance payment and a deposit are required, as is a handicap certificate. It is a good idea to check the tournament calendar before you go. ⊠ *Craigend Rd.* ☎ *01292/311555* ⊕ *www.royaltroon.com* ✉ *Old Course and Portland Course, £205 mid-Apr.–early Sept.; Old Course, £150 mid-Sept.–mid-Oct.* ⅄ *Old Course: 18 holes, 7208 yards, par 71; Portland Course: 18 holes, 6349 yards, par 72* ⊙ *Mid-Apr.–early Sept. and mid-Sept.–mid-Oct., Mon., Tues., and Thurs. for visitors.*

AYR AND ALLOWAY

6 miles south of Troon, 34 miles south of Glasgow.

The commercial port of Ayr is Ayrshire's chief town, a peaceful and elegant place with an air of prosperity. Poet Robert Burns was baptized in the Auld Kirk (Old Church) here and wrote a humorous poem about the Twa Brigs (Two Bridges) that cross the river nearby. Burns described Ayr as a town unsurpassed "for honest men and bonny lasses."

If you're on the Robert Burns trail, head for Alloway, on B7024 in Ayr's southern suburbs. A number of sights here are part of the **Burns National Heritage Park**, including the magnificent Robert Burns Birthplace Museum.

GETTING HERE AND AROUND

From Glasgow you can take the bus or train to Ayr; travel time is about an hour (a bit less by train). Drivers can use the A78 and A77 near the coast; a car would provide more flexibility to see the Burns sites around Alloway.

ESSENTIALS

Visitor Information Ayr Visitor Information Centre. ⊠ *22 Sandgate, Ayr* ☎ *01292/288688* ⊕ *www.visitscotland.com.*

EXPLORING
TOP ATTRACTIONS

Burns Cottage. In the delightful Burns Heritage Park, this thatched cottage is where Scotland's national poet lived for his first seven years. It has a living room, a kitchen, and a stable, one behind the other. The life and times of Burns, born in 1759, are beautifully and creatively illustrated in the fly-on-the-wall videos of daily life in the 18th century. The garden is lush with the types of vegetables the poet's father might have grown. Take the Poet's Path through the village to the Robert Burns Birthplace Museum, the spooky churchyard where Tam o'Shanter faced fearsome ghosts, and the Brig o' Doon. ⊠ *Greenfield Ave., Alloway* ☎ *0844/493–2601* ⊕ *www.burnsmuseum.org.uk* ✉ *£9, includes Burns Monument and Robert Burns Birthplace Museum* ⊙ *Apr.–Sept., daily 10–5:30; Oct.–Mar., daily 10–5.*

Fodor's Choice **Robert Burns Birthplace Museum.** Besides being a poet of delicacy and
★ depth, Robert Burns was also a rebel, a thinker, a lover, a good com-
panion, and a man of the countryside. This wonderful museum explains
why the Scots so admire this complex "man o' pairts." The imaginative displays present each of his poems in context, with commentaries
sensitively written in a modern version of the Scots language in which
he spoke and wrote. Headsets let you hear the poems sung or spoken.
The exhibits are vibrant and interactive, with touch screens that allow
you to debate his views on politics, love, taxation, revolution, and Scottishness. An elegant café offers a place to pause, while the kids can play
in the adjoining garden. Included in the ticket are the Burns Cottage,
a few minutes' walk down a Burns-themed walkway, and the Burns
Monument. ⊠ *Murdoch's Lone, Alloway* ☎ *0844/493-2601* ⊕ *www.
burnsmuseum.org.uk* ⊠ *£9, includes Burns Cottage and Burns Monument* ☉ *Apr.–Sept., daily 10–5:30; Oct.–Mar., daily 10–5.*

WORTH NOTING

Auld Kirk Alloway. Auld Kirk Alloway is where Tam o' Shanter, in Robert
Burns's great epic poem, unluckily passed a witches' revel—with Old
Nick himself playing the bagpipes—on his way home from a night of
drinking. Tam, in flight from the witches, managed to cross the medieval **Brig o' Doon** (*brig* is Scots for *bridge*; you can still see the bridge)
just in time. His gray mare, Meg, lost her tail to the closest witch. (Any
resident of Ayr will tell you that witches cannot cross running water.)
The church is in ruins, but the graveyard includes the tomb of Burns's
father, William. ⊠ *Murdoch's Lone, Alloway* ⊠ *Free.*

Bachelors' Club. About 8 miles northeast of Ayr is the Bachelors' Club, the
17th-century house—now fully restored—where Robert Burns learned to
dance, founded a debating and literary society, and became a Freemason.
⊠ *Sandgate St., Tarbolton* ☎ *0844/493-2146* ⊕ *www.nts.org.uk* ⊠ *£3.50*
☉ *Apr.–late Sept., daily 1:30–5:30; Oct., weekends 1:30–5:30.*

Burns Monument. This neoclassical structure, built in 1823, overlooks
the Brig o' Doon. You can climb to the top (with some care!). Entrance
is included in the Burns Museum ticket. ⊠ *Murdoch's Lone, Alloway*
⊕ *www.burnsmuseum.org.uk* ⊠ *£9, includes Burns Cottage and Robert Burns Birthplace Museum* ☉ *Apr.–Sept., daily 9:30–5; Oct.–Mar.,
daily 10–4.*

Dumfries House. Built in the 1750s by the Adam brothers, Dumfries
House has preserved unchanged the living conditions of the landed
aristocracy of the time. The restored house contains a large collection
of furniture by Chippendale that is original to the property, as well as
pieces by other great designers of the period. Run by a charity headed
by Prince Charles, the surrounding 2,000-acre estate is projected as a
site for a new eco-village and centers practicing historic crafts. Entry is
by guided tour only; booking is essential. The house is about 10 miles
east of Ayr. ⊠ *Cumnock* ☎ *01290/421742* ⊕ *www.dumfries-house.org.
uk* ⊠ *Admission by guided tour only: £9. Grounds are free to visitors*
☉ *Mar., Sun.–Fri. tours at 12:15 and 1:45; Apr.–Oct., Sun.–Fri. 11–3:30
(tours throughout the day); Nov.–Feb., weekend tours at 12:15 and 1:45.*

WHERE TO EAT AND STAY

$$

BRITISH

✕ **Brig o' Doon House.** Originally built in 1827, this attractive restaurant often has a piper by the door to greet hungry travelers. The setting is very Scottish, with tartan carpets, dark wood paneling, and buck heads mounted on the walls. The bar is a shrine to Robert Burns, and the surrounding gardens overlook the Brig o' Doon as well as a small, rushing river. The food keeps to the Scottish theme: try panfried scallops with citrus butter to start, and venison casserole with juniper berries and creamed potatoes or the haggis with neeps and tatties (served with a dram) as a main course. There are several rooms for rent upstairs. $ *Average main: £17* ⊠ *High Maybole Rd., Alloway* ☎ *01292/442466* ⊕ *www. brigodoonhouse.com.*

> ### REMEMBERING MR. BURNS
>
> Born in Ayrshire, Robert Burns (1759–96) is one of Scotland's treasures. The poet and balladeer had a style that was his and his alone. His most famous song, "Auld Lang Syne," is heard everywhere on New Year's Day. Burns's talent, charisma, and good looks made him an icon to both the upper and lower classes (and made him quite popular with the ladies). Today his birthday (January 25) is considered a national holiday; on "Burns Night" young and old alike get together for Burns Suppers and recite his work over neeps, tatties, and drams of the country's finest whisky.

3

$

ITALIAN

✕ **Cafe Le Monde.** This Italian-style café serves lunch and smaller bites to a mainly day-visitor crowd. The ciabattas and soups are well made and substantial, if not enormously adventurous, all served by attentive staff. $ *Average main: £10* ⊠ *36 Newmarket St., Ayr* ☎ *01292/611219.*

$$$$

HOTEL

FAMILY

🏨 **Trump Turnberry.** Turnberry has been synonymous with golf for a century and a half—its three great courses are among the highest rated in the world—and indeed golf is what brings most visitors to this luxury resort, which also caters to the partners and children of golfers with stunning facilities and cuisine. **Pros:** golfer's paradise; high level of luxury in food and accommodation. **Cons:** only for the deepest wallets; controversial renovations; advance golf reservations required. $ *Rooms from: £295* ⊠ *Maidens Rd., off A719, Turnberry* ☎ *01655/331000* ⊕ *www.turnberryresort.co.uk* ↻ *132 rooms* ❘❍❘ *Breakfast.*

GOLF

Girvan. Opened in 1902, scenic Girvan plays along a narrow coastal strip and a lush inland section next to the Water of Girvan—a challenging hazard at the 15th hole unless you're a big hitter. Unlike its illustrious neighbor Turnberry, Girvan is not a championship course, but it is a pleasant combination of links and parkland. And it does share with neighbors fine views of Ailsa Craig and the Clyde Estuary. ⊠ *40 Golf Course Rd., Girvan* ☎ *01465/714346* ⊕ *www.golfsouthayrshire.com* 🎫 *£17.50* ⛳ *18 holes, 5064 yards, par 64* ☼ *Daily.*

Prestwick Golf Club. Tom Morris helped to design this challenging Ayrshire coastal links course, which saw the birth of the British Open Championship in 1860. The first hole is reputed to be among the most challenging in Scotland, since the railway line runs along the length of the hole. But it doesn't get any easier after that. Some of its bunkers are especially threatening, and the bumps at the 5th are high enough to be called the Himalayas. Prestwick has excellent, fast rail links with Glasgow. There are a limited number of tee times on Saturday afternoon. ⊠ *2 Links Rd., Prestwick* ☎ *01292/477404* ⊕ *www.prestwickgc. co.uk* ⎘ *Apr.–Oct., £150 weekdays, £175 weekends; Nov.–Mar., £85* ⚑ *18 holes, 6544 yards, par 71* ⊙ *Daily.*

Fodor's Choice
★
Trump Turnberry. One of the most famous links courses in Scotland, Turnberry now bears the name of its new owner, Donald Trump. The main course, the iconic Ailsa Course, is open to the elements, and the 9th hole requires you to hit the ball over the open sea. The British Open was hosted here in 1977, 1986, 1994, and 2009. A second course, the Kintyre, is more compact, with tricky sloped greens. Five of the holes have sea views. There is also a 9-hole course, the Arran. ⊠ *Trump Turnberry Resort, Maidens Rd., off A719, Turnberry* ☎ *01655/331000* ⊕ *www.turnberryresort.co.uk* ⎘ *Ailsa, £250 weekdays, £275 weekends; Kintyre, May–Oct., £90, Nov.–Apr., £55* ⚑ *Ailsa: 18 holes, 7217 yards, par 70; Kintyre: 18 holes, 6921 yards, par 72* ⊙ *Daily.*

CULZEAN CASTLE AND COUNTRY PARK

12 miles south of Ayr, 50 miles south of Glasgow.

There's plenty to do at this popular spot between visiting the Adam-designed house and touring the extensive grounds.

GETTING HERE AND AROUND

Stagecoach buses run from Ayr to the park entrance; the nearest train station from Glasgow is at Maybole, 4 miles to the east, but there is Stagecoach bus service to the park entrance. Note that the park entrance is a mile walk from the castle visitor center.

EXPLORING

FAMILY
Fodor's Choice
★
Culzean Castle and Country Park. The dramatic cliff-top castle of Culzean (pronounced ku- *lain*) is the National Trust for Scotland's most popular property. Robert Adam designed the neoclassical mansion, complete with a walled garden, in 1777. The grounds are enormous, combining parkland, forests, and a beach looking out over the Atlantic Ocean; the surprisingly lush shrubberies reflect the warm currents that explain the mild climate. There are caves in the cliffs; tours are occasionally available. In the castle itself you can visit the armory, luxuriously appointed salons and bedchambers, and a nursery with its lovely cradle in a boat. Adams's grand double spiral staircase is the high point of its design. There's a free audio tour, and guided tours are available daily at 11 and 2:30. A short walk through the woods brings you to the visitor center with shops and a restaurant. ⊠ *Culzean Castle, A719, Maybole* ☎ *0844/493–2149* ⊕ *www.nts.org.uk* ⎘ *Park £10.50, park and castle £15.50* ⊙ *Park daily 9:30–sunset; castle Apr.–Oct., daily 10:30–5; last admission at 4.*

WHERE TO STAY

$$$$
HOTEL
▥ **Eisenhower Hotel.** It would be hard to imagine a more spectacular location for an overnight stay than the upper floors of Culzean Castle, which looks out towards Arran and the Atlantic Ocean. **Pros:** beautiful setting;

luxurious lodging; a strong sense of history. **Cons:** a little remote; rather formal; not for minimalists. $ *Rooms from: £250* ✉ *Culzean Castle, A719, Maybole* ☎ *0844/493–2149* ⊕ *www.culzean-eisenhower.com* ⇤ *6 rooms* ⦿ *Breakfast.*

SIDE TRIPS: THE CLYDE VALLEY

The River Clyde is (or certainly was) famous for its shipbuilding, yet its upper reaches flow through some of Scotland's most fertile farmlands, rich with crops of tomatoes and fruit. It's an interesting area with some museums, most notably at New Lanark, that tell the story of the growth of manufacturing.

GETTING HERE AND AROUND

If you're driving from Glasgow, head south on the M74 and turn on to the A72. This is the main road through the Clyde Valley, ending at Lanark. The A702 is the turnoff to Biggar. Train service runs from Glasgow Central Station to Lanark; for details check National Rail. There are no trains to Biggar, but there's a connecting bus from Hamilton to Biggar.

NATIONAL MUSEUM OF RURAL LIFE

9 miles south of Glasgow.

The effect of farming on the land and on people's lives is the focus of this museum near Glasgow.

EXPLORING

FAMILY

Fodor'sChoice

★

National Museum of Rural Life. This lovely museum, a 20-minute drive from Glasgow, is slightly off the beaten track but well worth the trip. Set in a rural area, it explores every aspect of the country's agricultural heritage. In a modern building resembling a huge barn you learn about how farming transformed the land, experience the life and hardships of those who worked it, and see displays of tools and machines from across the ages. Take a tractor ride to a fully functioning 1950s farmhouse. There are also some great exhibits geared toward children. ✉ *Wester Kittochside, Philipshill Rd., East Kilbride* ⟴ *From Glasgow take the M77 then the A726 at junction 4 to East Kilbride or the A725 from Blantyre to East Kilbride* ☎ *0300/123–6789* ⊕ *www.nms.ac.uk/rural* ▦ *£7* ⊗ *Daily 10–5.*

SUMMERLEE–MUSEUM OF SCOTTISH INDUSTRIAL LIFE

10 miles east of Glasgow.

A former ironworks is now a museum with a re-created mine and exhibits on both industry and the lives of workers.

EXPLORING

FAMILY

Summerlee–Museum of Scottish Industrial Life. On the site of the old Summerlee Ironworks, this vast and exciting museum re-creates a mine and the miners' rows (the cottages where miners and their families lived). An electric tram transports you here from the huge hall where

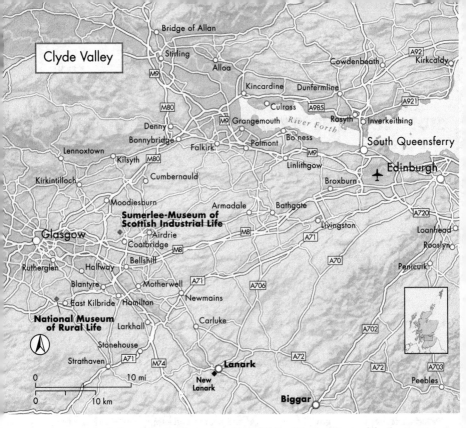

Clyde Valley

industrial machines vie with exhibits about ordinary life. Later you can stroll along the canal and take the kids to a fine playground. The drive from Glasgow takes around 15 minutes. ⊠ *Heritage Way, Coatbridge* ✚ *Take the M8 towards Edinburgh, exit at junction 8, and the A89 towards Coatbridge, then left at the roundabout in the town center* ☎ *01236/638460* ⊕ *www.visitlanarkshire.com/summerlee* ☒ *Free* ⊙ *Apr.–Oct., daily 10–5; Nov.–Mar., daily 10–4.*

LANARK

19 miles east of Glasgow.

Set in pleasing, rolling countryside, Lanark is a typical old Scottish town. It's now most often associated with its unique neighbor New Lanark, a model workers' community about a mile to the south.

GETTING HERE AND AROUND
If you're driving, take the M74 to the A72. The train from Glasgow Central Station takes 50 minutes or so.

ESSENTIALS
Visitor Information **Lanark Visitor Information Centre.** ⊠ *Horsemarket, Ladyacre Rd.* ☎ *01555/661661* ⊕ *www.visitscotland.com.*

EXPLORING

FAMILY

Fodor's Choice

★

New Lanark. Now a World Heritage Site, New Lanark was home to a social experiment at the beginning of the Industrial Revolution. Robert Owen (1771–1858), together with his father-in-law David Dale (1739–1806), set out to create a model industrial community with well-designed worker homes, a school, and public buildings. Owen went on to establish other communities on similar principles, both in Britain and in the United States. Robert Owen's son, Robert Dale Owen (1801–77), helped found the Smithsonian Institution.

After many changes of fortune, the mills eventually closed. One of the buildings has been converted into a visitor center that tells the story of this brave social experiment. You can also explore Robert Owen's house, the school, and a mill worker's house, and enjoy the Annie McLeod Experience, a fairground ride that takes you through the story of one mill worker's life. Other restored structures hold various shops and eateries; one has a rooftop garden with impressive views of the entire site. Another now houses the New Lanark Mill Hotel.

The River Clyde powers its way through a beautiful wooded gorge here, and its waters were once harnessed to drive textile-mill machinery. Upstream it flows through some of the finest river scenery anywhere in Lowland Scotland, with woods and spectacular waterfalls. ⊠ *New Lanark Rd., New Lanark* ☎ *01555/661345* ⊕ *www.newlanark.org* 🎟 *£8.50* ☉ *Oct.–Mar., daily 11–5; Apr.–Sept., daily 10–5.*

WHERE TO STAY

$

HOTEL

New Lanark Mill Hotel. Housed in a converted cotton mill in the 18th-century village of New Lanark, this hotel is decorated in a spare, understated style that allows the impressive architecture of barrel-vaulted ceilings and elegant Georgian windows to speak for itself. **Pros:** beautiful views of the river; large rooms; impressive spa. **Cons:** bland bar; some rooms can get cold; restaurant is the only one in the vicinity. $ *Rooms from: £94* ⊠ *New Lanark Rd., New Lanark* ☎ *01555/667200* ⊕ *www. newlanarkmillhotel.co.uk* 🛏 *38 rooms, 8 cottages* ⦵ *Breakfast.*

SHOPPING

Lanark has an interesting selection of shops within walking distance of each other; there are also some shops such as the Edinburgh Woollen Mill at New Lanark.

McKellar's. This shop sells Charles Rennie Mackintosh–inspired designs in gold and silver, as well as watches and clocks. ⊠ *41 High St.* ☎ *01555/661312* ⊕ *www.mckellarsjewellers.com.*

Strands. The amusingly named Strands carries yarns and knitwear, including Arran designs and one-of-a-kind creations by Scottish designers. ⊠ *8 Bloomgate* ☎ *01555/665757* ⊕ *www.strandsoflanark.co.uk.*

BIGGAR

34 miles southeast of Glasgow.

A pleasant town built of stone, Biggar is a rewarding place to spend an hour or two, out of all proportion to its size, thanks to an excellent collection of small, specialized museums. At Biggar you are near the headwaters of the Clyde, on the moors in the center of southern Scotland. The Clyde flows west toward Glasgow and the Atlantic Ocean, and the Tweed, only a few miles away, flows east toward the North Sea. There are fine views around Biggar to Culter Fell and to the Border Hills in the south.

GETTING HERE AND AROUND

From Glasgow, take the M74 and then the A72 to reach Biggar. On public transportation, your best option is a train to Lanark, where you can transfer to a bus bound for Biggar.

ESSENTIALS

Visitor Information **Biggar Visitor Information Centre.** ⊠ *155 High St.* ☎ *01899/221066.*

EXPLORING

Biggar and Upper Clydesdale Museum. Opened in 2015 after a major reorganization and rebuilding, the new Biggar and Upper Clydesdale Museum presents a fascinating view of Scotland's earlier history and its Victorian age. ⊠ *156 High St.* ☎ *01899/221050* ⊕ *www. biggarmuseumtrust.co.uk* ⊠ *£5* ☉ *Apr.–Oct., Tues.–Sat. 10–5, Sun. 1–5; Nov.–Mar., Sat. 10–5, Sun. 1–5.*

Biggar Gasworks. Built in 1839, the gasworks is a fascinating reminder of the efforts once needed to produce gas for light and heat. ⊠ *Gasworks Rd.* ☎ *01899/221050* ⊕ *www.historic-scotland.gov.uk* ⊠ *£1* ☉ *June–Sept., daily 2–5.*

FAMILY **Biggar Puppet Theatre.** Purves Puppets, famous for its "black box" puppetry, regularly performs at the Biggar Puppet Theatre. Before and after performances (£8), puppeteers lead hands-on tours (£3). One tour ducks backstage, while the other explores the puppet museum. These tours should be booked well in advance, as should tickets for very popular performances. ⊠ *8 Broughton Rd.* ☎ *01899/220631* ⊕ *www. purvespuppets.com.*

4

THE BORDERS AND
THE SOUTHWEST

4

Updated
by Mike
Gonzalez

In the Borders region, south of Edinburgh, are more stately homes, fortified castles, and medieval abbeys than in any other part of Scotland. This is also Sir Walter Scott territory, including his pseudo-baronial home at Abbotsford. The area embraces the whole 90-mile course of one of Scotland's great rivers, the Tweed. Passing woodlands luxuriant with game birds, the river flows in rushing torrents through this fertile land. To the west of the Borders is Dumfries and Galloway, an area of gentle coasts, forests, and lush hills, ideal country for walkers and cyclists, in close contact with the sea from the Solway Firth to the Atlantic coast.

For centuries the Borders was a battlefield, where English and Scottish troops remained locked in a struggle for its possession. At different times, parts of the region have been in English hands, just as slices of northern England (Berwick-upon-Tweed, for example) have been under Scottish control. The castles and fortified houses as well as the abbeys across the Borders are the surviving witnesses to those times. After the Union of 1707, fortified houses gradually gave way to the luxurious country mansions that pepper the area. And by the 19th century they had become grand country houses built by fashionable architects.

All the main routes between London and Edinburgh traverse the Borders, whose hinterland of undulating pastures, woods, and valleys is enclosed within three lonely groups of hills: the Cheviots, the Moorfoots, and the Lammermuirs. Hamlets and prosperous country towns dot the land, giving valley slopes a lived-in look, yet the total population is still sparse. The sheep that are the basis of the region's prosperous textile industry outnumber human beings by 14 to 1.

To the west is the region of Dumfries and Galloway, on the shores of the Solway Firth. It might appear to be an extension of the Borders, but the southwest has a history all its own. From these ports ships sailed to the Americas, carrying country dwellers driven from their land to make room for the sheep that still roam the hills across southern Scotland. Inland, the earth rises toward high hills, forest, and bleak but captivating moorland, whereas nearer the coast you can find pretty farmlands, small villages, and unassuming towns. The shoreline is washed by the North Atlantic Drift (Scotland's answer to the Gulf Stream), and first-time visitors are always surprised to see palm trees and exotic plants thriving in gardens and parks along the coast.

At the heart of the region is Dumfries, the "Queen o' the South." Once a major port and commercial center, its glamour is now slightly faded. But

TOP REASONS TO GO

Ancient abbeys: The great abbeys of the Border regions, and the Whithorn Priory and the wonderful Sweetheart Abbey in the Southwest, are mainly in ruins, but they retain an air of their former grandeur.

Outdoor activities: You can walk, bicycle, or even ride horses across Galloway or through the Borders. Abandoned railway tracks make good paths, and there are forests and moorlands if you prefer wilder country. World-class mountain bike trails cover the region.

Stately homes and castles: The landed aristocracy still lives in these grand mansions, and most of the homes are open to visitors. Try Floors Castle or the wonderful Traquair House in the east. Threave,

Drumnlarig, and the magical Caerlaverock Castle near Dumfries evoke grander times.

Literary Scotland: The Borders region has enough monuments dedicated to Sir Walter Scott to make him the focus of your visit. Abbotsford House, which he built for himself, is unmissable. The poet Robert Burns spent much of his working life in Dumfries.

Shopping: The sheep you see everywhere explain why so many locals became involved in textile production. Mill shops are abundant, and are well worth a visit for their wonderful woolens. Craft shops testify to the rebirth of ancient crafts like woodworking and pottery.

4

the memory of poet Robert Burns, who spent several years living and working here and who is buried in the town, remains very much alive.

GETTING ORIENTED

Once a battleground region separating Scotland and England, today the Borders area is a bridge between the two countries. This is a place of upland moors and hills, fertile farmland, and forested river valleys. Yet it also embraces the rugged coastline between Edinburgh and Berwick. It's rustic and peaceful, with century-old textile mills, abbeys, castles, and gardens. The area is a big draw for hikers and walking enthusiasts, too. The Borders region is also steeped in history, with Mary, Queen of Scots, a powerful presence despite the relatively short time she spent here.

The Borders. Borders towns cluster around and between two rivers—the Tweed and its tributary, the Teviot. These are mostly textile towns with plenty of personality, where residents take fierce pride in their local municipalities, The cut-down version of rugby (the Sevens), where teams consist of 7 rather than 15 players, brings the Borders towns into fierce (but friendly) rivalry. The Common Ridings, too, are unique to the Borders, as local people ride through the towns to commemorate a history of defending their local boundaries. The area's top attractions include Jedburgh Abbey, Floors Castle in Kelso, and Abbotsford House just outside Melrose.

Dumfries and Galloway. Easygoing and peaceful, towns in this southwestern region are usually very attractive, with wide streets and colorful buildings. The Solway Firth is a vast nature preserve, and the climate of the west sustains the surprising tropical plants at the Logan Botanic Gardens and the gardens at Threave Castle.

PLANNING

WHEN TO GO

Because many lodgings and some sights are privately owned and shut down from early autumn until early April, the area is less suited to off-season touring than some other parts of Scotland. The best time to visit is between Easter and late September. The region does look magnificent in autumn, especially along the wooded river valleys of the Borders. Late spring is the time to see the rhododendrons in the gardens of Dumfries and Galloway.

PLANNING YOUR TIME

The rail line that began operating in 2015 from Edinburgh's Waverley Station to Tweedbank, in the heart of the Borders, is helping to open up a fascinating region that has too often been seen as a corridor for travelers en route to the capital. Still, the easiest way to explore is with a car.

If you're driving north along the A1 toward Edinburgh, it's easy to take a tour around the prosperous Borders towns. Turn onto the A698 at Berwick-upon-Tweed, which will take you along the Scottish–English border toward Coldstream, and from there to Kelso, Jedburgh, Dryburgh, and Melrose. It's 36 miles from Jedburgh to Peebles, a good place to stay overnight. Another day might begin with a visit to Walter Scott's lovely Abbotsford House, and then some shopping in any of these prosperous towns.

To the west, Dumfries and Galloway beckon. From the A1, travel west on the A708 to Moffat and across the A74 toward Dumfries on the A70; from Glasgow take the A74 south to Beattock and pick up the A701 there. Two days would give you time to explore Burns sites and more in Dumfries. From Dumfries you can visit Sweetheart Abbey (8 miles away), Caerlaverock Castle (9 miles away), and Threave Gardens (20 miles away). Castle Douglas is a good place to stop for lunch. The A710 and A711 take you along the dramatic coastline of the Solway Firth. Farther west along the A75 are the towns of Newton Stewart and Portpatrick, and on the A714, Glen Trool. The region does not have very good rail links but there is good bus service, and by car it is a charming and compact region.

GETTING HERE AND AROUND

AIR TRAVEL

The nearest Scottish airports are at Edinburgh, Glasgow, and Prestwick (outside Glasgow).

BOAT AND FERRY TRAVEL

P&O European Ferries and Stena Line operate from Larne, in Northern Ireland, to Cairnryan, near Stranraer, several times daily. The crossing takes one hour on the Superstar Express, two hours on other ferries.

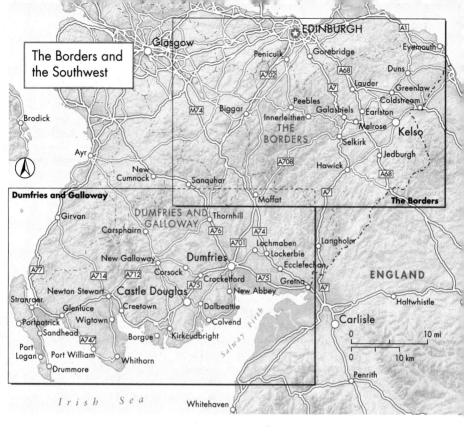

The Borders and
the Southwest

Boat and Ferry Contacts **P&O European Ferries.** ☎ *0800/130–0030* ⊕ *www.poferries.com.* **Stena Line.** ☎ *08447/707070* ⊕ *www.stenaline.co.uk.*

BUS TRAVEL

If you're approaching from the south, check with Scottish Citylink, National Express, or First about buses from Edinburgh and Glasgow. In the Borders, Firstborders and Perryman's Buses offer service within the region. Stagecoach Western is the main bus company serving Dumfries and Galloway.

Bus Contacts **First.** ☎ *01224/650100* ⊕ *www.firstgroup.com.* **Firstborders.** ☎ *01324/602200* ⊕ *www.firstborders.co.uk.* **National Express.** ☎ *0871/781-8181* ⊕ *www.nationalexpress.com.* **Perryman's Buses.** ☎ *01289/308719* ⊕ *www.perrymansbuses.co.uk.* **Scottish Citylink.** ☎ *0871/266-3333* ⊕ *www.citylink.co.uk.* **Stagecoach Western.** ☎ *0141/552-4961 in Glasgow, 01387/253496 in Dumfries* ⊕ *www.stagecoachbus.com.*

CAR TRAVEL

Traveling by car is the best and easiest way to explore the area. The main route into both the Borders and Galloway from the south is the M6, which becomes the M74 at the border. You can also take the scenic and leisurely A7 northwestward through Hawick toward Edinburgh, or the A75 and other parallel routes westward into Dumfries, Galloway, and the ferry ports of Stranraer and Cairnryan.

There are several other possible routes: starting from the east, the A1 brings you from the English city of Newcastle to the border in about an hour. The A1 has the added attraction of Berwick-Upon-Tweed, on the English side of the border, but traffic on the route is heavy. Moving west, the A697, which leaves the A1 north of Morpeth (in England) and crosses the border at Coldstream, is a leisurely back-road option. The A68 is probably the most scenic route to Scotland: after climbing to Carter Bar, it reveals a view of the Borders hills and windy skies before dropping into the ancient town of Jedburgh.

The best way to explore the region is to get off the main, and often crowded, arterial roads and onto the little back roads. You may occasionally be delayed by a herd of cows on their way to the milking parlor, or a pheasant fluttering across the road, but this is often far more pleasant than, for example, tussling on the A75 with heavy-goods vehicles rushing to make the Irish ferries.

TRAIN TRAVEL

Apart from the main London–Edinburgh line, there was no train service in the Borders until 2015, when a rail link from Edinburgh to Tweedbank, near Galashiels, began service. In the southwest, trains headed from London's Euston to Glasgow stop at Carlisle, just south of the border, and some also stop at Lockerbie. Trains between Glasgow and Carlisle stop at Gretna Green, Annan, and Dumfries. From Glasgow there is service on the coastal route to Stranraer.

First buses link Hawick, Selkirk, and Galashiels with train service at Carlisle, Edinburgh, and Berwick.

Train Contacts National Rail. ☎ *03457/484950* ⊕ *www.nationalrail.co.uk.* **ScotRail.** ☎ *0344/811–0141* ⊕ *www.scotrail.co.uk.*

RESTAURANTS

Until recently, most good restaurants in the region were located in hotels, but today things are beginning to change. Good independent eateries are popping up in small (and sometimes unlikely) towns and villages, and many of these new establishments specialize in fresh local ingredients. Seasonal menus are now popular in the area. It is important to remember that restaurants here usually serve dinner until 8:30 only.

HOTELS

From top-quality, full-service hotels to quaint 18th-century drovers' inns to cozy bed-and-breakfasts, the Borders has all manner of lodging options. Choices in Dumfries and Galloway may be a little less expensive than in the Borders (with the same full range of services). These days many establishments have a shifting scale and are willing to lower their rates depending on availability. *Hotel reviews have been shortened. For full reviews, see Fodors.com.*

WHAT IT COSTS IN POUNDS			
$	**$$**	**$$$**	**$$$$**
Restaurants	Under £15	£15–£19	£20–£25	Over £25
Hotels	Under £100	£100–£160	£161–£220	Over £220

Restaurant prices are the average cost of a main course at dinner or, if dinner is not served, at lunch. Hotel prices are the lowest cost of a standard double room in high season, including 20% V.A.T.

VISITOR INFORMATION
Visit Scottish Borders has offices in Jedburgh, Hawick, and Peebles. The Dumfries & Galloway Tourist Board can be found in Dumfries and Stranraer. Seasonal information centers are at Castle Douglas, Coldstream, Eyemouth, Galashiels, Gretna Green, Kelso, Kirkcudbright, Langholm, Melrose, Moffat, Newton Stewart, Sanquhar, and Selkirk.

Contacts Dumfries & Galloway Tourist Board. ⊠ *64 Whitesands, Dumfries* ☎ *01387/245550* ⊕ *www.visitscotland.com.* **Visit Scottish Borders.** ⊠ *Murray's Green, Jedburgh* ☎ *01835/863170* ⊕ *www.visitscotland.com.*

THE BORDERS

Although the Borders has many attractions, it's most famous for being the home base for Sir Walter Scott (1771–1832), the early-19th-century poet, novelist, and creator of *Ivanhoe,* who single-handedly transformed Scotland's image from that of a land of brutal savages to one of romantic and stirring deeds and magnificent landscapes. The novels of Scott are not read much nowadays—frankly, some of them are difficult to wade through—but the mystique that he created, the aura of historical romance, has outlasted his books. The ruined abbeys, historical houses, and grand vistas of the Borders provide a perfect backdrop.

A visit to at least one of the region's four great ruined abbeys makes the quintessential Borders experience. The monks in these powerful, long-abandoned religious orders were the first to work the fleeces of their sheep flocks, thus laying the groundwork for what is still the area's main manufacturing industry.

Borders folk take great pride in the region's fame as Scotland's main woolen-goods manufacturing area. Its main towns—Jedburgh, Hawick, Selkirk, Peebles, Kelso, and Melrose—retain an air of prosperity and confidence with their solid stone houses and elegant town squares. Although many of the mills have closed in recent years, the pride in local identity is evident in the fiercely contested Melrose Sevens rugby competition in April and the annual Common Ridings—local events commemorating the time when towns needed to patrol their borders—throughout June and July.

JEDBURGH

50 miles south of Edinburgh, 95 miles southeast of Glasgow, 14 miles northeast of Hawick.

The town of Jedburgh (*-burgh* is always pronounced *burra* in Scots) was for centuries the first major Scottish target of invading English armies. In more peaceful times it developed textile mills, most of which have since languished. The large landscaped area around the town's tourist information center was once a mill but now provides an encampment for the armies of modern tourists. The past still clings to this little town, however. The ruined abbey dominates the skyline, a reminder of the formerly strong governing role of the Borders abbeys.

GETTING HERE AND AROUND

By car from Edinburgh, you can take the A68 (about 45 minutes) or the A7 (about an hour). From Glasgow take the M8, then the A68 direct to Jedburgh (about two hours).

There are fairly good bus connections from all major Scottish cities to Jedburgh. From Edinburgh, direct routes to Melrose take about 2 hours. From Glasgow it takes 3½ hours to reach Melrose. From Melrose it's just 20 minutes to Jedburgh.

The new rail link will run between Edinburgh and Tweedbank, about 15 miles northwest of Jedburgh.

ESSENTIALS

Visitor Information **Jedburgh Visitor Centre.** ⊠ *Abbey Pl.* ☎ *01835/863170* ⊕ *www.visitscotland.com.*

EXPLORING
TOP ATTRACTIONS

FAMILY **Harestanes Countryside Visitor Centre.** Housed in a former farmhouse 4 miles north of Jedburgh, this visitor center portrays life in the Scottish Borders through art exhibitions and natural history displays. Crafts such as woodworking and tile-making are taught here, and finished projects are often on display. There's a gift shop and tearoom, and outside are meandering paths, quiet roads for bike rides, and the biggest children's play area in the Borders. There's plenty for children, including a fascinating puzzle gallery full of sturdy wooden games. It is also on one of the best-known walking routes in the Borders, the St. Cuthbert's Path. ⊠ *Junction of A68 and B6400, 4 miles north of Jedburgh* ☎ *01835/830306* ⊕ *www.scotborders.gov.uk* ⊠ *Free* ☉ *Apr.–Oct., daily 10–5.*

OFF THE
BEATEN
PATH
Hermitage Castle. To appreciate the famous 20-mile ride of Mary, Queen of Scots—she rushed to the side of her wounded lover, the Earl of Bothwell—travel southwest from Jedburgh to this, the most complete remaining example of the bare and grim medieval border castles. Restored in the early 19th century, it was built in the 13th century to guard what was at the time one of the important routes from England into Scotland. Local folklore maintains that a descendant of the original owner and notorious for diabolical excess, the 14th-century Lord Soulis was captured by the local populace, which wrapped him in lead and boiled him in a cauldron—a much better story than the reality, which

is that he died in Dumbarton Jail. ✉ *2 miles west of B6399, about 15 miles south of Hawick, Liddesdale* ☎ *01387/376222* ⊕ *www.historic-scotland.gov.uk/places* 🎟 *£4.50* 🕐 *Apr.–Sept., daily 9:30–5:30; last admission ½ hr before closing.*

Fodor's Choice **Jedburgh Abbey.** The most impressive of the Borders abbeys towers
★ above Jedburgh. Built by David I, king of Scots in the 12th century, the abbey was nearly destroyed by the English earl of Hertford's forces in 1544–45, during the destructive time known as the Rough Wooing. This was English king Henry VIII's (1491–1547) armed attempt to persuade the Scots that it was a good idea to unite the kingdoms by the marriage of his young son to the infant Mary, Queen of Scots (1542–87); the Scots disagreed and sent Mary to France instead. The story is explained in vivid detail at the visitor center , which also has information about the ruins and an audio tour. The arched abbey walls, the nave, and the cloisters still manage to give a sense of the power these buildings represented. ✉ *High St.* ☎ *01835/863925* ⊕ *www.historic-scotland.gov.uk/places* 🎟 *£5.50* 🕐 *Apr.–Sept., daily 9:30–5:30; Oct.–Mar., daily 10–4.*

Mary, Queen of Scots Visitor Centre. This *bastel* (from the French *bastille*) was the fortified town house in which, as the story goes, Mary stayed before embarking on her famous 20-mile ride to Hermitage Castle to visit her wounded lover, the Earl of Bothwell (circa 1535–78). Interesting displays relate the tale and illustrate other episodes in her life, from the rogues who surrounded her to her own reflections on her life. Some of her possessions are on display, as are tapestries and furniture of the period. The ornamental garden surrounding the house has ranks of pear trees leading down to the river. ✉ *Queen St.* ☎ *01835/863331* ⊕ *www.scotborders.gov.uk/museums* 🎟 *Free* 🕐 *Mar.–Nov., Mon.–Sat. 10–4:30, Sun. 10:30–4.*

WORTH NOTING
Jedburgh Castle Jail. This was the site of the Howard Reform Prison, established in 1820. It sits behind the front of the castle that previously stood in the same spot. Today you can inspect prison cells, rooms arranged with period furnishings, and costumed figures. Audiovisual displays recount the history of the Royal Burgh of Jedburgh. It's reputedly one of the most haunted buildings in the area. ✉ *Castlegate* ☎ *01835/864750* ⊕ *www.scotborders.gov.uk/museums* 🎟 *Free* 🕐 *Mar.–Oct., Mon.–Sat. 10–4:30, Sun. 1–4; last admission ½ hr before closing.*

THE COMMON RIDINGS

Borders communities have reestablished their identities through the gatherings known as the Common Ridings. Long ago it was essential that each town be able to defend its area, and this need became formalized in mounted gatherings to "ride the marches," or patrol the boundaries. The Common Ridings, which celebrate this history, possess much more authenticity than the concocted Highland Games so often taken to be the essence of Scotland. You can watch the excitement of clattering hooves and banners proudly displayed, but this is essentially a time for native Borderers.

4

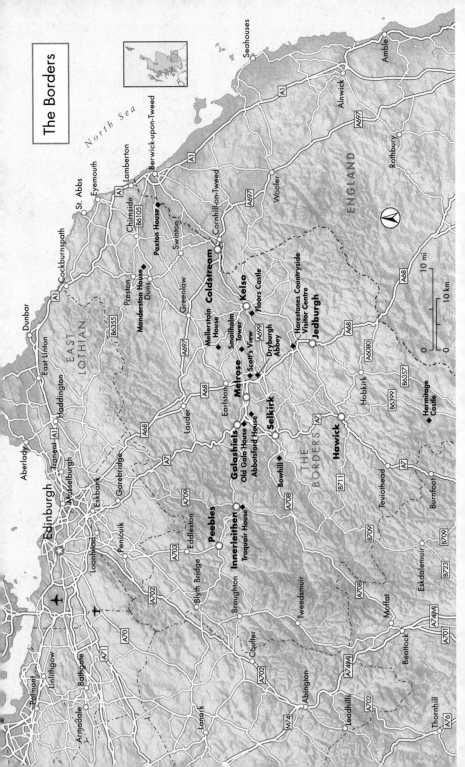

The Borders

North Sea

ENGLAND

EAST LOTHIAN

THE BORDERS

0   10 mi
0   10 km

WHERE TO EAT AND STAY

$$ SPANISH 🍴 **Forresters Restaurant.** The menu at this Spanish joint, above a bar close to the abbey reflects the years that the Scottish owners spent in Spain, as does the bright Mediterranean decor. The simple and authentic dishes have an occasional dramatic touch, like the *carne de chocolate* (literally, chocolate meat), a beef stew with a touch of cocoa. Tapas are generous, and cost between £6 and £8. [$] *Average main: £15* ✉ *23 Castlegate* ☎ *01835/862380* 🌐 *www.theforrestersrestaurantsb.com* 🕒 *Closed Mon.–Wed. July–Sept.; closed Sun.–Thurs. Oct.–Mar. No lunch.*

$ B&B/INN FAMILY 🏨 **Hundalee House.** This 18th-century manor house has richly decorated Victorian-style rooms with nice touches like four-poster beds and cozy fireplaces, and 15 acres of gardens and woods surround the B&B. **Pros:** fantastic views of apple orchards; hearty breakfasts; good children's facilities. **Cons:** farm aromas; far from shops and restaurants; rooms are quite small. [$] *Rooms from: £70* ✉ *Off A68* ✢ *1 mile south of Jedburgh* ☎ *01835/863011* 🌐 *www.accommodation-scotland.org* 🕒 *Closed Christmas, Jan.–Mar.* 🛏 *5 rooms* 🍽 *Breakfast.*

$ B&B/INN 🏨 **Meadhon House.** On a row of medieval buildings, Meadhon House is a charming 17th-century house with a history to match; rooms are bright and clean, with views onto the street or over the large and fragrant garden behind the house. **Pros:** central; pleasant rooms; welcoming atmosphere. **Cons:** rooms on the small side. [$] *Rooms from: £68* ✉ *48 Castlegate* ☎ *01835/862504* 🌐 *www.meadhon.co.uk* 💳 *No credit cards* 🛏 *5 rooms* 🍽 *Breakfast* ☞ *Cash only.*

SHOPPING

Edinburgh Woollen Mill. This shop has shelves bursting with sweaters, kilts, tartan knitwear, and scarves. It's a good place to stock up on gifts. ✉ *Bankend North, Edinburgh Rd.* ☎ *01835/864046* 🌐 *www.ewm.co.uk.*

Scottish Tradition. The knitwear and hats here are of the finest quality. Scottish Tradition also sells beautiful cashmere items, as well as Scottish tartan goods. ✉ *New Bongate Mill* ☎ *01835/863306.*

SPORTS AND OUTDOORS

Christopher Rainbow Tandem & Bike Hire. This shop rents tandem bikes, mountain bikes, and touring bikes. The location, between Jedburgh and Ancrum, makes it ideal for exploring the four abbeys, as well as the Tweed Cycleway and Borderloop Cycleway. The company provides tour itineraries, as well as extra services such as luggage forwarding. ✉ *8 Timpendean Cottages* ✢ *Between Jedburgh and Ancrum* ☎ *01835/830326* 🌐 *www.chrisrainbow.net.*

KELSO

12 miles northeast of Jedburgh.

One of the most charming Borders burghs, Kelso is often described as having a Continental flavor—some people think its broad, paved square makes it resemble a Belgian market town. The community has some fine examples of Georgian and Victorian Scots town architecture.

GETTING HERE AND AROUND

There are direct bus routes from Jedburgh to Kelso. Edinburgh has direct buses to Jedburgh; buses from Glasgow aren't direct. Your best option is to travel by car. From Jedburgh to Kelso take the A698, which is 12 miles, or about 20 minutes. Alternatively, the A699 is a scenic half-hour drive.

ESSENTIALS

Visitor Information Kelso Tourist Information Centre. ⊠ *Town House, The Square* ☎ *01573/228055* ⊕ *www.kelso.bordernet.co.uk.*

EXPLORING

Fodor's Choice ★ **Floors Castle.** The palatial Floors Castle, the largest inhabited castle in Scotland, is an architectural extravagance bristling with pepper-mill turrets. Not so much a castle as the ancestral seat of a wealthy and powerful landowning family, the Roxburghes, it stands on the "floors," or flat terrain, on the banks of the River Tweed. The enormous home was built in 1721 by William Adam (1689–1748) and modified by William Playfair (1789–1857), who added the turrets and towers in the 1840s. The interior rooms are crowded with valuable furniture, paintings, porcelain, and a strangely eerie circular room full of stuffed birds. Each room has a knowledgeable guide at the ready. The surrounding 56,000-acre estate is home to more than 40 farms. ⊠ *A6089* ☎ *01573/223333* ⊕ *www.floorscastle.com* ☒ *Grounds £4.50, castle and grounds £8.50* ☉ *May.–Sept., daily 10:30–5; Oct., daily 10:30-3:30. Last admission 1 hr before closing.*

Kelso Abbey. The least intact ruin of the four great abbeys, Kelso Abbey is just a bleak fragment of what was once the largest of the group. It was here in 1460 that the nine-year-old James III was crowned king of Scotland. On a main invasion route, the abbey was burned three times in the 1540s alone, on the last occasion by the English Earl of Hertford's forces in 1545, when the 100 men and 12 monks of the garrison were butchered and the structure all but destroyed. ⊠ *Bridge St.* ☎ *0131/668–8800* ☒ *Free* ☉ *Apr.–Dec., daily 24 hrs.*

Mellerstain House. One fine example of the Borders area's ornate country homes is Mellerstain House. Begun in the 1720s, it was finished in the 1770s by Robert Adam (1728–92) and is considered one of his finest creations. Sumptuous plasterwork covers almost all interior surfaces, and there are outstanding examples of 18th-century furnishings, porcelain and china, and paintings and embroidery. The beautiful terraced gardens (open an hour before the house itself) are as renowned as the house. ⊠ *Off A6089, 7 miles northwest of Kelso, Gordon* ☎ *01573/410225* ⊕ *www.mellerstain.com* ☒ *Gardens £5, house and gardens £8.50* ☉ *May–Sept., Fri.–Mon. 12:30–5; last admission 45 mins before closing.*

Fodor's Choice ★ **Smailholm Tower.** The characteristic Borders structure Smailholm Tower stands uncompromisingly on top of a barren, rocky ridge in the hills south of Mellerstain. The 16th-century peel was built solely for defense, and its unadorned stones contrast with the luxury of Mellerstain House. If you let your imagination wander in this windy spot, you can almost see the flapping pennants and rising dust of an advancing raiding party and hear the anxious securing of doors and bolts. Sir Walter Scott found this spot inspiring. His grandfather lived nearby, and the young Scott visited the tower often during his childhood. A museum displays costumed figures and tapestries relating to Scott's folk ballads. A free audio tour can be downloaded from the website. ✉ *Off B6404, 4½ miles south of Mellerstain House* ☎ *01573/460365* 🌐 *www.historic-scotland.gov.uk* 🎫 *£4.50* ⏲ *Apr.–Sept., daily 9:30–5:30; last admission at 5.*

WHERE TO EAT

$$ BRITISH 🍴 **Cobbles Inn.** A lively bar and restaurant just off the town square, Cobbles is much favored by locals. The bar menu is a good value serving burgers, salads, sandwiches, and a changing pasta dish or two as well as "Glaswegian nachos" (potato skins with sauces). Daily specials include a catch of the day, and the seafood chowder is a regular menu feature. Desserts are well made and come in generous portions. Reservations are advised for dinner, especially on weekends, when the restaurant closes at 8. [$] *Average main: £16* ✉ *7 Bowmont St.* ☎ *01573/223548* 🌐 *www.thecobbleskelso.co.uk.*

$ MEDITERRANEAN 🍴 **Oscar's Wine Bar and Restaurant.** Winner of numerous culinary and entrepreneurial awards, this establishment is a local favorite. The space is well lit, with bright yellow walls, contemporary furniture, and the work of local artists lining the walls. In season, try the smoked haddock crumble (as starter or main). The homemade banoffee pie (with banana, toffee, and cream) is to die for. The staff is attentive and well informed. [$] *Average main: £14* ✉ *35–37 Horsemarket* ☎ *01573/224008* 🌐 *www.oscars-kelso.com* ⏲ *Closed Tues. and Sun.*

WHERE TO STAY

$$ B&B/INN 🏨 **Edenwater House.** This handsome stone house overlooking Edenwater, a trout stream that runs into the River Tweed, has three well-appointed guest rooms, which afford superb views of the river and two of the Cheviot hills. **Pros:** excellent food; romantic atmosphere; peaceful surroundings. **Cons:** not good for families with small children; far from urban amenities. [$] *Rooms from: £120* ✉ *Off B6461, Ednam* ☎ *01573/224070* 🌐 *www.edenwaterhouse.co.uk* ⏲ *Restaurant closed Sun.–Wed.* 🛏 *3 rooms* 🍽 *Breakfast* ☞ *Reservations essential.*

$$ HOTEL Fodor's Choice ★ 🏨 **Ednam House Hotel.** People return again and again to this large, stately hotel on the banks of the River Tweed, close to Kelso's grand abbey and sprawling market square. **Pros:** great outdoor activities; atmospheric lobby; impressive restaurant. **Cons:** some rooms need a makeover. [$] *Rooms from: £158* ✉ *Bridge St.* ☎ *01573/224168* 🌐 *www.ednamhouse.com* ⏲ *Closed late Dec.–early Jan.* 🛏 *32 rooms* 🍽 *Breakfast.*

SHOPPING

John Moody. This shop sells soft cashmere and lambs wool sweaters, along with purses, scarves, and gloves. It's a real treat for knitwear fanatics, or those simply looking for something Scottish to keep them warm. ✉ *38 The Square* ☎ *01573/224400.*

COLDSTREAM

9 miles east of Kelso.

Three miles west of Coldstream, the England–Scotland border comes down from the hills and runs beside the Tweed for the rest of its journey to the sea. Coldstream itself is still a small town, with a mix of attractive 18th- and 19th-century buildings. Like Gretna Green, this was once a place where runaway couples from the south could come to get married in a time when the marriage laws of Scotland were more lenient than those of England. A plaque on the former bridge tollhouse recalls this fact.

The town is also celebrated in military history: in 1659 General Monck raised a regiment of foot guards here on behalf of his exiled monarch, Charles II of England (1630–85). Known as the Coldstream Guards, the successors to this regiment have become an elite corps in the British army.

GETTING HERE AND AROUND

There is no direct bus service from Jedburgh or Kelso. Your best bet is to drive. From Jedburgh, take the A68/A698/A697 (30 minutes). From Kelso, take the A698 (15 minutes).

ESSENTIALS

Visitor Information Coldstream Tourist Information Centre. ⊠ *76 High St.* ☎ *01890/882607* ⊕ *www.visitscotland.com.*

EXPLORING

FAMILY **Coldstream Museum.** In the former headquarters of the Coldstream Guards, the Coldstream Museum examines the history of the regiment and the community. You can see 18th-century marriage contracts, pieces of masonry from the village's lost medieval convent, weapons, uniforms, and photographs. A children's play area has toys and costumes, including a child-size guard uniform and a bearskin hat made by the regimental tailor. ⊠ *12 Market Sq.* ☎ *01890/882630* ⊕ *www.scotborders.gov.uk* ⊡ *Free* ⊙ *Mar.–Sept., Mon.–Sat. 10–4, Sun. 2–4; Oct., Mon.–Sat. 1–4.*

FAMILY **Hirsel and Homestead Museum.** This complex of farmyard buildings houses a museum and crafts center where the visitor can see artisans at work and buy their products. With extensive grounds—superb rhododendrons bloom here in late spring—this is a lovely spot for walkers, cyclists, and bird-watchers, whether they prefer a stroll through Dundock Wood or around the lake. The estate is open throughout the year. ⊠ *The Hirsel, A697* ☎ *01555/851536* ⊕ *www.dandaestates.co.uk* ⊡ *Free; £2.50 per car* ⊙ *Mar.–Oct., weekdays 10–5, weekends noon–5.*

OFF THE BEATEN PATH

Manderston House. Rebuilt by Sir James Miller, whose family made its fortune selling herring to Russia, Manderston is a masterful example of the no-expense-spared Edwardian country house. Designed by John Kinross, a young local architect, the original Georgian house from the 1790s was completely renovated between 1903 and 1905. The silver-plated staircase was modeled after the one in the Petit Trianon, at Versailles. Look for the collection of late-19th- and early-20th-century cookie tins. There's much to see downstairs in the kitchens, and outside, among a cluster of other buildings, is the octagonal, one-of-a-kind marble dairy where lunch, dinner, or afternoon tea can be arranged for groups. The 56-acre grounds are a combination of formal and wild gardens. ⌂ *Duns Rd., Duns ⚓ From Coldstream take the A6112 to Duns then the A 6105 east for 2 miles* ☎ *01361/882636* ⊕ *www.manderston. co.uk* ✉ *Grounds £6, house and grounds £10* ☉ *House: May–Sept., Thurs. and Sun. 1:30–5; last entry at 4:15. Gardens: May–Sept., Thurs. and Sun. 11:30–dusk.*

OFF THE BEATEN PATH

Paxton House. Stately Paxton House is a comely Palladian mansion designed in 1758 by James and John Adam, with interiors by their brother Robert. There's Chippendale and Trotter furniture, and the splendid Regency picture gallery has a magnificent collection of paintings. Access is by guided tour only. The garden is delightful, with a squirrel hide and a restored boathouse containing a museum of salmon fishing. The adjacent crafts shop and tearoom are open April to October, daily 9 to 5. There's also croquet in the gardens. The house is framed in 80 acres of woodland and riverside trails. ⌂ *B6461, Paxton ⚓ 15 miles northeast of Coldstream off the A698* ☎ *01289/386291* ⊕ *www. paxtonhouse.co.uk* ✉ *Grounds £4, house and grounds £6.84* ☉ *Mar.– Nov., daily 11–5. Guided tours at 11, 11:45, 12:30, 1:15, 2, and 3:30.*

WHERE TO EAT

$$

MODERN BRITISH

✕ **Wheatsheaf Hotel and Restaurant.** The Wheatsheaf is a dining establishment that also provides accommodations—an important distinction, according to the owner. You can enjoy an outstanding meal in the black-beamed bar, but the real treat is the formal restaurant. The starters are surprising and imaginative, like confit pork belly or the crab beignet, and the main dishes often combine the familiar with the unusual: loin of rabbit with carrot and cumin mousse, for example. Extend your stay in one of the 10 country-style bedrooms; room prices include breakfast. The inn is in Swinton, 6 miles north of Coldstream. Ⓢ *Average main: £19* ⌂ *Main St., Swinton* ☎ *01890/860257* ⊕ *www.wheatsheaf-swinton.co.uk* ☉ *Closed 1st 2 wks of Jan. No lunch* ⚲ *Reservations essential.*

MELROSE

24 miles west of Coldstream, 4 miles southeast of Galashiels.

Though it's small, there is nevertheless a bustle about Melrose, the perfect example of a prosperous Scottish market town and one of the loveliest in the Borders. It's set round a square lined with 18th- and 19th-century buildings housing myriad small shops and cafés. Despite its proximity to the much larger Galashiels, Melrose has rejected industrialization. You'll likely hear local residents greet each other by first name in the square.

GETTING HERE AND AROUND

Buses do go to Melrose. However, driving is the easiest, fastest, and most efficient way to travel here. From Coldstream, take the A699 (40 minutes). From Galashiels, take the A6091 (10 minutes).

ESSENTIALS

Visitor Information Melrose Tourist Information Centre. ⌂ *Priorwood Garden, Abbey St.* ☎ *01896/822283* ⊕ *www.visitscotland.com.*

EXPLORING
TOP ATTRACTIONS

Fodor'sChoice **Abbotsford House.** In this great house overlooking the Tweed, Sir Walter
★   Scott lived, worked, and received the great and the good in luxurious
salons. In 1811, the writer bought a farm on this site named Cartley-
hole, which was a euphemism for the real name, Clartyhole (*clarty* is
Scots for "muddy" or "dirty"). The name was surely not romantic
enough for Scott, who renamed the property after a ford in the nearby
Tweed used by the abbot of Melrose. Scott eventually had the house
entirely rebuilt in the Scottish baronial style. It was, of course, an expensive project, and Scott wrote feverishly to keep his creditors at bay. John
Ruskin, the art critic, disapproved, calling it an "incongruous pile," but
most contemporary visitors find it fascinating, particularly because of
its expansive views and delightful gardens.

The interior, reopened after extensive renovations in 2013, now includes
new areas of the house. A free audio tour guides you around the salon,
the wonderful circular study, and the library with its 9,000 leather-
bound volumes. If anyone redefined Scotland and woke the English
mind to its beauty and its past, albeit heavily romanticized, it was Scott.
The newly built visitor center houses displays about Scott's life, a gift
shop, and an upstairs restaurant serving lunch. To get here, take the
A6091 from Melrose and follow the signs for Abbotsford. ■TIP➔ **You
can also stay on the estate, in the Hope Scott Wing (£120).** ⊠ *B6360,
Galashiels ✛ Between Melrose and Tweedbank* ☎ *01896/752043*
⊕ *www.scottsabbotsford.co.uk* ✆ *House and gardens £8.75; gardens
only £3.50* ⊙ *Mar.,daily 10-4; Apr.–Sept., daily 10–5; Oct. and Nov.,
daily 10–4. Last admission 1 hr before closing.*

Fodor'sChoice **Melrose Abbey.** Just off Melrose's town square sit the ruins of Melrose
★   Abbey, one of the four Borders abbeys. "If thou would'st view fair Melrose aright, go visit it in the pale moonlight," wrote Scott in *The Lay
of the Last Minstrel,* and so many of his fans took the advice literally
that a sleepless custodian begged him to rewrite the lines. Today the
abbey is still impressive: a red-sandstone shell with slender windows,
delicate tracery, and carved capitals, all carefully maintained. Among
the carvings high on the roof is one of a bagpipe-playing pig. An audio
tour is included in the admission price. The heart of Robert the Bruce
is rumored to be buried here. ⊠ *Abbey St.* ☎ *01896/822562* ⊕ *www.
historic-scotland.gov.uk* ✆ *£5.50* ⊙ *Apr.–Sept., daily 9:30–5:30; Oct.–
Mar., daily 9:30–4:30; last admission ½ hr before closing.*

WORTH NOTING

Dryburgh Abbey. The final resting place of Sir Walter Scott and his wife,
and the most peaceful and secluded of the Borders abbeys, the "gentle
ruins" of Dryburgh Abbey sit on parkland in a loop of the Tweed. The
abbey, founded in 1150, suffered from English raids until, like Melrose, it
was abandoned in 1544. The style is transitional, a mingling of rounded
Romanesque and pointed early English. The north transept, where the
Haig and Scott families lie buried, is lofty and pillared, and once formed
part of the abbey church. ⊠ *St. Boswell's, B6404* ☎ *01835/822381*
⊕ *www.historic-scotland.gov.uk/places* ✆ *£5.50* ⊙ *Apr.–Sept., daily
9:30–5:30; Oct.–Mar., daily 10–4; last admission ½ hr before closing.*

The World of Sir Walter Scott

Sir Walter Scott (1771–1832) was probably Scottish tourism's best propagandist. Thanks to his fervid "Romantik" imagination, his long narrative poems—such as "The Lady of the Lake"—and a long string of historical novels, including *Ivanhoe, Waverley, Rob Roy,*and *The Heart of Midlothian,* the world fell in love with the image of heroic Scotland. Scott wrote of Scotland as a place of Highland wilderness and clan romance, shaping outsiders' perceptions of Scotland in a way that to an extent survives even today.

Scott was born in College Wynd, Edinburgh. A lawyer by training, he was an assiduous collector of old ballads and tales. "The Lay of the Last Minstrel," a romantic poem published in 1805, brought him fame. In 1811 Scott bought the house that was to become Abbotsford, his Borders mansion near Melrose.

Scott started on his series of Waverley novels in 1814, at first anonymously, and by 1820 had produced *Waverley, Guy Mannering, The Antiquary, Tales of My Landlord,* and *Rob Roy.* Between 1820 and 1825 there followed an additional 11 titles, including *Ivanhoe*

and *The Pirate.* Many of his verse narratives and novels had real-life settings, in particular the Trossachs, northwest of Stirling, an area that rapidly became, and still remains, popular with visitors.

Apart from his writing, Scott is also remembered for rediscovering the Honours of Scotland—the crown, scepter, and sword of state of the Scottish monarchs—in 1819. These symbols had languished at the bottom of a chest in Edinburgh Castle since 1707, when Scotland lost its independence. Today they're on display in the castle.

SCOTT SIGHTS

Abbotsford, Scott's home near Melrose in the Borders, is well worth a visit. Other houses associated with Scott can be seen in Edinburgh: 25 George Square, which was his father's house, and 39 Castle Street, where he lived from 1801 to 1826. The site of his birthplace, in College Wynd, is marked with a plaque. The most obvious structure associated with Scott in Edinburgh is the Scott Monument on Princes Street, which looks like a Gothic rocket ship with a statue of Scott and his pet dog as passengers.

Priorwood and Harmony Gardens. The National Trust for Scotland's Priorwood Gardens, next to Melrose Abbey, specializes in flowers for drying, and dried flowers are on sale in the shop. Next to the gardens is an orchard with some old apple varieties. The walled Harmony Garden, belonging to the lovely Georgian house at its heart, sits nearby opposite the abbey. It is also included in the entry price. ⊠ *Abbey St.* ☎ *0844/493–2257* ⊕ *www.nts.org.uk* ✉ *£3.50* ⊙ *Mar.–Oct., Mon.–Sat. 10–5, Sun. 1–5; Nov. and Dec., Mon.–Sat. 10–4.*

Scott's View. This is possibly the most photographed rural view in the south of Scotland. (It's almost as iconic as Eilean Donan Castle, far to the north.) The sinuous curve of the River Tweed and the gentle landscape unfolding to the triple peaks of the Eildons and then rolling out into the shadows beyond are certainly worth seeking out. ✉ *B6356, 3 miles north of Dryburgh, Dryburgh.*

Trimontium Roman Heritage Centre. Here you'll find such artifacts as tools, weapons, and armor retrieved from the largest Roman settlement in Scotland, which was at nearby Newstead. A blacksmith's shop, several examples of pottery, and scale models of the fort are also on display. A guided four-hour walk along the 5-mile trail to the site departs at 1:30 on Thursday (also on Tuesday in July and August). The cost is £3. ✉ *The Ormiston, Market Sq.* ☎ *01896/822651* ⊕ *www.trimontium.org. uk* ⌗ *£2* ☉ *Apr.–Oct., daily 10:30–4:30.*

WHERE TO EAT AND STAY

$$

ECLECTIC

✕ **Hergés on the Loch.** A wall of windows allows you to contemplate swans and ducks as they float serenely across Gunknowe Loch in the village of Tweedbank. This light and airy place has views of the lake from nearly every table, and if the weather allows, you can dine on the terrace. The elegant but understated food, well presented and served in generous portions, includes familiar dishes like steak-and-ale pie and oat-and-mustard-crusted loin of venison cooked pink and melt-in-your-mouth tender. The restaurant is named after the creator of Tintin, the beloved cartoon character whose statue oversees the drinkers in the comfortable bar area. Ⓢ *Average main: £15* ✉ *Tweedbank Dr., Tweedbank* ☎ *01896/759909* ⊕ *www.hergesontheloch.com.*

$$

BRITISH

Fodor's Choice

★

✕ **Hoebridge Inn.** Whitewashed walls, oak-beamed ceilings, and an open fire welcome you into this converted 19th-century bobbin mill. The cuisine is a blend of British and Mediterranean styles with occasional Asian influences. You might have lamb served with rosemary mashed potatoes and red-currant sauce or roast chicken breast with leeks and a grilled peach. Rabbit and guinea fowl also appear regularly on the menu. The inn lies in Gattonside, Melrose's across-the-river neighbor, but a 2-mile drive is required to cross to the other side; you can reach the inn more easily via a footbridge. Ⓢ *Average main: £17* ✉ *B6360, Gattonside* ☎ *01896/823082* ⊕ *www.thehoebridge.com* ☉ *Closed Sun. and Mon.* ⌓ *Reservations essential.*

$$

HOTEL

▦ **Burts Hotel.** This charming whitewashed building dating from the 18th century in the center of Melrose has individually decorated and different rooms filled with floral pastels. **Pros:** walking distance to restaurants and pubs; good menu in restaurant. **Cons:** some rooms are tiny; slightly overpriced for some rooms. Ⓢ *Rooms from: £140* ✉ *Market Sq.* ☎ *01896/822285* ⊕ *www.burtshotel.co.uk* ⇝ *20 rooms* ⦿ *Breakfast.*

$$

HOTEL

▦ **Dryburgh Abbey Hotel.** Mature woodlands and verdant lawns surround this imposing, 19th-century mansion, which is adjacent to the abbey ruins on a sweeping bend of the River Tweed. **Pros:** beautiful grounds; romantic setting. **Cons:** some rooms need to be freshened up; service can be on the slow side. Ⓢ *Rooms from: £115* ✉ *Off B6404, St. Boswells* ☎ *01835/822261* ⊕ *www.dryburgh.co.uk* ⇝ *36 rooms, 2 suites* ⦿ *Breakfast.*

NIGHTLIFE AND PERFORMING ARTS

Wynd Theatre. Concerts of folk, blues, jazz, or classical music are on the roster at the Wynd Theatre, which also hosts theatrical events and film screenings. ⊠ *3 Buccleuch St.* ☎ *01896/820028.*

SHOPPING

Abbey Mill. Take a break from sightseeing at Abbey Mill, where you'll find handwoven knitwear as well as homemade jams and fudge. There's also a wee tearoom. ⊠ *Annay Rd.* ☎ *01896/822138.*

GALASHIELS

5 miles northwest of Melrose.

A busy gray-stone Borders town, Galashiels is still active with textile mills and knitwear factories.

GETTING HERE AND AROUND

There is regular bus service from Melrose to Galashiels (20 minutes). You can also drive; from Melrose, take the B6374 or the A6091 (both 10 minutes).

EXPLORING

Old Gala House. Dating from 1583, Old Gala House is the former home of the lairds (landed proprietors) of Galashiels. It now serves as a museum with displays on the history of the building and the town, as well as a contemporary art gallery. You can trace your family history at a comprehensive genealogy facility. The house is a short walk from the town center. ⊠ *Scott Crescent* ☎ *01896/752611* ⊕ *www.galashiels. bordernet.co.uk/oldgalahouse* ☑ *Free* ⊙ *Apr.–Sept., Tues.–Sat. 10–4; July and Aug., Mon.–Sat. 10–4, Sun. 2–4; Oct., Tues.–Sat. 1–4.*

SELKIRK

6 miles southwest of Galashiels, 11 miles north of Hawick.

Selkirk is a hilly outpost with a smattering of antiques shops and an assortment of bakers selling Selkirk bannock (fruited sweet bread) and other cakes. It is the site of one of Scotland's iconic battles, Flodden Field, commemorated here with a statue in the town. Sir Walter Scott was sheriff (judge) of Selkirkshire from 1800 until his death in 1832, and his statue stands in Market Place. Selkirk is also near Bowhill, a stately home.

The town claims its Common Riding is the largest mounted gathering anywhere in Europe. More than 400 riders take part in the event in June. It's also the oldest Borders festival, with roots back to the Battle of Flodden in 1513.

GETTING HERE AND AROUND

If you're driving, take the A7 south to Galashiels. The scenic journey is less than 7 miles and takes around 10 minutes. First Edinburgh Bus offers a regular service between Galashiels and Selkirk.

ESSENTIALS

Visitor Information Selkirk Visitor Information Centre. ⊠ *Halliwell's House, Market Pl.* ☎ *01750/20054* ⊕ *www.visitscotland.com.*

EXPLORING
TOP ATTRACTIONS

Bowhill. Home of the Duke of Buccleuch, Bowhill dates from the 19th century and houses an outstanding collection of works by Gainsborough, Van Dyck, Canaletto, Reynolds, and Raeburn, as well as porcelain and period furniture. Access is by guided tour on specific days in summer. There is an excellent adventure playground for the kids and a 57-mile country ride for those who prefer horseback riding. A local stable hires out horses. ⊠ *Off A708, 3 miles west of Selkirk* ☎ *01750/22204* ⊕ *www.bowhill.org* ☞ *Grounds £4, house and grounds £10* ⊙ *Grounds Apr.–Sept., daily 10–5. House July–Sept. on specific dates by guided tour only.*

Sir Walter Scott's Courtroom. The historic courtroom, where Sir Walter Scott presided as sheriff from 1804 to 1832, contains a display examining his life, writings, and time on the bench. It uses models to recreate the atmosphere of a 19th-century Scottish court and includes an audiovisual presentation. His statue overlooks the comings and goings outside the court. ⊠ *Market Sq.* ☎ *01750/720761* ⊕ *www.scotborders. gov.uk* ☞ *Free* ⊙ *Mar., Apr., and Sept., weekdays 10–4, Sat. 11–3; May–Aug., Mon.–Sun. 11–3; Oct., Mon.–Sat. noon–3.*

Waverly Mill, Lochcarron of Scotland. You can take an informative guided tour of this world-renowned mill and also purchase some of the best woolen goods on offer, from knitwear to tartans and tweeds. The shop also sells Scottish jewelry. ⊠ *Dinsdale Rd.* ☎ *01750/726100* ⊕ *www. lochcarron.com* ⊙ *Tours Mon.–Thurs. at 10:30, 11:30, 1:30, and 2:30; visitor center Mon.–Sat. 9–5, Sun.11–4.*

WORTH NOTING

Halliwell's House Museum. Tucked off the main square, Halliwell's House Museum was once an ironmonger's shop, which is now re-created downstairs. Upstairs, an exhibit tells the town's story, illustrates the working lives of its inhabitants, and provides useful background information on the Common Ridings. ⊠ *Halliwell's Close, Market Pl.* ☎ *01750/20096* ⊕ *www.scotborders.gov.uk* ☞ *Free* ⊙ *Apr.–Oct., Mon.–Sat. 11–4, Sun. noon–3.*

Philiphaugh Salmon Centre. The site of a famous battle in 1645 in which the Scottish Covenanters drove off the pro-English armies under the Earl of Montrose, the Philiphaugh Salmon Centre is now devoted to more peaceful pursuits. Its salmon-viewing platforms and underwater cameras allow you to follow the life cycle of the salmon. There are also country walks and cycling routes to follow, and the Waterwheel Tea Room is open all year. A self-guided audio tour of the battlefield is available through the website. ⊠ *A708* ✛ *1 mile outside Selkirk on the A708* ☎ *01750/21766* ⊕ *www.salmonviewingcentre.com* ☞ *Free* ⊙ *Daily 10–4.*

WHERE TO EAT AND STAY

$ ✕ **Buon Gusto Ristorante.** A cozy, authentic Italian restaurant in the cen-
ITALIAN   ter of Selkirk, Buon Gusto has taken the tapas theme for its excellent lunch menu of Italian small dishes—£7.50 for two or £10.50 for three. The dinner menu has a selection of antipasti and a changing

list of homemade pasta. It's a welcome addition to Selkirk's dining scene. [$] *Average main: £10* ✉ *73 High St.* ☎ *01750/778174* 🌐 *www.buongustoristorante.co.uk* 🕒 *Closed Mon. and Tues.*

$$ HOTEL 🏨 **Best Western Philipburn House Hotel.** West of Selkirk, this alpine-style hotel enjoys a lovely setting among the woods and hills. **Pros:** pleasant rural setting; bright rooms; on-site parking. **Cons:** no elevator; restaurant closes rather early. [$] *Rooms from: £150* ✉ *Linglie Rd.* ☎ *01750/720747* 🌐 *www.bw-philipburnhousehotel.co.uk* 🛏 *12 rooms, 4 lodges* 🍴 *Breakfast.*

HAWICK

10 miles south of Selkirk, 14 miles southwest of Jedburgh.

Hawick (pronounced *hoyk*) is a busy town at the center of the region's textile industry, commemorated in the interesting Borders Textile Towerhouse. The Victorian buildings along its High Street recall the town's heyday. The largest community in the Borders, it's a good place to buy the delicate cashmere and wool goods that made the region famous. Hawick's Common Riding festival, held each June, draws onlookers from all over Scotland.

GETTING HERE AND AROUND

Driving here from Selkirk or Jedburgh is no trouble—it's a straight shot on major roads. There is also bus service from many of the other Borders towns.

ESSENTIALS

Visitor Information **Hawick Visitor Centre.** ✉ *Kirkstyle* ☎ *01450/373993* 🌐 *www.visitscotland.com.*

EXPLORING

FAMILY **Borders Textile Towerhouse.** In the former Drumlanrig Tower, this museum includes a good exhibition about the textile industry, once the lifeblood of the Borders. Plenty of interactive elements make it interesting for children as well. One room commemorates the demonstrations by textile workers who were demanding the right to vote in the 1880s. On the upper floor are up-to-the-minute fabrics that define the 21st century. Check out the shop, too. ✉ *1 Tower Knowe* ☎ *01450/377615* 🎟 *Free* 🕒 *Apr.–Oct., Mon.–Sat.10–4:30, Sun. noon–3; Nov.–Mar., Mon. and Wed.–Sat. 10–4.*

WHERE TO EAT

$ CAFÉ Fodor's Choice ★ 🍴 **Damascus Drum.** This lovely café and bookshop was established as a place to talk, tell stories, and buy beautiful Oriental rugs. Decorated in muted colors, the café is named for a traditional folktale. The menu includes Middle Eastern dishes alongside burgers. [$] *Average main: £8* ✉ *2 Silver St.* ☎ *07707/856123* 🌐 *www.damascusdrum.co.uk* 🕒 *No dinner.*

4

SHOPPING

Hawick Factory Visitor Centre. This is a good place to see knitwear in the making—literally. In the shop you can buy knitwear and cashmere goods for discounted prices. ⊠ *Trinity Mills, Duke St.* ☎ *01450/372510* ⊕ *www.hawico.com.*

White of Hawick. There's a room here exclusively dedicated to cashmere, and it's a good place to stock up on warm outerwear. White of Hawick also sells an extensive range of lambswool and knitted garments. ⊠ *Victoria Rd.* ☎ *01450/373206.*

INNERLEITHEN

17 miles northwest of Hawick.

Innerleithen is one of the larger Borders towns; you'll feel that you've entered a hub of activity when you arrive. It's also dramatically beautiful. Surrounded by hills and glens, the town is where the Tweed and Leithen Rivers join, then separate. Historically, Innerleithen dates back to pre-Roman times, and there are artifacts all around for you to see. Once a booming industrialized town of wool mills, today it's a great destination for outdoor activities including hiking, biking, and fly-fishing.

GETTING HERE AND AROUND

To drive to Innerleithen, take the A7 north from Hawick and then the A707 northwest from Selkirk. There are no trains between the two towns.

EXPLORING

FAMILY **Robert Smail's Printing Works.** Try your hand at printing the way it used to be done: painstakingly setting each letter by hand. Robert Smail's print shop, founded more than a century ago to produce materials for nearby factories, boat tickets, theater posters, and the local newspaper, is still a working print shop as well as a museum. Two great waterwheels once powered the presses, and they are still running. The guided tour, which includes making your own bookmark, takes 90 minutes. ⊠ *7–9 High St.* ☎ *01896/830206* ⊕ *www.nts.org.uk/Visits* ⊠ *£6.50* ☺ *Apr.–Oct., Fri.–Mon. noon–5, Sun. 1–5; last admission at 4:15.*

Fodor's Choice **Traquair House.** Said to be the oldest continually occupied home in Scotland, Traquair House has secret stairways and passages, a library with more than 3,000 books, and a bed said to be used by Mary, Queen of Scots, in 1566. You can walk freely through the rooms, and there is an explanatory leaflet in each as well as helpful guides hovering in the corridors. The top floor of the house is an interesting small museum. Outside is a reasonably scary maze, an adventure playground, and some lovely woodland walks as well as pigs, goats, and chickens. The 18th-century brew house still makes highly recommended ale. There is a café on the grounds near the beautiful walled garden. The Traquair Fair in August is the nearest you are likely to get to a medieval fair, and well worth the visit. You may even spend the night, if you wish. ⊠ *B709* ✛ *From the A70 some 6 miles south of Peebles, take the B709 for 7 miles; the car entrance into the house is in the village* ☎ *01896/830323* ⊕ *www.traquair.co.uk* ⊠ *Grounds £4, house* *and grounds £8.60* 🕐 *Apr.–Sept., daily 11–5; Oct., daily 11–4; Nov., weekends 11–3; last admission ½ hr before closing.*

WHERE TO STAY

$$$ B&B/INN 🏨 **Traquair House.** Staying in one of the guest rooms in the 12th-century wing of Traquair House is to experience a slice of Scottish history. **Pros:** stunning grounds; spacious rooms; great breakfast. **Cons:** nearly 2 miles to restaurants and shops; rooms fill up quickly in summer. [$] *Rooms from: £190* ✉ *B709* ☎ *01896/830323* 🌐 *www.traquair.co.uk* 🛏 *3 rooms* 🍴 *Breakfast.*

$$ B&B/INN 🏨 **Windlestraw Lodge.** This elegant bed-and-breakfast occupies a grand country home surrounded by extensive gardens. **Pros:** beautifully designed rooms; excellent dining. **Cons:** a bit expensive for what you get. [$] *Rooms from: £160* ✉ *9 Galashiels Rd., Walkerburn* ✥ *On the A72 between Galashiels and Innerleithen* ☎ *01896/870636* 🌐 *www.windlestraw.co.uk* 🛏 *5 rooms* 🍴 *Breakfast.*

4

PEEBLES

6 miles west of Innerleithen.

Thanks to its excellent though pricey shopping, Peebles gives the impression of catering primarily to leisured country gentlefolk. Architecturally, the town is nothing out of the ordinary, just a very pleasant burgh. Don't miss the splendid dolphins ornamenting the bridge crossing the River Tweed.

GETTING HERE AND AROUND

Because of its size and location, direct buses run from both Edinburgh and Glasgow to Peebles. There are also buses here from Innerleithen, though driving from here is more direct. (Take the A72; it's about a 10-minute drive.)

ESSENTIALS

Visitor Information Peebles Visitor Information Centre. ✉ *23 High St.* ☎ *01721/728095* 🌐 *www.visitscotland.com.*

EXPLORING

Neidpath Castle. A 15-minute walk upstream along the banks of the Tweed, Neidpath Castle perches artistically above a bend in the river. It comes into view as you approach through the tall trees. The castle is a medieval structure remodeled in the 17th century, with dungeons hewn from solid rock. You can return on the opposite riverbank after crossing an old, finely skewed railroad viaduct. Call ahead to arrange visits to the interior. ✉ *Off A72* ☎ *01875/870201* 🌐 *www.neidpathcastle.com* 🎟 *£3* 🕐 *By appointment only.*

Peebles War Memorial. The exotic, almost Moorish mosaics of the Peebles War Memorial are unique in Scotland, although most towns have a memorial to honor those killed in service. It's a remarkable tribute to the 225 Peebleans killed in World War II. ✉ *Chambers Quadrangle, High St.*

WHERE TO EAT

$ ✕ **Adam Room.** With a minstrels' gallery, crystal chandeliers, and tall
BRITISH windows with views over the Tweed, the dining room at the Tontine
FAMILY Hotel has a grand feel. It's a bit surprising, therefore, that it also serves
good home cooking at very reasonable prices. Local produce is used for
all the dishes, including the appetizing steak pie and the lamb rump, and
for the most part it remains within the traditional mold, though with
creative touches. There is also a good wine list. Bring along the kids,
as they have their own menu. $ *Average main: £14* ✉ *Tontine Hotel,
High St.* ☎ *01721/720892* ⊕ *www.tontinehotel.com.*

$ ✕ **Coltman's Delicatessen and Kitchen.** The dining room of this bright and
BISTRO airy eatery sits behind the deli counter, full of tempting tastes on its own.
The dining menu (dinner on weekends only) combines deli platters with
adventurous offerings like lamb with hazelnuts and monkfish with an
oxtail stew. Staff are friendly and welcoming. From Thursday to Saturday there is a set menu for £22.95 or £28.95 for two or three courses,
respectively. $ *Average main: £14* ✉ *71–73 High St.* ☎ *01721/720405*
⊕ *www.coltmans.co.uk* ⊙ *No dinner Sun.–Wed.*

$$$$ ✕ **Horseshoe Inn.** The opulent dining room at the Horseshoe has large
FRENCH gold-framed mirrors and heavy drapes to emphasize its grand style. The
prix-fixe menu (three courses for £50) is equally grand, combining a
globe artichoke starter with lemon-and-crab mayonnaise, with a main
dish of rump and shoulder of local lamb or grilled turbot with a bouillabaisse sauce. Lunch offers a three-course menu (£25) or a four-course
menu (£40). As you would expect, the pace echoes the surroundings and
the cuisine—slow with plenty of time to savor. If you elect to stay in the
area, the restaurant also has eight rooms en suite. $ *Average main: £30*
✉ *Horsehoe Inn, Eddleston* ☎ *01721/730225* ⊕ *www.horseshoeinn.
co.uk* ⊙ *Closed Mon. and Tues.* ⌂ *Reservations essential.*

WHERE TO STAY

$$$ ☷ **Cringletie House.** With medieval-style turrets and crow-step gables, this
HOTEL small-scale, peaceful retreat manages to be fancy *and* homey, Victorian
(it was built in the 1860s) and modern (flat-screen TVs). **Pros:** elegant
bedrooms; cozy fireplaces; decadent dining. **Cons:** some bedrooms have
low ceilings; atmosphere can be almost too quiet. $ *Rooms from: £165*
✉ *Edinburgh Rd.* ⊹ *Off the A703 north of Peebles* ☎ *01721/725750*
⊕ *www.cringletie.com* ⊙ *Closed Nov.–Feb.* ⊲ *13 rooms* ⦶ *Breakfast.*

$$ ☷ **Peebles Hydro.** One of the great "hydro hotels" built in the 19th
HOTEL century for those anxious to "take the waters," the family-friendly
FAMILY Peebles Hydro has comfortable if rather old-fashioned rooms. **Pros:**
plenty of activities; good children's programs; delicious breakfast. **Cons:**
can feel impersonal; some rooms have bland decor. $ *Rooms from:
£125* ✉ *Innerleithen Rd.* ☎ *01721/720602* ⊕ *www.peebleshydro.co.uk*
⊲ *132 rooms* ⦶ *Breakfast.*

$$ ☷ **Tontine Hotel.** A small and charming facade hides a spacious hotel that
HOTEL stretches back from Peebles High Street. **Pros:** centrally located; pleas-
ant rooms; welcoming staff. **Cons:** some rooms in the rear are quite
small; decor in some areas feels old-fashioned. $ *Rooms from: £100*
✉ *High St.* ☎ *01721/729732* ⊕ *www.tontinehotel.com* ⊲ *36 rooms*
⦶ *Breakfast.*

NIGHTLIFE AND PERFORMING ARTS

Eastgate Theatre. A year-round program of films, concerts, and theater as well as community activities for adults and children are on offer here. The theater also has a very pleasant café. ✉ *1 School Brae* ☎ *01721/725777* ⊕ *www.eastgatearts.com.*

SHOPPING

Be prepared for temptations at every turn as you browse the shops on High Street and in the courts and side streets leading off it.

Brevity. This tiny fashion boutique seems to cram an enormous amount of imaginative clothing into a small space. Younger designers, especially Italian, have their work on sale here, at very reasonable prices and presented with enormous enthusiasm by the owner. ✉ *50 High St.* ☎ *01721/724323.*

Caledonia. For anything and everything Scottish, from kilts to dirks and jams to tablecloths, look no further than Caledonia. ✉ *61 High St.* ☎ *01721/722343* ⊕ *caledonia.myshopify.com.*

Head to Toe. This shop stocks natural beauty products, handmade pine furniture, and handsome linens—from patchwork quilts to silk flowers. ✉ *43 High St.* ☎ *01721/722752.*

Keith Walter. Among the many jewelers on High Street, Keith Walter is a master of gold and silver who makes his creations on the premises. He also stocks jewelry made by other local designers. ✉ *28 High St.* ☎ *01721/720650* ⊕ *www.keithwalter28.com.*

DUMFRIES AND GALLOWAY

Galloway covers the southwestern portion of Scotland, west of the main town of Dumfries. Here a gentle coastline gives way to farmland and then breezy uplands that gradually merge with coniferous forests. Use caution when negotiating the A75—you're liable to find aggressive trucks bearing down on you as these commercial vehicles race for the ferries at Stranraer and Cairnryan. Things are far more relaxed once you leave the main highway; take the coastal A710/A711 instead. Dumfries and Galloway offer some of the most pleasant drives in Scotland—though the occasional herd of cows on the way to be milked is a potential hazard. The region now boasts two extraordinary public art projects—Charles Jencks's *Crawick Multiverse* and Andy Goldsworthy's *Striding Arches.*

GRETNA GREEN

10 miles north of Carlisle, England, 87 miles south of Glasgow, 92 miles southwest of Edinburgh.

The first town across the English–Scottish border, Gretna Green (not to be confused with nearby Gretna) was historically where runaway couples went to be married by the local blacksmith under Scotland's more lenient laws. No one could accuse the town of failing to exploit its reputation as the place to tie the knot. Although it is highly commercialized, it is still a favorite venue for weddings, even though the original reasons for going have long since changed.

GETTING HERE AND AROUND

From Glasgow you can reach Gretna Green via the M74 and A74; it's an hour-and-a-half drive. From Edinburgh, take the A74 (about two hours). Buses and trains travel daily to Gretna Green from Glasgow and Edinburgh.

ESSENTIALS

Visitor Information Gretna Green Tourist Information Centre. ☒ *Gretna Gateway Outlet Village, Glasgow Rd., Gretna* ☎ *01461/337834* ⊕ *www. gretnagreen.com.*

EXPLORING

Blacksmith's Shop. Today the 18th-century house of the village blacksmith, known as the "anvil priest," contains a collection of blacksmithing tools, as well as the anvil over which many weddings may have been conducted to symbolize the forging of the link between two people. The village was the first Scottish stop on the new coaching road from London to Edinburgh when the marriage laws in England became more restrictive than Scotland's, where, for a time at least, boys and girls in their early teens could marry without parental permission. Gretna Green was the first place runaway couples reached after crossing the border, hence its fame and the fact that over 1,000 couples a year still go there to marry. Today it also contains a shop and restaurant, as well as the Courtship Maze (£2), two rings that couples enter separately in the hope of finding each other. ☒ *Headless Cross* ☎ *01461/338441* ⊕ *www.gretnagreen.com* ☒ *Museum £3.50* ☾ *Apr. and May, daily 9–5:30; June–Sept., daily 9–6; Oct.–Mar., daily 9–5.*

RUTHWELL

21 miles west of Gretna Green, 83 miles south of Glasgow, 88 miles southwest of Edinburgh.

North of the upper Solway Firth the countryside is flat, fertile farmland. Progressing west, however, a pleasant landscape of low, round hills begins to take over, marked by some interesting historical features.

GETTING HERE AND AROUND

There is no train station in Ruthwell; however, buses—both local and national—do frequent the town. But the best way to get here is via car. From Glasgow, take the M74 then A74; the trip is just under two hours. From Edinburgh take the A74; your journey will take just over two hours.

EXPLORING

Fodor'sChoice **Caerlaverock Castle.** The stunningly beautiful moated Caerlaverock
★ Castle stands in splendid isolation amid the surrounding wetlands that form the Caerlaverock Nature Reserve. Built in a unique triangular design, this 13th-century fortress has solid-sandstone masonry and an imposing double-tower gatehouse. King Edward I of England (1239–1307) besieged the castle in 1300, when his forces occupied much of Scotland at the start of the Wars of Independence. A splendid

residence was built inside in the 1600s. Now largely in ruins, the interior is still very atmospheric, and the siege engines on the grounds give some sense of what medieval warfare was like. The castle has a pleasant café for coffee, cakes, or lunch. ⊠ *Off B725, 7 miles from Ruthwell* ☎ *01387/770244* ⊕ *www.historic-scotland.gov.uk/places* ⌨ *£5.50* ⊙ *Apr.–Sept., daily 9:30–5:30, last admission at 5; Oct.– Mar., daily 10–4, last admission at 3:30.*

Caerlaverock Wildfowl and Wetlands Centre. You can observe wintering wildfowl, including various species of geese, ducks, swans, and raptors, on the wetlands surrounding atmospheric Caerlaverock Castle. In summer, ospreys patrol the waters of this wild and beautiful place, the northernmost outpost of the Wildfowl and Wetlands Trust. The triops, the tadpole shrimp that is one of the oldest known species, lives in the aquarium here. Free guided walks are available in the afternoons throughout the year. ⊠ *Eastpark Farm, Off B725, Dumfries* ⊹ *9 miles southeast of Dumfries off the A75* ☎ *01387/770200* ⊕ *www.wwt.org. uk* ⌨ *£7.26* ⊙ *Daily 10–5.*

Ruthwell Parish Church. Inside Ruthwell Parish Church is the 8th-century Ruthwell Runic Cross, a sculpture placed here by the Christian monks expelled from Iona. Detailed biblical scenes carved onto its north and south faces and its carvings of vines, birds, and animals, are accompanied by verses from an Anglo-Saxon poem called "The Dream of the Rood," written in a language that had fallen out of use by the 12th century. Considered an idolatrous monument, it was removed and demolished by Church of Scotland zealots in 1642 but was later reassembled. ⊠ *Northern end of Kirklands Loaning.*

SPORTS AND OUTDOORS

Powfoot Golf Club. A pleasant mix of links and parkland holes, this course looks out across the Solway Firth. Its roughs and the tough thorny whins (local bushes with yellow flowers) make the course especially challenging, but it is the views from here that make it memorable and a pleasure to play. ⊠ *Off B724, Cummertrees, Annan* ☎ *01461/204100* ⊕ *www.powfootgolfclub.com* ⌨ *£40 weekdays, £46 weekends* ⚑ *18 holes, 6250 yards, par 71.*

DUMFRIES

15 miles northwest of Ruthwell, 76 miles south of Glasgow, 81 miles southwest of Edinburgh.

The River Nith meanders through Dumfries, and the pedestrian-only town center makes wandering and shopping a pleasure. Author J.M. Barrie (1860–1937) spent his childhood in Dumfries, and the garden of Moat Brae House is said to have inspired his boyish dreams in *Peter Pan*. But the town also has a justified claim to Robert Burns, who lived and worked here for several years. His house and his favorite *howff* (pub), The Globe Inn, are here, too, as is his final resting place in St. Michael's Churchyard.

The Dumfries & Galloway Tourist Board has a lodging service, and also sells golf passes for the region at £60 for three rounds.

GETTING HERE AND AROUND

Public transportation is a good option for reaching Dumfries—there's a good train station here, and most major Scottish cities have regular daily bus routes to the town. If you're driving from Ruthwell, take the B724. From Glasgow, take the M74 to the A701. From Edinburgh, take the A701.

ESSENTIALS

Visitor Information Dumfries & Galloway Tourist Board. ✉ *64 Whitesands* ☎ *01387/253862* ⊕ *www.visitscotland.com.*

EXPLORING

TOP ATTRACTIONS

Burns House. Poet Robert Burns lived here, on what was then called Mill Street, for the last three years of his life, when his salary from the customs service allowed him to improve his living standards. Many distinguished writers of the day visited him here, including William Wordsworth. The house contains some of his writings and letters, a few pieces of furniture, and some family memorabilia. ✉ *Burns St.* ☎ *01387/255297* ⊕ *www.dumgal.gov.uk* 🎫 *Free* ☉ *Apr.–Sept., Mon.– Sat. 10–5, Sun. 2–5; Oct.–Mar., Tues.–Sat. 10–1 and 2–5.*

OFF THE BEATEN PATH

Crawick Multiverse. This extraordinary land artwork by Charles Jencks, 45 minutes north of Dumfries, must surely become a focus for visitors to the region for many years to come. Jencks has transformed a 55-acre site, once an open-pit mine, into a beautiful and inspiring created landscape, at the heart of which are two grass spiral mounds that represent the Milky Way and the Andromeda Constellation. But they are simply the heart of a site where woodland, moor, mountain, and desert meet. Pause from time to time to look around as you climb through the different layers: the surrounding hills seem to shift and change. Local rocks have been lifted to form avenues and labyrinths across the site. As you look across from its highest point, it is as if you were looking in a mirror in which the skies were reflected on the earth, powerful and playful at the same time. Set aside two or three hours at least for the experience. ✉ *Crawick, by Sanquhar* ✛ *Take the A 75 towards Kirkconnel from Sanquhar, then turn on to the B740 (signposted Crawfordjohn)* ⊕ *www.crawickmultiverse.co.uk* 🎫 *£5* ☞ *Mar.–June, Sept., and Oct., daily 10–4; July and Aug., daily 10–6; Nov.–Feb. pedestrian access only* 🎫 *£5.*

OFF THE BEATEN PATH

Drumlanrig Castle. This spectacular estate is as close as Scotland gets to the treasure houses of England—which is not surprising, since it's owned by the dukes of Buccleuch, one of the wealthiest British peerages. Resplendent with romantic turrets, this pink-sandstone palace was constructed between 1679 and 1691 by the first Duke of Queensbury, who, after nearly bankrupting himself building the place, stayed one night and never returned. The Buccleuchs inherited the palace and soon filled the richly decorated rooms with a valuable collection of paintings by Holbein, Rembrandt, and Murillo. Because of the theft of a Leonardo da Vinci painting in 2003, all visits are conducted by guided tour. There's also a playground, a gift shop, and a tearoom. The grounds are varied and particularly suited to mountain biking; bikes can be hired

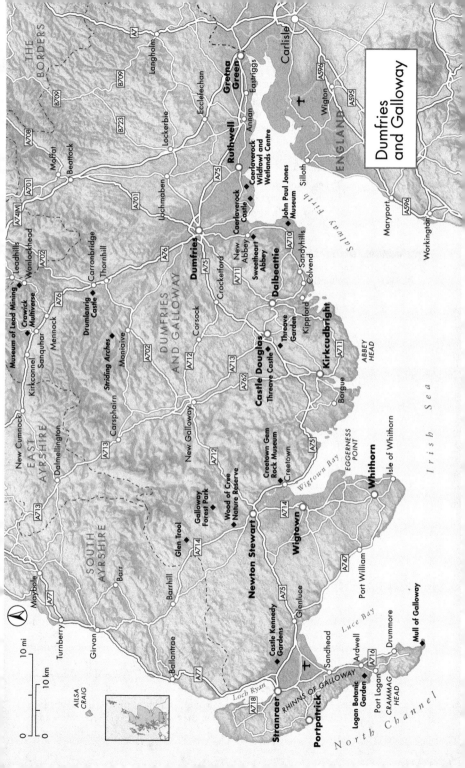

Dumfries and Galloway

at the castle. ✉ *Off A76, 18 miles northwest of Dumfries, Thornhill* ☎ *01848/600283* ⊕ *www.drumlanrig.com* ⛿ *Park £6, castle and park £10* ⊙ *Grounds Apr.–Sept., daily 10–5. Castle Mar.–Aug., daily 11–4.*

Robert Burns Centre. Not surprisingly, Dumfries has its own Robert Burns Centre, housed in a sturdy former mill overlooking the river. The center has an audiovisual program and an extensive exhibit on the life of the poet. There's a restaurant upstairs. ✉ *Mill Rd.* ☎ *01387/264808* ⛿ *Free* ⊙ *Apr.–Sept., Mon.–Sat. 10–5, Sun. 2–5; Oct.–Mar., Tues.–Sat. 10–1 and 2–5.*

St. Michael's Churchyard. When he died in 1796, poet Robert Burns was buried in a modest grave in St. Michael's Churchyard. English poet William Wordsworth, visiting a few years later, was horrified by the small gravestone and raised money to build this much grander monument. ✉ *39 Cardiness St.* ☎ *01387/253849.*

OFF THE BEATEN PATH

Striding Arches. This extraordinary piece of public landscape art by Andy Goldsworthy enriches the great natural amphitheater at Cairnhead in the southern uplands of Dumfries and Galloway. His three redsandstone arches stand 13 feet high and mark out the area, "striding" across the landscape. ✉ *Cairnhead Forest, near Moniaive* ✛ *Take the A702 (off the A76 at Thornhill) to Moniaive then the road to Benbuie until you reach The Byre. From there it is a walk to the viewpoint.* ☎ *07801/232229* ⊕ *www.stridingarches.com.*

Sweetheart Abbey. At the center of the village of New Abbey is the redtinted and roofless Sweetheart Abbey. The odd name is a translation of the abbey's previous name, St. Mary of the Dolce Coeur. The abbey was founded in 1273 by the Lady of Galloway, Devorgilla (1210–90), who, it is said, had her late husband's heart placed in a tiny casket that she carried everywhere. After she died, she was laid to rest in Sweetheart Abbey with the casket resting on her breast. The couple's son John Balliol (1249–1315) was the puppet king installed in Scotland by Edward of England when the latter claimed sovereignty over Scotland. After John's appointment the Scots gave him a scathing nickname that would stay with him for the rest of his life: Toom Tabard (Empty Shirt). ✉ *A710, 7 miles south of Dumfries, New Abbey* ☎ *01387/253849* ⊕ *www.historic-scotland.gov.uk* ⛿ *£4.50* ⊙ *Apr.–Sept., daily 9:30–5:30 (last admission at 5); Oct., daily 9:30–4:30; Nov.–Mar., Mon.–Wed. and weekends 10–4 (last admission at 3:30).*

WORTH NOTING

Dumfries Museum and Camera Obscura. A camera obscura is essentially a huge reflecting mirror that projects an extraordinarily clear panoramic view of the surrounding countryside onto an internal wall. The one at the Dumfries Museum is housed in the old Windmill Tower, built in 1836. The museum itself covers the culture and daily life of the people living in the Dumfries and Galloway region from the earliest times. ✉ *Rotchell Rd.* ☎ *01387/253374* ⛿ *Museum free; Camera Obscura £2.30* ⊙ *Museum Apr.–Sept., Mon.–Sat. 10–5; Oct.–Mar., Tues.–Sat. 10–1 and 2–5. Camera Obscura: Apr.–Sept., Mon.–Sat. 10–5, Sun. 2–5.*

Globe Inn. Poet Robert Burns spent quite a lot of time at the Globe Inn, where he frequently fell asleep in the tack room beside the stables. He later graduated to the upstairs bedroom where he slept with his wife, Jean Armour, and scratched some lines of poetry on the window. The room is preserved (or at least partly re-created) and the bar staff will happily show you around if you ask. ✉ *56 High St.* ☎ *01387/252335* ⊕ *www.globeinndumfries.co.uk* 🔲 *Free.*

John Paul Jones Museum. The little community of Kirkbean—blink and you'll miss it—is the backdrop for Arbigland Estate. It was in a cottage here, now the John Paul Jones Museum, in this bright green landscape that John Paul (1747–92), the son of an estate gardener, was born. He eventually left Scotland, added "Jones" to his name, and became the founder of the U.S. Navy. The cottage where he was born is furnished as it would have been when he was a boy. There is an informative video, which you watch in a reconstruction of his captain's cabin. Jones returned to raid the coastline of his native country in 1778, an exploit recounted in an adjoining visitor center. ✉ *Off A710, Kirkbean* ✛ *12 miles south of Dumfries* ☎ *01387/880613* ⊕ *www.jpj. demon.co.uk* 🔲 *£3.50* ☉ *Apr.–June and Sept., Tues.–Sun. 10–5; July and Aug., daily 10–5.*

OFF THE
BEATEN
PATH

Museum of Lead Mining. The Lochnell Mine was abandoned in 1861, after 150 years of operation. The isolated village of Warnlockhead, where it was located, has not changed a great deal since then—there was little alternative employment for the miners and their families. Their homes now form part of this museum re-creating their lives. The visitor center, housed in the old smithy, exhibits some of the minerals the mine yielded. The nearby Leadhills and Warnlockhead Narrow Gauge Railway runs on weekends throughout the summer and costs £4, with a 10% reduction for a joint ticket with the museum. ✉ *Off B797, Wanlockhead* ☎ *01659/74387* ⊕ *www.leadminingmuseum.co.uk* 🔲 *£7.75* ☉ *Apr.–Sept., daily 11–4:30.*

WHERE TO EAT

$ ✕ **Cavens Arms.** This lively, welcoming, traditional pub has a separate bar and dining area, comfortable seating, and a large selection of beers. The restaurant seems to always be busy, a testimony to the quality of its food (as well as the large portions). As for favorite dishes, grilled pork loin with fruity red cabbage vies with panfried sea bass with couscous. The excellent desserts are made on the premises. $ *Average main: £11* ✉ *20 Buccleuch St.* ☎ *01387/252896* ⚠ *Reservations not accepted.*

BRITISH

$$ ✕ **Hullabaloo.** Occupying the top floor of the Robert Burns Centre, itself an old mill, this restaurant serves a substantial and varied lunch and dinner menu. The melts are the highlight of the imaginative and very tasty lunch menu. The dinner menu is ambitious and equally varied, ranging from monkfish loin wrapped in Serrano ham to local lamb and vegetarian mole (a Mexican sauce). A separate, and interesting, vegan menu is available, too. The best tables are by the window overlooking the River Nith. $ *Average main: £16* ✉ *Robert Burns Centre, Mill Rd.* ☎ *01387/259679* ⊕ *www.hullabaloorestaurant.co.uk* ☉ *Closed Sun. No dinner Mon.* ⚠ *Reservations essential.*

BRITISH

WHERE TO STAY

$ HOTEL 🏨 **Cairndale Hotel.** Centrally located, the Cairndale has a Victorian Gothic appearance and spacious and comfortable rooms. **Pros:** central location; comfortable rooms; pool, sauna, and gym. **Cons:** a generally old-fashioned feel. [$] *Rooms from: £95* ✉ *132–6 English St.* ☎ *01387/354111* 🌐 *www.cairndalehotel.co.uk* 🛏 *91 rooms* 🍴 *Breakfast.*

$ B&B/INN 🏨 **Ferintosh Guest House.** Directly across from the train station, this handsome sandstone guesthouse sits on a leafy street in a quiet part of town. **Pros:** dog-friendly; great robes; helpful owners. **Cons:** no children under 10; some shared bathrooms. [$] *Rooms from: £66* ✉ *30 Lovers Walk* ☎ *01387/252262* 🌐 *www.ferintosh.net* 🛏 *6 rooms* 🍴 *Breakfast.*

$ HOTEL 🏨 **Holiday Inn.** With the secluded feel of a grand country hotel but less than 2 miles from the center of Dumfries, the Holiday Inn is on the Crichton Estate, once a hospital and then an education center, with lush plantings, rock gardens, and elegant Victorian buildings. **Pros:** beautiful setting; easy access to Dumfries; rooms for people with disabilities. **Cons:** slightly institutional feel; restaurant can be disappointing. [$] *Rooms from: £90* ✉ *Bankend Rd., Crichton* ☎ *01387/272410* 🌐 *holidayinndumfries.com* 🛏 *71 rooms* 🍴 *Breakfast.*

NIGHTLIFE AND PERFORMING ARTS

Dumfries & Galloway Arts Festival. This festival, celebrated every year since 1979, is usually held at the end of May at several venues throughout the region. ☎ *01387/260447* 🌐 *www.dgartsfestival.org.uk.*

Gracefield Arts Centre. With galleries hosting constantly changing exhibits, Gracefield Arts Centre also has a well-stocked crafts shop. A café serves lunch and snacks. ✉ *28 Edinburgh Rd.* ☎ *01387/262084* 🌐 *www.exploreart.co.uk* 🕒 *Tues.–Sat. 10–5.*

SHOPPING

Dumfries is the main shopping center for the region, with all the big-name chain stores as well as specialty shops.

Fodor's Choice ★ **Loch Arthur Creamery and Farm Shop.** Known for its high-quality dairy products, this lively and active farm in the charmingly named village of Beeswing has an expansive café and retail store selling a range of organic products. The farm work continues around the café, where they make bread, butcher their own meat, and cook the delicious food served here. The building itself has large windows opening directly on to the fields beyond. ✉ *A711, 6 miles from Dumfries, Beeswing* ☎ *01387/259669* 🌐 *www.locharthur.org.uk.*

SPORTS AND THE OUTDOORS

7stanes Mountain Biking. Dumfries and Galloway is something of a mecca for mountain bikers, offering trails and routes of every level of difficulty in beautiful and varying landscapes. This outfitter offers full equipment hire, skills training, advice, and local route maps organized by degree of difficulty. You can bring your own bike or rent one and ride gentle forest routes or tough hill climbs. There are seven centers across Dumfries and Galloway and the Borders; specific information on each is available on the comprehensive website. ✉ *Campbell House, Crichton Business Park, Bankend Rd.* ☎ *01721/721180* 🌐 *www.7stanesmountainbiking.com.*

G&G Cycle Centre. Bicycles can be rented from G&G Cycle Centre. The staff gives good advice on where to ride. ✉ *10–12 Academy St.* ☎ *01387/259483* ⏲ *Mon.–Sat. 9–5.*

DALBEATTIE

14 miles southwest of Dumfries, 89 miles south of Glasgow, 95 miles southwest of Edinburgh.

Like the much larger Aberdeen far to the northeast, Dalbeattie contains buildings constructed with local gray granite from the town's quarry. The well-scrubbed gray glitter makes Dalbeattie atypical of Galloway towns, where houses are usually painted in pastels. It is mainly a stopping point for visitors on their way to the Solway Firth.

4

GETTING HERE AND AROUND

There are no direct bus routes from Dumfries to Dalbeattie; your best mode of transport is car. From Dumfries, take the A711 (about 25 minutes). From Glasgow, take the M74, A74, then A701 (about 2 hours). From Edinburgh, take the A701 and A702 (about 2¼ hours).

WHERE TO STAY

$ B&B/INN 🏨 **Anchor Hotel.** This small, friendly hotel in the picturesque village of Kippford has wonderful views across the Solway Firth, and while the rooms are small and plainly furnished, all of them gaze out over the water. **Pros:** lovely location; friendly atmosphere; good pub food. **Cons:** small rooms; bar can be noisy at times. [$] *Rooms from: £70* ✉ *Main St., Kippford* ✣ *Take the A710 south from Dalbeattie and turn into Kippford (3 miles)* ☎ *01556/620205* 🌐 *www.anchorhotelkippford.co.uk* 🛏 *6 rooms* 🍴 *Breakfast.*

$ B&B/INN 🏨 **Kerr Cottage.** This 165-year-old house is holding up quite well, thank you very much—the fresh and spacious guest rooms have contemporary wood furniture, comfy beds, and large tiled bathrooms. **Pros:** close to biking and hiking trails; great storage space for outdoor gear; very reasonable price. **Cons:** no pets allowed; no children under 12. [$] *Rooms from: £70* ✉ *Port Rd.* ☎ *01556/612245* 🌐 *www.kerrcottage.co.uk* 🛏 *3 rooms* 🍴 *Breakfast.*

SPORTS AND THE OUTDOORS

Barend Riding School and Trekking Centre. At this riding school you'll be helped to a "horse-high" view of the beautiful coast and countryside. ✉ *A710, Sandyhills* ✣ *6 miles southeast of Dalbeattie* ☎ *01387/780533.*

Southerness Golf Club. Mackenzie Ross designed this course, the first built in Scotland just after World War II. Southerness is a long course, played over extensive links with fine views southward over the Solway Firth. The greens are hard and fast, and the frequent winds make for some testing golf. Thursday is reserved for women. ✉ *Southerness St., Southerness* ☎ *01387/880677* 🌐 *www.southernessgolfclub.com* 🎫 *£50 weekdays, £60 weekends* ⛳ *18 holes, 6110 yards, par 69* ✍ *Reservations essential.*

CASTLE DOUGLAS

6 miles west of Dalbeattie, 84 miles south of Glasgow, 90 miles south-west of Edinburgh.

A quaint town that sits beside Carlingwark Loch, Castle Douglas is a popular base for exploring the surrounding countryside. The loch sets off the city perfectly, reflecting its dramatic architecture of sharp spires and soft sandstone arches. Its main thoroughfare, King Street, has unique shops and eateries.

GETTING HERE AND AROUND

There's no train station in Castle Douglas, and buses from Dumfries make several stops along the way. The best way to get to Castle Douglas is by car. From Dalbeattie, take the A711/A745 (10 minutes). From Glasgow, take the A713 (just under 2 hours). From Edinburgh, take the A70 (2⅓ hours).

ESSENTIALS

Visitor Information Castle Douglas. ⊠ *Market Hill* ☎ *01556/502611* ⊕ *www.visitscotland.com.*

EXPLORING

Fodor's Choice ★ **Threave Castle.** This castle was an early home of the Black Douglases, who were the earls of Nithsdale and lords of Galloway. The imposing towers reflects well the Lord of Galloway who built it, Archibald the Grim, in the 14th century. Not to be confused with the mansion in Threave Gardens, the castle was dismantled in the religious wars of the mid-17th century, though enough of it remains to have housed prisoners from the Napoleonic Wars of the 19th century. It's a few minutes from Castle Douglas by car and is signposted from the main road. To get here, leave your car in a farmyard and make your way down to the edge of the river. Ring the bell (loudly) and, rather romantically, a boatman will come to ferry you across to the great stone tower looming from a marshy island in the river. ⊠ *A75, 3 miles west of Castle Douglas* ☎ *07711/223101* ⊕ *www.historic-scotland.gov.uk* ☞ *£4.50, includes ferry* ⊗ *Apr.–Sept., daily 10–4:30.*

Threave Garden. The National Trust for Scotland cares for the gently sloping parkland around the 1867 mansion built by William Gordon, a Liverpool businessman. The house, fully restored in the 1930s, gives a glimpse into the daily life of a prosperous family in the 19th century. The foliage demands the employment of many gardeners, many of them students at the National Trust's School of Heritage Gardening based on the estate, hence the variety of gardens you may find here. Entry to the house is by timed guided tour, and it's wise to book ahead. There's an on-site restaurant. ⊠ *South of A75* ✛ *1 mile west of Castle Douglas* ☎ *01556/502575* ⊕ *www.nts.org.uk/Visits* ☞ *Gardens £7.50, house and gardens £12.50* ⊗ *House (guided tours only) Apr.–Oct., Wed.–Fri. and Sun. 11–3:30. Gardens year-round, daily 10–5.*

WHERE TO EAT

$ CAFÉ **✕ The Café at Designs Gallery.** For a good balance of art and food, look no further. You'll find the freshest ingredients here, from soup to salads, sandwiches to quiches. Everything is made on-site, including the bread, and it's all organic. The soup of the day is always a good choice, as are the seasonal fruit pies. The café is downstairs, beneath the shop and gallery, and is full of light and wooden tables and chairs. You can also choose to sit in the conservatory or the lovely walled garden, if the weather allows. [$] *Average main: £7* ✉ *179 King St.* ☎ *01556/504552* 🌐 *www.designsgallery.co.uk* 🕒 *Closed Sun. and Mon. No dinner.*

SHOPPING

A.D. Livingston and Sons. Fine-furniture makers in wood and raffia, the Livingstons have a shop in the main street, and some of their fine work is displayed two doors down under an arch into a charming lane. ✉ *183 King St.* ☎ *01556/504234* 🌐 *www.livingstons-antiques.co.uk.*

By the Book. This well-stocked and (more importantly) well-organized secondhand bookshop on Castle Douglas's main shopping street has large windows that invite you in to browse, which you can do without interruption—there's bound to be something you want, though it may be in a box or under the table. ✉ *201 King St.* ☎ *01556/503338.*

Galloway Gems and Craft Centre and Outback Yarns. This glittery shop sells mineral specimens, polished stone slices, and a range of Celtic- and Nordic-inspired jewelry, as well as a bewildering range of craft materials of every kind. For fiber artists and sewers, it's a real find. ✉ *130–132 King St.* ☎ *01556/503254* 🌐 *outbackyarns.co.uk.*

SPORTS AND THE OUTDOORS

BICYCLING

Castle Douglas Cycle Centre. You can rent bicycles for everyone in the family from Castle Douglas Cycle Centre. It also handles repairs and service. ✉ *Church St.* ☎ *01556/504542* 🌐 *www.cdbikes.co.uk.*

BOATING

Galloway Activity Centre. With dinghies, kayaks, and canoes for rent, the Galloway Activity Centre on the banks of Loch Ken specializes in water sports. "Dry" sports include mountain biking, archery, and rock climbing. It's about 10 miles northwest of Castle Douglas. ✉ *Off A713* ✣ *10 miles northwest of Castle Douglas* ☎ *01644/420626* 🌐 *www.lochken.co.uk.*

KIRKCUDBRIGHT

9 miles southwest of Castle Douglas, 89 miles south of Glasgow, 99 miles southwest of Edinburgh.

Kirkcudbright (pronounced kir *-coo*-bray) is an 18th-century town of Georgian and Victorian houses, some of them washed in pastel shades and roofed with the blue slate of the district. In the early 20th century it became a haven for artists, and its L-shape main street is full of crafts and antiques shops.

GETTING HERE AND AROUND

Driving is your best and only real option. From Castle Douglas, take the A711 (15 minutes). From Glasgow, take the A713 (about 2 hours). From Edinburgh, take the A701 (about 2½ hours).

ESSENTIALS

Visitor Information **Kirkcudbright Tourist Information Centre.** ✉ *Harbour Sq.* ☎ *01557/330494* ⊕ *www.visitscotland.com.*

EXPLORING

Fodor'sChoice   **Broughton House.** The 18th-century Broughton House was the home of
★   the artist E. A. Hornel from 1901 until his death in 1933 and remains largely as it was in his time. Hornel was a member of the school of painters called the "Glasgow Boys" of the late 19th century. You can see many of his paintings in the gallery he had specially built onto the house to impress the guests and buyers who came to see his work. His use and love of color is nowhere more obvious than in the beautiful garden, which combines lawns, ponds, and formal and wild flower beds. The knowledgeable guides will gladly provide all the information you may need about the life and work of the painter. ✉ *12 High St.* ☎ *01557/330437* ⊕ *www.nts.org.uk* 💷 *£6.50* ⊘ *House and garden: Apr.–Oct., daily noon–5. Garden only: Feb. and Mar., weekdays 11–4.*

MacLellan's Castle. Conspicuous in the center of town are the stone walls of MacLellan's Castle, a once-elaborate castellated mansion dating from the 16th century. You can walk around the interior, still atmospheric even though the rooms are bare. The "Lairds Lug," behind the fireplace, allowed the *laird* (lord) to listen in to what his guests were saying about him. You can also get a glimpse of life below stairs in the vaults beneath the main staircase, where the kitchen is occupied by a couple of silent figures still waiting for the food to cook. There are lovely views over the town from the windows. ✉ *Off High St.* ☎ *01557/331856* ⊕ *www. historic-scotland.gov.uk* 💷 *£4.50* ⊘ *Apr.–Sept., daily 9:30–5:30; last admission at 5.*

Stewartry Museum. Stuffed with all manner of local paraphernalia, the delightfully old-fashioned Stewartry Museum allows you to putter and absorb as much or as little as takes your interest in the display cases. Stewartry is the former name of Kirkcudbright. ✉ *St. Mary St.* ☎ *01557/331643* ⊕ *www.dumgal.gov.uk* 💷 *Free* ⊘ *Mon.–Sat. 11–4.*

Tolbooth Arts Centre. In the 17th-century tollbooth (a combination town hall–courthouse–prison), the Tolbooth Arts Centre describes how the town attracted famous artists, among them E. A. Hornel, Jessie King, and Charles Oppenheimer. Some of their paintings are on display, as are works by contemporary artists. ✉ *High St.* ☎ *01557/331556* ⊕ *www. dumgal.gov.uk* 💷 *Free* ⊘ *Oct.–May, Mon.–Sat. 11–4; June–Sept., Mon.–Sat. 11–4, Sun. 2–5.*

WHERE TO EAT AND STAY

$$ ✕ **Artistas at the Selkirk Arms.** Paintings of Scotland, starched white
MODERN BRITISH   tablecloths, and giant windows overlooking the well-kept garden beckon you into this highly praised eatery. Locals love that the food is locally sourced and full of imagination. The traditional bar menu includes panfried lamb's liver and beer-batter fish-and-chips, while the unashamedly witty "Posh Nosh" brings together Vietnamese corn pancakes, picanha beef, and seafood cavatelli on one menu. Both are imaginative and delicious in their own ways. $ *Average main: £16*

✉ *Selkirk Arms, High St.* ☎ *01557/330402* 🌐 *www.selkirkarmshotel.co.uk* ✍ *Reservations essential.*

$$ HOTEL 🏨 **Selkirk Arms.** Bursting with charm, this elegant 18th-century hotel has a lot going for it—spacious rooms are individually decorated with cozy beds, contemporary wood furniture, and soft lighting. **Pros:** attentive service; massive breakfast; lively traditional pub. **Cons:** rooms closest to restaurant can be noisy; bar gets crowded during sporting events. [$] *Rooms from: £110* ✉ *High St.* ☎ *01557/330402* 🌐 *www.selkirkarmshotel.co.uk* 🛏 *16 rooms* 🍴 *Breakfast.*

NEWTON STEWART

18 miles northwest of Kirkcudbright, 77 miles southwest of Glasgow, 105 miles southwest of Edinburgh.

The bustling town of Newton Stewart is a good place to stop when touring the western region of Galloway. It's near some lovely outdoor areas.

GETTING HERE AND AROUND

Newton Stewart does not have a train station, but the town is served by regular buses from Glasgow and Edinburgh as well as local buses from neighboring towns. By car from Glasgow, take the A77 (about 2 hours). From Edinburgh, take the A702 (about 2¾ hours).

ESSENTIALS

Visitor Information **Newton Stewart Visitor Information Centre.** ✉ *Dashwood Sq.* ☎ *01671/402431* 🌐 *www.newtonstewart.org.*

EXPLORING

TOP ATTRACTIONS

Galloway Forest Park. You can walk or bicycle along the paths at the Galloway Forest Park through moorland and forests, by lochs and over hills—all contained within the 300 square miles of the forest. The Forestry Commission, which manages the forest, has three visitor centers at Glen Trool, Kirroughtree, and Clatteringshaws, where there are exhibits about the region's wildlife and a reconstruction of an Iron Age dwelling. The forest is designated as a Dark Sky Park, where low light pollution means it has exceptional stargazing. ✉ *A712, 7 miles northeast of Newton Stewart* ☎ *01671/402420* 🌐 *www.forestry.gov.uk/gallowayforestpark* 🎟 *Free* ⏲ *Daily.*

Glen Trool. With high purple-and-green hilltops shorn rock-bare by glaciers, and with a dark, winding loch and thickets of birch trees sounding with birdcalls, Glen Trool's setting almost looks more highland than the real Highlands. Note **Bruce's Stone,** just above the parking lot, marking the site where in 1307 Scotland's champion Robert the Bruce (King Robert I, 1274–1329) won his first victory in the Scottish Wars of Independence. To get here, follow the A714 north from Newton Stewart for about 15 minutes and turn right at the signpost for Glen Trool. A little road leads through increasingly wild woodland scenery to a parking lot. Only after you have climbed for a few minutes onto a heathery knoll does the full, rugged panorama become apparent. Driving is really the only way to get to Glen Trool. From Glasgow, take the A77 (about 2¼ hours). From Edinburgh, take the A702 (about

3 hours). ✉ *Off A714, Bargrennan* ☎ *01671/840302* 🌐 *www.forestry.gov.uk* 🎫 *Free* ⏱ *Visitor center daily 11–5.*

Wood of Cree Nature Reserve. Birders love the Wood of Cree Nature Reserve, managed by the Royal Society for the Protection of Birds. In the reserve you can see such species as the redstart, pied flycatcher, and wood warbler. To get there, take the minor road that travels north from Newton Stewart alongside the River Cree east of the A714. The entrance is next to a small parking area at the side of the road. ✉ *Off A714, 4 miles north of Newton Stewart* ☎ *01988/402130* 🌐 *www.rspb.org.uk* 🎫 *Donations accepted* ⏱ *Daily 24 hrs.*

GOLF GETAWAYS

There are more than 25 courses in Dumfries and Galloway and 21 in the Borders. The Freedom of the Fairways Pass (five-day pass, £129; three-day pass, £99) allows play on all 21 Borders courses and is available from the Scottish Borders Tourist Board at 🌐 *visitscotland.com/scottishborders-golfpass.* The Gateway to Golf Pass (six-round pass, £130; three-round pass, £90) is accepted by all clubs in Dumfries and Galloway. Available from 🌐 *visitscotland.com/dumfriesgalloway-golfpass.*

WORTH NOTING

Creetown Gem Rock Museum. In the village of Creetown outside Newton Stewart, the Creetown Gem Rock Museum has an eclectic mineral collection, a dinosaur egg, an erupting volcano, and a crystal cave. There's also an Internet café, a tearoom, and a shop selling stones and crystals—both loose and in settings. Entry is good for two weeks. ✉ *Chain Rd., off A75, Creetown* ☎ *01671/820357* 🌐 *www.gemrock.net* 🎫 *£4* ⏱ *Easter–Sept., daily 9:30–5:30; Sept.–Easter, daily 10–4; last admission ½ hr before closing.*

Machars. The Machars is the name given to the triangular promontory south of Newton Stewart. This is an area of pretty, rolling farmlands, yellow-gorse hedgerows, rich grazing for dairy cattle, and stony prehistoric sites. Fields are bordered by *dry stane dykes* (walls) of sharp-edge stones, and small hills and hummocks give the area its characteristic frozen-wave look, a reminder of the glacial activity that shaped the landscape.

WHERE TO STAY

$$ HOTEL 🏨 **Creebridge House Hotel.** Close to the river Cree and set among gardens and woodland, the Creebridge places the emphasis on comfort and quiet rural surroundings. **Pros:** practical center for exploring the area; comfort in a rural setting; within easy reach of Newton Stewart. **Cons:** slightly conservative feel. [$] *Rooms from: £140* ✉ *Minigaff* ☎ *01671/402121* 🌐 *www.creebridge.co.uk* 🛏 *18 rooms* 🍴 *Breakfast.*

WIGTOWN

7 miles south of Newton Stewart, 84 miles southwest of Glasgow, 111 miles southwest of Edinburgh.

More than 20 bookshops, mostly antiquarian and secondhand stores, have sprung up on the brightly painted main street of Wigtown, voted Scotland's national book town. The 10-day Wigtown Book Festival is held in late September and early October.

GETTING HERE AND AROUND

There is no train station in Wigtown, and you must make several transfers when traveling by bus to and from Scotland's larger cities. Driving is your best option. Take the A714 from Newton Stewart (15 minutes). From Glasgow, take the A77 (about two hours). From Edinburgh, take the A702 (about three hours).

EXPLORING

Fodor's Choice
★

Wigtown Book Festival. Held in late September and early October, the 10-day Wigtown Book Festival has readings, performances, and other events throughout town. ✉ *Wigtown* ☎ *01988/402036* ⊕ *www.wigtownbookfestival.com.*

SHOPPING

The Bookshop. One of the country's largest secondhand bookstores, the Bookshop offers temptingly full shelves. The narrow entrance, flanked by two tottering towers of books, belies the huge stock within, both upstairs and through to the rear of the shop. When you think you have reached the back of the shop, there is probably another room still to find. ✉ *17 N. Main St.* ☎ *01988/402499* ⊕ *www.the-bookshop.com.*

Old Bank Bookshop. Housed in the old Customs House and Bank dating from the 18th century, this fine secondhand bookshop has a cornucopia of books, from the antiquarian to the simply forgotten, in its five rooms. ✉ *7 S Main St., Wigtown* ☎ *01988/402111* ⊕ *oldbankbookshop.co.uk.*

WHITHORN

11 miles south of Wigtown, 94 miles southwest of Glasgow, 121 miles southwest of Edinburgh.

Known for its early Christian settlement, Whithorn is full of history. The main street is notably wide, with pretty pastel buildings nestled up against each other, their low doorways and small windows creating images of years long past. It's still mainly a farming community, but is fast becoming a popular tourist destination. Several scenes from the original *Wicker Man* were shot in and around the area. During the summer months, it's a popular place for festivals. The Isle of Whithorn, just beyond the town, is not an island at all but a fishing village of great charm.

GETTING HERE AND AROUND

There's no train station in Whithorn, and most of the buses are local (getting to main Scottish cities from Whithorn takes careful planning and several transfers). To drive from Wigtown, take the A746 (about

20 minutes). From Glasgow, take the A77 (about 2½ hours). From Edinburgh, take the A702 (about 3 hours).

EXPLORING

St. Ninian's Chapel. The Isle of Whithorn (a small fishing village, not an island) holds the ruins of St. Ninian's Chapel, where pilgrims who came by sea prayed before traveling inland to Whithorn Priory. Some people claim that this, and not Whithorn Priory, is the site of the Candida Casa. This 14th-century structure seems to have been built on top of a much older chapel. ✉ *Isle of Whithorn* 🌐 *www.historic-scotland.gov.uk* 🎫 *£4.50 (price includes Whithorn Priory and Whithorn Story and Visitor Centre).*

Whithorn Priory and Museum. The road that is now the A746 was a pilgrims' path that led to the royal burgh of Whithorn, where sat Whithorn Priory, one of Scotland's great medieval cathedrals, now an empty shell. It was built in the 12th century and is said to occupy the site of a former stone church, the Candida Casa, built by St. Ninian in the 4th century. As the story goes, the church housed a shrine to Ninian, the earliest of Scotland's saints, and kings and barons sought to visit the shrine at least once in their lives. As you approach the priory, observe the royal arms of pre-1707 Scotland—that is, Scotland before the Union with England—carved and painted above the *pend* (covered walkway). The museum houses stonework from the period, recently restored. ✉ *Off A746* 🌐 *www.whithornpriorymuseum.gov.uk* 🎫 *£4.50 (includes the Whithorn Story and Visitor Centre and St. Ninian's Chapel)* 🕒 *Apr.–Oct., daily 10:30–5.*

Whithorn Timescape. This center explains the significance of what is claimed to be the site of the earliest Christian community in Scotland. A museum has a collection of early Christian crosses. ✉ *45–47 George St.* ☎ *01988/500508* 🌐 *www.whithorn.com* 🎫 *£4.50 (includes the Whithorn Priory and St. Ninian's Chapel)* 🕒 *Apr.–Oct., daily 10:30–5; last tour at 4.*

WHERE TO EAT

$ BRITISH 🍴 **Steam Packet Inn.** This lovely, old-fashioned inn is always full, mainly because of its hearty, well-cooked food and good beer. Patrons also love the location, on the harbor of this quaint fishing village. You can walk the headland behind the pub to the rocky shore of the Solway Firth. Fish-and-chips and lamb shanks can be followed by some excellent house-made desserts. When weather permits you can eat at tables in the garden. If you like it so much you want to stay, there are also a couple of rooms. [$] *Average main: £13* ✉ *Harbour Row, Isle of Whithorn* ☎ *01988/500334* 🌐 *www.steampacketinn.co.uk.*

STRANRAER

31 miles northwest of Whithorn, 86 miles southwest of Glasgow via A77, 131 miles southwest of Edinburgh.

Stranraer has a lovely garden and is also the main ferry port to Northern Ireland—if you make a purchase in one of its shops, you may wind up with some euro coins from Ireland in your change.

GETTING HERE AND AROUND

Stranraer has a busy train station that serves all major lines and is directly accessible from Glasgow, and the buses are good as well (with many connections to smaller towns). If you're driving, take the A747 from Whithorn (about 45 minutes). From Glasgow, take the M77/A77 (two hours), and from Edinburgh, take the A77 (three hours).

ESSENTIALS

Visitor Information Stranraer **Visitor Information Centre.** ✉ 28 Harbour St. ☎ 01776/702595 ⊕ www. visitscotland.com.

HIKING THE SOLWAY FIRTH

Mostly undiscovered by travelers, the Solway Firth is a must for walkers, cyclists, bird-watchers, and stone-circle seekers. This lovely and protected inlet is a haven for a great variety of seabirds, which you can spot from the coastal paths that link Sandyhills, Rockcliffe, and Kippford. To get here, take the A710 from Dumfries, continuing on to the A711. Park where you choose and take the coastal path from any of the three villages.

4

EXPLORING

Fodor's Choice ★ **Castle Kennedy Gardens.** The lovely Castle Kennedy Gardens surround the shell of the original Castle Kennedy, which was burned in 1716. Parks scattered around the property were built by the second Earl of Stair in 1733. The earl was a field marshal and used his soldiers to help with the heavy work of constructing banks, ponds, and other major landscape features. When the rhododendrons are in bloom, the effect is kaleidoscopic. There's also a pleasant tearoom. ✉ *Castle Kennedy, 3 miles east of Stranraer on the A875* ☎ *01776/702024* ⊕ *www. castlekennedygardens.co.uk* ✆ *£5.50* ☉ *Easter–Oct., daily 10–5; Feb. and Mar., weekends 10–5.*

PORTPATRICK

8 miles southwest of Stranraer, 94 miles southwest of Glasgow, 139 miles southwest of Edinburgh.

The holiday town of Portpatrick lies across the Rhinns of Galloway from Stranraer. Once an Irish ferry port, Portpatrick's harbor eventually proved too small for larger vessels.

GETTING HERE AND AROUND

Direct buses travel between Portpatrick to Stranraer and some of the neighboring towns, but travel to and from the larger Scottish cities can prove more difficult. There is no train station in Portpatrick (though there is one in nearby Stranraer). Driving is probably your best bet. From Stranraer, take the A77; it's about a 15-minute journey. Take the M77/A77 from Glasgow (just over two hours) and the M8/A77 from Edinburgh (about three hours).

EXPLORING

Dunskey Castle. Just south of Portpatrick are the lichen-yellow ruins of 16th-century Dunskey Castle, accessible from a cliff-top path off the B7042. There is no access to the interior, and it is wise to stick to the path since the cliffs here are steep.

Logan Botanic Garden. One of the National Botanic Gardens of Scotland, the spectacular Logan Botanic Garden is a must-see for garden lovers. Displayed here are plants that enjoy the prevailing mild climate, especially tree ferns, cabbage palms, and other Southern Hemisphere exotica. There are free guided walks every second Tuesday of the month at 10:30 am; at other times there is a free audio guide. ✉ *Port Logan* ✣ *On B7065 14 miles south of Stranraer* ☎ *01776/860231* 🌐 *www.rbge.org.uk* 🎟 *£3.50* ⏲ *Mar. and Oct., daily 10–5; Apr.–Sept., daily 10–6.*

Mull of Galloway. If you wish to visit the southern tip of the Rhinns of Galloway, called the Mull of Galloway, follow the B7065/B7041 until you run out of land. The cliffs and seascapes here are rugged, and there's a lighthouse and a bird reserve.

Southern Upland Way. The village of Portpatrick is the starting point for Scotland's longest official long-distance footpath, the Southern Upland Way, which runs a switchback course for 212 miles to Cockburnspath, on the east side of the Borders. The path begins on the cliffs just north of the town and follows the coastline for 1½ miles before turning inland. 🌐 *www.southernuplandway.gov.uk.*

WHERE TO STAY

$ HOTEL 🏨 **Crown Portpatrick.** From the terrace of this simple small hotel in a working fishing village you can look out across the sea to Ireland while eating some delicious seafood. **Pros:** beautiful location; very good restaurant. **Cons:** Portpatrick is fairly remote. [$] *Rooms from: £90* ✉ *9 North Crescent* ☎ *01776/810261* 🌐 *www.crownportpatrick.com* 🛏 *12 rooms* 🍴 *Breakfast.*

FIFE AND ANGUS

Updated by
Shona Main

Breezy cliff-top walkways, fishing villages, and open beaches characterize Fife and Angus. They sandwich Scotland's fourth-largest—and often overlooked—city, Dundee. Scotland's east coast has only light rainfall throughout the year; northeastern Fife, in particular, may claim the record for the most sunshine and the least rainfall in Scotland, which all adds to the enjoyment when you're touring the coast or the famous golf center of St. Andrews.

Fife proudly styles itself as a "kingdom," and its long history—which really began when the Romans went home in the 4th century and the Picts moved in—lends some substance to the boast. From medieval times its earls were first among Scotland's nobility and crowned her kings. For many, however, the most historic event in the region was the birth of golf, in the 15th century, which, legend has it, occurred in St. Andrews, an ancient university town with stone houses and seaside ruins. The Royal & Ancient Golf Club, the ruling body of the game worldwide, still has its headquarters here.

Not surprisingly, fishing and seafaring have also played a role in the history of the East Neuk coastal region. From the 16th through 19th century a large population lived and worked in the small ports and harbors that form a chain around Fife's coast, which James V once called "a beggar's mantle fringed with gold." When the sun shines, this golden fringe—particularly at Tentsmuir, St. Andrews, and Elie—gleams like the beaches of Normandy. Indeed, the houses of the East Neuk villages have a similar character, with color-washed fronts, fishy weather vanes, outdoor stone stairways to upper floors, and crude carvings of anchors and lobsters on their lintels. All the houses are crowded on steep *wynds* (narrow streets), hugging pint-size harbors that in the golden era supported village fleets of 100 ships apiece.

North, across the Firth of Tay, lies the region of Angus, whose charm is its variety: in addition to its seacoast and pleasant Lowland market centers, there's also a hinterland of lonely rounded hills with long glens running into the typical Grampian Highland scenery beyond. One of Angus's interesting features, which it shares with the eastern Lowland edge of Perthshire, is its fruit-growing industry, which includes raspberries.

Known as the "City of Discovery" (after the RRS *Discovery,* a polar exploration vessel that set sail from this port in 1901), Dundee has a surprisingly sophisticated arts and cultural scene. The regeneration of the city's riverside means huge works are under way: beyond the fences building has begun on the ship-shape Victoria and Albert Museum. This aside, Dundee makes a good base from which to make a number of day trips.

TOP REASONS TO GO

St. Andrews: With its medieval streets, ruined cathedral and castle, and peculiarly posh atmosphere, St. Andrews is one of the most incongruous yet beguiling places in Scotland—even without its famous golf course.

Great golf: If you can't get on the Old Course in St. Andrews by ballot or by any other means, Fife and Angus have fabulous fairways aplenty, including the famous links course at Carnoustie.

East Neuk: As you take in crowstep-gabled fishermen's cottages, winding cobbled lanes, seaside harbor scenes, and lovely beaches, you can almost imagine the harsh lives of the hardworking Fifers who lived in tiny hamlets such as Crail, Anstruther, Pittenweem, and Elie. Today artists and visitors make it all pleasantly picturesque.

Dundee: This formerly industrial city is becoming better known for its vibrant arts, music, theater, restaurant, and nightlife scenes. It's in a spectacular natural setting by Britain's most powerful river, the Tay.

The glens: The long Angus glens (such as Glen Clova) that run into the wild Grampian Mountains are magical places beloved by outdoors enthusiasts and those just wanting to rediscover nature.

5

GETTING ORIENTED

Fife lies north of the Lothians, across the iconic bridges of the Firth of Forth. A headland, Fife's northeastern coast (or East Neuk) is fringed with golden sands, rocky shores, fishermen's cottages, and, of course, the splendor of St. Andrews, home of golf. Northwest of Fife and across the glorious Firth of Tay, the city of Dundee is undergoing a postindustrial reinvention. Its rural hinterland, Angus, hugs the city, which, stretching north toward the foothills of the Grampian Mountains, houses agricultural and fishing communities, and Glamis, one of Scotland's best-loved castles.

St. Andrews and East Neuk. St. Andrews isn't just a playground for golfers. This religious and academic center is steeped in history and prestige, with grand buildings, a palpable air of prosperity, and the cachet of being the place where a riveting 21st-century royal romance began. Beyond St. Andrews the colorful fishing villages of the East Neuk are a day-tripper's (and fish eater's) delight.

Dundee and Angus. Dundee has a knockout setting beside Britain's mightiest river, historical sights—including Captain Scott's ship, RRS *Discovery*—and a vibrant social life. The tree-lined country roads of the Angus heartlands roll through strawberry and raspberry fields to busy market towns, wee villages, and Glamis Castle.

PLANNING

WHEN TO GO

Spring in the Angus glens can be quite captivating, with the hills along Angus's northernmost boundary still covered in snow. Similarly, the moorland colors of autumn are appealing. However, Fife and Angus are really summer destinations, when most of the sights are open to visitors. St. Andrews hosts a number of international golf tournaments that effectively take over the town. Nongolfers may become incredibly frustrated when searching for accommodations or places to eat during these times, so check ahead.

PLANNING YOUR TIME

St. Andrews, 52 miles from Edinburgh, is not to be missed, for its history and atmosphere as much as for the golf; allot an overnight stop and at least a whole day if you can. The nearby East Neuk of Fife has some of Scotland's finest coastline, now becoming gentrified by the Edinburgh second-home set but still evoking Fife's past. A day's drive along A917 (allow for exploring and stops for ice cream and fish) will take you through the fishing villages of Elie, Pittenweem, Anstruther, and Crail. Dundee, with a rich maritime history and a grand museum, is an ideal base for a drive round the Angus towns of Arbroath, Kirriemuir, and Alyth; if you make a three-hour stop at Glamis Castle, this trip will take about a day.

GETTING HERE AND AROUND

AIR TRAVEL

Dundee Airport is off A85, 2 miles west of the city center. Air France operates a popular direct flight from London City Airport. If you are traveling to St. Andrews directly from Edinburgh Airport, the St. Andrews Shuttle offers transfers from £19.

BUS TRAVEL

Buses connect Edinburgh's St. Andrew Square bus station and Glasgow's Buchanan Street bus station to Fife and Angus. Megabus operates hourly service to Dundee from both Glasgow and Edinburgh. Stagecoach Fife serves Fife and St. Andrews, and Travel Dundee provides bus service in and around Dundee, Angus, and Fife. These services can be found on Dundee Travel Info or Traveline Scotland, websites that help you plan all public-transport journeys.

Stagecoach connects St. Andrews and Dundee to many of the smaller towns throughout Fife and Angus. A Day Rover ticket (£8.40 for Fife only) is a good value.

Bus Contacts Dundee Travel Info. ⊕ www.dundeetravelinfo.com. **Megabus.** ☎ 0900/160–0900 ⊕ uk.megabus.com. **Stagecoach.** ☎ 01382/313700 Dundee ⊕ www.stagecoachbus.com. **St. Andrews Shuttle.** ☎ 0790/248–8770 ⊕ www. standrewsshuttle.com. **Traveline Scotland.** ☎ 08706/200–2233 ⊕ www. travelinescotland.com.

CAR TRAVEL

The fastest route to Angus and northeast Fife is the M90 motorway from Edinburgh. Exit onto the A90 at Perth (45 minutes), and travel an additional 20 minutes to reach Dundee; 15 minutes later, you'll arrive in

St. Andrews. If you're coming from Fife, you can also take the A91 and the A914, and cross the Tay Bridge to reach Dundee. This is a slower route, but does take you through the heartland of Fife.

Fife and Angus cover a compact area, so getting around is straightforward. You can visit everything via a series of excursions off the main north–south artery, the A90/M90, which leads from Edinburgh to Aberdeen. From here you can easily make day trips to Edinburgh, Glasgow, or Perthshire. Aberdeenshire and the Central Highlands are not too far away either.

Fife is easy to navigate—although it can be difficult to find a place to park in St. Andrews. The most interesting sights are in the east, which is served by a network of cross-country roads. Angus is also an easy region to explore. It's serviced by a fast main road (the A90), a gentler road (the A92), and several rural roads that run between the Grampians and the A90.

TRAIN TRAVEL

ScotRail stops at Kirkcaldy, Cupar, Leuchars (for St. Andrews), Dundee, Broughty Ferry, Carnoustie, Arbroath, and Montrose.

Train Contact ScotRail. ☎ 0344/811–0141 ⊕ www.scotrail.co.uk.

RESTAURANTS

With an affluent population, St. Andrews supports several stylish hotel restaurants. Because it's a university town and popular tourist destination, there are also many good cafés and bistro-style restaurants. Bar lunches are the rule in large and small hotels throughout the region, and in seaside places the carry- *oot* (to-go) meal of fish-and-chips is an enduring tradition.

HOTELS

If you're staying in Fife, the obvious choice for a base is St. Andrews, with ample accommodations of all kinds. Another good option is the Howe of Fife, between Strathmiglo and Cupar, where there are some excellent country-house hotels, many with their own restaurants. Dundee and its hinterlands have a number of diverse accommodations, all of which offer good value. *Hotel reviews have been shortened. For full information, visit Fodors.com.*

WHAT IT COSTS IN POUNDS				
	$	$$	$$$	$$$$
Restaurants	Under £15	£15–£19	£20–£25	Over £25
Hotels	Under £100	£100–£160	£161–£220	Over £220

Restaurant prices are the average cost of a main course at dinner or, if dinner is not served, at lunch. Hotel prices are the lowest cost of a standard double room in high season, including 20% V.A.T.

VISITOR INFORMATION

The Arbroath, Dundee, and St. Andrews tourist offices are open year-round. Smaller tourist information centers operate seasonally in Anstruther, Brechin, Crail, Forfar, Kirriemuir, and Montrose.

ST. ANDREWS AND EAST NEUK

In its western parts Fife still bears the scars of heavy industry, especially coal mining, but these signs are less evident as you move east. Northeastern Fife, around the town of St. Andrews, seems to have played no part in the Industrial Revolution; instead, its residents earned a living from the grain fields or from the sea. Fishing has been a major industry, and in the past a string of Fife ports traded across the North Sea. Today the legacy of Dutch-influenced architecture, such as crowstep gables (the stepped effect on the ends of the roofs)—gives these East Neuk villages a distinctive character.

St. Andrews is unlike any other Scottish town. Once Scotland's most powerful ecclesiastical center as well as the seat of the country's oldest university and then, much later, the very symbol and spiritual home of golf, the town has a comfortable, well-groomed air, sitting almost smugly apart from the rest of Scotland. Its latest boast, being the town where Prince William first kissed Kate Middleton, has boosted university applications.

ST. ANDREWS

52 miles northeast of Edinburgh, 83 miles northeast of Glasgow.

Fodor'sChoice
★ It may have a ruined cathedral and a grand university—the oldest in Scotland—but the modern claim to fame for St. Andrews is mainly its status as the home of golf. Forget that Scottish kings were crowned here, or that John Knox preached here and that Reformation reformers were burned at the stake here. Thousands flock to St. Andrews to play at the Old Course, home of the Royal & Ancient Club, and to follow in the footsteps of Hagen, Sarazen, Jones, and Hogan.

The layout is pure Middle Ages: its three main streets—North, Market, and South—converge on the city's earliest religious site, near the cathedral. Like most of the ancient monuments, the cathedral ruins are impressive in their desolation—but this town is no dusty museum. The streets are busy, the shops are stylish, the gray houses sparkle in the sun, and the scene is particularly brightened during the academic year by bicycling students in scarlet gowns.

GETTING HERE AND AROUND

If you arrive by car, be prepared for an endless drive round the town as you look for a parking space. The parking lots around Rose Park (behind the bus station and a short walk from the town center) are your best bet. If you arrive by local or national bus, the bus station is a five-minute walk from town. The nearest train station, Leuchars, is 10 minutes away by taxi (£15) or bus (£2.75), both of which can be found outside the station. St. Andrews can be fully enjoyed on foot without too much exertion.

ESSENTIALS

Visitor Information St. Andrews. ⊠ *70 Market St.* ☎ *01334/472021* ⊕ *www. visitstandrews.com.*

EXPLORING

TOP ATTRACTIONS

Fodor'sChoice
★ **Bell Pettigrew Museum of Natural History.** Founded by Elsie Bell Pettigrew in memory of her husband James, a former professor of medicine, this fascinating collection of zoological specimens takes you from sea to jungle, mountain to sky. The antiquated manner of their presentation reminds you of their significance in an age when most of these creatures were still unknown to most people. In the handsome 16th-century St. Mary's Quadrangle, home to the St. Andrews University's divinity and psychology departments, it is dominated by a holm oak supposedly planted by Mary, Queen of Scots. ⊠ *Bute Medical Bldg., Queens Gardens, off South St.* ☎ *01334/463608* ⊕ *www.st-andrews.ac.uk/museum/ bellpettigrew* ⊠ *Free* ☉ *July and Aug., Tues. and Fri. 2–5; all other times by appointment (bellpett@st-andrews.ac.uk).*

British Golf Museum. This newly refurbished museum explores the centuries-old relationship between St. Andrews and golf and displays golf memorabilia from the 18th century to the 21st century. It's just opposite the Royal & Ancient Golf Club. ⊠ *Bruce Embankment* ☎ *01334/460046* ⊕ *www.britishgolfmuseum.co.uk* ⊠ *£6.50* ☉ *Apr.– Oct., Mon.–Sat. 9:30–5, Sun. 10–5; Nov.–Mar., daily 10–4.*

5

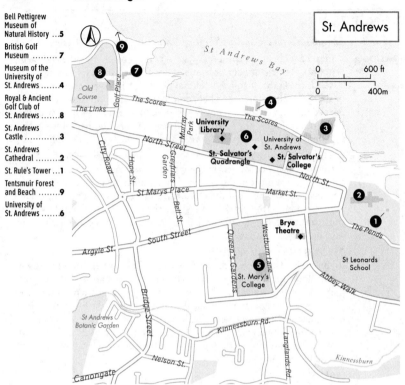

St. Andrews Castle. On the shore north of the cathedral stands ruined St. Andrews Castle, begun at the end of the 13th century. The remains include a rare example of a cold and gruesome bottle-shape dungeon, in which many prisoners spent their last hours. Even more atmospheric is the castle's mine and countermine. The former was a tunnel dug by besieging forces in the 16th century; the latter, a tunnel dug by castle defenders in order to meet and wage battle belowground. You can stoop and crawl into this narrow passageway—an eerie experience, despite the addition of electric light. The visitor center has a good audiovisual presentation on the castle's history. In the summer, the beach below is popular with sunbathers and rockpool investigators, weather permitting. ⊠ *N. Castle St.* ☎ *01334/477196* ⊕ *www.historic-scotland.gov. uk* ⊠ *£5.50, £7.20 with St. Andrews Cathedral and St. Rule's Tower* ☉ *Apr.–Sept., daily 9:30–5:30; Oct.–Mar., daily 9:30–4:30.*

St. Andrews Cathedral. These are the poignant remains of what was once the largest and most magnificent church in Scotland. Work on it began in 1160, and after several delays it was finally consecrated in 1318. The church was subsequently damaged by fire and repaired, but fell into decay during the Reformation. Only ruined gables, parts of the nave's south wall, and other fragments survive. The on-site museum helps you interpret the remains and gives a sense of what the cathedral must once

have been like. ⊠ *Off Pends Rd.*
☎ *01334/472563* ⊕ *www.historic-*
scotland.gov.uk 🎟 *£4.50, includes*
St. Rule's Tower; £7.20 includes
St Andrews Castle ⊙ *Apr.–Sept.,*
daily 9:30–5:30; Oct.–Mar., daily
9:30–4:30.

St. Rule's Tower. Local legend has
it that St. Andrews was founded
by St. Regulus, or Rule, who, acting under divine guidance, carried
relics of St. Andrew by sea from
Patras in Greece. He was shipwrecked on this Fife headland and

ICE CREAM TREATS

In summer the streets of St.
Andrews are full of people
walking around with a cone
or slider (a wafer ice cream
sandwich). Luvians (84 Market
Street) is like an old-fashioned
sweet shop, while Jannetta's (31
South Street) has a more modern
vibe. Which is best? Locals can't
decide, so you'll have to try both.

founded a church. The holy man's name survives in the cylindrical
tower, consecrated in 1126 and the oldest surviving building in St.
Andrews. Enjoy dizzying views of town from the top of the tower,
reached via a steep staircase. ⊠ *Off Pends Rd.* ☎ *01334/472563*
⊕ *www.historic-scotland.gov.uk* 🎟 *£4.20, includes St. Andrews Cathe-*
dral; £7.20 includes St. Andrews Castle ⊙ *Apr.–Sept., daily 9:30–5:30;*
Oct.–Mar., daily 9:30–4:30.

WORTH NOTING

Museum of the University of St. Andrews. With four galleries, the Museum
of the University of St. Andrews exhibits more than a few austere paintings from the 1600s all the way up to the present day. You'll also find
ecumenical regalia, decorative arts, and early scientific instruments
including Humphrey Cole's astrolabe of 1575. It also has sweeping
views over St. Andrews Bay. ⊠ *7A the Scores* ☎ *01334/461660* ⊕ *www.*
st-andrews.ac.uk/musa 🎟 *Free* ⊙ *Apr.–Oct., Mon.–Sat. 10–5, Sun.*
noon–4; Nov.–Mar., Thurs.–Sun. noon–4.

Royal & Ancient Golf Club of St. Andrews. The ruling house of golf worldwide is the spiritual home of all who play or follow the game. Founded
in 1754, its clubhouse on the dunes—open to members only, who must
be male—is a mix of classical, Victorian, and neoclassical styles; it's
adjacent to the famous Old Course. ⊠ *The Scores* ⊕ *www.randa.org.*

FAMILY **Tentsmuir Forest and Beach.** Just 2 miles east of Leuchars, this pine forest fringes the long, sandy Kinshaldy Beach. Popular with families,
beachcombers, and naturalists, it's 5 miles long and has enough space
for everyone. ⊠ *B945, Leuchars* ⊕ *www.tentsmuir.org* 🎟 *Parking £2*
⊙ *Daily 9–sunset.*

University of St. Andrews. Scotland's oldest university is the alma mater
of John Knox (Protestant reformer), King James II of Scotland, the
Duke and Duchess of Cambridge (William and Kate), and Chris Hoy,
Scotland's Olympic cyclist. Founded in 1411, the university's buildings
pepper the town. For the quintessential University of St. Andrews experience, **St. Salvator's Quadrangle** reveals the magnificence of this historic
institution. Looking out onto this impressive college green is the striking
St. Salvator's Chapel, founded in 1450. It bears the marks of a turbulent
past: the initials PH, carved into the paving stones under the bell tower,

are those of Patrick Hamilton, who was burned alive outside the chapel for his Protestant beliefs. ⊠ *St Mary's Pl.*

WHERE TO EAT

$$$$
CONTEMPORARY
Fodor's Choice
★

✕ **The Grange Inn.** Just 10 minutes outside town, this beautifully converted 17th century farmhouse surrounded by verdant fields is where Fife foodies flock. The dark-beamed, stone-walled interior is well lit, avoiding the gloom that often clutches old buildings. The prix-fixe menu offers exquisite versions of old Scot's standards—*cullen skink*, loin of venison—and these, too, benefit from a lightness of touch. There is a handsome bar but don't expect bar suppers: it is for the purposes of drinking only. $ *Average main: £30* ⊠ *Grange Rd.* ☎ *01334 /472670* ⊕ *www.thegrangeinn.com* ⊗ *Closed Mon. No dinner Sun.* ⚱ *Reservations essential.*

$
CONTEMPORARY
FAMILY

✕ **Playfair's Restaurant.** If all that sea air has made you ravenous, this restaurant under the Ardgowan Hotel offers great quality sustenance at decent prices. Their beef stovies (beef boiled with potatoes then mashed) served with oatcakes and haggis and neeps are singular examples of Scottish standards or try their simple grilled Isle of Lewis fish or Fife Ribeye steak. Vegetarians beware: they do cater for you but meat and fish are their thing. $ *Average main: £14* ⊠ *2 Playfair Terr., North St.* ✛ *Underneath the Ardgowan Hotel* ☎ *01334/472970* ⊕ *playfairsrestaurant.co.uk* ⊟ *No credit cards.*

$$$$
SEAFOOD

✕ **The Seafood Restaurant.** This stunning glass-walled building is perched on the banks of the West Sands. Once an open-air theater, the kitchen radiates a confidence and calm that contributes to the easy atmosphere. The prix-fixe menu is adventurous without being flashy: start with fat, juicy Shetland mussels, then move on to bream with peas. $ *Average main: £39.50* ⊠ *Bruce Embankment* ☎ *01334/479475* ⊕ *www.theseafoodrestaurant.com* ⚱ *Reservations essential.*

$
SEAFOOD

✕ **Tailend Restaurant.** The queue of customers outside might be a bit offputting but the sweet smell of fish-and-chips from St. Andrews's best "chipper" keeps them focused on the battered prize. There's a small but modish dining room or you can carry out, with your supper wrapped in last week's *St. Andrews Citizen*. The menu offers langoustine tails, seared scallops and a fish of the day, but you can't go wrong with their "humble haddock" and chips. To sit in, please be sure to book. $ *Average main: £11* ⊠ *130 Market St.* ☎ *01334/474070* ⊕ *www.thetailend.co.uk* ⚱ *Reservations essential* ⊟ *No credit cards.*

$
MODERN BRITISH

✕ **West Port Bar & Kitchen.** It's easy to forget that St. Andrews is a university town when the students are on summer break, but this modern bar and eatery remains vibrant and youthful year-round. The reasonably priced menu offers nicely prepared pub grub—everything from gourmet burgers to smoked haddock fishcakes—making this a satisfying stop for lunch or dinner. Upstairs are four bright B&B rooms that go for £95. $ *Average main: £12* ⊠ *170 South St.* ☎ *01334/473186* ⊕ *www.thewestport.co.uk.*

WHERE TO STAY

$$
B&B/INN

🖼 **Aslar Guest House.** This terraced town house dating from 1865 has large rooms with ornate cornicing and antique reproduction furniture. **Pros:** homey feel; great location; exceptional breakfast. **Cons:** books up quickly. $ *Rooms from: £100* ✉ *120 North St.* ☎ *01334/473460* ⊕ *www.aslar.com* ⮐ *6 rooms* ⦿ *Breakfast.*

$$$$ ⊞ **Fairmont St Andrews.** Two miles from St. Andrews, this modern hotel
HOTEL has spectacular views of the bay and two superb golf courses. **Pros:** spacious feel; excellent spa; golf at your doorstep. **Cons:** the huge atrium feels like a shopping center; paintings made to match the decor. $ *Rooms from: £280* ✉ *A917* ☎ *01334/837000* ⊕ *www.fairmont.com/standrews* ⮐ *192 rooms, 17 suites* ⦿ *Breakfast.*

$$$$ ⊞ **Old Course Hotel.** Regularly hosting international golf stars and jet-
HOTEL setters, the Old Course Hotel recently underwent a renaissance—the
Fodor's Choice guest rooms and public spaces have been reinvigorated, and the service
★ has warmed up. **Pros:** fabulous location and lovely views; unpretentious service; golfer's heaven. **Cons:** all the golf talk might bore non-golfers; spa is on the small side. $ *Rooms from: £390* ✉ *Old Station Rd.* ☎ *01334/474371* ⊕ *www.oldcoursehotel.co.uk* ⮐ *109 rooms, 35 suites* ⦿ *Breakfast.*

$$$ ⊞ **Rufflets Country House Hotel.** Ten acres of formal and informal gardens
HOTEL surround this creeper-covered country house just outside St. Andrews. **Pros:** attractive gardens; cozy drawing room; popular restaurant. **Cons:** too far to walk to St. Andrews; it's a venue for those celebrating. $ *Rooms from: £175* ✉ *Strathkinness Low Rd.* ☎ *01334/472594* ⊕ *www.rufflets.co.uk* ⮐ *23 rooms, 2 suites* ⦿ *Breakfast.*

$$$$ ⊞ **Scores Hotel.** Overlooking the St. Andrews shoreline, this pair of town
HOTEL houses keep good company—they sit next to the Royal & Ancient Golf Club of St. Andrews. **Pros:** rooms range from big to vast; the staff is motivated and happy to oblige; great location on the edge of the Old Course. **Cons:** reception area is uninspiring. $ *Rooms from: £250* ✉ *76 the Scores* ☎ *01334/472451* ⊕ *www.scoreshotel.co.uk* ▭ *No credit cards* ⮐ *36 rooms* ⦿ *Breakfast.*

NIGHTLIFE AND PERFORMING ARTS
PUBS
Central Bar. There are still some old-fashioned pubs to be found among the cocktail bars of St. Andrews, and this is one of the friendliest. You'll find a good range of beers (bottled and on tap) and decent pub food. ✉ *77 Market St.* ☎ *01334/478296.*

FILM
New Picture House Cinema. A lovely old cinema shows a well-chosen mix of Hollywood and independent films. ✉ *117 North St.* ☎ *01334/474902* ⊕ *http://nph.nphcinema.co.uk.*

SHOPPING
Artery. Artery sells work by local, Scottish, and British artists, including jewelry, ceramics, paintings, and intriguing handmade clocks. ✉ *43 South St.* ☎ *01334/478221.*

Balgove Larder. Here you'll discover a huge selection of Scottish items, from spurtles (for stirring your porridge) to tablet (sugary toffee) to big, thick sausages. In summer, the barn where they usually store the potatoes is transformed into a rustic steak house selling steak and chips for £15. ✉ *A91* ☎ *01334/898145* ⊕ *www.balgove.com.*

Mellis. This place is truly a cheese-lover's mecca. Look for a soft, crumbly local cheese called Anster. ✉ *149 South St.* ☎ *01334/471410* ⊕ *www. mellischeese.net.*

Rummage. A fascinating mix of old china, silver, linens and jewelry is mixed in with books and crafts. ✉ *138 South St.* ☎ *01334/478625* ⊕ *http://www.rummage-standrews.co.uk.*

GOLF

What serious golfer doesn't dream of playing at world-famous St. Andrews? Seven St. Andrews courses, all part of the St. Andrews Trust, are open to visitors, and more than 40 other courses in the region offer golf by the round or by the day.

ST. ANDREWS LINKS TRUST COURSES

St. Andrews Links Trust. For information about availability—there's usually a waiting list, which varies according to the time of year—contact St. Andrews Links Trust. Greens fees range from £80 to £175 for a round on the Old Course and from £8 to £120 for a round on the five other courses. ☎ *01334/466666* ⊕ *www.standrews.org.uk.*

Balgove Course. At the beginner-friendly Balgove Course you can turn up and tee off without prior reservation. ✉ *West Sands Rd., A91* ⊕ *www. standrews.org.uk* 🏌 *£8–£15* ⛳ *9 holes, 1520 yards, par 30.*

Castle Course. Designed by David McLay Kidd in 2008, the Castle Course hugs the rugged coastline and has jaw-dropping views. It's 2 miles from the town center. ✉ *A917* ⊕ *www.standrews.org.uk* 🏌 *£60– £120* ⛳ *18 holes, 6759 yards, par 71.*

Eden Course. The aptly named Eden Course, designed in 1914 by Harry S. Colt, winds through inland fields bordered with lovely foliage. It's a bit more forgiving compared to other St. Andrews courses. ✉ *West Sands Rd.* ⊕ *www.standrews.org.uk* 🏌 *£20–£45* ⛳ *18 holes, 6250 yards, par 70.*

Jubilee Course. This windswept course offers quite a challenge even for experienced golfers. When it opened in 1897 was intended for beginners, but the popularity of its seaside location encouraged the powers that be to convert it into a championship course. Many golfers say the 15th hole is one of the best in the sport. ✉ *West Sands Rd.* ⊕ *www. standrews.org.uk* 🏌 *£35–£75* ⛳ *18 holes, 6742 yards, par 72.*

New Course. Not exactly new—it opened in 1895—the New Course is rather overshadowed by the Old Course, but it has a firm following of golfers who appreciate the loop design. ✉ *West Sands Rd.* ⊕ *www. standrews.org.uk* 🏌 *£37–£75* ⛳ *18 holes, 6625 yards, par 71.*

Old Course. Believed to be the oldest golf course in the world, the Old Course was first played in the 15th century. Each year, more than 44,000 rounds are teed off, and no doubt most get stuck in one of its 112 bunkers. A handicap certificate and some very early morning waits for a possible tee off are required. ✉ *West Sands Rd.* ⊕ *www.standrews. org.uk* 🏌 *£80–£175* ⛳ *18 holes, 6721 yards, par 72.*

Strathtyrum Course. Those with a high handicap will enjoy this course, opened in 1993, without the worry or embarrassment of holding up more experienced golfers. ✉ *West Sands Rd., A91* ⊕ *www.standrews. org.uk* 🏌 *£15–£30* ⛳ *18 holes, 5620 yards, par 69.*

CRAIL

10 miles south of St. Andrews.

Fodor's Choice ★ The oldest and most aristocratic of East Neuk burghs, pretty Crail is where many fish merchants retired and built cottages. The town landmark is a picturesque Dutch-influenced town house, or *tolbooth*, which contains the oldest bell in Fife, cast in Holland in 1520. Crail may now be full of artists, but it remains a working harbor; take time to walk the streets and beaches and to sample fish by the harbor. ■ TIP→ **As you head into East Neuk from this tiny port, look about for market crosses, merchant houses, and little doocots (dovecotes, where pigeons were kept)—typical picturesque touches of this region.**

GETTING HERE AND AROUND

Stagecoach bus number 63 operates between Crail and St. Andrews. However, the number 95 takes 30 minutes, is more regular and also takes you to Anstruther, Pittenweem, and Lower Largo. Crail is about 15 minutes from St. Andrews by car via A917.

EXPLORING

Crail Museum and Heritage Centre. The story of this trading and fishing town can be found in the delightfully crammed Crail Museum and Heritage Centre, entirely run by local volunteers. There is a small tourist information desk within the center. ✉ *62–64 Marketgate* ☎ *01333/450869* 🌐 *www.crailmuseum.org.uk* 🎟 *Free* 🕒 *Apr. and May limited hrs, please check; June–Sept., Mon.–Sat. 11–4, Sun. 1–4.*

WHERE TO STAY

$ B&B/INN Fodor's Choice ★ 🏨 **Hazelton.** Beautifully polished wood, exquisitely restored period features, and gentle hues put the Hazelton head and shoulders above the typical seaside B&B. **Pros:** handsome building; excellent location; nothing is too much of a problem for the generous-spirited staff. **Cons:** a couple of the rooms are on the small side. [$] *Rooms from: £70* ✉ *29 Marketgate N* ☎ *01333/450250* 🌐 *www.thehazelton.co.uk* 💳 *No credit cards* 🕒 *Closed Jan.* 🛏 *5 rooms* 🍴 *Breakfast.*

WHERE TO EAT

$ SEAFOOD 🍴 **Lobster Store.** This hut on the pier, a hidden gem, sells beautifully cooked lobsters for £11–£16 each (depending on size) and other items at times, including lobster rolls. They'll crack the lobster for you to allow for easy eating on a nearby bench; there is no seating, but the lobster is wonderful. Hours can vary. [$] *Average main: £14* ✉ *34 Shoregate* ☎ 0133/450476 💳 *No credit cards.*

ANSTRUTHER

4 miles southwest of Crail.

Anstruther, locally called Ainster, has a lovely waterfront with a few shops brightly festooned with children's pails and shovels, a gesture to summer vacationers.

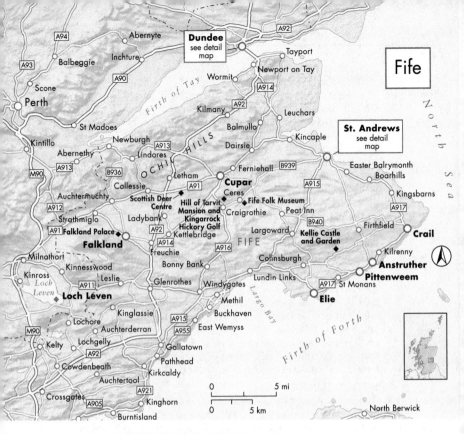

GETTING HERE AND AROUND

Strgecoach bus number 95 operates between St. Andrews, Crail, Anstruther, Pittenweem, and Lower Largo. Anstruther is 5 to 10 minutes from Crail by car via A917.

ESSENTIALS

Visitor Information Anstruther Tourist Information. ⊠ *Scottish Fisheries Museum, Harbour Head* ☎ *01333/311073* ⊕ *www.visitfife.com.*

EXPLORING

Fodor's Choice
★

Scottish Fisheries Museum. Facing Anstruther Harbor, the Scottish Fisheries Museum is inside a colorful cluster of buildings, the earliest of which dates from the 16th century. The museum illustrates the life of Scottish fisherfolk through documents, artifacts, model ships, paintings, and displays (complete with the reek of tarred rope and net). There are also floating exhibits at the quayside. There's a small desk here with tourism information. ⊠ *Harbourhead* ☎ *01333/310628* ⊕ *www.scotfishmuseum.org* ⌧ *£8* ⊙ *Apr.–Sept., Mon.–Sat. 10–5:30, Sun. 11–5; Oct.–Mar., Mon.–Sat. 10–4:30, Sun. noon–4:30; last admission 1 hr before closing.*

WHERE TO EAT

$ ✕ **Anstruther Fish Bar and Restaurant.**
SEAFOOD   Next door to the Scottish Fisheries
Fodor's Choice   Museum, this popular fish-and-chip
★   shop has space to eat, but most peo-
ple order take-out. Try Pittenweem-
landed prawns in batter or the catch
of the day, which could be mackerel
(line caught by the owners), hake,
or local crab. **$** *Average main: £8*
✉ *42–44 Shore St.* ☎ *01333/310518*
⊕ *www.anstrutherfishbar.co.uk*
▭ *No credit cards.*

$$$$ ✕ **The Cellar.** Entered through a
EUROPEAN   cobbled courtyard, this famously
unpretentious, old-fashioned restaurant has recently changed management: thankfully it is as good as
it ever was. Their three-course prix-
fixe meals are locally sourced yet
inventive, as is the style of the new
breed of Scots chefs: think Scots
gin-cured trout or Angus beef with
wild garlic spelt. **$** *Average main: £43* ✉ *24 E. Green* ☎ *01333/310378*
⊕ *www.thecellaranstruther.co.uk* ⊗ *Closed Mon. and Tues. No lunch
Wed.* ⚒ *Reservations essential.*

FIFE COASTAL PATH

Fife's green and undulating landscape includes the Lomond Hills,
to the west, which are easy to
climb and offer fabulous views of
both the Tay and Forth estuar-
ies. The Fife Coastal Path can be
bracing or an amble. The 7-mile
stretch between East Wemyss to
Lower Largo (four to six hours) is
the easiest going, with some of
it along the beaches of Elie. The
8-mile route between Pittenweem
to Fifeness (four to six hours) can
be rougher in patches, but takes
you through Anstruther and Crail.
Be sure to wear the right footwear and take a waterproof jacket.
For more information, contact
⊕ *www.fifecoastalpath.co.uk.*

NIGHTLIFE AND PERFORMING ARTS

Dreel Tavern. A 16th-century coaching inn, the Dreel Tavern is famous
for its hand-drawn ales. ✉ *16 High St. W* ☎ *01333/310727.*

SPORTS AND THE OUTDOORS

East Neuk Outdoors. The back roads of Fife make pleasant places for
biking. You can rent bicycles from East Neuk Outdoors, which also
has equipment for archery, climbing, and canoeing. ✉ *Cellardyke Park*
☎ *01333/311929* ⊕ *www.eastneukoutdoors.co.uk.*

PITTENWEEM

1½ miles southwest of Anstruther.

Many examples of East Neuk architecture serve as the backdrop for
the working harbor at Pittenweem. Look for the crowstep gables, white
harling (the rough mortar finish on walls), and red *pantiles* (roof tiles
with an S-shape profile). The *weem* part of the town's name comes from
the Gaelic *uaime*, meaning cave.

GETTING HERE AND AROUND

Stagecoach bus number 95 operates hourly between St. Andrews, Crail,
Anstruther, Pittenweem, and Lower Largo. Pittenweem is about five
minutes from Anstruther by car via A917.

EXPLORING

Kellie Castle and Garden. Dating from the 16th to 17th centuries and restored in Victorian times, Kellie Castle stands among the grain fields and woodlands of northeastern Fife. Four acres of pretty gardens surround the castle, which is in the care of the National Trust for Scotland. In summer you can buy berries grown in the walled garden, and baked goods are sold in the tearoom. ✉ *B9171, 3 miles northwest of Pittenweem* ☎ *01337 /720271* 🌐 *www.nts.org.uk* 🎟 *£10.50* 🕒 *Castle Apr., May, Sept., and Oct., Thurs.–Mon. noon–5, June–Aug., daily 10:30–5; garden daily 9–sunset.*

Pittenweem Arts Festival. There is nothing quite like August's Pittenweem Arts Festival. Exhibitions, which involve hundreds of local and international artists, take place in the town's public buildings and in private homes and gardens. It's a week of events, workshops, and live music. ☎ *01333/313903* 🌐 *www.pittenweemartsfestival.co.uk.*

St. Fillan's Cave. This town's cavern is called St. Fillan's Cave, which contains the shrine of St. Fillan, a 6th-century hermit who lived here. It's up a *pend* (alleyway) behind the waterfront. If the cave isn't open, ask at the Cocoa Tree on the High Street. Those who can are asked to make a donation of £1 to cover the upkeep of the site. ✉ *Cove Wynd* 🎟 *Free* 🕒 *Mon.–Sat. 10–5.*

WHERE TO EAT

$$$$ SEAFOOD

🍴 **16 West End.** The big sister of the Seafood Restaurant in St. Andrews, this eatery put St. Monans on Scotland's culinary map. The fixed-price menu has vegetarian and meat options, but with dishes like beetroot cured trout and stone bass and samphire in a crab-and-coconut broth, it's really for those looking for a new take on fish. [$] *Average main: £42* ✉ *16 West End, 2 miles west of Pittenweem, St. Monans* ☎ *01333/730327* 🕒 *Closed Mon. and Tues.* ✍ *Reservations essential.*

SHOPPING

Fodor's Choice ★

Pittenweem Chocolate Company. Open daily, this place stocks the most imaginative and comprehensive range of fine chocolates you'll find in this part of the world. There is also a lovely café, with cakes, drinks, light meals, and, of course, handmade chocolates from the Pittenweem Chocolate Company. ✉ *9 High St.* ☎ *01333/311495* 🌐 *www.pittenweemchocolate.co.uk* 🕒 *Daily 10–6.*

ELIE

5 miles south of Pittenweem.

To give it its full name, the Royal Burgh of Elie and Earlsferry is an old trading port with a handsome harbor that loops around one of the most glorious stretches of sand in the British Isles. Since Victorian times, when a railway (sadly defunct since the 1960s) linked it with the capital, Elie has been a weekend and summer retreat for the great and the good of Edinburgh. The beach to the south of the harbor is a mile long and has clean sands, clear waters, and just enough flotsam and jetsam to interest a beachcomber.

WHERE TO EAT

$ BRITISH 🍴 **Ship Inn.** Sports lovers visit Elie on Sunday to watch cricket matches played on the beach outside the Ship Inn. The staff fires up a barbecue and cooks simple fare, including fish, burgers, and chicken. On the side are salads and lots of chips. The relaxed atmosphere and the beauty of this slow, cerebral game makes for an afternoon you'll never forget, especially if the sun shines. [$] *Average main: £12* ✉ *The Toft* ☎ *01333/330246* 🌐 *www.ship-elie.com* 💳 *No credit cards.*

GOLF

Leven Links. A fine Fife course that has been used as a British Open qualifier, Leven Links has a whiff of the more famous St. Andrews, with a hummocky terrain and a tang of salt in the air. The 1st and 18th holes share the same fairway, and the 18th green has a creek running beside it. Saturday play must be booked at least a week in advance. ✉ *The Promenade, Leven* ☎ *01333/428859* 🌐 *www.leven-links.com* 🎟 *£55 weekdays, £60 weekends* 🏌 *18 holes, 6506 yards, par 71* 🕒 *Daily* ✍ *Reservations essential.*

Lundin Golf Club. One of a string of fantastic links courses, Lundin Golf Club is a worthy addition to any Scottish golfing itinerary. Designed by the great James Braid, the course is always in prime condition and the greens are a joy. The pick of the holes is the par-3 14th, played from an elevated tee back toward the sea. ✉ *Golf Rd., Lundin Links* ☎ *01333/320202* 🌐 *www.lundingolfclub.co.uk* 🎟 *£60 weekdays, £70 weekends* 🏌 *18 holes, 6371 yards, par 71* 🕒 *Daily.*

5

FALKLAND

24 miles northwest of Pittenweem, 15 miles northwest of Elie.

Fodor's Choice ★ One of the loveliest communities in Scotland, Falkland is a royal burgh of twisting streets and crooked stone houses.

GETTING HERE AND AROUND

Stagecoach bus number 64A connects Falkland to St. Andrews as well as Cupar and Ladybank (both of which are train stations on the Edinburgh to Dundee line). Falkland is about 15 minutes from Cupar and a half hour from St. Andrews by car via A91 and A912, or A91 to A914 to A912.

EXPLORING

Falkland Palace. A former hunting lodge of the Stuart monarchs, Falkland Palace dominates the town. The castle is one of the country's earliest examples of the French Renaissance style. Overlooking the main street is the palace's most impressive feature, the walls and chambers on its south side, all rich with buttresses and stone medallions, built by French masons in the 1530s for King James V (1512–42). He died here, and the palace was a favorite resort of his daughter, Mary, Queen of Scots (1542–87). The beautiful gardens behind Falkland Palace contain a rare survivor: a royal tennis court, built in 1539. In the gardens, overlooked by the palace turret windows, you may easily imagine yourself back at the solemn hour when James on his deathbed pronounced the doom of the house of Stuart: "It cam' wi' a lass and it'll gang wi a lass." ✉ *Main St.* ☎ *01337 /857397* ⊕ *www.nts.org.uk* 🎟 *£12.50* ◔ *Mar.–Oct., Mon.–Sat. 10–5, Sun. noon–5.*

LOCH LEVEN

10 miles southwest of Falkland.

Scotland's largest Lowland loch, Loch Leven is famed for its fighting trout. The area is also noted for abundant birdlife, particularly its wintering wildfowl. Mary, Queen of Scots, was forced to sign the deed of abdication in her island prison in the loch.

GETTING HERE AND AROUND

If you're driving from St. Andrews or Cupar, take A91 to Kinross and follow the signs from there. From Falkland, take A911.

EXPLORING

Vane Farm Nature Reserve. On the southern shore overlooking the loch, Vane Farm Nature Reserve, a visitor center run by the Royal Society for the Protection of Birds, provides information about Loch Leven's ecology. It's the best place in Britain to see lapwings, pink-footed geese, tufted ducks, and shovelers. ✉ *Rte. B9097, off M90 and B996* ☎ *01577/862355* ⊕ *www.rspb.org.uk* 🎟 *£5* ◔ *Daily 10–5.*

CUPAR

21 miles northwest of Loch Leven, 10 miles west of St. Andrews.

Cupar is a busy market town with several interesting sites, including a museum about Fife.

GETTING HERE AND AROUND

Cupar has a train station on the Edinburgh–Aberdeen line (which passes through Dundee), and there are trains almost every hour. Stagecoach buses serve the town as well. By car, you can reach Cupar from Loch Leven via M90 and A91; take A91 if you're traveling from St. Andrews.

EXPLORING

Fife Folk Museum. To learn more about the history and culture of rural Fife, visit the Fife Folk Museum. The life of local rural communities is reflected in artifacts and documents housed in a former weigh house and adjoining weavers' cottages. The museum is 3 miles southeast of Cupar via A916 and B939. ✉ *High St., Ceres* ☎ *01334/828180* ⊕ *www. fifefolkmuseum.org* 🎟 *£5* ◔ *Apr.–Oct., daily 10:30–4:30.*

Hill of Tarvit Mansion and Kingarrock Hickory Golf. On rising ground near Cupar stands the National Trust for Scotland's Hill of Tarvit House, a 17th-century mansion that was altered in the high-Edwardian style in the late 1890s and early 1900s by the Scottish architect Sir Robert Lorimer (1864–1929). The extensive wood and parklands offer an enjoyable place for a picnic or stroll, and the house itself is well worth a visit. Golfers will also want to play a round on the old Lorimer family course, the Hickory, which was brought back to life in 2008 after being ploughed up for agricultural use during World War II. ✉ *Off A916, 2 miles south of Cupar* ☎ *01334/653127* ⊕ *www.nts.org.uk*

£10.50 ⊘ House Apr.–Aug., Wed.–Sun. 1–5; Sept. and Oct., Wed.–Sun. 1–4; gardens daily 9:30–sunset.

FAMILY **Scottish Deer Centre.** At the Scottish Deer Centre, many types of deer can be seen at close quarters or on ranger-guided tours. There are falconry displays every two hours, woodland walks, and a café. The center, west of Cupar, is one of the few places you can spot the red squirrel. ⊠ *A91* ☎ *01337/810391* ⊕ *www.tsdc.co.uk* *£8.50 ⊘ July and Aug., daily 10–5:30; Sept.–June, daily 10–4:30.*

WHERE TO EAT AND STAY

$$$ ✕**Ostlers Close Restaurant.** Tucked away in an alley off the main street,
BRITISH this cottage-style restaurant with plain painted walls and stick-back chairs has earned a well-deserved reputation for top-quality cuisine that is imaginative without trying to be too trendy. Dishes are robust (try roast roe venison with a juniper sauce and Seville marmalade steamed pudding) but the portions are just right. It's so small that it's a good idea to reserve ahead. $ *Average main: £23* ⊠ *25 Bonnygate* ☎ *01334/655574* ⊕ *www.ostlersclose.co.uk ⊘ Closed Sun. and Mon. No lunch Reservations essential.*

$$$ **The Peat Inn.** With eight bright and contemporary two-room suites,
B&B/INN this popular "restaurant with rooms" is perhaps best known for its
Fodor'sChoice outstanding, modern, Scottish-style restaurant. **Pros:** exceptional res-
★ taurant; efficient but easygoing staff. **Cons:** booking ahead is essential; you need a car to get here. $ *Rooms from: £195* ⊠ *B941, at intersection of B940* ☎ *01334/840206* ⊕ *www.thepeatinn.co.uk ⊘ Closed Sun. and Mon. ⟿ 8 suites* ⏏| *Breakfast.*

GOLF

Ladybank Golf Club. Fife is known for its coastal courses, but this one provides an interesting inland layout. Although Ladybank, designed by Tom Morris in 1876, is on fairly level ground, the fir and birch trees and heathery rough give it a Highland flavor among the gentle Lowland fields. Qualifying rounds of the British Open are played here when the main championship is played at St. Andrews. ⊠ *A92, Annsmuir, Ladybank* ☎ *01337/830814* ⊕ *www.ladybankgolf.co.uk £25–£60 ⅄ 18 holes, 680 yards, par 71 ⊘ Daily Reservations essential.*

DUNDEE AND ANGUS

The small city of Dundee sits near the mouth of the River Tay surrounded by the farms and glens of rural Angus and the coastal grassy banks and golf courses of northeastern Fife. A vibrant, industrious city that's off the main tourist track, it plays a significant role in the biotech and computer-games industries. Dundee has a large student population, a lively arts and nightlife scene, and several historical and nautical sights. The city's transformation lies behind a mass of scaffolding and road diversions, as work continues on the first outpost of London's Victoria and Albert Museum, a repository of decorative arts, and the entire reconfiguration and rebuilding of the waterfront area.

Angus combines coastal agriculture on rich, red soils with dramatic inland glens that pierce their way into the foothills of the Grampian mountain range to the northwest. ■TIP→ **The main road from Dundee to Aberdeen—the A90—requires special care with its mix of fast cars and unexpectedly slow farm traffic.**

DUNDEE

14 miles northwest of St. Andrews, 58 miles north of Edinburgh, 79 miles northeast of Glasgow.

Dundee makes an excellent base for exploring Fife and Angus at any time of year. The West End—especially its main thoroughfare Perth Road—pulses with life, with intimate cafés and excellent bars. The Dundee Contemporary Arts center has gained the city some attention. As you walk the cobbled streets, you may glimpse the 1888 Tay Rail Bridge, and if you head southwest you can reach Magdalen Green, where landscape artist James McIntosh Patrick (1907–98) found inspiration from the views and ever-changing skyscapes. The popular comic strips *The Beano* and *The Dandy* were first published here in the 1930s, so statues by the Scottish sculptors Antony and Susie Morrow depicting Desperate Dan, Dawg, and a catapult-wielding Minnie the Minx were erected in the City Square.

GETTING HERE AND AROUND

The East Coast train line runs through the city, linking it to Edinburgh (and beyond, to London), Glasgow (and the West Coast of England), and Aberdeen, with trains to all every hour or half-hourly at peak times. Cheaper bus service is available to all these locations, as well as St. Andrews and several other towns in Fife and Angus.

If you're traveling by car, the A92 will take you north from Fife to Abroath and the Angus coast towns. The A90, from Perth, heads north to Aberdeen.

Most of the sights in Dundee are clustered together, so you can easily walk around the city. If the weather is bad or your legs are heavy, hail one of the many cabs on the easy-to-find taxi ranks for little more than a few pounds.

ESSENTIALS

Visitor Information Angus and Dundee Tourist Board. ⊠ *16 City Sq.* ☎ *01382/527527* ⊕ *www.angusanddundee.co.uk.*

EXPLORING

TOP ATTRACTIONS

Dundee Botanic Garden. This renowned botanical garden contains an extensive collection of native and exotic plants outdoors and in tropical and temperate greenhouses. There are some beautiful areas for picnicking, as well as a visitor center, an art gallery, and a coffee shop. ⊠ *Riverside Dr.* ☎ *01382/381190* ⊕ *www.dundee.ac.uk/botanic* ☑ *£3.90* ⊙ *Mar.–Oct., daily 10–4:30; Nov.–Feb., daily 10–3:30.*

FAMILY   **Dundee Contemporary Arts.** Between a 17th-century mansion and a cathedral, this strikingly modern building houses one of Britain's most exciting artistic venues. The two galleries house up to six shows a year by internationally acclaimed contemporary artists. There are children's and

Fodor's Choice
★

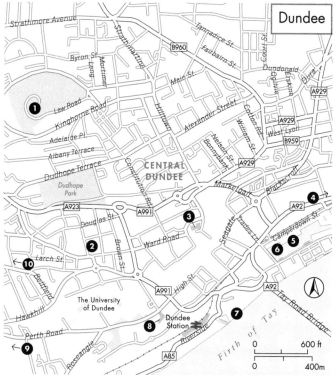

adult's workshops, special events and meet-the-artist events throughout the year. Two movie theaters screen mainly independent, revival, and children's films. There's also a craft shop and a buzzing café-bar that's open until midnight. ⊠ *152 Nethergate* ☎ *01382/909900* ⊕ *www.dca. org.uk* ⊠ *Free* ☉ *Fri.–Wed. 11–8, Thurs. 11–8.*

Fodor'sChoice
★

McManus Galleries. Dundee's principal museum and art gallery, housed in a striking Gothic Revival–style building, has an engaging collection of artifacts that document the city's history and the working, social, and cultural lives of Dundonians throughout the Victorian period and the 20th century. Its varied fine art collection includes paintings by Rossetti, Raeburn, and Peploe as well as thought-provoking yet accessible contemporary works and visiting exhibitions, often in connection with London's Victoria and Albert Museum. ⊠ *Albert Sq.* ☎ *01382/432350* ⊕ *www.mcmanus.co.uk* ⊠ *Free* ☉ *Mon.–Sat. 10–5, Sun. 12:30–4:30.*

FAMILY
Fodor'sChoice
★

RRS *Discovery*. Dundee's urban-renewal program—the city is determined to celebrate its industrial past—was motivated in part by the arrival of the RRS (Royal Research Ship) *Discovery,* the vessel used by Captain Robert F. Scott (1868–1912) on his polar explorations. The steamer was originally built and launched in Dundee; now it's a permanent resident. At Discovery Point, under the handsome cupola, the story of the ship and its famous expedition unfold; you can even feel the

Antarctic chill as if you were there. The ship, berthed outside, is the star: wander the deck, then explore the quarters to see the daily existence endured by the ship's crew and captain. ✉ *Discovery Quay, Riverside Dr.* ☎ *01382/309060* ⊕ *www.rrsdiscovery.com* 💷 *£9, £15.50 includes Verdant Works.* ⊙ *Apr.–Sept., Mon.–Sat. 10–6, Sun. 11–6; Oct.–Mar., Mon.–Sat. 10–5, Sun. 11–5; last admission 1 hr before closing.*

FAMILY **Verdant Works.** In a former jute mill, Verdant Works houses a multifaceted exhibit on the story of jute and the town's involvement in the jute trade. Restored machinery, audiovisual displays, and tableaux all bring to life the hard, noisy life of the jute worker. A light and airy café serves lovely little cakes. ✉ *W. Hendersons Wynd* ☎ *01382/309060* ⊕ *www.rrsdiscovery.com* 💷 *£9, £15.50 includes RRS Discovery* ⊙ *Apr.–Oct., Mon.–Sat. 10–6, Sun. 11–6; Nov.–Mar., Wed.–Sat. 10:30–4:30, Sun. 11–4:30.*

WORTH NOTING

OFF THE
BEATEN
PATH

Broughty Castle. Originally built to guard the Tay Estuary, Broughty Castle is now a museum focusing on fishing, ferries, and the history of the area's whaling industry. The canons and ramparts make for fine photo opportunities, and inside (up a very narrow stairway) are four floors of displays, including some of the lovely art collection of the Victorian inventor and engineer Sir James Orchar. To the north of the castle lies beautiful Broughty Ferry Beach, which, even in midwinter, is enjoyed by the locals; there is a regular bus service from Dundee's city center. ✉ *Castle Approach, 4 miles east of city center, Broughty Ferry* ☎ *01382/436916* ⊕ *www.leisureandculturedundee.com/broughty-castle* 💷 *Free* ⊙ *Apr.–Sept., Mon.–Sat. 10–4, Sun. 12:30–4; Oct.–Mar., Tues.–Sat. 10–4, Sun. 12:30–4.*

The Law. For sweeping views of the city, the Angus Glens to the north, and Fife's coastline to the south, head here. This hill (*law* means hill in Scottish) is actually an extinct volcano whose summit reaches 1,640 feet above sea level. A World War II memorial, parking lot, and seating area are at the top. ✉ *Law Rd.*

Mills Observatory. At the top of a thickly forested hill, Mills Observatory is the only full-time public observatory in Britain. There are displays on astronomy, space exploration, scientific instruments, and a 12-inch refracting telescope for night viewing of the stars and planets. ▪ **TIP→** Dundonians flock here when there's a solar or lunar event. If one happens during your visit, don't miss this universally happy experience. ✉ *Balgay Hill, 2 miles west of city center* ☎ *01382/435967* ⊕ *www.leisureandculturedundee.com/mills* 💷 *Free* ⊙ *Oct.–Mar., weekdays 4–10 pm, weekends 12:30–4; Apr.–Sept., Tues.–Fri. 11–5, weekends 12:30–4.*

North Carr Lightship. Moored next to the Unicorn, you'll see a strange red ship, the *North Carr Lightship*. After playing a significant role in World War II, Scotland's only remaining lightship was wrecked on the Fife shore during a storm in 1959; seven crew members were lost. The ship is currently closed for refurbishment, but is worth a look from the dock. ✉ *Broughty Ferry Harbour, Beach Crescent* ☎ *01382/562497.*

FAMILY Fodor's Choice ★ **Tay River Trips.** Taymara, the nonprofit group that looks after the *North Carr Lightship*, runs exhilarating dolphin-watching trips on its other vessels, the *Badger* and the *Marigot.* Excursions leave from Broughty Ferry Harbour and include a half-day trip along the River Tay to Perth or an hour around the mouth of the delta, where dolphins jump and play. Prior booking is essential. One-hour trips are £14, half-day trips are £36. ✉ *Broughty Ferry Harbour, Beach Cres.* ☎ *01382/562497* 🌐 *www.tayrivertrips.org.*

FAMILY ***Unicorn.*** It's easy to spot this 46-gun wood warship, as it's fronted by a figurehead of a white unicorn. This frigate has the distinction of being the oldest British-built warship afloat, having been launched in 1824 at Chatham, England. You can clamber right down into the hold, or see the models and displays about the Royal Navy's history. In the summer there are often jazz nights on board. The ship's hours vary in winter, so call ahead. ✉ *Victoria Dock, east of Tay Rd. bridge* 🌐 *www.frigateunicorn.org* 🎫 *£5* 🕓 *Apr.–Oct., daily 10–5; Nov.–Mar., Wed.–Fri. noon–4, weekends 10–5; last admission 30 mins before closing.*

5

WHERE TO EAT

$ INTERNATIONAL Fodor's Choice ★ 🍴 **D'Arcy Thomson.** Near the University of Dundee, the D'Arcy Thomson is named after the college's first professor of biology. Using beautiful zoological illustrations in its decor—from the tables to the bar—it's a refreshing mix of modern and traditional. An original use of Scottish ingredients works well, for example, catch of the day on braised nettles or venison chile. Leave room for the puddings such as rhubarb and custard tart. The service is diligent but relaxed. [$] *Average main: £10* ✉ *21–23 Old Hawkhill* ☎ *01382/622694* 🌐 *www.thedarcythompson.co.uk* 💳 *No credit cards.*

$$ BRITISH Fodor's Choice ★ 🍴 **Jute.** Downstairs at Dundee Contemporary Arts, this lively eatery serves breakfast at the bar, cocktails and snacks on the terrace in fine weather, or dinner in the open-plan dining area with its huge windows that offer views of artists at work in the printmakers studio. There are plenty of handsomely presented dishes, including roasted salmon with prawn, mussel-and-pea risotto, and champagne panna cotta. [$] *Average main: £15* ✉ *152 Nethergate* ☎ *01382/909246* 🌐 *www.jutecafebar.co.uk.*

$ CHINESE 🍴 **Manchurian Chinese Restaurant.** This family-run restaurant above a Chinese supermarket will not win any style awards (it feels a little like a hotel conference suite) but thanks to its food it has won a loyal following. The dishes taste fresh and light: from plump and fragrant dim sum to more unusual dishes such as bitter melon pork noodles and showstoppers such as their Taiwanese-style wine chicken pot. [$] *Average main: £14* ✉ *15a Gellatly St.* ☎ *01382/228822* 🌐 *www.manchuriandundee.com* 🕓 *Closed Wed.* ✍ *Reservations essential.*

$$ ITALIAN 🍴 **Piccolo.** This small basement eatery, with wooden tables and chairs and a quirky staff, attracts a diverse clientele. It serves surprisingly good pizzas, crepes, and their much-loved Dolce Vita, a fine plate of pappardelle with chicken and apricot in a creamy ginger-and-brandy sauce. [$] *Average main: £16* ✉ *21 Perth Rd.* ☎ *01382/201419* 🌐 *www.piccolodundee.co.uk* 🕓 *Closed Sun. and Mon.* ✍ *Reservations essential.*

$$$ ✕ **Playwright.** This stylish restaurant is one of the city's more expensive,
BRITISH   but it's worth the price to see the glass floor that looks into the wine
           cellar. The menu, including a prix-fixe lunch and pretheater menu, is
           well put together, offering interesting combinations of seasonal flavors.
           Start with squid risotto with broad beans, then move on to a perfectly
           presented roast duck breast with black cherries. There's a beautiful bar,
           too, for pre- or post-dinner tippling. The staff is laid-back but totally
           efficient. $ *Average main: £25* ⊠ *11 Tay Sq.* ☎ *01382/223113* ⊕ *www.
           theplaywright.co.uk* ⊙ *Closed Sun.* ⚖ *Reservations essential.*

$$$ ✕ **Sol y Sombra Tapas Bar.** It looks like an old Scottish pub and it is, but
TAPAS   the tapas and sangria are so authentic it'll make you feel as if you're
Fodor's Choice in España. There's no menu (you are asked if there is anything you
   ★   don't like) and for £21.50 a head you'll be served a steady stream of
           little dishes. Booking in advance is essential and one word of warning:
           don't go looking for a quiet romantic meal. $ *Average main: £21* ⊠ *27
           Gray St., Broughty Ferry* ☎ *01382/776941* ⚖ *Reservations essential*
           ▤ *No credit cards.*

WHERE TO STAY

$$ ⚏ **Apex City Quay.** Scandinavian-style rooms with easy chairs, plump bed-
HOTEL   ding, and flat-screen TVs with DVD players help you unwind at this
           contemporary quayside hotel. **Pros:** stylish rooms; lively, especially at
           weekends. **Cons:** outside is popular with seagulls, too; the bar is often
           mobbed. $ *Rooms from: £120* ⊠ *1 W. Victoria Dock Rd.* ☎ *01382/202404*
           ⊕ *www.apexhotels.com* ⇥ *145 rooms, 6 suites* �‖ *Breakfast.*

$$ ⚏ **Duntrune House.** Set among acres of tidy lawns and rustling trees,
B&B/INN   this mansion is a genteel contrast to the city. **Pros:** owners are keen
           genealogists and can offer advice to ancestor-seekers; the house and
           gardens are full of interest; tasty meals. **Cons:** might be too cluttered
           for some tastes; minimum two-night stay. $ *Rooms from: £100* ⊠ *Off
           A90, 5 miles northeast of Dundee, Duntrune* ☎ *01382/350239* ⊕ *www.
           duntrunehouse.co.uk* ⊙ *Closed Nov.–Feb.* ⇥ *3 rooms* �‖ *Breakfast.*

$$ ⚏ **Malmaison.** Not only has Malamaison brought life to a dilapidated
HOTEL   but much-loved Dundee landmark, it's done it with such style. **Pros:**
           beautifully restored old building; stylish rooms. **Cons:** pricey restaurant.
           $ *Rooms from: £110* ⊠ *44 Whitehall Cres.* ☎ *0844/693–0661* ⊕ *www.
           malmaison.com/locations/dundee/* ⇥ *86 rooms, 5 suites* �‖ *Breakfast.*

$ ⚏ **Shaftesbury Lodge.** Just off the Perth Road, this Victorian-era villa set
HOTEL   among well-tended shrubs is a find for those who like smaller, more inti-
Fodor's Choice mate hotels. **Pros:** first-rate service; fresh, well-maintained rooms; close,
   ★   but not too close, to the city. **Cons:** some bathrooms are small. $ *Rooms
           from: £90* ⊠ *I Hyndford St.* ☎ *01382/669216* ⊕ *www.shaftesburylodge.
           co.uk* ▤ *No credit cards* ⇥ *12 rooms* �‖ *Breakfast.*

NIGHTLIFE AND PERFORMING ARTS
BARS AND PUBS
Dundee's pub scene, centered in the West End–Perth Road area, is one
of the liveliest in Scotland.

Jute Cafe Bar. Better known as the bar at Dundee Contemporary Arts,
this places attracts film fans (the art-house cinema's entrance is next
door), students, and the well-heeled for European beers, wine, cocktails,

or coffee. It serves tasty bar snacks every night until 9:30. ✉ *152 Nethergate* ☎ *01382/909246* ⊕ *www.jutecafebar.co.uk.*

Ship Inn. Right on Broughty Ferry's promenade, this bright and breezy pub has a friendly atmosphere and great bar food. ✉ *121 Fisher St, Broughty Ferry* ☎ *01382/779176* ⊕ *www.theshipinn-broughtyferry.co.uk.*

Speedwell Bar. Called Mennie's by locals, the Speedwell Bar is in a mahogany-paneled building brimming with Dundonian characters. It's renowned for its superb cask beers. ✉ *165–168 Perth Rd.* ☎ *01382/667783* ⊕ *www.speedwell-bar.co.uk.*

MUSIC

Caird Hall. Caird Hall is one of Scotland's finest concert halls, staging a wide range of music and events. ✉ *City Sq.* ☎ *01382/434940* ⊕ *www.cairdhall.co.uk.*

Fodor's Choice **Clarks on Lindsay Street.** This busy bar hosts live music until the early ★ hours. Get in early to avoid the huge queues. ✉ *80 N. Lindsay St.* ☎ *01382/224925* ⊕ *www.clarksonlindsaystreet.com* ↝ *Closed Mon. and Tues.*

THEATER

Dundee Repertory Theatre. This is home to the award-winning Dundee Rep Ensemble and to Scotland's preeminent contemporary-dance group, Scottish Dance Theatre. Popular with locals, the restaurant and bar welcome late-night comedy shows and jazz bands. ✉ *Tay Sq.* ☎ *01382/223530* ⊕ *www.dundeerep.co.uk.*

SHOPPING

COFFEE AND TEA

J. Allan Braithwaite. This shop carries 13 types of freshly roasted coffees and more than 30 blended teas that you can pop into one of the quaint teapots you'll find here. ✉ *6 Castle St.* ☎ *01382/322693.*

JEWELRY

DCA. Just as you enter Dundee Contemporary Arts, the shop on the left sells artist-made jewelry, home ware, prints, and gifts. ✉ *DCA, 152 Nethergate* ☎ *01382/909240* ⊕ *dca.org.uk.*

Queen's Gallery. The Queen's Gallery has a compelling selection of jewelry, ceramics and paintings by Scottish artists. ✉ *160 Nethergate* ☎ *01382/220600.*

GOLF

East of Perthshire, near the city of Dundee, lies a string of demanding courses along the shores of the North Sea and inland into the foothills of the Grampian Mountains. Golfers who excel in windy conditions particularly enjoy the breezes blowing westward from the sea.

Camperdown Golf Course. For an alternative to the wild and windy east-coast links, try this magnificent municipal parkland course on the outskirts of Dundee. You can enjoy a game amid tree-lined fairways near the imposing Camperdown House. ■TIP→ **On a fine night in June or July, try the Twilight Session.** ✉ *Camperdown Park, Coupar Angus Rd.* ☎ *01382/431820* ⊕ *www.golfdundee.com/camperdown-golf-course* ⊕ *www.dundeecity.gov.uk/golf* 🎫£13–£35 ⛳ *18 holes, 6548 yards, par 71* ⊙ *Daily.*

Fodor's Choice **Carnoustie Golf Links.** The venue for the British Open in 1999 and 2007,
★ the coastal links around Carnoustie have challenged golfers since at
least 1527. Winners here have included many of the sport's biggest
names: Armour, Hogan, Cotton, Player, and Watson. There are three
courses, the most famous of which is the breathtaking Championship
Course, ranked among the very best in the world. The choice Burnside
course is full of historical interest and local color, as well as being tough
and interesting. The Buddon course, designed by Peter Allis and Dave
Thomas, is recommended for links novices. ⊠ *20 Links Parade, Carnoustie* ☎ *01241/802270* ⊕ *www.carnoustiegolflinks.co.uk* ⊠ *Championship, £160; Burnside, £44; Buddon, £44* ⚑ *. Championship Course:
18 holes, 6941 yards, par 72; Burnside Course: 18 holes, 6028 yards,
par 68; Buddon Course: 18 holes, 5420 yards, par 66* ☉ *Daily* ⚐ *Reservations essential.*

Panmure Golf Club. Down the road from the famous Carnoustie Golf
Links, this traditional course offers an excellent challenge with its
seaside setting, undulating greens, and sometimes excruciating—but
always entertaining—burrows. The signature 6th is named after British Open Championship winner Ben Hogan, who practiced here prior
to his triumphant tournament at Carnoustie in 1953. ⊠ *Burnside Rd.,
off Station Rd., Carnoustie* ☎ *01241/855120* ⊕ *www.panmuregolfclub.
co.uk* ⊠ *£25–£80* ⚑ *. 18 holes, 6551 yards, par 70* ☉ *Daily* ⚐ *Reservations essential.*

ARBROATH

15 miles north of Dundee.

You can find traditional boatbuilding in the fishing town of Arbroath. It
has several small curers and processors as well, and shops sell the town's
most famous delicacy, Arbroath smokies—whole haddock gutted and
lightly smoked. The town is also known for its association with the
Declaration of Arbroath, a key document in Scotland's history. A few
miles north along the coast is the old fishing village of Auchmithie, with
a beautiful little beach that you can walk to via a short path. The jagged,
reddish cliffs and caves are home to a flourishing seabird population.

GETTING HERE AND AROUND
The East Coast train line stops at Arbroath. The Abbey and Signal
Tower are all within walking distance, but you'll need a car to get to
Auchmithie. If you're driving from Dundee, take A92.

ESSENTIALS
Visitor Information Arbroath Tourist Information. ⊠ *Fish Market Quay, A92*
☎ *01241/872609* ⊕ *www.angusanddundee.co.uk.*

EXPLORING
Arbroath Abbey. Founded in 1178 and linked to the famous Declaration
of Arbroath, Arbroath Abbey is an unmistakable presence in the town
center; it seems to straddle whole streets, as if the town were simply
ignoring the red-stone ruin in its midst. Surviving today are remains of
the church, as well as one of the most complete examples in existence
of an abbot's residence. From here in 1320 a passionate plea was sent

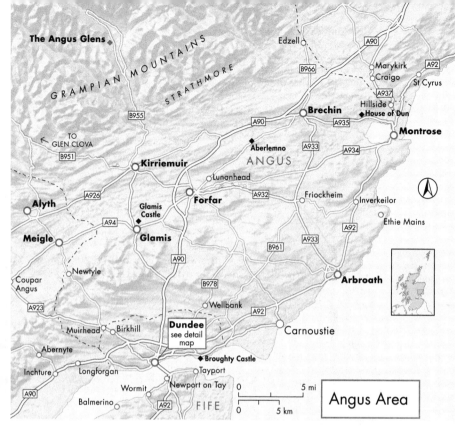

Angus Area

by King Robert the Bruce (1274–1329) and the Scottish Church to Pope John XXII (circa 1249–1334) in far-off Rome. The pope had until then sided with the English kings, who adamantly refused to acknowledge Scottish independence. The Declaration of Arbroath stated firmly, "It is in truth not for glory, nor riches, nor honours that we are fighting, but for freedom—for that alone, which no honest man gives up but with life itself." Some historians describe this plea, originally drafted in Latin, as the single most important document in Scottish history. The pope advised English king Edward II (1284–1327) to make peace, but warfare was to break out along the border from time to time for the next 200 years. The excellent visitor center recounts this history in well-planned displays. ⊠ *Abbey St.* ☎ *01241/878756* ⊕ *www.historic-scotland.gov.uk* ✉ *£5.50* ☾ *Apr.–Sept., daily 9:30–5:30; Oct.–Mar., daily 9:30–4:30.*

Signal Tower Museum. In the early 19th century, Arbroath was the base for the construction of the Bell Rock lighthouse on a treacherous, barely exposed rock in the Forth of Tay. A signal tower was built to facilitate communication with the builders working far from shore. That structure now houses the Signal Tower Museum, which tells the story of the lighthouse, built by Robert Stevenson (1772–1850) in 1811. The museum also houses a collection of items related to the history of the town, its customs, and the local fishing industry: look out for the 1813 Book of Signals and the witch's eye, a blue glass buoy hung from the window to ward off evil spirits. ⊠ *Ladyloan, west of harbor* ☏ *01241/435329* 🖃 *Free* ☉ *Tues.– Sat. 10–5.*

WHERE TO EAT

$ ✕ **Bellrock.** You can't go to Arbroath
FAST FOOD and not sample some fish-and-chips. Just across the road from the Signal Museum and painted in nautical white and blue, you can sit outside on the benches come the warmer days. They do all the classics, breaded or battered but if you are in the mood for something a little different, their spicy fish (in a spiced batter) has certainly won round discerning locals. $ *Average main: £9* ⊠ *33 Ladyloan* ☏ *01241/873656* ⊕ *www.thebellrock.com.*

$ ✕ **But 'n' Ben.** This homey restaurant serves lunches and dinners which
BRITISH offer a taste of quality Scottish home cooking, including Arbroath smokie
Fodor's Choice pancakes, mince and tatties, venison with rowan jelly, and rich moist
★ gingerbread, all at reasonable prices. It's next to Auchmithie's lovely shingle beach; a stroll here is the perfect way to work up an appetite or work off overindulgence. $ *Average main: £13* ⊠ *Ethie St., 3 miles off A92, Auchmithie* ☏ *01241/877223* ⊕ *www.butnbenauchmithie.co.uk* ☉ *Closed Tues.*

$ ✕ **Sugar and Spice.** Peruse the sweets of your childhood and reminisce
CAFÉ about the cakes your grandmother used to make in this combination café and sweet shop. Locals flock here to enjoy the meringues, sponges, and other desserts. There are soups and sandwiches for lunch and simple dishes like roast beef and Yorkshire pudding followed by clootie dumpling for dinner. Their homemade fudge makes a great souvenir for folks back home. $ *Average main: £9* ⊠ *9–13 High St.* ☏ *01241/437500* ⊕ *www.sugarandspicetearoom.co.uk* 🗀 *No credit cards.*

WHERE TO STAY

$$ 🏠 **The Brucefield.** This old manor house, set among well-tended grounds,
B&B/INN offers luxurious rooms for very reasonable rates. **Pros:** all the touches you'd expect in a five-star hotel; quality bedding; friendly owners. **Cons:** two-night minimum in high season; a 20-minute walk to the city center. $ *Rooms from: £110* ⊠ *Cliffburn Rd.* ☏ *01241/875393* ⊕ *www.brucefieldbandb.com* 🛏 *4 rooms* ⫯◯⫰ *Breakfast.*

$ 🏠 **Harbour Nights.** An excellent and somewhat plush budget option, this
B&B/INN B&B is right on the harbor, affording you the most authentic Arbroath stay possible. **Pros:** splendid seafront location; delicious breakfasts. **Cons:** only one room with a private bathroom; you must book far in advance. $ *Rooms from: £80* ⊠ *4 Shore* ☏ *01421/434343* ⊕ *www.harbournights.co.uk* 🛏 *5 rooms, 1 with bath* ⫯◯⫰ *Breakfast.*

LIGHTHOUSE BUILDERS

The name Stevenson is strongly associated with the building of lighthouses throughout Scotland. However, the family's most famous son was Robert Louis Stevenson (1850–94), who gravely disappointed his parents by choosing to be a writer instead of an engineer.

MONTROSE

14 miles north of Arbroath via A92.

An unpretentious and attractive town with a museum and a selection of shops, Montrose sits beside a wide estuary known as the Montrose Basin.

GETTING HERE AND AROUND

On the main East Coast train line and local bus route (the Stagecoach Strathtay 39 and 73 from Dundee and Arbroath), the town is easily accessed by public transportation. However, you'll need a car to get to attractions outside town.

ESSENTIALS

Visitor Information Montrose Tourist Information Point. ⊠ *Panmure Pl.* ☎ *01674/673232.*

EXPLORING

Fodor's Choice
★
House of Dun. The National Trust for Scotland's leading attraction in this area is the stunning House of Dun, which overlooks the Montrose Basin. The mansion was built in the 1730s for lawyer David Erskine, otherwise known as Lord Dun (1670–1755). Designed by architect William Adam (1689–1748), the house is particularly noted for its magnificently ornate plasterwork and curious Masonic masonry. Showing everything from Lady Dun's collection of embroidery to the working kitchens, this house tells the story of the Seat of Dun and the eminent family's history. The sprawling grounds have a restored hand-loom weaving workshop, plus an enchanting walled Victorian garden and wooded den. ⊠ *A935, 4 miles west of Montrose* ☎ *01674/810264* ⊕ *www.nts.org.uk/Visits* ⛶ *£10* ☉ *House: Mar.–June and Sept.–Aug , Wed.–Sun. noon–5; July and Aug., daily 11–5. Garden: daily 9–sunset.*

Montrose Basin Local Nature Reserve. Run by the Scottish Wildlife Trust, the Montrose Basin Local Nature Reserve hosts migrating geese, ducks, and swans. Several nature trails can take you up close to the reserve's residents if you're quiet. In October, at least 20,000 pink-footed geese arrive: come in the morning and the evening to see them fill the sky. ⊠ *Rossie Braes* ☎ *01674/676336* ⊕ *www.montrosebasin. org.uk* ⛶ *£4* ☉ *Visitor center Mar.–Oct., daily 10:30–5; Nov.–Feb., Fri.–Sun. 10:30–4.*

Montrose Museum. The town's museum—housed in a neoclassical building that also contains the tourist information center—exhibits some fascinating bequests by the local gentry, including an early-19th-century ship carved from bone by French prisoners in the Napoleonic war. ⊠ *Panmure Pl.* ☎ *01674/673232* ⊕ *archive.angus.gov.uk* ⛶ *Free* ☉ *Tues.–Sat. 10–5.*

WHERE TO EAT

$
CAFÉ
✕ **The Pavilion Cafe.** Bringing new purpose to an old bowling pavilion, this café's owner has freshly painted its clapboard, spruced up the delightful color-glazed fanlights, and gently restored many of the unusual features of this late Victorian beauty. Expect superfresh home bakes (the owner used to run the legendary Rosie's Bakehouse in Brechin): their seasonal fruit-festooned cream sponges are a treat. ⓢ *Average main: £6* ⊠ *Melville Gardens* ☎ *07801/138292* ▭ *No credit cards.*

BEAUTIFUL BEACHES

Scotland's east coast enjoys many hours of sunshine, compared with its west coast, and is blessed with lots of sandy beaches under the ever-changing backdrop of the sky. Take time to explore the beaches and walk along the coast for a change of pace whatever the time of year.

In Fife, Tentsmuir's Beach near St. Andrews is popular with kite flyers and horseback riders, and the famous and lovely West Sands in St. Andrews is where the running sequences in the movie *Chariots of Fire* were filmed. The small cove beach at Elie, south of Crail, hosts cricket matches in summer.

In Angus the beach at Broughty Ferry, near the city of Dundee, fills with families and children on weekends and during school holidays—even on the most blustery of days.

North of Arbroath lies Auchmithie Beach, more shingly (pebbly) than the others and offering a bracing breath of North Sea air. And finally, near the Montrose Basin you can discover the enchanting crescent of Lunan Bay, home to many species of seabirds.

BRECHIN

10 miles southwest of Montrose.

The small market town of Brechin has a cathedral that was founded around 1200 and contains an interesting selection of antiquities, including the Mary Stone, a Pictish relic.

GETTING HERE AND AROUND

Brechin is not on the East Coast train line but can be reached by bus from Montrose or Arbroath (the Stagecoach Strathtay number 30). It's on the A935, just off the main A90 road between Dundee and Aberdeen.

EXPLORING

Brechin Cathedral and Round Tower. The town's 10th-century Brechin Cathedral and Round Tower is on the site of a former Celtic monastery (priory of the Culdee monks) and has some unusual examples of medieval sculpture. The tower is one of only two on mainland Scotland. This type of structure is more frequently found in Ireland. ⊠ *6 Church St.* ☎ *01356/629360* ⊕ *www.brechincathedral.org* ⬛ *Free* ⊙ *Daily 9–5.*

Brechin Town House Museum. Located in the old courtroom which had cells in its cellars, the Brechin Town House Museum houses a small but interesting collection of objects from inhabitants of the area: from Bronze Age jewelry to a Jacobite sporran to a letter from a World War I soldier. There is a small tourist information desk within the museum. ⊠ *28 High St.* ☎ *01356/625536* ⊕ *archive.angus.gov.uk/history/museums/brechin* ⬛ *Free* ⊙ *Tues.–Sat. 10–5.*

WHERE TO EAT

$
CAFÉ
FAMILY
✕ **Brechin Castle Garden Centre.** Just off the A90, this small country park has a play area for children and an excellent café, serving door-stop sandwiches, tasty soups, and still-warm scones. ⓢ *Average main: £8* ⊠ *Haughmuir, Brechin* ☎ *01356/626813* ⊕ *www.brechincastlecentre.co.uk.*

THE ANGUS GLENS

25 miles southwest of Brechin.

You can rejoin the hurly-burly of the A90 for the return journey south from Montrose or Brechin; the more pleasant route, however, leads southwesterly on minor roads (there are several options) that travel along the face of the Grampians, following the fault line that separates Highland and Lowland. The **Angus Glens** extend north from points on A90. Known individually as the glens of Isla, Prosen, Clova, and Esk, these long valleys run into the high hills of the Grampians and some clearly marked walking routes. Those in Glen Clova are especially appealing.

Be aware that Thursday is a half day in Angus; many shops and attractions close at lunch.

GETTING HERE AND AROUND

You really need a car to reach the Angus Glens and enjoy the gentle (and not so gentle) inclines here. Glamis and Kirriemuir are both on the A928 (just off the A90), and the B955—which loops round at Glen Clova—is one of the loveliest Scottish roads to drive along, especially when the heather is blooming in late summer.

WHERE TO STAY

$ **Glen Clova Hotel.** Since the 1850s, the hospitality of this hotel has lifted
HOTEL the spirits of many a bone-tired hill walker. **Pros:** stunning location; great base for outdoor pursuits; spacious accommodations. **Cons:** lack of decent public transportation; people enjoying themselves in the bar can be noisy. $ *Rooms from: £90* ✉ *B955, Glen Clova* ☎ *01575/550350* ⊕ *www.clova.com* ➟ *10 rooms* ⊙| *Breakfast.*

KIRRIEMUIR

15 miles southeast of Brechin.

Kirriemuir stands at the heart of Angus's red-sandstone countryside and was the birthplace of the writer J. M. Barrie (1860–1937), best known abroad as the author of *Peter Pan* (a statue of whom you can see in the town's square).

GETTING HERE AND AROUND

A number of roads lead to Kirriemuir, but A928 (off A90), which also passes Glamis Castle, is one of the loveliest. Stagecoach Strathtay runs buses to this area; the 20 and 22 from Dundee are the most regular.

EXPLORING

J.M. Barrie's Birthplace. At the J. M. Barrie's Birthplace, the National Trust pays tribute to the man who sought to preserve the magic of childhood more than any other writer of his age. The house's upper floors are furnished as they might have been in Barrie's time, complete with domestic necessities, while downstairs is his study, replete with manuscripts and personal mementos. The outside washhouse is said to have served as Barrie's first theater. ✉ *9 Brechin Rd.* ☎ *0844/4932142* ⊕ *www.nts.org.uk/Property/J-M-Barries-Birthplace/* 🎫 *£6.50* ⊙ *Apr.– June, Sept., and Oct., Sat.–Wed. noon–5; July and Aug., daily 11–5.*

Kirriemuir Gateway to the Glens Museum. As is the style in Angus, the local museum doubles as the visitor center, meaning you can get all the information you need and admire a few stuffed birds and artifacts at the same time. Rock fans will appreciate the exhibit celebrating local lad made good (or rather bad), the late Bon Scott, lead singer of the rock band AC/DC. ✉ *32 High St.* ☎ *01575/575479* 🌐 *archive.angus.gov.uk* 🎫 *Free* 🕒 *Tues.–Sat. 10–5.*

WHERE TO EAT

$ CAFÉ 🍴 **88 Degrees.** If you're not in a rush (service can be slow), take time to savor excellent coffee, inventive sandwiches, pizzettes, cakes, and handmade chocolates at this appealing café and shop selling quality fare. Can't stop? Buy delicious cheese or chocolates to go, or pick up a cheese and apple scone, or whatever the creative baker is whipping up. [$] *Average main: £6* ✉ *17 High St.* ☎ *01575/570888* 💳 *No credit cards.*

FORFAR

7 miles east of Kirriemuir.

Forfar goes about its business of being the center of a farming hinterland without being preoccupied with (or even that interested in) tourism.

GETTING HERE AND AROUND

Buses are slow here. The quickest route is by car: take the A90 north, then the A926 turnoff. Alternatively, the A932/A933 route from Arbroath takes you through farmland and Angus villages.

EXPLORING

OFF THE BEATEN PATH **Aberlemno.** You can see excellent examples of Pictish stone carvings about 5 miles northeast of Forfar alongside the B9134. Carvings of crosses, angels, serpents, and other animals adorn the stones, which date from the 7th to the early 9th century. Note the stone in the nearby churchyard—one side is carved with a cross and the other side depicts the only known battle scene in Pictish art, complete with horsemen and foot soldiers.

Meffan Museum and Art Gallery. The high point of a visit to Fofar is the Meffan Museum and Art Gallery, which displays an interesting collection of Pictish carved stones and artifacts from the dark days of burning witches. Two galleries host frequently changing exhibitions by leading local and Scottish artists. The museum also houses a tourist information desk. ✉ *20 W. High St.* ☎ *01307/476482* 🌐 *archive.angus.gov.uk/history/museums/meffan* 🎫 *Free* 🕒 *Tues.–Sat. 10–5.*

GLAMIS

5 miles southwest of Forfar, 6 miles south of Kirriemuir.

Set in rolling countryside is the little village of Glamis (pronounced *glahms*), the highlight of which is nearby famous Glamis Castle.

GETTING HERE AND AROUND

The drive to Glamis Castle, along beech- and-yew-lined roads, is as majestic as the castle itself. Take the A90 north from Dundee, then off onto the A928. The village of Glamis can be reached by the Stagecoach Strathtay number 22, but service is rather infrequent.

EXPLORING

Fodor's Choice
★

Glamis Castle. One of Scotland's best known and most beautiful castles, Glamis Castle connects Britain's royalty through 10 centuries, from Macbeth (Thane of Glamis) to the late Queen Mother and her daughter, the late Princess Margaret, born here in 1930 (the first royal princess born in Scotland in 300 years). The property of the earls of Strathmore and Kinghorne since 1372, the castle was largely reconstructed in the late 17th century; the original keep, which is much older, is still intact. One of the most famous rooms in the castle is Duncan's Hall, the legendary setting for Shakespeare's *Macbeth*. Guided tours allow you to see fine collections of china, tapestries, and furniture. Within the castle is the delightful Castle Kitchen restaurant; the grounds contain a huge gift shop, a shop selling local produce, and a pleasant picnic area. ■**TIP**➔ **If you are looking to hear the pipes and see some Highland dancing and games of strength, the Strathmore Highland Games are held here around the second weekend of June. See www.strathmorehighlandgames.co.uk for more information.** ⊠ *A94, 1 mile north of Glamis* ☎ *01307/840393* ⊕ *www.glamis-castle.co.uk* ⊡ *£11* ⊗ *Mar.–Oct., daily 10-6.*

MEIGLE

7 miles southwest of Glamis, 11 miles northwest of Dundee.

The historic village of Meigle, nestled in the rich agricultural land of the Strathmore Valley, is well known to those with an interest in Pictish stones. Said to be built on an 11th-century Pictish monastery, the village has a number of elaborate Victorian buildings.

GETTING HERE AND AROUND

Meigle is an easy and pleasant drive from Glamis on the A94 (or from Dundee on the B954). The hourly Stagecoach Strathtay from Dundee (number 57) stops here.

EXPLORING

Meigle Sculptured Stone Museum. The town of Meigle, in the wide swathe of Strathmore, has one of the most notable collections of sculpted stones in western Europe, housed at the Meigle Sculptured Stone Museum. It consists of some 25 monuments from the Celtic Christian period (8th to 11th century), nearly all of which were found in or around the local churchyard. The large cross slab known as Meigle 2 shows Daniel in the lions' den. Local legend holds the slab marked the grave of Guinevere, wife of King Arthur; in the story, Arthur sentences her to death by being torn apart by wild animals. ⊠ *A94* ☎ *01828/640 612* ⊕ *www.historic-scotland.gov.uk* ⊡ *£4.50* ⊗ *Apr.–Sept., daily 9:30–5:30.*

ALYTH

10 miles west of Glamis, 15 miles northwest of Dundee.

Dating back to the Dark Ages, this market town was completely transformed by the Industrial Revolution, which lined its streets with mills and factories. The 20th century saw the closing of most of these companies, but the town had never forgotten its agricultural heritage. To this day it holds on to its rural appeal.

GETTING HERE AND AROUND

Just 4 miles farther along the B954 from Meigle, Alyth is also served by Stagecoach Strathtay number 57.

EXPLORING

Alyth Museum. This small but intriguing museum about the region's history displays an enviable collection of old photos and nearly every type of tool and implement put to use by the resourceful and hardy locals. ✉ *Commercial St.* ☎ *01828/633474* 🌐 *www.pkc.gov.uk/article/6474/Alyth-Museum* 🎟 *Free* 🕐 *May–Sept., Wed.–Sun. 1–5.*

WHERE TO STAY

$$ B&B/INN Fodor's Choice ★ 🏨 **Tigh Na Leigh.** This grand house, now a classy B&B, was originally built by the Earl of Airlie for his doctor. **Pros:** lovingly restored building; luxurious rooms; evening meals are available. **Cons:** only five rooms; books up quickly. [$] *Rooms from: £108* ✉ *22–24 Airlie St.* ☎ *01828/632372* 🌐 *www.tighnaleigh.com* 🛏 *5 rooms* 🍴 *Breakfast.*

THE CENTRAL HIGHLANDS

Updated
by Mike
Gonzalez

The Central Highlands are home to superb castles, moody mountains, and gorgeous glens that are best explored at a leisurely pace. The waters of Loch Lomond reflect the crags and dark woods that surround it, and attract those in search of a more romantic and nostalgic Scotland enshrined in the verses of the famous song that bears its name. When you finish a day of exploring, celebrate with a glass of one of the region's top-notch whiskies.

The Carse of Stirling, the wide plain guarded by Stirling Castle, was the scene of many important moments in Scotland's history—from the Roman invasion commemorated by the Antonine Wall, to the castles that mark the site of medieval kingdoms and the battles to preserve them. Look up at Stirling Castle from the valley and you can see why so many battles were fought over its possession.

North from Stirling, past Dunblane, are the Highland hills and valleys of the Trossachs, whose high peaks attract walkers and a tougher breed of cyclist. From Callander, a neat tourist town, the hills stretch westward to the "bonnie bonnie banks" of Loch Lomond. From the peaks of the Trossachs, on a good day, you can see Edinburgh Castle to the east and the tower blocks of Glasgow's housing projects to the west.

Farther north is Perth, once Scotland's capital; its wealthy mansions reflect the prosperous agricultural land that surrounds the city, and it is still an important market town today. Overlooking the River Tay, the city can reasonably claim to be the gateway to the Highlands, sitting as it does on the Highland Fault that divides Lowlands from Highlands. From Perth the landscape begins to change on the road to Pitlochry and the unforgiving moors of Rannoch.

For many years Stirling was the starting point for visitors from Edinburgh and Glasgow setting out to explore the Trossachs, with their lochs and hills hung with shaggy birch, oak, and pinewoods. The Victorians were drawn by the lyrical descriptions of the area by Romantic poets like Sir Walter Scott (1771–1832), who set his dramatic verse narrative of 1810, "The Lady of the Lake," in the landscape of the Trossachs.

For those in search of more dramatic landscapes, the Highland Fault line runs northeast above Perth, and into the old county of Angus and the high, rough country of Rannoch Moor and the towering Ben Lawers, near Killin, the ninth-highest peak in Scotland.

The region is full of reminders of heroic struggles, particularly against the English, from the monument to William Wallace to the field at Bannockburn (near Stirling), where Robert the Bruce took on the invader. In nearby Callander, Rob Roy MacGregor, the Scottish Robin Hood, lived (and looted and terrorized) his way into the storybooks.

TOP REASONS TO GO

Loch Lomond: You can see the sparkling waters of Scotland's largest loch by car, by boat, or on foot. A popular option is the network of bicycle tracks that creep around Loch Lomond and the Trossachs National Park, offering every conceivable terrain.

Castles: Choosing between Scotland's most splendid fortresses and mansions is a challenge. Among the highlights are Stirling Castle, with its palace built by James V, and Scone Palace, near Perth, with its grand aristocratic acquisitions. By contrast, Doune Castle is an atmospheric reminder of life in a fortification.

Great hikes: The way to experience the Central Highlands is to head out on foot. The fit and well equipped can "bag a Munro" (hills over 3,000 feet, named after the mountaineer who listed them). The less demanding woodland paths and gentle rambles of the Trossachs will stir even the least adventurous rambler.

Whisky tours and tastes: The Scots love their whisky, and what better way to participate in Scottish life and culture than to learn about the land's finest? There are some exceptional distilleries in this region, from the Edradour Distillery to Glenturret, home of the Famous Grouse.

Bike trails: This region claims excellent biking trails, ranging from a gentle pedal through Stirling to a wind-in-your-face journey on the Lowland/Highland Trail. Whatever your preference, biking is a beautiful way to tour the countryside.

6

ORIENTATION AND PLANNING

GETTING ORIENTED

The twin reference points for your trip are Stirling, an ancient historic town from whose castle you can see central Scotland laid out before you, and Perth, 36 miles away, the gateway to the Highlands. North from Stirling, you cross the fertile open plain (the Carse of Stirling) dotted with historic cathedral towns like Dunblane and Doune. The Trossachs are the Scotland of the Romantic imagination, lochs and woodland glens, drovers' inns and grand country houses. The small towns of the region, like Callander, Aberfoyle, and Pitlochry, are bases from which to explore this changing countryside. To the west lies Loch Lomond, along whose banks the road leads from industrial Glasgow to the hills and glens of the Highlands.

Stirling. Stirling is a city vibrant with history. The Old Town is quite a small area on the hill, and is worth covering on foot. Look down from the Stirling Castle crag that dominates the plains below and you can see the stages of its growth descending from the hill. The town is a good center from which to explore the changing landscape of central Scotland.

The Trossachs and Loch Lomond. This area is small, but incredibly varied—from dramatic mountain peaks that attract walkers and climbers, to the gentler slopes and forests that stretch from Perth eastward to Aberfoyle and the shores of Loch Lomond. The glens and streams that pepper the

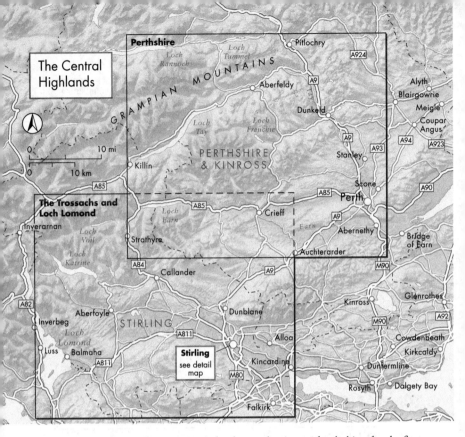

region create a romantic landscape that is a perfect habitat for the figure of Rob Roy McGregor—Robin Hood or bandit according to taste, but undeniably Scottish. Loch Lomond's western side is more accessible, if busier, than the east, but the views across the loch are spectacular.

Perthshire. The prosperous air of Perth, once the capital of Scotland, testifies to its importance as a port exporting wool, salmon, and whisky to the world. Scone Palace serves as a monument to that era. The route northward leads across the Highland Boundary and into the changing landscapes beyond Pitlochry to Rannoch Moor, where the wind sweeps across the hardy heather.

PLANNING

WHEN TO GO

The Trossachs and Loch Lomond are in some ways a miniature Scotland, from the tranquil east shore of Loch Lomond to the hills and glens of the Trossachs and the mountains of the Arrochar Alps to the west—and all within a few hours' drive. In spring and summer, despite the erratic weather, the area is always crowded; this is a good time to go. However, the landscape is notably dramatic when the trees are turning red and brown in autumn, and evening skies are spectacular. Scotland in winter has a different kind of beauty, especially for skiers and climbers.

■ TIP→ Carry clothes for wet and dry weather, as the weather can change quickly. Summer evenings attract midges; take some repellent.

PLANNING YOUR TIME

Scotland's beautiful interior is excellent touring country, though the cities of Stirling and Perth are worth your time, too; Stirling in particular is worth a day. Two (slightly rushed) days would be enough to explore the Trossachs loop, to gaze into the waters of Loch Venachar and Loch Achray. The glens, in some places, run parallel to the lochs, including those along Lochs Earn, Tay, and Rannoch, making for satisfying loops and round-trips. Loch Lomond is easily accessible from either Glasgow or Stirling, and is well worth exploring. Don't miss the opportunity to take a boat trip on a loch, especially on Loch Lomond or on Loch Katrine.

GETTING HERE AND AROUND

AIR TRAVEL

Perth and Stirling can be reached easily from the Edinburgh, Dundee, and Glasgow airports by train, car, or bus.

BUS TRAVEL

A good network of buses connects with the central belt via Edinburgh and Glasgow. For more information, contact Scottish Citylink or National Express. The Perth and Kinross Council supplies a map (available in tourist information centers) showing all public transport routes in Perthshire, marked with nearby attractions.

First, Scottish Citylink, and Stagecoach organize reliable service on routes throughout the Central Highlands.

Bus Contacts First. ☎ 08708/727271 ⊕ www.firstgroup.com. **National Express.** ☎ 08717/818181 ⊕ www.nationalexpress.com. **Scottish Citylink.** ☎ 0871/266–3333 ⊕ www.citylink.co.uk. **Stagecoach.** ☎ 01292/613502 ⊕ www.stagecoachbus.com.

CAR TRAVEL

You'll find easy access to the area from the central belt of Scotland via the motorway network. The M80 connects Glasgow to Stirling, and then briefly joins the M9 from Edinburgh, which runs within sight of the walls of Stirling Castle. From there the A9 runs from Stirling to Perth, and onward to Pitlochry; it is a good road but a little too fast for its own good (so take care). Perth can also be reached via the M90 over the Forth Bridge from Edinburgh. Three signed touring routes are useful: the Perthshire Tourist Route, the Deeside Tourist Route, and the Pitlochry Tourist Route, a beautiful and unexpected trip via Crieff and Loch Tay. Local tourist information centers can supply maps of these routes. Once you leave the major motorways, roads become narrower and slower, with many following the contours of the lochs. Be prepared for your journey to take longer than distances might suggest.

TRAIN TRAVEL

The Central Highlands are linked to Edinburgh and Glasgow by rail, with through routes to England (some direct-service routes from London take less than five hours). Several discount ticket options are available, although in some cases on the ScotRail system a discount card must be purchased before your arrival in the United Kingdom. Note that families with children and travelers under 26 or over 60 are eligible for significant discounts. Contact Trainline, National Rail, or ScotRail for details.

The West Highland Line runs through the western portion of the area. Services also run to Stirling, Dunblane, Perth, and Gleneagles; stops on the Inverness–Perth line include Dunkeld, Pitlochry, and Blair Atholl.

Train Contacts National Rail Enquiries. ☎ *03457/484950* ⊕ *www. nationalrail.co.uk.* **ScotRail.** ☎ *0344/811-0141* ⊕ *www.scotrail.co.uk.* **Trainline.** ☎ *0871/244-1545* ⊕ *www.thetrainline.com.*

RESTAURANTS

Regional country delicacies—loch trout, river salmon, lamb, and venison—appear regularly on even modest menus in Central Highlands restaurants. In all the towns and villages in the area, you will find simple pubs, often crowded and noisy, many of them serving substantial food at lunchtime and in the evening until about 9 (eaten balanced on your knee, perhaps, or at a shared table). It can be difficult to find a place to eat later than that, so plan ahead.

HOTELS

There is a wide selection of accommodations available throughout the region, especially in Stirling, Bridge of Allan, Callander, and Pitlochry. They range from bed-and-breakfasts to private houses with a small number of rooms to rural accommodation (often on farms). The grand houses of the past—family homes to the landed aristocracy—have for the most part become country-house hotels. Their settings, often on ample grounds, offer an experience of grand living—but there are also modern hotels in the area, for those who prefer 21st-century amenities. *Hotel reviews have been shortened. For full information, visit Fodors.com.*

WHAT IT COSTS IN POUNDS			
$	**$$**	**$$$**	**$$$$**
Restaurants	Under £15	£15–£19	£20–£25	Over £25
Hotels	Under £100	£100–£160	£161–£220	Over £220

Restaurant prices are the average cost of a main course at dinner or, if dinner is not served, at lunch, excluding tax. Hotel prices are the lowest cost of a standard double room in high season, including 20% V.A.T.

VISITOR INFORMATION

The tourist offices in Stirling and Perth are open year-round, as are offices in larger towns; others are seasonal (generally from April to October).

STIRLING

26 miles northeast of Glasgow, 36 miles northwest of Edinburgh.

Stirling is one of Britain's great historic towns. An impressive proportion of the Old Town walls can be seen from Dumbarton Road, a cobbled street leading to Stirling Castle, built on a steep-sided plug of rock. From its esplanade there is a commanding view of the surrounding Carse of Stirling. The guns on the castle battlements are a reminder of the military advantage to be gained from its position.

GETTING HERE AND AROUND

Stirling's central position in the area makes it an ideal point for travel to and from Glasgow and Edinburgh (or north to Perth and the Highlands) by rail or bus. The town itself is compact and easily walkable, though a shuttle bus travels to and from the town center up the steep road to Stirling Castle every 20 minutes. The Back Walk takes the visitor on a circuit around the base of the castle walls—set aside at least 30 minutes for a leisurely walk.

TIMING

The historic part of town is tightly nestled around the castle—everything is within easy walking distance. The National Wallace Monument (2 miles away) is on the outskirts of the town and can be reached by taxi or, for the more energetic, on foot.

ESSENTIALS

Visitor Information **Stirling Visitor Information Centre.** ⊠ *Old Town Jail, St. John St.* ☎ *01786/465019* ⊕ *www.visitscotland.com/stirling.*

6

EXPLORING

TOP ATTRACTIONS

FAMILY **Battle of Bannockburn Visitor Centre.** You can almost hear horses' hooves
Fodor's Choice and the zip of arrows in this 21st-century re-creation of the battle that
★ changed the course of Scotland's history. Robert the Bruce's defeat of the armies of the English king, despite a 2-to1-disadvantage, is the stuff of legend. Using the latest in 3-D technology, the battle rages across screens that ring the central hall. Participants on both sides speak directly to the visitor, courtesy of holograms. Later you can play a role in a Bannockburn battle game (reservations essential; age seven and over only) and perhaps alter the course of history. Bruce pursued the Scottish crown, ruthlessly sweeping aside enemies; but his victory here was masterful, as he drew the English horses into the marshy land around the new center where they sank in the mud. A circular monument commemorates the battlefield. This is a bold step in historical re-creation, and it works. ⊠ *Glasgow Rd., Bannockburn* ☎ *0844/493–2139* ⊕ *www. battleofbannockburn.com* 🎫 *£11.50* ⊙ *Mar.–Oct., daily 10–5:30; Nov.–Feb., daily 10–5.*

National Wallace Monument. This Victorian-era shrine to William Wallace (circa 1270–1305), the Scottish freedom fighter reborn as "Braveheart" in Mel Gibson's film of the same name, was built between 1856 and 1869. It sits on Abbey Craig, from which Wallace watched the English armies struggle across the old Stirling Bridge before attacking them and winning a major victory in 1297. A steep stone spiral staircase leads to the roof gallery, with views of the bridge and the whole Carse of Stirling. A less flamboyant version of Wallace's life is told in an exhibition and audiovisual presentation on the second floor. To reach the monument, follow the Bridge of Allan signs (A9) northward, crossing the River

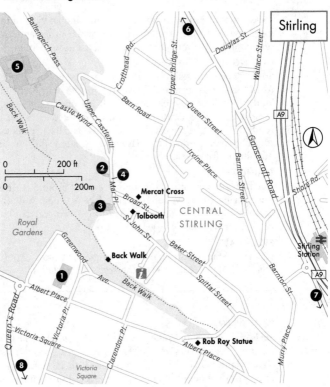

Forth by the New Bridge of 1832, next to the old one. The National Wallace Monument is signposted at the next traffic circle. From the car park a free shuttle will take you to the monument. ⊠ *Abbey Craig, Hillfoot Rd.* ☎ *01786/472140* ⊕ *www.nationalwallacemonument.com* 🖃 *£9.50* ⊘ *Apr.–June, Sept., and Oct., daily 10–5; July and Aug., daily 10–6; Nov.–Mar., daily 10:30–4.*

FAMILY

Fodor's Choice

★

Stirling Castle. Its magnificent strategic position on a steep-sided crag made Stirling Castle the grandest prize in the Scots Wars of Independence in the late 13th and early 14th centuries. Robert the Bruce's victory at Bannockburn won both the castle and freedom from English subjugation for almost four centuries. Take time to visit the **Castle Exhibition** in the Queen Anne Garden beyond the lower gate to get an overview of its long history and evolution as a stronghold and palace.

The daughter of King Robert I (Robert the Bruce), Marjory, married Walter Fitzallan, the high steward of Scotland. Their descendants included the Stewart dynasty of Scottish monarchs (Mary, Queen of Scots, was a Stewart, though she preferred the French spelling, *Stuart*). The Stewarts were responsible for many of the works that survive within the castle walls today. They made Stirling Castle their court and power base, creating fine Renaissance-style buildings that were never completely obliterated, despite reconstruction for military purposes.

Enter the castle through its outer defenses, which consist of a great curtained wall and batteries from 1708, built to bulwark earlier defenses by the main gatehouse. From this lower square the most conspicuous feature is the **Palace,** built by King James V (1512–42) between 1538 and 1542. The decorative figures festooning the ornate outer walls show the influence of French masons. An orientation center in the basement, designed especially for children, lets you try out the clothes and musical instruments of the time. Then you are led across a terrace to the newly refurbished **Royal Apartments,** which re-create the furnishings and tapestries found here during the reign of James V and his French queen, Mary of Guise. The queen's bedchamber contains copies of the beautiful tapestries in which the hunt for the white unicorn is clearly an allegory for the persecution of Christ. Overlooking the upper courtyard is the **Great Hall,** built by King James IV (1473–1513) in 1503. Before the Union of Parliaments in 1707, when the Scottish aristocracy sold out to England, this building had been used as one of the seats of the Scottish Parliament. It has since been restored to its original splendor, with sparse but impressive furnishings.

Among the later works built for regiments stationed here, the **Regimental Museum** stands out; it's a 19th-century baronial revival on the site of an earlier building. Nearby, the **Chapel Royal** is unfurnished. The oldest building on the site is the **Mint,** or **Coonzie Hoose,** perhaps dating as far back as the 14th century. Below it is an arched passageway leading to the westernmost section of the ramparts, the **Nether Bailey.** As you walk along the high walls beyond the arch, you'll have the distinct feeling of being in the bow of a warship sailing up the *carselands* (valley plain) of the Forth Valley.

To the castle's south lies the hump of the Touch and the Gargunnock Hills (part of the Campsie Fells), which diverted potential direct routes from Glasgow and the south. For centuries all roads into the Highlands across the narrow waist of Scotland led through Stirling. If you look carefully northward, you can still see the Old Stirling Bridge, once the lowest and most convenient place to cross the river, and the site of William Wallace's most famous victory. ⊠ *Castlehill* ☎ *01786/450000* ⊕ *www.historic-scotland.gov.uk/places* ✇ *£14.50, includes admission to Argyll's Lodging* ☉ *Apr.–Sept., daily 9:30–5:15; Oct.–Mar., daily 9:30–4:15.*

WORTH NOTING

Argyll's Lodging. A nobleman's town house built in three phases from the 16th century onward, this building is actually older than the name it bears—that of Archibald, the ninth Earl of Argyll (1629–85), who bought it in 1666. It served for many years as a military hospital. It has now been refurbished to show how the nobility lived in 17th-century Stirling. Specially commissioned reproduction furniture and fittings are based on the original inventory of the house's contents at that time. ⊠ *Castle Wynd* ☎ *01786/450000* ⊕ *www.historic-scotland.gov.uk/places* ✇ *£14.50, includes Stirling Castle* ☉ *Daily 9:30–5:15; last admission is at 4.*

Cambuskenneth Abbey. On the south side of the Abbey Craig, the scanty remains of this 13th-century abbey lie in a sweeping bend of the River Forth, with the dramatic outline of Stirling Castle as a backdrop. Important meetings of the Scottish Parliament were once held here, and King Edward I (1239–1307) of England visited in 1304. The abbey was looted and damaged during the Scots Wars of Independence in the late 13th and early 14th centuries. The reconstructed tomb of King James III (1452–88) can be seen near the outline of the high altar. ⊠ *Ladysneuk Rd.* ☎ *01667/460232* ⊕ *www.historic-scotland.gov.uk/places* ⊠ *Free* ☉ *May–Sept., daily 9:30–6.*

Church of the Holy Rude. The nave of this handsome church survives from the 15th century, and a portion of the original medieval timber roof can also be seen. This is the only Scottish church still in use to have witnessed the coronation of a Scottish monarch—James VI (1566–1625) in 1567. ⊠ *Top of St. John's St.* ☉ *Apr.–Sept., daily 11–4.*

Mar's Wark. These distinctive windowless and roofless ruins are the stark remains of a Renaissance palace built in 1570 by Lord Erskine (died 1572), Earl of Mar and Stirling Castle governor. The name means "Mar's work" or building. Look for the armorial carved panels, the gargoyles, and the turrets flanking a railed-off *pend* (archway). During the 1745 Jacobite rebellion, Mar's Wark was besieged and severely damaged, but its admirably worn shell survives. The ruins are enclosed by a fence, so you can view them only from the outside. ⊠ *Castle Wynd* ☎ *01667/460232* ⊕ *www.historic-scotland.gov.uk/places.*

Smith Art Gallery and Museum. This small but intriguing Romanesque-style museum, founded in 1874, details the history of the town through artworks and objects, the oldest of which are 7,000-year-old whale bones. A permanent exhibit traces the history of Stirling from its earliest days. There are also temporary exhibits and a café. ⊠ *Dumbarton Rd.* ☎ *01786/471917* ⊕ *www.smithartgalleryandmuseum.co.uk* ⊠ *Free* ☉ *Tues.–Sat. 10:30–5, Sun. 2–5.*

WHERE TO EAT

$
BRITISH
FAMILY
✕ Allanwater Cafe. Run by the Bechelli family for four generations, this light and airy café is a popular spot with locals. Try the traditional "fish tea"—here confusingly called "catch of the day"—which consists of fish-and-chips served with tea or coffee and bread and butter. This place is time-honored, tasty, and a good value. There's a tantalizing selection of Italian ice cream—if you have room. $ *Average main: £11* ⊠ *15 Henderson St., Bridge of Allan* ☎ *01786/833060* ⊕ *www. allanwatercafe.co.uk.*

$$
ECLECTIC
✕ Hermann's Restaurant. Run by Austrian Hermann Aschaber and his Glaswegian wife, the restaurant presents the cuisines of both countries. The Black Watch–tartan carpet and alpine murals are as successfully matched as the signature Scottish dishes like *cullen skink* (a fish-and-potato soup) and Austrian staples like Wiener schnitzel and cheese spaetzle. $ *Average main: £19* ⊠ *58 Broad St.* ☎ *01786/450632* ⊕ *www.hermanns-restaurant.co.uk.*

$$ ECLECTIC FAMILY 🍴 **River House.** Behind Stirling Castle, this restaurant sits by its own tranquil little loch and is built in the style of a Scottish *crannog* (ancient loch dwelling). It's relaxed and friendly, with tables on a deck overlooking the water. Local produce dominates the menu, yet the food reflects French and Mediterranean influences. Try the curried Scottish lamb with lime yogurt or the cod with a chorizo-and-chickpea stew. You can get here directly from the M9 motorway: follow the Stirling sign at Junction 10. From Aberfoyle it's on A84, or follow B8051 around the castle toward the Castle Business Park. [$] *Average main: £18* ✉ *Castle Business Park, B8051* ☎ *01786/465577* 🌐 *www.riverhouse-restaurant.co.uk.*

WHERE TO STAY

$ B&B/INN 🏨 **Castlecroft.** Tucked beneath Stirling Castle, this comfortable modern house welcomes you with freshly cut flowers and homemade breakfasts. **Pros:** great location; lovely views; hearty breakfasts. **Cons:** a little hard to find if you are not arriving directly from the motorway. [$] *Rooms from: £80* ✉ *Ballengeich Rd.* ☎ *01786/474933* 🌐 *www.castlecroft-uk.com* 🛏 *5 rooms* 🍽 *Breakfast.*

$ HOTEL 🏨 **Park Lodge Hotel.** This elegant 18th-century country-house hotel gives you a taste of French-inspired design and cuisine. **Pros:** great views of park; homey feel; recently renovated. **Cons:** too many floral prints. [$] *Rooms from: £95* ✉ *32 Park Terr.* ☎ *01786/474862* 🌐 *www.parklodge.net* 🛏 *9 rooms* 🍽 *Breakfast.*

$$ B&B/INN 🏨 **Portcullis Hotel.** This small hotel with a lively traditional pub scores above all on location: it is just outside the walls of Stirling Castle, and the views are spectacular, especially from rooms on the upper floors. **Pros:** excellent location close to the castle; fine views. **Cons:** can get very noisy; rooms are snug. [$] *Rooms from: £109* ✉ *Castle Wynd* ☎ *01786/472290* 🌐 *www.theportcullishotel.com* 🛏 *4 rooms* 🍽 *Breakfast.*

$$ B&B/INN 🏨 **Victoria Square Guest House.** Looking out over a pleasant grassy square, this rather grand Victorian house has been completely modernized in tasteful restrained colors; decorative notes such as William Morris wallpaper and brass chandeliers recall the house's origins. **Pros:** spacious, bright rooms; luxurious details; central and quiet location. **Cons:** no children under 12. [$] *Rooms from: £115* ✉ *12 Victoria Sq.* ☎ *01786/473920* 🌐 *www.victoriasquareguesthouse.com* 🛏 *7 rooms* 🍽 *Breakfast.*

$ B&B/INN 🏨 **West Plean.** More than 200 years old, this handsome, rambling B&B is part of a working farm. **Pros:** beautiful gardens; plenty of peace and quiet; huge and hearty breakfast. **Cons:** a little off the beaten track; a long walk to Stirling. [$] *Rooms from: £94* ✉ *Denny Rd.* ☎ *01786/812208* 🌐 *www.westpleanhouse.com* 🕒 *Closed Dec.* 🛏 *4 rooms* 🍽 *Breakfast.*

NIGHTLIFE AND PERFORMING ARTS

Macrobert Arts Centre. This arts center has a theater, gallery, and cinema with programs that range from films to pantomime. It's on the campus of the University of Stirling, off the A9 as you're heading toward Bridge of Allan. ⊠ *University of Stirling, W. Link Rd.* ☎ *01786/466666* ⊕ *www.macrobert.org.*

Tolbooth. Built in 1705, the Tolbooth has been many things: courthouse, jail, meeting place. At one time the city's money was kept here. It has retained its traditional Scottish steeple and gilded weathercock, and a newer tower lets you survey the surrounding country. Today it serves as an art gallery and a 200-seat theater. The bar is open for performances. ⊠ *Broad St.* ☎ *01786/274000* ⊕ *www.stirling.gov.uk/tolbooth.*

SHOPPING

CERAMICS AND GLASSWARE

Barbara Davidson Pottery. South of Stirling, Barbara Davidson Pottery is run by one of the best-known potters in Scotland. Demonstrations can be arranged by appointment. Signs point the way from the A9. ⊠ *Muirhall Farm, Muirhall Rd., Larbert* ☎ *01324/554430* ⊕ *www.barbara-davidson.com.*

Heart of Glass. This shop sells original works made by local glassblowers. ⊠ *14 Henderson St., Bridge of Allan* ☎ *01786/832137.*

CLOTHING

House of Henderson. A Highland outfitter, House of Henderson sells tartans, woolens, and accessories, and offers a made-to-measure kilt service. ⊠ *6–8 Friars St.* ☎ *01786/473681* ⊕ *www.houseofhenderson.co.uk* ☉ *Mon.–Sat. 9:30–5:30.*

Mill Trail. East of Stirling is Mill Trail country, along the foot of the Ochil Hills. A leaflet from any local tourist information center will lead you to the delights of a real textile mill shop and low mill prices—even on cashmere—at Tillicoultry, Alva, and Alloa.

GIFTS

Fotheringham Gallery. The upscale Fotheringham Gallery stocks fine jewelry and paintings. ⊠ *78 Henderson St., Bridge of Allan* ☎ *01786/832861* ⊕ *www.fotheringhamgallery.co.uk.*

Stirling Bagpipes. This small shop sells bagpipes of every type and at every price, including antiques by legendary craftspeople that are displayed in glass cases. In the room behind the shop, the owner lovingly turns the chanters and drones, but he will happily take time to talk you through the history of these instruments. ⊠ *8 Broad St.* ☎ *01786/448886* ⊕ *www.stirlingbagpipes.com.*

SHOPPING MALL

Stirling Arcade. Built in the 19th century, Stirling Arcade has about 20 shops selling everything from toys to fine clothing. ⊠ *King St.* ☎ *01786/450719* ⊕ *www.stirlingarcade.com.*

SIDE TRIP: FALKIRK

14 miles southeast of Stirling, along the M9 motorway.

Falkirk has a fascinating history. It was here, at the impressive Antonine Wall, that the Roman occupiers drove back the warlike Picts. You can visit parts of the wall and imagine the fierce battles over this strategic location.

In the late 18th century Falkirk was an important industrial town because of its network of canals linking Glasgow and Edinburgh. But with the arrival of the railways, Falkirk's fortunes flagged. The canals have been brought back to life with the £78 million Millennium Link Project, which added cycling and walking routes, the new Kelpies nature park, and the spectacular Falkirk Wheel, a boat lift.

GETTING HERE AND AROUND

The M9 from Stirling to Falkirk follows the widening estuary of the River Forth, the view dominated by the huge Grangemouth oil refinery in the distance.

EXPLORING

Antonine Wall. West of Falkirk, Bonnybridge is home to the most extensive remains of the Antonine Wall, a 60-mile-long Roman earthwork fortification that marked the northernmost limit of the Roman Empire. Built around AD 140 as a defense against the warlike Picts of the north, it was abandoned some 20 years later. A UNESCO World Heritage Site, the wall was site of a famous battle in 1298, when William Wallace was defeated by the English. To get here from Falkirk, take the A803 west. ✉ *Off A803, Bonnybridge* ✛ *2 miles west of Falkirk off the A803* ⊕ *www.historic-scotland.gov.uk/antoninewall* ✇ *Free* ☉ *Open 24 hrs.*

FAMILY   **Callendar House.** Near the town center, this grand country house gives you a glimpse of a family's daily life in the early 1800s. In the kitchen, local guides will explain cooking in the early 19th century and perhaps even offer you a sample. Entry is through an impressive wooden hallway, and the first-floor morning and drawing rooms are the grandest in the region. There are exhibits on the Romans and the Antonine Wall, as well as on the history of Falkirk. The second floor is a gallery space and houses the town's archives. The beautiful grounds, Callendar Park, offer lots of activities and are open all year. The house is something of a secret, but well worth a visit. ✉ *Callendar Park, off Callendar Rd.* ☎ *01324/590900* ⊕ *www.falkirkcommunitytrust.org* ✇ *Free* ☉ *Mon.– Sat. 10–5, Sun. 2–5.*

FAMILY   **Falkirk Wheel.** The only rotating boat lift in the world, the Falkirk Wheel
Fodor's Choice   links two major waterways, the Forth and Clyde Canal and the Union
★   Canal, between Edinburgh and Glasgow. This extraordinary engineering achievement lifts and lowers boats using four giant wheels shaped like Celtic axes; it can transport eight or more boats at a time from one canal to the other in about 45 minutes. As the wheel turns, you're transported up or down to the other canal. The Falkirk Wheel replaced 11 locks that were once the only way of moving between the two bodies of water. The site offers children's play areas, as well as children's canoes and bicycle rentals. An on-site office has information on canal boat

cruises. For those who prefer solid ground there are several canal path walkways to choose from. ⊠ *Lime Rd., Tamfourhill* ☏ *08700/500208* ⊕ *www.thefalkirkwheel.co.uk* 🎫 *£8.95* ☉ *Apr.–Oct., daily 10–5:30; Nov.–Mar., Wed.–Sun. 11–4.*

FAMILY
Fodor's Choice
★

The Kelpies. The Helix, a new country park on the edges of Falkirk with cycle and walking paths, play areas, and a wetland, is home to sculptor Andy Scott's extraordinary work *The Kelpies*, horse heads forged in steel, 85 and 98 feet high respectively. The largest works of art in Scotland sit at the center of the park, their beautiful heads framed against the Ochil Hills behind, paying homage to Falkirk's industrial past. The heads are modeled on Clydesdales, the huge draft horses that hauled barges along the canals before the advent of the railways. The guided tour (£4.95) will give you an insight into the area's past and take you inside the sculptures. ⊠ *The Helix, A9 and Falkirk Rd.* ✢ *From the A9, the M9, or through Falkirk, where the route is well signposted* ☏ *01324/506850* ⊕ *www.thehelix.co.uk.*

THE TROSSACHS AND LOCH LOMOND

Immortalized by Wordsworth and Sir Walter Scott, the Trossachs (the name means "bristly country") contains some of Scotland's loveliest forest, hills, and glens, well justifying the area's designation as a national park. The area has a special charm, combining the wildness of the Highlands with the prolific vegetation of an old Lowland forest. Its open ground is a dense mat of bracken and heather, and its woodland is of silver birch, dwarf oak, and hazel—trees that fasten their roots into the crevices of rocks and stop short on the very brink of lochs. There are also many small towns to visit along the way, some with their roots in a medieval world; others sprang up and expanded in the wake of the first tourists who came to Scotland in the late 19th century in search of wild country or healing waters. Dunblane has a magnificent cathedral; Doune's castle will make you stare in awe.

The most colorful season is fall, particularly October, a lovely time when most visitors have departed, and the hares, deer, and game birds have taken over. Even in rainy weather the Trossachs of "darksome glens and gleaming lochs" are memorable: the water filtering through the rocks by Loch Lomond comes out so pure and clear that the loch is like a sheet of glass.

The best way to explore this area is by car, by bike, or on foot; the latter two depend, of course, on the weather. Keep in mind that roads in this region of the country are narrow and winding, which can make for dangerous conditions in all types of weather.

DUNBLANE

6 miles north of Stirling.

The small, quiet town of Dunblane has long been an important religious center; it is dominated by its cathedral, which dates mainly from the

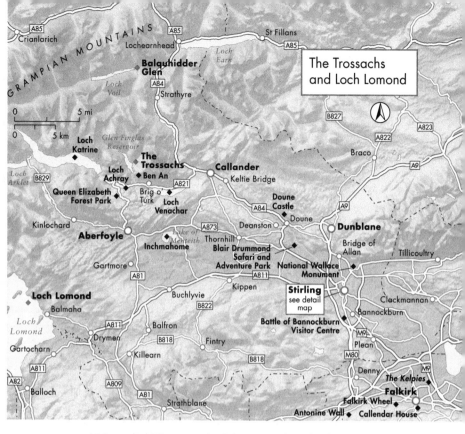

13th century. The town also boasts one of Scotland's most impressive libraries, the Leighton Library.

GETTING HERE AND AROUND
Dunblane station is on the main line to Perth and Inverness, and regular bus service links the town to Stirling. For drivers it is easily reached along the main A9 artery.

EXPLORING
FAMILY **Doune Castle.** No self-respecting Highland chief's attire was complete without an ornate pair of pistols made in Doune, 5 miles west of Dunblane. Today the community is more widely known for having one of the best-preserved medieval castles in Scotland. It's also a place of pilgrimage for fans of *Monty Python and the Holy Grail*, which was filmed here. Doune Castle is grim and high-walled, with a daunting central keep and echoing, drafty stairways up to the curtain-wall walk. The views make the climb well worthwhile. There is a good audio guide narrated by Monty Python's Terry Gilliam. ■ TIP→ **The best place to photograph this squat, walled fort is from the bridge, a little way upstream.** ⊠ *Castle Rd., Doune* ☎ *01786/841742* ⊕ *www.historic-scotland.gov.uk* ⌑ *£5.50* ⊙ *Apr.–Sept., daily 9:30–5:30; Oct., daily 9:30–4; Nov.–Mar., Sat.–Wed. 9:30–4.*

Dunblane Cathedral. The oldest part of Dunblane—with its narrow winding streets—huddles around this church's square. The cathedral was built by Bishop Clement in the early 13th century on the site of St. Blane's tiny 8th-century cell; with the Reformation of the 16th century, it ceased to be a cathedral. In 1996 it was the scene of a moving memorial service for the 15 children and one teacher killed in the local school by Thomas Hamilton. ⊠ *The Cross* ☎ *01667/460232* ⊕ *www.historic-scotland.gov.uk/places* ▧ *Free* ◷ *Apr.–Sept., Mon.–Sat. 9:30–12:30 and 1:30–5, Sun. 2–5; Oct.–Mar., Mon.–Sat. 9:30–4, Sun. 2–4.*

WHERE TO EAT AND STAY

$
BRITISH

✕ Old Churches House Brasserie. Housed in a row of 18th-century cottages directly opposite the cathedral, this pleasant and quiet bar-restaurant with modern flair serves a fairly conservative but carefully prepared menu, with specialties like steak-and-ale pie and haggis-stuffed chicken. The property also offers bed-and-breakfast accommodation. $ *Average main: £13* ⊠ *1 Kirk St.* ☎ *01786/823663* ⊕ *www.oldchurcheshouse.com.*

$$
ECLECTIC

✕ Sheriffmuir Inn. The road to Sheriffmuir from Dunblane is too narrow to be numbered, and you may be concerned you have taken a wrong turn until you reach this splendidly isolated, whitewashed inn. Inside there is a warm fire at a friendly bar filled with wooden furniture. The restaurant is slightly more formal and has views onto the moor beyond. Owner and chef Geoff Cook keeps to local produce wherever possible, but with a specialty in Japanese Wagyu beef burgers. The desserts are very tempting. $ *Average main: £15* ⊠ *Off A9* ☎ *01786/823285* ⊕ *www.sheriffmuirinn.co.uk.*

$$$$
HOTEL
Fodor'sChoice
★

Cromlix. A grand Victorian country house set on beautiful grounds, Cromlix House has been tastefully refurbished to maintain its atmosphere and create a sense of restrained luxury; you can easily imagine a weekend country party strolling through the trees or fishing on the private loch. **Pros:** luxurious facilities in a beautiful setting; lovely grounds for walking; comfortable beds. **Cons:** not much for children; a little hard to find. $ *Rooms from: £250* ⊠ *Kinbuck* ✤ *Just beyond the village of Kinbuck* ☎ *01786/822125* ⊕ *www.cromlix.com* ⇆ *10 rooms, 5 suites, 1 lodge* ⦿ *Breakfast.*

$$
HOTEL

DoubleTree by Hilton Dunblane Hydro. One of the grandes dames where Victorians would come to "take the waters," this hotel on sprawling grounds has retained its original building and the high style of its interior. **Pros:** fine views; lovely grounds; leisure center included in the rates. **Cons:** a slightly old-fashioned feel; some rooms are small; charge for Wi-Fi. $ *Rooms from: £139* ⊠ *Perth Rd.* ☎ *01786/822551* ⊕ *www.doubletreedunblane.com* ⇆ *200 rooms* ⦿ *No meals.*

CALLANDER

8 miles northwest of Doune.

A traditional Highland-edge resort, the little town of Callander bustles throughout the year, even during off-peak times, simply because it's a gateway to Highland scenery and Loch Lomond and the Trossachs National Park. As a result, there's plenty of window-shopping here, plus nightlife in pubs and a good selection of accommodations.

GETTING HERE AND AROUND

You can access Callander by bus from Stirling, Glasgow, or Edinburgh. If you're traveling by car from Stirling, take the M8 to Dunblane, then the A820 (which becomes the A84) to Callander. If you are coming from Glasgow, take the A81 through Aberfoyle to Callander; an alternative route (longer but more picturesque) is to take the A821 around Loch Venachar, then the A84 east to Callander.

ESSENTIALS

Visitor Information Callander Visitor Information Centre. ⊠ *52–54 Main St.* ☎ *01877/330342* ⊕ *www.visitscotland.com.*

EXPLORING

FAMILY
Fodor's Choice
★

Blair Drummond Safari and Adventure Park. As unlikely as it might seem in this gentle valley, the Blair Drummond Safari and Adventure Park is the place to see sea lions bobbing their heads above the water or monkeys swinging from the branches. Take a footbridge to Lemur Land or watch hawks and falcons in the "Birds of Prey" exhibit. Beware the llamas, who are more bad-tempered than they may appear. The enclosures are spacious, so the place doesn't feel like a zoo. There are rides, slides, and an adventure playground for the kids. ⊠ *Blair Drummond, Doune* ☎ *01786/841456* ⊕ *www.blairdrummond.com* 🎟 *£14.50* ⊙ *Mar.–Oct., daily 10–5:30.*

FAMILY
Hamilton Toy Collection. Crowded into this small house and shop on Callander's main street is one of the most extensive toy collections in Britain. The small rooms throughout the house are filled with everything from Corgi cars and an enormous number of toy soldiers, carefully organized by regiment, to Amanda Jane dolls and Beatles memorabilia. The collection of model railways has extended into the newly built tracks in the back garden. The museum is crowded and quirky, but full of reminders of everyone's childhood. ⊠ *111 Main St.* ☎ *01877/330004* ⊕ *www.thehamiltontoycollection.co.uk* 🎟 *£3* ⊙ *Apr.–Oct., Mon.–Sat. 10-4:30, Sun. noon–4:30.*

WHERE TO EAT

$
BRITISH

✕ **Lade Inn.** A mile from Callander, this traditional pub offers good, solid fare such as locally sourced steaks, burgers, and chicken as well as international dishes like tagines. The establishment specializes in ales, and there's an even larger selection at the shop next door. The staff is friendly and attentive, traditional music plays much of the time, and musicians break out their instruments weekend nights. $ *Average main: £14* ⊠ *Off A821, Kilmahog* ☎ *01877/330152* ⊕ *www.theladeinn.com.*

$
CAFÉ

✕ **Pip's Coffee House.** Come to this cheerful little place just off the main street for imaginative soups and salads, as well as exquisite Scottish home baking, including fresh scones. And then, of course, there's great coffee. $ *Average main: £8* ⊠ *21–23 Ancaster Sq.* ☎ *01877/330470* ⊙ *No dinner.*

6

$ MODERN BRITISH Fodor's Choice ★ 🍴 **Venachar Lochside.** There is a special pleasure in dining overlooking a loch, and this restaurant's glass wall affords a lovely panorama of the water and surrounding hills—a pleasant surprise given that all you see from the road is what seems to be a large shed, which could be easily missed. And the menu lives up to its surroundings. The emphasis is on fish—mussels, scallops, the excellent smoked-fish selection to start, and the trout with roast chorizo. If you have room, there is an array of cakes to follow. Don't miss it on the A821 about 6 miles from Callander at Brig o' Turk. [$] *Average main: £13* ✉ *Loch Venachar* ☎ *01877/330011* 🌐 *www.venachar-lochside.co.uk* 🕒 *No dinner Nov.–Mar. No dinner Thurs.–Sun. Apr.–Oct.* ✍ *Reservations essential.*

WHERE TO STAY

$ B&B/INN FAMILY 🏨 **Auchenlaich Farmhouse.** This unpretentious house on a working farm sits just outside Callander, with bright, comfortable rooms and lovely views. **Pros:** fine views; especially good for cyclists and walkers; economical. **Cons:** not all rooms are en suite. [$] *Rooms from: £75* ✉ *Keltie Bridge* ✣ *Just past Keltie Bridge at the end of a short farm road* ☎ *01877/331683* 🌐 *www.auchenlaichfarmhouse.co.uk* 🛏 *5 rooms* 🍽 *Breakfast* 💳 *No credit cards.*

$$ B&B/INN Fodor's Choice ★ 🏨 **Roman Camp.** Within a hundred yards of Callander's main street, pass through an unpretentious arch and you'll find this 17th-century hunting lodge surrounded by ornate gardens. **Pros:** beautiful grounds; luxurious rooms; close to everything in town. **Cons:** restaurant is expensive; no Internet in rooms. [$] *Rooms from: £160* ✉ *Off Main St.* ☎ *01877/330003* 🌐 *www.romancamphotel.co.uk* 🛏 *12 rooms, 3 suites* 🍽 *Breakfast.*

SHOPPING

Trossachs Woollen Mill. The Edinburgh Woollen Mill Group owns this mill shop in Kilmahog. It has a vast selection of woolens on display, including luxurious cashmere and striking tartan throws, and will provide overseas mailing and tax-free shopping. ✉ *Main St., Kilmahog* ☎ *01877/330178* 🌐 *www.ewm.co.uk* 🕒 *Mar.–Oct., daily 9–5; Nov., daily 9–4:30; Dec.–Feb., daily 9–4.*

SPORTS AND THE OUTDOORS

BICYCLING

Wheels. This friendly firm rents bikes of every sort by the hour, the half day, or the day. Most popular are the mountain bikes, which go for £20 per day. The staff will help you find the best mountain-bike routes around the Trossachs. ✉ *Invertrossachs Rd.* ☎ *01877/331100* 🌐 *www.wheelscyclingcentre.com.*

GOLF

Callander Golf Club. Designed by Tom Morris in 1890 and extended to 18 holes in 1913 by Willie Fernie, Callander has a scenic upland feel in a town well prepared for visitors. Pine and birch woods and hilly fairways afford fine views, especially toward Ben Ledi, and the tricky moorland layout demands accurate hitting off the tee. ✉ *Aveland Rd.* ☎ *01877/330090* 🌐 *www.callandergolfclub.co.uk* 🎟 *£30 weekdays, £40 weekends* ⛳ *18 holes, 5208 yards, par 66.*

HIKING

Bracklinn Falls. A walk is signposted from the east end of Callander's main street to the Bracklinn Falls, over whose lip Sir Walter Scott once rode a pony to win a bet.

Callander Crags. It's a 1½-mile walk through the woods up to the Callander Crags, with views of the Lowlands as far as the Pentland Hills behind Edinburgh. The walk begins at the west end of Callander's main street.

Pass of Leny. Just north of Callander, the mountains squeeze both the road and rocky river into the narrow Pass of Leny. An abandoned railway—now a pleasant walking or biking path—also goes through the pass, past Ben Ledi and Loch Lubnaig.

> ## GOLF IN THE TROSSACHS
>
> There are many beautiful golf courses within the Loch Lomond area and the Trossachs National Park. The National Park Golf Pass (£50 for three rounds, £80 for five) allows play at Callander, St. Fillans, Aberfoyle, Killin, and Buchanan Castle. The Loch Lomond Pass (£90 for three rounds) covers the Cardos, Helensburgh, and Buchanan Castle courses.

BALQUHIDDER GLEN

6

12 miles north of Callander.

A 20-minute drive from Callander, through the Pass of Leny and beyond Strathyre, is Balquhidder Glen (pronounced *bal*-kwidd-er), a typical Highland glen that runs westward. The glen has characteristics seen throughout the north: a flat-bottom U-shape profile, formed by prehistoric glaciers; extensive Forestry Commission plantings replacing much of the natural woodlands above; a sprinkling of farms; and, farther up the glen, hill roads bulldozed into the slopes to provide access for foresters. You may notice the boarded-up look of some of the area's houses, many of which are second homes for affluent residents of the south. The glen is also where Loch Voil and Loch Doune spread out, adding to the stunning vistas.

GETTING HERE AND AROUND

To reach Balquhidder Glen by car, take the A84 from Callander (signposted to Crianlarich) and turn left at Kingshouse. This road ends in the glen, so you will have to turn back and rejoin the A84 to continue your journey—but it's certainly worth the diversion.

EXPLORING

Grave of Rob Roy MacGregor. The area around Balquhidder Glen, known as the Braes (Slopes) of Balquhidder, was the home of the MacLarens and the MacGregors. The grave of Rob Roy MacGregor, the 18th-century Scottish outlaw hero and subject of the 1995 movie *Rob Roy*, is signposted beside Balquhidder village. The site of his house, now a private farm, is beyond the parking lot at the end of the road up the glen. The glen has no through road, though there is a right-of-way (on foot) from the churchyard where Rob Roy is buried, through Kirkton Glen and on to open grasslands and a lake.

WHERE TO STAY

$ 🎮 **MHOR 84 Motel.** For walkers and cyclists Balquhidder Glen is the
B&B/INN perfect place, especially since the opening of the new Rob Roy Way and
FAMILY this modest hotel, designed with the outdoor enthusiast in mind. **Pros:**
beautiful setting; great quality for the price; game room for kids. **Cons:**
a rather isolated spot. $ *Rooms from: £80* ☎ *01877/384646* ⊕ *www.
mhor.net* ⌿ *7 rooms* ❚❙❘ *No meals.*

$$$$ 🎮 **Monachyle MHOR.** Set on 2,000 acres of forests and moorland, this
HOTEL beautifully converted farmhouse sits in splendid isolation against a
Fodor'sChoice backdrop of mountains and views over Lochs Voil and Doine. **Pros:**
★ stunning scenery; delicious food; complimentary salmon and trout
fishing. **Cons:** you're isolated; rooms are on the small side. $ *Rooms
from: £265* ✉ *Off A84, Balquhidder* ☎ *01877/384622* ⊕ *www.mhor.
net* ⌿ *14 rooms* ❚❙❘ *Breakfast.*

THE TROSSACHS

10 miles west of Callander.

With its harmonious scenery of hill, loch, and wooded slopes, the Trossachs has been a popular touring region since the late 18th century, at
the dawn of the age of the Romantic poets. Influenced by the writings
of Sir Walter Scott, early visitors who strayed into the Highlands from
the central belt of Scotland admired this as the first "wild" part of
Scotland they encountered. Perhaps because the Trossachs represent the
very essence of what the Highlands are supposed to be, the whole of
this area, including Loch Lomond, is now protected as a national park.
Here you can find birch and pine forests, vistas down lochs where the
woods creep right to the water's edge, and, in the background, peaks
that rise high enough to be called mountains, though they're not as high
as those to the north and west.

GETTING HERE AND AROUND

To reach the Trossachs, take the A84 from Callander through the Pass
of Leny, then on to Crianlarich on the A85; from here you can continue
down the western shore of Loch Lomond or continue on toward Fort
William. Alternately, turn onto the A821 outside Callander and travel
past Loch Katrine through the Duke's Pass to Aberfoyle.

EXPLORING
TOP ATTRACTIONS

Fodor'sChoice **Ben An.** The parking lot by Loch Achray is the place to begin the ascent
★ of steep, heathery Ben An, which affords some of the best Trossachs
views. The climb requires a couple of hours and good lungs. The beginning of the path is near Loch Achray. ✉ *A821, Aberfoyle.*

FAMILY **Loch Katrine.** This loch was a favorite among Victorian visitors—mys-
Fodor'sChoice terious and wide and, at times, quite wild. Today it's the source of
★ Glasgow's freshwater. Take a cruise around the loch if time permits,
as the shores remain undeveloped and scenic. The steamship *Sir Walter Scott* and the motor launch *Lady of the Lake* sail from here several times a day. You can make the round-trip journey around the
loch, or head directly across to Stronachlachar and return by bicycle
on the lochside road. Boats depart several times a day between April

and October. There are café facilities and cycle-hire shops at the head of the loch; reservations are required if you're bringing a bike. ⊠ *Trossachs Pier, off A821, Aberfoyle* ☎ *01877/376316* ⊕ *www.lochkatrine.com* ⛴ *Sir Walter Scott £16 round-trip, £13.50 one way; Lady of the Lake £14 round-trip, £11.50 one way.*

WORTH NOTING

Brig o'Turk. A few minutes after it passes Loch Venachar, the A821 becomes muffled in woodlands and twists gradually down to the village of Brig o'Turk. (*Turk* is Gaelic for the Scots *tuirc*, meaning wild boar, a species that has been extinct in this region since about the 16th century.) ⊠ *A821, Brig o'Turk.*

Loch Achray. Stretching west of Brig o' Turk, Loch Achray dutifully fulfills expectations of what a verdant Trossachs loch should be: small, green, reedy meadows backed by dark plantations, rhododendron thickets, and lumpy hills, thickly covered with heather. ⊠ *A821, Brig o'Turk.*

Loch Venachar. The A821 runs west together with the first and gentlest of the Trossachs lochs, Loch Venachar. A sturdy gray-stone building, with a small dam at the Callander end, controls the water that feeds into the River Teith (and, hence, into the Forth). ⊠ *A821, Brig o'Turk.*

SCOTLAND BY BIKE

The region's big attraction for cyclists is the **Lowland/Highland Trail,** which stretches more than 60 miles and passes through Drymen, Aberfoyle, the Trossachs, Callander, Lochearnhead, and Killin. This route runs along former railroad-track beds, as well as private and minor roads, to reach well into the Central Highlands. Another almost completely traffic-free option is the roadway around Loch Katrine. Mountain bikes can tackle many of the forest roads and trails enjoyed by walkers. Almost every town along the route has cycle-hire shops. Avoid main roads, which can be busy with traffic.

ABERFOYLE

11 miles south of Loch Katrine, in the Trossachs.

This small tourist town has a somewhat faded air, and several of its souvenir shops have closed their doors. But the surrounding hills (some snowcapped) and the green slopes visible from the town are the reason so many visitors pause here before continuing up to Duke's Pass or on to Inversnaid on Loch Lomond. Access to nearby Queen Elizabeth Forest Park is another reason to visit.

GETTING HERE AND AROUND

The main route out of Glasgow, the A81, takes you through Aberfoyle and on to Callander and Stirling. There are regular buses from Stirling and Glasgow to Aberfoyle.

ESSENTIALS

Visitor Information Trossachs Discovery Centre. ⊠ *Main St.* ☎ *01877/382352* ⊕ *www.visitscotland.com.*

EXPLORING

FAMILY **Go Ape High Wire Forest Adventure.** Near the David Marshall Lodge, this is an exhilarating experience for thrill-seekers age 10 and over. After a short orientation course, you can travel 40 feet above the forest via zip lines and rope ladders. ✉ *Queen Elizabeth Forest Park, A821, 1 mile north of Aberfoyle* ☎ *0845/643–9215* 🌐 *www.goape.com* 🎟 *£31 (3 hrs), £25 (2 hrs)* ⏲ *Apr.–Oct., daily 9:30–4:30; Nov., Feb., and Mar., weekends 9–5.*

Fodor's Choice ★ **Inchmahome.** The 13th-century ruined priory on the tiny island of Inchmahome, on the Lake of Menteith, is a lovely place for a picnic. It was a place of refuge in 1547 for the young Mary, Queen of Scots. Between April and September, a ferry takes passengers to the island, now owned by the National Trust for Scotland. To get here, take the A81 to the B8034. The ferry jetty is just past the Port of Menteith. ✉ *Off A81* ✣ *4 miles east of Aberfoyle* ☎ *01786/450000* 🌐 *www.historic-scotland.gov.uk* 🎟 *Ferry £5.50* ⏲ *Apr.–Sept., daily 10–4:15; Oct., daily 10–3:15.*

Fodor's Choice ★ **Queen Elizabeth Forest Park.** For exquisite nature, drive north from Aberfoyle on the A821 and turn right at signposts to Queen Elizabeth Forest Park. Along the way you'll be heading toward higher moorland blanketed with conifers. The conifers hem in the views of Ben Ledi and Ben Venue, which can be seen over the spiky green waves of trees as the road snakes around heathery knolls and hummocks. There's another viewing area, and a small parking lot, at the highest point of the road. Soon the road swoops off the Highland edge and leads downhill.

At the heart of the Queen Elizabeth Forest Park, the **David Marshall Lodge** leads to four forest walks, a family-friendly bicycle route, and the 7-mile 3 Lochs Forest Drive, open April to October. Or you can sit on the terrace of the Bluebell Cafe and scan the forests and hills of the Trossachs. The visitor center has a wildlife-watch room where you can follow the activities of everything from ospreys to water voles. ✉ *Off A821, 1 mile north of Aberfoyle* ☎ *01877/382383* 🌐 *www.forestry.gov.uk/qefp* 🎟 *Free.*

FAMILY **Scottish Wool Centre.** With a vast range of woolen garments and knitwear, the Scottish Wool Centre also has a small café. Three times a day from April to September it presents an interactive "gathering" when dogs herd sheep and ducks in the large amphitheater, with a little help from the public. ✉ *Off Main St.* ☎ *01877/382850* 🎟 *Free* ⏲ *Feb.–Dec., daily 9:30–5:30; Jan., daily 10–4:30.*

WHERE TO EAT AND STAY

$ BRITISH 🍴 **Pier Cafe.** At the historic Stronachlachar Pier, this elegant coffee shop has a satisfying lunch menu and an expansive deck overlooking Loch Katrine. Cakes, scones, and soups are made on the premises. Many people get off the boat from Trossachs Pier here before cycling or walking along the road around the loch. [$] *Average main: £9* ✉ *B829, Stronachlachar* ☎ *01877/386374* 🌐 *www.thepiercafe.com* ⏲ *No dinner.*

$$ HOTEL Fodor's Choice ★ 🏨 **Lake of Menteith Hotel.** With its muted colors and simple but elegant rooms, this restful hotel emphasizes peace and quiet. **Pros:** elegant, unpretentious bedrooms; beautiful setting. **Cons:** not well signposted; not all rooms have lake views and those that do are more expensive.

[$] *Rooms from: £129* ✉ *Off A81* ☎ *01877/385258* 🌐 *www.lake-hotel.com* 🛏 *17 rooms* 🍴 *Breakfast.*

$$ HOTEL 🏨 **Macdonald Forest Hills Hotel.** A traditional Scottish country-house theme pervades this hotel, from the rambling white building itself to the wood-paneled lounges, log fires, and numerous sporting activities. **Pros:** stunning views; 20+ acres of grounds to explore; good children's programs. **Cons:** restaurant is pricey and food is average; some of the building looks run-down. [$] *Rooms from: £149* ✉ *B829, Kinlochard* ☎ *08448/799057* 🌐 *www.macdonaldhotels.co.uk/foresthills* 🛏 *56 rooms* 🍴 *Breakfast.*

GOLF

Aberfoyle Golf Club. This hilly course is set against the backdrop of Queen Elizabeth Forest Park. One of the area's many James Braid–designed parkland courses, it dates back to 1890. There are views of Ben Lomond and Stirling Castle from different points on the course, which is relatively short but varied and challenging even for quite experienced players, with several uphill shots and undulating ground. ✉ *Braeval* ☎ *01877/382493* 🌐 *www.aberfoylegolf.co.uk* 🎫 *£20 weekdays, £25 weekends* ⛳ *18 holes, 5158 yards, par 66.*

6

LOCH LOMOND

14 miles west of Aberfoyle.

The waters of Scotland's largest loch, which also happens to be one of its most beautiful, create a perfect reflection of the surrounding hills. You can cruise among its small islands or follow the low road that carries you from Glasgow to the beginning of the Highlands.

GETTING HERE AND AROUND

To reach Loch Lomond from Aberfoyle, take the A81 toward Glasgow, then the A811 to Drymen and then the B837 as far as it will take you. From Glasgow, take the A82 to the Balloch roundabout and either go right through Balloch for Drymen and the eastern shore, or continue along the A82 as it hugs the west bank all the way to Crianlarich.

You can drive, cycle, or walk along the 32 miles of Loch Lomond along its western shores, and watch the changing face of the loch as you go, or look up toward the shifting slopes of Ben Lomond.

ESSENTIALS

Visitor Information **Loch Lomond and the Trossachs National Park Headquarters.** ✉ *The Old Station, Balloch* ☎ *01389/722600* 🌐 *www.lochlomond-trossachs.org.*

EXPLORING

Fodor's Choice ★ **Loch Lomond.** Known for its "bonnie, bonnie banks," Loch Lomond is Scotland's largest loch in terms of surface area, and its waters reflect the crags that surround it. The song "The Banks of Loch Lomond" is said to have been written by a Jacobite prisoner incarcerated in Carlisle, England.

On the western side of the loch, the A82 follows the shore for 24 miles, continuing a further 7 miles to Crianlarich, passing picturesque Luss, which has a pier where you can hop aboard boats cruising along the loch, and Tarbert, the starting point for the *Maid of the Loch*. On the eastern side of the loch, take the A81 to Drymen, and from there the B837 signposted toward Balmaha, where you can hire a boat or take the ferry to the island of Inchcailloch. Once you're there, a short walk takes you to the top of the hill and a spectacular view of the loch. Equally spectacular, but not as wet, is the view from Conic Hill behind Balmaha. If you continue along the B837 beyond Rowardennan to where it ends at a car park, you can join the walkers at the beginning of the path up Ben Lomond. Don't underestimate this innocent-looking hill; go equipped for sudden changes in the weather.

> ## HIKE THE HIGHLAND WAY
>
> **West Highland Way.** The long-distance walkers' route, the West Highland Way, begins in Glasgow, running 96 miles from the Lowlands of Central Scotland to the Highlands at Fort William. Nearly 50,000 people discover the glens each year, climbing the hills and listening to birds singing in the tree canopy. This is not a difficult walk, but keep Scotland's ever-changing weather in mind. From Milngavie, in Glasgow, the route passes along the banks of Loch Lomond before snaking northward into the more demanding hills beyond and finishing at Fort William. ⊕ *www.west-highland-way.co.uk.*

WHERE TO EAT

$ ✕ **Coach House Coffee Shop.** This lively restaurant and café fits perfectly
BRITISH   into its surroundings with its cheerful, over-the-top Scottishness (Luss
Fodor's Choice   attracts large numbers of visitors because of its association with a favor-
★   ite TV soap opera). Long wooden tables, a large chimney with an open fire in the winter months, and a cabinet full of mouthwatering cakes baked by the owner create the atmosphere. Favorites include rich homemade soups and *stokies* (large round rolls filled to overflowing), as well as the ubiquitous haggis, served in king-size quantities. It's worth asking for tea served in ceramic teapots representing everything from dining rooms to telephone boxes (the pots are for sale in the shop). $ *Average main: £11 ⊠ Church Rd., Luss ☎ 01436/860341 ⊘ No dinner.*

$ ✕ **Drovers Inn.** The portions at this noisy, friendly inn are enormous,
BRITISH   which is just as well because many customers have returned from a day's walking on the nearby West Highland Way. Scottish staples like sausage and mash, minced beef, and haggis with mash and *neeps* (turnips) jostle for a place beside occasionally more adventurous dishes. The dining areas are hung with swords and modern copies of old paintings, but the best place to eat is the crowded bar. This is a genuine traveler's pub (hearty rather than elegant) with an appropriate range of whiskies and mounted animals presumably brought by earlier travelers. The bear at the door should not put you off (it is stuffed and very old). There is traditional music every weekend, and there are 30 rooms for rent. $ *Average main: £12 ⊠ A82, north of Ardlui, Inverarnan ☎ 01301/704234 ⊕ www.thedroversinn.co.uk.*

WHERE TO STAY

$ HOTEL **Balloch House.** Cute, cozy, and very Scottish, this small hotel offers tasty breakfasts and hearty pub meals like fish-and-chips and local smoked salmon for reasonable prices. **Pros:** beautiful building; recently refurbished; near shopping. **Cons:** noisy pinball machine next to bar; not all rooms have views. *[$] Rooms from: £86 ✉ Balloch Rd., Balloch ☎ 01389/752579 🌐 www.innkeeperslodge.com/loch-lomond 🛏 12 rooms 🍴 Breakfast.*

$$$ HOTEL **Cameron House.** There is little that you cannot do at this luxury resort hotel beside Loch Lomond, including taking to the water in a motorboat or riding a seaplane above the trees. **Pros:** beautiful grounds; away-from-it-all feel; good dining. **Cons:** prices are high; slightly difficult access from A82. *[$] Rooms from: £190 ✉ Loch Lomond, off A82, Alexandria ☎ 01389/755565 🌐 www.qhotels.co.uk 🛏 96 rooms, 7 suites 🍴 Breakfast.*

$$ HOTEL **Culcreuch Castle Hotel.** Set in vast and beautiful grounds, this authentic castle has its own loch for those wanting to fish and hills for those who prefer walking. **Pros:** historic building; expansive and beautiful grounds; good food at reasonable prices. **Cons:** a little remote; steep stairways; rather small shower rooms. *[$] Rooms from: £150 ✉ Off B822, Fintry ☎ 01360/860555 🌐 www.culcreuch.com 🛏 14 rooms 🍴 Breakfast.*

6

SHOPPING

Loch Lomond Shores. This lakeside shopping complex contains restaurants, pubs, and a visitor center. *✉ Ben Lomond Way, Balloch ☎ 01389/751031 🌐 www.lochlomondshores.com.*

SPORTS AND THE OUTDOORS

BOATING

FAMILY **Cruise Loch Lomond.** You can take tours year-round with Cruise Loch Lomond. From April to October boats depart from various ports around the loch, including Tarbet, Luss, Balmaha, and Inversnaid. There is also a Two-Loch Tour taking in Loch Lomond and Loch Katrine. From November to March the boats operate on demand. *✉ A82, Tarbet ☎ 01301/702356 🌐 www.cruiselochlomond.co.uk ☞ £9.50–£12.50.*

Macfarlane and Son. At this longtime favorite, boats with outboard motors rent for £60 per day. Rowboats rent for £10 per hour or £40 per day. From Balmaha, it is a short trip to the lovely island of Incailloch. Macfarlane's also runs a ferry to the island for £5 per person. *✉ Balmaha Boatyard, B837, Balmaha ☎ 01360/870214 🌐 www.balmahaboatyard.co.uk.*

GOLF

Buchanan Castle Golf Club. Surrounded by mature trees, the setting here is quiet and beautiful, framed by rivers and woods. Established in 1936, this parkland course sits less than 2 miles from the lovely village of Drymen. Although it is relatively young in terms of Scottish golf courses, it has some challenging moments, like the tall trees halfway along the fairways. A putting green is a nice touch. *✉ A809, Drymen ☎ 01360/660330 🌐 www.buchanancastlegolfclub.co.uk 🎫 £42 weekdays, £47 weekends 🏌 18 holes, 6131 yards, par 70.*

PERTHSHIRE

If Perthshire's castles invoke memories of past conflicts, the grand houses and spa towns here are testimony to the continued presence of a wealthy landed gentry. This is also a place for walking, cycling, and water sports. In some ways Perthshire is a crossing point between different Scottish landscapes and histories. Perthshire itself is rural, agricultural Scotland, fertile and prosperous. Its woodlands, rivers, and glens (and agreeable climate and strategic position) drew the Romans and later the Celtic missionaries. In fact, the motto of the capital city, Perth, is "the perfect center."

PERTH

36 miles northeast of Stirling, 43 miles north of Edinburgh, 61 miles northeast of Glasgow.

For many years Perth was Scotland's capital, and central to its history. One king (James I) was killed here, and the Protestant reformer John Knox preached in St. John's Kirk, where his rhetoric moved crowds to burn down several local monasteries. Perth's local whisky trade and the productive agriculture that surrounds the town have sustained it through the centuries. Its grand buildings, especially on the banks of the River Tay, testify to its continued wealth. The open parkland within the city (the Inches) gives the place a restful air, and shops range from small crafts boutiques to department stores. Impressive Scone Palace is nearby.

GETTING HERE AND AROUND

Perth is served by the main railway line to Inverness, and regular and frequent buses run here from Glasgow, Edinburgh, and Stirling. The central artery, the A9, passes through the city en route to Pitlochry and Inverness, while a network of roads opens the way to the glens and hills around Glen Lyon, or the road to Loch Lomond (the A85) via Crianlarich.

ESSENTIALS

Visitor Information Perth Visitor Centre. ⊠ *45 High St.* ☎ *01738/450600* ⊕ *www.visitscotland.co.uk.*

EXPLORING PERTH
TOP ATTRACTIONS

Elcho Castle. From the battlements of Elcho Castle you can see the River Tay stretching east and west. Built around 1560, the castle marks a transition period when these structures began to be built as grand houses rather than fortresses, and it's easy to see that Elcho was built for both comfort and defense. The well-preserved but uncluttered rooms let you imagine how life might have been here in the 17th century. The staircases still give access to all floors, and a flashlight is provided for the darker corners. The castle is open in summer only. ⊠ *Off A912* ✛ *Close to Rhynd* ☎ *01738/639998* ⊕ *www.historic-scotland.gov.uk/ places* ▦ *£4.50* ⊙ *Apr.–Sept., daily 9:30–5.*

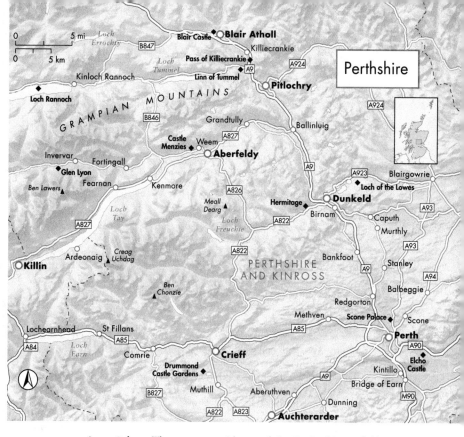

FAMILY
Scone Palace. The current residence of the Earl of Mansfield, Scone
Fodor's Choice Palace (pronounced *skoon*) is much more cheerful than the city's other
★ castles. Although it incorporates various earlier works, the palace today
has mainly a 19th-century theme, with mock castellations that were
fashionable at the time. There's plenty to see if you're interested in the
acquisitions of an aristocratic Scottish family: magnificent porcelain,
some sumptuous furniture, a fine collection of ivory, clocks, and 16th-
century needlework. Each room has a specialist guide who will happily
talk you through its contents and their associations. In one bedroom
hangs a portrait of Dido Elizabth Belle, a young black slave adopted by
the family, who became a well-known society beauty in the 1760s. A
coffee shop, restaurant, gift shop, and play area are on-site. The palace
has its own mausoleum nearby, on the site of a long-gone abbey on **Moot
Hill**, the ancient coronation place of the Scottish kings. To be crowned,
they sat on the Stone of Scone, which was seized in 1296 by Edward I of
England, Scotland's greatest enemy, and placed in the coronation chair
at Westminster Abbey, in London. The stone was returned to Scotland
in November 1996 and is now on view in Edinburgh Castle. Some
Scots hint darkly that Edward was fooled by a substitution and that the
real stone is hidden, waiting for Scotland to regain its independence.
✉ *Scone Palace, Braemar Rd.* ✛ *2 miles from Perth* ☎ *01738/552300*

🌐 *www.scone-palace.co.uk* 🎫 *£10.50* 🕑 *Apr.–Oct., daily 9:30–5, last admission at 4:30; Nov–Mar., Fri.–Sun. 10–4.*

WORTH NOTING

Fergusson Gallery. Originally a water works, this gallery's magnificent and newly restored dome and rotunda shelter a collection of 6,000 works—paintings, drawings, and prints—by the Scottish artist J. D. Fergusson (1874–1961) and his wife Margaret Morris, an artist in her own right and a pioneer of modern dance. Fergusson was the longest-lived member of the group called the Scottish Colourists, who took their inspiration from the French impressionist painters in their use of color and light. ✉ *Marshall Pl.* ☎ *01738/783425* 🌐 *www.pkc.gov.uk/museums* 🎫 *Free* 🕑 *Mon.–Sat. 10–5.*

Perth Art Gallery and Museum. The recently refurbished gallery has a wide-ranging collection including exhibits on natural history, local history, archaeology, and art and an important glass collection. It also has work by the great painter of animals Sir Edwin Landseer and some botanical studies of fungi by Beatrix Potter. ✉ *78 George St.* ☎ *01738/632488* 🌐 *www.pkc.gov.uk/perthmuseumandartgallery* 🎫 *Free* 🕑 *May–Oct., Tues.–Sun. 10–5; Nov.–Apr., Tues.–Sat. 10–5.*

Regimental Museum of the Black Watch. Some will tell you the Black Watch was a Scottish regiment whose name is a reference to the color of its tartan. An equally plausible explanation, however, is that the regiment was established to keep an undercover watch on rebellious Jacobites. The Gaelic word for black is *dubh,* meaning, in this case, "hidden" or "covert." A wide range of uniforms, weaponry, and marching banners are displayed. The castle is closed on the last weekend in June. ✉ *Balhousie Castle, Hay St.* ☎ *01738/638152* 🌐 *www.theblackwatch.co.uk* 🎫 *£7.50 (Guided tour £12.50)* 🕑 *Apr.–Oct., Mon.–Sat. 9:30–5, Sun. 10–4; Nov.–Mar., Mon.–Sat. 9:30–5.*

St. John's Kirk. This impressive cruciform-plan church dates from the 12th century; reformer John Knox preached a fiery sermon here in 1559. The interior was divided into three parts at the Reformation, but was restored to something closer to its medieval state by Sir Robert Lorimer in the 1920s. ✉ *St. John St.* ☎ *01738/633192* 🌐 *www.st-johns-kirk.co.uk* 🎫 *Free* 🕑 *Mar.–Sept., weekdays 10–4, Sun. services at 9:30 and 11.*

WHERE TO EAT AND STAY

$$$ BRITISH 🍴 **63 Tay Street.** Dine looking out on to the River Tay in this elegant restaurant that serves imaginative and creative fare with an emphasis on local produce. Try the asparagus and rabbit starter followed by the "happy" chicken with sweet pea and truffle velouté. On Saturdays only the full three-course menu (£42) is served. [$] *Average main: £24* ✉ *63 Tay St.* ☎ *01738/441451* 🌐 *www.63taystreet.com* ✍ *Reservations essential.*

$$ BRITISH 🍴 **Deans Restaurant.** The varied clientele reflects the broad appeal of noted chef Willie Deans's imaginative menu. The dinner menu combines creative starters like cheese-and-cauliflower soufflé with black pudding and a whisky cream and earthy main dishes with a Scottish flavor (venison, halibut, and lobster, for example). The restaurant is airy and pleasant, merging warm colors and rich woods, with comfortable

sofas for a pre-dinner drink. $ *Average main: £19* ✉ *77–79 Kinnoull St.* ☎ *01738/643377* ⊕ *www.letseatperth.co.uk* ⌕ *Reservations essential.*

$$
B&B/INN
🏨 **Parklands.** This stylish Georgian town house overlooking lush woodland has rooms with elegant furnishings and relaxing color schemes, as well as modern amenities like flat-screen TVs and wireless Internet. **Pros:** lovely rooms; lush setting; superb restaurants. **Cons:** some rooms have better views than others; more formal restaurant closed Sunday and Monday. $ *Rooms from: £129* ✉ *2 St. Leonard's Bank* ☎ *01738/622451* ⊕ *www.theparklandshotel.com* ⇱ *14 rooms* ⦿ *Breakfast.*

$
B&B/INN
🏨 **Sunbank House Hotel.** This early Victorian gray-stone mansion near Perth's Branklyn Gardens overlooks the River Tay and the city of Perth. **Pros:** reasonably priced; friendly staff; delicious local cuisine. **Cons:** some rooms are very small; you can hear traffic from the main road. $ *Rooms from: £90* ✉ *50 Dundee Rd.* ☎ *01738/624882* ⊕ *www. sunbankhouse.com* ⇱ *9 rooms* ⦿ *Breakfast.*

NIGHTLIFE AND PERFORMING ARTS

Perth Concert Hall. The city's main concert venue hosts musical performances of all types. ✉ *Mill St.* ☎ *017384/621031* ⊕ *www.horsecross.co.uk.*

Perth Repertory Theatre. The Victorian-era Perth Repertory Theatre stages plays and musicals. ✉ *185 High St.* ☎ *017384/621031* ⊕ *www. horsecross.co.uk.*

SHOPPING

CERAMICS

Perth is an especially popular hunting ground for china and glass.

Watsons of Perth. This shop has sold exquisite bone china and cut crystal since 1900. The staff can pack your purchase for shipment overseas. ✉ *163–167 High St.* ☎ *01738/639861* ⊕ *www.watsonsofperth.co.uk.*

JEWELRY AND ANTIQUES

Cairncross of Perth. The Romans coveted freshwater pearls from the River Tay. If you do, too, then head to Cairncross of Perth, where you can admire a display of some of the more unusual shapes and colors. Some of the delicate settings take their theme from Scottish flowers. ✉ *18 St. John's St.* ☎ *01738/624367* ⊕ *www.cairncrossofperth.co.uk* ⊗ *Closed Sun.*

Timothy Hardie. Antique jewelry and silver, including a few Scottish items, can be found at Timothy Hardie. ✉ *25 St. John's St.* ☎ *01738/633127* ⊕ *www.timothyhardie.co.uk.*

Whispers of the Past. This lovely shop has a collection of jewelry, china, and other gift items. ✉ *15 George St.* ☎ *01738/635472* ⊕ *whispers-of-the-past.weebly.com.*

DUNKELD

14 miles north of Perth.

The ruined cathedral above the town of Dunkeld marks its historic beginnings. The present town grew up around the main square, built by the Atholl family in the wake of the 1689 defeat of the Jacobite army (following its earlier victory in the Battle of Killiecrankie). The National Trust for Scotland has helped to maintain the houses with its Little Houses Project; it has a small exhibition above the Dunkeld and Birnam Tourist Information Centre (ask for the Heritage Trail leaflet). Crafts and interior-design shops dominate Atholl Street, which leads down to the River Tay.

The bridge across the River Tay takes you to Birnam Wood, where Shakespeare's Macbeth met the three witches who issued the prophecy about his death. Witty wooden notices lead you to the right tree, a gnarled hollow oak.

GETTING HERE AND AROUND
Dunkeld is on the A9 between Perth and Pitlochry. The town is also on the main train line to Inverness.

ESSENTIALS
Visitor Information **Dunkeld and Birnam Tourist Information Centre.** ⊠ *The Cross* ☏ *01350/727688* ⊕ *www.visitscotland.com.*

EXPLORING
FAMILY **Beatrix Potter Garden.** The garden celebrates the life and work of this much-beloved children's writer who, for many years, spent her family holidays in the area. You're free to walk around the enchanting garden where you can peep into the homes of Peter Rabbit and Mrs. Tiggy-Winkle, her best-known characters. The visitor center has a well-stocked shop, a small café, and an imaginative small exhibition on the writer's life and work (£1.50). ⊠ *Birnam Arts Centre, Station Rd., Birnam* ☏ *01350/727674* ⊕ *www.birnamarts.com* 🎟 *Free* ☉ *Exhibit daily 10–5.*

Hermitage. On the outskirts of Dunkeld, the Hermitage is a woodland walk that follows the River Braan. In the 18th century, the dukes of Atholl constructed two follies (fantasy buildings) here, **Ossian's Cave** and the awesome **Ossian's Hall,** above a spectacular—and noisy—waterfall. (Ossian was a fictional Celtic poet invented by James MacPherson in the 18th century for an era fascinated by the primitive past.) You'll also be in the presence of Britain's tallest tree, a Douglas fir measuring 214 feet. ⊠ *A9, 1 mile west of Dunkeld* ⊕ *www.nts.org.uk.*

FAMILY **Loch of the Lowes.** From the lochside hides at this Scottish Wildlife Trust reserve near Dunkeld, you can observe the area's rich birdlife through a powerful telescope. The main attractions are always the ospreys, one of Scotland's conservation success stories, which can be observed between March and August. But there is much to see throughout the year, like the great crested grebe at feeding stations. The enthusiastic staff will willingly describe what is happening around the center. ⊠ *Off A923* ✛ *About 2 miles northeast of Dunkeld off the A9* ☏ *01350/727337* ⊕ *scottishwildlifetrust.org.uk* 🎟 *£4* ☉ *Daily 10–5.*

WHERE TO EAT
$ ✕ **Taybank Hotel.** This spot overlooking the River Tay is a musical meet-
BRITISH   ing place owned by Scottish singer Dougie MacLean. Of course there's live music several nights a week. The walls are lined with instruments, which you're welcome to play. The bar serves good solid Scottish

food, including chicken breast cooked with bacon and kale and pot roast and bacon steaks with colcannon—mashed potatoes mixed with spring onions, a Scottish specialty. $ *Average main: £13* ⊠ *Tay Terr.* ☎ *01350/727340.*

SHOPPING

Jeremy Law of Scotland's Highland Horn and Deerskin Centre. Here you can purchase stag antlers and cow horns shaped into walking sticks, cutlery, and tableware. Deerskin shoes and moccasins and a collection of more than 200 different whiskies are also on offer. ⊠ *City Hall, Atholl St.* ☎ *0800/146780* ⊕ *www.moccasin.co.uk.*

PITLOCHRY

15 miles north of Dunkeld.

In the late 19th century Pitlochry was an elegant Victorian spa town, famous for its mild microclimate and beautiful setting. Today it is a busy tourist town, with wall-to-wall gift shops, cafés and B&Bs, large hotels, and a huge golf course. The town itself is oddly nondescript, but it's a convenient base from which to explore the surrounding hills and valleys.

GETTING HERE AND AROUND

The main route through central Scotland, the A9, passes through Pitlochry, as does the main railway line from Glasgow/Edinburgh to Inverness. From here the B8019 connects to the B846 west to Rannoch Moor or south to Aberfeldy.

ESSENTIALS

Visitor Information Pitlochry Visitor Information Centre. ⊠ *22 Atholl Rd.* ☎ *01796/472215* ⊕ *www.visitscotland.com.*

EXPLORING

TOP ATTRACTIONS

Edradour Distillery. If you have a whisky-tasting bent, visit Edradour Distillery, which claims to be the smallest single-malt distillery in Scotland (but then, so do others). There's a fun, informative tour of the distillery where you get to see how the whisky is made; you also get to savor a free dram at the end of the tour. ⊠ *A924, 2½ miles east of Pitlochry* ☎ *01796/472095* ⊕ *www.edradour.com* ✉ *Tours £7.50* ☉ *Apr.–Oct., Mon.–Sat. 10–4.*

Fodor's Choice **Loch Rannoch.** With its shoreline of birch trees framed by dark pines, ★ Loch Rannoch is the quintessential Highland loch. Fans of Robert Louis Stevenson (1850–94), especially of *Kidnapped* (1886), will not want to miss the last, lonely section of road. Stevenson describes the setting: "The mist rose and died away, and showed us that country lying as waste as the sea, only the moorfowl and the peewees crying upon it, and far over to the east a herd of deer, moving like dots." Loch Rannoch is off B846, 20 miles west of Pitlochry.

Pitlochry Dam and Fish Ladder. Most Scottish dams have salmon passes or ladders of some kind, enabling the fish to swim upstream to their spawning grounds. The Pitlochry Dam and Fish Ladder, just behind the main street and beside the Festival Theatre, leads into a glass-paneled pipe that allows the fish to observe the visitors. ✉ *Port Na Craig* ☎ *01796/473152* ⊕ *www.highlandperthshire.com* 🎟 *Free* ☉ *May–Oct., Mon.–Sat. 10–5, Sun. noon–5; Nov. and Dec., Mon.–Sat. 10–4, Sun. noon–4; Jan. and Feb., Mon.–Sat. 10–4.*

WORTH NOTING

Linn of Tummel. This series of marked walks along the river and through tall, mature woodlands, is a little north of Pitlochry. Above the Linn, the A9 rises on stilts and gives an exciting view of the valley.

Pass of Killiecrankie. Set among the oak woods and rocky river just north of the Linn of Tummel, the Pass of Killiecrankie was the site of a famous battle won by the Jacobites in 1689. The spot where a soldier escaped the battle by jumping across the river is now called the Soldier's Leap. The battle was noted for the death of the central Jacobite leader, John Graham of Claverhouse (1649–89), also known as Bonnie Dundee, who was hit by a stray bullet. After his death the rebellion petered out.

The National Trust for Scotland's visitor center at Killiecrankie explains the significance of this battle, which was the first attempt to restore the Stewart monarchy. ✉ *B8079, 3 miles north of Pitlochry* ☎ *01796/473233* ⊕ *www.nts.org.uk/visits* ☉ *Apr.–Oct., daily 10–5.*

WHERE TO EAT

$$
BRITISH
✕ **Moulin Hotel and Brewery.** This traditional pub with dark wooden interiors serves standard Scottish fare in large quantities. Venison, for example, is cooked in the brewery's own beer, and the haggis with neeps and tatties is predictable but good. This is a pleasant place, provided you are not too averse to the stuffed animals along the walls. The home-brewed beer is powerful, and during the afternoon you can visit the adjacent brewery. $ *Average main: £15* ✉ *11–30 Kirkmichael Rd.* ☎ *01796/472196* ⊕ *www.moulinhotel.co.uk.*

$$
BRITISH
✕ **Two Sisters Restaurant.** In the pleasant East Haugh House hotel, Two Sisters serves local produce in charming surroundings. The menu has a good range of fish dishes, including hake in salsa verde, mussels, and clams, as well as venison and pheasants "often shot by the chef"! The Fishermans Bar is a more casual eatery in the hotel. $ *Average main: £15* ✉ *East Haugh House* ✛ *1 mile south of Pitlochry* ☎ *01796/473121* ⊕ *www.easthaugh.co.uk* ⌗ *Reservations essential.*

WHERE TO STAY

$$$
HOTEL
FAMILY
🖼 **Atholl Palace Hotel.** A grand hotel in the best Victorian style, the Atholl Palace is a 19th-century vision of a medieval castle on 50 acres with views of hills and valleys. **Pros:** lovely grounds; lots for kids to do; high comfort. **Cons:** old-fashioned feel; long anonymous corridors. $ *Rooms from: £189* ✉ *A924* ☎ *01796/472400* ⊕ *www.athollpalace.com* 🛏 *106 rooms* ⊺⊙⊺ *Breakfast.*

$
B&B/INN
🖼 **Claymore Guest House.** One of the large Victorian houses set back from the main road, this B&B is a quiet refuge with spacious rooms with large windows. **Pros:** large, well-lit rooms with comfortable seating areas; dog-friendly. **Cons:** no children; slightly old-fashioned feel. $ *Rooms from: £80* ✉ *162 Atholl Rd.* ☎ *01796/472888* ⊕ *www.claymorehotel.com* 🛏 *10 rooms* ⊺⊙⊺ *Breakfast.*

$$$$ HOTEL Fodor's Choice ★ 🏨 **Green Park Hotel.** Set among woods and on the shores of Loch Faskally, Green Park is a genuinely luxurious country house hotel; most rooms have views over the loch or the gardens, and the most sought-after are those with a balcony on the second floor. **Pros:** great location; very attentive staff; country house comfort. **Cons:** a slightly conservative feel; very popular so books up early. [$] *Rooms from: £228* ✉ *Clunie Bridge Rd.* ✣ *5 mins from Pitlochry Centre on A924* ☎ *01796/473248* 🌐 *www.thegreenpark.co.uk* 🛏 *51 rooms* 🍴 *Some meals.*

$$$$ HOTEL 🏨 **Killiecrankie Hotel.** This neat oasis is set amid the wooded hills and streams of the Pass of Killiecrankie. **Pros:** lovely location; pleasant rooms. **Cons:** books up fast. [$] *Rooms from: £260* ✉ *B8079, Killiecrankie* ✣ *3 miles north of Pitlochry* ☎ *01796/473220* 🌐 *www.killiecrankiehotel.co.uk* 🛏 *10 rooms* 🍴 *Some meals* ☞ *Rates are for dinner, bed, and breakfast.*

NIGHTLIFE AND PERFORMING ARTS

Pitlochry Festival Theatre. This theater presents six plays each season, hosts Sunday concerts, and holds art exhibitions. It also has a café and restaurant overlooking the River Tummel. ✉ *Port Na Craig* ☎ *01796/484626* 🌐 *www.pitlochry.org.uk.*

GOLF

Blairgowrie Golf Club. Well known to native golfers looking for a challenge, the Blairgowrie Golf Club's Rosemount Course is laid out on rolling land in the pine, birch, and fir woods, which bring a wild air to the scene. There are, however, wide fairways and at least some large greens. If Rosemount is hosting a tournament, you can play on Lansdowne, another 18-hole course, or Wee, a 9-hole course. ✉ *Golf Course Rd., Blairgowrie* ☎ *01250/872622* 🌐 *www.theblairgowriegolfclub.co.uk* 🎫 *Rosemount, £605; Lansdowne, £65; Wee, £30* ⛳ *Rosemount: 18 holes, 6630 yards, par 72; Lansdowne: 18 holes, 6886 yards, par 72; Wee: 9 holes, 2327 yards, par 32.*

Pitlochry Golf Course. A decent degree of stamina is needed for the first three holes at Pitlochry, where steep climbs are involved. The reward is magnificent Highland scenery. Despite its relatively short length, this beautiful course has more than its fair share of surprises. The course offers golf with food packages and day tickets. ✉ *Golf Course Rd.* ☎ *01796/472792* 🌐 *www.pitlochrygolf.co.uk* 🎫 *Mar., Apr., Oct., and Nov.: £32 weekdays, £40 weekends; May–Sept.: £40 weekdays, £50 weekends* ⛳ *18 holes, 5681 yards, par 69.*

6

BLAIR ATHOLL

10 miles north of Pitlochry.

Where the Tilt and Garry rivers flow together, this small town sits in the middle of the Grampian Mountains. Here you'll find Blair Castle, one of Scotland's grandest grand houses.

GETTING HERE AND AROUND

Popular Blair Castle is just off the A9 Pitlochry-to-Inverness road, beyond the village of Blair Atholl. The village has a railway station that is on the main Inverness line.

EXPLORING

Fodor's Choice ★ **Blair Castle.** Its setting among woodlands and gardens, together with its war-torn past, make Blair Castle one of Scotland's most highly rated sights. The turreted white castle was home to successive dukes of Atholl and their families, the Murrays, one of the most powerful in the land. During the Jacobite rebellion of 1745 the loyalties of the Atholls were divided—a preserved piece of floor shows the marks of red-hot shot fired when the castle was under siege. In the end the supporters of the English king held off the rebels and were well rewarded for it. The dukes were allowed to retain a private army, the Atholl Highlanders. The castle entrance hall presents some of the dukes' collections of weapons, while a rich collection of furniture, china, and paintings occupies the family rooms. The grounds contain a 9-acre walled garden, an 18th-century folly, and a play area for children. ✉ *Off B8079* ☎ *01796/481207* ⊕ *www.blair-castle.co.uk* ✑ *Castle and gardens: Apr.–Oct., £10.50, grounds only: Apr.–Oct., £5.80; Nov.–Mar., free* ☉ *Apr.–Oct., daily 9:30–5:30; Nov.–Mar., weekends 10–4.*

SHOPPING

House of Bruar. An upscale shopping complex, the House of Bruar has a heavy emphasis on traditional tweeds and cashmeres. A large supermarket sells local produce and food, and a restaurant serves breakfast and lunch. When you're done shopping, take a walk up the path that crosses Bruar Falls, behind the complex. ✉ *Off A9, Pitlochry* ☎ *01796/483236* ⊕ *www.houseofbruar.com.*

ABERFELDY

15 miles southwest of Pitlochry, 25 miles southwest of Blair Castle.

The most dramatic thing about Aberfeldy is the high humpbacked bridge into the town, built by William Adam in 1733 and commissioned by General Wade, who marched through Scotland suppressing local resistance after the Jacobite rebellion. The town itself is rather sleepy, but this is a popular base for exploring the region. There's also a whisky distillery and plenty of local golf courses.

GETTING HERE AND AROUND

You can reach Aberfeldy from Dunkeld via the A9 and the A827. A longer but very pretty route is the A85 from Crieff, then through Killin on the A827. Aberfeldy is served by regular buses from Perth and Pitlochry.

ESSENTIALS

Visitor Information Aberfeldy Tourist Information Centre. ✉ *The Square* ☎ *01887/820276* ⊕ *www.visitscotland.com.*

EXPLORING

Castle Menzies. A 16th-century fortified tower house, Castle Menzies contains the **Clan Menzies Museum,** which displays many relics of the clan's history. The rooms have been carefully restored, including the bedroom where Bonnie Prince Charlie once took refuge. The castle stands west of Aberfeldy, on the opposite bank of the River Tay. ✉ *Aberfeldy Rd., Weem* ✛ *Off the B846* ☎ *01887/820982* ✑ *£6.50* ☉ *Apr.– Oct., Mon.–Sat 10:30–4:30, Sun. 2–4:30.*

Dewar's Aberfeldy Distillery. This established distillery offers tours that demonstrate how whisky is made (with a tasting at the end, of course); audio guides and interactive screens add to the appeal. There's also a worthwhile Heritage Center and a pleasant restaurant. The basic tours are £9.50, but there are more expensive tours for whisky experts, including cask tastings. ✉ *A827* ☎ *01887/822010* 🌐 *www.dewars.com* 🎟 *Basic tour £9.50; cask tasting tour £15* 🕒 *Apr.–Oct., Mon.–Sat. 10–6, Sun. noon–4; Nov.–Mar., Mon.–Sat. 10–4.*

Glen Lyon. One of central Scotland's most attractive glens, 34-mile-long Glen Lyon is also one of its longest. It has a rushing river, thick forests, and the typical big house hidden on private grounds. There's a dam at the head of the loch, a reminder that little of Scotland's scenic beauty is unadulterated. The winding road lends itself to an unrushed, leisurely drive, past the visitor center at the access to Ben Lawers, a popular climb, and on to Killin. ✉ *A827, 15 miles north of Aberfeldy.*

WHERE TO EAT

$ BRITISH 🍴 **Habitat Cafe.** This café offers excellent coffee and tea, sandwiches, and soup in the central square of Aberfeldy. Habitat takes great pride in its coffee making, with reason, and on a good day you can take your time looking out towards the hills from the handmade tables in the square. [$] *Average main: £9* ✉ *The Square* ☎ *01877/822944.*

SHOPPING

Aberfeldy Water Mill. This historic mill combines an excellent independent bookshop with a large children's section, a gallery with frequently changing exhibitions, and a café. ✉ *Mill St.* ☎ *01887/822896* 🌐 *www.aberfeldywatermill.com* 🕒 *Daily 10–5.*

John A Lacey. Watch for this house between Killin and Aberfeldy: its front room is a treasure trove of horn carving, from a full-masted galleon to knives in their sheaths. There are also deerskins for sale. Carver John Lacey has worked here for 30 years; he says the egg spoons are still the most popular items. ✉ *A827* ☎ *01567/820561.*

SPORTS AND THE OUTDOORS

FAMILY **Highland Safaris.** This center just outside Aberfeldy offers a full range of outdoor activities, from encounters with the red deer in the neighboring field to off-road driving, fishing, bike rental, and "safaris" into the nearby hills in Land Rovers or on foot. There is a shop and café on-site. ✉ *Aberfeldy* ✣ *2½ miles from Aberfeldy on B846* ☎ *01887/820071* 🌐 *www.highlandsafaris.net.*

KILLIN

24 miles southwest of Aberfeldy, 39 miles north of Stirling, 45 miles west of Perth.

Killin's setting near the Breadalbane Mountains at the end of Loch Tay (where the Falls of Dochart rush into the lake) gives the village an almost alpine flavor. You'll find a surprisingly diverse selection of crafts and woolen shops here, as well as a plethora of B&Bs.

6

GETTING HERE AND AROUND

Killin can be reached from Stirling via the A85 and A827, or from Aberfeldy via the A827, the winding road beside Loch Tay. The hop on/hop off bus service called the Ring of Breadalbane Explorer shuttles passengers between Killin, Aberfeldy, Crieff, Comrie, and Perth. The full circuit takes 3½ hours, and takes you through some of Scotland's loveliest landscapes. Buses run Tuesday, Wednesday, and Sunday from May to October; a £12 ticket is good for the whole day.

ESSENTIALS

Visitor Information Killin Tourist Information. ☎ *01786/459203.* **Rings of Breadalbane Explorer.** ☎ *01828/626262* 🌐 *www.breadalbane.org.*

EXPLORING

Falls of Dochart. Overlooked by a pine-clad islet, these white-water rapids are at the west end of Killin. ✉ *Off A827.*

Finlarig Castle. Across the River Dochart from Killin sit the ruins of Finlarig Castle, built by Black Duncan of the Cowl, a notorious Campbell laird. The castle grounds can be visited at any time, but be careful on the uneven stones. ✉ *Off A827.*

WHERE TO STAY

$ B&B/INN 🏨 **Breadalbane House.** This unpretentious but welcoming guesthouse in the center of Killin has small but comfortable rooms and reassuringly hearty breakfasts. **Pros:** a lovely location; friendly owners; easy parking. **Cons:** no young children allowed; limited public transport. [$] *Rooms from: £65* ✉ *Main St.* ☎ *01567/820134* 🌐 *www.breadalbanehouse.com* 🛏 *5 rooms* 🍴 *No meals.*

$$ B&B/INN 🏨 **Bridge of Lochay Hotel.** On the edge of Killin, this small, family-run hotel on the banks of the River Tay has a slightly old-fashioned feel, but the welcome you'll receive is friendly and warm. **Pros:** good base for exploring the area; welcoming atmosphere. **Cons:** basic rooms; slightly pricey for what it is. [$] *Rooms from: £115* ✉ *Aberfeldy Rd.* ☎ *01567/820272* 🌐 *www.bridgeoflochay.co.uk* 🛏 *10 rooms* 🍴 *Breakfast.*

SPORTS AND THE OUTDOORS

BICYCLING

Killin Outdoor Centre and Mountain Shop. If you want to explore the northern end of the Glasgow–Killin cycleway, this shop rents mountain bikes (£20 for four hours, £25 for 24 hours). Also available are canoes, crampons, snowshoes, and ice axes. ✉ *Main St.* ☎ *01567/820652* 🌐 *www.killinoutdoor.co.uk.*

GOLF

Killin Golf Club. Set in the Perthshire Highlands, this picturesque 9-hole golf course on the outskirts of Killin is regarded by those in the know as the most beautiful of its kind in Scotland. And despite being a smaller course, it is actually quite challenging. ✉ *Off A827* ☎ *01567/820312* 🌐 *www.killingolfclub.co.uk* 🎫 *£22 weekdays, £25 weekends (18 holes)* ⛳ *9 holes, 5066 yards, par 65.*

CRIEFF

25 miles southwest of Killin.

A spa and market town in the foothills of the Grampians, Crieff retains the prosperous air of its Victorian heyday. Its central square, where local farmers may once have gathered to trade, is still a lively center. For a different view of the town, you could climb Knock Hill, which is signposted from the town center.

GETTING HERE AND AROUND

Crieff once prospered because of the arrival of the railway. There is no station here today, but there are regular buses from Stirling and Glasgow. By car, take the A85 from Perth, or the A9, turning onto the A822 after Dunblane.

ESSENTIALS

Visitor Information Crieff Visitor Information Centre. ✉ *Muthill Rd.* ☎ *01764/654065* ⊕ *www.visitscotland.com.*

EXPLORING

Fodor'sChoice ★ **Drummond Castle Gardens.** These formal Victorian gardens celebrate family and Scottish heraldry. Combining the formal French and more relaxed Italian styles, the flower beds are planted and trimmed in the shapes of various heraldic symbols, such as a lion rampant and a checkerboard, associated with the coat of arms of the family that owns the castle. It's regarded as one of the finest of its kind in Europe, and it even made an appearance in the film *Rob Roy.* ✉ *Off A822, 6 miles southwest of Crieff* ☎ *01764/681433* ⊕ *www.drummondcastlegardens. co.uk* 🎟 *£5* ☉ *May, June, Sept., and Oct., daily 1–6; July and Aug., daily 11–6; last admission at 5.*

Glenturret Distillery. To discover the delights of whisky distilling, sign up for the "Famous Grouse Experience" at the Glenturret Distillery, which claims to be Scotland's oldest. A guide takes you through the distillery and to the bar where you can have a glass of Famous Grouse Finest (a blended whisky) and try your skill at "nosing." Here you learn how whisky is made and why time, water, soil, and air are so important to the taste. You might cap your tour with lunch in the Glenturret Cafe. Signs lead to the distillery on the west side of the town. ✉ *The Hosh, Comrie Rd.* ☎ *01764/656565* ⊕ *www.thefamousgrouseexperience.com* 🎟 *£10* ☉ *Mar.–Oct., daily 10–6, last tour at 4:30; Nov.–Feb., daily 10–5, last tour at 3:30.*

WHERE TO STAY

$$$$ HOTEL FAMILY **Crieff Hydro.** One of Scotland's great Victorian hydropathy centers, this grand hotel on 900 acres has been owned and run by the same family for more than 100 years. **Pros:** extensive grounds; variety of activities; particularly good for children. **Cons:** some rooms are rather dull; some activities are quite expensive. $ *Rooms from: £250* ✉ *Off A85* ☎ *01764/655555* ⊕ *www.crieffhydro.com* 🛏 *220 rooms* 🍽 *All-inclusive.*

SHOPPING

Crieff is a center for china and glassware.

Waterford Crystal. This factory shop sells Waterford, Dartington, and Wedgwood wares. ✉ *Muthill Rd.* ☎ *01764/654004.*

AUCHTERARDER

11 miles southeast of Crieff.

Famous for the Gleneagles Hotel (including its restaurant by Andrew Fairlie) and nearby golf courses, Auchterarder also has a flock of tiny antiques shops to amuse Gleneagles's golf widows and widowers.

GETTING HERE AND AROUND

Gleneagles Station is on the main Inverness line, while the A9 gives direct access to Gleneagles and Auchterarder via the A823.

ESSENTIALS

Visitor Information Auchterarder Visitor Information Centre. ✉ *90 High St.* ☎ *01764/663450* 🌐 *www.perthshire-scotland.co.uk.*

WHERE TO STAY

$$$$ HOTEL Fodor's Choice ★

🏨 **Gleneagles Hotel.** One of Britain's most famous hotels, Gleneagles is the very essence of modern grandeur, a vast, secret palace, that stands hidden in breathtaking countryside amid its world-famous golf courses. **Pros:** luxe rooms; numerous amenities; the three courses are a golfer's paradise. **Cons:** all this comes at a steep price. [$] *Rooms from: £405* ✉ *Off A823* ☎ *01764/662231* 🌐 *www.gleneagles.com* 🛏 *216 rooms, 13 suites* 🍴 *Some meals.*

GOLF

Fodor's Choice ★

Gleneagles. A part of golfing history, this sprawling resort hosted the Ryder Cup in 2014. The 18 holes of the King Course, designed by James Braid in 1919, have quirky names—many golfers have grappled with the tough 17th hole, known as the Warslin' Lea (Wrestling Ground). The beguiling Queen's Course mixes varied terrain, including woods and moors. Jack Nicklaus designed the PGA Centenary Course, which sweeps into the Ochil Hills and has views of the Grampians. The 9-hole Wee Course provides challenges for beginners and pros alike. This is also where you'll find the PGA National Academy, a good place to improve your skills. ✉ *A823* ☎ *01764/662231* 🌐 *www.gleneagles.com* 🎟 *Kings, Queens, and PGA Centenary courses, £155; Wee Course, £32* ⛳ *Kings: 18 holes, 6790 yards, par 71; Queens: 18 holes, 6790 yards, par 68; PGA Centenary: 18 holes, 6815 yards, par 72; Wee Course: 9 holes, 1418 yards, par 27.*

7

ABERDEEN AND
THE NORTHEAST

2Visit Fodors.com for advice, updates, and bookingsVisit Fodors.com for advice, updates, and bookings

Updated by
Shona Main

Here, in this granite shoulder of Grampian, are some of Scotland's most enduring travel icons: Royal Deeside, the countryside that Queen Victoria made her own; the Castle Country route, where fortresses stand hard against the hills; and the Malt Whisky Trail, where peaty streams embrace the country's greatest concentration of distilleries. The region's gateway is the city of Aberdeen, constructed of granite and now aglitter with new wealth and new blood drawn together by North Sea oil.

Located over 125 miles north of the *central belt* of Glasgow and Edinburgh, Aberdeen has historically been a fairly autonomous place. Even now it's perceived by many U.K. inhabitants as lying almost out of reach in the northeast. In reality, it's a 90-minute flight from London or a little more than two hours by car from Edinburgh. Its magnificent 18th- and early-19th-century city center amply rewards exploration. Yet even if this popular base for travelers vanished from the map, an extensive portion of the northeast would still remain at the top of many travelers' wish lists.

Balmoral, the Scottish baronial–style house built for Queen Victoria as a retreat, is merely the most famous castle in the area, and certainly not the oldest. There are so many others that in one part of the region a Castle Trail has been established. In later structures, such as Castle Fraser, you can trace the changing styles and tastes of each of their owners over the centuries. Grand mansions such as 18th-century Haddo House, with its symmetrical facade and elegant interior, surrender any defensive role entirely.

A trail leading to a more ephemeral kind of pleasure can be found south of Elgin and Banff, where the glens embrace Scotland's greatest concentration of malt-whisky distilleries. With so many in Morayshire, where the distilling is centered on the valley of the River Spey and its tributaries, there's now a Whisky Trail. Follow it, and visit other distilleries as well, to experience a surprising wealth of flavors.

The northeast's chief topographical attraction lies in the gradual transition from high mountain plateau—by a series of gentle steps through hill, forest, and farmland—to the Moray Firth and North Sea coast, where the word "unadulterated" is redefined. Here you'll find some of the United Kingdom's most perfect wild shorelines, both sandy and sheer cliff, and breezy fishing villages like Cullen on the Banffshire coast and Stonehaven, south of Aberdeen. The Grampian Mountains, to the west, contain some of the highest ground in the nation, in the area of the Cairngorms. In recognition of this area's special nature, Cairngorms National Park was created in 2003.

TOP REASONS TO GO

Glorious castles: With more than 75 castles, some Victorian and others dating back to the 13th century, this area has everything from ravaged ruins like Dunnottar to opulent Fyvie Castle. They still evoke the power, grandeur, and sometimes the cruelty of Scotland's past.

Fine distilleries: The valley of the River Spey is famous for its single-malt distilleries, including those connected by the signposted Malt Whisky Trail. You can choose from bigger operations such as Glenfiddich to the iconic Strathisla, where Chivas Regal is blended.

Seaside cities and towns: The fishing industry may be in decline, but the big-city port of Abderdeen and the colorful smaller fishing

towns of Stonehaven and Cullen in the northeast are great (and very different) places to soak up the seagoing atmosphere—and some seafood.

Great walking: There are all types of walking for all kinds of walkers, from the bracing but spectacular inclines of the Grampian Hills to the wooded gardens and grounds of Balmoral and Haddo House, to breath-stealing golden sands near towns such as Cullen.

Superb golf: The northeast has more than 50 golf clubs, some of which have championship courses. Less famous clubs, both inland and by the sea, have some amazing courses as well.

7

ORIENTATION AND PLANNING

GETTING ORIENTED

Aberdeen, on the North Sea in the eastern part of the region, is Scotland's third-largest city; many people start a trip here. Once you have spent time in the city, you may be inclined to venture west into rural Deeside, with its royal connections and looming mountain backdrop. To the north of Deeside is Castle Country, with many ancient fortresses. Speyside and the Whisky Trail lie at the western edge of the region, and are equally accessible from Inverness. From Speyside you might travel back east along the pristine coastline at Scotland's northeastern tip.

Aberdeen. Family connections or Royal Deeside often take travelers to this part of Scotland, but many are surprised by how grand and rich in history Aberdeen is. The august granite-turreted buildings and rose-lined roads make this a surprisingly pleasant city to explore; don't miss Old Aberdeen in particular.

Royal Deeside and Castle Country. Prince Albert designed Balmoral Castle for Queen Victoria, and so began the royal family's love affair with Deeside—and Deeside's love affair with it. However, this area has long been the retreat or the fortress of distinguished families, as the clutter of castles throughout the region shows. The majesty of the countryside also guarantees a superlative stop for everyone interested in history and romance.

The Northeast and the Malt Whisky Trail. For lovers of whisky, this is a favored part of Scotland to visit. Unique in their architecture, their ingredients, and the end product, the distilleries of Speyside are keen to share with you their passion for "the water of life." This region also has rolling hills and, to the north, the beautiful, wild coastline of the North Sea.

PLANNING

WHEN TO GO

May and June are probably the loveliest times to visit, but many travelers arrive from late spring to early fall. The National Trust for Scotland tends to close its properties in winter, so many of the northeast's castles are not open for off-season travel, though you can always see them from the outside. The distilleries are open much of the year, but check for the "silent month" when they close down for a holiday. That's often in August, but may vary.

PLANNING YOUR TIME

How you allocate your time may depend on your special interests—castles or whisky, for example. But even if you can manage only a morning or an afternoon, do not miss a walk around the granite streets of Old Aberdeen, and take in St. Nicholas Kirk, and a pint in the Prince of Wales pub. A trip southward to the fishing town of Stonehaven and the breathtaking cliff-top fortress of Dunnottar makes a rewarding afternoon. Royal Deeside, with a good sprinkling of castles and grandeur, needs a good two days; even this might be tight for those who want to lap up every moment of majesty at Balmoral, Crathes, Fraser, and Fyvie, the best of the bunch. A visit to malt-whisky country should include tours of Glenfiddich, Glenfarclas, Glenlivet, and Glen Grant distilleries, and although it's not technically a maker of malt whisky, Strathisla. Real enthusiasts should allot two days for the distilleries, and they shouldn't pass up a visit to Speyside Cooperage, one of the few remaining cooperages in the Scotland. Cullen and Duff House gallery in Banff, on the coast, can be done in a day before returning to Aberdeen.

GETTING HERE AND AROUND

AIR TRAVEL

The city is easy to reach from other parts of the United Kingdom as well as Europe. British Airways, bmi, EasyJet, and Flybe are some of the airlines with service to other parts of Britain. Aberdeen Airport—serving both international and domestic flights—is in Dyce, 7 miles west of the city center on the A96 (Inverness). The drive to the center of Aberdeen is easy via the A96 (which can be busy during rush hour).

Airport Contact Aberdeen Airport. ✉ *Dyce Dr., Dyce* ☎ *0844/481–6666* ⊕ *www.aberdeenairport.com.*

BOAT AND FERRY TRAVEL

Northlink Ferries has service between Aberdeen, Lerwick (Shetland), and Kirkwall (Orkney).

Boat and Ferry Contact Northlink Ferries. ✉ *Jamieson's Quay, Aberdeen* ☎ *0845/600–0449* ⊕ *www.northlinkferries.co.uk.*

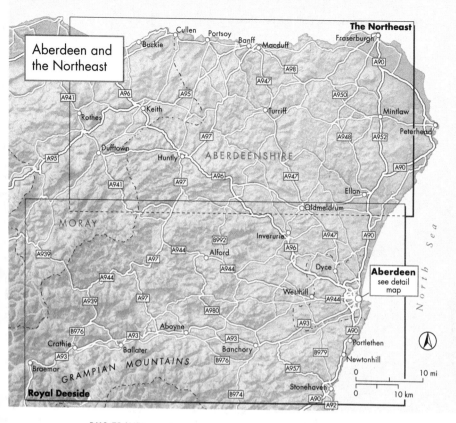

Aberdeen
see detail
map

BUS TRAVEL

Long-distance buses run to Aberdeen from most parts of Scotland, England, and Wales. Contact Megabus, National Express, and Scottish Citylink for bus connections with English and Scottish towns. There's a network of local buses throughout the northeast run by Stagecoach, but they can take a long time and connections are not always well timed.

Bus Contacts Megabus. ☎ 0900/160–0900 ⊕ uk.megabus.com. **National Express.** ☎ 08717/818178 ⊕ www.nationalexpress.com. **Scottish Citylink.** ☎ 0871/266–3333 ⊕ www.citylink.co.uk. **Stagecoach.** ✉ Union Square Bus Station, Guild St., Aberdeen ☎ 01224/591381 ⊕ www.stagecoachbus.com.

Traveline. ☎ 08706/200-2233 ⊕ www.travelinescotland.com.

CAR TRAVEL

A car is the best way to see the northeast. If you are coming from the south, take the A90, continuing on from the M90 (from Edinburgh) or the M9/A9 (from Glasgow), which both stop at Perth. The coastal route, the A92, is a more leisurely alternative, with its interesting resorts and fishing villages. The most scenic route, however, is the A93 from Perth, north to Blairgowrie and into Glen Shee. The A93 then goes over the Cairnwell Pass, the highest main road in the United Kingdom. This route isn't recommended in winter, when snow can make driving difficult.

Around the northeast roads can be busy, with speeding and erratic driving a problem on the main A roads.

TRAIN TRAVEL

You can reach Aberdeen directly from Edinburgh (2½ hours), Inverness (2½ hours), and Glasgow (3 hours). ScotRail timetables have full details. There are also London–Aberdeen routes that go through Edinburgh and the east-coast main line connecting Aberdeen to all corners of the United Kingdom.

Train Contact ScotRail. ⊠ *Aberdeen Railway Station, Guild St., Aberdeen* ☎ *0344/811–0141* ⊕ *www.scotrail.co.uk.*

RESTAURANTS

Partly in response to the demands of workers in the oil industry, restaurants have cropped up all over Aberdeen, and the quality of the food improves yearly. As in the rest of Scotland, this region is rediscovering the quality and versatility of the local produce. Juicy Aberdeen Angus steaks, lean lamb, and humanely reared pork appear on local menus, but despite this being the center of the fishing industry, most seafood available is still of the fish-and-chips variety. Restaurants like the Silver Darling in Aberdeen are spearheading a new interest in fish dishes, though, and old standards like *cullen skink* (a creamy smoked-fish soup) are increasingly on menus.

HOTELS

The northeast has some splendid country hotels with log fires and old Victorian furnishings, where you can also be sure of eating well. Many hotels in Aberdeen are in older buildings that have a baronial feel. The trend for serviced apartments has caught on here, with some extremely modish and good-value options for those who want a bit more privacy. This trend is now extending into Deeside, where it's been notoriously difficult to find good accommodations beyond some country-house hotels, even though it's a popular tourist spot. *Hotel reviews have been shortened. For full information, visit Fodors.com.*

WHAT IT COSTS IN POUNDS			
	$	$$	$$$	$$$$
RESTAURANTS	Under £15	£15–£19	£20–£25	Over £25
HOTELS	Under £100	£100–£160	£161–£220	Over £220

Restaurant prices are the average cost of a main course at dinner or, if dinner is not served, at lunch. Hotel prices are the lowest cost of a standard double room in high season, including 20% V.A.T.

VISITOR INFORMATION

The tourist information center in Aberdeen has a currency exchange, Internet access, and supplies information on all of Scotland's northeast. There are also year-round tourist information offices in Braemar and Elgin. In summer, also look for tourist information centers in Alford, Ballater, Banchory, Braemar, Elgin, and Stonehaven.

Contact Aberdeen Visitor Information Centre. ⊠ *23 Union St., Aberdeen* ☎ *01224/288828* ⊕ *www.aberdeen-grampian.com.*

ABERDEEN

As a gateway to Royal Deeside and the Malt Whisky Trail, Aberdeen attracts visitors, though many are eager to get out into the countryside. Today, though, the city's unique history is finally being recognized as more impressive than many Scots had previously realized, and Aberdeen is being rediscovered. Distinctive architecture, some fine museums, universities, and good restaurants, nightlife, and shopping add to the appeal of Scotland's third-largest city (population 217,000). Union Street is the heart of the city, but take time to explore the university and the pretty streets of Old Aberdeen.

In the 18th century local granite quarrying produced a durable silver stone that would be used boldly in the glittering blocks, spires, columns, and parapets of Victorian-era Aberdonian structures. The city remains one of the United Kingdom's most distinctive, although some would say it depends on the weather and the brightness of the day. The mica chips embedded in the rock look like a million mirrors in the sunshine. In rain (and there is a fair amount of driving rain from the North Sea) and heavy clouds, however, their sparkle is snuffed out.

The city lies between the Dee and Don rivers, with a working harbor that has access to the sea; it has been a major fishing port and is the main commercial port in northern Scotland. The North Sea has always been important to Aberdeen. In the 1850s the city was famed for its sleek, fast clippers that sailed to India for cargoes of tea. In the late 1960s the course of Aberdeen's history was unequivocally altered when oil and gas were discovered offshore, sparking rapid growth, prosperity, and further industrialization.

GETTING HERE AND AROUND

AIR TRAVEL Stagecoach Bluebird Jet Service 727 and First Aberdeen Bus 27 operate between the airport terminal and Union Square in the center of Aberdeen. Buses (£2.90 and £2.60 respectively) run frequently at peak times, less often at midday and in the evening; the journey time is approximately 40 minutes. Stagecoach Bluebird Bus 10 stops at Aberdeen Airport, either taking you into the city center or northwest to Elgin.

Dyce is on ScotRail's Inverness–Aberdeen route. The rail station is a short taxi ride from the terminal building (£10). Alternatively, the Jet Connect Service 80 operates between 06.30-6.30 (£1.50). The ride takes 12 minutes, and trains run approximately every two hours.

BUS TRAVEL First Aberdeen has easy and reliable service within the city of Aberdeen. Timetables are available from the tourist information center in Union Street.

Contact First Aberdeen. ☎ 01224/650000 ⊕ www.firstaberdeen.co.uk.

CAR TRAVEL Aberdeen is a compact city with good signage. Its center is Union Street, the main east–west thoroughfare, which tends to get crowded with traffic. Anderson Drive is an efficient ring road on the city's west side; be extra careful on its many traffic circles. It's best to leave your car in one of the parking garages (arrive early to get a space) and walk around, or use the convenient park-and-ride stop at the Bridge of Don, north of the city. Street maps are available from the tourist information center, newsstands, and booksellers.

TAXI TRAVEL   You can find taxi stands throughout the center of Aberdeen: at the railway station and at Back Wynd, Chapel Street, Dee Street, and Hadden Street. The taxis have yellow plates, meters, and might be saloon cars (sedans) or black cabs. They are great ways to travel between neighborhoods.

TRAIN TRAVEL   Aberdeen has good ScotRail service.

AROUND UNION STREET

Aberdeen centers on Union Street, with its many fine survivors of the Victorian and Edwardian streetscape. Marischal College, dating from the late 16th century, has many grand buildings that are worth exploring.

TOP ATTRACTIONS

FAMILY   **Aberdeen Maritime Museum.** This excellent museum, which incorporates
Fodor's Choice   the 1593 Provost Ross's House, tells the story of the city's relationship
★   with the sea, from early inshore fisheries to tea clippers and the North Sea oil boom. The information-rich exhibits include the bridge of a fishing boat and the cabins of a clipper, in addition to models, paintings, and equipment associated with the fishing, shipbuilding, and oil and gas industries. There's an excellent café downstairs and a museum shop with nautical but nice knickknacks. ⊠ *Ship Row* ☎ *01224/337700* ⊕ *www.aagm.co.uk* ⊠ *Free* ⊘ *Tues.–Sat. 10–5, Sun. noon–3.*

St. Nicholas Kirk. The original burgh church, the Mither Kirk, as this edifice is known, is not within the bounds of the early town settlement; that was to the east, near the end of present-day Union Street. During the 12th century the port of Aberdeen flourished, and there wasn't room for the church within the settlement. Its earliest features are its pillars—supporting a tower built much later—and its clerestory windows: both date from the 12th century. The East Kirk is closed for renovation work which has been extended due to the discovery of numerous skeletons, mainly children, that date back to the 12th century: the post-excavation work can be viewed from a large window in the Drum's Aisle. In the chapel, look for Shona McInnes's stained-glass window that commemorates the victims of the1989 Piper Alpha oil-rig disaster and a glass case containing two books. One lists the names of all those who've lost their lives in the pursuit of oil exploration in the North Sea; the second is empty, a testament to the many "unknown" workers whose deaths were never officially recorded. ⊠ *Union St.* ☎ *01224/643494* ⊕ *www.kirk-of-st-nicholas.org.uk* ⊠ *Free, but donations welcome* ⊘ *May–Sept., weekdays noon–4.*

WORTH NOTING

OFF THE
BEATEN
PATH   **Duthie Park.** These 44 acres were donated to the people of Aberdeen by a Miss Elizabeth Crombie Duthie in 1880. An excellent place to while away an afternoon, whether it be the sunniest or foulest day, it has a boating pond, bandstand, playgrounds, and a popular conservatory café selling creamy ice cream. In the beautifully tended Winter Gardens

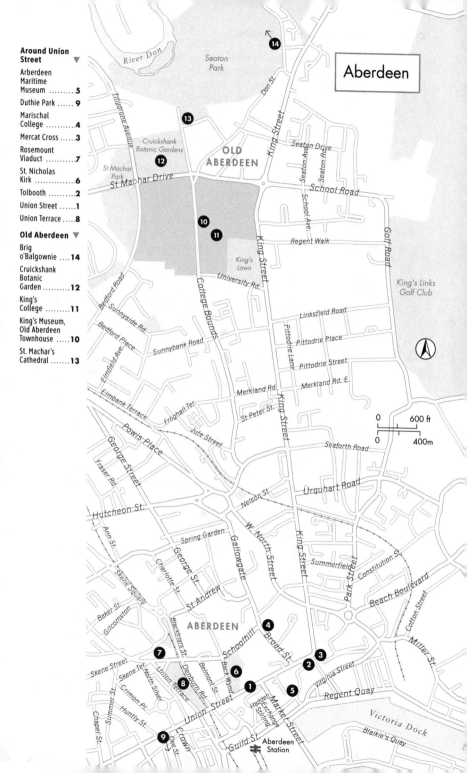

Aberdeen

River Don

Seaton Park

Cruickshank Botanic Gardens

OLD ABERDEEN

St Machar Park

St Machar Drive

King's Lawn

King's Links Golf Club

Don St.

King Street

Seaton Drive

Seaton Ave.

Seaton Drive

School Road

School Ave.

Regent Walk

Golf Road

University Rd.

Cottage Bounds

Bedford Road

Sunnyside Rd.

Bedford Place

Elmfield Ave.

Sunnybank Road

Linksfield Road

Pittodrie Lane

Pittodrie Place

Pittodrie Street

Merkland Rd.

King Street

Merkland Rd. E.

Elmbank Terrace

Froghall Ter.

Jute Street

St Peter St.

Seaforth Road

Powis Place

George Street

Fraser Rd.

Nelson St.

Urquhart Road

Hutcheon St.

Ann St.

Spring Garden

W. North Street

Gallowgate

George St.

Charlotte St.

Summerfield

King Street

Park Street

Constitution St.

Beach Boulevard

Cotton Street

Baker St.

Gilcomston

Skene Square

St Andrew

ABERDEEN

Schoolhill

Broad St.

Back Wynd

Blackfriars St.

Mitter St.

Skene Street

Skene Ter.

North Street

Union Terrace

Denburn Rd.

Belmont St.

Crimon Pl.

Union Street

Summer St.

Huntly St.

Crown St.

Dee St.

Guild St.

Market Street

Hadden Exchange Stafford

Regent Quay

Virginia Street

Victoria Dock

Blaikie's Quay

Aberdeen Station

0 ——— 600 ft
0 ——— 400m

(tropical and arid conservatories) are fishponds, free-flying birds, and turtles and terrapins among the luxuriant foliage and flowers. The park borders Aberdeen's other river, the Dee. ⊠ *Polmuir Rd., about 1 mile south of city center* 🎫 *Free* 🕐 *Gardens daily 8 am–1 hr before sunset.*

Marischal College. Founded in 1593 by the Earl Marischal (the keeper of the king's mares), Marischal College was a Protestant alternative to the Catholic King's College in Old Aberdeen. The two joined to form the University of Aberdeen in 1860. The spectacularly ornate work of the main university building is set off by the gilded flags, and this turn-of-the-20th-century creation is still one of the world's largest granite buildings. In 2011, the building's interior was rebuilt to house the city council. In keeping with the Aberdonian custom of never throwing anything away, the discarded materials have already been used in buildings around the city. The building works across the road are the controversial new Marischal Square development which will house shops, offices, and restaurants. ⊠ *Broad St.*

Mercat Cross. Built in 1686 and restored in 1820, the Mercat Cross (the term stems from "marketplace"), always the symbolic center of a Scottish medieval burgh, stands just beyond King Street. Along its parapet are 12 portrait panels of the Stewart monarchs. ⊠ *Justice and Marischal Sts.*

Rosemount Viaduct. Three silvery, handsome buildings on this bridge are collectively known by all Aberdonians as Education, Salvation, and Damnation. The **Central Library** and **St. Mark's Church** date from the last decade of the 19th century, and **His Majesty's Theatre** (1904–08) has been restored inside to its full Edwardian splendor. If you're taking photographs, you can choose an angle that includes the statue of Scotland's first freedom fighter, Sir William Wallace (1270–1305), in the foreground pointing majestically to Damnation. ⊠ *Aberdeen.*

FAMILY **Tolbooth.** The city was governed from this 17th-century building, which was also the burgh court and jail, for 200 years. Now a museum of crime and punishment, highly entertaining tour guides take you round its cells and dungeons and bring life and death to the various instruments of torture—including the "Maiden," a decapitating machine—making it a must-see for older kids. ⊠ *Castle St.* 📞 *01224/621167* 🌐 *www.aagm. co.uk* 🎫 *Free* 🕐 *July–Sept., Mon.–Sat. 10–5, Sun. noon–3.*

Union Street. This great thoroughfare is to Aberdeen what Princes Street is to Edinburgh: the central pivot of the city plan and the product of a wave of enthusiasm to rebuild the city in a contemporary style in the early 19th century. ⊠ *Aberdeen.*

Union Terrace. In the 19th-century development of Union Terrace stands a statue of Robert Burns (1759–96) addressing a daisy. Behind Burns are the **Union Terrace Gardens,** faintly echoing Edinburgh's Princes Street Gardens in that both separate the older part of the city, to the east, from the 19th-century development to the west. There are plans to build above the gardens and the railway lines, a move that will either be to Aberdeen's aesthetic benefit or its disgrace, depending on your viewpoint. ⊠ *Aberdeen.*

OLD ABERDEEN

Very much a separate area of the city, Old Aberdeen is north of the modern center and clustered around St. Machar's Cathedral and the many fine buildings of the University of Aberdeen. Take a stroll on College Bounds; handsome 18th- and 19th-century houses line this cobbled street in the oldest part of the city.

TOP ATTRACTIONS

Cruickshank Botanic Garden. Built on land bequeathed by Miss Anne Cruickshank in memory of her beloved brother Alexander, the 11-acre Cruickshank Botanic Garden at the heart of Old Aberdeen has a peaceful water garden and lush greens ideal for lounging—when the weather allows—and beautifully tended subtropical and alpine collections. Botanical tours are available. ⌧ *St. Machar Dr., at the Chanonry* ☎ *01224/272704* ⊕ *www.abdn.ac.uk/botanic-garden* ⌧ *Free* ☾ *Apr.– Sept., daily 9–7; Oct.–Mar., daily 9:30–4:30.*

Fodor's Choice ★ **King's College.** Founded in 1494, King's College is now part of the University of Aberdeen. Its **chapel,** built around 1500, has an unmistakable flying (or crown) spire. That it has survived at all was because of the zeal of the principal, who defended his church against the destructive fanaticism that swept through Scotland during the Reformation, when the building was less than a century old. Today the renovated chapel plays an important role in university life. Don't miss the tall oak screen that separates the nave from the choir, the ribbed wooden ceiling, and the stalls, as these constitute the finest medieval wood carvings found anywhere in Scotland. The **King's College Centre** has more information about the university. ⌧ *High St.* ☎ *01224/272660* ⊕ *www.abdn.ac.uk* ☾ *Weekdays 10:30–3:30.*

King's Museum, Old Aberdeen Townhouse. Across from the archway leading to King's College Chapel, this plain but handsome Georgian building was the center of all trading activity in the city before it became a grammar school, a Masonic lodge, and then a library. Now housing the university's museum, it hosts constantly changing exhibitions. It presents some impressive and often strange curiosities from the university's collection, from prehistoric flints to a tiger's penis. ⌧ *17 High St.* ☎ *01224/274300* ⊕ *www.abdn.ac.uk/kingsmuseum* ⌧ *Free* ☾ *Mon. and Wed.–Fri. 10–6, Tues. 10–7:30, Sat. 11–4.*

QUICK BITE

✕ **St. Machar Bar.** St. Machar Bar is a small, vibrant pub in the middle of the university campus, selling not just pints but also real *stovies* (a hot potato-based beef stew) or haggis bon bons (deep-fried panko-encrusted haggis balls) This is a great place to warm up or pass away the time with a newspaper if the weather is unbecoming. ⌧ *97 High St.* ☎ *01224/483079* ⊕ *www.themachar.com.*

Fodor's Choice ★ **St. Machar's Cathedral.** It's said that St. Machar was sent by St. Columba to build a church on a grassy platform near the sea, where a river flowed in the shape of a shepherd's crook. This beautiful spot, now the still-beating heart of Old Aberdeen, fits the bill. Although the cathedral was founded in AD 580, most of the existing building dates from the

7

15th and 16th centuries. Built as a fortified kirk, its twin towers and thick walls give it a sturdy standing: the former can be seen up close by climbing the spiral staircases to the upper floors which also affords an admirable view of the "body of the kirk" inside and graveyard outside. It lost its status as a cathedral during the Reformation, but now, a Presbyterian Church of Scotland church, its vibrant congregation has turned it into a welcoming and interesting place with some members on hand to tell you of its history. The stained-glass windows depicting the martyrdom of the saints and handsome heraldic ceiling are worth noting but it's the free (although donations are welcome) bookmarks with a humbling translation of the Lord's Prayer into the local Doric dialect that will stir the soul. ⊠ *Chanonry* ☎ *01224/485988* ⊕ *www. stmachar.com* ⊙ *Daily 9:30–4:30.*

✗ **Kilau Coffee.** Popular with students and academics alike, this cheerful café across from the cathedral offers loungy seating downstairs and table and chairs upstairs. Expertly made coffee is on offer, as well as cakes and snacks. It closes in the early evening; hours can vary. ⊠ *55–57 High St.* ☎ *01224/485510* ⊕ *www.kilaucoffee.wordpress.com* ⊙ *Closed Sun. No dinner.*

WORTH NOTING

Brig o'Balgownie. Until 1827, the only northern route out of Aberdeen was over the River Don on this single-arch bridge. It dates from 1314 and is thought to have been built by Richard Cementarius, Aberdeen's first provost. ⊠ *Seaton Park.*

WHERE TO EAT

$
BRITISH
FAMILY

✗ **Ashvale.** Ask anyone about this long-established place and the response will probably be overwhelmingly positive. Fish-and-chips are the specialty, and the secret-recipe batter is now the stuff of legend, although if you prefer your fish in a gluten-free batter or grilled, that's not a problem. Attempt the Whale—a gigantic fillet of battered cod—and you'll be rewarded with a free dessert. The decor is your basic wood-chairs-and-tables. $ *Average main: £12* ⊠ *42–48 Great Western Rd.* ☎ *01224/596981* ⊕ *theashvale.co.uk.*

$
MODERN BRITISH

✗ **Café 52.** Right in the historic Grassmarket, this artsy café-restaurant has an innovative menu, an atmospheric dining room with open kitchen, plus covered outdoor seating. Mackerel and watermelon salad, Persian marinated chicken, and bramble panna cotta are just a few of the options. No matter what you order, local produce makes it tasty and fresh. The handsome restaurant is in a silvery granite building with exposed-stone walls, huge windows, and shiny black tables. $ *Average main: £13* ⊠ *52 The Green* ☎ *01224/590094* ⊕ *www.cafe52.co.uk* ⊙ *No dinner Sun.*

$
BRITISH
FAMILY

✗ **Foodstory.** A friendly homespun café/eatery, Foodstory pulls a loyal crowd to graze on its healthy, freshly made breakfasts, lunches, and wonderful cakes. Expect a choice of organic breakfast/brunch choices: superfood porridge, scones, Aberdeenshire bacon rolls, and Ellon pork sausage. Lunch choices include a daily special light dish, soup, rolls, pies, wraps, and heaped salads. Recycled chairs, tables, wooden panels and tiles give it a homey kitchen-canteen feel. $ *Average main: £7* ⊠ *15 Thistle St.* ☎ *01224/622293* ⊕ *www.foodstorycafe.co.uk* ☉ *Closed Sun.*

$$ ✕**Moonfish.** This elegant yet relaxed seafood restaurant can be found
BRITISH along a medieval lane next to St. Nicholas Kirk. TV series *Masterchef* finalist Brian McLeish creates a changing, innovative menu, using seasonal produce from Aberdeenshire. Fishy mains may include freshly caught sea trout, halibut, or hake served with imaginative accompaniments such as celeriac with seaweed. The sophisticated atmosphere of the dining room is enhanced with striking landscape photography and somber lighting. A gin bar serves craft distillations and cocktails. $ *Average main: £16* ⊠ *9 Correction Wynd* ☎ *01224 /644166* ⊕ *www. moonfishcafe.co.uk* ⚷ *Reservations essential.*

$$$ ✕**Silver Darling.** Huge windows overlook the harbor and beach at this
SEAFOOD quayside favorite in a former customs house, long one of Aberdeen's
Fodor's Choice most acclaimed restaurants. As the name implies, the French-inspired fare
★ focuses on fish: a silver darling is a herring. Try the langoustine ravioli with hazelnut velouté for a starter, then move on to wild halibut steamed in seaweed, or sea bass with crushed ginger potatoes. $ *Average main: £25* ⊠ *North Pier, Pocra Quay* ☎ *01224/576229* ⊕ *thesilverdarling.co. uk* ☉ *Closed Sun. No lunch Sat.* ⚷ *Reservations essential.*

$$ ✕**Yatai.** It might seem odd ordering Japanese food in Aberdeen, but
JAPANESE considering the quality and quantity of fresh fish being landed on the
Fodor's Choice quayside each day it makes perfect sense. The slick facade and glowing
★ red interior might be a little intimidating at first, but the smiling staff is approachable, and, for the uninitiated, is happy to help you choose the right blend of flavors and textures. The place isn't cheap, but as far as Japanese food is concerned, it's not extortionate either: £9.50 for two Kushiyaki-style skewers of aged sirloin steak, £14 for nine pieces of sushi, miso soup, and salad. Japanese sake and beer are a treat. $ *Average main: £15* ⊠ *53 Langstane Pl.* ☎ *01224/592355* ⊕ *www.yatai.co.uk* ▭ *No credit cards* ☉ *Closed Sun. and Mon.* ⚷ *Reservations essential.*

WHERE TO STAY

$$ ⛫**Atholl Hotel.** With its many turrets and gables, this granite hotel recalls
HOTEL a bygone era but has modern amenities. **Pros:** family-run establishment; tasty restaurant; very pleasant staff. **Cons:** some rooms are a little generic; some bathrooms need updating. $ *Rooms from: £145* ⊠ *54 Kings Gate* ☎ *01224/323505* ⊕ *www.atholl-aberdeen.com* ⇨ *34 rooms* ⑂ *Breakfast.*

$$ ⛫**Bauhaus Hotel.** When the owner got his hands on this 1960s-era
HOTEL granite office block, he decided to pay homage to Walter Gropius, the founder of the Bauhaus movement, with a hotel in a clean-lined, modern style. **Pros:** great design; comfortable rooms; tasty eatery. **Cons:** beware the furniture's sharp corners; fake art on the walls—in a city with a great art school; nightlife noise at weekend. $ *Rooms from: £140* ⊠ *52–60 Langstane Pl.* ☎ *01224/212122* ⊕ *www.thebauhaus.co.uk* ⇨ *34 rooms, 5 suites* ⑂ *Breakfast; Some meals.*

$$ ⛫**City Wharf.** With one- to four-bedroom apartments at three downtown
RENTAL addresses, City Wharf offers fuss-free stays of any length in comfortable

surroundings. **Pros:** rates drop dramatically on weekends; all modern conveniences; passes to a nearby gym. **Cons:** no porters to help you with your bags; no restaurant; beware the seagulls. [$] *Rooms from: £150* ✉ *47 Regent Quay* ☎ *01224/589282* 🌐 *www.citywharfapartments.co.uk* 🛏 *22 apartments* 🍴 *Breakfast.*

$$ HOTEL 🏨 **Craibstone Suites.** On one of Aberdeen's most attractive squares, these 18 modern but comfortable suites come with fully equipped kitchens. **Pros:** great central location; feels more like an apartment than a hotel room. **Cons:** executive suites are small—go for the grand or superior suites if you need elbow room; the breakfast is pretty basic. [$] *Rooms from: £114* ✉ *15 Bon Accord Sq.* ☎ *01224/857950* 🌐 *www.craibstone-suites.co.uk* 🛏 *18 suites* 🍴 *Breakfast.*

$$ B&B/INN Fodor's Choice ★ 🏨 **The Jays Guest House.** Alice Jennings or her husband George will greet you at the front door of this granite house, a homey bed-and-breakfast they've run for 32 years. **Pros:** immaculate rooms; expert advice on city's sites; near Old Aberdeen and the University. **Cons:** no public areas; popular so book ahead. [$] *Rooms from: £100* ✉ *422 King St.* ☎ *01224/638295* 🌐 *www.jaysguesthouse.co.uk* 🛏 *10 rooms* 🍴 *Breakfast.*

$$$$ HOTEL 🏨 **Marcliffe Hotel and Spa.** Set on 11 wooded acres, this spacious, elegant country-house hotel combines old and new to impressive effect. **Pros:** the wooded environs means a stunning dawn chorus; well-trained and friendly staff. **Cons:** if you struggle to sleep, the dawn chorus; a little out of town. [$] *Rooms from: £270* ✉ *N. Deeside Rd.* ☎ *01224/861000* 🌐 *www.marcliffe.com* 🛏 *35 rooms, 7 suites* 🍴 *Breakfast.*

NIGHTLIFE AND PERFORMING ARTS

Aberdeen has a fairly lively nightlife scene revolving around pubs and clubs. Theaters, concert halls, arts centers, and cinemas are also well represented. The principal newspapers—the *Press and Journal* and the *Evening Express*—and *Aberdeen Leopard* magazine can fill you in on what's going on anywhere in the northeast. Aberdeen's tourist information center has a monthly publication with an events calendar.

PERFORMING ARTS

Aberdeen is a rich city, both financially and culturally.

FAMILY **Aberdeen International Youth Festival.** August sees the world-renowned Aberdeen International Youth Festival, which attracts 80 international acts—orchestras, choirs, dance troupes, and theater companies—who over nine days perform in 50 venues across the city and the region. ☎ *01224/213800* 🌐 *www.aiyf.org.*

ARTS CENTERS

ACT Aberdeen (Arts Centre and Theatre Aberdeen). The Arts Centre and Theatre Aberdeen is a mid-scale venue that hosts plays, musicals, poetry readings, and exhibitions by professional, amateur, and youth companies. ✉ *33 King St.* ☎ *01224/635208* 🌐 *www.aberdeenartscentre.org.uk.*

Lemon Tree. The Lemon Tree has an innovative and international program of dance, stand-up comedy, and puppet theater, as well as folk, jazz, and rock music. ✉ *5 W. North St.* ☎ *01224/641122* 🌐 *www.aberdeenperformingarts.com.*

Peacock Visual Arts. This gallery displays photographic, video, and slide exhibits of contemporary art and architecture. ✉ *21 Castle St.* ☎ *01224/639539* ⊕ *www.peacockvisualarts.com* ⊙ *Tues.–Sat. 9:30–5:30.*

CONCERT HALLS

His Majesty's Theatre. The Edwardian His Majesty's Theatre hosts performances on par with those in some of the world's biggest cities. It's a regular venue for musicals and operas, as well as classical and modern dance. The restaurant, called 1906, is popular with audiences and cast members alike. ✉ *Rosemount Viaduct* ☎ *01224/641122* ⊕ *aberdeenperformingarts.com.*

Music Hall. The Scottish National Orchestra and the Scottish Chamber Orchestra are regulars here, as are shows with a vibrant mix of Scottish traditional, folk, jazz, and roots. In addition, there's also comedy and literary events and, increasingly, demonstrations by celebrity chefs. ✉ *Union St.* ☎ *01224/641122* ⊕ *www.aberdeenperformingarts.com.*

FILM

The Belmont. Independent, foreign language, and classic films are screened at the Belmont. The basement café bar is a stylish place to hang out although it closes at 8 pm. ✉ *49 Belmont St.* ☎ *01224/343500* ⊕ *www.belmontfilmhouse.com.*

NIGHTLIFE

With a greater club-to-clubber ratio than either Edinburgh or Glasgow, Aberdeen offers plenty of loud music and dancing for a night out. There are also pubs and pool halls for those with two left feet. Pubs close at midnight on weekdays and 1 am on weekends; clubs go until 2 or 3 am.

BARS AND PUBS

Bottle Cap Brewery. Craft-brewery and feisty in-house ales are served alongside good pub grub. The handsome old stone warehouse stages frequent live music gigs. ✉ *10 Littlejohn St.* ☎ *01224/478080.*

Brewdog. Aberdeen's pioneering craft brewery–turned–global brand runs its flagship bar with suitable gusto and no lack of style. Barebrick warehouse interiors with lots of steel mean there's lots of noise and chatter flying around the cavernous space, oiled by a choice of over 100 craft beers. ✉ *17 Gallowgate* ☎ *01224 /631223* ⊕ *www.brewdog.com.*

CASC Bar. Located in the Merchant Quarter, CASC ups Aberdeen's oil-boom largesse, by adding a sophisticated atmosphere, a selection of malt whiskies, and Cuban cigars to the ubiquitous craft-beer list (over 150 from around the world). Cool industrial interiors and outside seating make it popular with groups. ✉ *7 Stirling St.* ☎ *01224 /212373* ⊕ *www.cascbar.co.uk.*

Cellar 35. Next to traditional boozer the Noose & Monkey, this intimate club space (capacity 80) is known for its live music and comedy. Most nights (check the latest listings on the website) there are local and visiting bands, DJ sets, or comedy. ✉ *35 Rosemount Viaduct* ☎ *01224 /640483* ⊕ *www.nooseandmonkey.com.*

Fittie Bar. Some pubs spend a fortune trying to re-create the warm atmosphere that the Fittie Bar comes by naturally. Located where the harbor stops and the old fishing village of Footdee (Fittie) begins, the pub tells the story of Aberdeen's fishing past, as will any of the salty dogs who drink there. ⊠ *18 Wellington St.* ☎ *01224/582911.*

Old Blackfriars. Old Blackfriars enjoys a nice location near the end of Union Street. The lighting is dim, and the big fireplace warms things up on a chilly evening, although it can get crowded as the night goes on. This cask-ale pub has a great selection—Belhaven St. Andrews Ale and Caledonian 80 top the list. ⊠ *52 Castle St.* ☎ *01224/581922* ⊕ *www. oldblackfriars-aberdeen.co.uk.*

Musa. With fabulously atmospheric surroundings within an old banana-ripening warehouse and adjoining church, Musa is a new vibrant food-and-drinking hole, as well as an arts hub. Alongside wonderfully quirky dining options and art exhibitions, there's often live music. ⊠ *33 Exchange St.* ☎ *01224 /571771* ⊕ *www.musaaberdeen.com.*

Fodor's Choice ★ **The Prince of Wales.** Dating from 1850, the Prince of Wales has retained its paneled walls and wooden tables. Still regarded as Aberdeen's most traditional pub, it's hardly regal, but good-quality food and reasonable prices draw the regulars back. ⊠ *7 St. Nicholas La.* ☎ *01224/640597.*

Fodor's Choice ★ **The Tippling House.** Aberdonian *bon viveurs* have taken this new subterranean and sophisticated late-night drinking den to their hearts and stomachs. It's a great place to escape and mingle and offers casual dining, innovative cocktails, craft beers, and spirits. ⊠ *4 Belmont St.* ⊕ *www.thetipplinghouse.com.*

SHOPPING

You can find most of the large national department stores in Union Square. The shopping malls of Bon Accord, St. Nicholas, and Trinity host mainly high-end chain stores, but Aberdeen has a few good specialty shops as well: Rosemount Viaduct and Belmont Street are worth a meander.

Aitkins. You can't leave Aberdeen without trying one of its famous *rowies* (or *butteries*), the fortifying morning roll. Aitkins Bakery is considered the finest purveyor of this local speciality. ⊠ *202 Holburn St.* ☎ *01224/582567.*

Alex Scott & Co. For Scottish kilts, tartans, crests, and other traditionally Scottish clothes (including a stunning "Scotland" hoodie), a good place to start is Alex Scott & Co. ⊠ *43 Schoolhill* ☎ *01224/643924* ⊕ *www. kiltmakers.co.uk.*

Books and Beans. This secondhand bookshop has its own little café. You're welcome to browse and sip at the same time. ⊠ *22 Belmont St.* ☎ *01224/646438* ⊕ *www.booksandbeans.co.uk.*

Candle Close Gallery. This shop has some strange and wonderful mirrors, clocks, ceramics, and jewelry that you're unlikely to see elsewhere. ⊠ *123 Gallowgate* ☎ *01224/624940* ⊕ *www.candleclosegallery.co.uk.*

Cocoa Ooze. Enjoy a cup of tea and a chocolate fondue before tasting and buying handmade chocolate gifts, such as chocolate-drenched cinder toffee and hand-rolled truffles. ⊠ *24/28 Belmont St.* ☎ *01224/467212* ⊕ *www.cocoa-ooze.co.uk.*

Colin Wood. This shop is the place to go for small antiques, interesting prints, and regional maps. ✉ *25 Rose St.* ☎ *01224/643019.*

Juniper. Here you'll find gifts, homeware, and souvenirs, perfect for friends and family back home. ✉ *35 Belmont St.* ☎ *01224/640480.*

Peapod. Check out vintage and retro clothing and homeware: think Bakelite, chichi cups and saucers, and 1920s cocktail dresses. ✉ *144 Rosemount Pl.* ☎ *01224/635710.*

Fodor's Choice
★
Teasel & Tweed. If you are in need of a Harris Tweed iPod cover, this is your place. All manner of homewares and accessories made by Scottish designers and craftspeople are on offer. Downstairs is the fabulous Yvi's House of Tea with their own blended teas and German waffles. ✉ *85 Rosemount Viaduct* ☎ *01224/652352.*

GOLF

Northeast Scotland is known for good golf. Despite the continuing outcry from locals and environmentalists, Donald Trump has "stabilized" the dynamic dune system that borders the Menie Estate, just north of Aberdeen and the Ythan Estuary, to create Trump International Golf Links. Just south of Aberdeen, Jack Nicklaus has been lined up to design a championship course at Ury Castle. The financial climate has delayed the project, though.

You can expect to pay £15 to £120 per round at the golf courses in and around Aberdeen. Make reservations at least 24 hours in advance. Some private courses restrict tee times for visiting golfers to certain days or hours during the week, so be sure to check that the course you wish to play is open when you want to play it.

Murcar Links Golf Club. Sea views and a variety of rugged terrain—from sand dunes to tinkling burns—are the highlights of this course, founded in 1909. It's most famous for breathtaking vistas at the 7th hole, appropriately called the Serpentine. Designer Archibald Simpson considered this course to be one of his finest. ✉ *Bridge of Don* ☎ *01224/704354* ⊕ *www.murcarlinks.com* 💷 *£100 weekdays, £125 weekends* ⛳ *18 holes, 6314 yards, SSS 73.*

Royal Aberdeen Golf Club. This venerable club, founded in 1780, is the archetypal Scottish links course: tumbling over uneven ground, with the frequently added hazard of sea breezes. Prickly gorse is inclined to close in and form an additional hurdle. The two courses are tucked behind the rough, grassy sand dunes, and there are surprisingly few views of the sea. One historical note: in 1783 this club originated the five-minute-search rule for a lost ball. A handicap certificate and letter of introduction are required. Visitors are only allowed on weekdays. ✉ *Links Rd., Bridge of Don* ☎ *01224/702571* ⊕ *www.royalaberdeengolf.com* 💷 *Balgownie, £156; Silverburn, £70* ⛳ *Balgownie: 18 holes, 6900 yards, par 71; Silverburn: 18 holes, 4021 yards, par 64* ⊙ *Daily* ⚠ *Reservations essential.*

Westhill Golf Club. This parkland course, founded in 1977, overlooks Royal Deeside and has a friendly clubhouse. This affable place is the most inexpensive in the area by far. ✉ *Westhill Heights, Westhill* ☎ *01224/740159* ⊕ *www.westhillgolfclub.co.uk* ✉ *£20* ⚐ *18 holes, 5849 yards, par 70.*

ROYAL DEESIDE AND CASTLE COUNTRY

Deeside, the valley running west from Aberdeen down which the River Dee flows, earned its "royal" appellation when discovered by Queen Victoria. To this day, where royalty goes, lesser aristocracy and freshly minted millionaires follow. Many still aspire to own a grand shooting estate in Deeside, and you may appreciate this yearning when you see the piney hills, purple moors, and blue river intermingling. As you travel deeper into the Grampian Mountains, Royal Deeside's gradual scenic change adds a growing sense of excitement.

There are castles along the Dee as well as to the north in Castle Country, another region that illustrates the gradual geological change in the northeast: uplands lapped by a tide of farms. All the Donside and Deeside castles are picturesquely sited, with most fitted out with tall slender turrets, winding stairs, and crooked chambers that epitomize Scottish baronial style. All have tales of ghosts and bloodshed, siege and torture. Many were tidied up and "domesticated" during the 19th century. Although best toured by car, much of this area is accessible either by public transportation or on tours from Aberdeen.

STONEHAVEN

15 miles south of Aberdeen.

This historic town near splendid Dunnottar Castle was once a popular holiday destination, with people including Robert Burns enjoying walks along the golden sands. The surrounding red-clay fields were made famous by Lewis Grassic Gibbon (real name James Leslie Mitchell), who attended school in the town and who wrote the seminal Scottish trilogy, *A Scots Quair,* about the people, the land, and the impact of World War I. The decline of the fishing industry emptied the harbor, but the town, being so close to Aberdeen, has begun to thrive again. It's now famous for its Hogmanay (New Year) celebrations, where local men swing huge balls of fire on chains before tossing them into the harbor.

GETTING HERE AND AROUND

Stagecoach Bluebird runs a number of buses to Stonehaven from Aberdeen, but numbers 107 and 109 are the fastest (50 minutes). Most trains heading south from Aberdeen stop at Stonehaven; there's at least one per hour making the 15-minute trip. Drivers should take A90 south and turn off at A957.

ESSENTIALS

Visitor Information Stonehaven Visitor Information Centre. ✉ *66 Allardyce St.* ☎ *01569/762806* ⊕ *www.aberdeen-grampian.com.*

EXPLORING

Fodor's Choice ★ **Dunnottar Castle.** It's hard to beat the cinematic-majesty of the magnificent cliff-top ruins of Dunnottar Castle, with its panoramic views of the North Sea. Building began in the 14th century, when Sir William Keith, Marischal of Scotland (keeper of the king's mares), decided to build a tower house to demonstrate his power. Subsequent generations added to the structure, and important visitors included Mary, Queen of Scots. The castle is most famous for holding out for eight months against Oliver Cromwell's army in 1651 and 1652, and thereby saving the Scottish crown jewels, which had been stored here for safekeeping. Reach the castle via the A90; take the Stonehaven turnoff and follow the signs. Wear sensible shoes, and allow about two hours. ✉ *Off A92* ☎ *01569/762173* 🌐 *www.dunnottarcastle.co.uk* 🎟 *£6* 🕒 *Easter–Sept., daily 9–6; Nov.–Easter, daily 10–sunset.*

FAMILY Fodor's Choice ★ **Stonehaven Open-Air Swimming Pool.** They were extremely popular in the 1930s, but the Stonehaven Open-Air Swimming Pool, an aging Art Deco gem, is one of only a few remaining outdoor heated pools in Scotland. Salty water from the North Sea is pumped in and warmed up to a toasty 28°C (82°F). Run by a local trust, this place is perfect for families. Wednesday's midnight swims (£6.90) let you float under the stars. ✉ *Queen Elizabeth Park, off A90* ☎ *01569/762134* 🌐 *www.stonehavenopenairpool.co.uk* 🎟 *£5.50* 🕒 *June and mid-Aug.–early Sept., weekdays 1–7:30, weekends 10–6; July and early Aug., weekdays 10–7:30, weekends 10–6.*

WHERE TO EAT AND STAY

$$ SEAFOOD 🍴 **The Ship Inn.** This former coaching inn is exactly where you want to take nourishment after a bracing walk from Dunnottar Castle (stop by the Visitor Information Centre for details of the coastal path). Refurbishment has taken away much of the history, but new-wood paneling and rattan chairs make it comfortable while the huge new windows provide viewsof the stunning harbor outside. The staff are friendly and knowledgeable about seafood: the crab-claw-and-mussel platter (£18) is worth the splurge. [$] *Average main: £16* ✉ *5 Shore Head* ☎ *01569/762617* 💳 *No credit cards.*

$ B&B/INN Fodor's Choice ★ 🏨 **Bayview B&B.** On the beach and down the lane from the town square, this contemporary bed-and-breakfast couldn't be in a more convenient location or have better views. **Pros:** spic-and-span rooms; right on the beach; fresh, modern design. **Cons:** standard rooms are smallish. [$] *Rooms from: £95* ✉ *Beachgate La.* ☎ *07791/224227* 🌐 *www.bayviewbandb.co.uk* 🛏 *3 rooms, 1 suite* 🍽 *Breakfast.*

SHOPPING

Fodor's Choice ★ **Aunty Betty's.** Even if the weather is lousy, this coffee, sweets, and ice cream shop confirms you are on your summer holidays. Grown-ups will love the gin-and-tonic or champagne sorbets: kids, the complimentary sprinkles. ✉ *The Promenade* ☎ *01569 /763656.*

Royal Deeside

North Sea

Stonehaven
Dunnottar Castle

Aberdeen
see detail map

Pitmedden Garden
Pitmedden

Castle Fraser

Drum Castle, Garden and Estate

Crathes Castle
Brig o'Feuch

BANCHORY

Kincardine O'Neil

Craigievar Castle

ALFORD
HOWE OF ALFORD

ABERDEENSHIRE

Kildrummy Castle
Glenbuchat Castle

LADDER HILLS

Queen's View

Ballater

Corgarff Castle

GLEN GAIRN

Balmoral Castle

Braemar Castle
Braemar
Linn of Dee

GRAMPIAN MOUNTAINS

ANGUS

Loch Muick

GLEN GELDER

GLEN MUICK

GLEN CLUNIE

River Dee

5 mi
5 km

Which Castle Is Right for You?

We admit it—there are almost too many castles in this part of Scotland. Because it's nearly impossible to see all of them, we've noted the prime characteristics of each to help you decide which you'd most like to visit.

■ **Balmoral:** The Queen's home, this is where Queen Victoria and the royal family fell in love with Scotland and all things Scottish. Expect baronial largesse and groomed grounds, though you don't see much inside.

■ **Balvenie:** This ruined castle is known for its indomitable bearing and verdant surroundings, right in the midst of the Malt Whisky Trail.

■ **Braemar:** Offering memorable insight into the lives of the Scottish landed gentry, this recently restored castle heaves with memorabilia and mementos of the fascinating Farquharsons, who still hold their clan gathering here.

■ **Corgarff:** You'll find a sober solitude out on the moorland, as well as 18th-century graffiti and the reconstructed barracks used by Jacobite troops in 1746 as they retreated north.

■ **Craigievar:** Highlights of this 17th-century castle are a magical forest, fairy-tale turrets, and the furnishings and possessions of the Forbes family that fill the house.

■ **Crathes:** Expect tight quarters, notable family portraits, and a network of walled gardens at this well-preserved seat of the Burnett family. Its adventure park keeps the kids occupied.

■ **Drum:** A fusion of architectural styles and some historic roses are notable at this castle, but it's the medieval chapel that stirs the senses.

■ **Dunnottar:** The dramatic, scene-stealing, cliff-top location of Mel Gibson's *Hamlet* (1991), the ruins of this 14th-century tower house by the sea are unbeatable.

■ **Fraser:** Considered the grandest castle in Aberdeenshire, Castle Fraser has opulent period furnishings and woodland walks that make for a rewarding day.

■ **Fyvie:** This 14th-century castle underwent a luxurious Edwardian makeover. Come here for an awesome art collection, rich interiors, and haunting history.

■ **Kildrummy:** This is the place for evocative ruins, some from the 13th century, and tales of a treacherous past. Its austere but poignant chapel is a must-see.

7

BANCHORY

15 miles west of Stonehaven, 19 miles west of Aberdeen.

Banchory is an immaculate town filled with pinkish granite buildings. It's usually bustling with ice-cream-eating strollers, out on a day trip from Aberdeen. Nearby are Crathes and Drum castles.

GETTING HERE AND AROUND

A car is by far the best way to get around the area; A93 is one of the main roads connecting the towns.

For those reliant on public transport, Stagecoach buses operate a number of services for towns along or just off A93 (Drum Castle, Banchory, Kincardine, Aboyne, Ballater, Balmoral, and Braemar).

ESSENTIALS

Visitor Information Banchory Visitor Information Centre. ☒ *Bridge St.* ☎ *01330/823784* ⊕ *www.aberdeen-grampian.com.*

EXPLORING
TOP ATTRACTIONS

FAMILY

Fodor's Choice

★

Crathes Castle. About 16 miles west of Aberdeen, Crathes Castle was once the home of the Burnett family and is one of the best-preserved castles in Britain. Keepers of the Forest of Drum for generations, the family acquired lands here by marriage and later built a castle, completed in 1596. The National Trust for Scotland cares for the castle, which is furnished with many original pieces and family portraits. Outside are grand yet lovingly tended gardens with calculated symmetry and flower-rich beds. Make sure you browse the Horsemill bookshop and sample the tasty baked goods in the tearoom. There's an adventure park for kids, and the staff organizes activities that are fun and educational. ☒ *Off A93* ☎ *01330/844525* ⊕ *www.nts.org.uk* ☒ *£12.50* ⊙ *Apr.–Oct., daily 10–4:45; Nov.–Mar., weekends 10:30–3:45; last admission 45 mins before closing.*

Drum Castle, Garden and Estate. This foursquare tower has an evocative medieval chapel that dates from the 13th century; like many other castles, it also has later additions up to Victorian times. Note the tower's rounded corners, said to make battering-ram attacks more difficult. Nearby, fragments of the ancient Forest of Drum still stand, dating from the days when Scotland was covered by great stands of oak and pine. The Garden of Historic Roses, open from April to October, lays claim to some old-fashioned roses not commonly seen today. Drum Castle is 8 miles east of Banchory and 11 miles west of Aberdeen. ■TIP→ **During the refurbishment of Aberdeen Art Gallery, selected works from its collection will be on display here until March 2017.** ☒ *Off A93* ☎ *01330/700334* ⊕ *www.nts.org.uk* ☒ *£12.50* ⊙ *Castle: Apr.–June and Sept., Thurs.–Mon. 11–4:45; July–Aug., daily 11–4:45; last entry 45 mins before closing time. Grounds: daily 9:30–sunset.*

FAMILY **Royal Deeside Railway.** Once the Royal line to the Balmoral estate, this railway line has recently reopened. Work to the station continues in earnest and the railway is now running passengers along a shortened scenic route either by diesel or, if you're lucky, by steam. The journey lasts around 15 to 20 minutes. If that's not enough, for a little extra you can purchase a Day Rover ticket to let you go back and forth all day. ☒ *Milton of Crathes* ☎ *01330/844416* ⊕ *www.deeside-railway.co.uk* ☒ *Return ticket £4 for diesel or £6 for steam; Day Rover £6 for diesel or £9 for steam* ⊙ *July and Aug., Wed. and weekends 11–4:15; other months, see website for details.*

WORTH NOTING

Brig o'Feuch. If you visit in autumn, drive for a mile along the B974 south of Banchory to the Brig o'Feuch (pronounced *fyooch,* the *ch* as in loch). The area around this bridge is pleasant, and the fall colors and foaming waters make for an attractive scene. Salmon leap in season (September to November and February and March). ✉ *B974.*

OFF THE BEATEN PATH

Kincardine O'Neil. The ruined kirk in this little village 9 miles west of Banchory on A93 was built in 1233 and once sheltered travelers: it was the last hospice before the Mounth, the name given to the massif that shuts off the south side of the Dee Valley. Beyond Banchory (and the B974), no motor roads run south until you reach Braemar (A93), though the Mounth is crossed by a network of tracks once used by Scottish soldiers, invading armies (including the Romans), and cattle drovers. Photography buffs won't want to miss the bridge at Potarch, just to the east.

OFF THE BEATEN PATH

Queen's View. To reach one of the most spectacular vistas in northeast Scotland—stretching across the Howe of Cromar to Lochnagar—take the B9094 due north from Aboyne, then turn left onto the B9119 for 6 miles.

WHERE TO STAY

$$ HOTEL Fodor's Choice ★

🏨 **Banchory Lodge.** Right on the River Dee, this Georgian lodge offers the lovely touches you expect at a luxury hotel—but with none of the faff or the cost. **Pros:** a warm welcome; great bar; excellent food and afternoon teas. **Cons:** popular for weddings. [$] *Rooms from: £130* ✉ *Dee St.* ☎ *01330/822625* 🌐 *www.banchorylodge.com* 🛏 *28 rooms* 🍴 *Breakfast* 💳 *No credit cards.*

$$$ HOTEL

🏨 **Raemoir House Hotel.** Dating from the 16th to 19th century, this baronial home 2 miles north of Banchory makes you feelas if you're on the set of a period drama. **Pros:** charming old building with extensive grounds; popular restaurant; staff is informal and efficient. **Cons:** pricey rates. [$] *Rooms from: £220* ✉ *Off A980, Raemoir* ☎ *01330/824884* 🌐 *www.raemoir.com* 🛏 *18 rooms* 🍴 *Breakfast.*

NIGHTLIFE AND PERFORMING ARTS

Fodor's Choice ★

Woodend Barn. Holding art exhibitions, film nights, and live performances, this arts venue packs a mean cultural punch for a renovated barn. Its excellent café bar serves simple dishes in a modern way. ✉ *Banchory* ☎ *1330/825431 box office, 1330 /826520 general enquiries* 🌐 *www.woodendbarn.com.*

BALLATER

22 miles west of Kincardine O'Neill, 43 miles west of Aberdeen.

The handsome holiday resort of Ballater, once noted for the curative properties of its waters, has profited from the proximity of the royals, nearby at Balmoral Castle. You might be amused by the array of "by royal appointment" signs proudly hanging from many of its various shops (even monarchs need bakers and butchers). Take time to stroll around this well-laid-out community. The railway station houses the tourist information center and a display on the glories of the Great North of Scotland branch railway line, closed in the 1960s along with so many others in this country.

The locals have long taken the town's royal connection in stride. To this day, the hundreds who line the road when the Queen and her family arrive for services at the family's parish church at Crathie are invariably visitors to Deeside—one of Balmoral's attractions for the monarch has always been the villagers' respect for royal privacy.

GETTING HERE AND AROUND

There's good train service to Aberdeen, but you'll need to catch a bus to get to this and other towns near A93. Stagecoach Bluebird buses numbers 201 and 202 operate hourly to all the main towns, including Ballater. Otherwise, it's an easy car trip.

ESSENTIALS

Visitor Information **Ballater Visitor Information Centre.** ⊠ *Albert Memorial Hall, Station Sq.* ☎ *01339/755306.*

EXPLORING

Balmoral Castle. The enormous parking lot is indicative of the public's appreciation of Balmoral Castle, one of Queen Elizabeth II's favorite family retreats. Only the formal gardens, the ballroom, and the carriage hall are on view, with their exhibitions of royal artifacts, commemorative china, and native wildlife. Thanks to Victoria and Albert, who built the house to Prince Albert's design, stags' heads abound, the bagpipes wailed incessantly, and the garish Stewart tartan was used for everything from carpets to chair covers. A more somber Duff tartan, black and green to blend with the environment, was later adopted.

Queen Elizabeth II follows her predecessors' routine in spending a holiday of about six weeks in Deeside, usually from mid-August to the end of September. During this time Balmoral is closed to visitors, including the grounds. You can take a guided tour in November and December; if the weather is crisp and bright, the estate is at its most dramatic and romantic. You're only allowed a peek inside, but the Royal Cottage is where Queen Victoria spent much of her time. You can see the table where she took breakfast and wrote her correspondence.

Around and about Balmoral, which is 7 miles west of Ballater, are some notable spots—Cairn O'Mount, Cambus O'May, and the Cairngorms from the Linn of Dee—that are home to golden eagles, Harris hawks, red squirrels, red deer, black and red grouse, and snow bunting, some of which may be seen on the quintessentially queen-like Landrover Safari Tour. Tempted by the setting? Balmoral Castle has a number of cottages (some very large) for rent by the week at certain times. They are atmospheric but can be basic (which believe it or not, is how the royal family like their holidays to be). ⊠ *A93* ☎ *01339/742534* ⊕ *www. balmoralcastle.com* 🖾 *£11* ⊙ *Apr.–July, daily 10–5; last admission 1 hr before closing. Guided tours on certain dates in Nov. and Dec.*

Loch Muick. A three- or four-hour walk takes you around glorious Loch Muick (Gaelic for "pig") and past Glas-alt Shiel, a favorite retreat of Queen Victoria's that you might recognize from the film *Mrs. Brown*. From Ballater, take the B976 over the River Dee before turning off at the sign for Glen Muick. Park at the Spittal of Loch Muick car park. The path around the loch is well signposted, although good boots are necessary for the stoney beach at the far side of the loch. The native red deer are quite common throughout the Scottish Highlands, but here is one of the best places to see them. ⊠ *Ballater.*

Balmoral, Queen Victoria's Retreat

Some credit Sir Walter Scott with having opened up Scotland for tourism through his poems and novels. But it was probably Queen Victoria (1819–1901) who gave Scottish tourism its real momentum when, in 1842, she first came to Scotland and when, in 1847—on orders of a doctor, who thought the relatively dry climate of upper Deeside would suit her—she bought Balmoral. The pretty little castle was knocked down to make room for a much grander house in full-blown Scottish baronial style, designed by her husband, Prince Albert (1819–61), in 1855. It had a veritable rash of tartanitis. Before long the entire Deeside and the region north were dotted with country houses and mock-baronial châteaux.

"It seems like a dream to be here in our dear Highland Home again," Queen Victoria wrote. "Every year my heart becomes more fixed in this dear Paradise." Victoria loved Balmoral more for its setting than its house,

so be sure to take in its pleasant gardens. Year by year Victoria and Albert added to the estate, taking over neighboring houses, securing the forest and moorland around it, and developing deer stalking and grouse shooting here.

In consequence, Balmoral is now a large property, with grounds that run 12 miles along the Deeside road. Its privacy is protected by belts of pinewood, and the only view of the castle from the A93 is a partial one, from a point near Inver, 2 miles west of the gates.

There's an excellent bird's-eye view of Balmoral from an old military road, now the A939, which climbs out of Crathie, northbound for Cockbridge and the Don Valley. This view embraces the summit of Lochnagar, in whose *corries* (hollows) the snow lies year-round and whose boulder fields the current Prince of Wales, Charles Windsor, so fondly and so frequently treads.

As you continue west into Highland scenery past Balmoral Castle, further pine-framed glimpses appear of the "steep frowning glories of dark Lochnagar," as it was described by the poet Lord Byron (1788–1824). Lochnagar (3,786 feet) was made known to an audience wider than hill walkers by the current Prince of Wales, who published a children's story, *The Old Man of Lochnagar*.

WHERE TO EAT

$

BISTRO

× **Rocksalt & Snails.** This cheeky little contemporary café bar, with its fancy metalwork interiors and solid wooden tables, has an interesting take on local produce, serving Heidi (goat meat) and Deerstalker (venison) pies and the abundant Rocksalt & Snails platter (with all kinds of salmon and trout). For sweetness there are huge scones or cakes and very good coffee or loose-leaf tea. $ *Average main: £9* ⊠ *2 Bridge St.* ☎ *07834 /452583* ▭ *No credit cards.*

WHERE TO STAY

$$ B&B/INN Auld Kirk. This strikingly renovated old church makes for an interesting stay. **Pros:** helpful team looks after you; pin-tidy bedrooms and public rooms. **Cons:** bar is popular with locals, so can get noisy; restaurant has reduced hours in winter. [$] *Rooms from: £110* ✉ *Braemar Rd.* ☎ *01339/755762* 🌐 *www.theauldkirk.com* 🛏 *7 rooms* 🍴 *Breakfast.*

$$$ HOTEL **Hilton Craigendarroch.** This grand old country house was, in its day, considered a luxury retreat for the oil-rich Aberdonians. **Pros:** a great pool and decent gym facilities; good amenities for kids; leafy location in Royal Deeside. **Cons:** if there's a conference, nonattending guests can feel lost among the crowds. [$] *Rooms from: £165* ✉ *Braemar Rd.* ☎ *01339/755558* 🌐 *www.hilton.co.uk/craigendarroch* 🛏 *40 rooms, 11 suites* 🍴 *Breakfast.*

$$ B&B/INN **No 45.** With plenty of period charm, this Victorian-era house offers old-fashioned hospitality and simple, understated comfort. **Pros:** unpretentious feel; good price; relaxing lounge. **Cons:** a few bedrooms on the small side. [$] *Rooms from: £120* ✉ *45 Braemar Rd.* ☎ *01339/755420* 🌐 *www.no45.co.uk* 💳 *No credit cards* 🛏 *8 rooms* 🍴 *Breakfast.*

$ B&B/INN Fodor's Choice ★ **Schoolhouse B&B.** Just outside the center of town, this solid, dependable B&B offers superior accommodations that are a bit unusual for Aberdeenshire. **Pros:** low-priced luxury; meticulously clean. **Cons:** if you're coming in high season book well in advance. [$] *Rooms from: £80* ✉ *Anderson Rd.* ☎ *01339/756333* 🌐 *www.school-house.eu* 🛏 *4 rooms* 🍴 *Breakfast.*

SHOPPING

Atholl Countrywear. At either location of Countrywear, men can find everything that's necessary for Highland country living, including fishing tackle, natty tweeds, and that flexible garment popular in Scotland between seasons: the body warmer. ✉ *15 and 35 Bridge St.* ☎ *01339/755453* 🌐 *www.athollcountrywear.co.uk.*

Byzantium. This long-standing boutique has a loyal following from all over the world who like their eclectic mix of clothing and accessories. ✉ *1–3 Bridge St.* ☎ *01339/755055.*

Deeside Books. Beyond the gifts section, veer to the right and you will find an interesting collection of old, out-of-print, and hard-to-find books about Scotland, which make splendid gifts for lovers of all things Scots. ✉ *18–20 Bridge St.* ☎ *01339/754080* 🌐 *www.deesidebooks.com.*

Dee Valley Confectioners. For a low-cost gift you could always see what's being boiled up at Dee Valley Confectioners, the region's top sweets maker. ✉ *Station Sq.* ☎ *01339/755499* 🌐 *www.dee-valley.co.uk.*

McEwan Gallery. A mile west of Ballater, the McEwan Gallery displays fine paintings, watercolors, prints, and books (many with a Scottish or golf theme) in an unusual house built by the Swiss artist Rudolphe Christen in 1902. ✉ *A939* ☎ *01339/755429* 🌐 *www.mcewangallery.com.*

GOLF

Ballater Golf Club. The mountains of Royal Deeside surround this course, which is laid out along the sandy flats of the River Dee. The club, originally opened in 1892, has a holiday atmosphere, and the shops and pleasant walks in nearby Ballater make this a good place for nongolfing partners. ✉ *Victoria Rd.* ☎ *013397/55567* ⊕ *www.ballatergolfclub.co.uk* 🖃 *£30 weekdays, £40 weekends* 👣 *18 holes, 6059 yards, par 70* ☉ *Daily.*

BRAEMAR

17 miles west of Ballater, 60 miles west of Aberdeen, 51 miles north of Perth via A93.

Synonymous with the British monarchy, due to its closeness to Balmoral, and with the famous Highland Games, this village is popular year-round as a base for walkers and climbers enjoying the Grampian Mountains. This very much reflects in the choice of accommodation available which is surprisingly basic. However, the purchase and overhaul of the Fife Arms by a Swiss art-dealing husband and wife—due to open early in 2017—suggests that the potential of Braemar has caught the eye of international developers. Meanwhile, there isn't really much else going on in Braemar, although the castle is well worth a couple of hours.

GETTING HERE AND AROUND

The town is on A93; there's bus service here, as to other towns on the road, but the closest train station is Aberdeen.

ESSENTIALS

Visitor Information **Braemar Visitor Information Centre.** ✉ *The Mews, Mar Rd.* ☎ *01339/741600* ⊕ *www.braemarscotland.co.uk.*

EXPLORING

Fodor'sChoice
★
Braemar Castle. On the northern outskirts of town, Braemar Castle dates from the 17th century, although its defensive walls, in the shape of a pointed star, came later. At Braemar (the *braes,* or slopes, of the district of Mar), the standard, or rebel flag, was first raised at the start of the unsuccessful Jacobite rebellion of 1715. About 30 years later, during the last Jacobite rebellion, Braemar Castle was strengthened and garrisoned by government troops. From the early 1800s the castle was the clan seat of the Farquharsons, who hold their clan reunion here every summer.

Thanks to the commitment of local volunteers, a remarkable 2008 renovation restored Braemar back to the home it would have been in the early 20th century, complete with all the necessary comforts and family memorabilia. A dozen rooms are on view, including the laird's day room with a plush day bed and the kitchen. ✉ *Off A93* ☎ *01339/741219* ⊕ *www.braemarcastle.co.uk* 🖃 *£8* ☉ *Apr.–June, Sept., and Oct., Wed.– Sun 10–5; July and Aug., daily 10–5.*

Braemar Highland Gathering. The village of Braemar is associated with the Braemar Highland Gathering, held the first Saturday in September. Although there are many such gatherings celebrated throughout Scotland, this one is distinguished by the presence of the royal family. Competitions and events include hammer throwing, caber tossing, and bagpipe playing. If you plan to attend, book your accommodations months in advance and be sure to buy tickets and, if necessary, your car parking ticket about six months in advance, as they do sell out.

THE HIGHLAND GAMES

They might not all be as royally attended as the Braemar Highland Gathering, but from spring to late summer across a wide swath of northern Scotland competitors gather to toss, pull, fling, and sing at various Highland events. No two games are the same, but many incorporate agricultural shows, sporting competitions, clan gatherings, or just beer in the sun. VisitScotland (🌐 *www.visitscotland.com*) has a list of them.

Which one to attend? Braemar stands tall on ceremony and tradition, and the chance of seeing royalty up close means it attracts visitors from far and wide. Dufftown Games (🌐 *www.dufftownhighlandgames.org*) is the most competitive, with its race up the nearby Ben Rinnes, while the most picturesque is the Lochcarron Games (🌐 *www.lochcarrongames.org.uk*), which are played and danced out under the massif of the Torridon hills.

✉ *Princess Royal and Duke of Fife Memorial Park, Broombank Terr.* 🌐 *www.braemargathering.org.*

Braemar Highland Heritage Centre. You can find out more about local lore at the Braemar Highland Heritage Centre, in a converted stable block in the middle of town. The center tells the history of the village with displays and a film. The tourist office and a gift shop are here, too. ✉ *The Mews, Mar Rd.* ☎ *01339/741944* 🎟 *Free* 🕓 *Jan.–May, Nov., and Dec., Mon.–Sat. 10:30–1:30 and 2–5, Sun. 1–4; June, Sept., and Oct., daily 9–5; July and Aug., daily 9–6.*

OFF THE BEATEN PATH

Linn of Dee. Although the main A93 slinks off to the south from Braemar, a little unmarked road will take you farther west into the hilly heartland. The road offers views over the winding River Dee and the blue hills before passing through the tiny hamlet of Inverey and crossing a bridge at the Linn of Dee. *Linn* is a Scots word meaning "rocky narrows," and the river's gash here is deep and roaring. Park beyond the bridge and walk back to admire the sylvan setting.

WHERE TO EAT AND STAY

$$ BRITISH 🍴 **Moorfield House Hotel.** While the dining room may be underwhelming and the menu limited, when your plate is set before you, you'll understand why this is considered one of the best eateries in Braemar. The chef—who learned his craft by catering for big groups—offers unpretentious yet superb home-style cooking. Simple main dishes like panfried fish with garden vegetables, followed by a dessert like a seasonal crumble, will satisfy even the most exacting gourmand. Upstairs there are six pleasant bedrooms with great views. [$] *Average main: £17* ✉ *Moorfield House Hotel, Chapel Brae* ☎ *013397/41244* 🌐 *www.moorfieldhousehotel.com* 💳 *No credit cards.*

$ CAFÉ 🍴 **Taste.** It's strangely difficult to eat like a queen in Braemar, but this chalet-style café serves her subjects well, with the tastiest, freshest soups and sandwiches (Scottish cheddar and homemade meat loaf are two options). You can order moist cakes and tasty lattes here, too.

$ *Average main: £6* ✉ *Auchendryne Sq.* ☎ *01339/741425* ⊕ *www. taste-braemar.co.uk* ▤ *No credit cards* ⊘ *Closed Sun. No dinner.*

$

B&B/INN

Fodor's Choice

★

☐ **Ivy Cottage.** A relative newcomer in Braemar, this B&B should up the game of its competitors. **Pros:** relaxing rooms; owners who go out of their way to make you feel at home. **Cons:** next to the church, so expect bells on Sunday morning. $ *Rooms from: £75* ✉ *Cluniebank Rd.* ☎ *01339/741642* ⊕ *www.ivycottagebraemar.co.uk* ▤ *No credit cards* ⤦ *3 rooms, 2 self-catering flats* ⦿ *Some meals.*

GOLF

Braemar Golf Course. The tricky 18-hole Braemar Golf Course, founded in 1902, is laden with foaming waters. Erratic duffers, take note: the compassionate course managers have installed, near the water, poles with little nets on the end for those occasional shots that may go awry. ✉ *Cluny Bank Rd.* ☎ *01339/741618* ⊕ *www.braemargolfclub.co.uk* ▤ *£26* ⚑ *18 holes, 4935 yards, par 65.*

CORGARFF CASTLE

23 miles northeast of Braemar, 14 miles northwest of Ballater.

This castle has a striking setting on the moors and some rebuilt military features that recall its strategic importance.

GETTING HERE AND AROUND
By car, take A939 and then follow signs.

EXPLORING
Corgarff Castle. Eighteenth-century soldiers paved a military highway north from Ballater to Corgarff Castle, an isolated tower house on the moorland with a star-shape defensive wall that's a curious replica of Braemar Castle. Corgarff was built as a hunting lodge for the earls of Mar in the 16th century. After an eventful history that included the wife of a later laird being burned alive in a family dispute, the castle ended its career as a garrison for Hanoverian troops. The troops were responsible for preventing illegal whisky distilling. Reconstructed barracks show what the castle must have been like when the Redcoats arrived in 1746. ✉ *Off A939, Corgarff* ☎ *01975/651460* ⊕ *www.historic-scotland.gov. uk* ▤ *£5.50* ⊘ *Apr.–Sept., daily 9:30–5:30; last admission 30 mins before closing.*

EN
ROUTE

Castle Trail. If you return east from Corgarff Castle to the A939/A944 junction and make a left onto the A944, the signs indicate that you're on the Castle Trail. The A944 meanders along the River Don to the village of Strathdon, where a great mound by the roadside turns out to be a *motte*, or the base of a wooden castle, built in the late 12th century. Although it takes considerable imagination to become enthusiastic about a grass-covered heap, surviving mottes have contributed greatly to the understanding of the history of Scottish castles. The A944 then joins the A97, and a few minutes later a sign points to **Glenbuchat Castle**, a plain Z-plan tower house. ⊕ *www.visitscotland.com/see-do/ itineraries/castles/scotlands-castle-trail.*

7

CLOSE UP

Language and the Scots

"Much," said Doctor Johnson, "may be made of a Scotchman if he be caught young." This quote sums up, even today, the attitude of some English people—confident in their English, the language of parliament and much of the media—toward the Scots language. The Scots have long been made to feel uncomfortable about their mother tongue, and until the 1970s (and in some private schools, even today) they were encouraged to mimic the dialect of the Thames Valley ("standard English") in order to "get on" in life.

LOWLAND SCOTS

The Scots language (that is, Lowland Scots, not Gaelic) was a northern form of Middle English and in its day was the language used in the court and in literature. It borrowed from Scandinavian, Dutch, French, and Gaelic. After a series of historical blows—such as the decamping of the Scottish court to England after 1603 and the printing of the King James Bible in English but not in Scots—it declined as a literary or official language. It survives in various forms but is virtually an underground language, spoken among ordinary folk, especially in its heartland, in the northeast.

You may even find yourself exporting a few useful words, such as *dreich* (gloomy), *glaikit* (acting and looking foolish), or *dinna fash* (don't worry), all of which are much more expressive than their English equivalents.

Some Scottish words are used and understood across the entire country (and world), such as *wee* (small), *aye* (yes), *lassie* (girl), and *bonny* (pretty). Regional variations are evident even in the simplest of greetings. When you meet someone in the Borders, *Whit fettle?* (What state are you in?) or *Hou ye lestin?* (How are you lasting?) may throw you for a loop; elsewhere you could hear *Hoo's yer doos?* (How are your pigeons?). If a group of Scots takes a fancy to you at the pub, you may be asked to *Come intil the body o the kirk*, and if all goes well, your departure may be met with a jovial farewell, *haste ye back* (return soon).

GAELIC

Scottish Gaelic, an entirely different language, is still spoken across the Highlands and Hebrides. There's also a large Gaelic-speaking population in Glasgow as a result of the Celtic diaspora—islanders migrating to Glasgow in search of jobs in the 19th century. Speakers of Gaelic in Scotland were once persecuted, after the failure of the 18th-century Jacobite rebellions. Official persecution has now turned to enthusiastic support, as the Gaelic lobby has won substantial public funds to underwrite television programming, public signage, and language classes for new learners.

One of the joys of Scottish television is watching Gaelic news programs on BBC Alba to see how the ancient language copes with such topics as nuclear energy, the Internet, and the latest band to hit the charts. A number of Gaelic words have been absorbed into English: *banshee* (a wailing female spirit), *galore* (plenty), *slob* (a slovenly person), and *brat* (a spoiled or unruly child).

To experience Gaelic language and culture in all its glory, you can attend the Royal National Mod—a competition-based festival with speeches, drama, and music, all in Gaelic—held in a different location every year.

KILDRUMMY CASTLE

18 miles northeast of Corgarff, 23 miles north of Ballater, 22 miles north of Aboyne.

The ancient ruins of Kildrummy Castle still show its history of expansion and reveal a variety of styles.

GETTING HERE AND AROUND

By car, take A97 off A93 (or the A980 if you're coming direct from Banchory). Be wary of the sign for Kildrummy Castle Garden and Hotel. You want the turn after this for Kildrummy Castle itself.

EXPLORING

Kildrummy Castle. Although in ruins, Kildrummy Castle is significant because it dates to the 13th century and has ties to the mainstream medieval traditions of European castle building. It shares features with Harlech and Caernarfon, in Wales, as well as with Château de Coucy, near Laon, France. Kildrummy underwent several expansions at the hands of England's King Edward I (1239–1307); the castle was back in Scottish hands in 1306, when it was besieged by King Edward I's son. The defenders were betrayed by Osbarn the Smith, who was promised a large amount of gold by the English forces. They gave it to him after the castle fell, pouring the molten metal down his throat, or so the ghoulish story goes. Kildrummy's prominence ended after the collapse of the 1715 Jacobite uprising. It had been the rebel headquarters and was consequently dismantled. Although the castle is almost completely ruined, its unadorned yet strangely moving chapel remains intact. ⊠ *A97, Kildrummy* ☎ *01975/571331* ⊕ *www. historic-scotland.gov.uk* 🖾 *£4.50* ⊙ *Apr.–Sept., daily 9:30–5:30.*

Kildrummy Castle Gardens. The Kildrummy Castle Gardens, behind the castle and with a separate entrance from the main road, are built in what was the original quarry for the castle. This sheltered bowl within the woodlands has a broad range of shrubs and alpine plants and a notable water garden. ⊠ *A97, Kildrummy* ☎ *01975/571203* ⊕ *www. kildrummy-castle-gardens.co.uk* 🖾 *£4.50* ⊙ *Apr.–Oct., daily noon–5.*

WHERE TO STAY

$$$ 🏨 **Kildrummy Castle Hotel.** A grand late-Victorian country house, this
HOTEL elegant lodging offers a peaceful stay and attentive service all seemingly from an age gone by. **Pros:** fabulous old hunting lodge; great views. **Cons:** there's no elevator, and you may need to go up a fair number of steps. 💲 *Rooms from: £165* ⊠ *A97, Kildrummy* ☎ *01975/571288* ⊕ *www. kildrummycastlehotel.com* ⊙ *Closed Jan.* 🍴 *16 rooms* 🍽️ *Breakfast.*

ALFORD

9 miles east of Kildrummy, 28 miles west of Aberdeen.

A plain and sturdy settlement in the Howe (Hollow) of Alford, this town gives those who have grown somewhat weary of castle-hopping a break: it has a museum instead. Craigievar Castle and Castle Fraser are nearby, though.

GETTING HERE AND AROUND

The town is on A944.

ESSENTIALS

Visitor Information **Alford Visitor Information Centre.** ✉ *Grampian Transport Museum, Montgarrie Rd.* ☎ *01975/562650* ⊕ *www.visitscotland.com/info/ services/alford-information-centre-p332251.*

EXPLORING

Fodor's Choice
★

Castle Fraser. The massive Castle Fraser is the ancestral home of the Frasers and one of the largest of the castles of Mar; it's certainly a contender as one of the grandest castles in the northeast. Although the well-furnished building shows a variety of styles reflecting the taste of its owners from the 15th through the 19th century, its design is typical of the cavalcade of castles in the region, and for good reason. This—along with many others, including Midmar, Craigievar, Crathes, and Glenbuchat—was designed by a family of master masons called Bell. There are plenty of family items, but don't miss the two Turret Rooms—one of which is the trophy room—and Major Smiley's Room. He married into the family but is famous for having been one of the escapees from Colditz (a high-security prisoner-of-war camp) during World War II. The walled garden includes a 19th-century knot garden, with colorful flower beds, box hedging, gravel paths, and splendid herbaceous borders. Have lunch in the tearoom or the picnic area. ✉ *Off A944, 8 miles southeast of Alford* ☎ *01330/833463* ⊕ *www.nts.org.uk* ✉ *£10.50* ⊙ *Apr. and June–Sept., Wed.–Sun. 11–5; July and Aug., daily 11–5; Oct., Wed.–Sun. noon–5; last admission 45 mins before closing.*

Craigievar Castle. Much as the stonemasons left it in 1626, Craigievar Castle has pepper-pot turrets that make it an outstanding example of a tower house. Striking and well preserved, it has many family furnishings, and the lovely grounds are worth exploring, too. Craigievar was built in relatively peaceful times by William Forbes, a successful merchant in trade with the Baltic Sea ports (he was also known as Danzig Willie). ✉ *A980, 5 miles south of Alford* ☎ *01339/883635* ⊕ *www.nts. org.uk* ✉ *£12.50* ⊙ *Apr.–June and Sept., Fri.–Tues. 11–4:45; July and Aug., daily 11–4:45.*

FAMILY
Fodor's Choice
★

Grampian Transport Museum. The entertaining and enthusiastically run Grampian Transport Museum specializes in road-based means of locomotion, backed up by an archives and library. Its collection of buses and trams is second to none, but the Craigievar Express, a steam-driven creation invented by the local postman to deliver mail more efficiently, is the most unusual. Look out for the Hillman Imp: if Scotland has a national car, this is it. There's a small café that offers tea, baked goods, and ice cream. ✉ *Montgarrie Rd.* ☎ *01975/562292* ⊕ *www. gtm.org.uk* ✉ *£9.50 (includes 2 children)* ⊙ *Apr.–Sept., daily 10–5; Oct., daily 10–4.*

THE NORTHEAST AND THE MALT WHISKY TRAIL

North of Deeside another popular area of this region lies inland, toward Speyside—the valley, or strath, of the River Spey—famed for its whisky distilleries, some of which it promotes in another signposted trail. Distilling Scotch is not an intrinsically spectacular process. It involves pure water, malted barley, and sometimes peat smoke, then a lot of bubbling and fermentation, all of which cause a number of odd smells. The result is a prestigious product with a fascinating range of flavors that you may either enjoy immensely or not at all.

Instead of closely following the Malt Whisky Trail, dip into it and blend visits to distilleries with some other aspects of the county of Moray, particularly its coastline. Whisky notwithstanding, Moray's scenic qualities, low rainfall, and other reassuring weather statistics are worth remembering. You can also sample the northeastern seaboard, including some of the best but least-known coastal scenery in Scotland.

DUFFTOWN

54 miles west of Aberdeen.

On one of the Spey tributaries, Dufftown was planned in 1817 by the Earl of Fife. Its simple cross layout with a square and a large clock tower (originally from Banff and now the site of the visitor center) is typical of a small Scottish town built in the 19th century. Its simplicity is made all the more stark by the brooding, heather-clad hills that rise around it. Dufftown is convenient to a number of distilleries.

GETTING HERE AND AROUND

To get here from Aberdeen, drive west on A96 and A920; then turn west at Huntly. It's not easy or quick, but you can take the train to Elgin or Keith and then the bus to Dufftown.

EXPLORING
TOP ATTRACTIONS

Fodor's Choice ★ **Balvenie Distillery.** Offering just a handful of tours each week, you'd think that Balvenie Distillery didn't want visitors. Yet as soon as you step into the old manager's office—now gently restored and fitted with knotted-elm furniture—you realize Balvenie just wants to make sure that all visitors get to see, smell, and feel the magic of the making of this malt. Balvenie is unusual because it has its own cooperage with six coopers hard at work turning the barrels. During the three-hour tour you'll see the mashing, fermentation, and distillation process, culminating in a five-malt tasting session. ⊠ *Balvenie St.* ☏ *01340/822210* ⊕ *www. thebalvenie.com* ⊠ *£35* ⊙ *Tours Mon.–Thurs. at 10 and 2, Fri. at 10.*

Fodor's Choice ★ **Glenfiddich Distillery.** Many make Glenfiddich Distillery their first stop on the Malt Whisky Trail. The independent company of William Grant and Sons Limited was the first to realize the tourist potential of the distilling process. The company began offering tours around the typical pagoda-roof malting buildings and subsequently built an entertaining

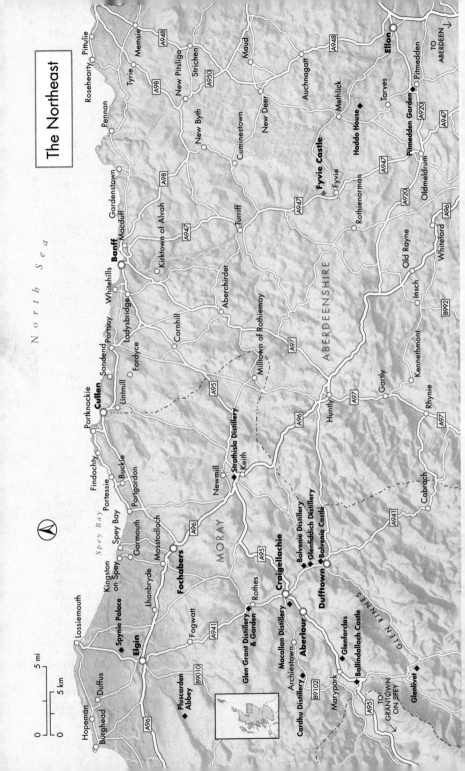

The Northeast

visitor center. Besides a free 20-minute tour of the distillery there's a two-hour in-depth Connoisseurs' Tour (£20; reserve ahead in summer) that includes a special nosing and tasting session. Check out the Malt Barn Bar, serving a limited but tasty menu, and look out for viewings of the current Glenfiddich Distillery Artists in Residence's work. ⊠ *A941, ½ mile north of Dufftown* ☎ *01340/820373* ⊕ *www.glenfiddich.com* 🎫 *£10* ⊘ *Daily 9:30–4.*

Strathisla Distillery. Whisky lovers should take the B9014 11 miles northeast from Dufftown—or alternatively, ride the Keith Dufftown Railway—to see one of Scotland's most iconic distilleries, the Strathisla Distillery, with its cobblestone courtyard and famous double pagoda roofs. Stretching over the picturesque River Isla, the Strathisla Distillery was built in 1786 and now produces the main component of the Chivas Regal blend. Guided tours take you to the mash house, tun room, and still house—all pretty much the same as they were when production began. The tour ends with a tasting session. ⊠ *Seafield Ave., Keith* ☎ *01542/783044* ⊕ *www.maltwhiskydistilleries.com* 🎫 *£7.50* ⊘ *Jan.–mid-Mar., weekdays 10–noon and 1–2; mid-Mar.–mid-Nov., Mon.–Sat. 9:30–5, Sun. noon–5.*

WORTH NOTING
Balvenie Castle. On a mound just above the Glenfiddich Distillery is this grim, gray, and squat curtain-walled castle. This ruined fortress, which dates from the 13th century, once commanded the glens and passes toward Speyside and Elgin. ⊠ *A941* ☎ *01856/761616* ⊕ *www. historic-scotland.gov.uk* 🎫 *£4.50* ⊘ *Apr.–Sept., daily 9:30–5:30; last entry ½ hr before closing.*

Fodor's Choice ★ **Keith and Dufftown Railway.** Leaving from Dufftown three times a day on weekends then returning from Keith, this restored locomotive lets you return to the age when trains were exciting, chugging 11 miles through forests, fields, and across rivers. It passes Drummuir Castle on its way to Keith, home of the Strathisla Distillery. The Buffer Stop restaurant car at the Dufftown Station serves snacks, scones, and tea. Reservations are a good idea. ⊠ *Dufftown Station, Station Rd.* ☎ *01340/821181* ⊕ *www. keith-dufftown-railway.co.uk* 🎫 *£6.50 or £10 return* ⊘ *Easter–Sept., weekends.*

Mortlach Church. Set in a hollow by the Dullan Water, Mortlach Church is thought to be one of Scotland's oldest Christian sites, perhaps founded by St. Luag, a contemporary of St. Columba, as early as AD 566. Note the weathered Pictish cross in the churchyard and the even older stone under cover in the vestibule, with a strange Pictish elephantlike beast carved on it. Though much of the church was rebuilt after 1876, some early work survives, including three lancet windows from the 13th century and a leper's squint (a hole extended to the outside of the church so that lepers could hear the service but be kept away from the rest of the congregation). ⊠ *Church St.*

WHERE TO STAY
$
B&B/INN
Castleview. Next to the babbling Burn of Mackalea, the tranquil Castleview has rooms that are quite small but beautifully dressed and well maintained. **Pros:** colorful garden; fabulous views; bountiful

CLOSE UP

Whisky, the Water of Life

Conjured from an innocuous mix of malted barley, water, and yeast, malt whisky is for many synonymous with Scotland. Clans produced whisky for hundreds of years before it emerged as Scotland's national drink and major export. Today those centuries of expertise result in a sublimely subtle drink with many different layers of flavor. Each distillery produces a malt with—to the expert—instantly identifiable, predominant notes peculiarly its own.

WHISKY TYPES AND STYLES

There are two types of whisky: malt and grain. Malt whisky, generally acknowledged to have a more sophisticated bouquet and flavor, is made with malted barley—barley that is soaked in water until the grains germinate and then is dried to halt the germination, all of which adds extra flavor and a touch of sweetness to the brew. Grain whisky also contains malted barley, but with the addition of unmalted barley and maize.

Blended whiskies, which make up many of the leading brands, usually balance malt- and grain-whisky distillations; deluxe blends contain a higher percentage of malts. Blends that contain several malt whiskies are called "vatted malts." Whisky connoisseurs often prefer to taste the single malts: the unblended whisky from a single distillery.

In simple terms, malt whiskies may be classified into "eastern" and "western" in style, with the whisky made in the east of Scotland, for example in Speyside, being lighter and sweeter than the products of the Western Isles, which often have a taste of peat smoke or even iodine.

The production process is, by comparison, relatively straightforward: just malt your barley, mash it, ferment it, and distill it, then mature to perfection. To find out the details, join a distillery tour, and be rewarded with a dram. Check out 🌐 *www.scotlandwhisky.com* for more information.

TASTING WHISKY

When tasting whisky, follow these simple steps. First, pour a dram. Turn and tilt the glass to coat the sides. Smell the whisky, "nosing" to inhale the heady aromas. If you want, you can add a little water and turn the glass gently to watch it "marry" with the whisky, nosing as you go. Take a wee sip and swirl it over your tongue and sense what connoisseurs call the "mouthfeel." Swallow and admire the finish. Repeat until convinced it's a good malt!

breakfasts. **Cons:** half-hour walk into town; not for anyone with a cat allergy. [$] *Rooms from: £80* ✉ *A920, 2½ miles east of Dufftown* ☎ *01340/820941* 🌐 *www.castleviewdufftown.com* 💳 *No credit cards* 🛏 *3 rooms* 🍴 *Breakfast.*

SHOPPING

Collector's Cabin. Two adjoining shops—one with Scottish silver, fossils, and book illustrations, the other with kilts, ceramics, and other curiosities—are filled with conversation starters. This is truly a trove worth delving into. ✉ *22 and 24 Balvenie St.* ☎ *01340/821393* 🕒 *Closed Wed.*

Dufftown Glassworks. This light and airy gallery sells interesting fused and painted glass, as well as prints and crafts by local makers. The adjoining café sells the best coffee in Dufftown, leaf tea, and a good selection of cakes from scones to lemon drizzle to gooey chocolate. ⊠ *16 Conval St.* ☎ *01340/821069* ⊕ *dufftownglassworks.com.*

CRAIGELLACHIE

4 miles northwest of Dufftown via A941.

Renowned as an angling resort, Craigellachie, like so many settlements on the River Spey, is sometimes enveloped in the malty reek of the local industry. Glen Grant is one of the distilleries nearby. The Spey itself is crossed by a handsome suspension bridge, designed by noted engineer Thomas Telford (1757–1834) in 1814 and now bypassed by the modern road.

GETTING HERE AND AROUND

The town is on A491; it's best to drive here, as public transportation is infrequent and complicated.

EXPLORING

Fodor'sChoice
★
Glen Grant Distillery & Garden. James Grant founded a distillery in 1840 when he was only 25, and it was the first in the country to be electrically powered. This place will come as a welcome relief to companions of dedicated Malt Whisky Trail followers, because in addition to the distillery there's a large and beautiful garden. It's planted and tended as Grant envisioned, with orchards and woodland walks, log bridges over waterfalls, a magnificent lily pond, and azaleas and rhododendrons in profusion. Using peculiarly tall stills and special purifiers that follow a design introduced over a century ago, Glen Grant produces a distinctive pale-gold whisky with an almost floral or fruity finish. The tour is excellent value, with perhaps the friendliest guides and certainly the most generous tastings. There's a coffee shop, too, selling huge scones. ⊠ *A941, Rothes* ☎ *01340/832118* ⊕ *www.glengrant.com* ✉ *£5* ⊙ *Apr–Oct., daily 9:30–4; Nov.–Mar., Mon.–Sat. 9:30–4, Sun. noon–5.*

Macallan Distillery. On the sprawling Easter Elchies Estate, Macallan Distillery offers unique whisky matured in sherry casks and, more recently, in oak bourbon casks. The tour lasts 1 hour and 45 minutes and, aiming to give you a full understanding of the six pillars of whisky making, it takes you from the still house to the warehouse where maturation takes place, finishing off with a nosing and tasting session. Booking is essential. ⊠ *Off B9102* ☎ *01304/872280* ⊕ *www.themacallan.com* ✉ *£15* ⊙ *Easter–Sept., Mon.–Sat. 9:30–6; Oct.–Easter, weekdays 9:30–5.*

Fodor'sChoice
★
Speyside Cooperage and Visitor Centre. A major stop on the Malt Whisky Trail, the huge Speyside Cooperage and Visitor Centre is a must for all whisky fans. Retired coopers will talk you through the making of the casks, a surprisingly physical and dramatic process that uses the same tools and skills employed for hundreds of years. Inside you can watch highly skilled craftspeople make and repair oak barrels used in the local whisky industry. The Acorn to Cask exhibit tells all about the ancient craft of coopering. There's a cottage café with

CHOOSING A DISTILLERY TOUR

Like whiskies, distillery tours are not the same, though you'll usually spend about an hour or two at each place. The company's history, size, and commercial savvy create different experiences. You should also investigate any special in-depth tours if you're willing to pay extra and spend more time. Here's a cheat sheet to help you choose a tour or two to suit your taste.

Balvenie: This distillery's tour is for those who want to understand and celebrate the details of distilling. No other distillery lets you see and smell the malting floor before watching the coopers turn their barrels.

Cardhu: Architecturally, the stocky buildings and proud towers of Cardhu, formerly an illicit still, seem to have a grim defiance. The tour gives you a great understanding of whisky's simple ingredients, including locally sourced spring water, and the process it undergoes.

Glen Grant: The distillery tour is good, but the gardens of Major Grant are sublime. He traveled the world collecting species and created a Victorian garden that has been gloriously restored.

Glenfarclas: This proud family-owned still may not provide the slickness of the Glenfiddich tour, but

the quiet passion of the still workers and their belief in their whisky is more powerful than a dram of the stuff.

Glenfiddich: Owned by the same family since day one, this distillery offers both entry-level and enthusiasts' tours that cover the older, more atmospheric buildings and the swankier visitor center.

Glenlivet: It's a beautiful drive to this, the first licensed distillery in the Highlands. You'll learn the fascinating story of Glenlivet's founder, George Smith.

Macallan: Situated on the green and pleasant Easter Elchies Estate, this vast distillery is dominated by a warehouse with row upon row of sherry casks imbuing this whisky with its sweetness.

Speyside Cooperage: Although this isn't a distillery, real whisky enthusiasts shouldn't miss a visit to one of the few remaining cooperages in Scotland. Watch the coopers at work and see just how much craft goes into making and treating these precious barrels.

Strathisla: Home of Chivas, not a malt but a fine blended whisky, this is perhaps one of the prettiest and most compact distilleries in the northeast and is delightfully situated on the River Isla.

huge cakes and sandwiches for those in need of sustenance. ✉ *Duff-town Rd.* ☎ *01340/871108* ⊕ *www.speysidecooperage.co.uk* 💷 *£3.50* 🕐 *Weekdays 9–4.*

WHERE TO EAT AND STAY

$$ ✕ **Copper Dog.** Exposed stonework and mismatched wooden chairs
BRITISH makes the restaurant of the Craigellachie Hotel feel cozy and informal. The menu is equally relaxed, with dishes such as locally produced gourmet sausages and rumble thumps (potato, cabbage, and onions) and an outstanding platter of Scottish cheeses with homemade chutney,

all of which can be matched with regional craft beers. [$] *Average main: £15* ✉ *Criagellachie Hotel, Victoria St.* ☎ *01340/881204* 🌐 *www.craigellachiehotel.co.uk.*

$$ HOTEL Fodor's Choice ★ **Craigellachie Hotel.** Locals gasped in horror when the owner of London nightclubs bought this hotel, but, in giving it a complete overhaul, it's won back its gentle Speyside charm lost over many years of piecemeal refurbishment. **Pros:** stylish decor down to the details; perfectly pitched service. **Cons:** popular, so book ahead; lots of weddings. [$] *Rooms from: £150* ✉ *Victoria St.* ☎ *01340/881204* 🌐 *www.craigellachiehotel.co.uk* 🛏 *28 rooms* 🍴 *Breakfast.*

$$ B&B/INN **Highlander Inn.** Don't be fooled by the rather alpine exterior: this very Scottish hotel prides itself on its whisky bar and its friendly welcome. **Pros:** simple accommodations; warm atmosphere; great bar. **Cons:** dated decor; could be rather too lively for some. [$] *Rooms from: £108* ✉ *Victoria St.* ☎ *01340/881446* 🌐 *www.whiskyinn.com* 🛏 *5 rooms* 🍴 *Breakfast.*

ABERLOUR

2 miles southwest of Craigellachie.

Aberlour, often listed as Charlestown of Aberlour on maps, is a handsome little burgh, essentially Victorian in style, though actually founded in 1812 by the local landowner. The names of the noted local whisky stills are Cragganmore, Aberlour, and Glenfarclas; Glenlivet and Cardhu are also nearby. Also in Aberlour is Walkers, famous for producing shortbread, tins of buttery, crumbly goodness, since 1898.

7

GETTING HERE AND AROUND

Aberlour is on A95; public transportation here is infrequent.

EXPLORING

Ballindalloch Castle. The family home of the Macpherson-Grants since 1546, Ballindalloch Castle—known as the Pearl of the North—is the quintessential castle you've probably seen in a miniseries made by the BBC. You can wander around the beautifully kept rooms and meticulously tended gardens at your leisure; you may even bump into the lord and lady of the manor, who live here all year. There's also a splendid tea shop offering large slices of cake. Anglers take note: The estate offers a limited number of permits for fishing on the banks of the Spey and the Avon. It's 8 miles southwest of Craigellachie. ✉ *Off A95* ☎ *01807/500205* 🌐 *www.ballindallochcastle.co.uk* 🎟 *£10.50* ⏲ *Easter–Sept., Sun.–Fri. 10–5 (last entry 45 mins before closing).*

Cardhu Distillery. The striking outline of Cardhu Distillery, whose main product lies at the heart of Johnnie Walker Blends, is set among the heather-clad Mannoch Hills. Established by John and Helen Cumming in 1811, it was officially founded in 1824 after distilling was made legal by the Excise Act of 1823. Today Cardhu is owned by the superbrewer Diageo (which tried to rename it Cardow, although the single malt is still known as Cardhu). Guides take you to the mashing, fermenting, and distilling halls, and they explain the malting process that now takes place on the coast at Burghead. Take time to walk around the attractive grounds or picnic there. Cardhu is 10 miles north of Glenlivet and 7 miles west of Aberlour. ⊠ *B1902, Knockando* ☎ *01340/875635* ⊕ *www.scotlandwhisky.com* 🕮 *£5–£14* 🕙 *Oct.–Apr., weekdays 11–3; May and June, weekdays 10–5; July–Sept., Mon.–Sat. 10–5, Sun. 11–4; last tour 1 hr before closing.*

Glenfarclas. In an age when most small distilleries have been taken over by multinationals, Glenfarclas remains family owned, passed down from father to son since 1865. That link to the past is most visible among its low buildings, where the retired still sits outside: if you didn't know what it was, you could mistake it for part of a submarine. The tours end with tastings in the superlative Ship Room, the intact lounge of an ocean liner called the *Empress of Australia*. An in-depth Connoisseur's Tour and tasting is available at 2 pm on Fridays in high season for £40 or, for £90, the Five Decades Tour & Tasting which is by appointment only. ⊠ *Off A95, Ballindalloch* ☎ *01807/500345* ⊕ *www.glenfarclas.co.uk* 🕮 *£5* 🕙 *Oct.–Mar., weekdays 10–4; Apr.–June, weekdays 10–5, July–Sept., weekdays 10–5, Sun. 10–4.*

Glenlivet. The famous Glenlivet was the first licensed distillery in the Highlands, founded in 1824 by George Smith. Today it produces one of the best-known 12-year-old single malts in the world. The free distillery tour reveals the inside of the huge bonded warehouse where the whisky steeps in oak casks. The tour has two aspects: the Spirit of the Glen examines how unique factors come together to make this nectar, and the 45-minute distillery tour looks at the dream of the distillery's founder. There is another tour—the Glenlivet Inspiration (£35)—and a tutored tasting session, the Legacy Experience (£60), for those who can't get enough. There's a coffee shop with baked goods and, of course, a whisky shop. Glenlivet is 10 miles southwest of Aberlour via A95 and B9008. ⊠ *Off B9008, Ballindalloch* ☎ *01340/821720* ⊕ *www.glenlivet. com* 🕮 *Free* 🕙 *Apr.–Oct., Mon.–Sat. 9:30–4, Sun. noon–4.*

WHERE TO EAT AND STAY

$
CAFÉ
✕**Old Pantry.** This pleasantly rustic corner restaurant overlooks Aberlour's tree-shaded central square. The kitchen serves—albeit sometimes slowly—everything from a cup of coffee with a sticky cake at teatime to a three-course spread of soup, roasted meat, and traditional pudding. 💲 *Average main: £9* ⊠ *The Square* ☎ *01340/871617* 🕙 *No dinner Oct.–May.*

$$
B&B/INN
Fodor's Choice
★
🖼**Cardhu Country House.** This once-abandoned manse (minister's house) looks as if it has always been loved and lived in: huge bedrooms with wooden floors, antique fireplaces, and large beds dressed in Harris tweed throws are married to contemporary bathrooms. **Pros:** period charm and modern comforts; tasty meals. **Cons:** you need a car to get here. 💲 *Rooms from: £120* ⊠ *Off B9102, Knockando* ☎ *01340/810895* ⊕ *www. cardhucountryhouse.co.uk* 🚫 *No credit cards* ⤶ *6 rooms* 🍽 *Breakfast.*

$$
B&B/INN
Fodor's Choice
★
🖼**Mash Tun.** Curvy yet sturdy, this former station hotel harks back to a time when Aberlour was a busy holiday destination on the Aberdeen–Aviemore train line. **Pros:** superb accommodations; tasty meals; great atmosphere in the restaurant and bar. **Cons:** book well ahead in summer. 💲 *Rooms from: £105* ⊠ *8 Broomfield Sq.* ☎ *01340/881771* ⊕ *www. mashtun-aberlour.com* ⤶ *4 rooms, 1 suite* 🍽 *Breakfast.*

SHOPPING

Speyside Pottery. A couple of miles west of Aberlour, look for Speyside Pottery, where Thomas and Anne Gough produce domestic stoneware in satisfying, sturdy traditional shapes. Call ahead for an appointment November to March. ✉ *A95, Ballindalloch* ☎ *01807/500338* ⊕ *www. speysidepottery.co.uk* ☉ *Apr.–Oct. daily 10–5.*

ELGIN

15 miles north of Craigellachie, 69 miles northwest of Aberdeen, 41 miles east of Inverness.

As the center of the fertile Laigh (low-lying lands) of Moray, Elgin has been of local importance for centuries. Sheltered by great hills to the south, the city lies between two major rivers, the Spey and the Findhorn. Beginning in the 13th century, Elgin became an important religious center, a cathedral city with a walled town growing up around the cathedral and adjacent to the original settlement.

Elgin prospered, and by the early 18th century it became a mini-Edinburgh of the north and a place where country gentlemen spent their winters. It even echoed Edinburgh in carrying out wide-scale reconstruction in the 18th century. Many fine neoclassical buildings survive today despite much misguided demolition in the late 20th century for better traffic flow. However, the central main-street plan and some of the older little streets and *wynds* (alleyways) remain.

GETTING HERE AND AROUND

Elgin is on the A96 road from Aberdeen to Inverness. The A941 runs north from the distillery area to the city. There's a train stop here on the line that links Aberdeen and Inverness: Aberdeen is 90 minutes away.

ESSENTIALS

Visitor Information Elgin Visitor Information Point. ✉ *Elgin Library, Cooper Park* ☎ *01343/562608.*

EXPLORING

TOP ATTRACTIONS

Elgin Cathedral. Cooper Park contains a magnificent ruin, the Elgin Cathedral, consecrated in 1224. Its eventful story included devastation by fire: a 1390 act of retaliation by bandit Alexander Stewart (circa 1343–1405), the Wolf of Badenoch. The illegitimate son of King David II (1324–71) had sought revenge for his excommunication by the bishop of Moray. The cathedral was rebuilt but finally fell into disuse after the Reformation in 1560. By 1567 the highest authority in the land, the regent earl of Moray, had stripped the lead from the roof to pay for his army. Thus ended the career of the religious seat known as the Lamp of the North. Some traces of the cathedral settlement survive—the gateway Pann's Port and the Bishop's Palace—although they've been drastically altered. ✉ *Cooper Park* ☎ *01343/547171* ⊕ *www.historic-scotland.gov. uk* 🎟 *£5.50; £7.20 with Spynie Palace* ☉ *Apr.–Sept., daily 9:30–5:30; Oct.–Mar., Sat.–Wed. 9:30–4:30; last admission ½ hr before closing.*

St. Giles Church. At the center of Elgin, the most conspicuous structure is St. Giles Church, which divides High Street. The grand foursquare building, constructed in 1828, exhibits the Greek Revival style: note the columns, the pilasters, and the top of the spire, surmounted by a representation of the Lysicrates Monument. ⊠ *High St.* ⊕ *www. elginstgileschurch.co.uk.*

WORTH NOTING

OFF THE
BEATEN
PATH

Pluscarden Abbey. Given the general destruction caused by the 16th-century upheaval of the Reformation, abbeys in Scotland tend to be ruinous and deserted, but at the 13th-century Pluscarden Abbey the ancient way of life continues. Monks from Prinknash Abbey near Gloucester, England, returned here in 1948, and the abbey is now a Benedictine community. Mass is at 9 (10 on Sunday) and is sung by the monks using Gregorian chant. ⊠ *Off B9010, 6 miles southwest of Elgin* ⊕ *www. pluscardenabbey.org* 🖼 *Free* ⊙ *Daily 4:30 am–8:30 pm.*

Spynie Palace. Just north of Elgin sits Spynie Palace, the impressive 15th-century former headquarters of the bishops of Moray. It has now fallen into ruin, though the top of the tower has good views over the Laigh of Moray. Find it by turning right off the Elgin–Lossiemouth road. ⊠ *Off A941* ☎ *01343/546358* ⊕ *www.historic-scotland.gov.uk* 🖼 *£4.50; £7.20 with Elgin Cathedral* ⊙ *Apr.–Sept., daily 9:30–6:30; Oct.–Mar., weekends 9:30–4:30; last admission ½ hr before closing.*

SHOPPING

Gordon and MacPhail. An outstanding delicatessen and wine merchant, Gordon and MacPhail also stocks rare malt whiskies. This is a good place to shop for gifts for your foodie friends. ⊠ *58–60 South St.* ☎ *01343/545110* ⊕ *www.gordonandmacphail.com.*

Johnstons of Elgin. This woolen mill has a worldwide reputation for its luxury fabrics, especially cashmere. The large shop stocks not only the firm's own products, but also top-quality Scottish crafts. There's a coffee shop on the premises. Free tours of the mill must be booked in advance. ⊠ *Newmill Rd.* ☎ *01343/554088* ⊕ *www.johnstonscashmere.com.*

GOLF

Moray Golf Club. Discover the relatively mild microclimate of what vacationing Victorians dubbed the Moray Riviera, as Tom Morris did in 1889 when he was inspired by the lay of the natural links. Henry Cotton's New Course (1979) has tighter fairways and smaller greens. A handicap certificate is required for the Old Course. ⊠ *Stotfield Rd., Lossiemouth* ☎ *01343/812018* ⊕ *www.moraygolf.co.uk* 🖼 *Old Course, £80; New Course, £30; joint ticket £90* 🏌 *Old Course: 18 holes, 6995 yards, par 71; New Course: 18 holes, 6008 yards, par 69* ⊙ *Daily.*

FOCHABERS

9 miles east of Elgin.

With its hanging baskets of fuchsia in summer and its perfectly mowed village square, Fochabers has a cared-for charm that makes you want to stop here, even just to stretch your legs. Lying just to the south of the River Spey, the former market town was founded in 1776 by the Duke of Gordon. The duke moved the village from its original site because it was too close to Gordon Castle. Famous today for being home to the Baxters brand of soups and jams, Fochabers is near some of the best berry fields: come and pick your own in the summer months.

GETTING HERE AND AROUND

Fochabers is not on the Inverness-to-Aberdeen train line, but there is an hourly bus service (Stagecoach Bluebird number 10) from Fochabers to Elgin. It's near the junction of A98 and A96.

EXPLORING

TOP ATTRACTIONS

Baxters Highland Village. A mile west of the center of Fochabers, you can see the works of a major local employer, Baxters of Fochabers. From Tokyo to New York, upmarket stores stock the company's soups, jams, chutneys, and other gourmet products—all of which are made here, close to the River Spey. Take home a can of Royal Game Soup, a favorite of the late Queen Mum. Watch cooking demonstrations, have a look at a re-creation of the Baxters' first grocery shop, or browse around the Best of Scotland, specializing in all kinds of Scottish products. A restaurant serves up an assortment of delectables. ⊠ *A96* ☎ *01343/820666* ⊕ *www.baxters.com* ✆ *Free* ⊘ *Daily 10–5.*

Fochabers Folk Museum & Heritage Centre. Once over the Spey Bridge and past the cricket ground (a very unusual sight in Scotland), you can find the symmetrical, 18th-century Fochabers village square. The old Pringle Church is now the home of the Fochabers Folk Museum, which boasts a fine collection of items relating to past life of all types of residents in the village and surrounding area. Exhibits include carts and carriages, farm implements, domestic labor-saving devices, and an exquisite collection of Victorian toys. ⊠ *High St.* ☎ *01343/821204* ⊕ *www.fochabers-heritage.org.uk* ✆ *Free* ⊘ *Easter–Oct., Tues.–Fri. 11–4, weekends 2–4.*

Gordon Chapel. One of the village's lesser-known treasures is the Gordon Chapel, which has an exceptional set of stained-glass windows by Pre-Raphaelite artist Sir Edward Burne-Jones. Look out for the Good Shepherd, carrying a newborn lamb around his neck. ⊠ *Castle St., just off The Square.*

WORTH NOTING

Earth Pillars. Consider diverting onto the road that runs south directly opposite the Fochabers Folk Museum. Leaving the houses behind for well-hedged country lanes, you can discover a Forestry Commission sign to the Earth Pillars. These curious eroded yet still vivid red sandstone pillars form the bank of the River Spey and are framed by tall-trunk pines.

Scottish Traditional Boat Festival. Take the A98 to the old fishing town of Portsoy, home of the ebullient Scottish Traditional Boat Festival one weekend in late June. The harbor fills with skiffs and rowboats, while the harborside hosts boatbuilders, crafts stalls promoting the work of knitters and weavers, cooking demonstrations—focusing on fish, of course—and street musicians. ⊠ *Portsoy* ⊕ *www.stbfportsoy.com.*

WHERE TO EAT

$$ ✕**Gordon Castle Walled Garden Cafe.** With light streaming through the
BRITISH large windows onto the wooden tables and rattan chairs, there is an
Fodor's Choice airiness and freshness to this new eatery. Fish landed just a few miles
★ away on the Moray coast is a good bet as are the well-hung steaks.
Either way be sure to finish with one of their seasonal fruit panna cotta:
there's elderflower in June and raspberry and strawberry in July and
August, all from the estate's walled gardens which you can visit. $ *Average main: £15* ✉ *Fochabers* ✛ *Just off A96, Fochabers Bypass Rd.*
☎ *01343/612333* ⊕ *www.gordoncastlescotland.com* ☉ *Sun.–Thurs.10–
8; Fri. and Sat.10–late* ▭ *No credit cards.*

SHOPPING

Frockabers. Here you'll find vintage clothing and accessories from hand-
embroidered '50s aprons to Harris tweed plus-fours worn for golf.
Wondering who once owned these clothes is entertainment in itself.
✉ *48 High St.* ☎ *0751/5107558 mobile.*

Just Art. If you're interested in works by local artists, head to Just Art,
a fine gallery with imaginative, often fun contemporary ceramics and
paintings. ✉ *64 High St.* ☎ *01343/820500* ⊕ *www.justart.co.uk.*

FAMILY **The Quaich.** While they do still sell some cards and gifts, it's the café
Fodor's Choice this place is loved for. Their tasty and filling breakfasts are popular
★ with those walking the Speyside Way but it's their easygoing abil-
ity to cater for everyone—from vegetarians to children (crayons and
paper are provided)—that makes this an excellent stop. ✉ *85 High St.*
☎ *01343/820981* ☉ *Closed Mon.*

Watt's Antiques. This shop has small collectables, jewelry, ornaments,
and china. ✉ *45 High St.* ☎ *01343/820077* ⊕ *www.wattsantiques.com.*

CULLEN

13 miles east of Fochabers, 3 miles east of Findochty.

Fodor's Choice Look for some wonderfully painted homes at Cullen, in the old fishing
★ town below the railway viaduct. The real attractions of this charming
little seaside resort, however, are its white-sand beach (the water is quite
cold, though) and the fine view west toward the aptly named Bowfiddle
Rock. In summer Cullen bustles with families carrying buckets and
spades and eating ice cream and chips.

A stroll past the small but once busy harbor reveals numerous fishers'
cottages, huddled together with small yards where they dried their nets.
Beyond these, the vast stretch of beach curves gently round the bay.
Above are the disused Victorian viaduct—formerly the Peterhead train
line—and the 18th-century town.

GETTING HERE AND AROUND
Cullen is on A98, on Cullen Bay.

EXPLORING
Seafield Street. The town has a fine *mercat* (market) cross and one main
street—Seafield Street—that splits the town. It holds numerous specialty
shops—antiques and gift stores, an ironmonger, a baker, a pharmacy, and
a locally famous ice-cream shop among them—as well as several cafés.

QUICK BITE

🍴 Ice Cream Shop. In summer it can seem as if everyone you see in Cullen is licking a cone from the Ice Cream Shop. There's only a handful of flavors but they are all made on-site. It also sells an abundance of sweets familiar to those who were kids in the '70s or '80s. ✉ *40 Seafield St.* ☎ *01542/840484.*

WHERE TO EAT AND STAY

$ CAFÉ Fodor's Choice ★ **🍴 Castle of Park.** Castle of Park was built in 1536 on the site of a stronghold established in the 13th century, and the Breakfast Room (from 10 to 4 pm) feels just like dining in the family quarters of a castle, with old-fashioned tablecloths and wooden dressers. Choose from delicious soups with homemade bread and a fine selection of thoroughly desirable cakes before walking it all off in the stunning gardens that include a labyrinth. They also have three beautifully furnished bedrooms (from £110 per night). [$] *Average main: £5* ✉ *Cornhill* ✥ *Just off the B9023* ☎ *01466/751595* 🌐 *www.castleofpark.co.uk* ⏲ *No dinner* 💳 *No credit cards.*

$ SEAFOOD **🍴 Linda's Fish & Chips.** This casual place serves the freshest fish, caught in nearby Buckie and cooked to crispy perfection (gluten-free batter is available, too). There's a seating area inside, but it's best for takeout. You can walk down the hill and head toward the harbor for some benches with sweeping views: a nice spot for a meal. [$] *Average main: £8* ✉ *54 Seafield St.* ☎ *01542/840202.*

$ SEAFOOD Fodor's Choice ★ **🍴 Rockpool.** A newer addition to the Cullen scene, this modish fish restaurant has remarkably reasonable prices for the quality of the food and size of the servings. Try the rich *cullen skink* (a creamy smoked-haddock soup), a pint glass of fat prawns served with mayo and oat bread, or some freshly fried squid with a lime sauce, all beautifully presented on wooden boards. It's also worth mentioning the lovingly crafted cupcakes and the happy staff that takes great delight in serving you your food. [$] *Average main: £8* ✉ *10 The Square* ☎ *01542/841397* 🌐 *www.rockpool-cullen.co.uk* 💳 *No credit cards* ⏲ *Closed Mon. No dinner.*

$ B&B/INN Fodor's Choice ★ **🏨 Academy House.** About 10 minutes from the seaside town of Cullen, this luxurious bed-and-breakfast in a handsome Victorian house was once the headmaster's house for the local secondary school. **Pros:** good home cooking; delightful setting; helpful owners, keen to help you find you way around. **Cons:** rooms book up fast. [$] *Rooms from: £80* ✉ *School Rd., Fordyce* ☎ *01261/842743* 🌐 *www.fordyceaccommodation.com* 💳 *No credit cards* 🛏 *2 rooms* 🍽 *Breakfast.*

SHOPPING

Abra Antiques. With surprisingly pleasing prices, Abra Antiques overflows with all kinds of trinkets, Victoriana, antiquarian books, and Scottish miscellany. ✉ *6 Seafield St.* ☎ *01542/840605* ⏲ *Closed Wed.*

BANFF

36 miles east of Elgin, 47 miles north of Aberdeen.

Midway along the northeast coast, overlooking Moray Firth and the estuary of the River Deveron, Banff is a fishing town of considerable

7

elegance that feels as though it's a million miles from tartan-clad Scotland. Part Georgian, like Edinburgh's New Town, and part 16th-century small burgh, like Culross, Banff is an exemplary east-coast salty town, with a tiny harbor and fine architecture. It's also within easy reach of plenty of unspoiled coastline—cliff and rock to the east, at Gardenstown (known as Gamrie) and Pennan, or beautiful little sandy beaches westward toward Sandend and Cullen.

GETTING HERE AND AROUND
Banff is on the A98 coastal road and at the end of the tree-lined A947 to Aberdeen. If you are relying on public transportation, Bus 325 from Aberdeen Bus Station takes two hours and gets you into Low Street, just five minutes from Duff House.

ESSENTIALS
Visitor Information **Banff Visitor Information Centre.** ⊠ *Collie Lodge, Low St.* ☎ *01261/812419.*

EXPLORING
Fodor'sChoice ★ **Duff House.** The jewel in Banff's crown is the grand mansion of Duff House, a splendid William Adam–designed (1689–1748) Georgian mansion. Used as a swish hotel in the Roaring Twenties before becoming a sanatorium and then a military base, it lay empty and mouldering for years before it was restored in 1995 by the National Galleries of Scotland. It exhibits many fine paintings, including works by El Greco, Sir Henry Raeburn, and Thomas Gainsborough. A good tearoom and a gift shop are on the ground floor. ⊠ *Off A98* ☎ *01261/818181* ⊕ *www.duffhouse.org.uk* ⊡ *£7.10* ⊙ *Apr.–Oct., daily 11–5; Nov.–Mar., Thurs.–Sun. 11–4; last admission 45 mins before closing.*

FAMILY **Macduff Marine Aquarium.** Across the river in Banff's twin town, Macduff, on the shore east of the harbor, stands the conical Macduff Marine Aquarium. A 250,000-gallon central tank and many smaller display areas and touch pools show the sea life of the Moray Firth and North Atlantic. Clearly run on a shoestring, this place wouldn't be half as good without the staff, who are knowledgeable, inventive, and engaging, especially with children, and there's always some creature to admire—the baby stingrays and octopus cause the most excitement—or watch being fed by divers. ⊠ *11 High Shore* ☎ *01261/833369* ⊕ *www.macduff-aquarium.org.uk* ⊡ *£6.50* ⊙ *Apr.–Oct., weekdays 10–4, weekends 11–5; Nov.–Mar., Sat.–Wed. 11–4.*

GOLF
Duff House Royal Golf Club. Just moments from the sea, this club combines a coastal course with a parkland setting. Close to the center of Banff, it's on the grounds of Duff House, a country-house art gallery in a William Adam–designed mansion. The club has inherited the ancient traditions of seaside play; golf records here go back to the 17th century. ⊠ *The Barnyards, off A98* ☎ *01261/812075* ⊕ *www.duffhouseroyal.com* ⊡ *£40 Apr.–Sept.; £20 Oct.–Mar.* ⟨ *18 holes, 6031 yards, par 68* ⊙ *Daily* ⚲ *Reservations essential.*

Fraserburgh Golf Club. According to parish records, the extensive links around this northeast fishing town have been used for golf since 1613;

the club is relatively new, having been founded in 1777. Be prepared for a steep climb and a tough finish on James Braid's 1922 redesigned Corbiehill Course. The 9-hole Rosehill Course provides a challenging warm-up. ✉ *B9033, off A90, Fraserburgh* ☎ *01346/516616* ⊕ *www. fraserburghgolfclub.org* 🖫 *Corbiehill, weekdays and weekends after 2 pm, £45, weekends until 2 pm, £55; Rosehill, £18* 🏌 *Corbiehill: 18 holes, 6308 yards, par 70; Rosehill: 9 holes, 4832 yards, par 66* ☉ *Daily.*

FYVIE CASTLE

18 miles south of Banff, 18 miles northwest of Ellon.

This castle mixes ancient construction with Edwardian splendor and includes excellent art. The grounds are also worth exploring.

GETTING HERE AND AROUND

If you're driving from Banff, take the A947 south for 20 minutes or so until you see the turnoff.

EXPLORING

Fodor's Choice ★ **Fyvie Castle.** In an area rich with castles, Fyvie Castle stands out as the most complex. Five great towers built by five successive powerful families turned a 13th-century foursquare castle into an opulent Edwardian statement of wealth. Some superb paintings are on view, including 12 works by Sir Henry Raeburn. There are myriad sumptuous interiors—the circular stone staircase is considered one of the best examples in the country—and delightfully laid-out gardens. A former lady of the house, Lillia Drummond, was apparently starved to death by her husband, who entombed her body inside the walls of a secret room. In the 1920s, when the bones were disrupted during renovations, a string of such terrible misfortunes followed that they were quickly returned and the room sealed off. Her name is carved into the windowsill of the Drummond Room. ✉ *Off A947, Turriff* ☎ *01651/819226* ⊕ *www.nts. org.uk* 🖫 *£12.50* ☉ *Apr.–June and Sept., Sat.–Wed. noon–5; July and Aug., daily 11–5; last admission 45 mins before closing.*

ELLON

32 miles southwest of Banff, 14 miles north of Aberdeen.

Formerly a market center on what was then the lowest bridging point of the River Ythan, Ellon, a bedroom suburb of Aberdeen, is a small town at the center of a rural hinterland. It's also well placed for visiting Fyvie Castle and Haddo House.

GETTING HERE AND AROUND

To get to Ellon, take the A947 from Banff or the A90 from Aberdeen; both routes take half an hour.

EXPLORING

Haddo House. Built in 1732, this elegant mansion has a light and graceful Georgian design, with curving wings on either side of a harmonious, symmetrical facade. The interior is late-Victorian ornate, filled with magnificent paintings (including works by Pompeo Batoni and Sir Thomas Lawrence) and plenty of objets d'art. Pre-Raphaelite stained-glass windows by Sir Edward Burne-Jones grace the chapel. Outside is a terrace garden with a fountain, and few yards farther is Haddo Country Park, which has walking trails leading to memorials about the Gordon family. Visits to the house are by prebooked tour only which are held at 11 and 2. ⊠ *Off B999, 8 miles northwest of Ellon* ☎ *01651/851440* ⊕ *www.nts.org.uk* ⊠ *£10* ☉ *Jan.–Mar., weekends 10–6; Apr.–Oct., daily 10–5; Nov.–Mar., weekends 10–4.*

Pitmedden Garden. Five miles west of Ellon, at Pitmedden, is an exquisite re-creation by the National Trust for Scotland of a 17th-century garden. Pitmedden Garden is best visited in summer, from July onward, when annual bedding plants—framed by precision-cut box hedging—form intricate formal patterns. The 100-acre estate also has woodland and farmland walks, as well as the Museum of Farming Life. ⊠ *Off A920, Pitmedden* ☎ *01651 / 843188* ⊕ *www.nts.org.uk* ⊠ *£6.50* ☉ *Garden, shop, museum, and tearoom May–Sept., daily 10–5:30; grounds daily 10–5:30; last entry ½ hr before closing.*

NIGHTLIFE AND PERFORMING ARTS

Haddo House. About 20 miles north of Aberdeen, Haddo House offers a range of events, from highbrow opera, recitals, ballet, and Shakespeare to puppet shows and planting parties in their marvellously laid-out grounds. The season runs from spring through fall. ⊠ *Off B999, Tarves* ☎ *01651 /851440* ⊕ *www.nts.org.uk.*

SHOPPING

Formartine's. More than a shop, with its restaurant, walks, and adventure playground, this food emporium is the place to buy Dee-caught smoked salmon, local cheeses like Cambus O'May and Devenick, and Aberdeenshire-brewed craft beers. ⊠ *Tarves* ✛ *Off B999, 5 miles west of Ellon* ☎ *01651 /851123* ⊕ *www.formartines.com.*

GOLF

Cruden Bay Golf Club. Sheltered behind extensive sand dunes, Cruden Bay offers a typical Scottish golf experience. The narrow channels and deep valleys on the challenging fairways ensure plenty of excitement. Like Gleneagles and Turnberry, this course owes its origins to an association with the grand railway hotels built in the heyday of steam. The hotel may be gone, but the course remains in fine shape. Weekend tee times are extremely limited; book months in advance. ⊠ *Aulton Rd., Cruden Bay* ☎ *01779/812285* ⊕ *www.crudenbaygolfclub.co.uk* ⊠ *Championship, £100; St. Olaf, weekdays £25, weekends £35* ⅃ *Championship: 18 holes, 6287 yards, par 70; St. Olaf: 9 holes, 2463 yards, par 32* ☉ *Daily* ⌲ *Reservations essential.*

ARGYLL AND THE ISLES

Updated
by Mike
Gonzalez

Argyll's rocky seaboard looks out onto islands that were once part of a single prehistoric landmass. Its narrow roads slow travel but give time to admire its lochs and woods, and the ruins that recall the region's dramatic past. Here, too, are grand houses like Brodick and Inveraray castles and elegant gardens such as Crarae. This is whisky country, too: the peaty aroma of Islay's malts are unmistakable. Yet all this is within three hours of Glasgow.

Divided in two by the long peninsula of Kintyre, western Scotland has a complicated, splintered coastline where you'll observe the interplay of sea, loch, and rugged green peninsula. The islands are breathtakingly beautiful, though they often catch the extremely wet weather arriving here from the Atlantic. It is common to experience four seasons in a day, as cliffs and woods suddenly and dramatically disappear in sea mists then reappear just as suddenly.

Ancient castles like Dunstaffnage and the ruined towers on the islands of Loch Awe testify to the region's past importance. Prehistoric peoples left their mark here in the stone circles, carved stones, and Bronze and Iron Age burial mounds around Kilmartin and on Islay and Arran. The gardens of Inveraray and Brodick castles, nourished by the temperate west-coast climate, are the pride of Argyll while the paths of Crarae's, south of Inveraray, wind through plantings of magnolias and azaleas.

The working people of Glasgow traditionally spent their family holidays on the Clyde estuary, taking day trips to Dunoon or Rothesay on the Isle of Bute. From Ardrossan, farther down the coast, ferries cruise to the prosperous and varied Isle of Arran.

Western Scotland's small islands have jagged cliffs or tongues of rock, long white-sand beaches, fertile pastures where sheep and cattle graze, fortresses, and shared memories of clan wars and mysterious beasts. Their cliff paths and lochside byways are a paradise for walkers and cyclists, and their whisky the ideal reward after a long day outside. While the islands' western coasts are dramatic, their more sheltered eastern seaboards are the location for pretty harbor towns like brightly painted Tobermory on Mull, or Port Ellen on Islay, with its neat rows of low whitewashed houses.

ORIENTATION AND PLANNING

GETTING ORIENTED

With long sea lochs carved into its hilly, wooded interior, Argyll is a beguiling interweaving of water and land. The Kintyre Peninsula stretches between the islands of the Firth of Clyde (including Arran)

TOP REASONS TO GO

Whisky, whisky, whisky: Whisky is everywhere, varying subtly in taste and character from distillery to distillery. The unmistakable peaty smell of the whiskies of Islay contrasts with the lighter whiskies of Arran and Oban.

Iona and its abbey: Maybe it's the remoteness that creates the almost mystical sense of history on Iona. From this early center of Scottish Christianity, evangelists traveled throughout Europe from the 6th century onward. It was also the burial place of Scottish kings, including Macbeth.

The great outdoors: Salmon and trout fill the lochs and rivers, while even bigger trophy fish await farther out to sea. Golfers have more than two-dozen courses to choose from, and cyclists and walkers will find every kind of terrain at hand.

Cool castles: Often poised on cliffs overlooking the sea, the region's castles tell the story of eight centuries of occupations, sieges, and conflicts between warring clan chiefs and nobles. Vikings, Scots, and the English fought for their possession.

Glorious gardens: Plants flourish in the mild Gulf Stream that brushes against this broken, western coastline. For vivid flowers, trees, birds, and butterflies, visit Crarae Garden, southwest of Inveraray. The Achamore House Gardens on the Isle of Gigha are a colorful extravaganza.

and the islands of the Inner Hebrides. Ferry services allow all kinds of interisland tours and can shorten mainland trips as well.

On land, you can take the A85 to Oban (the main port for ferries to Mull and other islands) past barren hills and into the forest of Argyll after Loch Lomond (and the A82) ends. The roads grow narrower as they wind around the banks of Loch Awe and Loch Etive. Alternatively, you can turn off the A82 at Arrochar and trace the longer route around Loch Fyne, once an active fishing center, to Inveraray and down the Argyll Peninsula to Campbeltown. Along the way you'll pass Kennacraig, where ferries sail to Islay and Jura.

Argyll. The twin peninsulas of Kintyre are thickly wooded areas broken up by long, pretty lochs. From Inverarary at the head of Loch Fyne, you can take in Auchindrain's re-created fishing village on the way to the Arran ferry. Or turn west toward Crinan and the prehistoric sites around Kilmartin, then travel northward toward Loch Awe and its intriguing island ruins. A short drive away is Oban, the busy resort where you catch the island ferries.

Arran. Touring this island will give you a glimpse in a day or two of the whole of Scotland in miniature. In the north, the forbidding Goatfell is a challenge that draws walkers and climbers. The island's wilder west coast attracts bird-watchers and naturalists, while the fertile south of the island contains nine lovely golf courses, leisurely walks, and Brodick Castle.

Islay and Jura. The smell of peat that hangs in the air on Islay is bottled in its famous whiskies. Aside from distilleries, the island's historical sites evoke a past in which these islands were far less remote. The whitewashed cottages along the coast of Islay line clean and beautiful beaches, many of them visited by a variety of wildlife. Jura is wilder and more dramatic, its twin mountains (the Paps) dominating its infertile moorland.

Isle of Mull and Iona. The pretty harbor of Tobermory, with its painted houses, is a relaxing base from which to explore the varied and beautiful island of Mull. Along Mull's west coast, spectacular cliffs and rocky beaches look out on to the Atlantic. From Craignure, the road crosses the sweeping green valleys of the Ross of Mull to Fionnphort and the ferry to the meditative island of Iona.

The Smaller Islands. These islands seem closer to the remoter Outer Hebrides than to the greener pastures of Mull or Arran. Abandoned by many of their original inhabitants, they are havens for birdlife, particularly Coll's giant dunes or the cliffs of Tiree. Colonsay's Kiloran Bay is open to the Atlantic's breakers, while Tiree's waves draw surfers from around the world.

PLANNING

WHEN TO GO

This part of the mainland is close enough to Glasgow to make it accessible year-round. Oban is just over two hours from the city by car (three hours by bus), but getting to the isles via ferries takes longer, and the crossings are less frequent. You can take advantage of quiet roads and plentiful accommodations in early spring and late autumn. The summer months of July and August can get very busy indeed; book accommodations and restaurants in advance during high season, or you might miss out. In winter, short daylight hours and winds can make island stays rather bleak.

This is a coastal region, buffeted by Atlantic winds and rains. The climate is erratic, and locals take a curious pride in the fact that the area often experiences several seasons in a single day. Come prepared with adequate clothing for the changing weather, including good walking shoes, waterproof outerwear, and sunscreen.

PLANNING YOUR TIME

You could easily spend a week exploring the islands alone, so consider spending at least a few nights in this region. Argyll and some island excursions make pleasant and easy side trips from Glasgow and Loch Lomond. Driving anywhere here takes a little longer than you'd think, so allow ample travel time. A leisurely day will take you to Inveraray, its castle, and the surrounding gardens (don't miss the folk museum at Auchindrain) before driving on to Kennacraig to take the ferry for Islay and Jura. Two or three days here will give you a sense of the history and varied landscapes of these stunning islands—and time for a distillery or two. If time is a constraint, begin in Oban and sail to Mull, returning the same day or the next to take in the Scottish Sea Life Sanctuary. If you can, drive around the beautiful Loch Awe on your way back to Glasgow.

Plan ahead: car ferries fill up in the summer months (there is usually no problem for foot passengers), and some of the smaller islands are served

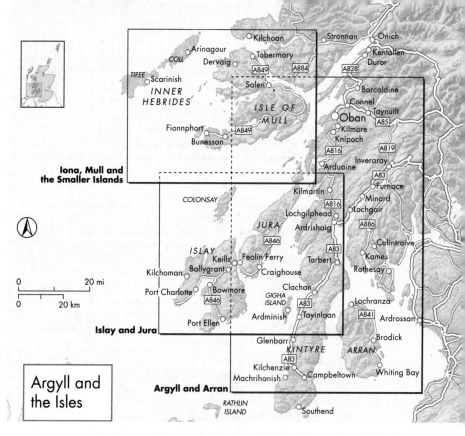

only once or twice a week. Bear in mind that it is not easy to find places to eat after 9 pm at any time of year—though you can usually find a place that will sell you a whisky until much later.

GETTING HERE AND AROUND

AIR TRAVEL

Flybe operates flights from Glasgow to Campbeltown, Islay, Tiree, and Mull. Hebridean Air Services flies between the small islands out of Oban.

Air Travel Contacts Flybe. ☎ 0871/700–2000 ⊕ www.flybe.com. **Hebridean Air Services.** ☎ 0845/805–7465 ⊕ www.hebrideanair.co.uk.

BOAT AND FERRY TRAVEL

Caledonian MacBrayne (CalMac) operates car-ferry and passenger services to and from the main islands. It is important to plan ahead when traveling to the islands in order to coordinate the connecting ferries; CalMac can advise you on this. Multiple-island tickets are available and can significantly reduce the cost of island-hopping.

CalMac ferries run from Oban to Mull, Lismore, Coll, and Tiree; from Kennacraig to Islay, Jura, and Gigha; from Ardrossan to Arran; and from Port Askaig on Islay to Feolin on Jura; as well as a number of shorter routes. Western Ferries operate between Dunoon, in Argyll, and Gourock, west of Glasgow. The ferry passage between Dunoon and Gourock is one frequented by locals; it saves a lot of time, and you can take your car across as well. Jura Passenger Ferry operates between Tayvallich (on the mainland) and Craighouse on Jura.

Ferry reservations are needed if you have a car; passengers traveling by foot do not need to make reservations.

Boat and Ferry Travel Contacts Caledonian MacBryne (*CalMac*). ☎ *0800/066–5000* ⊕ *www.calmac.co.uk.* **Jura Passenger Ferry.** ☎ *07768/450000* ⊕ *www.jurapassengerferry.com.* **Western Ferries.** ✉ *Dunoon* ☎ *01369/704452* ⊕ *www.western-ferries.co.uk.*

BUS TRAVEL

You can travel throughout the region by bus, but service here tends to be less frequent than elsewhere in Scotland. Scottish Citylink runs daily service from Glasgow's Buchanan Street Station to the mid-Argyll region and Kintyre; the trip to Oban takes about three hours. Several other companies provide local services within the region.

Bus Contacts Garelochhead Coaches. ☎ *01436/810200* ⊕ *www. garelochheadcoaches.co.uk.* **Islay Coaches.** ☎ *01496/840273* ⊕ *www.bmundell. co.uk.* **Royal Mail.** ☎ *03457/740740* ⊕ *www.royalmail.com/postbus.* **Scottish Citylink.** ☎ *0871/266–3333* ⊕ *www.citylink.co.uk.* **Stagecoach West Scotland.** ☎ *0871/200–2233* ⊕ *www.stagecoachbus.com.* **West Coast Motors.** ☎ *01586/552319* ⊕ *www.westcoastmotors.co.uk.*

CAR TRAVEL

Negotiating this area is easy except in July and August, when the roads around Oban may be congested. There are a number of single-lane roads, especially on the east side of the Kintyre Peninsula and on the islands, which require special care. Remember that white triangles indicate places where you can pass. You'll probably have to board a ferry at some point during your trip; nearly all ferries take cars as well as pedestrians.

From Glasgow, take the A82 and the A85 to Oban, the main ferry terminal for Mull and the islands (about 2½ hours by car). From the A82, take the A83 at Arrochar; it rounds Loch Fyne to Inveraray. From there you can take the A819 from Inveraray around Loch Awe and rejoin the Glasgow–Oban road. Alternatively, you can stay on the A83 and head down Kintyre to Kennacraig, the ferry terminal for Islay. Farther down the A83 is Tayinloan, the ferry port for Gigha. You can reach Brodick on Arran by ferry from Ardrossan, on the Clyde coast (M8/A78 from Glasgow); in summer you can travel to Lochranza from Claonaig on the Kintyre Peninsula, but there are very few crossings.

TRAIN TRAVEL

Oban and Ardrossan are the main rail stations; it's a three-hour trip from Glasgow to Oban. For information call ScotRail. All trains connect with ferries.

Train Contact ScotRail. ☎ *0344/811–0141* ⊕ *www.scotrail.co.uk.*

RESTAURANTS

Until recently this part of Scotland had few restaurants of distinction. That has changed, and more and more quality restaurants are opening and using the excellent local produce—fine fish and shellfish, lamb, and excellent venison, as well as game of many kinds. Most hotels and many guesthouses offer evening meals, and it may often be your best option to look to hotel restaurants, though the quality can vary. Bear in mind that most restaurants and pubs stop serving food by 9 pm; lunch usually ends at 2:30.

HOTELS

Accommodations in Argyll and on the isles range from country-house hotels to private homes offering a bed and breakfast. Most small, traditional, provincial hotels in coastal resorts have been updated and modernized, while still retaining personalized service. And though hotels often have a restaurant offering evening meals, the norm is to offer breakfast only. *Hotel reviews have been shortened. For full information, visit Fodors.com*

WHAT IT COSTS IN POUNDS				
	$	$$	$$$	$$$$
Restaurants	Under £15	£15–£19	£20–£25	Over £25
Hotels	Under £100	£100–£160	£161–£220	Over £220

Restaurant prices are the average cost of a main course at dinner or, if dinner is not served, at lunch. Hotel prices are the lowest cost of a standard double room in high season, including 20% V.A.T.

TOURS

BOAT TOURS

Getting out on the water is a wonderful way to see the landscape of the islands and also sea life.

Sea Life Surveys. Wildlife tours along the Argyll coast and around the islands are the specialty here, departing from Tobermory on Mull. Sea Life Surveys also organizes whale-watching tours as well as "Surf and Turf" tours, which include wildlife at sea and on land. ⊠ *A848, Tobermory* ☎ *01688/302916* ⊕ *www.sealifesurveys.com* ⊠ *From £30.*

Staffa Tours. This company organizes a number of tours to the smaller islands, with the emphasis on wildlife. Tours run from Mull, Ardnamurchan on the mainland, or from Iona. The three-hour trip to Staffa includes Fingal's Cave, commemorated by Mendelssohn in his famous overture. The island is uninhabited (by humans at least). With luck you may encounter dolphins on the way. They also run tours to the Treshnish islands, famous for the puffin colonies on Lunga. ⊠ *Railway Pier, Iona* ☎ *07831/885985* ⊕ *www.staffatours.com* ⊠ *From £30.*

Turus-Mara. Based on the island of Mull, Turus-Mara runs trips to Staffa, Iona, and the Treshnish islands, with an emphasis on wildlife. There are puffins and guillemots through the summer, seals until late in the year, and sometimes even basking sharks. Tours depart from

Ulva Ferry on the west coast of Mull, but there is a courtesy bus from Tobermory. ✉ *Penmore Mill, Dervaig* ☎ *01688/400242* ⊕ *www. turusmara.com* ✉ *From £30.*

BUS TOURS

Many of the bus companies in the area also arrange sightseeing tours, so check with them.

West Coast Tours. A range of bus tours in and around Oban and on Mull are available through West Coast Tours. They can also arrange combined bus and boat tours. ✉ *1 Queenspark Pl., Oban* ☎ *01631/566809* ⊕ *www.westcoasttours.co.uk* ✉ *From £7.*

VISITOR INFORMATION

The tourist offices in Lochgilphead, Tarbert, and Tobermory (Mull) are open April through October only; other offices are open year-round.

ARGYLL

Topographical grandeur and rocky shores are what make Argyll special. Try to take to the water at least once, even if your time is limited. The sea and the sea lochs have played a vital role in the history of western Scotland since the time of the war galleys of the clans. Oban is the major ferry gateway and transport hub, with a main road leading south into the Kintyre Peninsula.

OBAN

96 miles northwest of Glasgow, 125 miles northwest of Edinburgh, 50 miles south of Fort William, 118 miles southwest of Inverness.

It's almost impossible to avoid Oban when touring the west. Its waterfront has some character, but the town's main role is as a launch point for excursions into Argyll and for ferries to the islands. A traditional Scottish resort town, Oban has many music festivals, *ceilidhs* with Highland dancing, as well as all the usual tartan kitsch and late-night revelry in pubs and hotel bars. The Oban Distillery offers tours and a shop. Still, there are more exciting destinations just over the horizon, on the islands and down into Kintyre.

GETTING HERE AND AROUND

From Glasgow, the A82 along Loch Lomond meets the A85 at Crianlarich. Turn left and continue to Oban. In summer the center of Oban can become gridlocked with ferry traffic, so leave yourself time for the wait. Alternatively, the A816 from Lochgilphead enters Oban from the less crowded south. Train services run from Glasgow to Oban (ScotRail); Scottish Citylink runs buses from Glasgow to Oban several times a day.

ESSENTIALS

Visitor Information Oban Tourist Information Centre. ✉ *3 North Pier* ☎ *01631/563122* ⊕ *www.oban.org.uk.*

EXPLORING

TOP ATTRACTIONS

Fodor'sChoice **Dunstaffnage Castle.** Standing high atop volcanic rock, Dunstaffnage
★ commands the hills and lochs that surround it. That is why this 13th-
century castle was so strategic and contested by those battling for control of the kingdom of Argyll. From the walk along the walls you have
outstanding views across the **Sound of Mull** and the **Firth of Lorne.** A small
well-illustrated guidebook (£2.50) lets you take your own guided tour,
but there are storyboards throughout the building that give you a sense
of how it was used across the ages. In the woods is the ruined chapel of
St. Cuthbert, built by the Macdougall clan at the same time as the castle.
⊠ *Off A85* ☎ *01631/562465* ⊕ *www.historic-scotland.gov.uk/places*
💷 *£4.50* ♡ *Apr.–Sept., daily 9:30–5:30, last admission 5; Oct.–Mar.,*
Mon.–Wed. and weekends 10–4, last admission 3:30.

FAMILY **Ocean Explorer Centre.** On the Firth of Lorn, this imaginative venture lets
you get a look under the sea. Hands-on exhibits include microscopes
where you can observe tiny algae and a live undersea camera where you
can see what's happening below the waves. Part of a scientific research
center, it's educational, but also accessible and fun. There is a bright
little café and a shop with books on marine science and other topics. It's
2 miles from Oban—follow the signs for nearby Dunstaffnage Castle.
⊠ *Kirk Rd.* ☎ *01631/559123* ⊕ *www.oceanexplorercentre.org* 💷 *Free*
♡ *Apr.–Oct., weekdays 10–5; Nov.–Mar., weekdays 9:30–4:30.*

FAMILY **Scottish Sea Life Sanctuary.** On the shores of Loch Creran, this marine
sanctuary is part aquarium where you can get an up-close look at everything from sharks to stingrays, and part animal rescue facility. Adorable
otters and seals receive rehabilitation here before being released back
into the wild. Kids will appreciate the adventure playground. The restaurant serves morning coffee, a full lunch menu, and afternoon tea. To
get here, drive north from Oban for 10 miles on the A828; West Coast
Motors also provide regular bus service. ■ TIP➜ Book online for significantly cheaper tickets. ⊠ *Barcaldine, off A828, Connel* ☎ *01631/720386*
⊕ *www.sealsanctuary.co.uk* 💷 *£13.20* ♡ *Daily 10–4; last admission 1*
hr before closing.

WORTH NOTING

Oban Distillery. One of Scotland's oldest and smallest distilleries was
founded in 1794, several years before the town where it now stands.
It produces a well-known 14-year-old malt which, according to those
who know, has a taste somewhere between the smoky Islay whiskies
and the softer sweeter Highland varieties—a distinctive West Highland
flavor. ⊠ *Stafford St.* ☎ *01631/572004* ⊕ *www.discovering-distilleries.*
com/oban 💷 *Basic tour £8* ♡ *Mar.–June, Oct., and Nov., daily 10–5;*
July–Sept., weekdays 9:30–7:30, weekends 9:30–5; Dec., weekdays
12:30–4 (last tour 75 mins before closing).

WHERE TO EAT

$$$ ✕ **Ee-usk.** This clean-lined restaurant's name means "fish" in Gaelic, and
SEAFOOD it has earned quite a reputation for serving excellent dishes made with
the freshest fish and shellfish delivered directly from Oban's harbor.
The signature creations use appealingly simple sauces; try oven-baked

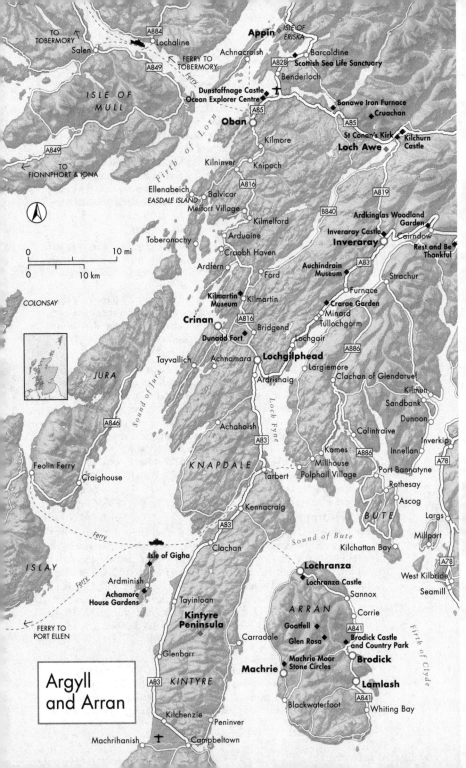

wild halibut with creamed leeks or the full-scale seafood platter. On clear days, there are nice views of the islands through the large glass windows. Children under 12 are not admitted for dinner. $ *Average main: £20* ⊠ *North Pier* ☎ *01631/565666* ⊕ *www.eeusk.com* ⊗ *Closed Sun.* ⚠ *Reservations essential.*

$$
BRITISH
✕ **Hawthorn Restaurant.** This charming restaurant with white walls and modern furnishings has a rural setting; some of the surrounding crofts are still working farms. Although it's just a few miles from Oban, from where it gets its fish, the restaurant feels quite remote. Fish shares a menu with local lamb and pork belly with scallops and salsa verde. $ *Average main: £19* ⊠ *Keil Crofts, Benderloch* ✛ *6 miles north of Oban off the main A816, after crossing the Connel Bridge* ☎ *01631/720777* ⊕ *www. hawthorn-restaurant.co.uk* ⊗ *No lunch Mon.–Thurs. No dinner Mon. Apr.–Oct.; no dinner Mon.–Thurs. Nov.–Mar.*

$
CAFÉ
✕ **Kitchen Garden.** Directly across the road from the ferry port, this delicatessen serves good homemade soups, paninis, and sandwiches, as well as freshly baked cakes. The service is sometimes a little slow; prices are reasonable and the location is quite convenient. $ *Average main: £10* ⊠ *North Pier, 14 George St.* ☎ *01631/566332* ⊕ *www. kitchengardenoban.co.uk* ⊗ *No dinner.*

$
SEAFOOD
Fodor's Choice
★
✕ **Oban Seafood Hut.** Literally a hut directly on the pier, this eatery is famous for fresh fish and shellfish. Belly up to the open-air wooden tables and benches and try the crab sandwich or the local oysters. This is fine fare at rock-bottom prices. $ *Average main: £8* ⊠ *CalMac Pier* ☎ *No phone* ⊕ *www.obanseafoodhut.co.uk* ▭ *No credit cards.*

WHERE TO STAY

$
B&B/INN
🏠 **Glenburnie House.** At this typical seafront guesthouse in a Victorian house with fine views over Oban Bay, most rooms are spacious and comfortable, if slightly overdecorated in traditional style. **Pros:** centrally located; good sea views. **Cons:** too many flowery fabrics for some tastes; slightly expensive for what you get; no elevator. $ *Rooms from: £90* ⊠ *Esplanade* ☎ *01631/562089* ⊕ *www.glenburnie.co.uk* ⊗ *Closed Dec.–Feb.* ⇆ *12 rooms* ⦿ *Breakfast.*

$
B&B/INN
🏠 **Kilchrenan House.** Just a few minutes from the town center, this Victorian-era stone house has been transformed into a lovely bed-and-breakfast. **Pros:** great sea views; tasteful attention to detail. **Cons:** some bedrooms may be too colorfully decorated for some tastes; attic rooms have a slanting roof; credit cards not accepted for one-night stays. $ *Rooms from: £78* ⊠ *Corran Esplanade* ☎ *01631/562663* ⊕ *www.kilchrenanhouse. co.uk* ⊗ *Closed Dec. and Jan.* ⇆ *13 rooms* ⦿ *Breakfast.*

$$$$
HOTEL
🏠 **Manor House Hotel.** On the coast near Oban, this 1780 stone house—once the home of the duke of Argyll—has wonderful sea views and a convenient location. **Pros:** excellent restaurant; near all necessary amenities; nice garden overlooking the bay. **Cons:** smallish bedrooms; no children under 12. $ *Rooms from: £245* ⊠ *Gallanach Rd.* ☎ *01631/562087* ⊕ *www.manorhouseoban.com* ⇆ *11 rooms* ⦿ *Breakfast.*

8

BICYCLING

Oban Cycles. This shop rents bikes of various sorts starting at £15 for a full day. The area round Oban is good cycling country, and the staff is happy to advise you on routes. ✉ *87 George St.* ☎ *01631/566033.*

APPIN

The little peninsula of Appin, a 20-minute drive from Oban, is a charming, well-kept secret. Just 2 miles along a narrow road from the main Fort William route (A828), the bay opens to Lismore and the sea. Castle Stalker, a privately owned castle on the water, sits magnificently in the center of the picture, a symbol of ancient coastal Scotland. This is an excellent, uncrowded base for walking, fishing, water sports, and cycling. The Appin Rocks, on the headland, are frequently visited by seals.

GETTING HERE AND AROUND

From Oban, follow the A828 around Loch Creran and take the left turn to Port Appin just beyond Tynribbie. Continue for just over 2 miles to the old pier. From the port, the passenger ferry runs to the island of Lismore throughout the year. Steamers once plied the waters of Loch Linnhe, but today the largest boats here are those taking workers to the quarries of Kingairloch.

WHERE TO EAT AND STAY

$$$ SEAFOOD ✕ **Pierhouse Hotel and Restaurant.** The round towers of the old pier mark the entrance to this restaurant, appealingly situated on the water's edge beside the jetty. The restaurant serves the freshest seafood; try its signature platter of lobster (caught at the pier's edge), scallops, mussels, and langoustine. The restaurant is small and lively, and the public bar beside it is pleasantly animated, filled with walkers and water-sports enthusiasts headed to or returning from Lismore. The Pierhouse also has quite small, but clean and comfortable rooms. The hotel is a good base for exploring the region, and it's also a nice place to relax and watch the changing moods of the loch. [$] *Average main: £21* ✉ *Port Appin* ☎ *01631/730302* 🌐 *www.pierhousehotel.co.uk.*

$$$$ HOTEL Fodor's Choice ★ 🏨 **Airds Hotel and Restaurant.** The old ferry inn for travelers visiting Lismore now houses this luxurious small hotel; rooms are stylish and restrained, with superb views either toward the sea or the woods behind. **Pros:** fabulous views from the breakfast room; spare boots for the unprepared; beautiful location. **Cons:** quite an expensive option. [$] *Rooms from: £330* ✉ *A828, Port Appin* ☎ *01631/730236* 🌐 *www.airds-hotel.com* 🛏 *9 rooms, 2 suites, 1 cottage* 🍴 *Some meals.*

$$$$ HOTEL Fodor's Choice ★ 🏨 **Isle of Eriska.** A severe, baronial-style granite facade belies the sense of welcome within this hotel, set on its own island 10 miles north of Oban and accessible by a bridge from the mainland; the rooms are individually furnished and luxurious in their detail, and a range of outdoor activities are available, as are a spa, pools, and gyms. **Pros:** exceptional food; good service; refuge of peace and quiet. **Cons:** in the middle of nowhere; few choices when it comes to dining out; very expensive. [$] *Rooms from: £340* ✉ *Off A828, Benderloch* ☎ *01631/720371* 🌐 *www.eriska-hotel.co.uk* 🛏 *25 rooms* 🍴 *Some meals.*

LOCH AWE

18 miles east of Oban.

Measuring more than 25 miles long, Loch Awe is Scotland's longest stretch of freshwater. Its northwest shore is quiet; forest walks crisscross the Inverliever Forest here. At the loch's northern end tiny islands, many with ruins, pepper the water. One, Inishail, is home to a 13th-century chapel.

GETTING HERE AND AROUND

From Oban the A85 will bring you to the head of Loch Awe and the small town of the same name. Turn onto the B845 at Taynuilt to reach the loch's northern shore, or continue through the forbidding Pass of Brander and turn onto the A819 to get to the southern shore. From here you can continue on to Inveraray, or drive along the loch on the B840.

EXPLORING

TOP ATTRACTIONS

Bonawe Iron Furnace. This beautifully reconstructed site shows a different face of this mainly agricultural region. The ironworks were very advanced for their time, and an elaborate exhibit takes you through the different stages of the production process. During the Napoleonic Wars it began making cannonballs, and these provided firepower for Admiral Lord Nelson's ships at the Battle of Trafalgar in 1805. The local graveyard, at Taynuilt, has a monument to Nelson raised by the workers. The majority of the workers were Gaelic-speaking peasants who were responsible for collecting the wood from the surrounding forests to make charcoal. Those who worked in Bonawe were mostly Englishmen who arrived on the cargo boats used to transport the iron. ⊠ *Off B845, Bonawe* ☎ *01866/822432* ⊕ *www.historic-scotland.gov. uk* 🎫 *£4.50* ⊗ *Apr.–Sept., daily 9:30–5:30.*

Cruachan. This fascinating engineering achievement is all the more dramatic for being hidden in a landscape that gives no hint of its presence. Inside Ben Cruachan you find yourself in a massive man-made cavern containing the vast turbines and machinery that supply so much of western Scotland's electricity. Take in the hands-on exhibit at the visitor center, then travel by bus ½ mile into the "hollow mountain," past the tropical plants that grow near the vast generating hall. ⊠ *A85, Dalmally* ☎ *01866/822618* ⊕ *www.visitcruachan.co.uk* 🎫 *£7* ⊗ *Apr.–Oct., daily 9:30–4:45; Nov.–Mar., weekdays 9:30–3:45.*

Rest and Be Thankful. Not advice for a good life in this case but the name of a beautiful point on the road to Oban, the A83. The A819 south to Inveraray initially runs alongside Loch Awe, but soon leaves these pleasant banks to turn east and join the A83, between Oban and Loch Lomond to Glasgow. Some 10 miles before Tarbert, where the road joins the A82 at Loch Lomond, the road twists and turns through an almost alpine landscape to this high point. The car park at what is called "The Rest" is a perfect viewpoint, before returning to the A83 as it continues along the banks of Loch Fyne ⊠ *A83* ✛ *10 miles northwest of Tarbert.*

8

WORTH NOTING

Kilchurn Castle. A striking ruined fortress at the northeastern end of Loch Awe, the castle was built in the 15th century and rebuilt in the 17th century. Airy vantage points amid the towers have fine panoramas of the surrounding Highlands and loch. It's 2½ miles west of Dalmally, accessible by foot along an old railway line near A85. ✉ *Off A85, west of the junction with A819, Dalmally* ☎ *01866/833333* 🌐 *www.historic-scotland.gov.uk/places* 🎫 *Free* 🕓 *Apr.–Sept, daily.*

St. Conan's Kirk. This striking stone-built church on the banks of Loch Awe has a medieval air about it, but in fact it was completed in 1930 by amateur architect Walter Campbell. It was built with the boulders strewn across the area, rather than quarried stone, and it looks rough and almost incomplete. But its interior is impressive. Light filters in through modern stained-glass windows, and wood and stone carvings are scattered throughout, not to mention the effigy of Robert the Bruce lying on a stone catafalque that contains a fragment of bone taken from Bannockburn. It's on the A85, about 18 miles from Oban. ✉ *A85, Lochawe* ☎ *01838/200298* 🌐 *www.stconanskirk.org.uk* 🎫 *Free.*

WHERE TO STAY

$$$ HOTEL Fodor'sChoice ★ 🏨 **Taychreggan Hotel.** The tranquillity of this lovely country-house hotel echoes the stillness of nearby Loch Awe: from many of the rooms and the restaurant you can gaze out over the water, or for an even better vantage point, take a stroll through the surrounding gardens. **Pros:** lovely setting; high level of comfort; wonderful meals. **Cons:** Wi-Fi only in public rooms; off the beaten track. [$] *Rooms from: £163* ✉ *Off B845, Kilchrenan* ☎ *01866/833211* 🌐 *www.taychregganhotel.co.uk* 🛏 *18 rooms* 🍴 *Breakfast.*

INVERARAY

21 miles south of Loch Awe, 61 miles north of Glasgow, 29 miles west of Loch Lomond.

Fodor'sChoice ★ The town is a sparkling fishing village with cute shops, attractions, and the haunted Campbell Castle all within walking distance. There are lovely views of the water and plenty of fishing boats to watch; several worthwhile gardens and museums are nearby, too. On the approaches to Inveraray, note the ornate 18th-century high bridge that carries the road along the loch side. This is your first sign that Inveraray is not just a jumble of houses; in fact, much of it was designed as a planned town in the mid-18th century for the third Duke of Argyll, whose castle dominates the town.

GETTING HERE AND AROUND

If you're driving from Oban, take the A85 and the A819 beyond Loch Awe (the village). From Glasgow, take the A82, turn on to the A83 at Arrochar, and make the long drive around Loch Fyne.

ESSENTIALS

Visitor Information Inveraray Tourist Information Centre. ✉ *Front St.* ☎ *01499/302063* 🌐 *www.visitscotland.com.*

EXPLORING

TOP ATTRACTIONS

Ardkinglas Woodland Garden. Rambling over 12,000 acres, one of Britain's finest collections of conifers is set off by rhododendron blossoms in early summer. You can find the garden around the head of Loch Fyne, about 10 miles east of Inveraray. There's a wild woodland walk beyond the garden; both are open all year. The house, regarded as architect Sir Robert Lorimer's masterpiece, is only open to visitors on Fridays between April and October. ⊠ *Ardkinglas Estate, Cairndow* ☎ *01499/600261* ⊕ *www.ardkinglas.com* ⊡ *£5* ☼ *Daily sunrise–sunset.*

Fodor'sChoice
★

Auchindrain Museum. Step a few centuries back in time at this open-air museum, a rare surviving example of an 18th-century communal tenancy farm. About 250 years ago, there were several thousand working communities like Auchindrain. Auchindrain was the last of them, its final tenant leaving in 1963. Today the bracken-thatch and iron-roof buildings, about 20 in all, give you a feel for early farming life in the Highland communities. Several houses are furnished and tell the story of their occupants. A tearoom is open morning to afternoon. ⊠ *Auchindrain* ⊕ *Off A83 about 6 miles south of Inveraray* ☎ *01499/500235* ⊕ *auchindrain.org.uk* ⊡ *£5.95* ☼ *Apr.–Oct., daily 10–5, last admission 4; Nov.–Mar., weekdays 10–2.*

Crarae Garden. Well worth a visit for plant lovers is this 100-acre garden, where magnolias, azaleas, and rhododendrons flourish in the moist, lush environment around Crarae Burn (a burn is a small stream). A rocky gorge and waterfalls add appeal, and the flowers and trees attract several different species of birds and butterflies. The gardens are 10 miles southwest of Inveraray off the A83. ⊠ *Off A83* ☎ *0844/493–2210* ⊕ *www.nts.org.uk* ⊡ *£6.50* ☼ *Garden: daily 9:30–sunset. Visitor center: Apr.–Oct., daily 10–5; last admission at 4:30.*

8

Inveraray Castle. The current seat of the Chief of the Clan Campbell is a smart, grayish-green turreted stone house with a self-satisfied air. Set among well-tended grounds, it contains displays of luxurious furnishings and interesting art, as well as a huge armory. Built between 1743 and 1789, the castle has spires on the four corner turrets that give it a vaguely French look. Fans of *Downton Abbey* will recognize it as the fictional Duneagle Castle of Season Three's finale. Tours of the castle follow the history of the powerful Campbell family and how it acquired its considerable wealth. There is a tearoom for snacks and light lunches. You can hike around the extensive estate grounds, but wear sturdy footwear. ⊠ *Off A83* ☎ *01499/302203* ⊕ *www.inveraray-castle.com* ⊡ *£10* ☼ *Apr.–Oct., daily 10–5:45, last admission at 5.*

WORTH NOTING

FAMILY
Inveraray Jail. In this old jail, realistic courtroom scenes, carefully re-created cells, and other paraphernalia give you a glimpse of life behind bars in Victorian times—and today. Actors represent some of the jail's most famous occupants. The site includes a Scottish crafts shop. ⊠ *Main St.* ☎ *01499/302381* ⊕ *www.inverarayjail.co.uk* ⊡ *£10.95* ☼ *Apr.–Oct., daily 9:30–6; Nov.–Mar., daily 10–5; last admission 1 hr before closing.*

WHERE TO EAT AND STAY

$$
SEAFOOD
✕ **Loch Fyne Oyster Bar and Restaurant.** The flagship location of a popular chain, this well-regarded seafood spot 10 miles northeast of Inverary sits surrounded by hills at the head of Loch Fyne, with beautiful views in both directions. Polished wood and maritime artworks help set the mood. The dishes are generally simple and unpretentious—try the fish and shellfish soup, or the roast salmon with asparagus, broad beans, and pea salad. Don't miss the oysters, either in the restaurant or in the adjacent shop. Arrive early, as the place closes at 8, and reserve in advance. $ *Average main: £19* ⊠ *Clachan Farm, A83, Cairndow* ☎ *01499/600482* ⊕ *www.lochfyne.com* ⌂ *Reservations essential.*

$$
SEAFOOD
✕ **Samphire Seafood Restaurant.** This new restaurant in the center of Inveraray is quickly gaining a reputation for excellent seafood cookery, though it also serves meat and vegetarian dishes. It is small and comfortable, without pretensions. Favorites include the seafood pie and the Taste of the Loch extravaganza, which includes everything that Loch Fyne produces (and a little more). $ *Average main: £18* ⊠ *6A Arkland* ☎ *01499/302321* ⊕ *www.samphireseafood.com* ⊘ *Closed Sun. and Mon.* ⌂ *Reservations essential.*

$
HOTEL
Fodor's Choice
★
🏨 **The George Hotel.** The Clark family has run this 18th-century former coaching inn at the heart of Inveraray for six generations, and that's reflected in the warmth of the welcome you'll receive. **Pros:** excellent restaurant; atmospheric bars; economical compared with other hotels in the area. **Cons:** too much tartan for some; unattractive reception area; Wi-Fi in public areas only. $ *Rooms from: £80* ⊠ *Main St. E* ☎ *01499/302111* ⊕ *www.thegeorgehotel.co.uk* ⇱ *17 rooms* ⦿| *Breakfast.*

LOCHGILPHEAD

26 miles south of Inveraray.

Lochgilphead, the largest town in this region, looks best when the tide is in, as Loch Gilp (really a bite out of Loch Fyne) reveals a muddy shoreline at low tide. With a series of well-kept, colorful buildings along its main street, this neat little town is worth a look though other areas may have more appeal for travelers.

GETTING HERE AND AROUND
From Inveraray continue south for 24 miles along the A83, which follows the bank of the Loch Fyne.

SHOPPING
Highbank Collection. The factory shop here sells hand-painted pottery and glassware, colorful ceramics, and model wooden boats, as well as plenty of rather eccentric Loch Ness Monster memorabilia. ⊠ *Highbank Industrial Estate, off A816* ☎ *01546/602044* ⊕ *www.highbank.co.uk.*

CRINAN

10 miles northwest of Lochgilphead.

Crinan is synonymous with its canal, the reason for this tiny community's existence and its mainstay. The narrow road beside the Crinan

Hotel bustles with yachting types waiting to pass through the locks, bringing a surprisingly cosmopolitan feel to such an out-of-the-way corner of Scotland. Also accessible from Crinan is the worthwhile Kilmartin House Museum.

GETTING HERE AND AROUND

To reach Crinan, take the A816 Oban road north from Lochgilphead for about a mile, then turn left on to the B841 at Cairnbaan.

EXPLORING

Crinan Canal. This canal opened in 1801 to let fishing vessels reach Hebridean fishing grounds without making the long haul south around the Kintyre Peninsula. At its western end the canal drops to the sea in a series of locks, the last of which is beside the Crinan Hotel. Today it's popular with pleasure boats traveling to the west coast.

Fodor'sChoice ★ **Kilmartin Museum.** For an exceptional encounter with early Scottish history, start at this museum 8 miles north of Crinan and then explore some of the more than 300 ancient monuments within a 6-mile radius. Exhibits provide information about the stone circles and avenues, burial mounds, and carved stones dating from the Bronze Age and earlier that are scattered nearby. Beginning in 2016, visitors can take part in excavations and visit various sites in the area with museum staff. There is also a nice tearoom in the museum. Nearby **Dunadd Fort,** a rocky hump rising out of the level ground between Crinan and Kilmartin, was once the capital of the early kingdom of Dalriada, founded by the first wave of Scots who migrated from Ireland around AD 500. Clamber up the rock to see a basin, a footprint, and an outline of a boar carved on the smooth upper face of the knoll. ⊠ *A816, Kilmartin* ☎ *01546/510278* ⊕ *www.kilmartin.org* ⊠ *£5* ☉ *Mar.–Oct., daily 10–5:30; Nov. and Dec., daily 11–4.*

WHERE TO STAY

$$
B&B/INN
Allt-Na-Craig. A location on the edge of the village and overlooking Loch Fyne distinguishes this stone Victorian house set in lovely gardens. **Pros:** atmospheric; good food and views; Wi-Fi throughout the hotel. **Cons:** you're pretty isolated, so it helps to have a car. $ *Rooms from: £110* ⊠ *Tarbert Rd., 4 miles south of Lochgilphead, Ardrishaig* ☎ *01546/603245* ⊕ *www.allt-na-craig.co.uk* ⤳ *5 rooms, 1 cottage* ⦿ *Breakfast.*

$$
HOTEL
Crinan Hotel. One of a group of houses around the last loch of the Crinan Canal, the hotel has a dramatic setting overlooking the Sound of Jura and Craignish Point. **Pros:** elevator to rooms on upper floors; good restaurants. **Cons:** Wi-Fi in public areas only. $ *Rooms from: £130* ⊠ *Off B841* ☎ *01546/830261* ⊕ *www.crinanhotel.com* ⤳ *20 rooms* ⦿ *Breakfast.*

KINTYRE PENINSULA

52 miles south of Lochgilphead (to Campbeltown).

Rivers and streams crisscross this long, narrow strip of green pasturelands and hills stretching south from Lochgilphead.

GETTING HERE AND AROUND

Continue south on the A83 (the road to Campbeltown) to Tarbert. Some 4 miles farther along the A83 is Kennacraig, where you catch the ferry to Islay. Beyond that is the pier at Tayinloan; CalMac ferries run from here to the Isle of Gigha.

Flybe operates flights from Glasgow to Campbeltown.

ESSENTIALS

Air Travel Contact Campbeltown Airport. ⊠ *Off A83, Campbeltown* ☎ *01586/553797* ⊕ *www.hial.co.uk.*

Visitor Information Campbeltown Information Centre. ⊠ *Mackinnon House, The Pier, Campbeltown* ☎ *01586/552056* ⊕ *www.visitscotland.com.* **Tarbert Information Centre.** ⊠ *Harbour St., Tarbert* ☎ *01880/820429* ⊕ *www.visitscotland.com.*

EXPLORING

Achamore House Gardens. One relic of the Isle of Gigha's aristocratic legacy is the Achamore House Garden, which produces lush shrubberies with spectacular azalea displays in late spring. Its variety is explained by the island's warm microclimate. For a nimble day trip, take the 20-minute ferry to Gigha from Tayinloan and walk right over to the gardens. The gardens are managed by the Gigha Community Trust; the house itself is privately owned. ⊠ *Achamor House, Isle of Gigha* ☎ *01583/505275* ⊕ *www.isle-of-gigha.co.uk* ⚑ *£6* ☉ *Daily sunrise–sunset.*

Isle of Gigha. Barely 7 miles long, this sheltered island between Kintyre and Islay has sandy beaches and rich wildlife. The island was long favored by British aristocrats as a summer destination. Ferries make the 20-minute trip from Tayinloan on the mainland. The Archamore Gardens are a high point of a visit. ⊠ *Isle of Gigha* ☎ *01583/505392* ⊕ *www.gigha.org.uk.*

Tarbert. A name that appears throughout the Highlands, Tarbert is the Gaelic word for "place of portage," and a glance at the map tells you why it was given to this little town with a workaday waterfront: Tarbert sits on the narrow neck of land between East and West Loch Tarbert, where long ago boats were actually carried across the land to avoid looping all the way around the peninsula. The town's visitor center is on Harbour Street. ⊕ *www.visitscotland.com.*

GOLF

Machrihanish Golf Club. Many enthusiasts discuss this course in hushed tones—its out-of-the-way location has made it something of a golfer's Shangri-la. It was laid out in 1876 by Tom Morris on the links around the sandy Machrihanish Bay. The drive off the first tee is across the beach to reach the green—an intimidating start to a memorable series of holes. There is also a 9-hole course, The Pans. ⊠ *Off B843, Machrihanish* ☎ *01586/810277* ⊕ *www.machgolf.com* ⚑ *£65 Apr.–Oct., £30 Nov.–Mar.* ⚑ *Championship Course: 18 holes, 6235 yards, par 70; The Pans: 9 holes (out), 2376 yards, par 34* ⚑ *Reservations essential.*

ARRAN

Approaching Arran by sea, you'll first see the forbidding Goatfell (2,868 feet) in the north, then the green fields of the south. It is this contrast and varied geography that has led visitors to describe Arran as "Scotland in Miniature." The island's temperate climate allows tropical plants to grow, and this relative warmth probably attracted the ancient cultures whose stone circles still stand on the island. This weather also explains why it has long been a favorite resort getaway for Glasgow's residents, who come here to walk, climb Goatfell, play golf on Arran's nine courses, observe the rich birdlife, or simply enjoy the sea.

GETTING HERE AND AROUND

Caledonian MacBrayne runs regular car and passenger ferries that cross the Firth of Clyde from Ardrossan (near Saltcoats) to Brodick throughout the year (crossing takes just under an hour). There is also a small ferry from Claonaig on the Kintyre Peninsula to Lochranza during the summer months.

Connecting trains run to the ferry at Ardrossan from Glasgow's Queen Street station. Stagecoach runs regular local bus services around the island. Exploring the island by car is easy, as the A841 road circles it.

BRODICK

1 hour by ferry from Ardrossan.

Arran's largest village, Brodick, has a main street that is set back from the promenade and the lovely bay. Beyond that, it is really little more than a gateway to the rest of the island.

GETTING HERE AND AROUND

You can reach Brodick from Ardrossan by ferry. From Brodick the A841 circles the island; head south to reach Lamlash, north to reach Lochranza. The String Road crosses the island between Brodick and Machrie.

ESSENTIALS

The information center, opposite the landing point for the Ardrossan Ferry, has an accommodation desk as well as tourist information. Ask for the very nice illustrated map of Arran.

Visitor Information

Brodick Information Centre. ⊠ *The Pier* ☎ *01770/303774* ⊕ *www.visitscotland.com.*

EXPLORING

Fodor'sChoice **Brodick Castle and Country Park.** On the north side of Brodick Bay, this
★ reddish sandstone structure is surrounded by lush woods, gardens, and parks. Several rooms are open to the public between March and October, both in the original 16th-century castle and in the Victorian additions that nicely illustrate the Hamilton family's opulent lifestyle. The large downstairs kitchen reveals how servants lived, and the 87 stag heads on the stairs are a slightly disturbing reminder of how the aristocracy spent their leisure time. The vast gardens, open all year, are filled with rhododendrons and azalea. A café serves homemade cakes

and coffee for breakfast as well as a light lunch menu, and if the weather permits, you can sit at tables outside and look out over the bay.

The country park here includes the 2,867-foot **Goatfell,** the highest peak in Arran. The beautiful upland landscape is more challenging to explore than it seems, so it's important to go prepared, but the views from the peak merit the effort to get there. Year-round access is from the country park or from Cladach on the A841. ✉ *Off A841, 1 mile north of Brodick Pier* ☎ *0844/493–2152* 🌐 *www.nts.org.uk* 🎟 *Castle and gardens £12.50* 🕒 *Castle: Apr. and Oct., daily 11–3; May–Sept., daily 11–4. Garden: Apr. and Oct., daily 10–4; May–Sept., daily 10–5. Country park: open daily year-round.*

Glen Rosa. Here you can stroll through a long glen glimpsing the wild ridges that beckon so many outdoors enthusiasts. To get here from A841, drive a short way along String Road and turn right at the signpost into the glen. The road soon becomes unpassable; park the car and wander on foot. ✉ *Off String Rd.*

Isle of Arran Heritage Museum. This charming small museum documents life on the island from ancient times to the present. The buildings include a cottage, a 1940s schoolroom, and outbuildings with displays of agricultural equipment as well as prehistoric life, farming, fishing, and other aspects of the island's social history. There are play areas for kids and a pleasant tearoom. ✉ *Rosaburn, A841* ☎ *01770/302636* 🌐 *www.arranmuseum.co.uk* 🎟 *£4* 🕒 *Apr.–Oct., daily 10:30–4:30; last admission 4.*

WHERE TO EAT

$$ BRITISH 🍴 **Brodick Brasserie.** This brasserie next to the Brodick Bar may be a forbidding dull brown from the outside, but inside pleasant aromas waft and a lively atmosphere prevails. The restaurant serves prix-fixe menus for lunch (£13.50 with a drink) and dinner (£17.50). The daily menu is on a blackboard and includes imaginative venison and monkfish dishes as well as standards like salmon with hollandaise sauce and potatoes dauphinoise. Like many places in the west of Scotland, hours are restricted so it is well worth booking ahead. [$] *Average main: £16* ✉ *Alma Rd.* ☎ *01770/302169* 🌐 *www.brodickbar.co.uk* ✍ *Reservations essential.*

$$ SEAFOOD 🍴 **Creelers.** It would be hard to find fresher seafood than at Creelers. The shellfish served in the restaurant will often have been caught that day by the owners' own boat. The restaurant's name comes from the "creels," or baskets, used to gather shellfish. The restaurant serves a range of delicious smoked fish from its own smokery next door, as well as other fish and meat dishes. Try the Arran scallops with cauliflower and lobster or the halibut with a mussel chowder sauce. The restaurant does not sell wine but you can bring your own bottle (£3.50 corkage). [$] *Average main: £19* ✉ *The Paddock, A841* ☎ *01770/302810* 🌐 *www.creelers.co.uk* 🕒 *Closed Sun.* ✍ *Reservations essential.*

SHOPPING

Arran's shops are well stocked with locally produced goods. The Home Farm is a popular shopping area with several shops and a small restaurant.

Arran Aromatics. This is one of Scotland's best known suppliers of scents, soaps, and perfumes of every kind. The shop is filled with pleasant smells, and between May and September a tour of the soap factory is available every Thursday evening. Children can make their own soap (£6.50) or dip a candle at the back of the shop. ✉ *Home Farm, A841* ☎ *01770/302595* ⊕ *www.arranaromatics.com.*

Isle of Arran Cheese Company. Arran is famous for its cheeses, especially its cheddar and its Arran blue; stop here to sample and buy handmade Scottish cheeses. ✉ *The Home Farm, A841* ☎ *01770/302788* ⊕ *www. arranscheeseshop.co.uk.*

SPORTS AND THE OUTDOORS

Arran Adventure Company. Arran offers wonderful low-level walks as well as hill walking on Goatfell. The east of the island is generally calmer than the wild west coast, with its varied birdlife. All these activities, as well as mountain biking, gorge walking, and sea kayaking, are organized by Arran Adventure Company. ✉ *Shore Rd.* ☎ *01770/302244* ⊕ *auchrannie.co.uk* ⊘ *Closed Nov.–Mar.*

LAMLASH

4 miles south of Brodick.

With views offshore to Holy Island, which is now a Buddhist retreat, Lamlash has a breezy seaside-holiday atmosphere. To reach the highest point accessible by car, go through the village and turn right beside the bridge onto Ross Road, which climbs steeply from a thickly planted valley, **Glen Scorrodale,** and yields fine views of Lamlash Bay. From Lamlash you can explore the southern part of Arran: 4 miles to the southwest, **Whiting Bay** has a pleasant well-kept waterfront and a range of hotels and guesthouses. If you travel another 6 miles, you'll reach the little community of **Lagg,** which sits peacefully by the banks of the Kilmory Water.

GETTING HERE AND AROUND

You can reach Lamlash by driving south from Brodick on the A841. The town is also served by Stagecoach buses.

WHERE TO STAY

$
B&B/INN
🔲 **Lagg Hotel.** Arran's oldest inn is an 18th-century lodge with fireplaces in the common rooms and 11 acres of gardens and grounds that meander down to the river. **Pros:** beautiful gardens; warming fireplaces; nice local feel. **Cons:** floral designs everywhere; some rooms are small; Wi-Fi in public areas only. 💲 *Rooms from: £95* ✉ *A841, Kilmory* ☎ *01770/870255* ⊕ *www.lagghotel.com* ⇗ *13 rooms* ⦿ *Breakfast.*

SHOPPING

Patterson Arran. The store is famous for its preserves and marmalades, as well as its mustards. ✉ *The Old Mill, A841* ☎ *01770/600606* ⊕ *www. paterson-arran.com.*

MACHRIE

10 miles west of Brodick, 11 miles north of Lagg.

The area surrounding Machrie, home to a popular beach, is littered with prehistoric sites: chambered cairns, hut circles, and standing stones dating from the Bronze Age.

GETTING HERE AND AROUND

The quick route to Machrie is via the String Road (B880) from Brodick; turn off onto the Machrie Road 5 miles outside Brodick. A much longer but stunning journey will take you from Brodick, north to Lochranza, around the island to Machrie, and down the island's dramatic west coast, a distance of some 28 miles.

EXPLORING

Machrie Moor Stone Circles. From Machrie, a well-surfaced track takes you to a grassy moor by a ruined farm, where you can see the Machrie Moor Stone Circles: small, rounded granite-boulder circles and much taller, eerie red-sandstone monoliths. Out on the bare moor, the lost and lonely stones are very evocative, well worth a walk to see if you like the feeling of solitude. The stones are about 1½ miles outside Machrie; just follow the "Historic Scotland" sign pointing the way. The ground is boggy so go prepared.

WHERE TO EAT

$ ✕ **Cafe Thyme.** The road from Lochranza to Machrie follows the wilder
TURKISH west coast where seabirds and wildlife abound. It would be all too easy to miss the sign for Cafe Thyme on the left, but it is well worth watching for it. This bright and pleasant restaurant sitting above the road about a mile and a half inland, next to the Old Byre Visitor Centre, offers a surprising and delicious combination of Scottish and Turkish flavors (an expression of the owners' backgrounds) as well as fine views out to sea. Look for meze as well as *pides* (Turkish pizza)—try the haggis-and-cheese or crayfish-and-olive combinations. Parents will appreciate the huge play area fully visible from the restaurant. $ *Average main: £12* ✉ *Old Byre Visitor Centre* ☎ *01770/840608* ⊕ *www.oldbyre.co.uk/cafethyme* ⊘ *No dinner Oct.–Apr.* ⚑ *Reservations essential.*

SHOPPING

Old Byre Showroom. This shop sells sheepskin goods, hand-knit sweaters, leather goods, and rugs; Simon Thorborn's Pottery, which sits beside it, offers the chance to paint your own cups and plates. ✉ *Auchencar Farm, A841, 2 miles north of Machrie* ☎ *01770/840227* ⊕ *www.oldbyre.co.uk.*

LOCHRANZA

11 miles north of Brodick.

The road to Lochranza exposes another face of Arran: muddy, rocky beaches line one side, while the other has views of the sweeping slopes up to Goatfell and Caisteal Abhail (2,735 feet), whose stark granite peaks dominate the skyline of the north of the island. The variety of birdlife here is striking, which is why ornithologists flock to Arran in the off-season.

Arran's only distillery, the sparkling Isle of Arran Distillery, is in Lochranza, nestled in the hills overlooking Lochranza Bay.

GETTING HERE AND AROUND

Lochranza is north of Brodick via the A841.

EXPLORING

Isle of Arran Distillery. The open aspect and closeness to the sea explains the taste of Arran's well-respected single malt, light and airy and with the scent of sea and fields. The round white building housing the distillery sits comfortably among fields and hills in the nothernmost part of the island. The tours take the visitor through the process of creating whisky, with a small or slightly larger tasting depending on the level. The basic tour ends with a dram. The CASKS café-restaurant is a comfortable place for a long lunch. ✉ *Distillery Visitor Centre* ☎ *01770/830264* 🌐 *www.arranwhisky.com* 🎫 *Tours £7.50.*

Lochranza Castle. This ruined castle is quite picturesque, sitting as it does on a grassy bank framed by the bay. You'll often see deer grazing nearby or seals swimming in the bay. The ground-floor rooms and a few upstairs can be visited during the summer months. This is said to have been the landing place of Robert the Bruce when he returned from Rathlin Island in 1307 to start the campaign that won Scotland's independence. ✉ *Off A841* ☎ *0131/668–8800* 🌐 *www.historic-scotland.gov.uk* 🎫 *Free* 🕒 *Apr.–Sept., daily 9:30–5:30.*

WHERE TO STAY

$ 🏨 **Apple Lodge.** A charming whitewashed building that once served as a
B&B/INN pastor's house, this lodge beneath the hills at the edge of Lochranza has elegant landscaped gardens and a reputation for good home cooking. **Pros:** lovely setting on the outskirts of Lochranza; charming gardens. **Cons:** dinner not always available; no children under 12; credit cards not accepted. [$] *Rooms from: £78* ✉ *Apple Lodge, A841* ✣ *On the main road from Broddick into Lochranza, as you enter the village and before the distillery* ☎ *01770/830229* 🌐 *www.applelodgearran.co.uk* 💳 *No credit cards* 🕒 *Closed mid-Dec.–mid-Jan.* 🛏 *4 rooms, 1 suite* 🍴 *Breakfast.*

ISLAY AND JURA

Islay has a different character from the rest of the islands that make up the Hebrides. In contrast to areas where most residents live on crofts (small plots generally worked by people in their spare time), Islay's western half in particular has large, self-sustaining farms. Many of the island's wildlife preserves, historical sites, and beautiful beaches are also on the western side of the island. It's dangerous to swim at the coastal beaches, but the white-sand beaches around Loch Indaal are safe and clean. The southeast, by contrast, is mainly an extension of the island of Jura's inhospitable quartzite hills. Islay is particularly known for its birds, including the rare chough (a crow with red legs and beak) and, in winter, its barnacle geese. Its eight distilleries produce Islay's characteristically peaty malt whiskies, and most welcome visitors. They charge a fee for tours, which you can usually credit toward any whisky purchases.

BOWMORE

On Islay: 11 miles north of Port Ellen.

Bowmore, Islay's capital, is a good base for touring because it's central to Islay's main routes. A tidy town, its grid pattern was laid out in 1768 by local landowner Daniel Campbell, of Shawfield. Main Street stretches from the pier head to the commanding parish church, built in 1767 in an unusual circular design—so the devil could not hide in a corner.

GETTING HERE AND AROUND

Flybe flights from Glasgow to Islay Airport take 40 minutes; the airport is 5 miles north of Port Ellen. The trip by CalMac ferry from Kennacraig to Port Ellen takes about 2½ hours; ferries also travel less frequently to Port Askaig. From Port Ellen it is 10 miles on the A846 to reach Bowmore; drivers should use caution during the first mile out of Port Ellen, as the road is filled with sharp turns. The rest of the route is straight but bumpy, because the road is laid across peat bog. The ferry to Feolin on Jura departs from Port Askaig; the crossing takes five minutes.

Bus service is available on the island through Islay Coaches and Royal Mail; comprehensive timetables are available from the tourist information center.

ESSENTIALS

Air Travel Contact Islay Airport. ⊠ *A846, Glenegedale* ☎ *01496/302022* ⊕ *www.hial.co.uk.*

Visitor Information Bowmore Visitor Information Centre. ⊠ *The Square* ☎ *01496/305165* ⊕ *www.visitscotland.com.*

EXPLORING

Bowmore Distillery. Whisky lovers can tour this 1779 distillery, which has an appealing spot near the water's edge. The more expensive Craftsman's Tour, costing £55 per person, is best for those who fancy themselves experts; otherwise tours cost £6, and all must be booked in advance. ⊠ *School St.* ☎ *01496/810441* ⊕ *www.bowmore.com* ⌦ *£6 tour* ⊗ *Visitor center: Easter–Sept., Mon.–Sat. 9–5; Oct.–Mar., weekdays 9–5, Sat. 9–12:30. Tours: Easter–Sept., Mon.–Sat. at 10, 11, 2, 3, and 3:30, Sun. at 1 and 2; Oct.–Mar., weekdays at 10:30 and 3, Sat. at 9:30.*

Islay Woollen Mill. In a wooded hollow by the river, this mill has a fascinating array of machinery that proud owners Gordon and Sheila Covell will be happy to show you. A shop sells high-quality products that were woven on the premises. All the tartans and tweeds worn in the film *Braveheart* were woven here. ⊠ *A846* ✛ *3 miles outside Bridgend, off the main road to Port Askaig* ☎ *01496/810563* ⊕ *www. islaywoollenmill.co.uk* ⌦ *Free* ⊗ *Mon.–Sat. 10–5.*

WHERE TO EAT

$ ✕**Bowmore Taste of Islay.** This fairly new café-restaurant beside the Bowmore Distillery (and owned by it) serves sandwiches, soups, salads, and cakes through the day in pleasant and bright surroundings. Unusual for a café but hardly surprising in this neck of the woods, it also has a whisky menu. In the summer months the café also serves dinner, including haddock chowder, steaks, lamb burgers, and a chicken breast

BRITISH

ISLAY'S WHISKIES

In terms of population, Islay has more whisky distilleries than anywhere else in the world. They are all quite close to the sea, and visits almost always take you through some spectacular scenery.

Which of the local whiskies you prefer depends on your fondness for the distinctive scent of peat, the boggy material used for fertilizers and fires and whose smoke tints the island's air. The distilleries on the southeast coast of the island—including Laphroaig, Lagavulin, and Ardbeg—have the strongest taste of peat. You're allowed to add a little water when you enjoy a dram. The western distilleries—such as Bowmore, Bruichladdich, and Caol Ila—have that characteristic peaty

scent, but they are lighter and more flowery because they are often matured in sherry barrels. And Bunnahabhain, which looks out on to Jura, is unusually free of that characteristic Islay flavor.

All the distilleries offer basic tours for a few pounds and more expensive specialized tours geared toward whisky connoisseurs. These include reasonably priced taster tours, where you sample several top-notch whiskies, as well as more expensive tours that let you sip whiskies that are available nowhere else. The Islay Festival of Music and Malt ⊕ www.islayfestival.com, the last week in May, brings large numbers of whisky lovers to the island.

sandwich. $ *Average main: £12* ✉ *School St.* ☎ *01496/810491* ⊕ *www.bowmore.com* ⊗ *Closed Dec.–Mar. Closed Sun. and Mon. Apr.–Nov.*

$$
SEAFOOD
✕ **Harbour Inn.** The cheerfully noisy bar of this harborside inn is frequented by off-duty distillery workers who are happy to rub elbows with travelers and exchange island gossip. The recently refurbished restaurant and small hotel (seven rooms) offers a rather more upmarket experience. The dinner menu features local produce, especially the fruits of the sea—oysters, langoustines, mussels—in an elegant dining room looking out onto the water. It is now also owned by the Bowmore Distillery. $ *Average main: £18* ✉ *The Square* ☎ *01496/810330* ⊕ *www.harbour-inn.com* ⇄ *7 rooms* ❑ *Breakfast.*

SHOPPING

Islay Whisky Shop. If you haven't time to visit all of Islay's distilleries, let alone those elsewhere, you can do worse than visit this shop with its enormous collection of whiskies. The owner is enthusiastic and extremely knowledgeable and will take you on a mini-tour around his shelves. ✉ *Shore St.* ☎ *01496/810684* ⊕ *www.islaywhiskyshop.com.*

PORT CHARLOTTE

On Islay: 11 miles west of Bowmore.

A delightful conservation village (meaning an area of architectural or historical interest) at the head of Loch Indaal on Islay, Port Charlotte is home to the Museum of Islay Life, the charming Natural History Trust, and safe, sandy beaches. South of Port Charlotte, the A847 continues along the wild landscape of the Rhinns of Islay. The road ends

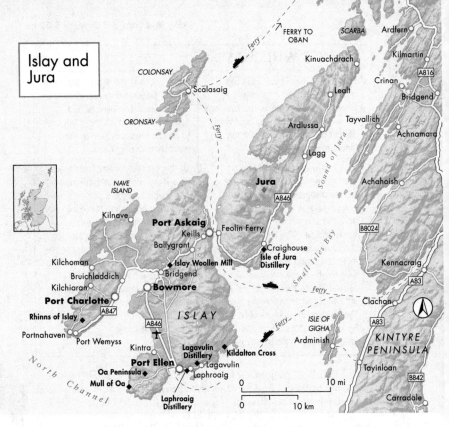

Islay and Jura

COLONSAY
Scalasaig
ORONSAY
NAVE ISLAND
Kilnave
Kilchoman
Bruichladdich
Kilchiaran
Port Charlotte
A847
Rhinns of Islay
Portnahaven
Port Wemyss
Kintra
North Channel

FERRY TO OBAN
SCARBA   Ardfern
Kinuachdrach   Kilmartin
                              A816
Lealt   Crinan
                        Bridgend
Tayvallich
Ardlussa   Achnamara
Lagg
Sound of Jura
Jura   Achahoish
A846
Port Askaig   Feolin Ferry   B8024
Keills
Ballygrant
Islay Woollen Mill
Bridgend   Isle of Jura Distillery   Kennacraig
Bowmore   Craighouse   A83
ISLAY   Clachan
A846   Small Isles Bay   A83
Ferry   ISLE OF GIGHA
Lagavulin Distillery   Kildalton Cross   KINTYRE PENINSULA
Port Ellen   Ardminish
Lagavulin   Tayinloan   B842
Oa Peninsula   Laphroaig
Mull of Oa
Laphroaig Distillery
0   10 mi
0   10 km
Carradale

at **Portnahaven** and its twin, **Port Wemyss**, where pretty white cottages built in a crescent around the headland belie the harsh lives of the fisher families who live and work here.

GETTING HERE AND AROUND
To reach Port Charlotte from Bowmore, take the A846 via Bridgend and then the A847, Portnahaven Road. Islay Coaches and Royal Mail buses also travel here from Bowmore.

EXPLORING
Museum of Islay Life. A converted church is home to this local museum, a haphazard but authentic collection of local artifacts, photographs, and memorabilia. There is also a local history archive. ⊠ *A847* ☎ *01496/850358* ⊕ *www.islaymuseum.org* 🎫 *£3.50* ☉ *Apr.–Oct., weekdays 10–5.*

FAMILY **Natural History Centre.** With its exhibits about the island's wildlife, the Natural History Centre has lots of hands-on activities for kids. It's a great stop on rainy days, and tickets are valid for a week. On Monday and Friday there are nature rambles, and family activities are offered throughout July and August. ⊠ *Main St.* ☎ *01496/850288* ⊕ *www. islaynaturalhistory.org* 🎫 *£3* ☉ *May–Oct., daily 10–4.*

Rhinns of Islay. South of Port Charlotte, the A847 continues along the wild landscape of the Rhinns of Islay. The road ends at **Portnahaven** and its twin, **Port Wemyss**. Planned at the same time, the two villages share a church, but with separate entrances. From Portnahaven you can often see gray seals on the rocks below. And there is a small pub here, too, easily mistaken for a private house. Return to Port Charlotte via the bleak, unclassified road that loops north and east, passing by the recumbent stone circle at Coultoon and the ruined chapel at Kilchiaran along the way. The strange whooping sound you may hear as you turn away from Portnahaven comes from Scotland's first wave-powered generator, sucking and blowing as it supplies electricity for both villages. It's well worth the climb down to the shore to see it in action.

WHERE TO STAY

$$$ HOTEL 🏨 **Port Charlotte Hotel.** Once a row of fishermen's cottages and with views over a sandy beach, this whitewashed Victorian hotel has been lovingly restored. **Pros:** beautiful location; lovely restaurant; views over the water. **Cons:** slightly expensive; rooms are quite small; can be a little noisy from the bar. [$] *Rooms from: £210* ✉ *Main St.* ☎ *01496/850360* 🌐 *www.portcharlottehotel.co.uk* 🛏 *10 rooms* 🍴 *Breakfast.*

PORT ELLEN

On Islay: 11 miles south of Bowmore.

Islay's sturdy community of Port Ellen was founded in the 1820s, and much of its architecture dates from the following decades. It has a harbor (ferries stop here), a few shops, and a handful of inns. The road traveling east from Port Ellen (the A846 to Ardbeg) passes three top distilleries and makes a pleasant afternoon's "whisky walk." All three distilleries offer tours, but you should call ahead for an appointment; there may be no tours on weekends at times.

GETTING HERE AND AROUND

It is likely that Port Ellen will be your port of arrival on Islay. From here you can travel north to Bowmore, along the A846 before turning northwest towards Bridgend and Port Askaig.

EXPLORING

TOP ATTRACTIONS

Islay Festival of Music and Malt. The last week in May, large numbers of whisky lovers descend on the island for this festival, the heart of which is Port Ellen. Distilleries all over Islay offer special events, and traditional music performances and ceilidhs take place all over Islay. Hotels and ferries (and the distilleries of course) are full to overflowing, so book well ahead. ✉ *Port Ellen* 🌐 *www.islayfestival.com.*

Lagavulin Distillery. The whisky produced here is certainly distinctive—it has the strongest peaty scent (the mark of Islay whisky) of all the island malts. Warehouse demonstrations take place daily at 10:30 year-round, and distillery tours are given early December through August; call ahead to make reservations. ✉ *A846* ☎ *01496/302400* 🌐 *www.discovering-distilleries.com* 🎟 *Distillery tour £6; warehouse demonstration £23*

8

⏲ *Tours: Apr.–Aug., daily at 9:30, 11:30, and 3:30; Dec.–Feb., Mon.–Sat. at 12:30; Feb., weekdays at 12:30; Mar., daily 9:30 and 12:30.*

Laphroaig Distillery. The whisky produced here is one of the most unusual in the Western Isles, with a tangy, peaty, seaweed-and-iodine flavor. The visitor center is free, and a basic tour costs £5. Call ahead for these and more expensive tour options. The distillery is a little less than a mile from Port Ellen. ✉ *A846* ☎ *01496/302418* 🌐 *www.laphroaig.com* 🎟 *£5* ⏲ *Mar.–Oct., daily 9:45–5; Nov.–Feb., daily 9:45–4:30.*

WORTH NOTING

Kildalton Cross. About 8 miles northeast of Port Ellen is one of the highlights of Scotland's Celtic heritage. After passing through a pleasantly rolling, partly wooded landscape, take a narrow road (it's signposted "Kildalton Cross") from Ardbeg. This leads to a ruined chapel with surrounding kirkyard, in which stands the finest carved cross anywhere in Scotland: the 8th-century Kildalton Cross. Carved from a single slab of epidiorite rock, the ringed cross is encrusted on both sides with elaborate designs in the style of the Iona school. The surrounding grave slabs date as far back as the 12th and 13th centuries. Recently a table with tea and biscuits has appeared here, with an honor box—for the visitor: a charming touch. ✉ *Port Ellen* 🌐 *www.historic-scotland.gov.uk.*

Oa Peninsula. The southern Oa Peninsula, west of Port Ellen, is a region of caves that's rich in smuggling lore. At its tip, the Mull of Oa, is a monument recalling the 650 men who lost their lives in 1918 when the British ships *Tuscania* and *Otranto* sank nearby. Bring good, strong walking shoes. ✉ *Port Ellen.*

WHERE TO STAY

$$$ HOTEL 🏨 **The Islay Hotel.** This charming refurbished hotel overlooking Port Ellen's harbor has large, bright rooms decorated in muted contemporary colors. **Pros:** central location; bright, welcoming interior; friendly staff. **Cons:** can get crowded. [$] *Rooms from: £180* ✉ *Charlotte St.* ☎ *01496/300109* 🌐 *www.theislayhotel.com* 🛏 *13 rooms* 🍴 *Breakfast.*

SPORTS AND THE OUTDOORS

GOLF

Machrie Golf Links. This course would be a lot more crowded if it were a little more accessible. Set among sand dunes and with views across a fine bay, it was designed in 1891 by Willie Campbell. It has changed very little since, apart from some minor changes in the 1970s.The dunes pose their own challenges, especially if you are gazing out to sea at the time. ✉ *Off A846, 4 miles from Port Ellen* ☎ *01496/302310* 🌐 *www.machrie.net* 🎟 *£65* ⛳ *18 holes, 5894 yards, par 71.*

HORSEBACK RIDING

Ballivicar Pony Trekking. The company leads horseback-riding trips on nearby beaches and into the surrounding countryside. ✉ *Ballivicar Farm, off A846* ☎ *01496/302251* 🌐 *www.islay-farm-accommodation.co.uk.*

PORT ASKAIG

On Islay: 11 miles northeast of Bowmore.

Serving as the ferry port for Jura and receiving ferries from Kenna-craig, Port Askaig is a mere cluster of cottages. Uphill, just outside the village, a side road travels along the coast, giving impressive views of Jura on the way. There are distilleries near here, too; make appointments for tours.

GETTING HERE AND AROUND

Traveling from Bowmore, you can reach Port Askaig (where the road ends) via A846. The village is also served by local buses.

EXPLORING

Bunnahabhain Distillery. Established in 1881, the Bunnahabhain (pronounced Boon-a-hain) Distillery sits on the shore, with dramatic views across to the Paps of Jura. This is one of the milder single malts on Islay, since peat enters its production process for only a few summer weeks. The distillery tour is informative and enthusiastic. You can upgrade to a more elaborate tour when you reserve ahead. ⊠ *A846* ☎ *01496/840646* ⊕ *www.bunnahabhain.com* ◷ *£7* ◷ *Tours: Apr., Mon.–Sat. at 10, 11:30, 1, 2:30; May.–Oct., Mon.–Sat. at 10, 11:30, 1, 2:30, and 4, Sun. at 11, 12:30, and 2; Nov.–Mar, weekdays by appointment 10–4:30.*

WHERE TO STAY

$$

B&B/INN

Kilmeny Country House. This luxurious bed-and-breakfast is on a 300-acre farm, but the rooms are so elegantly furnished that the place feels more like a hotel. **Pros:** elegant and quiet; great breakfast. **Cons:** easy to miss; up a farm road. Ⓢ *Rooms from: £135* ⊠ *A846, Ballygrant* ✛ *Signposted off the A846 to Port Askaig just before the village of Ballygrant* ☎ *01496/840668* ⊕ *www.kilmeny.co.uk* ⏎ *4 rooms* ◉ *Breakfast.*

8

JURA

5 minutes by ferry from Port Askaig.

The rugged, mountainous landscape of the island of Jura—home to only about 200 people—looms immediately east of Port Askaig, across the Sound of Islay: a perfect landscape for walkers. Jura has only one single-track road (the A846), which begins at Feolin, the ferry pier. It climbs across moorland, providing scenic views of the island's most striking feature, the Paps of Jura, three breast-shaped rounded peaks. The ruined Claig Castle, on an island just offshore, was built by the Lords of the Isles to control the sound. The island has no cash machines, so plan ahead.

Jura House lies between Feolin and Craighouse, the island's only village, some 8 miles away (its walled gardens are open to the public for part of the year). Jura's solitude attracted George Orwell to the remote farmhouse at Barnhill, where he completed his famous novel *1984*.

GETTING HERE AND AROUND

The Port Askaig–Feolin car ferry takes five minutes to cross the Sound of Islay, and there is a passenger-only ferry during the summer from Tayvallich on Argyll to Craighouse. Bus service is also available from Craighouse and Inverlussa.

EXPLORING

Isle of Jura Distillery. The community of Craighouse has the island's only distillery, producing malt whisky since 1810. Phone ahead to reserve your place on a tour. ✉ *Craighouse* ☎ *01496/840681* 🌐 *www.jurawhisky.com* 🎫 *Tours £6* 🕓 *Apr.–Sept, Mon.–Sat., tours at 11 and 2; Oct.–Mar., tours by appointment weekdays 10–2.*

Kinuachdrach. The settlement of Kinuachdrach once served as a crossing point to Scarba and the mainland. To get to Kinuachdrach after crossing the river at Lealt, follow the track beyond the surface road for 5 miles. The coastal footpath to Corryvreckan lies beyond, over the bare moors. This area has several enticements: the first is the house at **Barnhill** (not open to the public) where George Orwell wrote *1984*; the second, for wilderness enthusiasts, is the whirlpool of the **Gulf of Corryvreckan,** where Orwell nearly drowned. And then there is the unspoiled coastal scenery. A 20-mile round-trip, this is a good walk, drive, or taxi trip. ✉ *Jura.*

WHERE TO STAY

$ HOTEL 🏨 **Jura Hotel.** This hotel has a lot going for it, including great views, a handy location, and pleasant gardens—a good thing, considering it's the only show in town for both lodging and dining (the hotel automatically books your evening meal when you book a room). **Pros:** good views across the bay; spacious rooms; next door to distillery. **Cons:** some shared bathrooms; unreliable Wi-Fi. [$] *Rooms from: £99* ✉ *A846, Craighouse* ☎ *01496/820243* 🌐 *www.jurahotel.co.uk* 🛏 *17 rooms, 11 with bath* 🍴 *Breakfast.*

ISLE OF MULL AND IONA

Though its economy has historically been built on agriculture, fishing, and whisky distilling, today the Isle of Mull relies on tourism dollars—which makes sense, because there are many wonderful things to see here. The landscapes range from the pretty harbor of Tobermory and the gentle slopes around Dervaig to the dramatic Atlantic beaches on the west. In the south, the long road past the sweeping green slopes of the Ross of Mull leads to Iona, a year-round attraction. On the Isle of Mull, hotel restaurants will serve nonguests and are sometimes the only option.

GETTING HERE AND AROUND

Ferries to Mull are run by the ubiquitous Caledonian MacBrayne. Its most frequent car-ferry route to Mull is from Oban to Craignure (45 minutes). Two shorter routes are from Lochaline on the Morvern Peninsula to Fishnish (15 minutes), or Kilchoan (on the Adrnamurchan Peninsula) to Tobermory (15 minutes). These ferries do not accept reservations, and the Lochaline ferry does not run on Sunday. West Coast

Tours serves the east coast, running between Tobermory, Craignure, and Fionnphort (for the ferry to Iona).

CRAIGNURE

On Mull: 40-minute ferry crossing from Oban, 15-minute ferry crossing to Fishnish (5 miles northwest of Craignure) from Lochaline.

Craignure, little more than a pier and some houses, is close to the well-known Duart Castle. Reservations for the year-round ferries that travel from Oban to Craignure are advisable in summer. The ferry from Lochaline to Fishnish, just northwest of Craignure, does not accept reservations and does not run on Sunday.

GETTING HERE AND AROUND

The arrival point for the 40-minute ferry crossing from Oban, Craignure is the starting point for further travel on Mull northwest toward Salen and Tobermory, or toward Fionnphort and the Iona ferry to the southwest.

ESSENTIALS

Visitor Information **Craignure Information Centre.** ✉ *The Pierhead* ☎ *01680/812377* 🌐 *www.visitscotland.com.*

EXPLORING

Duart Castle. The 13th-century Duart Castle stands dramatically atop a cliff overlooking the Sound of Mull. The ancient seat of the Macleans, it was ruined by the Campbells in 1691 but restored by Sir Fitzroy Maclean in 1911. Inside you can visit the dungeons and state rooms, then climb the keep for a view of the waterfront. Below are the rocks where the *Swan,* a vessel sent by Oliver Cromwell to kidnap the 10-year-old clan chief, sank in 1653. Nearby stands the **Millennium Wood,** planted with groups of Mull's indigenous trees. To reach Duart by car, take the A849 and turn left around the shore of Duart Bay. From Craignure's ferry port, there is a direct bus that takes you to the castle in about 10 minutes. ✉ *A849, 3 miles southeast of Craignure* ☎ *01680/812309* 🌐 *www.duartcastle.com* 🎫 *£6* 🕒 *Apr., Sun.–Thurs. 11–4; May–mid-Oct., daily 10:30–5.*

WHERE TO STAY

$ B&B/INN 🏨 **Craignure Inn.** This 18th-century drovers inn, in a whitewashed building a short walk from the ferry pier, has a lively bar that often hosts local musicians. **Pros:** lively bar scene; hearty local food; expansive views. **Cons:** live music can get loud; bar can get very busy. [$] *Rooms from: £82* ✉ *A849, near the ferry pier* ☎ *01680/812305* 🌐 *www.craignure-inn.co.uk* 🛏 *3 rooms* 🍴 *Breakfast.*

DERVAIG

On Mull: 27 miles northwest of Craignure, 60 miles north of Fionnphort.

A pretty riverside village, Dervaig has a circular, pointed church tower that is reminiscent of the Irish-Celtic style of the 8th and 9th centuries. The Bellart is a good trout- and salmon-fishing river, and Calgary Bay, 5 miles away, has one of the best beaches on Mull.

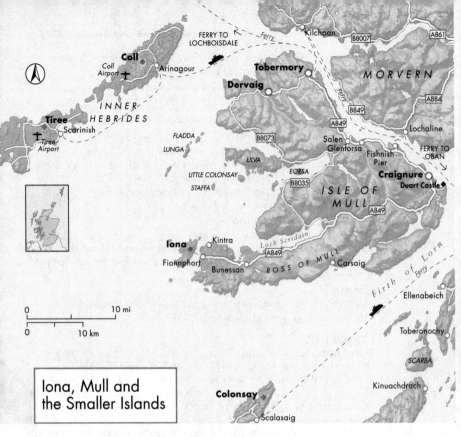

Iona, Mull and
the Smaller Islands

GETTING HERE AND AROUND
You can reach Dervaig from Craignure via the A849. From Salen, take
the B8073, and from Tobermory, take the B8073.

EXPLORING
Old Byre Heritage Centre. At this museum, an audiovisual presentation on
the history of the region is one of the highlights. The tearoom's whole-
some fare, particularly the homemade soup, is a boon to travelers, as is
the craft shop. You'll see signs for the center on the B8073, just before
Dervaig. ⊠ *Off B8073* ☎ *01688/400229* ⊕ *www.old-byre.co.uk* 🖾 *£4*
⊙ *Easter–Oct., Wed.–Sun. 10:30–6:30; last admission at 5:30.*

TOBERMORY

On Mull: 5 miles northeast of Dervaig, 21 miles north of Craignure.

Fodor's Choice Founded as a fishing station, Tobermory is now a lively tourist center
★ and a base for exploring Mull. The town is famous throughout Scotland
and beyond for its crescent of brightly painted houses around the harbor.

GETTING HERE AND AROUND
The most frequent service to Mull is via the Oban-Craignure ferry.
Tobermory is 21 miles from Craignure along the A849/848 (via Salen).

ESSENTIALS

Visitor Information Mull Information Centre. ⊠ *Ledaig Car Park* ☎ *01680/302875* ⊕ *www.exploremull.co.uk.*

WHERE TO EAT AND STAY

$$ ✕ **Café Fish.** This restaurant's location has certainly contributed to its
SEAFOOD success—it's perched on the pier at the end of Tobermory. The own-
Fodor'sChoice ers pride themselves on the freshness of their fish; they have their own
★ boat and bring in their own seafood each day. The fish is served simply,
grilled with a slice of lemon, to let the natural flavors speak for them-
selves. Diver-harvested scallops are served with vermouth and orange
juice over rice. Other popular dishes include fish stew and the langous-
tines and squat lobster (not really a lobster—it's related to crab) served
with garlic butter and granary bread. $ *Average main: £18* ⊠ *The Pier*
☎ *01688/301253* ⊕ *www.thecafefish.com* ⏱ *Closed Jan.–mid-Mar.*
⌕ *Reservations essential.*

$$ ☶ **Highland Cottage.** Set on the hill above the harbor, this family-run hotel
B&B/INN prides itself on its elegant rooms and the imaginative dishes in its dining
room. **Pros:** comfortable hotel; attentive owners; high-quality dining.
Cons: rooms are a bit small; no children under 10. $ *Rooms from:*
£150 ⊠ *Breadalbane St.* ☎ *01688/302030* ⊕ *www.highlandcottage.*
co.uk ↳ *6 rooms* ⏥ *Breakfast.*

$$ ☶ **Tobermory Hotel.** Made up of five former fishermen's cottages, this
HOTEL lodging on Tobermory's waterfront has a warm, intimate feel. **Pros:**
FAMILY adorable cottage setting with fireplace; toys for children. **Cons:**
small rooms; small bathrooms. $ *Rooms from: £136* ⊠ *Main St.*
☎ *01688/302091* ⊕ *www.thetobermoryhotel.com* ⏱ *Closed Nov.–Mar.*
↳ *18 rooms* ⏥ *Breakfast.*

$$ ☶ **Western Isles Hotel.** This grand hotel from the Victorian era looks
HOTEL down on Tobermory from its wonderful location overlooking the Sound
of Mull; it suffered a period of neglect, but is now being refurbished
and restored to its former elegance. **Pros:** the view is brilliant; spacious
public rooms; great food. **Cons:** some rooms look onto the car park;
rooms vary in size. $ *Rooms from: £100* ⊠ *Off B882* ☎ *01688/302012*
⊕ *www.westernisleshotel.co.uk* ↳ *26 rooms* ⏥ *Breakfast.*

NIGHTLIFE AND PERFORMING ARTS

Mull Theatre. The renowned Mull Theatre, founded in 1966, once prided
itself on being the smallest theater in the United Kingdom. Today it
has grown in size and in stature, and its productions tour not only the
islands, but the whole of Scotland. It's wise to book ahead. ⊠ *Druimfin,*
Salen Rd. ☎ *01688/302828* ⊕ *www.mulltheatre.com.*

IONA

5 minutes by ferry from Fionnphort (Mull), which is 36 miles west of
Craignure.

The ruined abbey on Iona gives little hint that this was once one of
the most important Christian religious centers in the land. The price-
less *Book of Kells* (now in Dublin) was illustrated here, and it was the
monks of Iona who spread Christian ideas across Scotland and the

north. The abbey was founded in the year 563 by the fiery and argumentative Columba (circa 521–97) after his expulsion from Ireland. Until the 11th century, many of Scotland's kings and rulers were buried here, their tombstones still visible inside the abbey. While few visitors venture beyond the pier and the abbey, there are several tranquil paths around the island.

GETTING HERE AND AROUND

Caledonian MacBrayne's ferry from Fionnphort departs at regular intervals throughout the year (£4.50 round-trip). Timetables are available on the Caledonian MacBrayne website. Note that cars are not permitted; there's a parking lot by the ferry at Fionnphort.

EXPLORING

Fodor's Choice ★ **Iona Abbey.** Overseen by St. Columba, who traveled here from Ireland, Iona was the birthplace of Christianity in Scotland in the 6th century. It survived repeated Norse sackings before falling into disuse around the time of the Reformation. Restoration work began at the beginning of the 20th century. Today the restored buildings serve as a spiritual center under the jurisdiction of the Church of Scotland. Guided tours by the Iona Community, an ecumenical religious group, begin every half hour in summer and on demand in winter. ✉ *Iona* ☎ *01681/700793* 🌐 *www.iona.org.uk* 🎫 *£7.10* 🕒 *Apr.–Sept., daily 9:30–5:30; Oct.–Mar., daily 9:30–4:30.*

WHERE TO STAY

$$ HOTEL 🏨 **St. Columba Hotel.** Rooms in this 1846 manse are very simply decorated, but all those on the front have glorious views across the Sound of Iona to Mull (and are more expensive). **Pros:** it's all about what's good for the earth and soul; nice log fires; Wi-Fi throughout the hotel. **Cons:** no TVs; basic decor. [$] *Rooms from: £127* ✉ *Next to cathedral, about ¼ mile from the ferry pier* ☎ *01681/700304* 🌐 *www.stcolumba-hotel.co.uk* 🕒 *Closed Nov.–Mar.* 🛏 *27 rooms* 🍴 *Breakfast.*

SHOPPING

Iona Community Shop. The shop carries Celtic-inspired gift items, as well as sheet music, songbooks, and CDs. It also sells local crafts and the Wild Goose publications of the Iona Community. ✉ *Across from Iona Abbey* ☎ *01681/700404* 🌐 *www.iona.org.uk.*

Low Door. This shop attached to the St. Columba Hotel sells locally produced jams, chutneys, and other artifacts as well as cookery books. ✉ *Beside St. Columba Hotel* ☎ *01681/700483* 🌐 *www.stcolumba-hotel.co.uk.*

THE SMALLER ISLANDS

The smaller islands, sometimes known as the Southern Hebrides, may seem quite remote but were once important centers of power and production. Successively depopulated by force or by emigration to Glasgow's industries or the promise of the Americas, the islands still survive on fishing, cattle and sheep raising, and, of course, whisky production. Their Gaelic language is vibrant once again, but their populations remain small. For the visitor, the experience is one of open, often barely populated landscapes and a slightly brooding sense of history.

TIRE

4-hour sail from Oban, via Coll.

Archaeological sites and good surfing make this windy island popular in summer.

GETTING HERE AND AROUND

Caledonian MacBrayne runs ferries to Tiree via Coll, four times a week (Tuesday, Thursday, Saturday, and Sunday). You can also fly here from Glasgow on Flybe or from Oban on Hebridean Air Services. On Tiree the Royal Mail postbus (which carries mail and passengers) runs an infrequent service around the island; there is a shared taxi service (☎ *01879/220311*), which you should book ahead of your arrival. An alternative is to rent a bike from **Skerryvore House** (☎ *01879/220268*).

ESSENTIALS

Air Travel Contact Tiree Airport. ⊠ *Off B8065* ☎ *01879/220456* ⊕ *www.hial.co.uk.*

EXPLORING

Tiree. A fertile, low-lying island with its own microclimate, Tiree is windswept, but has more hours of sunshine per year than any other part of the British Isles. Long, rolling Atlantic swells make it a favorite with surfers, and summer visitors can raise the population to the nearly 4,500 it supported in the 1830s. Among Tiree's several archaeological sites are a large boulder near Vaul covered with more than 50 Bronze Age cup marks, and an excavated *broch* (stone tower) at Dun Mor Vaul. It has one hotel and is served by the CalMac ferry from Oban. ⊕ *www.isleoftiree.com.*

COLL

3-hour sail from Oban.

Good birding and a number of ancient sites are among the attractions on Coll.

GETTING HERE AND AROUND

Caledonian MacBrayne runs ferries to Coll on Tuesday, Thursday, Saturday, and Sunday. You can also fly here from Oban on Hebridean Air Services. There is no public transportation on Coll, but you can rent a bike (☎ *01879/230333*) or use the island's one taxi (☎ *01879/230402*).

EXPLORING

Coll. Unlike their neighbors in nearby Tiree, Coll's residents were not forced to leave the island in the 19th century. Today half of the island's sparse population lives in its only village, Arinagour. Its coasts offer extraordinarily rich birdlife, particularly along the beautiful sandy beaches of its southwest. Coll is even lower lying than Tiree but also rockier and less fertile. The island is rich in archaeology, with standing stones at Totronald, a cairn at Annagour, and the remains of several Iron Age forts around the island. The keep of Breachacha Castle, a former stronghold of the Maclean clan on the south end of Coll, dates back to 1450. It is not open to the public, but you may view it from the road near Uig. ⊕ *www.visitcoll.co.uk.*

COLONSAY

2½-hour sail from Oban.

Less bleak than Coll and Tiree, Colonsay is one of Scotland's quietest, most unspoiled, and least populated islands. It is partly wooded, with a fine quasi-tropical garden at Colonsay House and a great variety of wildlife.

GETTING HERE AND AROUND

Caledonian MacBrayne ferries run to Colonsay on Monday, Wednesday, Friday, and Sunday. The island of Oronsay lies half a mile away and can be reached at certain times across a natural causeway. There is a limited postbus service on Colonsay; bikes can be rented from **A. McConnel** (☎ *01951/200355*).

EXPLORING

Colonsay. The beautiful beach at Kiloran Bay on Colonsay is an utterly peaceful place even at the height of summer. The standing stones at Kilchattan Farm are known as Fingal's Limpet Hammers. Fingal, or Finn, MacCoul is a warrior of massive size and strength in Celtic mythology. Standing before the stones, you can imagine Fingal wielding them like hammers to cull equally large limpets from Scotland's rocky coast. The island's social life revolves around the bar at the 19th-century Colonsay Hotel, 100 yards from the ferry pier. The adjacent island of Oronsay with its ruined cloister can be reached at low tide via a 1½-mile wade across a sandy sound. ⊕ *www.colonsay.org.uk.*

9

INVERNESS AND AROUND THE GREAT GLEN

Visit Fodors.com for advice, updates, and bookings

Updated by
Jack Jewers

Defined by its striking topography, the Great Glen brings together mountains and myths, history and wild nature—then lets you wash it all down with a dram of the world's finest whisky. Inverness is the gateway to an area in which the views from almost every twist and bend in the circuitous roads may take your breath away. There's also plenty here for history buffs, including Culloden Moor, where the last battle fought on British soil ended the hopes of the tragically outgunned Jacobite rebels in 1746.

The Great Glen Fault runs diagonally through the Highlands of Scotland and was formed when two tectonic plates collided, shoving masses of the crust southwest toward the Atlantic Ocean. Over time the rift broadened into a glen, and a thin line of lochs now lies along its seam. The most famous of these is deep, murky Loch Ness, home to the elusive Loch Ness monster.

The city of Inverness has a growing reputation for excellent restaurants, and from here nearly everything in the Great Glen is an easy day trip. Just south of the city the 13th-century ruined Urquhart Castle sits on the shores of Loch Ness. In Fort Augustus, the Caledonian Canal joins Inverness to Fort William via a series of 29 locks. At the western end of the canal, Ben Nevis, Britain's highest mountain, rises sharply. The Nevis Range, like Cairngorms National Park to the east, is ideal for walking, climbing, and mountain biking through the hills and glens.

Fort William makes a good base for exploring Glencoe, an awe-inspiring region that was also the scene of another notoriously murky episode in Scottish history: the Glencoe Massacre of 1692. It's an area where history seems to be imprinted on the landscape, and it remains desolate, with some of the steepest, most atmospheric hills in Scotland.

Just north of Fort William the Road to the Isles offers impressive coastal views. The Small Isles of Rum and Eigg create a low rocky skyline across the water. Near the start of this road lies Glenfinnan, where in 1745 Bonnie Prince Charlie rallied his Jacobite troops. The surrounding Morayshire coast is home to a more pastoral landscape, and 14th-century Cawdor Castle and its gardens have an opulent air. Nearby Brodie Castle has an awe-inspiring library and art collection.

Impressive long, sandy beaches stretch out along the coast from the towns of Nairn and Findhorn. Finally, the Malt Whisky Trail begins in Forres and follows the wide, fast River Spey south until it butts against the Cairngorm Mountains and the old Caledonian forests, with their diverse and rare wildlife.

TOP REASONS TO GO

Castles, fortresses, and battlefields: Hear stories of the Highland people and famous figures like Bonnie Prince Charlie, and absorb the atmosphere of castles and battlefields, at Culloden Moor, Cawdor and Brodie castles, Fort George, and Glencoe.

Hill walking and outdoor activities: The Great Glen is renowned for its hill walking. Some of the best routes are around Glen Nevis, Glencoe, and on Ben Nevis, the highest mountain in Britain. It's not just hiking: Glenmore Lodge in the Cairngorms offers everything from kayaking to mountain biking to ice climbing.

Wild landscapes and rare wildlife: Spot rare plants and beasts including tiny least willow trees and golden eagles in the near-arctic tundra of Cairngorms National Park.

Whisky tours: The two western-most distilleries on the Malt Whisky Trail are in Forres. Benromach is the smallest distillery in Moray and has excellent tours; Dallas Dhu is preserved as a museum. You can strike out from here to nearby distilleries in Speyside (⇨ *see Chapter 7*).

Boat trips: There are many ferries to the Small Isles (or to Skye) from Arisaig and Mallaig. You can also go Nessie-watching on Loch Ness or hire a small boat and travel the Caledonian Canal.

ORIENTATION AND PLANNING

GETTING ORIENTED

If Inverness is the center point of a compass, the Great Glen spreads out to the east, south, and west. To the east stretches the Morayshire coast, populated with castles, distilleries, and beaches. Head southeast and you hit the Cairngorms National Park and other nature preserves. The A82 heads south from Inverness, hugging the west side of Loch Ness. Nearby are the contemplative ruins at Urquhart Castle and the interesting locks of the Caledonian Canal. Farther southwest, Fort William can be a good base for day trips to the foreboding and steep mountain pass of Glencoe.

Inverness and Nearby. From the small city of Inverness, just about anywhere in the Great Glen is a day trip. Spend your days exploring Culloden Moor, Brodie Castle, or Cawdor Castle. There are long, walkable beaches at Nairn and Findhorn.

Speyside and the Cairngorms. Speyside is best known for its whisky distilleries, and those who enjoy a good dram often follow the Whisky Trail. In and around the Cairngorms there are mountains, lochs, rivers, and dozens of cycling and walking paths that make it tailor-made for outdoors enthusiasts.

Loch Ness, Fort William, and Nearby. Have a go trying to spot Nessie from the banks of Loch Ness. For something wilder, base yourself at Fort William and take in the spectacular scenery of Glencoe and Glen Nevis. If you dare, climb Britain's highest peak, Ben Nevis. The Road to the Small Isles, known for larger-than-life figures both old (the Bonnie Prince) and new (Harry Potter), has classic views across water to rocky islands perched on blue seas.

PLANNING

WHEN TO GO
Late spring to early autumn is the best time to visit the Great Glen. If you catch good weather in summer, the days can be glorious. Unfortunately summer is also when you will encounter midges (tiny biting insects: keep walking, as they can't move very fast). Winter can bring a damp chill, gusty winds, and snow-blocked roads, although many Scots value the open fires and the warming whisky that make the off-season so appealing.

PLANNING YOUR TIME
The Great Glen is an enormous area that can easily be broken into two separate trips. The first would be based in or near Inverness, allowing an exploration of Speyside, the Cairngorms, Cawdor and Brodie castles, and perhaps a few whisky-distillery tours. The second moves through the cloud-laden Glencoe and down through the moody Rannoch Moor, or toward the Road to the Isles; you could stay near Glencoe or in Fort William. To do the area justice you probably need at least three days.

For those with more time, a trip around the Great Glen could be combined with forays north into the Northern Highlands, east toward Aberdeen and the rest of the Malt Whisky Trail, southeastward to the Central Highlands, or south to Argyll.

GETTING HERE AND AROUND
AIR TRAVEL
Inverness Airport has flights from London, Edinburgh, and Glasgow. Domestic flights covering the Highlands and islands are operated by easyJet and Flybe. Fort William has bus and train connections with Glasgow, so Glasgow Airport can be a good access point.

BUS TRAVEL
A long-distance Scottish Citylink service connects Glasgow and Fort William. Inverness is also well served from the central belt of Scotland. Discount carrier Megabus (book online to avoid phone charges) has service to Inverness from various cities.

Traveling around the Great Glen area without a car is challenging if not impossible, especially in the more rural areas. Stagecoach Highlands serves the Great Glen and around Fort William. A handful of postbus services (run by the postal service) can help get you to a few of the more remote corners of the area, although just a few seats are available on each bus.

Bus Contacts Megabus. ☎ *0900/160–0900* ⊕ *www.megabus.com.* **Royal Mail Post Buses.** ☎ *0345/774–0740* ⊕ *www.royalmail.com.* **Scottish City-link.** ☎ *0871/266–3333* ⊕ *www.citylink.co.uk.* **Stagecoach Highlands.** ☎ *01463/233371* ⊕ *www.stagecoachbus.com.*

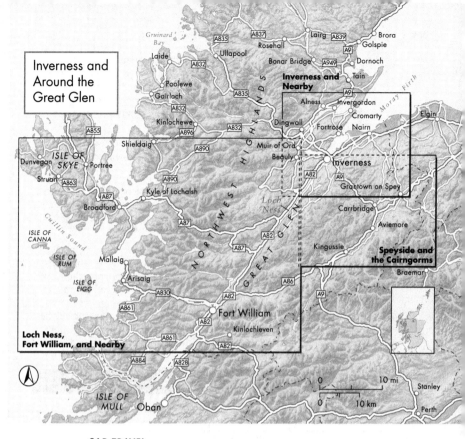

Inverness and Around the Great Glen

CAR TRAVEL

As in all areas of rural Scotland, a car is a great asset for exploring the Great Glen, especially because the best of the area is away from the main roads. You can use the main A82 from Inverness to Fort William, or use the smaller B862/B852 roads to explore the much quieter east side of Loch Ness. Mallaig, west of Fort William, is reached via a new road, but there are still a few narrow and winding single-lane roads, which require slower speeds and concentration.

In the Great Glen the best sights are often hidden from the main road, which is an excellent reason to favor peaceful rural byways and to avoid as much as possible the busy A96 and A9, which carry much of the traffic in the area.

TRAIN TRAVEL

ScotRail has connections from London to Inverness and Fort William (including overnight sleeper service), as well as reliable links from Glasgow and Edinburgh. There's train service between Glasgow (Queen Street) and Inverness, via Aviemore, which gives access to the heart of Speyside.

Although there's no rail connection among towns within the Great Glen, this area has the West Highland Line, which links Fort William to Mallaig. This train, run by ScotRail, remains the most enjoyable way to experience the rugged hills and loch scenery between these two places. The Jacobite Steam Train is an exciting summer (mid-May to mid-October) option on the same route.

Train Contacts Jacobite Steam Train. ☎ *0844/850–4685* ⊕ *www. westcoastrailways.co.uk.* **ScotRail.** ☎ *0344/811–0141* ⊕ *www.scotrail.co.uk.*

RESTAURANTS

Inverness, Aviemore, and Fort William have plenty of cafés and restaurants in all price ranges. Inverness has particularly diverse dining options. Outside the towns there are many country-house hotels serving superb meals.

HOTELS

In the Great Glen, towns have a range of accommodations ranging from cozy inns to expansive hotels; in more remote areas your choice will usually be limited to smaller establishments. Because this is an established vacation area, you should have no trouble finding a room for a night; however, the area is quite busy in the peak season and the best places book up early. In Inverness, you may find it more appealing to stay outside the city center or in the nearby, pretty countryside. *Hotel reviews have been shortened. For full information, visit Fodors.com.*

WHAT IT COSTS IN POUNDS			
	$	$$	$$$	$$$$
Restaurants	Under £15	£15–£19	£20–£25	Over £25
Hotels	Under £100	£100–£160	£161–£220	Over £220

Restaurant prices are the average cost of a main course at dinner or, if dinner is not served, at lunch. Hotel prices are the lowest cost of a standard double room in high season, including 20% V.A.T.

TOURS

Inverness Tours. This outfitter runs the occasional boat cruise but they're mainly known for their very good tours around the Highlands in well-equipped vehicles, which are led by expert guides and heritage enthusiasts. However, they price per minibus, not per person, so while they're quite a bargain for parties of six or seven, they're less appealing for small groups. It may be possible to get single tickets if another group is willing to sell their unused space. ☎ *01667/455699* ⊕ *www. invernesstours.com* 🖼 *From £150.*

J.A. Johnstone. At the more luxurious end of the scale, this company offers chauffeur-driven tours of the Highlands in air-conditioned Mercedes sedans. Tours are completely tailored to what you want to see, although the guides have an encyclopedic knowledge of the region. The company also runs multiday tours of the Scottish regions, and they can help booking accommodations along the way. ☎ *01463/798372* ⊕ *www.jajcd.com* 🖼 *From £360.*

INVERNESS AND NEARBY

At the center of this region is Inverness, a small but appealing city that makes a useful gateway to the Great Glen. It has an increasingly strong range of restaurants and accommodations, but its cultural offerings remain more or less limited to what is happening at the Eden Court Theatre and the live music at a few good pubs.

East of Inverness, the infamous Culloden Moor still looks desolate on most days, and you can easily imagine the fierce, brief, and bloody battle that took place here in 1746 that ended in final, catastrophic defeat for the Jacobites and their quest to restore the exiled Stewarts to the British throne. Because Jacobite tales are interwoven with landmarks throughout this entire area, you will get much more out of this storied landscape if you first learn something about this thorny but colorful period of Scottish history. The Morayshire coast boasts many long beaches and some refined castles (Cawdor and Brodie) that are definitely worth a visit. Moving east along the inner Moray Firth, you might be tempted by Benromach distillery in Forres, a taste of what you can find farther south if you follow the Malt Whisky Trail.

INVERNESS

176 miles north of Glasgow, 109 miles northwest of Aberdeen, 161 miles northwest of Edinburgh.

It's not the prettiest or the most charming Scottish city, but with a few attractions and some reliably good hotels and restaurants, Inverness makes a practical base for exploring a region that has a lot to offer. From here you can fan out in almost any direction for interesting day trips: east to Moray and the distilleries near Forres, southeast to the Cairngorms, and south to Loch Ness. Throughout its past the town was burned and ravaged by Highland clans competing for dominance.

GETTING HERE AND AROUND

You can easily fly into Inverness Airport, as there are daily flights from London, Bristol, Birmingham, Manchester, and Belfast. However, there are also easy train and bus connections from Glasgow Airport. Scottish Citylink has service here, and Megabus has long-distance bus service from Edinburgh and Glasgow. ScotRail runs trains here from London, Edinburgh, Glasgow, and other cities.

Once you're here, you can explore much of the city on foot. A rental car makes exploring the surrounding area much easier. But if you don't have a car, there are bus and boat tours from the city center to a number of places in the Great Glen.

An unusual option from Inverness is a day trip to Orkney. John O'Groats Ferries runs day tours from Inverness to Orkney, daily from May through September. They cost £32 round-trip.

ESSENTIALS

Airport Contact Inverness Airport. ✉ *Dalcross* ☎ *01667/464000* ⊕ *www.hial. co.uk/inverness-airport.*

Boat Contact John O'Groats Ferries. ☎ *01955/611353* ⊕ *www.jogferry.co.uk.*

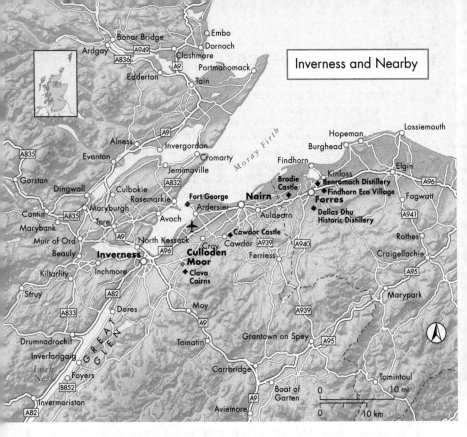

Inverness and Nearby

Bus Contact **Inverness Coach Station.** ✉ *Margaret St.* ☎ *01463/233371.*

Visitor Information **Inverness.** ✉ *Castle Wynd* ☎ *01463/252401* ⊕ *www.inverness-scotland.com.*

EXPLORING

TOP ATTRACTIONS

Fort George. After the fateful battle at Culloden, the nervous government in London ordered the construction of a large fort on a promontory reaching into the Moray Firth. Fort George was started in 1748 and completed some 20 years later. It's one of the best-preserved 18th-century military fortifications in Europe. At its height it housed 1,600 men and around 30,000 pounds of gunpowder. The on-site Highlanders Museum gives you a glimpse of the fort's history. The fort is 14 miles northeast of Inverness. ✉ *Old Military Rd., Ardersier* ☎ *01667/460232* ⊕ *www.historic-scotland.gov.uk* 🎟 *£9* ⊙ *Apr.–Sept., daily 9:30–5:30; Oct.–Mar., daily 10–4:30; last admission 45 mins before closing.*

Inverness Castle. One of Inverness's few historic landmarks is reddish sandstone Inverness Castle (now the local Sheriff Court), nestled above the river off Castle Road on Castle Hill. The current structure is Victorian, built after a former fort was blown up by the Jacobites in the

1745 campaign. The castle isn't open to the public, but you are free to wander the grounds. ⊠ *41 Castle St.*

WORTH NOTING

Inverness Cathedral. This handsome Victorian cathedral, dating from 1869, has two unique claims to fame; in addition to being the northernmost cathedral in the British Isles, it was, more significantly, the first cathedral to be built in Britain after the Reformation. The twin-turreted exterior of the building is made from characteristically reddish local Tarradale stone. Inside it follows a medieval layout, with the addition of an unusual patterned wooden floor. Check out the beautiful white marble font, carved in the shape of a seated angel. ⊠ *Ardross St.* ☎ *01463/233535* ⊕ *moray.anglican.org/inverness-cathedral* ☜ *Free* ⊙ *Daily 6–5; times vary in winter.*

FAMILY **Inverness Museum and Art Gallery.** The small but excellent Inverness Museum and Art Gallery covers archaeology, art, local history, and the natural environment in its lively displays. The museum is also home to the Highland Photographic Archive. ⊠ *Castle Wynd* ☎ *01463/237114* ⊕ *www.highlifehighland.com/inverness-museum-and-art-gallery* ☜ *Free* ⊙ *Apr.–Oct., Tues.–Sat. 10–5.*

Phoenix Boat Trips. With two-hour trips by boat from Inverness harbor into the Moray Firth, Phoenix Boat Trips offers you the chance to see dolphins in their breeding areas. The modern, ex-naval SWIFT vessels depart daily at 10 and 1:30, with additional evening trips on certain dates in summer. Sailing times may be affected by bad weather. Tickets cost £30. ⊠ *Inverness Marina, Longman Dr.* ☎ *0770/316–8097* ⊕ *www.inverness-dolphin-trips.co.uk.*

WHERE TO EAT

$$ ✕ **Cafe 1.** Consistently recommended by locals as one of the best res-
MODERN BRITISH taurants in the area, Cafe 1 really practices what they preach in terms
Fodor's Choice of sustainable, local produce. Taking inspiration from such big names
★ as Blue Hill in New York, the restaurant has recently started rearing its own herds to provide the Hebridean lamb and Highland beef on their menu, maybe served with a simple order of chips (thick-cut fries) and a sweet whisky-and-mustard sauce. The atmosphere is casual, and the prices, though high for Inverness, won't raise too many eyebrows among those used to city dining. The tiny bar at the front has a great view of the castle. $ *Average main: £17* ⊠ *75 Castle St.* ☎ *01463/226200* ⊕ *www. cafe1.net* ⊙ *Closed Sun.*

$ ✕ **Dores Inn.** Off a pretty country road on the eastern shore of Loch
BRITISH Ness, this low-slung, white-stone eatery is the perfect place to stop for lunch or dinner. The menu is a combination of well-prepared old favorites—fish-and-chips, perhaps, or neeps and tatties (turnips and potatoes)—together with steaks, lamb, and seafood. It's busy during the summer and on weekends, so be sure to book ahead. For dessert, try the local ice cream (handmade on the "Black Isle" peninsula), served with fresh berry compote. $ *Average main: £12* ⊠ *Off B862, Dores* ☎ *01463/751203* ⊕ *www.thedoresinn.co.uk.*

9

$$ BISTRO FAMILY 🍴 **Fig and Thistle Bistro.** This intimate little restaurant has been packing in the crowds nightly since it opened in 2015. Modern bistro fare is presented stylishly but without fuss—goat cheese and fig tart on a bed of oakleaf lettuce to start, perhaps, followed by some perfectly poached local salmon, or roast duck with blackberries and garden veggies. Or you could have a simple burger and chips, served with homemade slaw. Try the mango crème brûlée for dessert (if you can resist the chocolate profiteroles). The atmosphere is lively and the staff run things effortlessly well—but you'll need a reservation, especially on weekends. [$] *Average main: £15* ✉ *4A Stephens Brae* ☎ *01463/712422* ⏲ *Closed Sun. No lunch Mon.*

FISHING

The Great Glen is laced with rivers and lochs where you can fly-fish for salmon and trout. The fishing seasons are as follows: salmon, from early February through September or early October (depending on the area); brown trout, from March 15 to September 30; sea trout, from May through September or early October; rainbow trout year-round. Sea angling from shore or boat is also possible. Tourist centers can provide information on locations, permits, and fishing rights.

$$ ITALIAN 🍴 **Riva.** Facing Inverness Castle, Riva has views over the River Ness from its window seats. The dining room has subtly lighted deep-red walls lined with black-and-white photographs of Italian cityscapes. Tasty Italian dishes include pasta carbonara (with eggs, cream, and pancetta), as well as more unusual concoctions like tagliatelle with smoked salmon and a tomato cream sauce. There is a separate pizzeria upstairs from the main dining room. [$] *Average main: £15* ✉ *4–6 Ness Walk* ☎ *01463/237377* 🌐 *www.rivarestaurant.co.uk* ⏲ *No lunch Sun.*

$$$ BRASSERIE Fodor's Choice ★ 🍴 **Rocpool Restaurant.** Another perennial, the Rocpool has a frequently changing menu of modern bistro classics, with a few international twists. Local seafood is a specialty—John Dory from Kinlochbervie Bay served with seasonal vegetables, or monkfish and prawns cooked in chile and cilantro, for example. ■ TIP→ **The early evening menu is an exceptional value, at just £18 for two courses.** The wine list is excellent; for a splurge, try the deliciously dark and fruity Meerlust Stellenbosch with a plate of local steak or lamb. [$] *Average main: £21* ✉ *1 Ness Walk* ☎ *01463/717274* 🌐 *www.rocpoolrestaurant.com* ⏲ *Closed Sun.*

WHERE TO STAY

There are many places to stay in Inverness, but if your goal is to explore the countryside, a hotel outside the center may be a good choice.

$ B&B/INN 🏨 **Atholdene House.** This family-run stone villa dating from 1879 extends a warm welcome with a roaring fire. **Pros:** free Wi-Fi; friendly, family-run atmosphere; check-in until 9 pm, later than most small B&Bs. **Cons:** you have to choose breakfast the night before; small bedrooms; two-night minimum in summer. [$] *Rooms from: £85* ✉ *20 Southside Rd.* ☎ *01463/233565* 🌐 *www.atholdene.com* 🛏 *9 rooms* 🍽 *Breakfast.*

$ B&B/INN 🏨 **Avalon.** A 20-minute walk from the city center, this neat and modern B&B is a rare find. **Pros:** friendly and well run; good-size rooms. **Cons:** slightly far outside the city; minimum stay on some dates; not for families with very young kids (they must be "old enough to sleep in a room of their own"). $ *Rooms from: £75* ⊠ *79 Glenarquhart Rd.* ☎ *01463/239075* ⊕ *www.inverness-loch-ness.co.uk* ⤶ *6 rooms* ¶⊖¶ *Breakfast.*

$ ⊞ **Bluebell House.** Each room at Bluebell House has sturdy oak fur-
B&B/INN nishings, including a downstairs bedroom with a full-curtained four-
poster bed and a curved chaise lounge. **Pros:** large rooms; decadent
furnishing; great hosts. **Cons:** smallish bathrooms; no windows in
bathrooms. $ *Rooms from: £95* ⊠ *31 Kenneth St.* ☎ *01463/238201*
⊕ *www.bluebell-house.com* ⤶ *4 rooms* ¶⊖¶ *Breakfast.*

$$$ ⊞ **Bunchrew House Hotel.** This 17th-century baronial mansion, its tur-
HOTEL rets reflected in a glassy lake, looks like something from a Scottish
fairy tale. **Pros:** beautiful setting; atmospheric building; good restaurant.
Cons: some rooms could do with refurbishment. $ *Rooms from: £180*
⊠ *Off A862, about 3 miles west of Inverness* ☎ *01463/234917* ⊕ *www.
bunchrew-inverness.co.uk* ⤶ *16 rooms* ¶⊖¶ *Breakfast.*

$ ⊞ **Moyness House.** On a quiet residential street with well-trimmed hedges
B&B/INN a few minutes from downtown Inverness, this lovely Victorian villa was
once the home of Scottish author Neil M. Gunn (1891–1973), known
for short stories and novels that evoke images of the Highlands, such
as *Morning Tide, Highland River,* and *Butcher's Broom.* **Pros:** beautiful building; lovely garden; great location near the river. **Cons:** public
rooms a bit fussy for some; books up quickly; harsh cancellation policy. $ *Rooms from: £78* ⊠ *6 Bruce Gardens* ☎ *01463/233836* ⊕ *www.
moyness.co.uk* ⤶ *6 rooms* ¶⊖¶ *Breakfast.*

$$ ⊞ **Strathness House.** Standing on the banks of the River Ness, this
B&B/INN 12-room guesthouse is a quick walk from the well-regarded Eden Court
Theatre and the rest of the attractions of the city center. **Pros:** overlooks
the river; close to the city center; free Wi-Fi. **Cons:** parking can be dif-
ficult. $ *Rooms from: £105* ⊠ *4 Adross Terr.* ☎ *01463/232765* ⊕ *www.
strathnesshouse.com* ⤶ *12 rooms* ¶⊖¶ *Breakfast.*

$$ ⊞ **Trafford Bank.** A 15-minute walk from downtown Inverness, this
B&B/INN delightful little B&B makes for a practical but stylish base. **Pros:** wel-
coming atmosphere; stylish rooms; relaxing vibe. **Cons:** rooms on the
small side. $ *Rooms from: £120* ⊠ *96 Fairfield Rd.* ☎ *01463/241414*
⊕ *www.traffordbankguesthouse.co.uk* ⤶ *5 rooms* ¶⊖¶ *Breakfast.*

NIGHTLIFE AND PERFORMING ARTS
BARS AND LOUNGES

Blackfriars Pub. Blackfriars Pub, built in 1793, prides itself on its cask-
conditioned ales. You can enjoy one to the accompaniment of regular live entertainment including jazz nights and *ceilidhs* (a traditional
mix of country dancing, music, and song). ⊠ *93–95 Academy St.*
☎ *01463/233881.*

Hootananny. An odd combination of Scottish pub, concert hall, and
Thai restaurant, Hootananny is one of the best places in the region
to hear live music. The excellent pub has a warm atmosphere and
serves food that comes highly recommended by locals. Several bands
play each Saturday evening and a few during the week, too—check
the website for listings. ⊠ *67 Church St.* ☎ *01463/233651* ⊕ *www.
hootananny inverness.co.uk.*

9

THEATER

Eden Court Theatre. The varied program at this popular local theater includes films, music, comedy, ballet, and even pantomime. Check out the art gallery and the bright café, and take a walk around the magnificent Bishop's Palace. ⊠ *Bishops Rd.* ☎ *01463/234234* ⊕ *www.edencourt.co.uk.*

SHOPPING

Although Inverness has the usual indoor shopping malls and department stores, the most interesting goods are in the specialty outlets in and around town.

BOOKSTORES

Leakey's Secondhand Bookshop. This shop claims to be the biggest secondhand bookstore in Scotland. When you get tired of leafing through the 100,000 or so titles, climb to the mezzanine café and study the cavernous church interior. Antique prints and maps are housed on the balcony. ⊠ *Greyfriars Hall, Church St.* ☎ *01463/239947.*

CLOTHING

Duncan Chisholm. This shop specializes in Highland dress and tartans. Mail-order and made-to-measure services are available. ⊠ *47–51 Castle St.* ☎ *01463/234599* ⊕ *www.kilts.co.uk.*

GALLERIES

Castle Gallery. The excellent Castle Gallery sells contemporary paintings, sculpture, prints, and crafts. It also hosts frequently changing exhibitions by up-and-coming artists. ⊠ *43 Castle St.* ☎ *01463/729512* ⊕ *www.castlegallery.co.uk.*

Riverside Gallery. Paintings, etchings, and prints of Highland landscapes, as well as abstract and representational contemporary work by Highland artists are available at the Riverside Gallery. ⊠ *11 Bank St.* ☎ *01463/224781* ⊕ *www.riverside-gallery.co.uk.*

LOCAL SPECIALTIES

The Chocolate Place. To-die-for Belgian chocolates, completely free of artificial preservatives, are handmade at this delightfully sweet little family-run store. In addition to a wide variety of indulgent treats, they also sell a range of dairy and gluten-free chocolates, and a few chocolate-related souvenirs ("chocolate fund" piggy bank, anyone?) ⊠ *15 Chapel St.* ☎ *01463/232684* ⊕ *www.thechocolateplace.co.uk.*

Highland Wineries. Fruit liqueurs, jams, pickles, and other delicacies made from unusual Scottish ingredients can be bought from this shop at Moniack Castle. Anyone for a glass of silver birch wine? ⊠ *A862, 7 miles west of Inverness, Kirkhill* ☎ *01463/831283* ⊕ *www.highlandwineries.co.uk.*

SHOPPING CENTER

Victorian Market. Don't miss the colorful Victorian Market, built in 1870. The atmospheric indoor space houses more than 40 privately owned specialty shops. ⊠ *Academy St.* ☎ *01463/724273.*

GOLF

Fodor's Choice
★ **Castle Stuart Golf Links.** Opened in 2009, this course overlooking the Moray Firth is already considered one of Scotland's finest, hosting the Scottish Open in 2011. Expect undulating fairways and extensive bunkers that test your mettle. The 210-yard 17th hole provides perilous cliff-top play; the wind can defeat the canniest player. The art deco–inspired clubhouse offers stunning views of the water. ⊠ *B9039* ☎ *01463/796111* ⊕ *www.castlestuartgolf.com* 💷 *£190 May–Oct., £140 Apr. and Nov.* ⅃ *18 holes, 6553 yards, par 72* ⊗ *Apr.–Nov., daily.*

Inverness Golf Club. Established in 1883, and partly designed by famous British Open champion and course designer James Braid, Inverness Golf Club welcomes visitors to its parkland course 1 mile from downtown. The tree-lined course overlooking the Beauly Firth presents some unique challenges to keep even experienced golfers on their toes. ⊠ *Culcabock Rd.* ☎ *01463/239882* ⊕ *www.invernessgolfclub.co.uk* 💷 *£38 Apr., £50 May–Sept., £28 Oct., £20 Nov.–Mar.* ⅃ *18 holes, 6256 yards, par 69.*

Torvean Golf Course. This municipal course has one of the longest par-5 holes (565 yards) in the north of Scotland. There are quite a few water hazards, including the Caledonian Canal. One of the most challenging sections is Torvean Hill, a famous local landmark colloquially known as the "Hill of Bean"—partly in reference to its history (the "Bean" is thought to be the 11th-century St. Bean)—but also as a wry nod to what the foolhardy may assume its gradient amounts to. ⊠ *Glenurquhart Rd.* ☎ *01463/225651* ⊕ *www.torveangolfclub.co.uk* 💷 *£35 weekdays, £40 weekends* ⅃ *18 holes, 5784 yards, par 68.*

CULLODEN MOOR

8 miles east of Inverness.

Culloden Moor was the scene of the last battle fought on British soil—and to this day its name is enough to invoke raw and tragic feelings in Scotland. Austere and windswept, it's also a place of outstanding natural beauty.

GETTING HERE AND AROUND

Driving along the B9006 from Inverness is the easiest way to Culloden Moor, and there's a large car park to handle many visitors. Local buses also run from Inverness to the battlefield.

EXPLORING

Clava Cairns. Not far from Culloden, on a narrow road southeast of the battlefield, are the Clava Cairns, dating from the Bronze Age. In a cluster among the trees, these stones and monuments form a large ring with underground passage graves that are reached via a tunnel. Helpful placards put everything into historical context. ⊠ *B851, Culloden* 💷 *Free* ⊗ *Open 24 hrs.*

Fodor's Choice
★ **Culloden Moor.** Here, on a cold April day in 1746, the hopelessly outgunned Jacobite forces of Bonnie Prince Charlie were destroyed by King George II's army. The victorious commander, the Duke of Cumberland (George II's son), earned the name of the "Butcher" of Cumberland for the bloody reprisals carried out by his men on Highland families,

CLOSE UP

Bonnie Prince Charlie

His life became the stuff of legend. Charles Edward Louis John Casimir Silvester Maria Stuart—better known as Bonnie Prince Charlie, or the Young Pretender—was born in Rome in 1720. The grandson of ousted King James II of England, Scotland, and Ireland (King James VII of Scotland) and son of James Stuart, the Old Pretender, he was the focus of Jacobite hopes to reclaim the throne of Scotland. Charles was charming and attractive, and he enjoyed more than the occasional drink.

In 1745 Charles led a Scottish uprising to restore his father to the throne. He sailed to the Outer Hebrides with only a few men but with promised support from France. When that support failed to arrive, he sought help from the Jacobite supporters, many from the Highland clans, who were faithful to his family. With 6,000 men behind him, Charles saw victory in Prestonpans and Falkirk, but the tide turned when he lied to his men about additional Jacobite troops waiting south of the border. When these fictitious troops did not materialize, his army retreated to Culloden where, on April 16, 1746, they were massacred.

Charles escaped to the Isle of Benbecula, where he met and is rumored to have fallen in love with Flora MacDonald. After he had hidden there for a week, Flora dressed him as her maid and brought him to sympathizers on the Isle of Skye, who helped him escape to France.

Scotland endured harsh reprisals from the government after the rebellion. As for Charles, he spent the rest of his life in drunken exile, taking the title Count of Albany. In 1772 he married Princess Louise of Stolberg-Gedern, only to separate from her eight years later. He died a broken man in Rome in 1788.

Jacobite or not, caught in the vicinity. In the battle itself, the duke's army—greatly outnumbering the Jacobites—killed up to 2,000 soldiers. (The victors, by contrast, lost just 50). It was the last battle to be fought on British soil. The National Trust for Scotland has re-created a slightly eerie version of the battlefield as it looked in 1746 that you can explore with a guided audio tour. An innovative visitor center enables you to get closer to the sights and sounds of the battle and to interact with the characters involved. A new viewing platform helps (literally) put things into perspective from on high. Academic research and technology have helped re-create the Gaelic dialect, song, and music of the time. There's also a good on-site café. ⊠ B9006, Culloden ☎ 0844/493–2159 ⊕ www.nts.org.uk/Culloden ⊡ £11 ⊙ Visitor center: Apr., May, Sept., and Oct., daily 9–5:30; June–Aug., daily 9–6; Nov.–late Dec., Feb., and Mar., daily 10–4. Battlefield open year-round.

NAIRN

12 miles east of Culloden Moor, 17 miles east of Inverness, 92 miles west of Aberdeen.

This once-prosperous fishing village has something of a split personality. King James VI (1566–1625) once boasted of a town so large the residents at either end spoke different languages. This was a reference to Nairn, whose fisherfolk, living by the sea, spoke Lowland Scots, whereas its uptown farmers and crofters spoke Gaelic. Nearby is Cawdor Castle, loaded with history. East of Nairn pier is a long beach, great for a stroll.

GETTING HERE AND AROUND

A car gives you the most flexibility, but Nairn is close to Inverness (via B9006/B9091), and regular local buses serve the town.

EXPLORING

FAMILY Fodor's Choice ★ **Cawdor Castle.** Shakespeare's Macbeth was the Thane of Cawdor (a local officer of the crown), but the sense of history that exists within the turreted walls of Cawdor Castle is certainly more than fictional. Cawdor is a lived-in castle, not an abandoned, decaying structure. The earliest part is the 14th-century central tower; the rooms contain family portraits, tapestries, fine furniture, and paraphernalia reflecting 600 years of history. Outside the walls are sheltered gardens and woodland walks. Children will have a ball exploring the lush and mysterious Big Wood, with its wildflowers and varied wildlife. There are lots of creepy stories and fantastic tales amid the dank dungeons and drawbridges. If the castle sounds appealing, keep in mind that the estate has cottages to rent. ✉ *B9090, 5 miles southwest of Nairn, Cawdor* ☎ *01667/404401* 🌐 *www.cawdorcastle.com* 🎟 *Castle £10.50; grounds only £5.75* 🕒 *May–early Oct., daily 10–5:30.*

Nairn Museum. The fishing boats have moved to larger ports, but Nairn's historic flavor has been preserved at the Nairn Museum, in a handsome Georgian building in the center of town. Exhibits emphasize artifacts, photographs, and model boats relating to the town's fishing past. A genealogy service is also offered. A library in the same building has a strong local-history section. ✉ *Viewfield House, Viewfield Dr.* ☎ *01667/456791* 🌐 *www.nairnmuseum.co.uk* 🎟 *£3* 🕒 *Apr.–Oct., weekdays 10–4:30, Sat. 10–1.*

WHERE TO STAY

$$$ B&B/INN Fodor's Choice ★ 🏨 **Boath House.** Built in the 1820s, this stunning Regency manor house is surrounded by 20 acres of lovingly nurtured gardens. **Pros:** excellent dining; beautiful 20-acre grounds; relaxed atmosphere. **Cons:** some airplane noise; breakfast (significantly) extra. [$] *Rooms from: £220* ✉ *A96, Auldearn* ☎ *01667/454896* 🌐 *www.boath-house.com* 🛏 *8 rooms* 🍴 *No meals.*

SHOPPING

Auldearn Antiques. It's easy to spend an hour wandering around an old church filled with furniture, fireplaces, architectural antiques, and linens. The converted farmsteads have tempting antique (or just old) chinaware and textiles. ✉ *Dalmore Manse, Lethen Rd., 3 miles east of Nairn, Auldearn* ☎ *01667/453087* 🌐 *www.auldearnantiques.co.uk.*

Brodie Countryfare. Visit Brodie Countryfare only if you're feeling flush: you may covet the unusual knitwear, quality designer clothing and shoes, gifts, and toys, but they are *not* cheap. The excellent restaurant, on the other hand, is quite inexpensive. ✉ *On A96, Brodie, Forres* ☎ *01309/641555* 🌐 *www.brodiecountryfare.com.*

9

GOLF

Nairn's courses are highly regarded by golfers and are very popular, so book far in advance.

Nairn Dunbar Golf Club. Founded in 1899, Nairn Dunbar Golf Club is a difficult course with gorse-lined fairways and lovely sea views. ■TIP→ **Ask about the special rate Nairn ticket, which allows you to play both this and the similarly named Nairn Golf Club for the bargain rate of £140 from May to September (£105 in April, £110 in October).** The special tickets are valid for four days. ✉ *Lochloy Rd.* ☎ *01667/452741* ⊕ *www. nairndunbar.com* 🎫 *£55 (£40 after 4 pm) Apr.–Sept., £40 (£30 after 4 pm) Mar. and Oct., £25 (£10 after 2 pm) Nov.–Feb.* 🏌 *18 holes, 6765 yards, par 72.*

Nairn Golf Club. Well regarded in golfing circles, the Nairn Golf Club dates from 1887 and is the regular home of Scotland's Northern Open. Huge greens, aggressive gorse, a beach hazard for five of the holes, a steady prevailing wind, and distracting views across the Moray Firth make play on the Championship Course unforgettable. The adjoining 9-hole Cameron Course is ideal for a warm-up or a fun round for the family. ✉ *Seabank Rd.* ☎ *01667/453208* ⊕ *www.nairngolfclub.co.uk* 🎫 *Championship Course, £110; Cameron Course, £30* 🏌 *Championship Course: 18 holes, 6774 yards, par 72; Cameron Course: 9 holes, 1634 yards, par 29* ⊗ *Daily* ⚐ *Reservations essential.*

FORRES

10 miles east of Nairn.

The burgh of Forres is everything a Scottish medieval town should be, with a handsome tolbooth (the former courthouse and prison) and impressive gardens as its centerpiece. It's remarkable how well the old buildings have adapted to their modern retail uses. With two distilleries—one still operating, the other preserved as a museum—Forres is a key point on the Malt Whisky Trail. Brodie Castle is also nearby. Just 6 miles north you'll find Findhorn Ecovillage, and a sandy beach stretches along the edge of the semi-enclosed Findhorn Bay, which is excellent bird-watching territory.

GETTING HERE AND AROUND

Forres is easy to reach by car from Inverness on the A96. Daily ScotRail trains run here from Inverness and Aberdeen.

EXPLORING
TOP ATTRACTIONS

Brodie Castle. This medieval castle was rebuilt and extended in the 17th and 19th centuries. Fine examples of late-17th-century plasterwork are preserved in the Dining Room and Blue Sitting Room; an impressive library and a superb collection of pictures extend into the 20th century. The castle is about 24 miles east of Inverness, making it a good day trip. ✉ *Off A96, Brodie* ☎ *0844/493–2156* ⊕ *www.nts.org.uk* 🎫 *Castle £10.50, grounds free* ⊗ *Castle: Apr., daily 10:30–4:30; May, June, Sept., and Oct., Sun.–Thurs. 10:30–4:30; July and Aug., daily 10:30–5. Last tour 1 hr before closing. Grounds: daily, 10:30–sunset.*

Dallas Dhu Historic Distillery. The final port of call on the Malt Whisky Trail, the Dallas Dhu Historic Distillery was the last distillery built in the 19th century and was still in operation until the 1980s. Today it holds a small museum that tells the story of Scotland's national drink. ⊠ *Mannachie Rd.* ☎ *01309/676548* 🖃 *£6* ⊙ *Apr.–Sept., daily 9:30–5:30 (last admission at 5); Oct.–Mar., Sat.–Wed. 10–4 (last admission at 3).*

WORTH NOTING

Benromach Distillery. The smallest distillery in Moray, Benromach was founded in 1898. It's now owned by whisky specialist Gordon and MacPhail, and it stocks a vast range of malts. An informative hourly tour ends with a tutored nosing and tasting. ⊠ *Invererne Rd.* ☎ *01309/675968* ⊕ *www.benromach.com* 🖃 *£6* ⊙ *May and Sept., Mon.–Sat. 9:30–5 (last tour 3:30); June–Aug., Mon.–Sat. 9:30–5 (last tour 3:30), Sun. noon–4 (last tour 3); Oct.–Dec. and Feb.–Apr., weekdays 10–4 (last tour 3).*

Findhorn Ecovillage. This education center is dedicated to developing "new ways of living infused with spiritual values." Drawing power from wind turbines, locals farm and garden to sustain themselves. A tour affords a thought-provoking glimpse into the lives of the ultraindependent villagers. See homes made out of whisky barrels, and the Universal Hall, filled with beautiful engraved glass. The Phoenix Shop sells organic foods and handmade crafts, and the Blue Angel Café serves organic and vegetarian fare. ⊠ *The Park, off B9011, 6 miles from Forres, Findhorn* ☎ *01309/690311* ⊕ *www.findhorn.org* 🖃 *Free; tours £8* ⊙ *Visitor center May–Sept., weekdays 10–5, weekends 1–4; Oct.–Apr., weekdays 10–5. Tours Apr., Oct., and Nov., Mon., Wed., and Fri. at 2; May–Sept., Fri.–Mon. and Wed. at 2.*

Sueno's Stone. At the eastern end of town stands Sueno's Stone, a 22-foot-tall pillar of stone carved with the ranks of soldiers from some long-forgotten battle. Nobody can quite agree on how old it is or what battle it marked, but it is generally believed to have been erected between AD 600 and 1000. ⊠ *Findhorn Rd.* 🖃 *Free.*

SPORTS AND THE OUTDOORS

Findhorn Bay Beach. Along the edge of Findhorn Bay you'll find a long stretch of beach, great for an afternoon by the sea. You can reach the beach through the dunes from the northern end of the Findhorn Ecovillage, or park at the edge of the village of Findhorn for a shorter stroll. There are public restrooms, but few other amenities. **Amenities:** toilets. **Best for:** solitude; walking. ⊠ *Off B89011, Findhorn.*

SPEYSIDE AND THE CAIRNGORMS

The Spey is a long river, running from Fort Augustus to the Moray Firth, and its fast-moving waters make for excellent fishing at many points along the way. They also give Speyside malt whiskies a softer flavor than those made with peaty island water. The area's native and planted pine forests draw many birds each spring and summer, and people come for miles to see the capercaillies and ospreys.

Defining the eastern edge of the Great Glen, Cairngorms National Park provides sporty types with all the adventure they could ask for, including walking, kayaking, rock climbing, and even skiing, if the winter is cold enough. The park has everything but the sea: craggy mountains, calm lochs, and swift rivers. While the unremarkable town of Aviemore may put off some travelers, the Cairngorms are truly stunning.

BOAT OF GARTEN

6 miles northeast of Aviemore.

In the peaceful village of Boat of Garten, the scent of pine trees mingles with an equally evocative smell—that of steam trains. You can take a nostalgic steam train trip on the Strathspey Steam Railway between Aviemore and Boat of Garden. Close to Cairngorms National Park, Boat of Garten is building a reputation as a great place to stay while exploring the region.

GETTING HERE AND AROUND

This charming town is an easy drive from Inverness or Aviemore via the A9 and the A95. It's also serviced by local buses, and some people travel here on the Strathspey Steam Train.

EXPLORING

FAMILY **Landmark Forest Adventure Park.** About 4 miles northwest of Boat of Garten, the Landmark Forest Adventure Park has nature trails, a fire tower you can climb, and plenty of more adventurous attractions to keep younger ones entertained. Among the amusements are the Wonder Wood, where tricks like forced perspective are used to befuddle your senses; a heart-stopping parachute jump simulator; and raft rides of varying degrees of, well, wetness. You could easily spend half a day here. The park is open year-round, but most attractions close in winter. To get to Carrbridge, take the quiet B9153 rather than the crowded A9. ✉ *B9153, Carrbridge* ☎ *0800/731–3446* 🌐 *www.landmarkpark.co.uk* 🎫 *Apr.–Oct., £17.30; Nov.–Mar., £5.75* ⏲ *Late Mar.–mid-July and mid-Aug.–late Sept., daily 10–5 or 6 (varies daily); mid-July–mid-Aug., daily 10–7; late Sept.–late Mar., daily 10–5.*

Loch Garten Nature Reseve. Set in the heart of Abernethy Forest, the Loch Garten Nature Reserve offers a glimpse of the osprey, a large fishing bird that comes here to breed. The reserve, one of the last stands of ancient Scots pines in Scotland, attracts a host of birds, including the bright crossbill and the crested tit. You might also spot the rarely seen red squirrel. The sanctuary is administered by the Royal Society for the Protection of Birds. ✉ *Off B970, 1 mile east of Boat of Garten, Nethy Bridge* ☎ *01479/831476* 🌐 *www.rspb.org.uk* 🎫 *£5* ⏲ *Apr.–Aug., daily 10–6; last admission 1 hr before closing.*

FAMILY **Strathspey Steam Railway.** The oily scent of smoke and steam hangs faintly in the air near the authentically preserved train station in Boat of Garten. Travel in old-fashioned style and enjoy superb views of the high and often white domes of the Cairngorm Mountains. Breakfasts, lunches, and special dinners are served on board from March to October and in December. ■ TIP→ **For the full experience, avoid booking on**

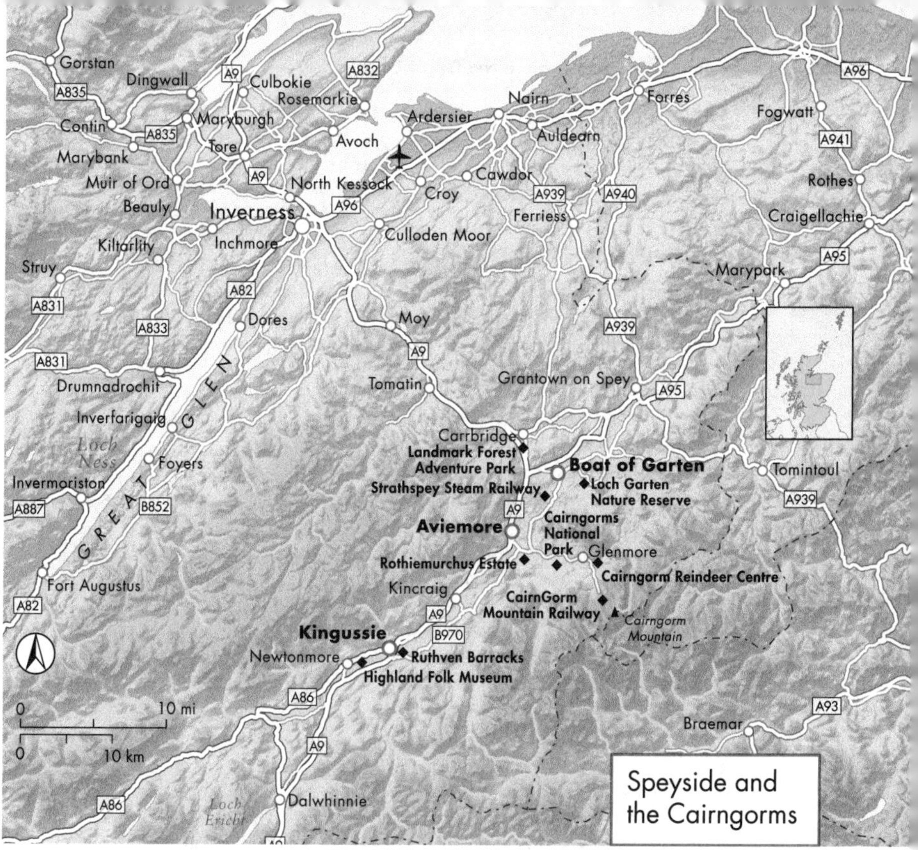

Sundays outside of the high season—less romantic diesel engines are generally used on Sundays after mid-September. ✉ *Boat of Garten Station, Spey Ave.* ☎ *01479/810725* 🌐 *www.strathspeyrailway.co.uk* 🎟 *£14.50 round-trip.*

WHERE TO STAY

$$ HOTEL 🏨 **Mountview Hotel.** An old hunting lodge perched in the hills of Nethybridge, this hotel boasts great views out over the valley. **Pros:** stunning setting; pretty views; good restaurant. **Cons:** some shared bathrooms. [$] *Rooms from: £130* ✉ *B970, Nethy Bridge* ☎ *01479/821515* 🌐 *www.mountviewhotel.co.uk* 🛏 *12 rooms* 🍴 *Breakfast.*

SHOPPING

Boat of Garten Post Office. Cheerfully run by Beth and David Woolsey, this local post office doubles as a gift shop and general store. With fruit, chocolate, cheese, freshly baked breads, and hot pies, it's a great place to stock up for a day hiking in the hills. ✉ *Dershar Rd.* ☎ *01479/831527.*

SPORTS AND THE OUTDOORS

BICYCLING

Cairngorm Bike & Hike. This small, well-stocked shop rents well-maintained bikes, offers a good selection of lightweight backpacks, and has all sorts of outdoor gear—everything you'll need for your biking excursions around the Cairngorms. ✉ *Boat of Garten Station, Spey Ave.* ☎ *01479/831745* ∰ *www. cairngormbikeandhike.co.uk.*

GOLF

Fodor'sChoice ★ **Boat of Garten Golf Club.** This is one of Scotland's greatest "undiscovered" courses. Boat of Garten, which dates to the late 19th century, was redesigned and extended by James Braid in 1932, and each of its 18 holes has a strong Highland feel. Some cut through birch wood and heathery rough, and most have long views to the Cairngorms. An unusual feature is the preserved steam railway that runs alongside part of the course. ✉ *Nethybridge Rd.* ☎ *01479/831282* ∰ *www. boatgolf.com* 🏷 *£45 weekdays, £49 weekends* ⚑ *18 holes, 5876 yards, par 70* ⚑ *Reservations essential.*

> **BOAT OF GARTEN'S FERRY**
>
> A ferry that once linked both sides of the River Spey gave its name to Boat of Garten. The first official record of the ferry is in 1662, although it had probably been there longer. The village itself did not appear until the coming of the railway, in 1868, when cottages sprang up between the railway line and the ferry crossing. When it was time to pick a name, the ferry seemed like a good symbol for the locale. Not long after that, bridges were built across the River Spey, and demand for the little ferry disappeared. The name, on the other hand, stuck.

AVIEMORE

6 miles southwest of Boat of Garten, 30 miles south of Inverness.

At the foot of the Cairngorms, the once-quiet Aviemore now has all the brashness and boxiness of a year-round holiday resort. In the summer months it's filled with walkers, cyclists, and rock-climbers, so it's a convenient place for stocking up on supplies. However, many of the smaller villages nearby are quieter places to stay. ■ TIP→ **Be forewarned: this region can get very cold above 3,000 feet, and weather conditions can change rapidly, even in the middle of summer.**

GETTING HERE AND AROUND

The A9, Scotland's major north–south artery, runs past Aviemore. From Boat of Garten, take the B970. The town is serviced by regular trains and buses from Inverness.

ESSENTIALS

Visitor Information Aviemore Visitor Information Centre. ✉ *7 Grampian Rd.* ☎ *01479/810930* ⊕ *visitcairngorms.com.*

EXPLORING

Fodor'sChoice ★ **CairnGorm Mountain Railway.** A funicular railway to the top of Cairn Gorm (the mountain that gives its name to the region), the CairnGorm Mountain Railway operates daily, year-round, and affords sweeping views across the Cairngorms and the broad valley of the Spey. At the top is a visitor center and restaurant. The round-trip journey takes about half an hour. Reservations are recommended. ✉ *B970* ☎ *01479/861261* ⊕ *www.cairngormmountain.co.uk* 🏷 *£11.50* ☼ *Daily, around 10:20–4.*

Fodor's Choice ★ **Cairngorms National Park.** A rugged wilderness of mountains, moorlands, glens, and lochs, the sprawling Cairngorms National Park, established in 2003, takes in more than 1,700 square miles. Past Loch Morlich, at the high parking lot on the exposed shoulders of the Cairngorm Mountains, are dozens of trails for hiking and cycling. This is a massive park, encompassing small towns as well as countryside, but a good place to start exploring is the main visitor center in Aviemore. The staff can dispense maps, expert advice on the best trails, and also information on guided walks and other activities. (There are additional Cairngorms visitor centers in Braemar, Glenmore, Ballater, Tomintoul, Newtonmore, and Grantown-on-Spey.) Because much of the best scenery in the park is off-road—including ancient pine forests and open moorland—a particularly good way to cover ground in the park is on a pony trek. The **Rothiemurchus Estate** leads guided hacks for riders of all levels of ability. The park is a haven for rare wildlife: a full 25% of Britain's endangered species have habitats in the park. Birding enthusiasts come here to look (and listen) for the Scottish crossbill—the only bird completely unique to Britain. Weather conditions in the park change abruptly, so be sure to bring cold-weather gear, particularly if you plan on hiking long distance. ⊠ *Visitor Information Centre, 7 The Parade, Grampian Rd.* 🕿 *01479/810930* ⊕ *cairngorms.co.uk* ⊗ *Apr.–June, Mon.–Sat. 9–6, Sun. 10–5; July and Aug., Mon–Sat. 9–6:30, Sun. 9:30–6; Sept. –Mar., Mon.–Sat. 9–5, Sun. 10–4.*

FAMILY **Cairngorm Reindeer Centre.** On the high slopes of the Cairngorms, you may see the reindeer herd that was introduced here in the 1950s. The reindeer are docile creatures that seem to enjoy human company. Ranger-led visits to the herd are offered at least once a day from February to December, weather permitting. From June to August you can also accompany rangers on gentle half-day treks through the mountains. From April through December a small herd of young reindeer are cared for at a paddock near the visitor center; you can visit (and pet them) for a small fee. Bring waterproof gear, as conditions can be wet and muddy. ⊠ *Glenmore Forest Park, B970, 6 miles east of Aviemore* 🕿 *01479/861228* ⊕ *www.cairngormreindeer.co.uk* 🖂 *£13.50; paddock £3.50* ⊗ *Visitor center: Feb.–Dec., daily 10–5. Visits to herd: Feb.–Apr. and Sept.–Dec. at 11; May and June at 11 and 2:30; July and Aug. at 11, 2:30, and 3:30.*

Fodor's Choice ★ **Rothiemurchus Estate.** This excellent activity center is among the best in the Cairngorms. It offers a host of organized outdoor diversions, including guided pony rides, mountain biking, fishing, gorge swimming, and white-water rafting. They also offer ranger-guided safaris to see the park's rare and endangered wildlife, including red squirrels and "hairy heilan coos" (Highland slang for Highland cattle—docile, yaklike creatures). The Rothiemurchus Centre is the best place to get oriented and book activities; it also has a handy restaurant and a well-stocked shop selling plenty of fresh produce from the estate. One of the most beautiful parts of the estate is a nature reserve called **Loch an Eilein**. There are great low-level paths around the tree-rimmed loch—perfect for bikes—or longer trails to Glen Einich. A converted cottage beside Loch an Eilein serves as a visitor center, art gallery, and craft store. ⊠ *Rothiemurchus*

9

CLOSE UP

Cairngorms National Park

At the heart of Britain's largest national park (nearly 1,750 square miles of countryside) is a wild arctic landscape that sits on a granite plateau. Five of Scotland's nine 4,000-feet-high mountains are found in this range, and there are 13 more over 3,000 feet. These rounded mountains, including Cairn Gorm (meaning "blue hill" in Gaelic) and Ben Macdui, the second highest in Britain at 4,295 feet, were formed at the end of the last ice age. The Larig Ghru Pass, a stunning U-shape glen, was carved by the retreating glacier.

Hikers, underestimate this landscape at your peril: the fierce conditions often found on the Cairngorms plateau have claimed many lives. Make sure you are well prepared and inform someone of your planned route and estimated return time.

The environment supports rare arctic-alpine and tundra plant and animal species (a full quarter of Britain's endangered species are found here) including flora such as the least willow and alpine blue-sow thistle, and birds such as the ptarmigan, Scottish crossbill, and dotterel. Lower down the slopes, terrain that was once filled with woodland is now characterized by heather, cotton grass, and sphagnum moss. This open expanse allows visitors to glimpse animals such as the golden eagle, roe deer, or red deer.

Fragments of the ancient Caledonian forest (largely Scots pine, birch, and rowan) remain and are home to pine martens, red squirrels, and capercaillie (a large grouse). Studding these forests are dramatic glens and the Rivers Spey, Don, and Dee, which are home to Atlantic salmon, otters, and freshwater pearl mussels.

Centre, on B970, Inverdruie ☎ *01479/812345* ⊕ *www.rothiemurchus. net* ✉ *Free* ⊙ *Rothiemurchus Centre: daily 9:30–5:30; Loch an Eilein Visitor Centre: daily 9–dusk; Gallery: Easter–Oct., daily 10–4:30.*

WHERE TO EAT

$ ✕ **Mountain Café.** On the main street in Aviemore, the Mountain Café is
CAFÉ   a useful pit stop for a hearty lunch or afternoon snack. Its all-day breakfasts are somewhat famed locally; they also serve good sandwiches, burgers, salads, and the like. Leave room for the cakes, which are made on the premises (and won a national award in 2014). There are great views of the Cairngorm Mountains from the dining room. $ *Average main: £10* ✉ *111 Grampian Rd.* ☎ *01479/812473* ⊕ *mountaincafe-aviemore.co.uk* ⊙ *No dinner.*

$$ ✕ **Old Bridge Inn.** Across a pedestrian bridge from Aviemore station, this
MODERN BRITISH   old-style bar and conservatory restaurant serves what many locals call the best pub food in Aviemore. The simple fare includes local favorites like Shetland ling (a type of fish native to these waters) or Speyside beef. Order some crispy, golden roasted potatoes on the side if they're on offer. The bar serves a wide selection of local brews, and there's often live music playing. Roaring fires are very welcome in a place that can have cool nights any time of year. $ *Average main: £17* ✉ *Dalfaber Rd.* ☎ *01479/811137* ⊕ *www.oldbridgeinn.co.uk* ⌖ *Reservations essential.*

SPORTS AND THE OUTDOORS

G2 Outdoor. The wide range of adventures at G2 Outdoor includes white-water rafting, gorge walking, and rock climbing. The company offers a family float trip on the River Spey in summer, and in winter runs ski courses. ⊠ *Dalfaber Industrial Estate, Off Dalfaber Dr.* ☎ *01479/811008* ⊕ *www.g2outdoor.co.uk.*

Glenmore Lodge. In Cairngorms National Park, this is a good center for day and residential courses on rock and ice climbing, hiking, kayaking, ski touring, mountain biking, and more. Some classes are aimed at kids over 14. There are superb facilities, such as an indoor climbing wall. ⊠ *Signposted on B970, Glenmore* ✛ *About 9 miles east of Aviemore* ☎ *01479/861256* ⊕ *www.glenmorelodge.org.uk.*

Mikes Bikes. This small bike shop stocks all the gear you might need to take advantage of the many paths around Aviemore. It also rents and repairs bikes. Prices start at £15 for four hours. ⊠ *Myrtlefield Shopping Centre, Grampian Rd.* ☎ *01479/810478* ⊕ *www.aviemorebikes.co.uk.*

KINGUSSIE

13 miles southwest of Aviemore.

Set in a wide glen, Kingussie is a pretty town east of the Monadhliadh Mountains. With great distant views of the Cairngorms, it's perfect for those who would prefer to avoid the far more hectic town of Aviemore.

GETTING HERE AND AROUND

From Aviemore, Kingussie is easy to reach by car via the A9 and the A86.

EXPLORING

FAMILY **Highland Folk Museum.** Explore reconstructed Highland buildings, including a Victorian-era schoolhouse, and watch tailors, clock makers, and joiners demonstrating their trades at this museum. Walking paths (or old-fashioned buses) take you to an 18th-century township that includes a feal house, made of turf, and a weaver's house. Throughout the museum there are hands-on exhibitions like a working quern stone for grinding grain. ⊠ *Kingussie Rd., Newtonmore* ☎ *01540/673551* ⊕ *www.highlandfolk.com* 🖸 *Free* ☉ *Late Mar.–Aug., daily 10:30–5:30; Sept. and Oct., daily 11–4:30.*

Ruthven Barracks. Looking like a ruined castle on a mound, Ruthven Barracks is redolent with tales of "the '45" (as the last Jacobite rebellion is often called). The defeated Jacobite forces rallied here after the battle at Culloden, but then abandoned and blew up the government outpost they had earlier captured. You'll see its crumbling, yet imposing stone outline as you approach. ⊠ *B970, ½ mile south of Kingussie* ☎ *01667/460232* ⊕ *www.historic-scotland.gov.uk* 🖸 *Free.*

WHERE TO EAT AND STAY

$$$$ ╳**The Cross at Kingussie.** This former tweed mill, with a narrow river
BRITISH running alongside its stone walls, is set in 4 acres of woodlands. The
Fodor$Choice intimate dining room, where the stone walls have been painted a creamy
★ white, is warmed by a crackling fireplace. The fixed-price menus are smart and bold, with dishes such as local halibut with blue cheese tortellini, or roast duck with turnips cooked in maple syrup. Each dish reveals

9

an intimate knowledge of textures and flavors. If you like it here so much you don't want to leave, there are also rooms available starting at £110 per night. $ *Average main: £55* ✉ *Tweed Mill Brae, Ardbroilach Rd.* ☎ *01540/661166* ⊕ *www.thecross.co.uk* ✆ *Closed Jan. No dinner Sun. and Mon.*

$
CAFÉ
FAMILY
Fodor'sChoice
★

✕ **The Potting Shed.** Seasonal fruits and smooth cream top many of the delectable desserts at this cake shop on Main Street in Kingussie. Taught by his Norwegian mother, John Borrowman makes sponges that are rich and light and contain no butter or fat (although you can't say the same thing about the rich cream they're topped with). The shop also offers gluten-free options that use almonds in place of flour, and these are by no means lacking in richness or flavor. There's a cake with a description that simply reads "just an awful lot of chocolate." An accompanying wide selection of coffees and teas makes this an excellent place to stop and plan your next activity. $ *Average main: £5* ✉ *Main St.* ☎ *01540/651287* ⊕ *www.inshriachnursery.co.uk* ✆ *Closed Mon. and Tues. No dinner.*

> **BIKING THE GLEN**
>
> A dedicated bicycle path, created by Scotland's National Cycle Networks, runs from Glasgow to Inverness, passing through Fort William and Kingussie. Additionally, a good network of back roads snakes around Inverness and toward Nairn. The B862/B852, which runs by the southeast side of Loch Ness, has little traffic and is a good bet for cyclists. Stay off the A9, however, as it's busy with vehicular traffic on both sides of Aviemore. The very busy A82 main road, along the northwest bank of Loch Ness via Drumnadrochit, is for the same reason not recommended for cyclists.

$
B&B/INN

🛏 **Coig Na Shee.** This century-old Highland lodge has a warm and cozy atmosphere, and each of its spacious bedrooms is unique, with well-chosen furnishings and soothing color schemes. **Pros:** quiet location; great walks from house; kids up to 16 can share with parents for £20 (including breakfast). **Cons:** a bit out of the way; car needed to get here; no children under eight. $ *Rooms from: £90* ✉ *Laggan Rd., Newtonmore* ☎ *01540/670109* ⊕ *www.coignashee.co.uk* ⇝ *5 rooms* ❑ *Breakfast.*

LOCH NESS, FORT WILLIAM, AND NEARBY

Compared with other lochs, Loch Ness is by no means known for its beauty, but it draws attention for its famous monster. Heading south from Inverness, you can travel along the loch's quiet east side or the more touristy west side. A pleasant morning can be spent at Urquhart Castle, in the tiny town of Drumnadrochit, or a bit farther south in the pretty town of Fort Augustus, where the Caledonian Canal meets Loch Ness. As you travel south and west, the landscape opens up and the Nevis Range comes into view.

From Fort William you can visit the dark, cloud-laden mountains of Glencoe and the desolate stretch of moors and lochans at Rannoch Moor. Travelers drive through this region to experience the landscape, which changes at nearly every turn. It's a brooding, haunting area that's worth a visit in any season.

The Road to the Isles, less romantically known as the A830, leads from Fort William to the coastal towns of Arisaig, Morar, and Mallaig, with access to the Small Isles of Rum, Eigg, Canna, and Muck. From here you can also visit the Isle of Skye (⇨ *see Chapter 10*) via the ferry at Mallaig.

DRUMNADROCHIT

14 miles south of Inverness.

A tourist hub at the curve of the road, Drumnadrochit is not known for its style or culture, but it attracts plenty of people interested in searching for mythical monsters. There aren't many good restaurants, but there are some decent-enough hotels.

GETTING HERE AND AROUND

It's easy to get here from Fort Augustus or Inverness via the A82, either by car or by local bus.

EXPLORING

Jacobite Cruises. The company runs morning and afternoon cruises on Loch Ness to Urquhart Castle and other destinations throughout the region. The harbor is 5 miles northeast of Drumnadochit via the A82. Prices start at about £14. ⊠ *Clansman Harbour, A82* ☎ *01463/233999* ⊕ *www.jacobite.co.uk.*

Loch Ness. From the A82 you get many views of the formidable and famous Loch Ness, which has a greater volume of water than any other Scottish loch, a maximum depth of more than 800 feet, and—perhaps you've already heard?—a monster. Early travelers who passed this way included English lexicographer Dr. Samuel Johnson (1709–84) and his guide and biographer, James Boswell (1740–95), who were on their way to the Hebrides in 1783. They remarked at the time about the poor condition of the population and the squalor of their homes. Another early travel writer and naturalist, Thomas Pennant (1726–98), noted that the loch kept the locality frost-free in winter. Even General Wade—remembered for destroying much of Hadrian's Wall in England—came here, his troops blasting and digging a road up much of the eastern shore. None of these observant early travelers ever made mention of a monster. Clearly, they had not read the local guidebooks. ⊠ *Drumnadrochit.*

FAMILY **Loch Ness Centre & Exhibition.** If you're in search of the infamous monster, the Loch Ness Centre & Exhibition documents the fuzzy photographs, the unexplained sonar readings, and the sincere testimony of eyewitnesses. It's said that the loch's huge volume of water has a warming effect on the local weather, making the loch conducive to mirages in still, warm conditions—but you'll have to make up your own mind. From Easter to October you can also take hourly cruises of the loch (£15). The cruises leave from the little craft store at the Loch Ness Lodge Hotel in Drumnadrochit; no prebooking allowed. ⊠ *On A82* ☎ *01456/450573* ⊕ *www.lochness.com* ☎ *£7.50* ☉ *Easter–June, daily 9:30–5:45; July and Aug., daily 9:30–6:45; Sept. and Oct., daily 9:30–5:45; Nov.–Easter, daily 10–4:15; last admission 45 mins before closing.*

Urquhart Castle. About 2 miles southeast of Drumnadrochit, this castle is a favorite Loch Ness monster–watching spot. This romantically

CLOSE UP

"Nessie": The Loch Ness Monster

Tall tales involving some kind of beast inhabiting the dark waters of Loch Ness go all the way back to St. Columba in the 7th century AD—but, for the most part, the legend of "Nessie" is a disappointingly modern one. In 1933, two vacationing Londoners gave an intriguing account to a newspaper, describing a large, unidentifiable creature that slithered in front of their car before plunging into the loch. Later that year, a local man, Hugh Gray, took the first purported photograph of the monster—and Nessie fever was born. The pictures kept coming—none of them *too* clear, of course—and before long the resident monster turned into boon for the local tourism industry. Fortunately for them, the age of camera phones has not dented Nessie's popularity; you don't have to search far on the Internet to find all sorts of photos of something—*anything*—that must surely be the monster, if you only squint a little. But does anybody seriously believe in it? Well... no. But like all good legends, there is just enough doubt to keep the campfire tales alive. In 2006 declassified documents even revealed that, in the 1980s, Prime Minister Margaret Thatcher considered plans to declare the Loch Ness monster a protected species, as a safeguard against the hordes of bounty hunters she feared would descend should it ever be proven to exist.

broken-down fortress stands on a promontory overlooking the loch, as it has since the Middle Ages. Because of its central and strategic position in the Great Glen line of communication, the castle has a complex history involving military offense and defense, as well as its own destruction and renovation. The castle was begun in the 13th century and was destroyed before the end of the 17th century to prevent its use by the Jacobites. A visitor center gives an idea of what life was like here in medieval times. ✉ *A82* ☎ *01456/450551* 🌐 *www.historic-scotland.gov.uk/places* 🎟 *£8.50* 🕒 *Apr.–Sept., daily 9:30–6; Oct., daily 9:30–5; Nov.–Mar., daily 9:30–4:30; last admission 45 mins before closing.*

WHERE TO STAY

$$$ B&B/INN Fodor's Choice ★ 🏨 **Loch Ness Lodge.** Run by siblings Scott and Iona Sutherland, Loch Ness Lodge is an exquisite place: opulent, classy, and welcoming. **Pros:** excellent staff; superb views; lovely rooms. **Cons:** near a busy road; no restaurant; don't confuse it with a (lesser) hotel of the same name in Drumnadrochit. [$] *Rooms from: £210* ✉ *A82, Brachla* ☎ *01456/459469* 🌐 *www.loch-ness-lodge.com* 🛏 *7 rooms* 🍴 *Some meals.*

EN ROUTE

A more leisurely alternative to the fast-moving traffic on the busy A82, and one that combines monster-spotting with peaceful road touring, is the **B862** south from Inverness and along the east bank of Loch Ness. Take the opportunity to view the waterfalls at Foyers and the peaceful, reedy Loch Tarff. Descend through forests and moorland until the road runs around the southern tip of Loch Ness. The half-hidden track beside the road is a remnant of the military road built by General Wade.

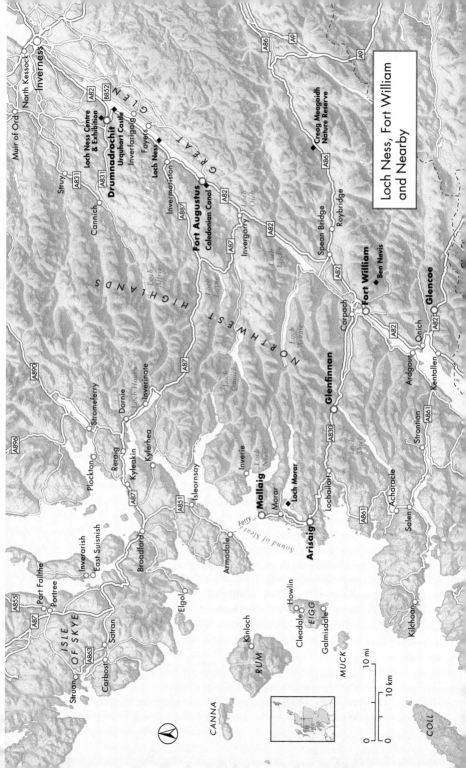

Loch Ness, Fort William and Nearby

FORT AUGUSTUS

19 miles south of Drumnadrochit, 33 miles south of Inverness, 31 miles northeast of Fort William.

The best place to see the locks of the Caledonian Canal is Fort Augustus, at the southern tip of Loch Ness. This bustling small town is a great place to begin walking and cycling excursions, or to sit by the canal watching the locks fill and empty as boats sail between Loch Lochy, Loch Oich, and Loch Ness.

Fort Augustus itself was captured by the Jacobite clans during the 1745 rebellion. Later the fort was rebuilt as a Benedictine abbey, but the monks no longer live here.

GETTING HERE AND AROUND

Fort Augustus is an easy drive from Inverness or Invergarry on the A82. Buses run frequently, as this is a busy tourist destination.

EXPLORING

Caledonian Canal. The canal, which links the lochs of the Great Glen—Loch Lochy, Loch Oich, and Loch Ness—owes its origins to a combination of military and political pressures that emerged at the time of the Napoleonic Wars with France. In short: Britain needed a better and faster way to move naval vessels from one side of Scotland to the other. The great Scottish engineer Thomas Telford (1757–1834) surveyed the route in 1803. The canal, which took 19 years to complete, has 29 locks and 42 gates. Telford ingeniously took advantage of the three lochs that lie in the Great Glen, which have a combined length of 45 miles, so that only 22 miles of canal had to be constructed to connect the lochs and complete the waterway from coast to coast. Along the canal stunning vistas open up: mountains, lochs, and glens, and to the south, the profile of Ben Nevis. At the newly renovated visitor center in Fort Augustus you can learn all about this historic engineering feat, and take a picturesque walk along the towpath. ⊠ *Ardchattan House, canal-side* ⊕ *www.scottishcanals.co.uk* ✉ *Free* ⊙ *Visitor center daily 9–6.*

FAMILY   **Clansman Centre.** In a handsome Victorian building, the Clansman Centre is a small museum full of stirring tales about life in this region. A guide plays the role of a 17th-century clansman, regaling you with stories about how his kinsmen lived in those wild days, as he shows you around his humble turf house. It's cheesy, informative fun. The well-stocked gift shop sells Celtic jewelry, traditional Highland garb, and ceremonial armor. ⊠ *Canal-side* ☎ *01320/366444* ⊕ *www.scottish-swords.com* ✉ *Free* ⊙ *Apr.–Oct., daily 10–6.*

OFF THE
BEATEN
PATH

Creag Meagaidh Nature Reserve. A stretch of the A86, quite narrow in some places, hugs the western shore of Loch Laggan. It has superb views of the mountainous heartlands to the north, and, over the silvery spine of hills known as the Grey Corries, culminates with views of Ben Nevis to the south. In summertime the reserve is a nesting ground for peregrine falcons and golden eagles. Halfway along the loch is the Creag Meagaidh Nature Reserve, a sublime picnic spot and a good base for walks into the restored woodland below the spectacular ice-carved crags of Coire Ardair. There are basic facilities like parking lots and restrooms, but no visitor center. ✉ *Off A86, Kinloch Laggan, New-tonmore* ☎ *01528/544265* ⊕ *www.nnr-scotland.org.uk/creag-meagaidh* 📧 *Free* ⊙ *Open 24 hrs.*

WHERE TO STAY

$$ 🏨 **Glengarry Castle Hotel.** Tucked away in Invergarry, this rambling baro-**HOTEL** nial mansion is just south of Loch Ness and within easy reach of the Great **Fodor's**Choice Glen's most popular sights. **Pros:** atmospheric building and gardens; ★ good-value take-out lunches; family rooms available. **Cons:** no elevator. Ⓢ *Rooms from: £135* ✉ *On A82, Invergarry* ☎ *01809/501254* ⊕ *www. glengarry.net* ⊙ *Closed mid-Nov.–mid-Mar.* 🔄 *26 rooms* 🍴 *Breakfast.*

FORT WILLIAM

16 miles north of Glencoe, 69 miles southwest of Inverness, 108 miles northwest of Glasgow, 138 miles northwest of Edinburgh.

As its name suggests, Fort William originated as a military outpost, first established by Oliver Cromwell's General Monk in 1655 and refortified by George I (1660–1727) in 1715 to help combat an uprising by the turbulent Jacobite clans. It remains the southern gateway to the Great Glen and the far west. It's not Scotland's most charming or authentic town, but it's got several good hotels and makes a convenient base for exploring the surrounding countryside.

GETTING HERE AND AROUND

From Glasgow (to the south) and Inverness (to the north), the A82 takes you the entire way. From Edinburgh, take the M9 to the A84. This empties into the A85, which connects to the A82 that takes you to Fort William. Roads around Fort William are well maintained, but mostly one lane in each direction. They can be very busy in summer.

A long-distance Scottish Citylink bus connects Glasgow and Fort William. ScotRail has trains from London, as well as connections from Glasgow and Edinburgh. It also operates a train service three times a day between Fort William and Mallaig.

9

ESSENTIALS

Visitor Information Fort William Tourist Information Centre. ✉ *15 High St.* ☎ *01397/701801* ⊕ *www.visitscotland.com.*

EXPLORING

Ben Nevis. The tallest mountain in the British Isles, 4,406-foot Ben Nevis looms over Fort William, less than 4 miles from Loch Linnhe. A trek to its summit is a rewarding experience, but you should be fit and well prepared—food and water, map and compass, first-aid kit, whistle, hat, gloves, and warm clothing (yes, even in summer) for starters—as the unpredictable weather can make it a hazardous hike. Ask for advice at the local tourist office before you begin.

Fodor's Choice **Jacobite Steam Train.** The most relaxing way to take in the landscape ★ of birch- and bracken-covered wild slopes is by rail. The best ride is on the Jacobite Steam Train, a spectacularly scenic 84-mile round-trip that runs between Fort William and Mallaig. You'll see mountains, lochs, beaches, and islands along the way. There are two trips a day (weekdays only outside high season). ⊠ *Station Sq.* ☎ *0844/850–4685* ⊕ *www.westcoastrailways.co.uk* 🎫 *£34* ⊘ *Mid-May–late June and late Sept.–late Oct., weekdays 10:15 and 2:30; late June–late Sept., daily 10:15 and 2:30.*

Nevis Range Gondola. Those who want to climb a mountain, without the need for hiking boots and an iron will, will prefer to make the journey in a gondola. These cable cars rise nearly 2,000 feet to the summit of Aonach Mor, part of the Nevis range. The journey takes about 15 minutes, and needless to say the views of the Great Glen are incredible—but definitely not for those without a head for heights. Call ahead for times, especially in winter—the published opening hours are a little confusing. ⊠ *A82* ☎ *01397/705825* ⊕ *www.nevisrange.co.uk* 🎫 *£12* ⊘ *Apr.–June and Sept., daily 10–5; July and Aug., daily 9:30–6; Oct.–mid-Nov. and Jan.–Mar., weekdays 10–4. Hrs may change according to daylight and weather conditions.*

Fodor'sChoice **West Highland Museum.** In the town center, the small but fascinating
★ West Highland Museum explores the history of Prince Charles Edward Stuart and the 1745 rebellion. Included in the museum's folk exhibits are a costume and tartan display and an excellent collection of Jacobite relics. One of the most intriguing objects here is a tray decorated with a distorted image of Bonnie Prince Charlie that only becomes visible when reflected in a wine glass or goblet. This elaborate ruse enabled clandestine supporters among the nobility to raise a (treasonous) toast without fear of discovery. ⊠ *Cameron Sq.* ☎ *01397/702169* ⊕ *www. westhighlandmuseum.org.uk* 🎫 *Free* ⊘ *Apr.–Oct., Mon.–Sat. 10–5; Mar., Nov., and Dec., Mon.–Sat. 10–4.*

WHERE TO EAT

$$ ✗ **Crannog Seafood Restaurant.** With a reputation for quality and simplic-
SEAFOOD ity, this restaurant on the town pier serves outstanding seafood. Fishing
Fodor'sChoice boats draw up on the shores of Loch Linnhe and deliver their catch
★ straight to the kitchen. The menu might include fillet of hake with a pistachio nut crust, or seared salmon served with seasonal vegetables. From the window seats you can watch the sun setting on the far side of the loch. The lunch special, two courses for £15, is a particularly good value. ∎ TIP➔ **During the summer, the restaurant runs daily cruises of Loch Linnhe that cost £25, last 90 minutes, and include lunch back at the restaurant afterwards.** 🖺 *Average main: £18* ⊠ *The Pier* ☎ *01397/705589* ⊕ *www.crannog.net.*

$ ✗ **Lochaber Farm Shop Cafe.** The lovely café at this friendly farm-and-
CAFÉ crafts store makes for a perfect pit stop if you're visiting Ben Nevis. The shop, which overlooks the mountain, sells produce from Lochaber farm, also put to great use in tasty light lunches—free-range chicken soup, perhaps, or sandwiches filled with local beef or ham. The homemade cakes are legendary. It's at the Lochabar Rural Complex, 6 miles north of Fort William, off A82; take the turnoff for the Aonach Mor Ski Centre. 🖺 *Average main: £7* ⊠ *Lochabar Rural Complex, Torlundy* ☎ *01397/708686* ⊕ *www.lochaberfarmshop.com* ⊘ *Closed Mon. and Tues. No dinner.*

WHERE TO STAY

$$ ⛉ **Crolinnhe.** An elegant Victorian house with colorful gardens, this
B&B/INN exceptionally comfortable B&B overlooks Loch Linnhe, yet is only a
Fodor's Choice 10-minute walk from town. **Pros:** stunning loch views; great breakfasts;
★ comfortable rooms. **Cons:** final payment only by cash or check. Ⓢ *Rooms
from: £130* ⊠ *Grange Rd.* ☎ *01397/702709* ⊕ *www.crolinnhe.co.uk*
🖃 *No credit cards* ⊗ *Closed Nov.–Easter* ⤢ *3 rooms* ⧚⊙⧚ *Breakfast.*

$$ ⛉ **The Grange.** This meticulously renovated Victorian villa stands in
B&B/INN pretty gardens a 10-minute walk from downtown. **Pros:** amazing loca-
Fodor's Choice tion; great attention to detail; elegant lounge with plenty of books. **Cons:**
★ no restaurant; not suitable for families with younger children. Ⓢ *Rooms
from: £140* ⊠ *Grange Rd.* ☎ *01397/705516* ⊕ *www.grangefortwilliam.
com* ⊗ *Closed Oct.–Mar.* ⤢ *3 rooms* ⧚⊙⧚ *Breakfast.*

$$$$ ⛉ **Inverlochy Castle Hotel.** A red-granite Victorian mansion turned luxury
HOTEL boutique hotel, Inverlochy Castle stands on 50 acres of woodlands in
the shadow of Ben Nevis, with striking scenery on every side; prices
are high, but you could have a meal here to take in the ambience. **Pros:**
spectacular setting; sumptuous public areas; top restaurant; children
under seven free (when sharing with parents). **Cons:** pricey; must dress
up for dinner. Ⓢ *Rooms from: £465* ⊠ *A82* ☎ *01397/702177* ⊕ *www.
inverlochycastlehotel.com* ⊗ *Closed Jan. and Feb.* ⤢ *14 rooms, 3
suites* ⧚⊙⧚ *Breakfast.*

$ ⛉ **Myrtle Bank Guest House.** This sweet, cheerful guesthouse is in a con-
B&B/INN verted Victorian villa on the banks of Loch Linnhe. **Pros:** great views;
friendly owners; convenient location. **Cons:** ground floor rooms don't
have such nice views; breakfast finishes early; some shared bathrooms.
Ⓢ *Rooms from: £80* ⊠ *Achintore Rd.* ☎ *01397/702034* ⊕ *www.
myrtlebankguesthouse.co.uk* ⤢ *25 rooms* ⧚⊙⧚ *Breakfast.*

SHOPPING

The majority of shops here are along High Street, which in summer
attracts bustling crowds intent on stocking up for excursions to the west.

Ellis Brigham Mountain Sports. This shop can help you get kitted out for your
outdoor adventures. ⊠ *St. Marys Hall, Belford Rd.* ☎ *01397/706220*
⊕ *www.ellis-brigham.com.*

Nevisport. This shop has been selling outdoor supplies, maps, and travel
books for more than 40 years. ⊠ *High St.* ☎ *01397/704921* ⊕ *www.
nevisport.com.*

SPORTS AND THE OUTDOORS

BICYCLING

Nevis Range Mountain Bike Track. For a thrilling ride down Ben Nevis,
take the gondola up to the beginning of the Nevis Range Mountain Bike
Track and then shoot off on a 2,000-foot descent. The lift costs £13.50.
It's open mid-May to mid-September, weather permitting. (Also closed
on certain dates for races; call ahead to check). Bike rentals are available near the gondola. ⚠ **Remember, though, that this is seriously mountainous territory and is only recommended for hard-core cyclists.** ⊠ *A82*
☎ *01397/705825* ⊕ *bike.nevisrange.co.uk.*

9

GOLF

Fort William Golf Club. This excellent course has spectacular views of Ben Nevis (indeed, it partly occupies its lower slope). The Highland course appeals to beginners and experts alike, drawn as much for the beautiful setting as the thoroughly reasonable green fees. Watch out for the treacherous 4th hole—it looks simple, but a fierce prevailing wind will test even the most practiced swing. ⊠ *Torlundy* ☎ *01397/704464* ⊕ *www. fortwilliamgolf.co.uk* ⊿ *£25, full day £30* ⚘ *18 holes, 6217 yards, par 70.*

HIKING

This area—especially around Glen Nevis, Glencoe, and Ben Nevis—is popular with hikers; however, routes are not well marked, so contact the Fort William tourist information center before you go. The center will provide you with expert advice based on your interests, level of fitness, and hiking experience.

Fodor's Choice
★
Glen Nevis. For a walk in Glen Nevis, drive north from Fort William on the A82 toward Fort Augustus. On the outskirts of town, just before the bridge over the River Nevis, turn right up the road signposted Glen Nevis. About 8 miles along this road is a parking lot where a footpath leads to waterfalls and a steel-cable bridge (1 mile), and then to Steall, a ruined croft beside a boulder-strewn stream (a good picnic place). You can continue up the glen for some distance without danger of becoming lost, so long as you stay on the path and keep the river to your right. Watch your step going through the tree-lined gorge. The return route is back the way you came.

GLENCOE

16 miles south of Fort William, 92 miles north of Glasgow, 44 miles northwest of Edinburgh.

Fodor's Choice
★
Glencoe is both a small town and a region of stunning grandeur, with high peaks and secluded glens. Dramatic scenery is the main attraction here; it's as awesomely beautiful for a drive as it is for a hike. The A82—the main route through Glencoe—can get surprisingly crowded in high season, but it's one of the great scenic drives in Scotland. This area, where wild, craggy buttresses loom darkly over the road, has a special place in the folk memory of Scotland: the glen was the site of an infamous massacre in 1692, still remembered in the Highlands for the treachery with which soldiers of the Campbell clan, acting as a government militia, treated their hosts, the MacDonalds. According to Highland code, in his own home a clansman should give shelter even to his sworn enemy. In the face of bitter weather, the Campbells were accepted as guests by the MacDonalds. Apparently acting on orders from the British crown, the Campbells turned on their hosts and murdered them. The Massacre of Glencoe has gained an unlikely resurgence of fame in recent years, since it was revealed to be the historical basis for the so-called "Red Wedding" in George R.R. Martin's popular books (and HBO series) *Game of Thrones.*

GETTING HERE AND AROUND

Glencoe is easily accessed by car via the A82. ScotRail trains and regional buses arrive from most of Scotland's major cities.

EXPLORING

Visitor Center at Glencoe. The National Trust for Scotland's Visitor Center at Glencoe tells the story of the MacDonald massacre, and has excellent displays about this area of outstanding natural beauty. You can also get expert advice about hiking trails. ✉ *Off A82, 1 mile south of Glencoe Village* ☎ *0844/493–2222* 🌐 *www.glencoe-nts.org.uk* 🎫 *Exhibition £6.50* ⏲ *Late Mar.–Oct., daily 9:30–5:30; Nov.–late Mar., Thurs.–Sun. 10–4. Last admission 45 mins before closing.*

WHERE TO STAY

$$$$ B&B/INN Fodor's Choice ★ 🏨 **Glencoe House.** Peaceful surroundings, jaw-dropping views, and the friendliest of welcomes await you at this former Victorian hunting lodge. **Pros:** beautiful landscape; superb restoration; lovely hosts. **Cons:** very expensive; few facilities. [$] *Rooms from: £340* ✉ *Glencoe Lochan* ☎ *01855/811179* 🌐 *www.glencoe-house.com* 🛏 *7 rooms* 🍴 *No meals.*

SPORTS AND THE OUTDOORS

FAMILY **Glencoe Activities.** This popular outdoor center west of Glencoe offers a long list of high-energy activities, from rock climbing to white-water rafting, and even hair-raising vertical canyon explorations complete with 500-foot descents. However, there's a welcome twist here—they also cater to those with more limited mobility (or less adventurous souls). Guided Segway tours (£35) last 50 minutes and take you through some spectacular scenery, with stunning mountain views and even a trail along a stretch of Loch Leven. ✉ *Dragon's Tooth Golf Course, off A828* ☎ *01855/811695* 🌐 *www.glencoeactivities.com* ⏲ *Daily 9–5.*

GLENFINNAN

10 miles west of Fort William, 26 miles southeast of Mallaig.

Perhaps the most visitor-oriented stop on the route between Fort William and Mallaig, Glenfinnan has much to offer if you're interested in Scottish history. Here the National Trust for Scotland has capitalized on the romance surrounding the story of the Jacobites and their attempts to return a Stewart monarch and the Roman Catholic religion to a country that had become staunchly Protestant. It was at Glenfinnan that the rash adventurer Bonnie Prince Charlie gathered his meager forces for the final Jacobite rebellion of 1745–46.

GETTING HERE AND AROUND

If you're driving from Fort William, travel via the A830. For great views, take a ride in the Jacobite Steam Train, which you can catch in Fort William.

EXPLORING

Glenfinnan Monument. One of the most striking monuments in Britain, the Glenfinnan Monument commemorates the place where Bonnie Prince Charlie raised his standard. The tower, which was built in 1815, overlooks Loch Shiel; note, however, that the figure on the top is a Highlander, not the Prince himself. The story of his ill-fated campaign is told in the nearby visitor center. You have to pay a small access fee when the center is open, but in truth it's just as picturesque when seen from the car park. ■ **TIP→ The view down Loch Shiel from the Glenfinnan Monument**

is one of the most photographed in Scotland. ✉ *A830* ☎ *0844/493–2221* 🌐 *www.nts.org.uk* 🎫 *Exhibition or tour £3.50; combined ticket £7* 🕓 *Visitor center: late Mar.–June, Sept., and Oct., daily 10–5; July and Aug., daily 9:30–5. Monument: late Mar.–June, daily 10–5; July and Aug., daily 9:30–5. Last admission 30 mins before closing.*

Glenfinnan Viaduct. The 1,248-foot-long Glenfinnan Viaduct was a genuine wonder when it was built in 1897, and remains so today. The railway's contractor, Robert MacAlpine (known among locals as "Concrete Bob") pioneered the use of concrete for bridges when his company built the Mallaig extension, which opened in 1901. In more recent times the viaduct became famous for its appearance in the Harry Potter films. The viaduct can be seen on foot; about half a mile west of the railway station in Glenfinnan, on the A380 road, is a small parking lot. Take the footpath from here; you'll reach the viaduct in about ½ mile. ✉ *A380.*

WHERE TO STAY

$$ HOTEL 🏨 **Glenfinnan House.** This handsome hotel on the shores of Loch Shiel was built in the 18th century as the home of Alexander MacDonald VII of Glenaladale, who was wounded fighting for Bonnie Prince Charlie; it was transformed into an even grander mansion in the 19th century. **Pros:** fabulous setting; atmospheric dining experience. **Cons:** some shared bathrooms. [$] *Rooms from: £150* ✉ *A830* ☎ *01397/722235* 🌐 *www.glenfinnanhouse.com* 🕓 *Closed mid-Nov.–mid-Mar.* 🛏 *14 rooms* 🍴 *Breakfast.*

EN ROUTE

As you get closer to **Arisaig** along A830, you'll be able to spot Eigg, a low island marked by the dramatic black peak of An Sgurr. Beyond Eigg is the larger Rum, with its range of hills and the Norse-named, cloud-capped Rum Coullin looming over the island. The breathtaking seaward views should continue to distract you from the road beside Loch nan Uamh (from Gaelic, meaning "cave" and pronounced *oo*-am). This loch is associated with Prince Charles Edward Stuart's nine-month stay on the mainland, during which he gathered a small army, marched as far south as Derby in England, alarmed the king, retreated to unavoidable defeat at Culloden in the spring, and then spent a few months as a fugitive in the Highlands. A cairn by the shore marks the spot where the prince was rescued by a French ship; he never returned to Scotland.

ARISAIG

15 miles west of Glenfinnan.

Considering its small size, Arisaig, gateway to the **Small Isles,** offers a surprising choice of high-quality options for dining and lodging. To the north of Arisaig the road cuts across a headland to reach a stretch of coastline where silver sands glitter with the mica in the local rock; clear water, blue sky, and white sand lend a tropical flavor to the beaches—when the sun is shining.

From Arisaig try to visit a couple of the Small Isles: **Rum, Eigg, Muck,** and **Canna,** each tiny and with few or no inhabitants. Rum serves as a wildlife reserve, while Eigg has the world's first solely wind-, wave-, and solar-powered electricity grid.

GETTING HERE AND AROUND

From Glenfinnan, you reach Arisaig on the A830, the only road leading west. The Fort William–Mallaig train also stops here.

EXPLORING

Arisaig Marine. Along with whale-, seal-, and bird-watching excursions, Arisaig Marine runs a boat service from the harbor at Arisaig to the islands from May to September. You can also charter a fast motor yacht, which can take up to 12 passengers around the Small Isles and farther afield. They also have a handy gift shop and café. ✉ *Arisaig Harbour* ☎ *01687/450224* ⊕ *www.arisaig.co.uk* ✉ *Round-trip fares from £10.*

WHERE TO EAT AND STAY

$$$
FRENCH
✕ **Old Library.** On the waterfront, this 1722 barn has been converted into a fine, reasonably priced restaurant. Expect fairly simple, but tasty plates of local fish and meats, prepared in a French-bistro style—lamb shank, sirloin, or perhaps a fillet of buttery hake, served with seasonal veggies. If you're lucky you may also be offered a few local specialties, including *cullen skink,* a thick and tasty kind of fish soup. Make a night of it in one of the six cozy, contemporary guest rooms for around £125 for a double. 🄢 *Average main: £22* ✉ *A30* ☎ *01687/450651* ⊕ *www. oldlibrary.co.uk.*

$$
B&B/INN
🛏 **Arisaig Hotel.** A coaching inn built in 1720, this hotel is close to the water and has magnificent views of the Small Isles. **Pros:** good-value restaurant; lots of life and music in the bar; amazing views of the bay. **Cons:** the main bar is noisy for some. 🄢 *Rooms from: £110* ✉ *A830* ☎ *01687/450210* ⊕ *www.arisaighotel.co.uk* 🛏 *13 rooms* ❪⃝❫ *Breakfast.*

$$
HOTEL
Fodor'sChoice
★
🛏 **Arisaig House.** An open-arms welcome and stunning views of the Isle of Skye await you at this wonderful mansion. **Pros:** beautiful views; lovely hosts; outstanding food. **Cons:** a bit isolated. 🄢 *Rooms from: £135* ✉ *Beasdale* ☎ *01687/450730* ⊕ *www.arisaighouse.co.uk* 🛏 *4 rooms, 6 suites* ❪⃝❫ *Some meals.*

9

MALLAIG

8 miles north of Arisaig, 44 miles northwest of Fort William.

After the approach along the coast, the workaday fishing port of Mallaig itself is somewhat anticlimactic. It has a few shops, and there's some bustle by the quayside when fishing boats unload or the ferry departs: this is the departure point for the southern ferry connection to the Isle of Skye, the largest island of the Inner Hebrides.

Mallaig is also the starting point for day cruises up the Sound of Sleat, which separates Skye from the mainland. The sound offers views into the rugged Knoydart region and its long, fjordlike sea lochs: Lochs Nevis and Hourn. The area to the immediate north and west beyond Loch Nevis, one of the most remote in Scotland, is often referred to as the Rough Bounds of Knoydart.

GETTING HERE AND AROUND

The Fort William–Mallaig train is by far the best way to travel to Mallaig, because you can relax and enjoy the stunning views. But road improvements on the A830 beyond Fort William make the drive far less taxing and time-consuming than it used to be.

EXPLORING

Caledonian MacBrayne. This company runs scheduled service and cruises from Mallaig to Skye, the Small Isles, and Mull. You can buy round-trip tickets to single islands or "hopscotch" tickets that allow you to visit several in one go. Round-trip prices start at around £30 for a car and £7 per adult, but can rise to several times that depending on how far you're going. The ferries depart from several different points along the coast; the port at Mallaig also has a booking office. ⊠ *Mallaig Harbour* ☎ *0800/066–5000* ⊕ *www.calmac.co.uk.*

Knoydart Ferry. For year-round cruises to Loch Nevis, Inverie, and Tarbert, contact this company, which also runs £10 lunchtime cruises during the summer months. ⊠ *Mallaig Harbour* ☎ *01687/462233* ⊕ *www. knoydart-ferry.co.uk.*

Loch Morar. A small, unnamed side road just south of Mallaig leads east to an even smaller road that will bring you to Loch Morar, the deepest of all the Scottish lochs (more than 1,000 feet). The next deepest point is miles out into the Atlantic, beyond the continental shelf. The loch is said to have a resident monster, Morag, which undoubtedly gets less recognition than its famous cousin Nessie. Whether that means you have more chance of getting her to appear for a photograph, we can't say. ⊠ *Loch Morar.*

THE NORTHERN
HIGHLANDS AND
THE WESTERN ISLES

Updated
by Mike
Gonzalez

Wild and remote, the Northern Highlands and the Western Isles of Scotland have a timeless grandeur. Dramatic cliffs, long beaches, and craggy mountains that rise up out of moorland like islands in a sea heighten the romance and mystery. Well-preserved Eilean Donan Castle marks a kind of gateway to the Isle of Skye, famous for the brooding Cuillin Mountains and forever associated with Bonnie Prince Charlie. Jurassic-era sites (dinosaurs left their prints here), prehistoric ruins, crumbling castles, and abandoned crofts (small farms) compress the whole span of history in the islands.

In Sutherland and Caithness in northern Scotland, the roads hug the coast, dipping down toward beaches and up again to give stunning views over the ocean or across rippled, desolate stretches of heather moorland toward the impressive and singular profiles of mountains like Ben Hope and Suilven. These twisted, undulating roads—many of them single-track—demand that you shift down a gear, pause to let others pass, and take the time to do less and experience more of the rough-hewn beauty. If you're lucky, you may see an otter fishing along the coast, an eagle soaring overhead, or catch sight of deer with their antlers jutting above the horizon.

Sutherland was once the southern land belonging to the Vikings, and some names reflect this. Cape Wrath got its name from the Viking word *hvarth*, meaning "turning point," and Suilven translates as "pillar." The Isle of Skye and the Outer Hebrides are referred to as the Western Isles, and remain the stronghold of the Gaelic language. Skye is often called Scotland in miniature because the terrain shifts from lush valleys in the south, to the rugged girdle of the Cuillin Mountains, and then to the steep cliffs that define the northern coast. A short ferry journey away, moody Harris lays claim to the brilliant golden sands of Luskentyre. To the north, Lewis boasts incredible prehistoric sites, including the lunar-aligned Calanais Standing Stones and Dun Carloway (an Iron Age circular tower), as well as a lighthouse that looks ready to tip into the Atlantic.

Depending on the weather, a trip to the Northern Highlands and the Western Isles can feel like a tropical getaway or a blustery, rain-drenched holiday where this much-touted phrase makes sense: "There's no such thing as bad weather, just inappropriate clothing."

TOP REASONS TO GO

Skye, the misty island: The landscape ranges from the lush, undulating hills and coastal tracks of Sleat in the Garden of Skye to the deep glens that cut into the saw-toothed peaks of the Cuillin Mountains. Farther north are stunning geological features like the Old Man of Storr and Kilt Rock.

Seafood: Sample fresh seafood like Bracadale crab, Dunvegan Bay langoustines, and Sconser king scallops, as well as the local smoked salmon, lobster, and oysters.

Coastal walks: There are no wilder places in Britain to enjoy an invigorating coastal walk than on the islands of Lewis, Harris, and the Uists. Expect vast swaths of golden sand set against blue bays, or—when the weather is rough—giant waves crashing against the rocks.

Wildlife viewing: Seals, deer, otters, as well as an abundance of birdlife can be seen throughout the Northern Highlands and Western Isles. Don't miss a boating foray to the Handa Island bird reserve, off Scourie.

Single-track roads: In the Northern Highlands, take a drive on single-track roads like Destitution Road, north of Gairloch, which lead through the most dramatic scenery in Britain. The area is a primeval landscape where strange craggy mountains, with Gaelic and Nordic names like An Teallach, Suilven, and Stac Pollaidh, jut out of vast, desolate moorlands dotted with lochans (small lochs).

ORIENTATION AND PLANNING

GETTING ORIENTED

Moving north and west from Inverness toward land's end at John O'Groats, this rugged landscape includes the old counties of Ross and Cromarty (sometimes called Easter and Wester Ross), Sutherland, and Caithness; together they constitute the northernmost portion of mainland Scotland. To the west, to get to Skye, you can travel from Kyle of Lochalsh across the Skye Bridge or take a short summer ferry ride from Mallaig to Armadale. From Skye you can hop from island to island, taking the ferry from Uig to Tarbert, then south from Leverburgh to Lochmaddy and the Uists.

10

The Northern Landscapes. North of Inverness, northwest Scotland is known for its dramatic coastlines and desolate landscapes. It's no wonder that this part of the country has been designated as Scotland's first UNESCO Geopark. You'll want to explore Stoer Point Lighthouse, the beaches north of Lochinver, and islandlike hills such as Suilven. The single-track road from Lairg to Tongue, near Durness, is particularly dramatic.

Torridon. A few hours' drive west of Inverness, Torridon has cool glens, mirrorlike lochs, impressive mountains, and tantalizing glimpses across to the Isle of Skye. Single-track roads lead to lighthouses on promontories battered by the sea. Glen Torridon is worth a visit.

Isle of Skye. Scotland's most famous island is home to the 11 peaks of the Cuillin Mountains, the quiet gardens of Sleat, and the dramatic peninsulas of Waternish and Trotternish. You can take a day trip to Skye, but it's worth spending a few days exploring its shores.

The Outer Hebrides. Extending about 130 miles from north to south, this archipelago is reached by ferry from the mainland and from the Isle of Skye. Lewis has wonderful historic attractions, such as the Calanais Standing Stones, sandy beaches, and traditional "black houses." Harris is flat and wild, but its beaches are untouched and glorious. The Uists are dotted with old cairns and ruined forts and chapels. Barra is so small you can easily walk from one end to the other.

PLANNING

WHEN TO GO

The Northern Highlands and islands are best seen from May to September. The earlier in the spring or later in the autumn you go, the greater the chances of your encountering the elements in their extreme form, and the fewer attractions and accommodations you will find open. Even tourist-friendly Skye closes down almost completely by the end of October. As a final deciding factor, you may not want to take a western sea passage in a gale, a frequent occurrence in the winter months.

PLANNING YOUR TIME

The rough landscape of the Highlands and Islands, as this region is sometimes called, means that this is not a place you can rush through. It could take eight busy days to do a coastal loop and also see some islands. Single-track roadways, undulating landscapes, and eye-popping views will slow you down. You can base yourself in a town like Ullapool or Portree, or choose a B&B or hotel (of which there are many) tucked into the hills or sitting at the edge of a sea loch. If you have only a couple of days, head directly to the Isle of Skye and the other islands off the coast. They attract hordes of tourists, and for good reason, yet you don't have to walk far to find yourself in wild places, often in solitude. Sunday is a day of minimal activity here; restaurants, bars, and shops are closed, as are many sites.

You could combine a trip to the Northern Highlands with forays into the Great Glen (including Inverness and Loch Ness) or up to Orkney (there are day trips from John O'Groats) and the Shetland Islands.

GETTING HERE AND AROUND
AIR TRAVEL

On a map, this area may seem far from major urban centers, but it's easy to reach. Inverness has an airport with direct links to London, Edinburgh, Glasgow, and Amsterdam.

The main airports for the Northern Highlands are Inverness and Wick (both on the mainland). Loganair and Flybe have direct air service from Edinburgh and Glasgow to Inverness and from Edinburgh to Wick. You can fly from London Gatwick, Luton Airport (near London), or Bristol to Inverness on one of the daily easyJet flights. British Airways also has a service from Gatwick. Loganair and Flybe operate flights to and among the islands of Barra, Benbecula, Harris, and Lewis in the Outer Hebrides.

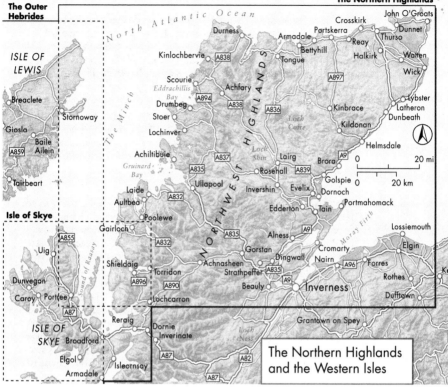

The Northern Highlands and the Western Isles

Airport Contact Inverness Airport. ✉ *Old Military Rd., Dalcross*
☎ *01667/464000* ⊕ *www.hial.co.uk/inverness-airport.html.*

BOAT AND FERRY TRAVEL

Ferry services are generally reliable, weather permitting. Car and passenger ferries run from Ullapool to Stornoway, from Oban to Castlebay and Lochboisdale, and from Uig (on the Isle of Skye) to Tarbert and Lochmaddy. The Island Hopscotch planned-route ticket and the Island Rover pass, both offered by Caledonian MacBrayne (known locally as CalMac) give considerable reductions on interisland ferry fares; it is worth calling ahead and asking for the best route plan.

Boat and Ferry Contact Caledonian MacBrayne. ☎ *08000/665000* ⊕ *www. calmac.co.uk.*

BUS TRAVEL

Scottish Citylink and National Express run buses to Inverness, Ullapool, Thurso, Scrabster, and Wick. There are also connections between the ferry ports of Tarbert and Stornoway; consult the local tourist information center for details. Buses can be a good way to see this region, but they don't run frequently.

Stagecoach Highlands provides a bus service in the region. On the Outer Hebrides several small operators run regular routes to most towns and

10

villages. The post-bus service—which also delivers mail—becomes increasingly important in remote areas. It supplements the regular bus service, which runs only a few times per week. A full timetable of services for the Northern Highlands (and the rest of Scotland) is available from the Royal Mail. Traveline Scotland, a handy website, provides timetables and a journey planner to help you navigate around Scotland. There's an app, too.

Bus Contacts National Express. ☎ *0871/781–8181* ⊕ *www.nationalexpress. com.* **Royal Mail Postbuses.** ☎ *0845/774–0740* ⊕ *www.royalmail.com/postbus.* **Scottish Citylink.** ☎ *0871/266–3333* ⊕ *www.citylink.co.uk.* **Stagecoach Highlands.** ☎ *01463/233371* ⊕ *www.stagecoachbus.com.* **Traveline Scotland.** ☎ *08706/082608* ⊕ *www.travelinescotland.com.*

CAR TRAVEL

Because of the infrequent bus service and sparse railway stations, a car is definitely the best way to explore this region. The winding single-lane roads demand a degree of driving dexterity, however. Local rules of the road require that when two cars meet, whichever driver reaches a passing place first must stop and allow the oncoming car to continue (this may entail a bit of backing up). Drivers always wave, as a courtesy and as a genuine greeting. Cars driving uphill have priority, and small cars tend to yield to large commercial vehicles. Never park in passing places, and remember you can also pull into them to allow traffic behind you to pass. On bad days, you encounter trucks at the most awkward of spots. On good days, single-track driving can be relaxing, with a lovely pace of stopping, waving, moving on. Note that in this sparsely populated area distances between gas stations can be considerable, so it is wise to fill your tank when you see one.

TRAIN TRAVEL

Main railway stations in the area include Oban (for ferries to Barra and the Uists) and Kyle of Lochalsh (for Skye) on the west coast, as well as Inverness (for points north to Thurso and Wick). There's direct service from London to Inverness and connecting service from Edinburgh and Glasgow. For information contact National Rail or ScotRail.

Train Contacts National Rail. ☎ *08457/484950, 44207/278–5240 from abroad* ⊕ *www.nationalrail.co.uk.* **ScotRail.** ☎ *0344/811–0141* ⊕ *www.scotrail.co.uk.*

TOURS

There are fascinating boat tours from a number of places around the coast, including seal- and bird-watching trips. Inland, tours of castles, distilleries, fishing lochs, and hill-walking routes are available locally.

J.A. Johnstone Chauffeur Drive. Take a private or small-group tour with J.A. Johnstone. Day trips are available, but they specialize in multi-day trips. Prices are individually negotiated and include knowledgeable driver-guides. ☎ *01463/798372* ⊕ *www.jajcd.com* ✉ *From £320.*

Rabbie's Trail Burners. This outfitter organizes tours throughout the Highlands, starting from a number of places. In small, comfortable buses, tours range from one to several days. ☎ *0131/226–3133* ⊕ *www. rabbies.com* ✉ *From £34.*

Scotland Tours. Choose from among a range of bus tours for a range of budgets, from one to eight days. The company is Highland-owned, and the guides know their region well. ☎ *0131/226–1414* ⊕ *www.scotlandtours.com* ✉ *From £39.*

RESTAURANTS

Northern Scotland has many excellent restaurants where talented chefs use locally grown produce. Most country-house inns (a good choice if you're looking for a restaurant) and pubs serve reliable, hearty seafood and meat-and-potatoes meals. The Isle of Skye has the most, and the most expensive, restaurants, many of them quite good. But you can find tasty meals almost everywhere, although in more remote regions you may have to drive some distance to find them. Remember that locals eat early, and few restaurants serve dinner after 9 or 9:30.

HOTELS

Charming, earthy, inexpensive inns and a few excellent luxury hotels will welcome you after a day of touring the Highlands. There are many B&Bs in the area, and they often book up far in advance. Some require a minimum two-day stay in high season.

In the more remote parts of Scotland your best lodging option may be to rent a cottage or house. Besides allowing you to make your own meals and to come and go as you please, it can also be less expensive. VisitScotland (⊕ *www.visitscotland.com*), the official tourism agency, lists many cottages and even rates them with stars, just like hotels. *Hotel reviews have been shortened. For full information, visit Fodors.com.*

WHAT IT COSTS IN POUNDS			
	$	**$$**	**$$$**	**$$$$**
Restaurants	Under £15	£15–£19	£20–£25	Over £25
Hotels	Under £100	£100–£160	£161–£220	Over £220

Restaurant prices are the average cost of a main course at dinner or, if dinner is not served, at lunch. Hotel prices are the lowest cost of a standard double room in high season, including 20% V.A.T.

10

VISITOR INFORMATION

The tourist information centers at Dornoch, Dunvegan, Durness, Portree, Stornoway, Tarbert, and Ullapool are open year-round, with limited winter hours at Dunvegan, Durness, and Ullapool.

Seasonal tourist information centers are at Bettyhill, Broadford (Skye), Castlebay (Barra, Outer Hebrides), Gairloch, Helmsdale, John O'Groats, Kyle of Lochalsh, Lairg, Lochboisdale (South Uist, Outer Hebrides), Lochcarron, Lochinver, Lochmaddy (North Uist, Outer Hebrides), North Kessock, Shiel Bridge, Thurso, and Uig.

Information Highlands of Scotland Tourist Board. ☎ *01463/234353* ⊕ *www.visitscotland.com.*

THE NORTHERN LANDSCAPES

Wester Ross and Sutherland, the northernmost part of Scotland, have some of the most distinctive mountain profiles and coastal stretches in all of Scotland. The rim roads around the wilds of Durness overlook rocky shores, and the long beaches are as dramatic as the awe-inspiring and desolate cross-country routes like Destitution Road in Wester Ross.

ULLAPOOL

238 miles north of Glasgow.

Ullapool is an ideal base for hiking throughout Sutherland and taking wildlife and nature cruises, especially to the Summer Isles. By the shores of salty Loch Broom, the town was founded in 1788 as a fishing station to exploit the local herring stocks. There's still a smattering of fishing vessels, as well as visiting yachts and foreign ships. When their crews fill the pubs, Ullapool has a cosmopolitan feel. The harbor area comes to life when the Lewis ferry arrives and departs.

GETTING HERE AND AROUND
A desolate but well-maintained stretch of the A835 takes you from Inverness to Ullapool.

ESSENTIALS
Visitor Information Ullapool Visitor Centre. ⊠ *7 and 8 W. Argyle St.* ☎ *01854/612987.*

EXPLORING
Ceilidh Place. Ullapool's cultural focal point is Ceilidh Place, an excellent venue for concerts and other events throughout the year (*ceilidh* is the Gaelic word for a local dance). It started out as a small café, and over the years has added space for performers, an excellent bookshop specializing in Scottish writing, and a handful of rooms for those who want to spend the night. It's a great place for afternoon coffee or a wee dram in the evening. ⊠ *14 W. Argyle St.* ☎ *01854/612103* ⊕ *www.theceilidhplace.com.*

Corrieshalloch Gorge. For a thrilling touch of vertigo, don't miss Corrieshalloch Gorge, 12 miles south of Ullapool, just off the A835. Draining the high moors, the Falls of Measach plunge 150 feet into a 200-foot-deep, thickly wooded gorge. There's a suspension-bridge viewpoint and a heady atmosphere of romantic grandeur, like an old Scottish print come to life. A short walk leads from a parking area to the viewpoint.

Falls of Rogie. Just north of Contin you'll find the Falls of Rogie. Walk down through the woods from the car park 2 miles west of the village to the interestingly bouncy suspension bridge that overlooks the falls and gives a fine view of the waters below. ⊠ *A835, 35 miles south of Ullapool, Contin.*

Ullapool Museum. Films, photographs, and audiovisual displays tell the story of the area from the Ice Age to modern times, including the "klondyking" period between 1970 and 1990 when foreign boats filled the loch to fish the mackerel. There's an ongoing exhibition on weather, climate change, and the environment. The building was designed by

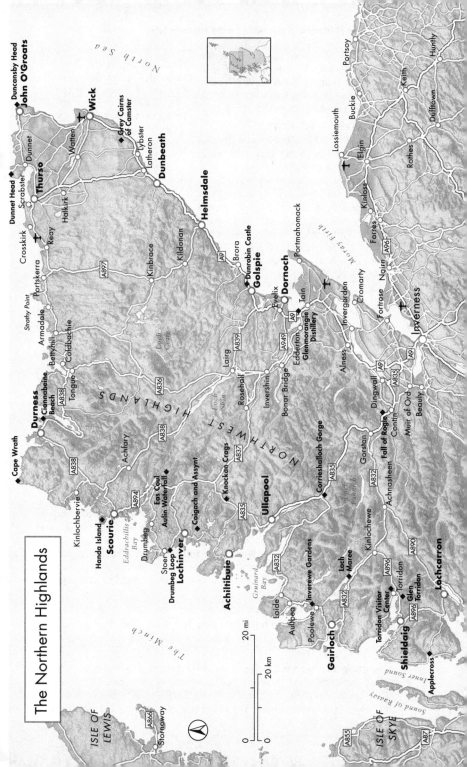

The Northern Highlands

North Sea

The Minch

ISLE OF LEWIS

ISLE OF SKYE

Sound of Raasay

Inner Sound

John O'Groats
Duncansby Head
Wick
Grey Cairns of Camster
Dunbeath
Thurso
Dunnet Head
Scrabster
Dunnet
Watten
Crosskirk
Reay
Portskerra
Halkirk
Lybster
Latheron
Helmsdale
Kinbrace
Kildonan
Brora
Dunrobin Castle
Golspie
Dornoch
Portmahomack
Edderton
Tain
Fearn
Glenmorangie Distillery
Lairg
Rosehall
Invershin
Bonar Bridge
Ardgay
Alness
Invergordon
Cromarty
Fortrose
Nairn
Inverness
Lossiemouth
Elgin
Kinloss
Forres
Rothes
Dufftown
Keith
Buckie
Portsoy
Huntly
Moray Firth

Durness
Cape Wrath
Clennabeine Beach
Kinlochbervie
Handa Island
Scourie
Drumbeg
Eddrachillis Bay
Stoer
Drumbeg Loop
Lochinver
Eas Coul Aulin Waterfall
Coigach and Assynt
Knockan Crags
Ullapool
Achfary
Tongue
Coldbackie
Bettyhill
Armadale
Strathy Point
Loch Loyal
Loch Naver
Loch Shin
NORTHWEST HIGHLANDS
Corrieshalloch Gorge
Loch Fannich
Garve
Contin
Dingwall
Strathpeffer
Muir of Ord
Beauly
Fall of Rogie
Achnasheen
Kinlochewe
Loch Maree
Inverewe Gardens
Poolewe
Aultbea
Laide
Gruinard Bay
Achiltibuie
Gairloch
Shieldaig
Torridon Visitor Center
Glen Torridon
Torridon
Applecross
Lochcarron

A855
A87
A866
A838
A894
A837
A835
A832
A896
A890
A832
A835
A836
A838
A897
A9
A949
A839
A9
A835
A862
A832

20 mi
20 km

Thomas Telford and dates from the early 19th century. ✉ *7 and 8 W. Argyle St.* ☎ *01854/612987* 🌐 *www.ullapoolmuseum.co.uk* 🎟 *£3.50* ⏰ *Apr.–Oct., Mon.–Sat. 10–5.*

GET HOOKED IN THE HIGHLANDS

The possibilities for fishing are endless in Sutherland, as a glance at the loch-covered map suggests. Brown trout and salmon are abundant. You can fish from the banks of Loch Garve, 35 miles south of Ullapool, or Loch Assynt, 5 miles east of Lochinver, from March to October. Boat fishing is popular on Loch Maree, southeast of Gairloch and north of Poolewe, from May to October. Fishing permits are available at local post offices and shops; some hotels have their own fishing rights but most will arrange fishing permits for you.

WHERE TO STAY

$$ HOTEL 🏨 **Ceilidh Place.** It advertises "rooms to let," but what this place really offers is simple and elegant accommodations, many with beamed ceilings and views of Loch Broom. **Pros:** quiet comfort; wonderful views; great for music lovers. **Cons:** decor a little tired. [$] *Rooms from: £100* ✉ *14 W. Argyle St.* ☎ *01854/612103* 🌐 *www.theceilidhplace.com* 🛏 *13 rooms* 🍴 *Breakfast.*

$ HOTEL 🏨 **Royal Hotel.** This longtime favorite has a great location and beautiful views over Ullapool Harbor and Loch Broom, so be sure to request a balcony room in advance. **Pros:** a short walk to Ullapool; good breakfasts. **Cons:** sometimes very crowded and a little noisy; rooms at the rear have no views. [$] *Rooms from: £90* ✉ *Garve Rd.* ☎ *01854/612181* 🌐 *www.royalhotel-ullapool.com* 🛏 *55 rooms* 🍴 *Breakfast.*

$$ B&B/INN 🏨 **Tanglewood House.** Sitting on a headland overlooking Loch Broom with a beautiful view over the water, this hotel is a mile from Ullapool but feels much more remote. **Pros:** lovely setting; pretty gardens. **Cons:** a steep drive down to the house. [$] *Rooms from: £104* ✉ *Off A835* ☎ *01854/612059* 🌐 *www.tanglewoodhouse.co.uk* 🛏 *3 rooms* 🍴 *Breakfast.*

ACHILTIBUIE

25 miles northwest of Ullapool.

Off the beaten track, Achiltibuie is a small coastal community set at the foot of magnificent mountains. It looks out over the Summer Isles, whose history dates back to Viking raids. Cruises leave from a small jetty just west of Achiltibuie and take you to the largest and only inhabited island, Tanera Mhor, where you can buy special Summer Isle stamps—Tanera Mhor is the only Scottish island to have a private postal service.

GETTING HERE AND AROUND

Achiltibuie is a two-hour drive from Inverness, much of it on the quick A835, with the last 15 miles on an occasionally daunting single-track road.

EXPLORING

Coigach and Assynt. Drive north of Ullapool on the A835 into Coigach and Assynt, and you enter a different kind of landscape. The mountains punch out of the heathered terrain and seem to shift their position, hiding behind one another. Even their names seem different from those of the *bens* (mountain peaks or high hills) elsewhere: Cul Mor, Cul Beag, Stac Pollaidh, Canisp, Suilven. Some owe their origins to Norse words rather than to Gaelic—a reminder that Vikings used to sail this northern seaboard. Much of this area lies within the North West Highlands Geopark. Loch Assynt itself is strangely beautiful, peppered with tiny wooded islands.

WHERE TO STAY

$$$
HOTEL
Fodor's Choice
★

Summer Isles Hotel. Halfway along a road that ends at the sea, this remote gem is built into a small hill and contemplates the mystical Summer Isles. **Pros:** stunning views; peaceful location; good food. **Cons:** not much to do nearby. $ *Rooms from: £179 ⊠ Achiltibuie Rd.* ☎ *01854/622282* ⊕ *www.summerisleshotel.com* ⊗ *Closed Nov–Mar.* ↝ *6 rooms* ⫶⊙⫶ *Breakfast.*

SPORTS AND THE OUTDOORS

Stach Pollaidh. For a great afternoon of walking, ascend the dramatic hill of Stach Pollaidh (pronounced "stack polly"), about 10 miles east of Achiltibuie. The clearly marked path climbs for a bit and then curves around to the right and takes you on a loop with incredible views over Sutherland, north to Suilven, and west to the Summer Isles. About halfway around the hill, a steeper path takes you to the start of the ridge. Only very experienced rock climbers should continue from here, as the route requires rock climbing in very exposed conditions. But not to worry, because from the west side of the looped path you can see the pinnacled pitch of Stach Pollaidh. Start your walk from a car park about 5 miles from A835. ⊠ *Off A835, Dornie.*

LOCHINVER

18 miles north of Achiltibuie, 38 miles north of Ullapool.

Lochinver is a very pretty quiet shoreside community of whitewashed cottages, with lovely beaches to the north, a harbor used by the west-coast fishing fleet, and a couple of good dining and lodging options. Behind the town the mountain Suilven rises abruptly. Take the cul-de-sac, **Baddidarroch Road,** for a great photo opportunity. Lochinver is a perfect base for exploring Sutherland.

10

GETTING HERE AND AROUND

To get to Lochinver, take A835/A837 north from Ullapool.

ESSENTIALS

Visitor Information Assynt Visitor Centre. ⊠ *Main St.* ☎ *01571/844194* ⊕ *www.discoverassynt.co.uk.*

EXPLORING

Drumbeg Loop. Bold souls spending time at Lochinver may enjoy the interesting single-track B869 Drumbeg Loop to the north of Lochinver—it has several challenging hairpin turns along with breathtaking views. The junction is on the north side of the River Inver bridge on the outskirts of the village, signposted as "Stoer" and "Clashnessie." Just beyond the scattered community of Stoer, a road leads west to **Stoer Point Lighthouse.** If you're an energetic walker, you can hike across the short turf and heather along the cliff top for fine views west towards the Isle of Skye. There's also a red-sandstone sea stack: the **Old Man of Stoer.** This makes a pleasant excursion on a long summer evening.

Eas Coul Aulin Waterfall. With a drop of 685 feet, this is the longest waterfall in the United Kingdom. A rugged hike leads to the falls, which are at the head of Loch Glencoul. Start from the car park off A894, approximately 17 miles east and north from Lochinver. In summer, cruises (£25) from Kylesku Old Ferry Pier offer a less taxing alternative. ✉ *A894, 3 miles southeast of Kylesku Bridge.*

WHERE TO EAT AND STAY

$ BRITISH 🍴 **An Cala Cafe at the Lochinver Mission.** An abandoned fishermen's mission (a place where fishermen stayed while in port), at the far end of town near the harbor, now houses this pleasant café serving lunch, soup, sandwiches, and home baking. The specials often include fish freshly delivered from the harbor. The building also contains the local archives, a marine center, and a bunkhouse with 14 places. [$] *Average main: £9* ✉ *Culag Park* ☎ *01571/844324* 🌐 *www.lochinvermission.org.uk* 💳 *No credit cards.*

$ B&B/INN 🏨 **Davar.** Well known for its fine views across Lochinver Bay, this guest house has been carefully restored to its former glory after a period of decline. **Pros:** lounge filled with books and games; wonderful mountain views. **Cons:** too small for some travelers. [$] *Rooms from: £70* ✉ *A837* ☎ *01571/844501* 🌐 *www.davar-lochinver.co.uk* 🕒 *Closed Dec.–Mar.* 🛏 *4 rooms* 🍽 *Breakfast.*

$$$$ HOTEL 🏨 **Inver Lodge Hotel.** In a commanding location on a hillside above Lochinver, this modern hotel has stunning views of the sea and smart guest rooms decorated in contemporary colors and traditional mahogany furniture. **Pros:** cozy public room with a fireplace; refreshing sauna; great fishing nearby. **Cons:** drab exterior; not good for families with children. [$] *Rooms from: £280* ✉ *Iolaire Rd.* ☎ *01571/844496* 🌐 *www.inverlodge.com* 🛏 *21 rooms* 🍽 *Breakfast.*

$ B&B/INN 🏨 **Tigh Na Sith.** Set just above the bay at Lochinver, this B&B wins rave reviews for its warm welcome. **Pros:** great hosts; fantastic views. **Cons:** room at back doesn't have a view; shared dining table for breakfast may not suit everyone. [$] *Rooms from: £79* ✉ *A837* ☎ *01571/844352* 🌐 *www.tighnasith.com* 🛏 *3 rooms* 🍽 *Breakfast.*

SHOPPING

Achins Book & Craft Shop. On the Lochinver–Achiltibuie road, this shop is a great place to find Scottish books on natural history, hill walking, and trout fishing. It also sells craft items—knitwear, tweeds, and pottery—along with works by local artists and recordings of traditional music. The shop and pleasant café are open daily from 10 to 5 (except for Sunday from October to March). ✉ *Off B869, Inverkirkaig* ☎ *01571/844262.*

Highland Stoneware. The huge sofa and television composed entirely of broken crockery are a witty introduction to the beautiful ceramic made at Highland Stoneware. The potters and decorators work behind the shop, and visitors are encouraged to watch. The shop displays the range of work they produce, all of it in some way echoing Highland themes. ✉ *Baddidarroch* ☎ *01571/844376* 🌐 *www.highlandstoneware.com.*

SCOURIE

28 miles north of Lochinver.

Scourie is a small settlement catering to visitors—fisherfolk especially—with a range of accommodations. The bay-side town makes a good base for a trip to the bird sanctuary on Handa Island.

GETTING HERE AND AROUND

From Lochinver, take the A837, which becomes the A894 as you turn north.

EXPLORING

Fodor's Choice ★ **Handa Island.** Just off the coast of Scourie is Handa Island, a bird sanctuary that shelters huge seabird colonies, especially impressive at nesting time. You can gaze at more than 200,000 birds nesting on spectacular cliffs, including guillemots, razorbills, great skuas, kittiwakes, and even the odd puffin from the towering sandstone vantage point of Stack an Seabhaig (Hawk's Stack). This remarkable reserve, administered by the Scottish Wildlife Trust, is open only in spring and summer. It can be reached by a small open boat from Tarbert; contact the tourist information center in Lochinver or Durness for details. Sturdy boots, a waterproof jacket, and a degree of fitness are needed to walk the path around the island. ☎ *07780/967800 ferry* 🌐 *scottishwildlifetrust.org.uk.*

WHERE TO STAY

$$ B&B/INN Fodor's Choice ★ 🏨 **Eddrachilles Hotel.** This longtime favorite has one of the best views of any lodging in Scotland—toward the tiny islands of Badcall Bay. (If you're entranced, you can explore them by boat.) The hotel sits on 320 acres of private moorland and is just south of the Handa Island bird sanctuary. **Pros:** attractive garden; stunning shoreline nearby; close to bird sanctuary. **Cons:** restaurant's quality can vary; service sometimes disappoints. [$] *Rooms from: £110* ✉ *Off A894* ☎ *01971/502080* 🌐 *www.eddrachilles.com* 🕒 *Closed early Oct.–late Mar.* 🛏 *11 rooms* 🍴 *Breakfast.*

$$ HOTEL Fodor's Choice ★ 🏨 **Kylesku Hotel.** This charming hotel looking out over Loch Glendhu and toward Eas Coul Aulin, Scotland's highest waterfall, has a professional staff, excellent food, and a warm, relaxed atmosphere. **Pros:** stunning views; great staff; delicious food. **Cons:** some old-building quirks; two attic rooms are small, but cheaper. [$] *Rooms from: £150* ✉ *Off A894, Drumbeg* ☎ *01971/502231* 🛏 *11 rooms* 🍴 *Breakfast.*

$$ HOTEL 🏨 **Scourie Hotel.** This family-run hotel in the center of Scourie is something of an Eden for those who love fishing: it has fishing rights over 46 lochs and rods available to guests. **Pros:** the place for people who love fishing; comfortable public rooms; welcoming atmosphere. **Cons:** fairly basic rooms; Wi-Fi in public areas only (and intermittently). [$] *Rooms from: £135* ✉ *Off A894, Scourie* ☎ *01971/502396* 🌐 *www.scouriehotel.com* 🛏 *21 rooms* 🍴 *Breakfast.*

DURNESS

27 miles north of Scourie, 55 miles north of Lochinver.

The sudden patches of green surrounding the village of Durness, on the north coast, are caused by the richer limestone outcrops among the acid moorlands. Here you'll find the country's highest cliff, Clo Mor.

GETTING HERE AND AROUND

Past Scourie, the A894 becomes the A838 as you head north. The road to Durness is often a single lane in each direction.

ESSENTIALS

Visitor Information Durness Information Centre. ✉ *Sangomore* ☎ *01971/511368* ⊕ *www.durness.org.*

EXPLORING

Cape Wrath. If you've made it this far north, you'll probably want to go all the way to Cape Wrath, a rugged headland at the northwest tip of Scotland. The white-sand beaches, impressive dunes covered in marram grass, and crashing seas of nearby Balnakeil Bay make it an exhilarating place to visit. As this land is owned by the Ministry of Defence (it is listed as an area for air force training), you can't drive your own vehicle. From May through September, a small boat ferries people here from Keoldale, 2 miles outside Durness; once you're across the sea inlet called the Kyle of Durness, a minibus will then take you to the lighthouse. Call ahead or check departure times on the board at the jetty. ☎ *01971/511284* ⊕ *www.visitcapewrath.com.*

Ciannabeine Beach. This must be one of Scotland's most beautiful beaches, a sweep of sand caught in the embrace of 10,000-year-old rocks, cracked and ancient like aging guards protecting the place. There is a car park opposite and a path down to the beach itself. You will recognize it by the white house just beyond, once the village school. **Amenities:** parking (free). **Best for:** swimming; walking. ✉ *Durness* ⊹ *Off the A838, 10 miles after Durness.*

Clo Mor. The highest mainland cliffs in Scotland, including 920-foot Clo Mor, lie between the Kyle and Cape Wrath.

Smoo Cave. This spectacular cavern, hollowed out of the limestone by rushing water, can be reached via a steep cliff stairway from the Smoo Cave car park. Explanatory boards at the top of the stairs tell the history of those who lived and used the caves in much earlier times. Also worth exploring are the number of wonderful sandy beaches found as you head east to Tongue, especially the one at Sango Bay. Boat tours around the Kyle of Durness run daily from April through September. ⊕ *www.smoocave.org.*

WHERE TO EAT AND STAY

$ **Cocoa Mountain.** A must for those with a sweet tooth, this "chocolate
CAFÉ bar" serves up world-class truffles and stunningly rich hot chocolate made with chocolate from its next-door chocolate "factory." There are sandwiches and cake, too, and coffee if you feel overwhelmed by chocolate. The factory (beside the café) sources the beans from around the world, but makes the final product here. $ *Average main:*

£9 ⊠ 8 Balnakeil ⚓ Northwest of Durness ☎ 01971/511233 ⊕ www. cocoamountain.co.uk.

$$ 🏨 **Tongue Hotel.** With open fireplaces in its public areas and hunting
HOTEL lodge–style rooms, the Tongue Hotel makes a great base for exploring
this most northern coast of the Scottish mainland. **Pros:** welcoming
atmosphere; stunning views; relaxing public rooms. **Cons:** a car neces-
sary to make the most of this area. 💲 *Rooms from: £110 ⊠ On A838,
near Lairg, Tongue ☎ 01847/611206 ⊕ www.tonguehotel.co.uk ⇦ 19
rooms ⦿ Breakfast.*

SHOPPING

Balnakeil Craft Village. Artisans sell pottery, leather, weavings, paintings,
and more from their studios at Balnakeil Craft Village. It is rather a
strange place, housed as it is on an unnamed road running northwest
from Durness in a collection of shabby former military buildings framed
by dramatic views of Balnakeil Bay. There are galleries, workshops, and
a range of crafts. The village is open April through October, and while
hours vary, most shops here are open daily from 10 to 5, and even later
on summer evenings. ⊠ *Balnakeil ☎ 01971/511777.*

Sculpture Croft. You come across this odd garden of delights on an open
moorland route, in the village of Laid. Strange ceramic plants appear
at the roadside, and the path to Lotte Glob's pottery gallery reveals
more scattered across the landscape. Her work reflects and adds to the
landscape, using natural shapes and forms and building patterns into
the rocks themselves. ⊠ *A838, 105 Laid, Loch Eriboll ☎ 01971/511727
⊕ www.lotteglob.co.uk.*

THURSO

74 miles east of Durness.

The town of Thurso is quite substantial for a community so far north. In
town are the Thurso Heritage Museum and Old St. Peter's Kirk, which
dates back to the 12th century. There are also fine beaches, particularly
at Dunnet Bay, and great seabird watching at Dunnet Head.

GETTING HERE AND AROUND

A car remains the best way to see this region, although local buses and
the post bus run on most days. At Tongue the A838 becomes the A836.

ESSENTIALS

Visitor Information Thurso Information Centre. ⊠ *Riverside Rd.*
☎ *01847/893155 ⊕ www.visitscotland.com.*

EXPLORING

Caithness Horizons. This rich museum explores life in the county of Caith-
ness from the dawn of history to the present, from Picts and Vikings
to the controversial Dounreay Nuclear Research Establishment. There
is also a café and shop. ⊠ *Old Town Hall, High St. ☎ 01847/896508
⊕ www.caithnesshorizons.wordpress.com ⊗ Apr.–Sept., Mon.–Sat.
10–6, Sun. 11–4; Oct.–Mar., Mon.–Sat. 10–6.*

10

Dunnet Head. Many people make the trip to Dunnet Head, the northernmost point of mainland Britain. Dunnet Head Lighthouse, built in 1831, still stands here. As a bonus, there are fine views over the sea to Orkney. ⊠ *Off B855.*

WHERE TO STAY

$$$ ⊡ **Forss Country House Hotel.** Don't be fooled by the stark exterior, as
B&B/INN this house dating from 1810 is a charming place to stay. **Pros:** large guest rooms; lots of outdoor activities; hearty meals. **Cons:** heavy old doors make a racket. $ *Rooms from: £175* ⊠ *Forss, 4 miles west of Thurso* ☎ *01847/861201* ⊕ *www.forsshousehotel.co.uk* ⇨ *14 rooms* ⦿ *Breakfast.*

BICYCLING

Wheels Cycle Shop. At the Wheels Cycle Shop, the staff rents bikes and gives advice on the best routes. ⊠ *35 High St.* ☎ *01847/896124.*

JOHN O'GROATS

21 miles east of Thurso.

The windswept little outpost of John O'Groats is usually taken to be the northernmost community on the Scottish mainland, though that is not strictly accurate, as an exploration of the network of roads between Dunnet Head and John O'Groats will confirm. From the harbor you can take a boat to see the dolphins and seals that live beneath the coastal cliffs. Or you can seek out Duncansby Head, where you can watch the puffins and guillemots. This is nature, wild and untouched. The little town has charms of its own, including a crafts center with high-quality shops selling knitwear, candles, and gifts.

GETTING HERE AND AROUND

Traveling east from Thurso, take the coast-hugging A836.

EXPLORING

Duncansby Head. Head to Duncansby Head for spectacular views of cliffs and sea stacks by the lighthouse—and puffins, too. It's on the coastal road east of town.

John O'Groats Ferries. Sailing from John O'Groats Harbor, this company takes you on 90-minute cruises past spectacular cliff scenery and birdlife into the Pentland Firth, to Duncansby Stacks, and to the island of Stroma. Trips cost £18 and are available daily at 2:30 between June and August. Between May and September the company also offers day trips to Orkney for £56. ⊠ *County Rd., John o' Groats* ☎ *01955/611353* ⊕ *www.jogferry.co.uk.*

NIGHTLIFE AND PERFORMING ARTS

Lyth Arts Centre. In a Victorian-era school building, the Lyth Arts Centre serves as a cultural hub. From April to November, professional music and theater companies fill the schedule and locals fill the seats. There are also exhibitions of contemporary fine art. Lyth is located between Wick and John O'Groats. ⊠ *Off A9, Lyth* ☎ *01955/641434* ⊕ *www.lytharts.org.uk.*

WICK

17 miles south of John O'Groats, 22 miles southeast of Thurso.

Wick is a substantial town that was built on its fishing industry. The town itself is not very appealing, but it does have the gaunt, bleak ruins of **Castle Sinclair** and **Castle Girnigoe** teetering on a cliff top 3 miles north of the town.

GETTING HERE AND AROUND

From Thurso, the A836 follows the coast to John O'Groats and becomes the A99 as you head south. An alternative route, the A882, cuts away from the coast.

EXPLORING

Wick Heritage Centre. To learn how this town grew, visit the Wick Heritage Centre. The locals who run it are real enthusiasts, and they will take you through the history of the town from its founding by the Vikings through its heyday as a leading herring port in the 1860s. The collection includes everything from fascinating fossils to 19th-century toys. It includes the Johnstone Collection of over 100 years of the town's history in photographs taken by a family of local photographers. There's also an art gallery and terraced gardens that overlook the town. ✉ *18–27 Bank Row* ☏ *01955/605393* ⊕ *www.wickheritage.org* 🎫 *£4* ⊙ *Easter–Oct., Mon.–Sat. 10–3:45.*

EN ROUTE

Grey Cairns of Camster. The extraordinary Grey Cairns of Camster, two Neolithic chambered cairns dating from 4000 BC to 3000 BC, are among the best preserved in Britain. **Camster Round Cairn** is 20 yards in diameter and 13 yards high, and **Camster Long Cairn** reaches nearly 77 yards in length. Some 19th-century excavations revealed skeletons, pottery, and flint tools in the round cairn's internal chamber. If you don't mind dirty knees, you can crawl into the chambers in both cairns. ✉ *Off A9, 10 miles south of Wick* ☏ *01667/460232* ⊕ *www.historic-scotland.gov.uk* 🎫 *Free* ⊙ *Open all yr.*

DUNBEATH

10

21 miles south of Wick.

A tiny coast village, Dunbeath is bordered by moors on one side, the sea on the other. A few interesting museums make it worth a stop.

GETTING HERE AND AROUND

South of Wick, Dunbeath can be reached via the A9. This coast-hugging route, crowded with Orkney ferry traffic, can be quite daunting because of the steep drop-offs when heading south.

EXPLORING

Dunbeath Heritage Centre. The moors of Caithness roll down to the sea at Dunbeath, where you find a former school that houses the Dunbeath Heritage Centre. Inside are photographs and domestic and crofting artifacts that relay the area's history from the Bronze Age up to the present. It's particularly helpful to those researching family histories. ✉ *Off A9* ☏ *01593/731233* ⊕ *www.dunbeath-heritage.org.uk* 🎫 *£3* ⊙ *Apr.–Sept., Sun.–Fri. 10–5; Oct.–Mar., weekdays 11–3.*

HELMSDALE

15 miles south of Dunbeath.

Helmsdale is a fascinating fishing village with a checkered past. It was a busy Viking settlement and then the scene of an aristocratic poisoning plot before it was transformed into a 19th-century village to house some of the people removed from their land to make way for sheep. These "clearances," perpetrated by the Duke of Sutherland, were among the area's most inhumane.

GETTING HERE AND AROUND

Helmsdale is one of the few towns on this part of the coast that has a daily train service from Inverness. However, a car will allow you to see more in the surrounding area. Get here via the coastal A9 or the inland A897.

EXPLORING

FAMILY **Timespan Heritage Centre.** This thought-provoking mix of displays, artifacts, and audiovisual materials portrays the history of the area from the Stone Age to the 1869 gold rush in the Strath of Kildonan. There's a geology exhibit in the garden and a tour of the Kildonan gold rush site. The complex also includes a café and an art gallery that often hosts visiting artists and changing exhibitions. ⊠ *Dunrobin St.* ☎ *01431/821327* ⊕ *www.timespan.org.uk* ⊠ *£4* ☉ *Mar.–Oct., Mon.–Sat. 10–5, Sun. noon–5; Nov.–Feb., Sat. 11–4, Tues. 2–4; last admission 1 hr before closing.*

GOLSPIE

18 miles south of Helmsdale.

The little coastal town of Golspie is worth a stop if you're heading for Dunrobin Castle. It has a number of shops and accommodations.

GETTING HERE AND AROUND

Golspie can be reached by train from Inverness, and in summer the train also stops at Dunrobin Castle. Drivers should use the A9.

EXPLORING

Dunrobin Castle. The Scottish home of the dukes of Sutherland is flamboyant Dunrobin Castle, an ancient seat developed by the first duke into a 19th-century white-turreted behemoth. As well as lavish interiors, there are summer falconry demonstrations and Versailles-inspired gardens. Trains so fascinated the duke that he built his own railroad in the park and staffed it with his servants. The first duke has a controversial legacy; he was responsible for the brutal Sutherland Clearances of 1810 to 1820, when people were removed from their farms to make room for sheep to graze. ⊠ *Off A9* ☎ *01408/633177* ⊕ *www.dunrobincastle. co.uk* ⊠ *£10.50* ☉ *Apr., May, Sept., and early Oct., Mon.–Sat. 10:30–4:30, Sun. noon–4:30; June–Aug., daily 10–5.*

SHOPPING

Orcadian Stone Company. A geological exhibition at this shop spans 3 billion years and includes some of the world's oldest rocks. The shop is open from Easter to October and for three weeks before Christmas. ⊠ *Main St.* ☎ *01408/633483* ⊕ *www.orcadianstone.co.uk.*

DORNOCH

10 miles south of Golspie, 40 miles north of Inverness.

A town of sandstone houses, tiny rose-filled gardens, and a 13th-century cathedral with stunning traditional and modern stained-glass windows, Dornoch is well worth a visit. It's noted for golf: you may hear it referred to as the St. Andrews of the North, but because of the town's location so far north, the golf courses here are delightfully uncrowded. Royal Dornoch is the jewel in its crown, praised by the world's top golfers.

GETTING HERE AND AROUND

From Inverness, take the A9 north to Dornoch. Be cautious, as it's often busy with ferry traffic.

ESSENTIALS

Visitor Information Dornoch Information Centre. ⊠ *Sheriff Court House, Castle St.* ☎ *01862/810594* ⊕ *www.visitscotland.com.*

EXPLORING

OFF THE BEATEN PATH

Glenmorangie Distillery. The light color and delicate floral taste of the Speyside whiskies is exemplified in Glenmorangie, one of the best known of the Highland whiskies. You can tour the distillery to see how that taste is achieved. It's 8 miles south of Dornach across the Dornach Firth. ⊠ *A9, Tain* ✛ *Near Tain on the A9 from Inverness* ☎ *01862/892477* ⊕ *www.glenmorangie.com* 🎟 *Tour £5* ⊙ *Apr.–Aug., daily 10–4; Sept. and Oct., Mon.–Sat. 10–3; Nov.–Mar., weekdays 10–2.*

WHERE TO EAT AND STAY

$$

BRITISH

✕ **Sutherland House.** Just off the main square, the Sutherland House restaurant has a feeling of intimacy in its two separate rooms, reinforced by the enthusiastic reception that guests receive as they arrive. The menu is imaginative, with some unusual combinations dreamed up by the chef, who's also the owner's son. Seafood dominates, as you would expect, but the chicken with a Glenmorangie whisky sauce and the pork medallions in a Cajun sauce are a delight. $ *Average main: £15* ⊠ *Argyle St.* ☎ *01862/811023* ⊕ *www.sutherland-house.net* ⌃ *Reservations essential.*

$$

HOTEL

🏰 **Dornoch Castle Hotel.** A genuine late-15th-century castle, once sheltering the bishops of Caithness, this hotel blends the quite old and the more modern. **Pros:** grand exterior; lovely gardens; friendly hotel staff. **Cons:** a few rooms need a lick of paint. $ *Rooms from: £129* ⊠ *Castle St.* ☎ *01862/810216* ⊕ *www.dornochcastlehotel.com* ⇆ *24 rooms* ⦿ *Breakfast.*

$

B&B/INN

🏰 **Strathview Lodge.** Just a few miles north of Dornoch, this B&B sits high above the road with a wonderful view of Loch Fleet. **Pros:** beautiful location; comfortable and warm rooms; attentive owners. **Cons:** sign for the B&B not easy to spot. $ *Rooms from: £72* ⊠ *Cambusavie* ☎ *01408/634286* ⊕ *www.strathview-dornoch.co.uk* ⇆ *3 rooms* ⦿ *Breakfast.*

SHOPPING

Jail Dornoch. It's rare that people might want to enter a jail, but in this case it has been transformed into an elegant craft- and gift-shopping precinct. The cells now house cards, children's clothes, and some beautiful leather and woolen gifts—a far happier use than their original role. ✉ *Castle St.* ☎ *01862/810555* 🌐 *www.jail-dornoch.com.*

GOLF

Fodor's Choice ★ **Royal Dornoch Golf Club.** The legendary Championship Course, laid out by Tom Morris in 1886, has fast raised greens with views of mountains and white sandy beaches. In the springtime, yellow gorse adds to the wild beauty. The Struie Course provides more sea views and challenging golf for players of every level. It's less than an hour's drive north of Inverness Airport. ✉ *Golf Rd.* ☎ *01862/810219* 🌐 *www.royaldornoch.com* 🎟 *Championship, £120; Struie, £45* ⛳ *Championship: 18 holes, 6711 yards, par 70; Struie: 18 holes, 6265 yards, par 71* ⏲ *Daily* ✍ *Reservations essential.*

TORRIDON

Located far to the west of Scotland, Torridon has a grand, rugged, and wild air that feels especially remote, yet it's just a few hours' drive from Inverness before you reach Kinlochewe, near the east end of Glen Torridon. The western side is equally spectacular. Walking trails and mountain panoramas abound. Torridon is a wonderful place to visit if you want to tackle one of the legendary peaks here—Beinn Alligin, Liathach, and Beinn Eighe—or if you enjoy outdoor activities like kayaking, climbing, or mountain biking. The A890, which runs from the A832 into the heart of Torridon, is a single-lane road in some stretches, with plenty of open vistas across the deserted heart of northern Scotland.

LOCHCARRON

66 miles west of Inverness.

Strung along the shore, the village of Lochcarron has some attractive croft buildings, a couple of churches (one an 18th-century ruin set in a graveyard), a golf club, and some handy shops.

GETTING HERE AND AROUND

To drive here from Inverness, take the A9 as it becomes the A835, A832, and then the A890. The single-track road skirts both steep mountains and lochs.

WHERE TO EAT

$ CAFÉ 🍴 **Bealach Cafe and Gallery.** This lovely café and gallery offers sandwiches, soups, and fine home baking against a background of mountains and the steepest road ascent in Britain, the Bealach na Ba (from which it gets its name). All this can be viewed through the café's large windows or from the outside deck if weather allows. The walls exhibit the work of local artists. [$] *Average main: £9* ✉ *Termapress, Kishorn* ✛ *On the A896, 2 miles before Lochcarron* ☎ *01520/733436* 🌐 *www.thebealach.co.uk* ⏲ *No dinner. Closed Mon.*

SHOPPING

Lochcarron Weavers. Watch a weaver producing pure-wool tartans that can be bought here or at the company's other outlets in the area. There's also a café. ⊠ *Mid Strome* ☎ *01520/722212* ⊕ *www.lochcarron.co.uk.*

SHIELDAIG

16 miles northwest of Lochcarron.

Just west of the southern coast of Upper Loch Torridon is Shieldaig, a village that sits in an attractive crescent overlooking a loch of its own, Loch Shieldaig. For an atmospheric evening foray, walk north toward Loch Torridon, at the northern end of the village by the church. The path—fairly well made, though hiking shoes are recommended—leads to exquisite views and tiny rocky beaches.

GETTING HERE AND AROUND

Shieldaig is on the A896 between Lochcarron and Kinlochewe.

EXPLORING

OFF THE BEATEN PATH

Applecross. The tame way to reach this small community facing Skye is by a coastal road from near Shieldaig. The exciting route turns west off the A896 a few miles farther south and then a series of hairpin turns corkscrews up the steep wall at the head of a corrie (a glacier-cut mountain valley), over the **Bealach na Ba** (Pass of the Cattle). There are spectacular views of Skye from the bare plateau on top, and you can brag afterward that you've been on what is probably Scotland's highest drivable road.

Fodor's Choice ★

Glen Torridon. The scenic spectacle of Glen Torridon lies east of Shieldaig as you follow the A896 from Shieldaig to Kinlochewe. Some say that Glen Torridon has the finest mountain scenery in Scotland. It consists mainly of the long gray quartzite flanks of **Beinn Eighe** and **Liathach**, with its distinct ridge profile that looks like the keel of an upturned boat.

FAMILY

Torridon Visitor Center. The National Trust for Scotland operates a visitor center that explains the ecology and geology of the area. A small deer museum has displays on these quintessentially Scottish beasts. ⊠ *A896, Achnasheen* ☎ *01445/791221* ⊕ *www.nts.org.uk/property/torridon* ⊠ *Free* ⊗ *Visitor center: Easter–Sept., daily 10–6; museum: daily 9–5.*

10

WHERE TO STAY

$$$$
HOTEL

Torridon Hotel. The Victorian Gothic turrets of this former hunting lodge promise atmosphere and grandeur. **Pros:** breathtaking location; center for outdoor activities; more than 300 malts in the bar. **Cons:** isolated location; quite pricey. $ *Rooms from: £340* ⊠ *A896, Achnasheen* ☎ *01445/700300* ⊕ *www.thetorridon.com* ⊃ *18 rooms* ⊗| *Breakfast.*

$$
B&B/INN

Torridon Inn. A more affordable option than the grand Torridon Hotel, this lodging makes a great base for exploring the area. **Pros:** pleasant wood-clad decor; eco-friendly vibe; reasonable rates. **Cons:** service sometimes erratic; sometimes noisy. $ *Rooms from: £110* ⊠ *A896, Achnasheen* ☎ *01445/700300* ⊕ *www.thetorridon.com/inn* ⊃ *12 rooms* ⊗| *Breakfast.*

GAIRLOCH

38 miles north of Shieldaig.

Aside from its restaurants and lodgings, peaceful Gairloch has one further advantage: lying just a short way from the mountains of the interior, this small oasis often escapes the rain clouds that can cling to the high summits. You can enjoy a round of golf here and perhaps stay dry, even when the nearby Torridon Hills are deluged.

GETTING HERE AND AROUND
From Ullapool, this coastal town can be reached via A832.

EXPLORING

Fodor'sChoice ★ **Destitution Road.** The road between Gairloch and the Corrieshalloch Gorge initially heads north and passes coastal scenery with views of Gruinard Bay and its white beaches, then woodlands around Dundonnell and Loch Broom. Soon the route traverses wild country: the toothed ramparts of the mountain An Teallach (pronounced tyel-lack) are visible on the horizon. The moorland route you travel is known chillingly as Destitution Road. At Corrieshalloch the road, A832, joins the A835 for Inverness.

Gairloch Heritage Museum. This little museum's exhibits cover prehistoric times to the present. It's also a source for genealogical research—by appointment with the curator. ⊠ *A832, at B8031* ☎ *01445/712287* ⊕ *www.gairlochheritagemuseum.org* ⧉ *£4* ⊙ *Apr.–Oct., weekdays 10–5, Sat. 11–3.*

Fodor'sChoice ★ **Inverewe Gardens.** A highlight of the area, Inverewe Gardens has lush plantings tucked away behind a dense barrier of trees and shrubs. This is all thanks to the warm North Atlantic Drift, which takes the edge off winter frosts. Inverewe is sometimes described as subtropical, but this inaccuracy irritates the head gardener; do not expect coconuts and palm trees here. Instead, look for rarities like the blue Himalayan poppy. There is also a restaurant, open the same times as the gardens. ⊠ *A832, 6 miles northeast of Gairloch, Poolewe* ☎ *01445/781200* ⊕ *www.nts. org.uk* ⧉ *£10.50* ⊙ *June–Aug., daily 9:30–6; Sept., daily 10:30–5; Oct., daily 10:30–4; Nov.–Mar. daily 10–3; Apr., daily 10–5.*

Fodor'sChoice ★ **Loch Maree.** Southeast of Gairloch stretches one of Scotland's most scenic lochs, Loch Maree. Its harmonious environs, with tall Scots pines and the mountain Slioch looming as a backdrop, witnessed the destruction of much of the tree cover in the 18th century. Iron ore was shipped in and smelted using local oak to feed the furnaces. Oak now grows here only on the northern limits of the range. Scottish Natural Heritage has an information center and nature trails by the loch and in the Beinn Eighe Nature Reserve. Red-deer sightings are virtually guaranteed; locals say the best place to spot another local denizen, the endangered pine marten (a member of the weasel family), is around the trash containers in the parking turnoffs.

WHERE TO STAY

$$ HOTEL **Dundonnell Hotel.** This family-run hotel set on the roadside by Little Loch Broom is quite remote, but with the mountains of An Leachall rising up behind, it couldn't be more picturesque. **Pros:** fabulous scenery;

plenty of outdoor activities; good dining options. **Cons:** bland exterior; decor not to everyone's taste. [$] *Rooms from: £100* ✉ *A832, 30 miles northeast of Gairloch, Dundonnell* ☎ *01854/633204* 🌐 *www.dundonnellhotel.com* 🛏 *28 rooms* 🍴 *Breakfast.*

ISLE OF SKYE

Fodor's Choice ★ The misty isle, Skye is full of romance and myth, lush gardens and steep, magnetic mountains (a compass is useless in the Cuillin Mountains). It ranks near the top of most visitors' must-see lists: the romance of Prince Charles Edward Stuart (1720–88), known as Bonnie Prince Charlie, combined with the Cuillin Mountains and their proximity to the mainland, all contribute to its popularity.

Today Skye remains dramatic, mysterious, and mountainous, an island of sunsets that linger brilliantly until late at night, and of beautiful, magical mists. Much photographed are the old crofts, one or two of which are still inhabited. It also has an increasingly impressive range of accommodations and some excellent restaurants that show off the best in the island's produce and culinary talent.

To reach Skye, you can cross over the bridge spanning the narrow channel of Kyleakin, between Kyle of Lochalsh and Kyleakin, or in summer you can take the more romantic trip via boats between Mallaig and Armadale or the little old ferry between Glenelg and Kylerhea. You can tour comfortably around the island in two or three days, but a bit longer would allow time for some hiking or some sea kayaking.

Orientation is easy: in the north, follow the roads that loop around the peninsulas of Waternish and Trotternish; in the south, enjoy the road running the length of the Sleat Peninsula. There are some stretches of single-lane road, but with attention and care none pose a problem.

KYLE OF LOCHALSH

55 miles west of Inverness, 120 miles northwest of Glasgow.

This little town is the mainland gateway to Skye. Opened in 1995, the bridge transformed not only travel to Skye but the very seascape itself. The most noticeable attraction, though (in fact, almost a cliché), is not in Kyle at all, but 8 miles farther east at Dornie—Eilean Donan Castle.

10

GETTING HERE AND AROUND

From the north, you reach Kyle of Lochalsh via the A890 or A896; from the south, take the A87. Trains travel here from Inverness, but the journey requires changing trains several times.

EXPLORING

Brightwater Visitor Centre. *Ring of Bright Water,*Gavin Maxwell's much-loved account of his work with otters on the island of Eilean Ban , off the coast of Skye at Kyleakin, is commemorated here. There's an exhibit illustrating his work; wildlife tours that promise otters, seals, and lots of birds; and plenty of interactive activities. The center itself is actually on Skye, just over the bridge from Kyle of Lochalsh, and includes a 155-year-old lighthouse designed by Robert Louis

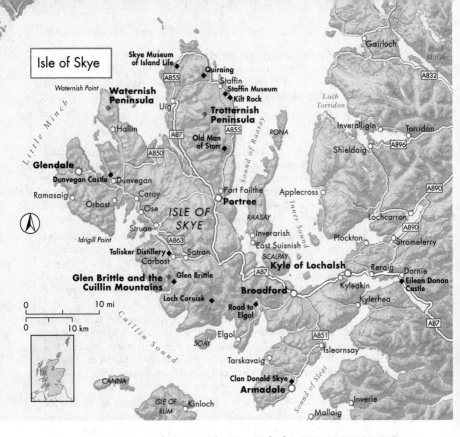

Isle of Skye

Skye Museum of Island Life
Quiraing
Staffin
Staffin Museum
Kilt Rock
Waternish Point
Waternish Peninsula
Uig
Trotternish Peninsula
Hallin
Old Man of Storr
Glendale
Dunvegan Castle
Dunvegan
Ramasaig
Caroy
Orbost
Ose
Port Failthe
Portree
Struan
ISLE OF SKYE
Idrigill Point
Talisker Distillery
Satran
Carbost
Glen Brittle and the Cuillin Mountains
Glen Brittle
Loch Coruisk
Broadford
Road to Elgol
Elgol
Tarskavaig
Clan Donald Skye
Armadale
Kinloch
ISLE OF RUM
CANNA
SOAY
Gairloch
Loch Torridon
Inveralligin
Torridon
Shieldaig
Applecross
RAASAY
Inverarish
East Suisnish
SCALPAY
Kyle of Lochalsh
Reraig
Dornie
Eilean Donan Castle
Kyleakin
Kylerhea
Plockton
Stromeferry
Lochcarron
Isleornsay
Inverie
Mallaig

Little Minch
Sound of Raasay
RONA
Inner Sound
Cuillin Sound
Sound of Sleat

0   10 mi
0   10 km

Stevenson's father. ✉ *The Pier, Kyleakin* ☎ *01599/530040* ⊕ *www. eileanban.org* ⛶ *Free* ⊙ *Apr.–Oct., Mon.–Sat. 9–5, Sun. 10–4.*

Fodor's Choice **Eilean Donan Castle.** Guarding the confluence of lochs Long, Alsh, and
★ Duich stands that most picturesque of all Scottish castles, Eilean Donan
Castle, perched on an islet connected to the mainland by a stone-arched
bridge. Dating from the 14th century, this romantic icon has all the
massive stone walls, timber ceilings, and winding stairs that you could
ask for. Empty and neglected for years after being bombarded by frig-
ates of the Royal Navy during an abortive Spanish-Jacobite landing
in 1719, it was almost entirely rebuilt from a ruin in the early 20th
century. The kitchen re-creates the busy scene before a grand banquet,
and the upper floors show how the castle was transformed into a grand
house. Now the hero of travel brochures, Eilean Donan has appeared in
many Hollywood movies and TV shows. There's a shop and a coffee-
house for the many visitors. ✉ *A87, Dornie* ☎ *01599/555202* ⊕ *www. eileandonancastle.com* ⛶ *£7* ⊙ *Feb. and Mar., daily 10–5; Apr., May, and Oct.–Dec., daily 10–6; June and Sept., daily 9:30–6; July and Aug., daily 9–6; last admission 1 hr before closing.*

WHERE TO STAY

$$ B&B/INN **Glenelg Inn.** Looking out over the Sound of Sleat, the Glenelg Inn's pleasant, contemporary rooms are furnished in wood and cane and are bright and clean. **Pros:** lively atmosphere; nice views; pleasant rooms. **Cons:** no sea views in some rooms; out-of-the-way location. [$] *Rooms from: £120* ✉ *Kirkton* ☎ *01599/522273* 🌐 *www.glenelg-inn.com* 🛏 *7 rooms* 🍴 *Breakfast.*

BROADFORD

8 miles west of Kyle of Lochalsh via Skye Bridge.

One of the larger of Skye's settlements, Broadford lies along the shore of Broadford Bay, which has on occasion welcomed whales to its sheltered waters.

GETTING HERE AND AROUND

Broadford is on the main road crossing the Isle of Skye, the A87.

ESSENTIALS

Visitor Information **Broadford Tourist Information Centre.** ✉ *The car park, off A87* ☎ *01471/822361* 🌐 *www.visitscotland.com.*

EXPLORING

FAMILY Fodor's Choice ★ **Misty Isle Boat Trips.** For fantastic views of the Cuillin Mountains and the Inner Hebrides, book a place on one of the Misty Isle Boat Trips. The expansive scenery around Loch Coruisk is some of the most spectacular in Scotland. Round-trip journeys depart from the town of Elgol, and booking ahead is essential. Prices vary, but a cruise to a seal colony costs £15. Private charters are available. ✉ *Elgol jetty, Sealladh na Mara, Elgol* ☎ *01471/866288* 🌐 *www.mistyisleboattrips.co.uk* 🎫 *From £15* ⏲ *Mon.–Sat. at 9, 10:15, 11, 12:35, 2:15, 3:50, 5:15.*

OFF THE BEATEN PATH

Road to Elgol. The B8083 leads from Broadford to one of the finest views in Scotland. This road passes through **Strath Suardal** and little **Loch Cill Chriosd** (Kilchrist) by a ruined church. You can appreciate breathtaking views of the mountain called **Bla Bheinn** as the A881 continues to Elgol, a gathering of crofts along this road that descends to a pier. Admire the heart-stopping profile of the Cuillin peaks from the shore, or, at a point about halfway down the hill, you can find the path that goes toward them across the rough grasslands. ✉ *Elgol.*

OFF THE BEATEN PATH

Bella Jane. Take a boat trip on the *Bella Jane* toward Loch Coruisk, where you'll be able to see seals. The three-hour round-trip excursions, available April to October (and sometimes beyond), cost £24 per person. ✉ *Elgol jetty, B8083, Elgol* ☎ *01471/866244* 🌐 *www.bellajane.co.uk* ☞ *Sailings at 9, 10:45, 12:15, and 2.*

FAMILY **Skye Serpentarium.** You can observe and handle snakes, frogs, lizards, and tortoises at the Skye Serpentarium, in the town center. It's also a refuge for wayward, worldly reptiles. ✉ *The Old Mill, off A87* ☎ *01471/822209* 🌐 *www.skyeserpentarium.org.uk* 🎫 *£4.50* ⏲ *Easter–Oct., Mon.–Sat. 10–5; July and Aug., daily 10–5.*

10

WHERE TO EAT AND STAY

$$ SEAFOOD 🍴 **Creelers of Skye.** Don't be put off by the shack that Creelers appears to be; inside is a celebrated seafood restaurant of quality. Its pan-roasted sea bass and its seafood gumbo are outstanding, but Creelers's signature dish is a true extravagance: bouillabaisse at £62 for two, an homage to great French cooking. It also serves nonseafood dishes like lamb, beef, and vegetarian choices. [$] *Average main: £19* ✉ *Lower Harrapool* ☎ *01471/822281* 🌐 *www.skye-seafood-restaurant.co.uk* 🕒 *Closed Sun.* ✍ *Reservations essential.*

$$$ HOTEL 🏨 **Broadford Hotel.** Though few of the rooms look directly out to sea, this comfortable hotel's dining room does have lovely views over Broadford Bay, and its simply decorated rooms are a pleasant place to lay your head. **Pros:** good base for touring the island; near the village; free Wi-Fi throughout. **Cons:** no elevator; rather dark public areas. [$] *Rooms from: £164* ✉ *Torrin Rd.* ☎ *01471/822204* 🌐 *www.broadfordhotel.co.uk* 🛏 *11 rooms* 🍽 *Breakfast.*

ARMADALE

17 miles south of Broadford, 43 miles south of Portree, 5 miles (ferry crossing) west of Mallaig.

Rolling moorlands, scattered with rivers and lochans, give way to enchanting hidden coves and scattered waterside communities here in **Sleat,** the southernmost part of Skye.

GETTING HERE AND AROUND

The Mallaig-Armadale ferry arrives here. There's a short (and beautiful) road to the southwest, while the main road heads east following the stunning coast.

EXPLORING

Clan Donald Skye. Walk the lush, extensive gardens at Armadale Castle Gardens and the Museum of the Isles and you take in magnificent views across the Sound of Sleat to Knoydart and the Mallaig Pennisula. The museum tells the story of the Macdonalds and their proud title—the Lords of the Isles—with the help of an excellent audiovisual presentation. In the 15th century the clan was powerful enough to threaten the authority of the Stewart monarchs of Scotland. There's a gift shop, restaurant, library, and center for genealogy research. Also on the grounds are high-quality accommodations in seven cottages with kitchen facilities. Access is from Armadale Pier, where signs indicate the different forest walks that are available. ✉ *Off A851, ½ mile north of Armadale Pier* ☎ *01471/844305* 🌐 *www.clandonald.com* 🎫 *Gardens free, museum £8.50* 🕒 *Gardens: daily dawn–dusk; museum: Apr.–Oct., daily 9:30–5:30; last admission 30 mins before closing.*

WHERE TO STAY

$$$$ HOTEL 🏨 **Duisdale House Hotel.** Set in 35 acres of mature woodlands and gardens, this former mansion has a lovely hillside location with views to the sea. **Pros:** nicely refurbished rooms; expansive views; excellent staff. **Cons:** nautical decor might not suit everyone; very expensive. [$] *Rooms*

from: £308 ✉ *Off A851, Isleornsay* ☎ *01471/833202* 🌐 *www.duisdale.com* 🛏 *18 rooms* 🍴 *Breakfast.*

$$$ HOTEL Fodor's Choice ★ 🏨 **Hotel Eilean Iarmain.** Built on a small peninsula dotted by a quiet lighthouse, this hotel has an unforgettable location. **Pros:** wonderful waterfront location; plenty of sporting activities; superb wine list. **Cons:** some unattractive renovations. [$] *Rooms from: £170* ✉ *Off A851* ☎ *01471/833332* 🌐 *www.eileaniarmain.co.uk* 🛏 *12 rooms, 4 suites* 🍴 *Breakfast.*

$$$$ HOTEL 🏨 **Kinloch Lodge.** A luxurious hotel with an equally luxurious restaurant, Kinloch Lodge overlooks the tidal Loch na Dal. The historic buildings date from the 17th century, while the newer South House has the best views and has been solidly built with comfort and relaxation in mind. **Pros:** historic property; interior full of character; great afternoon tea. **Cons:** pricey rooms and dining. [$] *Rooms from: £340* ✉ *Off A851, Isleornsay* ☎ *01471/833333* 🌐 *www.kinloch-lodge.co.uk* 🛏 *15 rooms* 🍴 *Some meals.*

SHOPPING

Fodor's Choice ★ **Ragamuffin.** A friendly place, this well-stocked shop specializes in designer knitwear. In winter the staff might make you a cup of coffee while you browse, then mail your purchases back home for you. ✉ *Armadale Pier, off A851* ☎ *01471/844217* 🌐 *www.ragamuffinloves.blogspot.co.uk.*

PORTREE

43 miles north of Armadale.

Portree, the population center of the island, is a pleasant place clustered around a small and sheltered bay. Although not overburdened by historical features, it's a good touring base with a number of good shops and an excellent bakery.

GETTING HERE AND AROUND

The biggest town on Skye, Portree is well served by local buses and by a well-maintained road, the A87.

ESSENTIALS

Visitor Information **Portree Information Centre.** ✉ *Bayfield House, Bayfield Rd.* ☎ *01478/614906.*

EXPLORING

Tigh na Coille: Aros. On the outskirts of town is Tigh na Coille: Aros (*tigh na coille* is Gaelic for "house of the forest," and *aros* means "home" or "homestead"), a visitor center that screens occasional films and exhibits local artworks. The café is spacious but on the expensive side. ✉ *Viewfield Rd.* ☎ *01478/613649* 🌐 *www.aros.co.uk* 🎟 *Free* 🕒 *Daily 10–5.*

WHERE TO EAT

$ BRITISH 🍴 **Café Arriba.** Up a steep flight of stairs, the laid-back café has window seats with great views over Portree Harbour. Using only local produce (whatever is "fresh, local, and available"), this is a good option for no-frills eating. Good choices include locally caught scallops, creamy summer risotto, and, on the lighter side, salad with freshly baked bread.

The Northern Highlands and the Western Isles

CLOSE UP

Clans and Tartans

Whatever the origins of the clans—some with Norman roots, intermarried into Celtic society; some of Norse origin, the product of Viking raids on Scotland; others traceable to the monastic system; yet others possibly descended from Pictish tribes—by the 13th century the clan system was at the heart of Gaelic tribal culture. By the 15th century the clan chiefs of the Scottish Highlands were a threat even to the authority of the Stewart monarchs.

The word *clann* means "family" or "children" in Gaelic, and it was the custom for clan chiefs to board out their sons among nearby families, a practice that helped to bond the clan unit and create strong allegiances.

THE CLAN SYSTEM

The clan chiefs' need for strong men-at-arms, fast-running messengers, and bards for entertainment, and the preservation of clan genealogy, was the probable origin of the Highland Games, still celebrated in many Highland communities each year, and which are an otherwise rather inexplicable mix of sports, music, and dance.

Gradually, by the 18th century, increasing knowledge of Lowland agricultural improvements, and better roads into the Highlands that improved communication of ideas and "southern" ways, began to weaken the clan system. The Battle of Culloden marked the death of the clan system, as the victorious English armies banned the kilt and the pipes and claimed the land of the rebellious clan chiefs. And when the new landowners introduced the hardy Cheviot breed of sheep and changed farming activity, the Highlands were transformed forever and the Highlanders,

and especially the islanders, began the long journey into emigration in the 1750s. By the 1820s, landowners paid people to leave.

TARTAN REVIVAL

Tartan's own origins as a part of the clan system are disputed; the Gaelic word for striped cloth is *breacan*—piebald or spotted—so even the word itself is not Highland. However, when cloth was locally spun, woven, and dyed using plant derivatives, each neighborhood would have different dyestuffs. In this way, combinations of colors and favorite patterns of the local weavers could become associated with an area and therefore clan. Between 1746 and 1782 the wearing of tartan was generally prohibited. By the time the ban was lifted, many recipes for dyes and weaving patterns had been forgotten.

It took the influence of Sir Walter Scott, with his romantic (and fashionable) view of Highland history, to create the "modern myth" of clans and tartan. Sir Walter engineered George IV's visit to Scotland in 1822, which turned into a tartan extravaganza. The idea of one tartan or group of tartans "belonging" to one particular clan was created at this time—literally created, with new patterns dreamed up and "assigned" to particular clans. Queen Victoria and Prince Albert reinforced the tartan culture later in the century and with it the revival of the Highland Games.

Clan Tartan Centre. You may be able to find a clan connection with expertise such as that available at the Clan Tartan Centre, which is part of the James Pringle Shopping Village in Leith Mills. ⊠ *70–74 Bangor Rd., Leith, Edinburgh* ☎ *0131/5535161.*

It has an especially varied vegetarian menu and hearty breakfasts available daily until 4:30. [$] *Average main: £10* ✉ *Quay Brae, Quay St.* ☎ *01478/611830* 🌐 *www.cafearriba.co.uk.*

$$$ BRITISH 🍴 **Scorrybreac Restaurant.** This tiny restaurant—it seats about 20—overlooking Portree Harbour has created something of a sensation in the short time it's been here. The vibe is relaxed and informal, while the cooking is imaginative and varied, creating some unexpected marriages like coffee-crusted venison or coconut and hake. All the ingredients are locally sourced and very Scottish, enlivened with a French touch. Leave room for the excellent desserts. The menu is £35 for three courses. [$] *Average main: £20* ✉ *7 Bosville Terr.* ☎ *01478/612069* 🌐 *www.scorrybreac.com* ✍ *Reservations essential.*

WHERE TO STAY

$$$ HOTEL 🏨 **Cuillin Hills Hotel.** This Victorian-era hunting lodge looks down on Portree and the brightly painted houses around the harbor. **Pros:** Portree a short stroll away; good breakfast menu; attentive service. **Cons:** rooms at back overpriced; restaurant sometimes very busy; no elevator. [$] *Rooms from: £210* ✉ *Off A855* ☎ *01478/612003* 🌐 *www.cuillinhills-hotel-skye.co.uk* 🛏 *29 rooms* 🍽 *Breakfast.*

$$ B&B/INN 🏨 **Peinmore House.** A former manse (the minister's house), Peinmore House has views north over Portree Bay, and, on a clear day, all the way to the Old Man of Storr; to the south you can spy the moody Cuillins. **Pros:** tranquil location; great breakfast. **Cons:** rather pricey; car required to get here. [$] *Rooms from: £150* ✉ *Off B883, 2 miles south of Portree* ☎ *01478/612574* 🌐 *www.peinmorehouse.co.uk* 🛏 *4 rooms* 🍽 *Breakfast.*

$$ B&B/INN Fodor's Choice ★ 🏨 **The Spoons.** After years of running a luxury estate for others, Marie and Ian Lewis put their considerable talents to work at the Spoons. **Pros:** top-notch breakfasts; perfect base for exploring; bucolic setting. **Cons:** books up quickly; no children under 14. [$] *Rooms from: £145* ✉ *75 Aird Bernisdale, Skeabost Bridge* ☎ *01470/532217* 🌐 *www.thespoonsonskye.com* 🛏 *3 rooms* 🍽 *Breakfast.*

$ B&B/INN 🏨 **Viewmount Guest House.** Set in extensive gardens overlooking the bay, this pink house stands out on the main road near the southern entrance of Portree. Many of the large detached houses—typical seaside homes—that line the road into town have become B&Bs. Viewmount's owners are friendly and welcoming, the facilities homey and unfussy. The house has four well-kept rooms in the main house and a separate chalet for those in search of extra privacy. Pets are welcome. this pink house stands out on the main road near the southern entrance of Portree. **Pros:** cheerful owners; unpretentious but comfortable rooms; ample parking. **Cons:** close to the main road; not good for those not fond of animals. [$] *Rooms from: £76* ✉ *Viewfield Rd.* ☎ *01478/612570* 🌐 *www.viewmount-skye.co.uk* 🛏 *5 rooms* 🍽 *Breakfast.*

SHOPPING

Isle of Skye Soap Company. This shop stocks soaps, essential oils, and other nice-smelling gifts. ✉ *Somerled Sq.* ☎ *01478/611350* 🌐 *www.skye-soap.co.uk.*

TROTTERNISH PENINSULA

16 miles north of Portree.

As A855, the main road, goes north from Portree, cliffs rise to the left. They're actually the edge of an ancient lava flow, set back from the road and running for miles. Fossilized dinosaur bones have been uncovered at the base of these cliffs. Don't forget to look up: you might spot a sea eagle, identifiable by the flash of its white tail.

GETTING HERE AND AROUND

From Portree, take the twisting, undulating A855 as it follows the coast.

EXPLORING

TOP ATTRACTIONS

Old Man of Storr. Along the dramatic road around the Trotternish Peninsula, a gate beside a car park marks the beginning of the climb to the Old Man of Storr. Give yourself at least three hours to explore this 2,000-foot-high volcanic pinnacle with spectacular views from the top. △ The weather here changes very quickly, so be prepared.

Quiraing. A geological formation of rocky crags and stacks, the spectacular Quiraing dominates the horizon about 5 miles beyond Kilt Rock. For a closer view of this area's strange pinnacles, make a left onto a small road at Brogaig by Staffin Bay. There's a parking lot near the point where this road breaches the ever-present cliff line. The road is very narrow and rough, so drive cautiously. The rambler's trail is on uneven, stony ground, and it's a steep scramble up to the rock formations. In ages past, stolen cattle were hidden deep within the Quiraing's rocky jaws.

Skye Museum of Island Life. Not far from the tip of the Trotternish Peninsula, the Skye Museum of Island Life brings the old crofting ways vividly to life. Included in the displays and exhibits are documents and photographs, reconstructed interiors, and implements. Flora Macdonald, who assisted Bonnie Prince Charlie, is buried nearby. ⊠ *Off A855, Kilmuir* ☎ *01470/552206* ⊕ *www.skyemuseum.co.uk* ⊡ *£2.50* ⊘ *Easter–Oct., Mon.–Sat. 9:30–5.*

WORTH NOTING

Kilt Rock. From Portree, the A855 travels past neat white croft houses and forestry plantings to Kilt Rock, which got its odd name because the sheer rock is ridged like a pleated kilt. Everyone on the tour circuit stops here to peep over the edge at the viewing platform.

Staffin Museum. Built on the foundations of an 1840s schoolhouse, this single-room museum is a labor of love of builder Dugald Ross, who first saw the fossilized dinosaur prints as a boy and as an adult saved them from rough seas. You'll also find objects saved from shipwrecks, agricultural implements, and some old photographs. It is highly individual and perhaps slightly eccentric, but fascinating. Opening hours are erratic; contact Dugald Ross before you go. ⊠ *6 Ellishadder, Staffin* ☎ *01470/562321* ⊕ *borve.net/staffin-museum.co.uk* ⊡ *£2* ⊘ *Apr.– Sept., Mon.–Sat. 9–5.*

WHERE TO EAT AND STAY

$$$ BRITISH 🍴 **The Glenview Skye Pie Cafe.** On the Trotternish Peninsula between Portree and Staffin, a renovated croft building houses this gem of a "restaurant with rooms." With wood floors and cheerfully painted walls, the simple, chic decor allows the older building's charms to flourish. The well-considered menu (£29 for two courses, £35 for three) includes locally sourced offerings like Skye shellfish broth and poached Uist salmon. If you like the place so much you want to stay, rooms are available from £95. [$] *Average main: £20* ✉ *A855, Culnacnoc, Portree* ☎ *01470/562248* 🌐 *skyepiecafe.co.uk* 💳 *No credit cards* 🕒 *Closed weekends. No dinner* ✍ *Reservations essential.*

$$$ HOTEL Fodor'sChoice ★ 🏨 **Flodigarry Country House Hotel.** With spectacular coastal views, Flodigarry retains the feel of a grand country house, with antique furnishings and beautifully finished wood throughout. **Pros:** spectacular views; a good base for walking; free Wi-Fi. **Cons:** steep road down; expensive rates; no room TVs. [$] *Rooms from: £205* ✉ *A855, Staffin* ☎ *01470/552203* 🌐 *www.flodigarry.co.uk* 🛏 *15 rooms* 🍽 *Breakfast.*

$ B&B/INN 🏨 **Glenview.** A whitewashed converted croft just off the Staffin road, Glenview is comfortable and warm (literally with a fire in the lounge) and unabashedly old-fashioned. **Pros:** comfortable and quiet; great breakfast. **Cons:** rather remote; old-fashioned plumbing. [$] *Rooms from: £95* ✉ *Culnacnoc, Portree* ☎ *01470/562248* 🌐 *glenviewskye.co.uk* 🛏 *3 rooms* 🍽 *Breakfast.*

WATERNISH PENINSULA

20 miles northwest of Portree.

The northwest corner of Skye has scattered crofting communities and magnificent coastal views. In the Hallin area look westward for an islet-scattered sea loch with small cliffs rising from the water—and looking like miniature models of full-size islands.

GETTING HERE AND AROUND

From Portree, follow the A850 to the Waternish Peninsula.

EXPLORING

Skye Skyns. A 10-minute tour of this working tannery gives excellent insight into the process of salting, washing, and preparing sheepskins. You'll learn the source of such phrases as "on tenterhooks" and "stretched to the limits." There are sheepskins in many forms for you to buy. ✉ *17 Lochbay, Waternish* ☎ *01470/592237* 🌐 *www.skyeskyns.co.uk.*

WHERE TO EAT

$$$$ SEAFOOD 🍴 **Loch Bay Seafood Restaurant.** On the waterfront stands a distinctive black-and-white restaurant. This relaxed place is where the island's top chefs unwind on their nights off, so you know the food must be good. The seafood is freshly caught and simply prepared, the goal being to enhance the natural flavors of the ingredients rather than overwhelm the senses with extraneous sauces. The menu offers a range of fish dishes, including halibut, sea bass, and Wester Ross salmon. Dinner is a three-course menu for £35. [$] *Average main: £35* ✉ *Off B886, Stein* ✣ *Near fishing jetty*

☎ 01470/592235 🌐 www.lochbay-seafood-restaurant.co.uk ⏲ Closed Oct.–Easter and Sun.–Tues. No lunch ✍ Reservations essential.

SHOPPING

Edinbane Pottery. You can buy pottery here with quirky designs and paintings of the local flora and fauna. *✉ Off A850, Edinbane ☎ 01470/582234 🌐 www.edinbane-pottery.co.uk.*

GLENDALE

2 miles south of Dunvegan.

Glendale is a region rich in flora and fauna: otters, seals, and dolphins can be spotted off its rocky coast, and white-tailed sea eagles soar above. Dunvegan Castle is just at the region's eastern edge.

GETTING HERE AND AROUND

Traveling south from Dunvegan, the B884 road twists and curves along the coast. It can feel quite isolated in bad weather or after dark.

EXPLORING

Fodor's Choice ★ **Dunvegan Castle.** In a commanding position above a sea loch, Dunvegan Castle has been the seat of the chiefs of Clan MacLeod for more than 700 years. Though the structure has been greatly changed over the centuries, a gloomy ambience prevails, and there's plenty of family history on display, notably the Fairy Flag—a silk banner, thought to be originally from Rhodes or Syria and believed to have magically saved the clan from danger. Enthusiastic guides take you through several rooms, and an interesting collection of photos hangs in the lower corridors. Make time to visit the gardens, with their water garden and falls, fern house, walled garden, and various viewing points. There's a café beside the car park. Boat trips from the castle to the nearby seal colony run mid-April through September. *✉ Junction of A850 and A863, Dunvegan ☎ 01470/521206 🌐 www.dunvegancastle.com 🎫 Castle and gardens £11; gardens only £8; seal trips £6 ⏲ Apr.–Oct., daily 10–5:30 (last admission at 5).*

WHERE TO EAT AND STAY

$$$$ MODERN BRITISH Fodor's Choice ★ 🍴 **Three Chimneys.** On Loch Dunvegan, this old building with thick stone walls holds a restaurant that has become a top destination for serious foodies. The kitchen serves consistently daring, well-crafted food, and the chef's belief in Scottish ingredients is clear in what is on offer: Glendale salad leaves, West Coast fruits de mer, and Mallaig monkfish, for example. Dinner is a five-course fixed-price extravaganza (£65); lunch is three courses for £37, with the same array of local products. **TIP→ Reservations are essential; book well ahead and reconfirm the day before.** There are six luxurious (and pricey) guest rooms at the nearby House Over-By. *[$] Average main: £65 ✉ B884, Colbost ☎ 01470/511258 🌐 www.threechimneys.co.uk ⏲ No lunch Sun. ✍ Reservations essential ☞ No children under nine years old at dinner.*

$ B&B/INN 🏨 **Roskhill House.** A 19th-century croft house that once housed the local post office, this pretty white hotel feels like a home away from home. **Pros:** great breakfasts; friendly and helpful hosts; cozy lounge with fireplace; free Wi-Fi. **Cons:** very small place; books up well in advance.

[$] *Rooms from: £96* ✉ *A863, 3 miles south of Dunvegan, Roskhill* ☎ *01470/521317* 🌐 *www.roskhillhouse.co.uk* 🛏 *5 rooms* 🍴 *Breakfast.*

SHOPPING

Skye Silver. Gold and silver jewelry with Celtic themes are a specialty of Skye Silver. More unusual pieces that reflect the natural forms of the seashore and countryside: silver-coral earrings, silver-leaf pendants, and sea-star earrings. It's near Dunvegan. ✉ *The Old School, B884, Colbost* ☎ *01470/511263* 🌐 *www.skyesilver.com.*

GLEN BRITTLE AND THE CUILLIN MOUNTAINS

28 miles southeast of Glendale.

Fodor's Choice ★ The gentle slopes of the valley called Glen Brittle are a gateway to the dramatic peaks and ridges of the Cuillin Mountains. The lower slopes are fine for walkers and weekend climbers, but the higher ridges are strictly for the serious mountaineers.

GETTING HERE AND AROUND

Glen Brittle extends off the A863/B8009 on the west side of the island.

EXPLORING

Glen Brittle. You can safely enjoy spectacular mountain scenery in Glen Brittle, with some fine views of the Cuillin Mountains (which are not for the casual walker, as there are many steep and dangerous cliff faces). The drive from Carbost along a single-track road is one of the most dramatic in Scotland and draws outdoorsy types from throughout the world. At the southern end of the glen is a murky-color beach, a campground, and the chance for a gentle stroll amid the foothills. ✉ *Off A863 and B8009.*

Talisker Distillery. The only distillery on the Isle of Skye, Talisker produces a sweet, light single malt that has the typical peaty aroma of island whiskies, but is a bit less intense. Robert Louis Stevenson called Talisker "the king of drinks," and the inhabitants of Skye are very proud of it. Classic tours take about 45 minutes, while two-hour tasting tours are usually available Monday, Tuesday, Thursday, and Friday. Book ahead, as the tours are very popular. ✉ *B8009, Carbost* ☎ *01478/614308* 🌐 *www.discovering-distilleries.com/talisker* 🎟 *£8* ⏲ *Apr., May, and Oct., Mon.–Sat. 9:30–5 (last tour at 4); June and Sept., Mon.–Sat., 9:30–5, Sun. 11–5; July and Aug., weekdays 9:30–5:30, Sat. 9:30–5, Sun. 11–5; Nov.–Mar., weekdays 10–4:30.*

THE OUTER HEBRIDES

The Outer Hebrides—the Western Isles in common parlance—stretch about 130 miles from end to end and lie about 50 miles from the Scottish mainland. This splintered archipelago extends from the Butt of Lewis in the north to the 600-foot Barra Head on Berneray in the south, whose lighthouse has the greatest arc of visibility in the world. In the Hebrides, clouds cling to the hills, and rain comes in squalls. Any trip here requires protection from the weather and a conviction that a great holiday does not require the sun.

The Isle of Lewis and Harris is the northernmost and largest of the group. The island's only major town, Stornoway, is on a nearly land-locked harbor on the east coast of Lewis; it's probably the most convenient starting point for a driving tour of the islands if you're approaching the Western Isles from the Northern Highlands. Lewis has some fine historic attractions, including the Calanais Standing Stones—a truly magical place. The Uists are known for their rare, plentiful wildlife.

Just south of the Sound of Harris is the Isle of North Uist, rich in monoliths, chambered cairns, and other reminders of a prehistoric past. Benbecula, sandwiched between North and South Uist, is in fact less bare and neglected-looking than its bigger neighbors to the north. The Isle of South Uist, once a refuge of the old Catholic faith, is dotted with ruined forts and chapels; in summer its wild gardens burst with alpine and rock plants. Eriskay Island and a scattering of islets almost block the 6-mile strait between South Uist and Barra, an isle you can walk across in an hour.

Harris tweed is available at many outlets on the islands, including some of the weavers' homes; keep an eye out for signs directing you to weavers' workshops. Sunday on the islands is observed as a day of rest, and nearly all shops and visitor attractions are closed. One result is that often the only place to eat is hotel restaurants.

ISLE OF LEWIS

53 miles from Ullapool via ferry.

The history of Lewis stretches back 5,000 years, as archaeological sites scattered across the island attest. Here the Highland past persists in the Gaelic that is spoken everywhere, and the clan names are still borne by most of its inhabitants. The main town is Stornoway.

GETTING HERE AND AROUND

Three main routes radiate from Stornoway to give access to the Isle of Lewis. The A859 leads south to Harris, the A858 travels west via Dalbeg to where it meets the A857 near Brue. The A857 leads north from Stornoway to the island's northernmost point at Port of Ness.

STORNOWAY

2½-hr ferry trip from Ullapool.

The port capital for the Outer Hebrides is Stornoway, the only major town on Lewis. The island's cultural center, it has an increasing number of good restaurants.

ESSENTIALS

The ferry docks at Stornoway, and there's an airport. It's best to have a car to explore the island, but there are also infrequent local buses.

Airport Contact Stornoway Airport. ✉ *A866* ☎ *01851/707400* ⊕ *www.hial. co.uk/stornoway-airport/.*

Visitor Information Stornoway Information Centre. ✉ *26 Cromwell St.* ☎ *01851/703088* ⊕ *www.visitscotland.com.*

EXPLORING

An Lanntair Arts Centre. The fabulous An Lanntair Arts Centre hosts exhibitions of contemporary and traditional art. There are frequent traditional musical and theatrical events in the impressive auditorium. There's also a cinema, a gift shop, and a restaurant serving international and Scottish fare. ✉ *Kenneth St.* ☎ *01851/703307* 🌐 *www.lanntair.com* 🎫 *Free* 🕓 *Mon.–Sat. 10 am–late.*

WHERE TO EAT AND STAY

$$$ MODERN BRITISH 🍴 **Digby Chick.** This local favorite is a great destination on a rainy night. The solid wood floors and white tablecloths brighten the spirits. The seasonal food is hearty even in the middle of summer, with scallops and pea puree, mustard-and-maple-roasted duck breast, and pistachio-and-sesame-crusted monkfish. Sweet-toothed desserts include raspberry soufflé mousse with ginger shortcake and frozen white chocolate parfait. This is fine dining at its most relaxed. [$] *Average main: £22* ✉ *5 Bank St.* ☎ *01851/700026* 🌐 *www.digbychick.co.uk* 🕓 *Closed Sun.*

$$$ B&B/INN 🏨 **Broad Bay House.** It's not in town, but you won't miss the hustle and bustle once you see the great views of the water from Broad Bay House, and besides, it's a perfect base for walking or touring. **Pros:** pure luxury; great coastal walks; fantastic evening meals. **Cons:** no kids under 12; sea views in only one room; not cheap; car required. [$] *Rooms from: £179* ✉ *B895, 7 miles north of Stornoway* ☎ *01851/820990* 🌐 *www.broadbayhouse.co.uk* 🛏 *4 rooms* 🍽 *Breakfast.*

SHOPPING

Harris Tweed Artisans Cooperative. Stylish and quirky hand-crafted tweed clothing, hats, and accessories, all made by local artists, are available here. ✉ *40 Point St.*

BICYCLING

AD Cycle Centre. When you rent a bike here you also get valuable advice on where to ride, including a route to Tolsta that takes in five stunning beaches before reaching the edge of moorland. ✉ *67 Kenneth St.* ☎ *01851/704025* 🌐 *www.stornowaycyclehire.co.uk.*

PORT OF NESS

30 miles north of Stornoway.

The stark, windswept community of Port of Ness cradles a small harbor squeezed in among the rocks.

GETTING HERE AND AROUND

From Stornoway, take the A857 to the Port of Ness.

EXPLORING

Fodor's Choice ★ **Black House.** In the small community of Arnol, the Black House is a well-preserved example of an increasingly rare type of traditional Hebridean home. Once common throughout the islands—even into the 1950s—these dwellings were built without mortar and thatched on a timber framework without eaves. Other characteristic features include an open central peat hearth and the absence of a chimney—hence the soot and the designation *black*. On display inside are many of the house's original furnishings. Opposite is the White House, built later when houses were no longer allowed to accommodate humans and animals together. The site is 21 miles southwest of Port of Ness; head

The Outer Hebrides

North Atlantic Ocean

Butt of Lewis Lighthouse
Port of Ness

Borgh Pottery

Barvas
Black House
Arnol
Gearrannan Dalbeg
Dun Carloway
Aird Uig
Breaclete
Timsgarry
Calanais Standing Stones
A866
Stornoway
Giosla
Archmore
Baile Ailein

Isle of Lewis
Aribruach

The Minch

FERRY TO
ULLAPOOL

Cliasmol
Amhuinnsuidhe Castle

Losgaintir
Tarbert
Seilebost

← TO
ST. KILDA

Isle of Harris
Northton
Leverburgh
Brusda
Roghadal
Dun an Stichar
St. Clement's Church
Eilean Siar
Ferry

Trinity Temple
North Uist
Lochmaddy
Waternish Point
Balranald Nature Reserve
Taigh Chearsabhagh
A855
Staffin
Barpa Langass Chambered Cairn
Uig
Cairinis
MONACH ISLANDS
Little Minch
Hallin
A87
Sound of Raasay
RONA

BENBECULA
Dunvegan
ISLE OF SKYE
Ardmore
Ramasaig
Caroy
Portree
Applecross
Inner Sound

Loch Druidbeg National Nature Reserve
Struan
Idrigill Point

South Uist
Kildonan Museum and Heritage Centre
A87
Broadford
Daliburgh
Lochbaghasdail

Cuillin Sound
Elgol
Isleornsay
Eriskay
ERISKAY
Sea of the Hebrides
CANNA
Tarskavaig

Borve
BARRA
Castlebay
Armadale
SANDRAY
ISLE OF RUM
PEBBAY
MINGULAY
BERNERAY

0   20 mi

0   20 km

FERRY TO
OBAN

south on the A857 and pick up the A858 at Barvas. ⊠ *Off A858, Arnol* ☎ *01851/710395* ⊕ *www.historic-scotland.gov.uk* 🖃 *£4* ☉ *Apr.–Sept., Mon.–Sat. 9:30–5:30; Oct.–Mar., Mon., Tues., and Thurs.–Sat. 10–4.*

Butt of Lewis Lighthouse. At the northernmost point of Lewis stands the Butt of Lewis Lighthouse, designed by David and Thomas Stevenson (of the prominent engineering family whose best-known member was not an engineer at all, but the novelist Robert Louis Stevenson). The structure was first lighted in 1862. The adjacent cliffs provide a good vantage point for viewing seabirds, whales, and porpoises. ⊠ *B8014* ✛ *Northwest of Port of Ness.*

SHOPPING

Borgh Pottery. Here you can buy attractive hand-thrown studio pottery made on the premises, including lamps, vases, mugs, and dishes. ⊠ *Fivepenny House, A857, Borve* ☎ *01851/850345* ⊕ *www.borgh-pottery. com* ☉ *Mon.–Sat. 9:30–6.*

EN ROUTE

Dun Carloway. One of the best-preserved Iron Age *brochs* (circular stone towers), a fortified residence of a type exclusive to Scotland, Dun Carloway dominates the scattered community of Carloway. The mysterious tower was probably built around 2,000 years ago as protection against seaborne raiders. The nearby Dun Broch Centre explains more about the broch and its setting. ⊠ *Off A857, Carloway.*

EN ROUTE

Gearrannan. Up a side road north from Carloway, Gearrannan is an old black-house village that has been brought back to life as a living museum with excellent guided tours evoking its past. For a unique experience, some of the restored houses can be rented. There is also a shop and café. ⊠ *Off A858, Carloway* ✛ *25 miles west of Stornoway* ☎ *01851/643416* ⊕ *www.gearrannan.com.*

CALANAIS STANDING STONES

15 miles west of Stornoway.

The group of stones at this ancient site is mysterious but evocative.

GETTING HERE AND AROUND

Take the A858 to reach Calanais.

10

EXPLORING

Fodor's Choice ★ **Calanais Standing Stones.** The west coast of Lewis is rich in prehistoric sites, the most famous of which are these impressive stones. Probably positioned in several stages between 3000 BC and 1500 BC, the grouping consists of an avenue of 19 monoliths extending northward from a circle of 13 stones, with other rows leading south, east, and west. Ruins of a cairn sit within the circle on the east side. Researchers believe they may have been used for astronomical observations, but you can create your own explanations. The visitor center has an exhibit on the stones, a gift shop, and a tearoom. ⊠ *Calanais Visitor Centre, Calanais, Callanish* ☎ *01851/621422* ⊕ *www.callanishvisitorcentre.co.uk* 🖃 *£2.50* ☉ *Apr., May, Sept., and Oct., Mon.–Sat. 10–6; June–Aug., Mon.–Sat. 9.30–8; Nov.–Mar., Tues.–Sat. 10–4.*

ISLE OF HARRIS

36 miles from the Isle of Lewis via the A859.

For most people, Harris is forever linked to tweed. Woven here and on nearby islands, the tweed has colors that echo the tones of the landscape. The dramatic mountains of the northern part of the island give way in the south to the *machairs*, the grassy plains typical of this region, and the spectacular beaches that gleam in the famous sunsets.

> ### THE BONNIE PRINCE
>
> At the Battle of Culloden, George II's army outnumbered that of Prince Charles Edward Stuart. After the battle, Bonnie Prince Charlie wandered over the Highlands. He escaped to the isles of Harris and South Uist, where he met Flora Macdonald (1722–90), who took him, disguised as her maid, "over the sea to Skye."

GETTING HERE AND AROUND

The A859 is the main artery through Harris. From Tarbert you can follow the A859 to Leverburgh (21 miles), where you can catch ferries bound for Newtonferry in North Uist. The single-track road down the east coast is known as the Golden Road.

TARBERT

47 miles south of Calanais.

The main port of Harris, Tarbert has some good shops and a few worthwhile sights. **Traigh Luskentyre,** roughly 5 miles southwest of Tarbert, is a spectacular example of Harris's tidy selection of beaches—2 miles of yellow sands adjacent to **Traigh Seilebost** beach, with superb views northward to the hills of the Forest of Harris. The narrow Golden Road, on the west coast, follows the coast and offers some glorious views.

GETTING HERE AND AROUND

The ferry from Uig on the Isle of Skye arrives at Tarbert once or twice daily. Having a car makes travel on Harris much easier, but with careful planning local buses can make for an excellent trip.

ESSENTIALS

Visitor Information Tarbert Information Centre. ⊠ *Pier Rd.* ☎ *01859/502011* ⊕ *www.visitscotland.com.*

EXPLORING

Amhuinnsuidhe Castle. Turreted Amhuinnsuidhe Castle (pronounced avun- *shooee*) was built in the 1860s by the earls of Dunmore as a base for fishing and hunting in the North Harris deer forest. The castle, which is now an exclusive resort, stands about 10 miles northwest of Tarbert. ⊠ *B887, Amhuinnsuidhe* ☎ *01859/560200* ⊕ *www. amhuinnsuidhe.com.*

WHERE TO EAT AND STAY

$$$$
BRITISH
Fodor's Choice
★

✕ **Scarista House.** Hearty, well-seasoned food is what you'll find here, particularly local catches like Sound of Harris langoustine and perfectly pitched desserts like tarte tartin; dinner is £43.50 for three courses. Stunning views from the dining room extend across a sloping golf course to a crescent-shape beach and the sea beyond. ■ TIP➔ **Try to see it at sunset, when it's at its most beautiful.** The building, previously a manse (the minister's house), sits in splendid isolation, but it's made cozy with heavy curtains, sturdy sofas and chairs, and an open fire. Coffee and petits fours are delivered to you in the comfortable library. The house also has rooms for rent. $ *Average main: £45* ⊠ *A859, Sgarasta Gheag* ✛ *15 miles south of Tarbert* ☏ *01859/550238* ⊕ *www.scaristahouse. com* ⊘ *No lunch* ⚒ *Reservations essential.*

$ ✕ **Skoon Art Café.** Along a twisting road south of Tarbert, this café
CAFÉ in a renovated croft house has a simple, delicious menu that changes daily. The limited number of dishes includes carrot-and-fennel soup, smoked salmon, oatcakes and cheese, and mouthwatering cakes, all made on the premises. You can also buy one of the owner's paintings. Check for seasonal hours, which vary. $ *Average main: £8* ⊠ *4 Geocrab* ☏ *01859/530268* ⊕ *www.skoon.com* ⊟ *No credit cards* ✛.

$$ ⊡ **Hotel Hebrides.** A small boutique hotel with lovely gardens, Hotel
HOTEL Hebrides overlooks loch and harbor immediately above the arrival point for the ferry. **Pros:** wonderful location; comfortable bedrooms. **Cons:** some rooms small; sea views from only some rooms. $ *Rooms from: £140* ⊠ *Pier Rd.* ☏ *01859/502364* ⊕ *www.hotel-hebrides.com* ↩ *21 rooms* ⦿ *Breakfast.*

LEVERBURGH
21 miles south of Tarbert.

Named after Lord Leverhulme, who bought Lewis and Harris in 1917 with an eye to developing its local industries, Leverburgh is now the ferry port for North Uist. Nearby Northton has several attractions, and St. Clement's Church at Rodel is particularly worth a visit.

GETTING HERE AND AROUND
Leverburgh is on the A859 between Tarbert and Rodel.

EXPLORING
Seallam! Visitor Centre and Co Leis Thu? Genealogical Research Centre The center is where you can trace your Western Isles ancestry. Photographs and interpretive signs describe the history of Harris and its people. The owners organize guided walks and cultural evenings weekly between May and September. ⊠ *Off A859, Northton* ☏ *01859/520258* ⊕ *www. hebridespeople.com* 🎟 *£2.50* ⊘ *Mon.–Sat. 10–5.*

10

St. Clement's Church. At the southernmost point of Harris is the community of Rodel, where you can find St. Clement's Church, a cruciform church standing on a hillock. The most impressive pre-Reformation church in the Outer Hebrides, it was built around 1500 and contains the magnificently sculptured tomb (1528) of the church's builder, Alasdair Crotach, MacLeod chief of Dunvegan Castle. ⊠ *A859, 3 miles south of Leverburgh, Rodel* ⊕ *www.historic-scotland.gov.uk.*

OFF THE
BEATEN
PATH

St. Kilda. About 15 miles to the west of Harris lies the abandoned island of St. Kilda. Dependent on the flesh of the fulmar, the cliff-dwelling seabird, the population of this most westerly of all the islands lived in the harshest conditions. By 1930 the 30 remaining inhabitants left forever their village on the small plain above the immense cliffs where they had once climbed in search of the fulmar. Cruises to this frozen-in-time place depart from Leverburgh and take three hours; you then have four hours to wander the island. Costing about £190, the tours are operated by Kilda Cruises (*www.kildacruises.co.uk*) and Sea Harris (*www.seaharris.co.uk*).

WHERE TO EAT AND STAY

$ MODERN BRITISH **Anchorage Restaurant.** Perched at the southernmost tip of the Island of Harris, this lively restaurant looks across the Sea of Hebrides toward North Uist. It's a great place to grab a bite before hopping aboard the ferry, which departs from the harbor nearby. The menu ranges from burgers and sandwiches to local langoustines and scallops. Booking ahead is recommended. **TIP→ The restaurant itself is open unusually late for the islands, as is the bar, which is something of a refuge in these parts.** *Average main: £13* *Pier Rd.* *01859/520225.*

$$ B&B/INN **Pairc an t-Srath Guest House.** Set back from the main road, this white house is comfortable and quirky, and the elegant but unpretentious rooms are decorated in restful colors. **Pros:** lovely views of the coast; very good breakfasts. **Cons:** rooms quite small; perhaps too many animal statues. *Rooms from: £104* *Off A859, Borve* *01859/550386* *www.paircant-srath.co.uk* *4 rooms* *Breakfast.*

SHOPPING

Hebrides Art. This lovely gallery features the work of Alisdair and Lesley Wiseman, who run the place, and stocks a wide range of other artworks with a Hebridean theme. The on-site café serves sandwiches and wonderful homemade cakes; watch the birdlife on Luskintyre beach through the gallery's wide windows as you eat them. *Seilebost, Borve* *01859/550338* *www.hebridesart.co.uk.*

NORTH UIST

8 miles south of Rodel via ferry from Leverburgh.

Stunning coastal scenery and ancient ruins are the main draws on North Uist. You'll find art throughout the island: at the end of roads or paths or on the shore, only visible from a boat. Be sure to visit the camera obscura (an old-fashioned projector) at the Uist Outdoor Centre just beyond the ferry terminal. Its watery images are evocative and a bit eerie.

GETTING HERE AND AROUND

You can get to North Uist by ferry from Harris, the Isle of Skye, or from one of the other islands. Public transport is infrequent, so a car (or a bike) is the most reliable way to travel.

EXPLORING

TOP ATTRACTIONS

Dun an Sticar. At Newtonferry (Port nan Long) stands the remains of what was reputed to be the last inhabited broch in North Uist, Dun an Sticar. This defensive tower, reached by a causeway over the loch, was abandoned when the Vikings arrived in the 9th century and then reoccupied by Hugh Macdonald, a descendant of Macdonald of Sleat, until he reached an unpleasant end in 1602.

Taigh Chearsabhagh. Set right on the shore, the well-run Taigh Chearsabhagh has two separate exhibition spaces, a working print shop, and a permanent exhibition in which life on North Uist is brilliantly described. The café serves a selection of cakes and soup, as well as excellent French-press coffee. ⊠ *North Uist, Lochmaddy* ✛ *A865* ☎ *01870/603970* ⊕ *www.taigh-chearsabhagh.org* ➤ *£3 museum entry* ⊙ *Apr.–Oct., Mon.–Sat. 10–5, Sun. 10–3.*

WORTH NOTING

Balranald Nature Reserve. Run by the Royal Society for the Protection of Birds, the Balranald Nature Reserve shelters large numbers of waders and seabirds who inhabit the rock foreshore and the marshland behind it. It's on the west side of North Uist. ⊠ *Off A865, Hougharry* ✛ *3 miles northwest of Bayhead* ☎ *01463/715000* ⊕ *www.rspb.org.uk* ➤ *Free* ⊙ *Reserve open year-round; visitor center Apr.–Aug., daily 9–6.*

Barpa Langass Chambered Cairn. Dating from the 3rd millennium BC, the Barpa Langass Chambered Cairn is the only chambered cairn in the Western Isles known to have retained its inner chamber fully intact. You can peek inside, but don't venture too far without a light. It sits close to the A867 between Lochmaddy and Clachen.

Trinity Temple (*Teampull na Trionaid*). You can explore the ruins of Trinity Temple (Teampull na Trionaid), a medieval college and monastery said to have been founded in the 13th century by Beathag, daughter of Somerled, the progenitor of the Clan Donald. The ruins stand 8 miles southwest of Lochmaddy, off the A865.

SOUTH UIST

34 miles south of Newtonferry (on North Uist) via Grimsay, Benbecula, and three causeways.

Carpets of wildflowers in spring and early summer, superb deserted beaches, and historical connections to Flora Macdonald and Bonnie Prince Charlie head the list of reasons to visit this island.

GETTING HERE AND AROUND

You can travel the length of South Uist along Route A865, making short treks off this main road on your way to Lochboisdale, on the southeast coast of the island. At Lochboisdale you can catch ferries to Barra, the southernmost principal island of the Outer Hebrides, or to Oban, on the mainland.

EXPLORING

Kildonan Museum and Heritage Centre. In the 1950s and 1960s local priest Father John Morrison collected South Uist artifacts, displayed today at the Kildonan Museum and Heritage Centre. On your left when you enter is a simple exhibition with concise and unsentimental descriptions of living on South Uist that reads, "However we interpret it there is nothing surer than that history has as much to do with the present as the past." The simple details, like how people filled their mattresses or the names for the tools they used in their houses, are what make this place interesting. ⊠ *A865, Kildonan* ☎ *01878/710343* ⊕ *www.kildonanmuseum.co.uk* ➤ *£2* ⊙ *Easter–Oct., daily 10–5.*

Loch Druidibeg National Nature Reserve. One of only two remaining British native—that is, nonmigrating—populations of greylag geese make their home at Loch Druidibeg National Nature Reserve in a fresh and brackish loch environment. Stop at the warden's office for information about access and nature trails. ✉ *Off A865, Stilligarry* ☎ *01870/620238* 🌐 *www.snh.gov.uk*.

WHERE TO STAY

$ B&B/INN 🏨 **Polochar Inn.** With its own standing stone surviving the rough winds off the sea, the Polochar Inn sits at the southern end of South Uist. **Pros:** wild and remote location; reasonable rates; free Wi-Fi throughout. **Cons:** some rooms smaller than others. [$] *Rooms from: £90* ✉ *A865, Lochboisdale* ☎ *01878/700215* 🌐 *www.polocharinn.com* 🛏 *11 rooms* 🍴 *Breakfast.*

SHOPPING

Hebridean Jewellery. Much of the Celtic-influenced jewelry at Hebridean Jewellery is made in the workshop, which you can tour. A café serves excellent espresso, rich cakes, and tasty soups. ✉ *Off A865, Iochdar* ☎ *01870/610288* 🌐 *www.hebrideanjewellery.co.uk*.

ORKNEY AND
SHETLAND ISLANDS

Updated by
Shona Main

A Scandinavian heritage gives the 170 islets that make up Orkney and Shetland a history and an ambience different from that of any other region of Scotland. Both Orkney and Shetland are essentially austere and bleak, but they have awe-inspiring seascapes, fascinating seabirds, remarkable ancient ruins, and genuinely warm, friendly people. Although a trip to these remote islands requires time and effort, your reward will be a unique experience.

An Orcadian has been defined as a farmer with a boat, whereas a Shetlander has been called a fisherman with a croft (small farm). Orkney, the southern archipelago, is greener and is rich with artifacts that testify to the many centuries of continuous settlement here: stone circles, burial chambers, ancient settlements, and fortifications. UNESCO has recognized the key remains as a World Heritage Site called the Heart of Neolithic Orkney.

North of Orkney, Shetland, with its ocean views and sparse landscapes—trees are a rarity because of ever-present wind—seems even more remote. However, don't let Shetland's desolate countryside fool you: it has a wealth of historic interest and is far from being a backwater. Oil money from local mineral resources and its position as a crossroads in the northern seas for centuries have helped make Shetland a busy, thriving community that wants for little.

For mainland Scots, visiting these islands is a little like traveling abroad without having to worry about a different language or currency. Neither has yet been overrun by tourism, but the people of Orkney and Shetland will be delighted that you have come so far to see their islands and learn a little of their extraordinary past.

ORIENTATION AND PLANNING

GETTING ORIENTED

Ten miles from Caithness in Scotland, Orkney is made up of 70 islands, of which 10 are inhabited. A number of ferries travel to ports on the Mainland, the main island of Orkney, including its administrative center, Kirkwall, where an airport serves Scotland's larger cities. The primary road is essentially a loop that passes near the key historic sites. The Mainland is linked to the southern island of South Ronaldsay by way of the Barricades.

About 125 miles north of Orkney lies the spiny outline of Shetland, comprising 100 islands. Sumburgh has the main airport, and 25 miles north is Lerwick, the island's "capital" and a port linking the island to Scotland and Orkney. South Mainland, half an hour from Lerwick,

TOP REASONS TO GO

Standing stones and ancient sites: Among the many Neolithic treasures in Orkney are the Ring of Brodgar, a 3,000-year old circle of standing stones, and Skara Brae, the remarkable remains of a village uncovered on the grounds of delightful Skaill House. In Shetland, Jarlshof has been the home to different societies since the Bronze Age. Don't miss Mousa Broch and Clickimin Broch in Shetland, two Iron Age towers.

Music and arts festivals: The Shetland Folk Festival in May is a fiddling shindig that attracts musicians and revelers from around the world. Orkney's St. Magnus Festival is less of a pub crawl and more of a highbrow celebration of classical music, poetry, and performance.

Seabirds, seals, and more: These islands have some of the planet's

most important colonies of seabirds, with millions clinging to colossal cliffs. You're guaranteed to see seals and may spot dolphins, orcas, or porpoises. In Shetland, Noss, and Eshaness, nature reserves are prime spots, or you can check out the puffins by Sumburgh Head.

Pure relaxation: There's a much more laid-back approach to life on these islands than on the mainland. Shetlanders are particularly renowned for their hospitality and are often happy to share stories and tips that will enrich your adventure.

Outdoor activities by the coast and ocean: The rugged terrain, beautiful beaches, and unspoiled waters make a perfect backdrop for invigorating strolls, sea fishing, diving, or exploring the coastline and sea lochs by boat.

has prehistoric sites. Less than an hour north of Lerwick are dramatic landscapes such as Eshaness. Ferries go beyond the Mainland to Yell and Unst, the latter Britain's most northerly point.

Orkney. The towns of Stomness and Kirkwall have sights and museums testifying to Orkney's rich past, including Kirkwall's Norman St. Magnus Cathedral. For many people, though, they're a prelude to impressive Neolithic sites around the Mainland: Maeshowe, Skara Brae, the Ring of Brodgar, and others. Beyond the Mainland, explore sights such as Scapa Flow on Hoy, which reveals the islands' role in two world wars.

Shetland. A descent at Sumburgh's airport provides stunning views of a shining white lighthouse, bird-crammed cliffs, and golden bays. Lerwick has the excellent Shetland Museum, and nearby on the South Mainland are the prehistoric sites of Jarlshof, Old Scatness, and Mousa Broch. Worth exploring to the north are the lunarlike Ronas Hill and wave-lashed Eshaness. Unst, the island farthest north, is worth the journey for wide-open ocean views and superb bird-watching at Hermaness National Nature Reserve.

PLANNING

WHEN TO GO

Although shivering, wind-flattened visitors braving Orkney and Shetland's winter are not unheard of, the travel season doesn't really start until May, and it runs until September. June is one of the most popular months for both islands. The bird colonies are at their liveliest in early summer, which is also when the long northern daylight hours allow you plenty of sightseeing time. Shetland's northerly position means that it has only four or five hours of darkness around the summer solstice, and on a clear night it doesn't seem to get dark at all. Beware the changeable weather even in summer: it could be 75°F one day and then hail the next. Many sights close in September, and by October wilder gales will be mixed with snow flurries one minute and glorious sunshine the next. If you are determined to brave the elements, take into account that there are only six hours of daylight in winter months. More importantly, there can be thick mist and high winds at Sumburgh and Kirkwall airports even in July, meaning flights cannot take off for days, although they will put you on the Northlink boat if there's space. Bear this in mind when planning flight connections.

Shetland's festival of fire, Up-Helly-Aa, is held the last Tuesday of each January. The spectacle of Lerwick overrun by Vikings, with torches aflame and a huge Viking longship, is wildly popular. Book at least a year in advance if you want to get a bed for the night.

PLANNING YOUR TIME

Orkney and Shetland require at least a couple of days each if you're to do more than just scratch the surface. The isles generate their own laid-back approach to life, and once here, you may want to take it slowly.

A good clutch of the key sites of Mainland Orkney can be seen in a day, if you have a car and are disciplined, but to really get the most out of them, take two days. You can do the Kirkwall sights in a morning before heading to the Italian Chapel on South Ronaldsay in the afternoon. This allows a whole day for Stomness, a town caught in the most poignant of time warps, and the archaeological sites of Maeshowe, the Ring of Brodgar, Skara Brae, and Skaill House and Gurness Broch. To include Birsay, plan your day round the tides.

Since getting to Shetland isn't easy, you may want to spend three or four days here. The sites on the South Mainland—Jarlshof, Scatness, the Crofhouse Museum, St. Ninian's Isle, and Mousa Broch—take the best part of a day, although sailing times for Mousa must be factored into your schedule. Lerwick and its lanes and spectacular museum is a good day, and can be supplemented with a trip to the Bonhoga Gallery in Weisdale. It's a good idea to take a whole day to explore the north of the islands, including Eshaness and Tangwick Haa, although a car or a guide who drives will be necessary. Ferry times allow for a mad dash round the northern islands of Yell and Unst, but you will see more if you book an overnight stay.

GETTING HERE AND AROUND

AIR TRAVEL

Loganair, Scotland's national airline, provides regular service to Sumburgh in Shetland and Kirkwall in Orkney from Edinburgh, Glasgow, Aberdeen, and Inverness. Tickets are very expensive, even if booked well in advance; although register with Flybe and you will get notice of reduced prices. Because of the isolation of Orkney and Shetland, there's also a network of interisland flights, through Directflight in Shetland and Loganair in Orkney. These flights are run by a friendly staff and are as reliable as the weather allows them to be.

Airline Contacts Directflight. ☎ *01595/840246* ⊕ *www.directflight.co.uk.* **Flybe.** ☎ *0371/700–2000 (0)1392–6831–52 if outside the U.K.* ⊕ *www.flybe. com.* **Loganair.** ☎ *01856/872494* ⊕ *www.loganair.co.uk.*

BOAT AND FERRY TRAVEL

Northlink operates ferries—locally known as "the boat"—from Aberdeen to Kirkwall in Orkney and Lerwick in Shetland. These leave Aberdeen harbor each evening (or every second night for Kirkwall), arriving at Kirkwall at 11 pm and Lerwick at 7:30 am the next day. These top-notch services have recliner seats for the budget traveler or clean, compact cabins in single, double, or four-berth combinations. There's a shop, a cinema, two bars, and two restaurants (one self-service and one table service) on each boat.

If you're arriving in Aberdeen on Sunday morning and plan on meeting a train, note that the station does not open until 9 am. Northlink allows you to stay in your cabin or the restaurant until 9:30 am.

An alternate way of reaching Orkney is the Northlink ferry from Scrabster to Stromness. There is also a ferry from John O'Groats to Burwick, operated by John O'Groats Ferries, with up to four daily departures May through September. The fastest and smoothest sail is by catamaran from Gills Bay, Caithness, to St. Margaret's Hope on Orkney. Operated by Pentland Ferries, it has three daily departures.

In both Orkney and Shetland, the local council runs the interisland ferry networks (Orkney Ferries and Shetland Island Ferries) to the outer islands. Northlink Ferries has service between Lerwick on Shetland and Kirkwall on Orkney. ■TIP→ **Always book ferry tickets in advance.**

Ferry Contacts John O'Groats Ferries. ☎ *01955/611353* ⊕ *www.jogferry. co.uk.* **Northlink Ferries.** ☎ *0845/6000449* ⊕ *www.northlinkferries.co.uk.* **Orkney Ferries.** ☎ *01856/872044, 01856/872044 hotline for sailing information* ⊕ *www.orkneyferries.co.uk.* **Pentland Ferries.** ☎ *0800/6888998* ⊕ *www. pentlandferries.co.uk.* **Shetland Island Ferries.** ☎ *01595/244200* ⊕ *www. shetland.gov.uk/ferries.*

BUS TRAVEL

Scottish Citylink and Stagecoach operate buses to Aberdeen where you can get a plane, ferry, or connecting bus to the ferries at John O'Groats, Gills Bay, or Scrabster. John O'Groats Ferries operates the Orkney Bus, a direct express coach from Inverness to Kirkwall (via ferry) that runs daily from June to early September.

The main bus service on Orkney is operated by Stagecoach and on Shetland by ZetTrans (although buses are run by small operators).

Bus Contacts John O'Groats Ferries. ☎ 01955/611353 ⊕ www.jogferry. co.uk. **National Express.** ☎ 08717/818178 ⊕ www.nationalexpress.co.uk. **Scottish Citylink.** ☎ 0871/266–3333 ⊕ www.citylink.co.uk. **Stagecoach.** ☎ 01856/878014 ⊕ www.stagecoachbus.com. **ZetTrans.** ☎ 01595/744868 ⊕ www.zettrans.org.uk.

CAR TRAVEL

The most convenient way of getting around these islands is by car, especially if your time is limited. Roads are well maintained and traffic is nearly nonexistent, although speeding cars can be a problem. Orkney has causeways—the Barricades—connecting some of the islands, but in some cases these roads take fairly roundabout routes.

You can transport your rental car from Aberdeen, but for fewer than five days it's usually cheaper to rent a car from one of Shetland and Orkney's agencies. Most are based in Lerwick, Shetland, and Kirkwall, Orkney, but airport pickups are easily arranged.

Local Car Rental Contacts Bolts Car and Minibus Hire. ⊠ 26 North Rd., Lerwick ☎ 01595/693636 ⊕ www.boltscarhire.co.uk. **Orkney Car Hire.** ⊠ Junction Rd., Kirkwall ☎ 01856/872866 ⊕ www.orkneycarhire.co.uk. **Star Rent-a-Car.** ⊠ 22 Commercial Rd., Lerwick ☎ 01595/692075 Lerwick, 01950/460444 Sumburgh Airport ⊕ www.starrentacar.co.uk. **W. R. Tullock.** ⊠ Castle Garage, Castle St., Kirkwall ☎ 01856/875500 ⊕ www.orkneycarrental.co.uk.

TRAIN TRAVEL

There are no trains on Orkney or Shetland, but you can take the train to Aberdeen or Thurso and then take a ferry to the islands.

Train Contact ScotRail. ☎ 0344/811–0141 ⊕ www.scotrail.co.uk.

RESTAURANTS

Kirkwall has an increasing number of good cafés and restaurants, as does Lerwick, but both islands now have memorable spots beyond the main towns, from cafés and fish-and-chips spots to some fancier restaurants. Orkney and Shetland have first-class seafood, and in pastoral Orkney the beef is lauded and in Shetland the heather- or seaweed-fed lamb. Orkney is famous for its cheese and its fudge; a glug of its Highland Park malt whisky or some Skull Splitter Ale is also worth trying. Shetlanders are also now brewing their own and make much of their natural edible resources of seaweed-fed lamb and mussels, while making ice cream and smoking fish in a variety of ways. Some bakeries create their own version of bannocks—a scone-type baked item you eat with salt beef, mutton, or jam—but Johnson and Wood (otherwise known as the Voe bakery), available in shops across the islands, takes the biscuit.

HOTELS

Accommodations in Orkney and Shetland are on par with mainland Scotland, with a growing range of stylish bed-and-breakfasts that might suit some travelers better than the bigger hotels that rely and therefore focus on business customers, which in Shetland—with the oil and the building of a major gas plant—are many. Although standards are improving, the islands still do not offer luxury accommodations. To experience a simpler stay, check out the unique "camping *böds*" in Shetland—old cottages providing inexpensive, basic lodging (log fires, cold water, and sometimes no electricity). For details, contact the Shetland Tourist Information Centre. *Hotel reviews have been shortened. For full information, visit Fodors.com.*

WHAT IT COSTS IN POUNDS				
	$	$$	$$$	$$$$
Restaurants	Under £15	£15–£19	£20–£25	Over £25
Hotels	Under £100	£100–£160	£161–£220	Over £220

Restaurant prices are the average cost of a main course at dinner or, if dinner is not served, at lunch. Hotel prices are the lowest cost of a standard double room in high season, including 20% V.A.T.

TOURS

Cycharters. John Tulloch offers a day trip to Foula, a remote Shetland island, on his boat, the MV *Cyfish*, on Wednesday. ✉ *Scalloway Harbour, Scalloway* ☎ *01595/810887* ⊕ *www.cycharters.co.uk* ✉ *From £50.*

Fodor's Choice ★ **Island Trails.** Local tour guide and crofter James Tait offers tours steeped in the social history of Shetland, giving you a lively account, and no doubt many an introduction, to Shetland and its people. Opt for a guided tour around St. Ninian's Isle or a bespoke day's tour of the island. ☎ *01950/950228* ⊕ *www.island-trails.co.uk* ✉ *From £20.*

Seabirds-and-Seals. Using underwater roving cameras, a trip on the MV *Dunter* lets you see all the wildlife, above and below water, as it takes you around Noss Nature Reserve, just off the Island of Bressay in Shetland. From April to September, trips leave Lerwick's Victoria Pier daily at 10 am and 2 pm. ☎ *07595/540224* ⊕ *www.seabirds-and-seals.com* ✉ *From £45.*

Shetland Nature. Here you'll find richly informed tours that cover a lot of ground while quietly tracking Shetland's otters, birds, and the unique wildflowers of the Islands. Photographers are specially catered to. ☎ *01957/710000* ⊕ *www.shetlandnature.net* ✉ *From £45.*

Wildabout. They provide well-organized and informative tours of the Neolithic and WW2 sites on Orkney. ☎ *01856/877737* ⊕ *www.wildaboutorkney.com* ✉ *From £59.*

VISITOR INFORMATION

The Orkney visitor center in Kirkwall is open all year. The Shetland visitor center, in Lerwick, stays open year-round; there's also a desk for Visit Shetland in the Sumburgh Airport.

Visitor Information Visit Orkney. ☎ *01856/230300* ⊕ *www.visitorkney.com.* **Visit Shetland.** ⊕ *www.shetland.org.*

ORKNEY

If you're touring the north of Scotland, the short boat trip to Orkney offers the chance to step outside the Scottish history you've experienced on the mainland. Prehistoric sites such as the Ring of Brodgar, and the remnants of Orkney's Viking-influenced past, are in dramatic contrast to that of the mainland. The Orkney Islands may have a population of just 20,000, but a visit reveals the islands' cultural richness. In addition, Orkney's continued reliance on farming and fishing reminds you how some things can stay the same despite technological advances. At Maeshowe, for example, it becomes evident that graffiti is not solely an expression of today's youths: the Vikings left their marks here way back in the 12th century. ■ TIP➜ You can purchase the Historic Scotland Orkney Explorer Pass joint-entry ticket (£18) at the first site you visit; the ticket costs less than paying separately for entry into each site.

STROMNESS AND THE NEOLITHIC SITES

1¾ hrs north of Thurso on Scotland's mainland, via ferry from Scrabster.

On the southwest of the Mainland, on the shore of Hamnavoe, is Stromness, a remarkably attractive fishing town seemingly so unsullied by modernity that it evokes an uncomplicated way of life long gone. Walk past the old-fashioned shops and austere cottages that line the main street and you'll understand why local poet and novelist George Mackay Brown (1921–96) was inspired and moved by its sober beauty.

With its ferry connection to Scrabster in Caithness, Stromness makes a good base for visiting the western parts of Orkney, and the town holds several points of interest. It was once a key trading port for the Hudson's Bay Company, and the Stromness Museum displays artifacts from those days. Nearby are three spectacular ancient sites, the Ring of Brodgar, Maeshowe, and Skara Brae at Skaill House.

GETTING HERE AND AROUND

Stromness is at the end of the A965 and can be reached by one of the many buses from Kirkwall.

Stagecoach buses 7 and 8 link Kirkwall, the Ring of Brodgar, and Skara Brae and Skaill House with Kirkwall. Altogether there are three bus services there and three back per day, so plan accordingly.

ESSENTIALS

Visitor Information Stromness Tourist Information Centre. ⊠ *Pier Head, Stromness* ☎ *01856/850716* ⊕ *www.visitorkney.com.*

EXPLORING

TOP ATTRACTIONS

Fodor'sChoice **Pier Arts Centre.** At the striking Pier Arts Centre, a gallery in a former mer-
★   chant's house and adjoining buildings, huge sheets of glass offer tranquil harbourside views and combine with space-maximizing design to make the best use of every shard of natural light and inch of wall to display the superb permanent collection. The more than 100 20th- and 21st-century paintings and sculptures include works by Barbara Hepworth and Douglas Gordon, and edgy temporary exhibitions showcase international

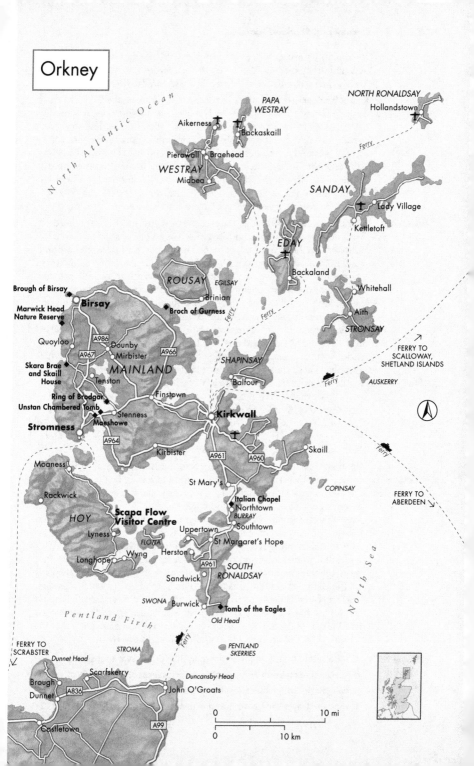

Orkney

North Atlantic Ocean

NORTH RONALDSAY
Hollandstown

PAPA WESTRAY

Aikerness
Backaskaill

Pierowall   Braehead
WESTRAY
Midbea

SANDAY

Lady Village

Kettletoft

EDAY

Backaland

ROUSAY   EGILSAY

Brinian

Whitehall

Aith

STRONSAY

Brough of Birsay

Marwick Head
Nature Reserve

Birsay

Broch of Gurness

Quoyloo

A986   Dounby
Mirbister

A967   A966

Skara Brae
and Skaill
House

MAINLAND

Tenston

SHAPINSAY

Balfour

FERRY TO
SCALLOWAY,
SHETLAND ISLANDS

AUSKERRY

Ring of Brodgar

Unstan Chambered Tomb

Stenness

Finstown

Stromness   Maeshowe

Kirkwall

A964

Kirbister

A961   A960

Skaill

COPINSAY

Moaness

St Mary's

FERRY TO
ABERDEEN

Rackwick

HOY

Scapa Flow
Visitor Centre

Italian Chapel
Northtown
BURRAY
Southtown

Uppertown

Lyness   FLOTTA

St Margaret's Hope

Longhope   Wyng   Herston

A961   SOUTH
RONALDSAY

Sandwick

SWONA   Burwick

Tomb of the Eagles

Old Head

North Sea

Pentland Firth

PENTLAND
SKERRIES

FERRY TO
SCRABSTER

STROMA

Dunnet Head

Duncansby Head

Scarfskerry

Brough

Dunnet   A836

John O'Groats

Castletown   A99

0   10 mi

0   10 km

contemporary artists such as Damien Hirst. A chic shop sells design products and art books. ⊠ *28–30 Victoria St., Stromness* ☎ *01856/850209* ⊕ *www.pierartscentre.com* ✉ *Free* ⊙ *Tues.–Sat. 10:30–5.*

Ring of Brodgar. About 5 miles northeast of Stromness, the Ring of Brodgar is a magnificent circle of 36 Neolithic standing stones (originally 60) surrounded by a henge, or deep ditch. When the fog descends over the stones—a frequent occurrence—their looming shapes seem to come alive. The site dates to between 2500 and 2000 BC. Though the original use of the circle is uncertain, it's not hard to imagine strange rituals taking place here in the misty past. The stones stand between Loch of Harray and Loch of Stenness. ⊠ *B9055, Stromness* ☎ *01856/841815* ⊕ *www.historic-scotland.gov.uk* ✉ *Free* ⊙ *Year-round.*

Fodor's Choice ★ **Skara Brae and Skaill House.** After a fierce storm in 1850, the laird of Breckness, William Graham Watt, discovered this cluster of Neolithic houses at the bottom of his garden. The houses, first occupied around 3000 BC and containing stone beds, fireplaces, dressers, and cupboards, are the most extensive of their kind in northern Europe and provide real insight into this ancient civilization. A reconstruction of one house can be seen in the visitor center, which displays artifacts from the site and hosts an excellent café. Skara Brae stands on the grounds of **Skaill House**, a splendid, intriguing mansion built by the Bishop of Orkney in the 1600s. His descendants, the lairds of Breckness, along with the various ladies of the manor, added to the house and to the eclectic furnishings. These sites offer a joint ticket in summer months that's well worth the price: the juxtaposition of different societies thousands of years apart that shared the same corner of Orkney makes a fascinating visit. ⊠ *B9056, 8 miles north of Stromness, Stromness* ☎ *01856/841815* ⊕ *www.historic-scotland.gov.uk* ✉ *Skara Brae £6.10, Skara Brae and Skaill House £7.10* ⊙ *Skara Brae Apr.–Sept., daily 9:30–5:30; Oct.– Mar., daily 9:30–4:30. Skaill House Apr.–Sept., daily 9:30–5:30.*

FAMILY **Fodor's** Choice ★ **Stromness Museum.** The enchanting Stromness Museum has the feel of some grand Victorian's private collection but has, in fact, been community owned since it opened in 1837. Its crammed but utterly fascinating exhibits on fishing, shipping, and whaling are full of interesting trinkets from all over the world that found their way to this small Orcadian town because of its connections with the Hudson's Bay Shipping Company. The company recruited workers in Stromness between the late 18th and 19th centuries as they were considered more sober and therefore more reliable than other Scots. Also here are model ships and displays on the German fleet that was scuttled on Scapa Flow in 1919. Upstairs, don't miss the beguiling, traditionally presented collection of birds and butterflies that are native to the British Isles. ⊠ *52 Alfred St., Stromness* ☎ *01856/850025* ✉ *£5 (allows as many visits as you like within a week)* ⊙ *Nov.–Mar., Mon.–Sat. 11–3:30; Apr.–Oct., daily 10–5.*

QUICK BITE

✕ **Julia's Café Bistro.** Right on the quayside, this casual spot serves the cakes that make you forget about calories. Expect huge slices of lemon drizzle, coffee layer, raspberry cream, and other cakes, as well as scones and traybakes (cakes baked in pans and cut up). Baked potatoes, quirky salads, and quiches round out the savory side of the menu, while real espresso and cappuccino seal the deal. ⊠ *20 Ferry Rd., Stromness* ☎ *01856/850904* ⊕ *www.juliascafe.co.uk* ☉ *No dinner.*

WORTH NOTING

Maeshowe. The huge burial mound of Maeshowe, circa 2500 BC, measures 115 feet in diameter and contains an enormous burial chamber. It was raided by Vikings in the 12th century, and Norse crusaders found shelter here, leaving a rich collection of runic inscriptions. Outside you see a large, grassy mound; the stunning interior of the chambered tomb has remarkably sophisticated stonework. This site is 6 miles northeast of Stromness and 1 mile from the Ring of Brodgar. Call early on the day of your visit to reserve a spot on the hourly tours. ⊠ *A965, Stromness* ☎ *01856/761606* ⊕ *www.historic-scotland.gov.uk* ⊟ *£5.50* ☉ *Apr.–Sept., daily 9:30–5; Oct.–Mar., daily 10–4.*

WHERE TO STAY

$$
HOTEL

Merkister Hotel. After a long day taking in the sights, the gentle lap of Loch Harray, which the Merkister overlooks, soothes the soul. **Pros:** endless coffee in the lounge and library; notable restaurant. **Cons:** some small rooms. $ *Rooms from: £120* ⊠ *A965, Harray, Birsay* ☎ *01856/771366* ⊕ *www.merkister.com* ⤴ *16 rooms* ⦿ *Breakfast.*

$$
B&B/INN

Fodor's Choice
★

Mill of Eyrland. White-painted stone walls, country antiques, and the rippling sound of a stream running beneath the windows make for an evocative stay at this former mill dating from 1861. **Pros:** the old grinding stones are a stunning focal point in the lounge; beautiful views out to Scapa Flow. **Cons:** difficult to find; breakfast is served at one big table, so be prepared to socialize. $ *Rooms from: £100* ⊠ *Off A964, Stenness* ☎ *01856/850136* ⊕ *www.millofeyrland.co.uk* ⊟ *No credit cards* ⤴ *4 rooms* ⦿ *Breakfast.*

SPORTS AND THE OUTDOORS

DIVING

The cool, clear waters of Scapa Flow and eight sunken ships that were part of Germany's fleet during World War I make for an unparalleled diving experience. Several companies organize trips to Scapa Flow and other nearby dive sites.

Scapa Scuba. Dives with Scapa Scuba are from its boat, the MV *Radiant Queen*. A day's diving around wrecks near the Churchill Barriers costs £140 per day. ⊠ *Lifeboat House, Dundas St., Stromness* ☎ *01856/851218* ⊕ *www.scapascuba.co.uk.*

BIRSAY

12 miles north of Stromness, 25 miles northwest of Kirkwall.

Birsay itself is a small collection of houses, but some interesting historic and natural sites are nearby.

GETTING HERE AND AROUND

The village is on A966; a car is the easiest way to see the nearby sites.

EXPLORING

Broch of Gurness (Aikerness Broch). Gurness Broch, an Iron Age tower built between 500 BC and 200 BC, stands more than 10 feet high and is surrounded by stone huts, indicating that this was a village. The tower's foundations and dimensions suggest that it was one of the biggest brochs in Scotland, and the remains of the surrounding houses are well preserved. ☒ *A966, 8 miles east of Birsay* ☎ *01856/751414* ⊕ *www. historic-scotland.gov.uk* ☒ *£5.50* ☉ *Apr.–Sept., daily 9:30–5:30; Oct. daily 9:30–4:30.*

Brough of Birsay. A Romanesque church can be seen at the Brough of Birsay, a tidal island with the remains of an early Pictish and then Norse settlement. (*Brough* is another word for burgh.) The collection of roofless stone structures on the tiny island, close to Birsay, are accessible only at low tide by means of a concrete path that winds across the seaweed-strewn bay. The path is slippery, so boots are essential. To ensure you won't be swept away, check the tides with the tourism office in Kirkwall or Stromness before setting out. ■TIP→ **The cliffs at the far side of the Island are stunning but be very careful as you look for puffins.** ☒ *A966* ☎ *01856/841815* ⊕ *www.historic-scotland.gov.uk* ☒ *£4.50* ☉ *June–Sept., daily 9:30–5:30.*

Marwick Head Nature Reserve. The Royal Society for the Protection of Birds tends the remote Marwick Head Nature Reserve, where in spring and summer the cliffs are draped in wildflowers like campion and thrift, and resound with thousands of nesting seabirds like cormorants, kittiwakes, and guillemots. The Kitchener Memorial, recalling the 1916 sinking of the cruiser HMS *Hampshire* with Lord Kitchener aboard, sits atop a cliff. Access to the reserve, which is unstaffed, is along a path north from Marwick Bay. ☒ *Off B9056, 4 miles south of Birsay* ☎ *01856/850176* ⊕ *www.rspb.org.uk* ☒ *Free* ☉ *Daily 24 hrs.*

KIRKWALL

16 miles east of Stromness.

In bustling Kirkwall, the main town on Orkney, there's plenty to see in the narrow, winding streets extending from the harbor. The cathedral and some museums are highlights.

GETTING HERE AND AROUND

Kirkwall is a ferry port and also near Orkney's main airport. Its sights are all near one another. Visitors to the Highland Park Distillery might want to hop on the T11 Kirkwall Circular or get a taxi (about £7).

ESSENTIALS

Visitor Information **Kirkwall Visitor Information Centre.** ☒ *Travel Centre, W. Castle St.* ☎ *01856/872856* ⊕ *www.visitorkney.com.*

EXPLORING

TOP ATTRACTIONS

OFF THE BEATEN PATH

Italian Chapel. During World War II, 550 Italian prisoners of war were captured in North Africa and sent to Orkney to assist with the building of the Churchill Barriers, four causeways that blocked entry into Scapa Flow, Orkney's great natural harbor. Using two corrugated-iron Nissan huts, the prisoners, led by Domenico Chiocchetti, a painter-decorator from the Dolomites, constructed this beautiful and inspiring chapel in memory of their homeland. The elaborate interior frescoes were adorned with whatever came to hand, including bits of metal, colorful stones, and leftover paints. ✉ *A961, 7 miles south of Kirkwall* ⛅ *Free* ☉ *Daily dawn–dusk.*

FAMILY **Orkney Museum.** With artifacts from the Picts, the Vikings, and other ancient peoples, this museum in Tankerness House (a former residence) has the entire history of Orkney crammed into a rabbit warren of rooms. It's not easily accessible for those with disabilities but with the help of staff, can be done. The setup may be old-fashioned, but some artifacts—especially those from everyday Orcadian life in the 19th century—are riveting. Lovely gardens around the back provide a spot to recoup after a history lesson. ✉ *Broad St.* ☎ *01856/873191* ⛅ *Free* ☉ *May–Sept., Mon.–Sat. 10:30–5; Oct.–Apr., Mon.–Sat. 10:30–12:30 and 1:30–5.*

Orkney Wireless Museum. The lifetime collection of Jim MacDonald, a radio operator during World War II, tells the story of wartime communications at Scapa Flow, where thousands of service members were stationed; they used the equipment displayed to protect the Home Fleet. Run by volunteers, the museum also contains many handsome 1930s wireless radios and examples of the handicrafts produced by Italian prisoners of war. ✉ *Kiln Corner, Junction Rd.* ☎ *01856/871400* ⊕ *www.owm.org.uk* ⛅ *£3* ☉ *Apr.–Sept., Mon.–Sat. 10:30–4:30, Sun. 2:30–4:30.*

St. Magnus Cathedral. Founded by the Norse earl Jarl Rognvald in 1137 and named for his uncle, this grand red-and-yellow sandstone cathedral was mostly finished by 1200, although more work was carried out during the following 300 years. The cathedral is still in use and contains some fine examples of Norman architecture, although traces of later styles are found here and there. The ornamentation on some of the tombstones in the church is particularly striking. At the far end to the left is the tomb of the tragically discredited Dr. John Rae, the Victorian-era Orcadian adventurer and unsung hero who discovered the final section of the Northwest Passage in Canada but was decried for his reporting that the British men of the Franklin expedition, overwhelmed by starvation, had resorted to cannibalism: an assertion that has since been proved true. ✉ *Broad St.* ☎ *01856/874894* ⊕ *www.stmagnus.org* ☉ *Apr.–Sept., Mon.–Sat. 9–6, Sun. 2–6; Oct.–Mar. weekdays 9–1 and 2–5.*

Tomb of the Eagles. In 1958, while looking for stones for diking, local farmer Ronnie Simison found and excavated this chambered cairn, packed with 340 human skulls that were 5,000 years old. The lack of other bones suggests that the skulls were taken after the bones had been picked clean by birds. The tomb, however, gets its name from the 70 talons of sea eagles and their remains found among the skulls. The walk to the tomb is a mile through fields and then along spectacular cliffs. Access to the tomb is by way of a trolley. This can be messy if it's muddy and a no-go for those with mobility problems, but it's not as uncomfortable or claustrophobic as you'd imagine. The visitor center, still run by Ronnie Simison, is full of exhibits. ✉ *Off A961, 22 miles south of Kirkwall, St.*

Margaret's Hope ☎ *01856/831339* ⊕ *www.tomboftheeagles.co.uk* ✉ *£7*
🕑 *Mar., daily 10–noon; Apr.–Oct., daily 9:30–5:30.*

WORTH NOTING

Bishop's and Earl's Palaces. The Bishop's Palace dates to the 12th century when St. Magnus Cathedral was built. In 1253 this was the site of King Hakon IV of Norway's death, marking the end of Norwegian rule over Sudreyjar (the Southern Hebrides). It was rebuilt in the late 15th century, and a round tower was added in the 16th century. The nearby Earl's Palace was built in 1607 for Earl Patrick Stewart, the much despised Earl of Orkney and Shetland who bound the people of both into terrible, inescapable poverty. While his name is still mud, his Orcadian residence is considered one of the finest examples of Renaissance architecture in Scotland. The great hall with its magnificent fireplace may be a ruin, but it evokes the splendor of its age. ✉ *Palace Rd.* ☎ *01856/871918* ⊕ *www.historic-scotland.gov.uk* ✉ *£4.50* 🕑 *Apr.–Sept., daily 9:30–5:30; Oct., daily 9:30–4:30.*

Fodor's Choice **Highland Park Distillery.** Having come this far, you'll have earned a dram
★ of the local single malt at Scotland's northernmost distillery. It was founded around the turn of the 19th century by Magnus Eunson, a church officer who dabbled in illicit stilling. The tour is highly recommended and takes you through the essential aspects of this near-sacred process, from the ingredients to the hand turning of the malt, the peating in the peat kilns, the mashing, and finally the maturation in oak casks. This smoky, peaty malt can be purchased all over Orkney, as well as from the distillery's austere shop. ✉ *Holm Rd.* ☎ *01856/874619* ⊕ *www.highlandpark.co.uk* ✉ *£7.50* 🕑 *Apr. and Sept., weekdays 10–5; May–Aug., Mon.–Sat. 10–5, Sun. noon–5; Oct.–Mar., weekdays 1–5.*

Unstan Chambered Tomb. This intriguing burial chamber lies within a 5,000-year-old cairn. Access to the tomb by trolley can be awkward for those with mobility problems. ✉ *A964, 7½ miles west of Kirkwall* ☎ *01856/841815* ⊕ *www.historic-scotland.gov.uk* ✉ *Free* 🕑 *Apr.–Sept., daily 9:30–5:30; Oct.–Mar., daily 9:30–4:30.*

WHERE TO EAT

$ ✕**Cafelolz.** If you've been indulging in too much fish-and-chips, this café
CAFÉ with its bountiful and inventive salads will make you feel healthy and nourished yet full. For those seeking something sweet, their award-winning baking—with huge muffins, tall cakes, and crunchy macaroons, much of which is gluten-free—and excellent coffee will liven up even the dankest Orkney afternoon. Please note they close at 5 pm. $ *Average main: £9* ✉ *21 Albert St.* ☎ *01856/877714* 🖃 *No credit cards.*

$$$$ ✕**The Creel.** This outstanding "restaurant with rooms" on the island of
MODERN BRITISH South Ronaldsay sits right on the waterfront of one of Orkney's loveliest harbors at St. Margaret's Hope. The imaginative modern Scottish cuisine (£40 for three courses) uses the freshest Orcadian seafood, seaweed-fed lamb, and locally grown vegetables. The inn's charm lies partly in the fuss-free approach to hospitality that makes everyone feel welcome. Three simple guest rooms overlook the bay. Note that the drive to Kirkwall is a long one, especially in the dark. $ *Average main: £40* ✉ *Front*

Rd., 13 miles south of Kirkwall, St. Margaret's Hope ☎ *01856/831311* 🌐 *www.thecreel.co.uk* ⏲ *Closed Oct.–Mar.* ✍ *Reservations essential.*

$ ITALIAN Fodor's Choice ★ 🍴 **Lucano.** This trattoria-style Italian restaurant has been taken to the heart of Orcadians who keep it busy all year round. It's simply stylish, with a tile floor, wooden tables, red chairs, and chalkboard menus on the wall. From pizza (£9) to classic pasta dishes (£11)—with fulsomely meaty carbonara and Bolognese and very tasty vegetarian *burro e salvia* (butter and sage) and pesto—to excellent *secondi piatti* (£15) such as chicken in rosemary, it's got something for every appetite. The ice cream puddings finish you off nicely. [$] *Average main: £11* ✉ *31–33 Victoria St.* ☎ *01856/875687* 🌐 *www.lucanokirkwall.com* 💳 *No credit cards.*

$ CAFÉ 🍴 **The Reel.** Orkney's musical tradition is alive and fiddling, but never more so than at this café and restaurant. As you eat, young Orcadians run up the stairs with their violin cases to the music school, where all sorts of sprees and shindigs are held in the performance spaces. The eating is cheap and hearty: expect big bowls of soup, doorstop-size sandwiches with inventive fillings, and slices of sponge cake. It becomes more like a pub on a Friday or Saturday night, with locally brewed ales and, of course, live music. [$] *Average main: £6* ✉ *3 Castle St.* ☎ *01856/871000* 🌐 *www.wrigleyandthereel.com* 💳 *No credit cards.*

WHERE TO STAY

$$ HOTEL 🏨 **Foveran Hotel.** About 34 acres of grounds surround this modern, ranch-style hotel overlooking Scapa Flow, about 3 miles southwest of Kirkwall. **Pros:** expansive grounds; efficient service; food that's cooked to perfection. **Cons:** exterior looks a bit institutional; you must book the popular restaurant ahead. [$] *Rooms from: £105* ✉ *Off A964* ☎ *01856/872389* 🌐 *www.thefoveran.com* 🛏 *8 rooms* 🍽 *Breakfast.*

$$ B&B/INN 🏨 **The Shore.** Right on the harbor, this friendly hotel above a pub has surprisingly modern bedrooms with small but chic bathrooms. **Pros:** clean and well-maintained bedrooms; friendly if slow staff. **Cons:** pricey for an inn; bars can be noisy; cars tearing up the main road outside may disturb sleep. [$] *Rooms from: £115* ✉ *Shore St.* ☎ *01856/872200* 🌐 *www.theshore.co.uk* 🛏 *10 rooms* 🍽 *Breakfast.*

$$ B&B/INN 🏨 **West End Hotel.** Built in 1824 by a retired sea captain, the West End Hotel once served as Kirkwall's first hospital. **Pros:** great location; helpful owners. **Cons:** no tubs, just showers; some rooms are small. [$] *Rooms from: £100* ✉ *Main St.* ☎ *01856/872368* 🌐 *www.westendkirkwall.co.uk* 💳 *No credit cards* 🛏 *10 rooms* 🍽 *Breakfast.*

NIGHTLIFE AND PERFORMING ARTS

St. Magnus Festival. The region's cultural highlight is Kirkwall's St. Magnus Festival, usually held the third week in June. Its impressive program includes distinguished orchestral, operatic, and choral artists. Orkney also hosts an annual folk festival at the end of May. ☎ *01856/871445* 🌐 *www.stmagnusfestival.com.*

SHOPPING

Judith Glue. At Judith Glue you can purchase designer knitwear with traditional patterns, as well as handmade crafts and hampers of local produce. The shop is also home to the Orkney Real Food Cafe. ✉ *25 Broad St.* ☎ *01856/874225* 🌐 *www.judithglue.com.*

Island Festivals

In the middle of the long winter, at the end of January, Shetlanders celebrate their Viking culture with the **Up-Helly-Aa Festival,** which—for the men—involves dressing up as Vikings, parading with flaming torches, and then burning a replica of a Viking longship, followed by one or sometimes two nights of carousing. Women play hostess in the halls, feeding and quenching the thirsts of those involved, and dancing with them. The **Shetland Folk Festival,** held in April, and October's **Shetland** **Accordion and Fiddle Festival** both attract large numbers of visitors.

Orkney's **St. Magnus Festival,** a celebration focusing on classical music, is based in Kirkwall and is usually held the third week in June. Orkney also hosts a jazz festival in April, an annual folk festival at the end of May, the unique Boys' Ploughing Match in mid-August, and The Ba' (ball; street rugby-football played by the Uppies and Doonies residents of Kirkwall) on Christmas and New Year's Day.

The Longship. Don't miss The Longship, which sells a huge array of Ola Gorrie's original designs in gold and silver jewelry with Celtic and Norse themes. They also stock knitwear from Hume Sweet Hume and the Isle of Auskerry and ceramics from Westray Pottery. Their wineshop in the courtyard sells locally brewed craft beers such as Dark Island, Northern Light, and the Sneaky Wee Orkney Stout. ⊠ *11 Broad St.* ☎ *01856/888790* ⊕ *www.thelongship.co.uk.*

The Orcadian Bookshop. The publisher of the local newspaper, *The Orcadian,* also manages this store, a good place to find books about the history of Orkney, its wildlife, and folklore. ⊠ *50 Albert St.* ☎ *01856/878888* ⊕ *www.orcadian.co.uk.*

SPORTS AND THE OUTDOORS
BICYCLING
Cycle Orkney. For £12.50 a day bicycles can be rented from Cycle Orkney, which is open year-round. ⊠ *Tankerness La.* ☎ *01856/875777* ⊕ *www.cycleorkney.com.*

FISHING
Merkister Hotel. The Merkister Hotel, on Loch Harray, arranges fishing trips. All your equipment, including boats, is available to rent. ⊠ *A965, Harray, Birsay* ☎ *01856/771366* ⊕ *www.merkister.com.*

SCAPA FLOW VISITOR CENTRE

On Hoy, 14 miles southwest of Kirkwall, 6 miles south of Stromness.

On the beautiful island of Hoy, Scapa Flow Visitor Centre explores the strategic and dramatic role that this sheltered anchorage played in two world wars.

GETTING HERE AND AROUND

The car ferry from Houton (7 miles east of Stromness) takes 25 minutes to reach Lyness on Hoy and the visitor center. The ferry costs around £22 round-trip for a regular-size car and £7 round-trip per passenger.

ESSENTIALS

Ferry Contacts Orkney Ferries. ☎ *01856/872044* ⊕ *www.orkneyferries.co.uk.*

EXPLORING

Scapa Flow Visitor Centre. Military history buffs will appreciate the Scapa Flow Visitor Centre, which displays military vehicles and guns from both world wars. You'll also find equipment salvaged from the German boats scuttled off the coast. In the plain but poignant graveyard here, British and German personnel both rest in peace. If you want to take your car over to Hoy, book well in advance with Orkney Ferries, as this is a popular route. The visitor center is a short walk from the ferry terminal on the island of Hoy. ⊠ *Off B9047, Lyness* ☎ *01856/791300* ⊕ *www.scapaflow.co.uk* ☞ *Free* ☉ *Mar., Apr., and Oct. weekdays 9-4:30; May–Sept., Mon.–Sat. 9–4:30, Sun. 10:30–3:30.*

SHETLAND

The Shetland coastline is an incredible 900 miles because of the rugged geology and many inlets; there isn't a point on the islands farther than 3 miles from the sea. Lerwick is the primary town, but the population of 22,000 is scattered across the 15 inhabited islands.

In general, the prehistoric treasures such as Jarlshof and Mousa Broch are in the South Mainland. For the geological marvels of the islands, Ronas Hill and Eshaness, visit the North Mainland. The social history of the islands is told most comprehensively in the Shetland Museum and in the lanes of Lerwick. Wherever your interest, you'll see and hear an island that buzzes with music, life, and history.

LERWICK

14 hrs by ferry from Aberdeen.

Founded by Dutch fishermen in the 17th century, Lerwick today is a busy town and administrative center. Handsome stone buildings—known as lodberries—line the harbor; they provided loading bays for goods, some of them illegal. The town's twisting flagstone lanes and harbor once heaved with activity, and Lerwick is still an active port today. This is also where most visitors to Shetland dock, spilling out of cruise ships, allowing passengers to walk around the town.

GETTING HERE AND AROUND

The town center of Lerwick is 1 mile south of Holmsgarth, the terminal for the ferry from Aberdeen. You can take a bus from Holmsgarth to the center or to the bus station for travel to Sumburgh or Scalloway. Car rentals can be arranged to meet you at the ferry terminal. Lerwick is small and compact, and the bus network, overseen by ZetTrans, offers hourly bus service around town.

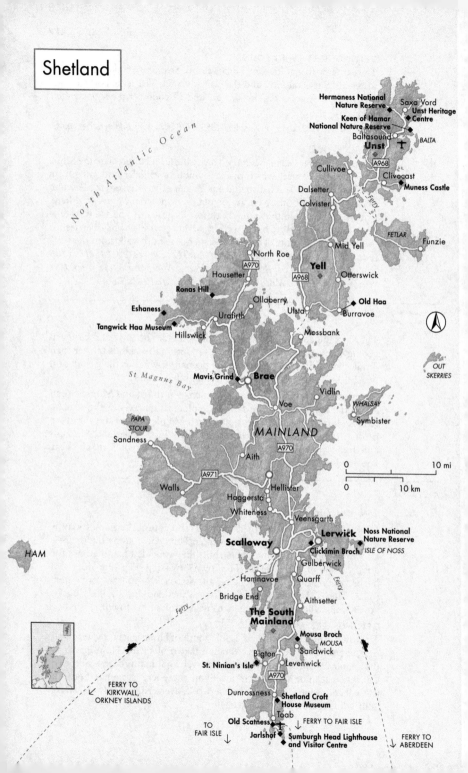

Shetland

North Atlantic Ocean

Hermaness National
Nature Reserve
Saxa Vord
**Unst Heritage
Centre**
Keen of Hamar
National Nature Reserve
BALTA
Baltasound
Unst
A968
Cullivoe
Clivocast
Dalsetter
Muness Castle
Colvister
FETLAR
Mid Yell
Funzie
North Roe
Yell
A970
Housetter
A968
Otterswick
Ronas Hill
Ollaberry
Old Haa
Ulsta
Eshaness
Urafirth
Burravoe
Tangwick Haa Museum
Hillswick
Mossbank
St Magnus Bay
Mavis Grind
Brae
Vidlin
WHALSAY
Voe
*OUT
SKERRIES*
MAINLAND
Symbister
*PAPA
STOUR*
Sandness
Aith
A970
A971
Walls
Hellister
Haggersta
Whiteness
Veensgarth
10 mi
Lerwick
**Noss National
Nature Reserve**
0
10 km
Scalloway
Clickimin Broch
ISLE OF NOSS
Gulberwick
Hamnavoe
Quarff
HAM
Bridge End
Aithsetter
Ferry
**The South
Mainland**
Mousa Broch
MOUSA
Bigton
Sandwick
St. Ninian's Isle
Levenwick
Ferry
A970
Dunrossness
**Shetland Croft
House Museum**
Toab
FERRY TO FAIR ISLE
Old Scatness
FERRY TO
KIRKWALL,
ORKNEY ISLANDS
Jarlshof
**Sumburgh Head Lighthouse
and Visitor Centre**
TO
FAIR ISLE
FERRY TO
ABERDEEN

ESSENTIALS

Transportation Contacts **Boddam Cabs.** ☎ *01950/460111* ⊕ *www. boddamcabs.co.uk.*

Visitor Information **Lerwick Visitor Information Centre.** ✉ *Market Cross* ☎ *08701/693434* ⊕ *visit.shetland.org/lerwick.*

EXPLORING

TOP ATTRACTIONS

Clickimin Broch. A stone tower on the site of what was originally an Iron Age fortification, Clickimin Broch makes a good introduction to these mysterious buildings. It was possibly intended as a place of retreat and protection in the event of attack. South of the broch are vivid views of the cliffs at the south end of the island of Bressay, which shelters Lerwick Harbor. ✉ *Off A970, 1 mile south of Lerwick* ☎ *01856/841815* ⊕ *www.historic-scotland.gov.uk* ⊠ *Free* ⊘ *Daily 24 hrs.*

Fort Charlotte. This artillery fort was built in 1665 to protect the Sound of Bressay from the invading Dutch. They seized it in 1673 and razed the fort to the ground. They were soon chased out of Shetland and the fort was rebuilt in 1781. ✉ *Market St.* ☎ *01856/841815* ⊕ *www. historic-scotland.gov.uk* ⊠ *Free* ⊘ *Apr.–Sept., daily 9:30–6:30; Oct.– Mar., daily 9:30–4:30.*

Fodor's Choice
★

Mareel. Next to the Shetland Museum, the bold and beautiful—although somewhat brutal around the back—Mareel is Shetland's adventurous and ambitious arts center. It has a live performance space attracting national and international musicians, two cinemas showing art-house and mainstream films, and a café and bar area that showcases local crafts, acoustic musicians, and some very drinkable Shetland beers. ✉ *North Ness* ☎ *01595/745555* ⊕ *www.mareel.org.*

FAMILY
Fodor's Choice
★

Shetland Museum. On the last remaining stretch of the old waterfront at the restored Hay's Dock, the striking Shetland Museum, with its sail-like tower, is the area's cultural hub and a stimulating introduction to local history. The two-story space is filled with displays about archaeology, textiles, and contemporary arts. Standout exhibits include depictions of the minutiae of everyday Shetland life across the centuries, the last remaining *sixareen* (a kind of fishing boat), and the collection of lace shawls donated by Shetland families. The museum is also a wonderful place to hang out; look for vintage vessels moored in the dock and seals that pop up to observe everyone at the glass-fronted café-restaurant terrace. ✉ *Hay's Dock, Commercial Rd.* ☎ *01595/695057* ⊕ *www. shetland-museum.org.uk* ⊠ *Free* ⊘ *Mon.–Sat.10–5, Sun. noon–5.*

WORTH NOTING

OFF THE
BEATEN
PATH

Noss National Nature Reserve. The island of Noss (which means "nose" in old Norse) rises to a point called the Noup. The smell and noise of the birds that live on the vertiginous cliffs can assault the senses. Residents nest in orderly fashion: black and white guillemots (45,000 pairs) and razorbills at the bottom; gulls, gannets, cormorants, and kittiwake in the middle; fulmars and puffins at the top. If you get too close to their chicks, some will dive-bomb from above. To get here, take a ferry from Lerwick to Bressay, then an inflatable boat to Noss. Mid-May to mid-July is the best time to view breeding birds. No matter when you visit, be sure to wear waterproof clothing and sensible shoes. ✉ *Noss* ☎ *01595/693345* 🌐 *www.nnr-scotland.org.uk* 🎟 *Free* 🕒 *Late Apr.–late Aug., daily 11–5.*

SHETLAND FIDDLING

Held in high regard both here and afar, Shetland's musicians have folks tapping their feet. At the Shetland Folk Festival, Fiddle Frenzy, and the Fiddle and Accordion Festival you can catch big names like Fiddler's Bid and Hom Bru, and, if you're lucky, the internationally known Shetland fiddler Aly Bain and accordionist Phil Cunningham. For something more informal, just wander into one of Lerwick's pubs.

WHERE TO EAT

$ CAFÉ Fodor's Choice ★ 🍴 **Fjarå.** Sitting on rocks on the ebb (or *Fjara* in Faroese) of Brewick Bay, the views from this large wooden-and-glass house allow you to look at otters and seals between courses. The menu is very simple: big breakfasts, coffees and cake, or soup and sandwiches made with soft homemade bread during the day, as well as fish-and-chips. In the evening there's Shetland lamb or a big sharing platter of meat, cheese, and bread. [$] *Average main: £12* ✉ *Sea Road* ☎ *01595/697388* 🌐 *www.fjaracoffee.com* ☞ *Mon.–Thurs. 8–10, Fri. and Sat. 8–midnight, Sun.10–10* 💳 *No credit cards.*

$$ BRITISH Fodor's Choice ★ 🍴 **Hay's Dock.** In the Shetland Museum, this airy, glass-fronted café and restaurant serving reasonably priced lunches and somewhat pricier dinners has proved popular. Chunky wooden tables fitted with glass panels allow you to see the artwork featured on top. Good lunch picks include the seafood chowder; in the evening, try Shetland lamb shoulder marinated in spiced yogurt or local salmon with green-pea risotto. [$] *Average main: £17* ✉ *Hay's Dock, off Commerical Rd.* ☎ *01595/741569* 🌐 *www.haysdock.co.uk* 🕒 *No dinner Sun or Mon.* ✍ *Reservations essential.*

$ CAFÉ Fodor's Choice ★ 🍴 **The Peerie Shop Cafe.** Who would believe you could get such good cappuccino at 60 degrees north? Round the back of the popular Lerwick knitwear shop is a modish, consistently good café that sells filled sponge cakes, lip-smackingly good soups, and, yes, the best coffee on the islands. It's always busy and Shetlanders do like to talk, so be prepared to hang around for a table during lunchtime. Alas, the café closes at 6. [$] *Average main: £6* ✉ *Esplanade* ☎ *01595/692817* 🌐 *www.peerieshop.co.uk* 🕒 *Closed Sun. No dinner.*

WHERE TO STAY

$ B&B/INN 🏨 **Alder Lodge Guest House.** Occupying a bank building dating from the 1830s, this guesthouse sits on a quiet street within easy reach of Lerwick's shops, pubs, and harbor. **Pros:** comfortable beds; superb location; child-friendly. **Cons:** booked solid in the summer months. [$] *Rooms from: £80* ✉ *8 Clairmont Pl.* ☎ *01595/695705* 🌐 *www.alderlodgeguesthouse.com* 💳 *No credit cards* 🛏 *11 rooms* 🍽 *Breakfast.*

$$ B&B/INN 🏨 **Kveldsro House Hotel.** If a fussy bed-and-breakfast doesn't suit you, try the plain but pleasing Kveldsro House, tucked away behind the town's main thoroughfare. **Pros:** minutes from the city center; cheery bar. **Cons:** generic hotel furniture; some walls are a bit thin. [$] *Rooms from: £138* ✉ *Greenfield Pl., off Commerical St.* ☎ *01595/692195* 💳 *No credit cards* 🛏 *17 rooms* 🍽 *Breakfast.*

SHOPPING

Anderson & Co. On Commercial Street, Anderson & Co. carries hand-knittted cardigans, jumpers, accessories, and woven throws. ✉ *60–62 Commercial St.* ☎ *01595/693714* ⊕ *shetlandknitwear.com.*

Ninian. Traditional and funky handmade scarves, clothing, throws, ceramics, and beautiful children's toys are found at Ninian. ✉ *80 Commercial St.* ☎ *01595/696655* ⊕ *www.ninianshetland.co.uk.*

Fodor's Choice ★ **Peerie Shop.** The Peerie (Shetland for small) Shop sells a colorful mix of knitwear, cards, ceramics, and interesting—and, yes, small—miscellanea. ✉ *Esplanade* ☎ *01595/692816* ⊕ *www.peerieshop.co.uk.*

Fodor's Choice ★ **Shetland Times.** The best bookshop within a radius of about 250 miles, the *Shetland Times,* the islands' newspaper and publisher, stocks a good selection of travel guides and local history titles. ✉ *71–79 Commercial St.* ☎ *01595/695531* ⊕ *www.shetlandtimes.co.uk/shop.*

SHETLAND PONIES

The squat and shaggy Shetland pony has been a common sight for more than 12 centuries. Roaming wild over the hills, the pony evolved its long mane and dense winter coat. The animals stand between 28 and 42 inches tall, which made them ideal for working in cramped coal-mine tunnels in the 1850s, when child labor was restricted. They became a popular pet for the aristocracy in the late 19th century; many believe this helped save the breed. Today a studbook society protects the purity of the stock, and you'll see ponies at equine events and all over the island, chomping the grass.

THE SOUTH MAINLAND

14 to 25 miles south of Lerwick via A970.

The narrow 3- or 4-mile-wide stretch of land that reaches south from Lerwick to Sumburgh Head has a number of fascinating ancient sites (and an airport) as well as farmland, wild landscapes, and dramatic ocean views.

GETTING HERE AND AROUND

Arriving in Sumburgh by plane offers stunning views of Sumburgh Head and its golden sands. A fairly regular bus makes the hour-long trip between the airport and Lerwick, and it's also easy to drive here if you're based in Lerwick. You can rent a car from the airport or take a taxi. Jarlshof and Scatness are both within walking distance of the terminal.

ESSENTIALS

Visitor Information Sumburgh Tourist Information Centre. ✉ *Sumburgh Airport Terminal, A9070, Virkie* ☎ *01950/460905* ⊕ *www.shetland.org.*

EXPLORING
TOP ATTRACTIONS

Fodor's Choice ★ **Mousa Broch.** Sandsayre Pier in Sandwick is the departure point for the passenger ferry to the tiny isle of Mousa, where you can see Mousa Broch, a fortified Iron Age stone tower rising about 40 feet high. The massive walls give a real sense of security, which must have been reassuring for islanders subject to attacks from ship-borne raiders. Exploring this beautifully preserved, curved-stone structure, standing on what feels like an untouched island, makes you feel as if you're back in 100 BC. From April to September, the ferry (£16 round-trip) departs for the island one or twice each afternoon. From May to July there are dusk boat trips (£20 round-trip) to catch the tiny storm petrels as they return from their day feeding at sea to their nests in the walls of the broch. The sight of them swarming in the half-light is something you'll never forget. ⊠ *Sandsayre Pier, off A970, 14 miles south of Lerwick, Sandwick* ☎ *07901/872339 ferry* ⊕ *www.mousa.co.uk.*

FAMILY
Fodor'sChoice
★
Shetland Croft House Museum. Five miles south of Sandwick this 19th-century thatched house reveals the way of life of rural Shetlanders, which the traditionally attired attendant will be delighted to discuss with you. The peat fire casts a glow on the box bed, the resting chair, and the wealth of domestic implements, including a hand mill for preparing meal and a straw "keshie" for carrying peat. One building made from an upturned boat was used for storing and drying fish and mutton: huts like this inspired the design of the new Scottish Parliament. If you're lucky, the museum's curator may be making bannocks from his homegrown and home-milled flour. ⊠ *East of A970, South Voe, Dunrossness* ☎ *01590/695057* ⊕ *www.shetland-museum.org.uk* ⊠ *Donations welcome* ⊙ *Mid-Apr.–Sept., daily 10–5.*

WORTH NOTING

FAMILY
Jarlshof. In 1897, a huge storm blew away 4,000 years of sand to expose the extensive remains of Bronze Age, Iron Age, Pictish, and Viking buildings; prehistoric wheelhouses; and earth houses that represented thousands of years of continuous settlement. It's a large and complex site, and you can roam the remains freely. The small visitor center is packed with facts and figures, and illustrates Jarlshof's more recent history as a medieval farmstead and home of the 16th-century Earl of Orkney and Shetland, "cruel" Patrick Stewart, who enslaved the men of Scalloway to build Scalloway Castle. ⊠ *Sumburgh Head, off A970, Virkie* ☎ *01950/460112* ⊕ *www.historic-scotland.gov.uk* ⊠ *£5.50* ⊙ *Apr.–Sept., daily 9:30–5:30; Oct.–Mar., daily 9:30–dusk.*

FAMILY
Old Scatness. Ongoing excavations at Old Scatness have uncovered the remains of an Iron Age village, including one building that still has a roof. The digs continue, but enthusiastic and entertaining guides, most in costume, tell stories that breathe life into the stones and the middens. They also show how the former residents made their clothes and cooked their food, including their staple dish: the ghastly seaweed porridge. Open on Fridays only. ⊠ *Off A970, Virkie* ☎ *01595/694688* ⊕ *www.shetland-heritage.co.uk/amenitytrust* ⊠ *£5* ⊙ *May–Aug., Fri. 10–5, last tour 4:30.*

Fodor'sChoice
★
St. Ninian's Isle. It was on St. Ninian's Isle that a schoolboy helping archaeologists excavate the ruins of a 12th-century church discovered the St. Ninian treasure, a collection of 28 silver objects dating from the 8th century. This Celtic silver is housed in the Museum of Scotland in Edinburgh (a point of controversy), but good replicas are in the Shetland Museum in Lerwick. Although you can't see the silver, walking

over the causeway of golden sand (called a tombolo or *ayre)* that joins St. Ninian's Isle to the Mainland is an unforgettable experience. From Sumburgh, head 8 miles north on A970 and B9122, then turn left at Skelberry.

PUFFINS AND MORE

Every summer more than a million birds alight on the cliff faces in Shetland to nest, feeding on the coastal fish and sand eels. Bird-watchers can spot more than 20 species, from tiny storm petrels to gannets with 6-foot wingspans. Popular with visitors are the puffins, with their short necks, striped beaks, and orange feet. Look for them on the cliffs at Sumburgh Head near the lighthouse, 2 miles south of Sumburgh Airport. The visitor center has a wealth of information about nesting sites, as well as live puffin cams during breeding season.

FAMILY Fodor's Choice ★ **Sumburgh Head Lighthouse and Visitor Centre.** Designed by Robert Stevenson—grandfather of the writer Robert Louis—this was built in 1921 and was the first lighthouse in Shetland. Sir Walter Scott was very taken with the location and based his novel *The Pirate*on the nearby landmarks of Jarlshof and Fitful Head. The recent refit has brought the stories of the Old Radar Hut—crucial during WWII—and the engine room with its deep booming foghorn back to life while a Marine Life Centre has excellent displays on the birds, fish, and sea mammals found around the cliffs. If you walk round the dry-stone dikes, you will hear and probably see puffins, guillemots, and fulmars breeding, feeding, and fighting on the rocks, but if it's wet and wild, the circular Education Suite with its jaw-dropping panorama will give you drama enough. ✉ *Sumburgh Head, Sumburgh* ☎ *01950/461966* 🌐 *www.sumburghhead.com* 🎟 *£6.*

WHERE TO STAY

$ B&B/INN Fodor's Choice ★ 🏨 **Hayhoull B&B.** This restful bed-and-breakfast has big rooms that are well designed and a dining room and lounge with beautiful views of St. Ninian's Isle and Foula. **Pros:** next to the bus stop for Lerwick; in friendly village next to the magical St. Ninian's Isle. **Cons:** two rooms share a shower room; 4 miles to the nearest pub or restaurant. [$] *Rooms from: £60* ✉ *Off B9122, Bigton* ☎ *01950/422206* 🌐 *www.bedandbreakfastshetland.com* 💳 *No credit cards* 🛏 *4 rooms* 🍴 *Breakfast.*

SHOPPING

Fodor's Choice ★ **Nielanell.** The designs here are rich in texture, color, and shape, but it's the philosophy behind the knitwear—she makes them for the day you feel at your worst—that makes them so desirable. Most of the pieces are multiwear, meaning you get three pieces for the price of one. ✉ *Hoswick* ☎ *01950/431413* 🌐 *www.nielanell.com.*

SCALLOWAY

6 miles west of Lerwick, 21 miles north of St. Ninian's Isle.

On the west coast of Mainland Island is Scalloway, which preceded Lerwick as the capital of the region. During World War II Scalloway was the port for the "Shetland Bus," a secret fleet of boats that carried

British agents to Norway to perform acts of sabotage against the Germans, who were occupying the country. On the return trips, the boats would carry refugees back to Shetland. As you approach the town from the A970, look for the information board, which overlooks the settlement and its castle.

GETTING HERE AND AROUND

The town is 10 minutes by car from Lerwick, or you can get one of the fairly regular buses or even a taxi (£12).

EXPLORING

Scalloway Museum. This modern museum tells some fascinating stories about Scalloway and it's well-traveled locals. There is a section dedicated to the exploits of the Shetland Bus, the WW II resistance movement which operated between Norway and Shetland, and cabinet upon cabinet of maritime artifacts donated by locals. ✉ *Castle St.* ☎ *01595/880734* 🌐 *www.scallowaymuseum.org* 🎟 *£2* 🕑 *Apr.–Sept., Mon.–Sat. 11–4; Sun. 2–4.*

Scalloway Castle. This waterfront fortress was built in 1600 by Patrick Stewart, Earl of Orkney and Shetland. He was hanged in 1615 for his cruelty and misdeeds, and the castle was never used again. To enter, retrieve the key from the Scalloway Museum. You may explore these handsome ruins to your heart's content. ✉ *A970* ☎ *01856/841815* 🌐 *www.historic-scotland.gov.uk* 🎟 *Free* 🕑 *Daily.*

WHERE TO STAY

$$ B&B/INN Fodor's Choice ★ 🏨 **Scalloway Hotel.** Facing the harbor, this traditional stone lodging has fine views, especially at sunset. **Pros:** thoughtfully put together bedrooms; memorable meals from the restaurant. **Cons:** can get booked up in advance. $ *Rooms from: £120* ✉ *Main St.* ☎ *01595/880444* 🌐 *www.scallowayhotel.com* 💳 *No credit cards* 🛏 *4 rooms* 🍴 *Breakfast.*

WEISDALE

9 miles north of Lerwick.

This tiny place is less a village than a group of houses, but it does have a worthwhile gallery.

GETTING HERE AND AROUND

Take A971 from Lerwick. The number 9 bus weekdays runs three times a day; the trip from Lerwick is 20 minutes.

EXPLORING

Bonhoga Gallery. Built in 1855 using stones from the Kergord estate's "cleared" (forcibly evicted) crofts, Weisdale Mill is now the Bonhoga Gallery, a contemporary art space showing quirky exhibitions by local, national, and international artists. Downstairs is a well-appreciated café that looks over the Weisdale burn. ✉ *B9075* ☎ *01595/745750* 🌐 *www.shetlandarts.org* 🕑 *Tues., Wed., Fri., and Sat. 10:30–5:30; Thurs: 10:30–7:30; Sun. 11:30–5:30.*

SHOPPING

Shetland Jewellery. This shop sells gold and silver Nordic- and Celtic-inspired jewelry, desk knives, and belt buckles made in the on-site workshop. ✉ *Sound Side* ☎ *01595/830275.*

BRAE

15 miles north of Weisdale, 24 miles north of Lerwick.

A thriving community, Brae is where you can see the spoils of Shetland's oil money. The rugged moorland and tranquil *voes* (inlets) of Brae are the home of Busta House, one of the best hotels on the island.

GETTING HERE AND AROUND

There are buses from Lerwick to Brae, but the spread-out sights make it impossible to really see this area without a car. A970 is the main road, and B9078 will take you through Hillswick and to Eshaness.

EXPLORING

OFF THE BEATEN PATH

Eshaness and Ronas Hill. About 15 miles north of Brae are the rugged, forbidding cliffs around **Eshaness**; drive north and then turn left onto B9078. On the way, look for the striking sandstone stacks or pillars (known as the Drongs) in the bay that resemble a Viking galley under sail. Then return to join the A970 at Hillswick and follow an ancillary road from the head of Ura Firth. This road provides vistas of rounded, red **Ronas Hill,** the highest hill in Shetland.

Mavis Grind. North of Brae the A970 meanders past Mavis Grind, a strip of land so narrow you can throw a stone—if you're strong—from the Atlantic, in one inlet, to the North Sea, in another. Keep an eye out for sea otters, which sometimes cross here.

OFF THE BEATEN PATH

Tangwick Haa Museum. After viewing the cliffs at Eshaness, call in at Tangwick Haa Museum, the 17th-century home of the Cheynes, now packed full with photographs, household items, and knitting, farming, and fishing equipment from the 18th to early 20th century. Upstairs is the Laird's Room—a traditional sitting room of the 19th century and a room of curiosities, including whale eardrums. Downstairs—next to the help-yourself café—there are rows of folders: ask one of the staff to let you hear what's in them and you will be rewarded with the soft, gentle voices of local elders telling you of life lived in Shetland. ✉ *Off B9078, Tangwick* ☎ *01806/503389* 🌐 *www.tangwickhaa.org.uk* 🎟 *Free* 🕒 *Apr.–Sept., daily 11–5.*

WHERE TO EAT AND STAY

$ BRITISH

🍴 **Braewick Café.** With a stunning position overlooking the Drongs (rocky columns standing in the sea), this eatery's famously large portions are popular with visitors and Shetlanders alike. Browse the local crafts in the shop while waiting for a crispy battered-fish supper, or just sit back on the sofas by the huge picture window and watch the dramatic sea and sky. Don't pass up the many tempting home-baked desserts like sponges, cheesecakes, and giant scones. [$] *Average main: £10* ✉ *Off B9078, Eshaness* ☎ *01806/503345* ☞ *Mon.–Sat. 10–5; Sun. lunch must be booked.*

$ ✕ **Frankie's Fish & Chips.** Proudly claiming to be the northernmost fish-
SEAFOOD   and-chip shop in Britain, this "chipper" is also the best of its kind on the
Fodor's Choice   islands. The combination of super-fresh seafood—skate wings, squid,
★   and crab legs—light and crispy batter, and low prices means Frankie's
is everything a chip shop could be. Try the local mussels: you'll not find
any that are fatter or juicier in the United Kingdom. Sit on the deck
or in the lovely dining room with views toward Busta Voe. $ *Average
main: £9* ✉ *A970* ☎ *01806/522700* ⊕ *www.frankiesfishandchips.com.*

$$ ▦ **Busta House.** Dating from the 16th century, Busta House—built by
HOTEL   the well-heeled but ill-fated Gifford family—is one of the few grand
Fodor's Choice   houses of Shetland. **Pros:** truly haunting atmosphere; charming pub-
★   lic rooms; lovely grounds. **Cons:** noisy plumbing; some rooms are a
tight fit. $ *Rooms from: £125* ✉ *Off A970* ☎ *01806/522506* ⊕ *www.
bustahouse.com* ⤵ *22 rooms* ⦿| *Breakfast.*

YELL

11 miles northeast of Brae, 31 miles north of Lerwick.

A desolate-looking blanket bog cloaks two-thirds of the island of Yell,
creating an atmospheric landscape to pass through on the way to Unst
to the north.

GETTING HERE AND AROUND

Although you will see the odd walker or cyclist, a car is needed to
explore the northern isles. To get to Yell, take A970 or B9076 and
catch the ferry from Toft to Ulsta. On Yell, B9081 runs through Bur-
ravoe and up the east side and joins the A968, which leads to Gutcher
and the ferry to Unst.

EXPLORING

Old Haa (*hall*). The oldest building on the island, Burravoe's Old Haa
is known for its crow-stepped gables (the stepped effect on the ends of
the roofs), typical of an early-18th-century Shetland merchant's house.
There's an earnest memorial to Bobby Tulloch, the great Shetland natu-
ralist (1929–96), and the displays in the upstairs museum tell the story
of the wrecking of the German ship, the *Bohus,* in 1924. A copy of the
ship's figurehead is displayed outside the building. The Old Haa serves
light meals with home-baked buns, cakes, and other goodies and also
acts as a kind of unofficial information center. A crafts shop is on the
premises, too. ✉ *Burravoe* ☎ *01957/702431* ⊕ *www.bobbytulloch.com*
✉ *Free* ⊙ *Apr.–Sept., Tues.–Sat. 10–4, Sun. 2–5.*

UNST

49 miles north of Lerwick.

Unst is the northernmost inhabited island in Scotland, a remote and
special place, especially for nature lovers and those who want to experi-
ence a community on the edge of faraway. On a long summer evening,
views north to Muckle Flugga, with only the ocean beyond, are incom-
parable. If you're a bird-watcher, head to the Hermaness and Keen of
Hamar nature reserves.

11

GETTING HERE AND AROUND

A ferry (take the A968 at the village of Mid Yell to Gutcher) crosses the Bluemull Sound to Unst. A car is best for exploring, though there is limited bus service, including from Lerwick; taxis are an option. The island has some B&B and house-rental options if you choose to linger.

EXPLORING

Hermaness National Nature Reserve. The Hermaness National Nature Reserve, a bleak moorland ending in rocky cliffs, is prime bird-watching territory. About half the world's population (6,000 pairs) of great skuas, called "bonxies" by locals, are found here. These sky pirates attack anything that strays near their nests, including humans, so keep to the paths. Thousands of other seabirds, including more than 50,000 puffins, nest on the cliffs, about an hour's walk from the reserve entrance. Gray seals gather in caves at the foot of the cliffs in fall, and offshore, dolphins and occasionally whales (including orcas) can be seen on calm days.

A path meanders across moorland and climbs up a gentle hill, from which you can see, to the north, a series of tilting offshore rocks; the largest of these sea-battered protrusions is **Muckle Flugga**, meaning "big, steep-sided island," on which stands a lighthouse. The lighthouse was built by engineer Thomas Stevenson, whose son, the great Scottish writer Robert Louis Stevenson, used the outline of Unst for his map of Treasure Island. Muckle Flugga is the northernmost point in Scotland.

The visitor center has leaflets that outline a walk; mid-May to mid-July is the best time to visit. To get here from Haroldswick, follow the B9086 around the head of Burrafirth to the signposted car park. ⊠ *B9086, Burrafirth* ☏ *01957/693345* ⊕ *www.nnr-scotland.org.uk* ⊠ *Free* ☉ *Mid-Apr.–mid-Sept., daily 9–5.*

Keen of Hamar National Nature Reserve. The rare and unusual flora here includes Edmonston's Chickweed, hoary whitlow grass and Norwegian sandwort, to name just a few. Near Baltasound, it's just off the A968, on the road past the famous **Unst Bus Shelter** (with its award-winning themed decor, the work of young locals). Please tread lightly and take care on the cliff-top paths. ⊹ *Off A968* ☏ *01595/693345* ⊕ *www.snh.gov.uk.*

Muness Castle. Scotland's northernmost castle was built just before the end of the 16th century and has circular corner towers. It is a ruin but has notable architectural details. ⊠ *B9084, Uyeasound* ⊕ *www.historic-scotland.gov.uk* ⊠ *Free* ☉ *Daily 24 hrs.*

Unst Heritage Centre. The unique and colorful history of the people of Unst is told in this fascinating assemblage of artifacts, tools, photographs, and reconstructions—there's a classroom and a *ben* or "good" end (sitting room) of a croft house—and will leave you with a never-forgotten visual memory of the ways in which the locals learned, crofted, knitted, fished, and worshipped through the last two centuries. The adjoining **Boat Haven** has a fleet of fishing and sailing boats from over the years and narratives of community life. ⊠ *Beach Rd., Haroldswick* ☏ *01957/711528* ⊕ *www.unstheritage.com* ⊠ *£2* ☉ *May–Sept., Mon.–Sat. 11–4, Sun. 2–4.*

WHERE TO EAT AND STAY

$ × **Victoria's Vintage Tea Rooms.** Run by a Devon girl, who knows a thing
CAFÉ or two about cream teas, this vintage-style café tested its appeal and
FAMILY cakes by being a "pop up." However, it has now found a permanent
base and is doing a roaring trade right on the water at Haroldswick.
The Shetland smoked salmon on Skibhoul (the local baker) bread is a
sandwich worth getting excited about as are their cakes, especially their
Victoria Sponge and scones. And the coffee is as good as you'd get in
Rome—but with the added attraction of gray seals and otters outside
the window. $ *Average main: £5* ⊠ *Old Haroldswick Shop, Harolds-
wick* ☎ *01957/711885* ⊕ *victoriasvintagetearooms.co.uk* ۩ *Closed Sun.
No dinner* ⊟ *No credit cards.*

$ ⊡ **The Baltasound Hotel.** This old Victorian house-hotel feels a little like
B&B/INN a work in progress which, coming into new ownership, it is. **Pros:** staff
make a real effort to make you feel at home; good quality considering
there's no competition; it has Wi-Fi, which works. **Cons:** if you can't
sleep in daylight, bring a sleep mask in midsummer. $ *Rooms from: £90*
⊠ *Baltasound* ☎ *01957/711334* ⊕ *www.baltasoundhotel.co.uk* ↩ *24
rooms* ⭤ *Breakfast* ⊟ *No credit cards.*

SHOPPING

Skibhoul Bakery. The bread from Skibhoul is so popular that large ship-
ments of it head south to the rest of the Isles on a Thursday. They're also
famous for their Oceanic sea salt oatcakes and Balta Biscuits. There's a
small self-serve café so you can taste their wares. ⊠ *Northside, Baltasound* ☎ *01957/711444.*

BICYCLING

Unst Cycles Hire. There's a few hilly bits but there are miles of road in
Unst made for cycling. Bikes cost £7.50 per day of £10 for an electric bike. ⊠ *Northbase Information Centre, Saxa Vord, Haroldswick*
☎ *01957/711393* ⊕ *www.unstcyclehire.co.uk.*

UNDERSTANDING
SCOTLAND

CHRONOLOGY

CHRONOLOGY

7000 BC   Hunter-gatherers move into the north of Scotland after the ice sheets of the last Ice Age recede; these travelers leave arrowheads and bone implements as testimony to their passing.

ca. 6000 BC   First settlers arrive, bringing farming methods with them. They leave their mark at Skara Brae in Orkney.

ca. 3000 BC   Neolithic migration from Mediterranean: "chambered cairn" people in north (such as the Grey Cairns of Camster). "Beaker people" erect the standing stone circles, like those at Callanish on the Isle of Lewis.

ca. 300 BC   Iron Age: arrival of Celtic peoples from the south and from Ireland; "Gallic forts" and "brochs" (towers) built, like the tower at Mousa in Shetland.

79–89   Julius Agricola (AD 40–93), Roman governor of Britain, invades Scotland; Scots tribes defeated at the battle of Mons Graupius (thought to be somewhere in the Grampians). Roman forts built at Inchtuthil and Ardoch.

123   Hadrian's Wall is built to mark the northern limit of the Roman Empire.

142   Emperor Antoninus Pius (86–161) orders the defensive Antonine Wall built between the Firths of Forth and Clyde, as the Romans continue their attempt to invade beyond Hadrian's Wall.

185   Antonine Wall abandoned.

392   St. Ninian (ca. 360–432), a Briton and a Christian, sends out a first Christian mission to the Picts from his chapel at Whithorn.

400–500   Tribes of Celtic origin, including the Scotti, emigrate from Ireland to present-day Argyllshire and establish the kingdom of Dalriada. The Pictish kingdom extends as far south as Fife. The Britons, meanwhile, occupy an area between Dumbarton and Carlisle.

400–843   Four kingdoms exist in Scotland: Dalriada (Argyllshire), the kingdom of the Picts (Aberdeenshire down to Fife and the Highlands excepting Argyllshire), Strathclyde (southwest Scotland), and the Lothians (Edinburgh and the Borders).

563   Columba, (ca. 521–97), a Gaelic-speaking Scotti, establishes the monastery at Iona. It will become a major center for the evangelization of Scotland and farther afield.

843   Kenneth MacAlpin, king of Dalriada, unites with the Picts while remaining king. In this way the embryonic Kingdom of Scotland (first called Alba, later Scotia) is born, with its capital at Scone.

780–1065   Scandinavian invasions; the Hebrides remain Norse until 1263, Orkney and Shetland until 1472.

1018   Malcolm II (ca. 953–1034) brings the Lothians into the Kingdom of Scotland and (temporarily) repels the English.

1034   Duncan (d. 1040), king of Strathclyde, ascends the throne of Scotland and unification is complete.

1040   Duncan is slain by his rival, Macbeth (d. 1057), whose wife has a claim to the throne.

1057 Malcolm III (ca. 1031–93), known as Canmore (Big Head), murders Macbeth and assumes the throne. The House of Canmore now assumes the Scottish crown and introduces a feudal landowning system into the country.

1093 Death of Malcolm's English-born queen, St. Margaret (1046–93), who brought Roman Catholicism to Scotland.

1099 Donald III becomes the last king of Scots to be buried on the island of Iona.

1124–53 David I (ca. 1082–1153), *sair sanct* (sore saint), builds the abbeys of Jedburgh (1118), Kelso (1128), Melrose (1136), and Dryburgh (1150) and brings Norman culture to Scotland.

1200 The Royal Burghs, or towns, of Stirling, Edinburgh, and Berwick are established with certain rights and privileges in trade. The Highland clans are largely excluded from power.

1250 Queen Margaret, wife of Malcolm III, is canonized, becoming Scotland's first (and only) royal saint.

1290 Death of Alexander III, great-great-grandson of David I. The heir is his granddaughter, Margaret, Maid of Norway (1283–90). She dies at sea on her way from Norway to claim the Scottish throne and marry the future Edward II (1284–1327), son of Edward I of England (1239–1307). The Scots naively ask Edward I, subsequently known as the Hammer of the Scots, to arbitrate between the remaining 13 claimants to the throne. Edward chooses John Balliol (1249–1315) over his ambitious rival Robert the Bruce.

1295 Under continued threat from England, John Balliol switches allegiance and signs Scotland's first treaty with England's enemy, France. This came to be known as "the Auld Alliance." The wine trade flourishes.

1297 While Robert the Bruce now sides with the English, William Wallace (ca. 1270–1305) leads an uprising against the English. His army is made up of peasants and the lower nobility like himself. It is in part a reaction against the extreme cruelty of the English armies under Edward I. The wealthy nobles, for their part, do not resist because many of them have lands in both England and Scotland.

1305 Wallace, betrayed and captured by the English, is executed.

1306–29 Reign of Robert the Bruce (1274–1329), later to become King Robert I, who turns again against the English. He defeats Edward II (1284–1327) at Bannockburn, 1314. The Declaration of Arbroath (1320) affirms Scottish sovereignty, which is eventually recognized by the Treaty of Northampton, 1328.

1329 After the death of Bruce, the nobles fight wars against one another for 50 years. The attempt by the new ruling house, the Stewards, or Stuarts, to control the situation largely fails.

1371 Robert II (1316–90), the first Stewart monarch and son of Robert the Bruce's daughter Marjorie and Walter the Steward, is crowned in 1371, but the struggle between the crown and Scottish barons (later dramatized in several of Sir Walter Scott's novels) continues for another century. Sporadic warfare with the English also continues during this time.

1383   Bishop Wardlaw of Glasgow is the first Scot to be made a cardinal.

1411   University of St. Andrews founded.

1451   University of Glasgow founded.

1488–1513   Reign of James IV (1473–1513). The Renaissance reaches Scotland. The Golden Age of Scots poetry includes Robert Henryson (ca. 1425–1508), William Dunbar (ca. 1460–1530), Gavin Douglas (1474–1522), and the king himself.

1495   University of Aberdeen founded.

1507   Andrew Myllar and Walter Chapman set up first Scots printing press in Edinburgh.

1513   After invading England in support of the French, James IV is slain at Flodden Field.

1542   Henry VIII (1491–1547), king of England, defeats James V (1512–42) at Solway Moss. The dying James, hearing of the birth of his daughter, Mary, declares: "It came with a lass [Marjorie Bruce] and it will pass with a lass."

1542–67   Reign of Mary, Queen of Scots (1542–87). She becomes queen at one year old, and her mother is appointed regent. At six she is married to the heir to the French throne. Romantic, Catholic, and with an excellent claim to the English throne, Mary proved to be no match for her barons, John Knox (1513–72), or her cousin Elizabeth I (1533–1603) of England.

1560   Mary returns to Scotland from France after the death of her husband, Francis II of France, at the same time that Catholicism is abolished in favor of Protestantism. She finds a Scotland dominated by a Protestantism influenced by the fiery John Knox.

1565   Mary marries Lord Darnley (1545–67), a Catholic but a self-indulgent consort.

1567   Darnley is murdered at Kirk o' Field and Mary marries one of the conspirators, the Earl of Bothwell (ca. 1535–78). Driven from Scotland, she appeals to Elizabeth, who imprisons her. Mary's son, James (1566–1625), is crowned James VI of Scotland.

1582   University of Edinburgh is founded.

1587   Elizabeth orders the execution of Mary.

1600   Charles I is born in Scotland.

1603   Elizabeth dies without issue; James VI is crowned James I of England, uniting the two crowns. But the parliaments remain separate for another century.

1638   National Covenant challenges Charles I's personal rule.

1639–41   Crisis. The Scots and then the English parliaments revolt against Charles I (1600–49).

1643   Solemn League and Covenant establishes Presbyterianism as the Church of Scotland (the Kirk). In England, Parliament rises against Charles I, who had summoned it after 11 years in the hope it would grant him resources for war. Civil War in England.

1649   Charles I beheaded. Oliver Cromwell (1599–1658) made Protector.

1650–52   Cromwell roots out Scots Royalists.

1658   The first Edinburgh–London coach is established. The journey takes two weeks.

1660   1660 Restoration of Charles II (1630–85). Episcopalianism reestablished in Scotland; Covenanters are persecuted and their army attacked by Highland soldiers.

1688   The unpopular James VII of Scotland (and II of England, Scotland, and Ireland) flees to France.

1688–89   Glorious Revolution; James VII and II (1633–1701), a Catholic, deposed in favor of his daughter Mary (1662–94) and her husband, William of Orange (1650–1702). Supporters of James (known as Jacobites) defeated at Killiecrankie. Presbyterianism reestablished.

1692   Highlanders who were late in taking oath to William and Mary massacred at Glencoe.

1695   The first bank in Scotland, the Bank of Scotland, is founded.

1698–1700   Attempted Scottish colony at Darien (on the Isthmus of Panama) fails. Many of the Scottish nobility face bankruptcy, and are therefore open to overtures from an English government anxious to unite the Scottish and English parliaments.

1707   Union of English and Scots parliaments under Queen Anne (1665–1714), the last Stuart monarch; deprived of French wine trade, Scots turn to whisky.

1714   Queen Anne dies; George I (1660–1727) of the House of Hanover, descended from a daughter of James VI and I, is crowned.

1715   First Jacobite Rebellion. James II's son, James Edward Stuart, agrees to undertake an invasion of England. His supporter, the Earl of Mar (1675–1732), the leader of the attempted Rising, is defeated.

1730–90   Scottish Enlightenment. The Edinburgh Medical School is the best in Europe; David Hume (1711–76) and Adam Smith (1723–90) redefine philosophy and economics. In the arts, Allan Ramsay the elder (1686–1758) and Robert Burns (1759–96) refine Scottish poetry; Allan Ramsay the younger (1713–84) and Henry Raeburn (1756–1823) rank among the finest painters of the era. Edinburgh's New Town, developed in the 1770s and including designs by the brothers Adam (Robert, 1728–92; James, 1730–94), provides a fitting setting.

1736   The first public theater in Scotland is opened in Carruber's Close in Edinburgh.

1745–46   Last Jacobite Rebellion. Bonnie Prince Charlie (1720–88), grandson of James II, is defeated at Culloden by the armies of the Duke of Cumberland. He escapes across the water to the Isle of Skye before eventually returning to France. The wearing of the kilt, the use of tartan, and the playing of bagpipes are now banned, and the clans of the north are finally crushed. James Watt (1736–1819), born in Greenock, is granted a patent for his steam engine.

1760   Thomas Braidwood (1715–1806) opens the first school for people who cannot hear or speak in Great Britain, in Edinburgh.

1771   Birth of Walter Scott (1771–1832), Romantic novelist.

1778   First cotton mill, at Rothesay.

1788   Death of Bonnie Prince Charlie in Rome.

1790   Forth and Clyde Canal opened.

1800–50   Highland Clearances: increased rents and the conversion of farms to sheep pasture lead to mass expulsions of the peasants and their forced migration to North America and elsewhere. Meanwhile, the Lowlands industrialize; Catholic Irish immigrate to factories of Glasgow and the southwest.

1807   The first museum in Scotland, the Hunterian Museum, is founded.

1822   Visit of George IV to Scotland, the first British monarch to make such a trip since Charles I. Sir Walter Scott orchestrates the visit, and almost single-handedly invents Scotland's national costume: the formal kilt, tartan plaid, and jacket.

1831   The first passenger rail service in Scotland opens on the line between Glasgow and Garnkirk.

1832   Parliamentary Reform Act expands the franchise, redistributes seats.

1837   1837 Victoria (1819–1901) ascends to the British throne.

1842   Edinburgh–Glasgow railroad opened.

1846   Edinburgh–London railroad opened.

1848   Queen Victoria buys estate at Balmoral as her Scottish residence. Andrew Carnegie emigrates from Dunfermline to Pittsburgh.

1860   The first British Open golf championship is held in Scotland, at Prestwick.

1884–85   Gladstone's Reform Act gives the majority of men over 21 the right to vote. Office of Secretary for Scotland authorized.

1886   Scottish Home Rule Association founded.

1888   Scottish Labour Party founded by Keir Hardie (1856–1915); he later forms the Independent Labour Party (1893)

1890   Forth Rail Bridge opened.

1896   The Glasgow subway opens.

1901   Death of Queen Victoria.

1904–31   One million Scots emigrate to Canada, the United States, New Zealand, Australia, and elsewhere.

1919   Rent strikes across Scotland. Troops are sent to Glasgow as thousands gather in the city's George Square to demand a shorter working week.

1928   Equal Franchise Act gives the vote to women. Scottish Office established as governmental department in Edinburgh. John Logie Baird gives the first demonstration of television. Alexander Fleming, a Scot, discovers penicillin. Death of architect and designer Charles Rennie Mackintosh.

1930   Unemployment in Scotland reaches 25%.

1931   Depression hits industrialized Scotland severely.

1933   The first press stories alleging that there is a monster in Loch Ness. They have continued ever since.

1934   Scottish National Party formed.

1938   The world's largest luxury liner, the *Queen Elizabeth,* is launched on the Clyde.

1939   The first German air raids of World War II on Scotland are made on the Forth Estuary.

1941   The town of Clydebank is bombed by German planes attacking the shipyards: 1,000 people are killed.

1945   Two Scottish Nationalists elected to Parliament.

1947   The Edinburgh International Festival, with events in all the performing arts, is launched.

1950   The Stone of Destiny, on which the kings of Scotland were traditionally crowned, is stolen from Westminster Abbey in London and returned to Scotland. It is found a year later, in Arbroath.

1951   The People's Festival, an alternative to the official Edinburgh Festival, launched. It later becomes the Fringe.

1959   Finnart Oil Terminal, Chapelcross Nuclear Power Station, and Dounreay Fast Breeder Reactor opened.

1970   British Petroleum strikes oil in the North Sea.

1973   Britain becomes a member of the European Economic Community (formerly known as the Common Market).

1974   Eleven Scottish Nationalists elected as members of Parliament. Old counties reorganized and renamed as new regions and districts.

1975   The first Scottish oil pumped ashore from the North Sea. "It's Scotland's Oil" becomes a slogan used by Nationalists.

1979   Referendum on devolution—the creation of a separate Scotland: 33% in favor, 31% against; 36% don't vote. Britain's Labour government had imposed a minimum vote of 40%.

1980   The Singer Sewing Machine factory in Clydebank, one of the largest factories in the world, closes with the loss of 25,000 jobs.

1981   Europe's largest oil terminal opens at Sullom Voe, Shetland.

1988   Pan Am flight 103 brought down by a terrorist bomb over Lockerbie.

1992   Increasing attention focused on Scotland's dissatisfaction with rule from London. Poll shows 50% of Scots want independence.

1997   The Labour Party wins the general election in May. For the first time not one Conservative is returned from Scotland. A referendum in Scotland votes in favor of the establishment of a Scottish parliament (with restricted powers). The first successful cloning of an animal in the world is achieved with the birth of Dolly the Sheep in Edinburgh.

1999   Scotland elects its first parliament in 300 years. There are 129 Members of the Scottish Parliament.

2002   The Millennium Link—the restoration of the canal link between Glasgow and Edinburgh—is completed at a cost of £78 million. It includes the Falkirk Wheel, the world's only rotating boat lift.

2004   The Scottish Parliament Building opens for business in a building whose modern design by Spanish architect Enric Miralles causes controversy.

2007   Alex Salmond, leader of the Scottish National Party, becomes the First Minister of Scotland heading a minority government.

2009   The country endures recession as part of the international economic upheaval.

2011   The Scottish National Party under Alex Salmond wins an absolute majority in the Scottish parliamentary elections. In January 2012 he proposes the question for the referendum on Scottish independence that he wants to hold in fall 2014.

2013   Scot Andy Murray wins the Wimbledon tennis championship.

2014   Commonwealth Games open in Glasgow in July. Independence referendum is defeated on September 18, with 55.3% voting no and a massive voter turnout of 84.6%.

TRAVEL SMART
SCOTLAND

GETTING HERE AND AROUND

■ AIR TRAVEL

Scotland's main hubs are Glasgow, Prestwick (near Glasgow), Edinburgh, Inverness, and Aberdeen. Glasgow and Prestwick are the gateways to the west and southwest, Edinburgh the east and southeast, Aberdeen and Inverness the north. All these cities have excellent bus and train transportation services and well-maintained roads that link them with each other and other cities within Scotland. Taxis are also an efficient and reliable option, but they are three to four times the cost of going by public transport.

Traveling by air is straightforward in Scotland. Security is heavy but efficient. You can often breeze through check-in lines by using your airline's online check-in option or bag drop, but confirm this ahead of time.

Flying time to Glasgow and Aberdeen is 6½ hours from New York, 7½ hours from Chicago, 9½ hours from Dallas, 10 hours from Los Angeles, and 21½ hours from Sydney. Flying time to Edinburgh is 7 hours from New York, 8 hours from Chicago, 10 hours from Dallas, 10½ hours from Los Angeles, and 22 hours from Sydney. Not all airlines offer direct flights to Scotland; many go via London. For those flights allow an extra four to five hours of travel (two to three for the layover in London plus an additional hour or two for the duration of the flight).

Smoking is prohibited on all flights.

Airline-Security Issues Transportation Security Administration. ⊕ *www.tsa.gov.*

AIRPORTS

The major international gateways to Scotland are Glasgow Airport (GLA), about 7 miles outside Glasgow, and Edinburgh Airport (EDI), 7 miles from the city. Both offer connections for dozens of European cities and regular flights to London's Gatwick (LGW) and Heathrow (LHR)

airports. Aberdeen Airport (ABZ) has direct flights to most major European cities. Prestwick (PIK) has direct flights to most major British and European cities at discounted rates. Inverness (INV) offers direct flights in and around the United Kingdom.

Airport tax is included in the price of your ticket. Generally the tax for economy tickets within the United Kingdom from European Union countries is £13. For all other flights it is £71. For first- and club-class flights from the United Kingdom and European Union the tax is £26; for all other destinations it's £142.

All Scottish airports offer typical modern amenities: restaurants, cafés, shopping (from clothes to food to tourist trinkets), sandwich and salad bars, pubs, pharmacies, bookshops, and newsstands; some even have spas and hair salons. Glasgow is the largest, most interesting airport when it comes to a delayed flight. Good food and shopping options abound—try Discover Glasgow for Scottish-inspired goods—and if you're in need of some tranquillity, head for the Relaxation Station for a clothed massage, no reservation necessary.

There are plenty of hotels near all airports, and all airports also have Internet access.

Airport Information Aberdeen Airport. ☎ *0844/481–6666* ⊕ *www.aberdeenairport. com.* **Edinburgh Airport.** ☎ *0844/448–8833* ⊕ *www.edinburghairport.com.* **Glasgow Airport.** ☎ *0844/481–5555* ⊕ *www. glasgowairport.com.* **Glasgow Prestwick Airport.** ☎ *0871/223–0700* ⊕ *www. glasgowprestwick.com.* **Inverness Airport.** ☎ *01667/464000* ⊕ *www.hial.co.uk/ inverness-airport.*

GROUND TRANSPORTATION

The best way to get to and from the airport based on speed and convenience is by taxi. All airport taxi stands are just outside the airport's front doors and are well marked with clear signs. Most taxis have a set price when going to and from the airport to the city center but will turn on the meter at your request. Ask the driver to turn on the meter to confirm the flat-rate price.

If you're traveling with a large party, you can request a people carrier to transport everyone, luggage included. Luggage is included in the taxi fare; you should not be charged extra for it.

If you're traveling alone, a more economical transfer option is public transportation. Buses travel between city centers and Glasgow, Edinburgh, Aberdeen, and Inverness airports. Trams travel between Edinburgh Airport and the city center; trains go direct to Glasgow Prestwick Airport. All are fast, inexpensive, and reliable. *For more information and specific contacts, refer to the Orientation and Planning sections at the beginning of chapters.*

TRANSFERS BETWEEN AIRPORTS

Scottish airports are relatively close to one another and all are connected by a series of buses and trains. Flights between airports add hours to your journey and are very expensive (between £200 and £400). The best way to travel from one airport to another is by bus, train, car, or taxi. Normally you must take a combination of bus and train, which is easy and—if you travel light—quite enjoyable.

From Edinburgh Airport you can take the Citylink Air (£11.40) bus direct to Glasgow Airport in 1 hour. For those wanting to see Edinburgh and have time on their hands, take a tram (£5) or bus (£4.50) to the city center and then a train to Glasgow city center (£13.50) and a shuttle bus to Glasgow Airport (£6.50). This journey should take you less than two hours. Taxis are fast but costly. The price of a taxi from Edinburgh Airport to Glasgow Airport is around £90, a good choice if you're traveling with a few people. Renting a car would be a good choice if you want to get from Edinburgh to, say, Aberdeen Airport and you're traveling

with a few people. Otherwise, take a bus to the city center and then take a train. *For specific information, see the Orientation and Planning section at the start of appropriate chapters.*

FLIGHTS

Scotland has a significant air network for a small country. Contact British Airways or British Airways Express for details on flights from London's Heathrow Airport or from Glasgow, Edinburgh, Aberdeen, and Inverness to the farthest corners of the Scottish mainland and to the islands. *See individual chapters for information on flying to various islands.*

Among the low-cost carriers, Virgin has service from Heathrow; and easyJet flies from London Luton/Gatwick/Stansted to and between Glasgow, Edinburgh, Aberdeen, and Inverness, plus to and from Belfast. Flybe has services to Sumburgh (Shetland) and Kirkwall (Orkney) from Aberdeen, Inverness, Glasgow, and Edinburgh, where you can continue on to Bristol, Cardiff, Exeter, Manchester, Newquay, and Southampton. Flybe also runs the Dundee-London Stansted route.

Major Airline Contacts British Airways. ☎ 800/247–9297 in U.S., 0844/493–0787 in U.K. ⊕ www.britishairways.com. **Delta Airlines.** ☎ 800/221–1212 in U.S., 0871/221–1222 in U.K. ⊕ www.delta.com. **KLM.** ☎ 866/434–0320 in U.S., 020/7660–0293 in U.K. ⊕ www.klm.com. **United Airlines.** ☎ 800/864–8331 in U.S., 0845/607–6760 in U.K. ⊕ www.united.com. **US Airways.** ☎ 800/428–4322 in U.S., 0845/600–3300 in U.K. ⊕ www.usairways.com. **Virgin Atlantic.** ☎ 800/862–8621 in U.S., 0344/209–7770 in U.K. ⊕ www.virgin-atlantic.com.

From London to Edinburgh and Glasgow easyJet. ☎ 0843/104–5000 ⊕ www.easyjet.com. **Ryanair.** ☎ 0871/246–0000 in U.K. ⊕ www.ryanair.com.

Within Scotland Flybe. ☎ 0371/700–2000 ⊕ www.flybe.com.

AIRLINE TICKETS

The least expensive airfares to Scotland are often priced for round-trip travel and must usually be purchased in advance. Airlines generally allow you to change your return date for a fee; most low-fare tickets, however, are nonrefundable.

If you intend to fly to Scotland from London, take advantage of the current fare wars on internal routes—notably among London's four airports and between Glasgow and Edinburgh. Among the cheapest fares are those from easyJet, which offers bargain fares from London Luton/Gatwick/Stansted (all with good rail links from central London) to Glasgow, Edinburgh, Aberdeen, and Inverness. However, British Airways now offers competitive fares on some flights.

■ BIKE TRAVEL

Bicycling in Scotland is variable. The best months for cycling are May, June, and September, when the roads are often quieter and the weather is usually better. Because Scotland's main roads are continually being upgraded, bicyclists can easily reach the network of quieter rural roads in southern and much of eastern Scotland, especially Grampian. In a few areas of the Highlands, notably in northwestern Scotland, the rugged terrain and limited population have resulted in the lack of side roads, making it difficult—sometimes impossible—to plan a minor-road route in these areas.

Several agencies now promote routes for recreational cyclists. These routes are signposted, and agencies have produced maps or leaflets showing where they run. Perhaps best known is the Glasgow–Loch Lomond–Killin Cycleway. VisitScotland has advice on a site dedicated to cycling.

BIKING ORGANIZATIONS

The Cyclists' Touring Club publishes a members' magazine, route maps, and guides. Sustrans is a nonprofit organization dedicated to providing environmentally friendly routes for cyclists. Active Scotland, part of the national tourism agency, has a great list of bike routes ranked by area and difficulty.

TRANSPORTING BIKES

Although some rural bus services will transport cycles if space is available, don't count on getting your bike on a bus. Check well in advance with the appropriate bus company.

You can take bicycles on car and passenger ferries in Scotland, and it's usually not necessary to book in advance. Arrive early so that your bike can be loaded through the car entrance.

ScotRail strongly advises that you make a train reservation for you and your bike at least one month in advance. On several trains reservations are compulsory.

Bike Maps and Information ActiveScotland. ☎ 0845/859–1006 ⊕ active.visitscotland.com. **Cyclists' Touring Club.** ☎ 0844/736–8450 ⊕ www.ctc.org.uk. **Sustrans.** ☎ 0131/346–1384 ⊕ www.sustrans.org.uk.

■ BOAT AND FERRY TRAVEL

Because Scotland has so many islands, plus the great Firth of Clyde waterway, ferry services are of paramount importance. Most ferries transport vehicles as well as foot passengers, although a few smaller ones are for passengers only.

It's a good idea to make a reservation ahead of time, although reservations are not absolutely necessary. Most travelers show up on the day of departure and buy their tickets from the stations at the ports. Keep in mind that these are working ferries, not tourist boats. Although journeys are scenic, most people use these ferries as their daily means of public transportation to and from their hometowns.

The main operator is Caledonian MacBrayne, known generally as CalMac. Services extend from the Firth of Clyde in the south, where there's an extensive network, right up to the northwest of Scotland and all the Hebrides. CalMac sells an 8-day or 15-day Island Rover runabout ticket, which is ideal for touring holidays in the islands, as well as an island-hopping plan called Island Hopscotch. Fares can range from £4 to £6 for a short trip to almost £50 for a longer trip with several legs.

The Dunoon–Gourock route on the Clyde is served by Western Ferries (for cars) and Argyll Ferries (for passengers and cycles only).

Northlink Ferries operates a car ferry for Orkney between Scrabster, near Thurso, and Stromness, on the main island of Orkney; and between Aberdeen and Kirkwall, which is also on the mainland of Orkney. Northlink also runs an efficient ferry to Lerwick, Shetland, and Kirkwall, Orkney. The journey to Lerwick is overnight, but comfortable cabins are available. These ferries can be busy in summer, so book well in advance.

Traveler's checks (in pounds), cash, and major credit cards are accepted for payment. *See the Orientation and Planning sections of each chapter for more details about ferry services.*

Information Argyll Ferries. ☎ 0800 /066–5000 ⊕ www.argyllferries.co.uk. **Caledonian MacBrayne.** ☎ 0800/066–5000 ⊕ www.calmac.co.uk. **Northlink Ferries.** ☎ 0845/600–0449 ⊕ www.northlinkferries.co.uk. **Western Ferries.** ☎ 01369/704452 ⊕ www.western-ferries.co.uk.

▌BUS TRAVEL

Long-distance buses usually provide the cheapest way to travel between England and Scotland; fares may be as little as a third of the rail fares for comparable trips and are cheaper if you buy in advance. However, the trip is not as comfortable as by train (no dining cart, smaller bathrooms, less spacious seats), and travel takes longer. Glasgow to London by nonstop bus takes 8 hours, 45 minutes; by train it takes about 5 hours, 30 minutes. Scotland's bus (short-haul) and coach (long-distance) network is extensive. Bus service is comprehensive in cities, less

so in country districts. Express service links main cities and towns, connecting, for example, Glasgow and Edinburgh to Inverness, Aberdeen, Perth, Skye, Ayr, Dumfries, and Carlisle; or Inverness with Aberdeen, Wick, Thurso, and Fort William. Express service is very fast, and fares are reasonable. Scottish Citylink, National Express, and Megabus are among the main operators; there are about 20 in all. The Royal Mail Post Bus provides a valuable service—generally twice-daily—in the Highlands, Argyll, and Bute and the Western Isles. All buses are nonsmoking.

The London terminal is Victoria Coach Station for National Express and Megabus, which now offers a Gold service: a sleeper coach with seats that fold down into beds.

DISCOUNTS AND DEALS
On Scottish Citylink, the Explorer Passes offer complete freedom of travel on all services throughout Scotland. Three permutations give 3 days of travel out of a 5-day period, 5 days of travel out of 10, and 8 days of travel out of 16. They're available from Scottish Citylink offices, and cost £41, £62, and £93 respectively.

National Express offers discounted seats on buses from London to more than 50 cities in the United Kingdom, including Glasgow and Aberdeen. Tickets range from £12 to £50, but only when purchased online. Megabus (order tickets online), a discount service, has similarly competitive prices between major cities throughout Scotland, including Aberdeen, Dundee, Glasgow, Inverness, and Perth.

Travelers ages 16 to 26 are eligible for 33.33% reductions with the Young Persons Coachcard (£10).

FARES AND SCHEDULES
Contact Traveline Scotland for information on all public transportation and timetables.

For town, suburban, or short-distance journeys, you buy your ticket on the bus, from a pay box, or from the driver. You need exact change. For longer journeys—for example, Glasgow–Inverness—it's usual (and a good idea; busy routes and times can book up) to reserve a seat online.

PAYING

Credit cards are accepted at most bus stations.

Bus Information Traveline Scotland.
☎ 0871/200–2233 ⊕ www.travelinescotland.com.

Bus Lines Megabus. ☎ 0900/160–0900 ⊕ www.megabus.co.uk. **National Express.** ☎ 0871/781–8181 ⊕ www.nationalexpress. com. **Royal Mail Post Bus.** ⊕ www.royalmail. com. **Scottish Citylink.** ☎ 0871/266–3333 ⊕ www.citylink.co.uk.

▌ CAR TRAVEL

If you plan to stick mostly to the cities, you will not need a car. All cities in Scotland are either so compact that most attractions are within easy walking distance of each other (Aberdeen, Dundee, Edinburgh, Inverness, and Stirling) or are accessible by an excellent local public transport system (Glasgow). And there is often good train or bus service from major cities to nearby day-trip destinations. Bus tours are a good option for day trips.

Once you leave Edinburgh, Glasgow, and the other major cities, a car will make journeys faster and much more enjoyable than trying to work out public-transportation connections to the farther-flung reaches of Scotland (though it is possible, if time consuming, to see much of the country by public transportation). A car allows you to set your own pace and visit off-the-beaten-path towns and sights most easily.

In Scotland your own driver's license is acceptable. International driving permits (IDPs) are available from the American Automobile Association and, in the United Kingdom, from the Automobile Association and Royal Automobile Club. These international permits, valid only in conjunction with your regular driver's license,

are universally recognized; having one may save you a problem with local authorities.

GASOLINE

Expect to pay a lot more for gasoline, about £5.50 a gallon (from £1.13 to £1.20 a liter) for unleaded. It's about 10p a liter higher in remote rural locations, even in the oil-producing region around Shetland. The British imperial gallon is about 20% more in volume than the U.S. gallon—approximately 4.5 liters. Pumps dispense in liters, not gallons. Most gas stations are self-service and stock unleaded, super-runleaded, and LRP (replacing four-star) plus diesel; all accept major credit cards.

PARKING

On-street parking is a bit of a lottery in Scotland. Depending on the location and time of day, the streets can be packed or empty of cars. In the cities you must pay for your on-street parking by getting a sticker from a parking machine; these machines are clearly marked with a large *P*. Make sure you have the exact change; the cost is around £3 for two hours, but can vary considerably from central to suburban zones, especially in Edinburgh and Glasgow. Put the parking sticker on the inside of your windshield. Parking lots are scattered throughout urban areas and tend to be more or less the same price as on-street parking.

The local penalty for illegally parked cars is generally £60 (£30 if paid within 14 days).

ROAD CONDITIONS

A good network of superhighways, known as motorways, and divided highways, known as dual carriageways, extends throughout Britain. In remote areas of Scotland where the motorway hasn't penetrated, travel is noticeably slower. Motorways shown with the prefix *M* are mainly two or three lanes in each direction, without any right-hand turns. These are the roads to use to cover long distances, though inevitably you'll see less of the countryside. Service areas are at most about an hour apart.

Dual carriageways, usually shown on a map as a thick red line (often with a black line in the center) and the prefix "a" followed by a number perhaps with a bracketed "t" (for example, "a304[t]"), are similar to motorways, except that right turns are sometimes permitted, and you'll find both traffic lights and traffic circles along the way. The vast network of other main roads, which typical maps show as either single red A roads, or narrower brown B roads, also numbered, are for the most part the old roads originally intended for horses and carriages. Travel along these roads is slower than on motorways, and passing is more difficult. On the other hand, you'll see much more of Scotland. The A9, Perth to Inverness, is a particularly dangerous road with the worst road accident record in Scotland because of the stopping and starting on the dual carriageway.

Minor roads (shown as yellow or white on most maps, unlettered and unnumbered) are the ancient lanes and byways of Britain, roads that are not only living history but a superb way of discovering hidden parts of Scotland. You have to drive slowly and carefully. On single-track (one-lane) roads, found in the north and west of Scotland, there's no room for two vehicles to pass, and you must use a passing place if you meet an oncoming car or tractor, or if a car behind wishes to overtake you. Never hold up traffic on single-track roads.

FROM	TO	DRIVING TIME
Edinburgh	Glasgow	1 hour
Glasgow	Stirling	¼ hour
Stirling	Dundee	1¼ hours
Dundee	Aberdeen	1½ hours
Aberdeen	Inverness	2¾ hours
Inverness	Glasgow	3½ hours
Edinburgh	Inverness	3¼ hours
Glasgow	Dundee	1¾ hours

ROADSIDE EMERGENCIES

For aid if your car breaks down, contact the 24-hour rescue numbers of either the Automobile Association or the Royal Automobile Club. If you're a member of the AAA (American Automobile Association) or another association, check your membership details before you travel; reciprocal agreements may give you free roadside aid.

Emergency Contacts in the U.K. Automobile Association (AA). ☎ 0800/887766 ⊕ www.theaa.com. Royal Automobile Club (RAC). ☎ 0844/891-3111 ⊕ www.rac.co.uk.

Emergency Contacts in the U.S. American Automobile Association (AAA). ☎ 800/564-6222 ⊕ www.aaa.com.

RULES OF THE ROAD

The most noticeable difference for most visitors is that when in Britain, you drive on the left and steer the car on the right. Give yourself time to adjust to driving on the left—especially if you pick up your car at the airport. One of the most complicated questions facing visitors to Britain is that of speed limits. In urban areas it's generally 30 mph, but it's 40 mph on some main roads, as indicated by circular red-rimmed signs. In rural areas the official limit is 60 mph on ordinary roads and 70 mph on divided highways and motorways. Traffic police can be hard on speeders, especially in urban areas. Driving while using a cell phone is illegal, and the use of seat belts is mandatory for passengers in front and back seats. Service stations and newsstands sell copies of the Highway Code (£2.50), which lists driving rules and has pictures of signs. It's also available online at ⊕ www.direct.gov.uk.

Drunk-driving laws are strictly enforced and penalties are heavy. Be aware that the legal alcohol limit is lower than in the rest of the United Kingdom: just 50 mg in every 100 ml of blood. That equates to just under a pint of beer or glass of wine for an average male, and half a pint or a small glass of wine for a woman. To be safe, avoid any alcohol if you're driving.

CAR RENTAL

You can rent any type of car you desire; however, in Scotland cars tend to be on the smaller side. Many roads are narrow, and a smaller car saves money on gas. Common models are the Renault Clio, Ford Focus, and Vauxhall Corsa. Four-wheel-drive vehicles aren't a necessity. Most cars are manual, not automatic, and come with air-conditioning, although you rarely need it in Scotland. If you want an automatic, reserve ahead.

When you're returning the car, allow an extra hour to drop it off and sort out any paperwork. If you're traveling to more than one country, make sure your rental contract permits you to take the car across borders and that your insurance policy covers you in every country you visit.

Rates in Glasgow begin at £25 a day and £130 a week for an economy car with a manual transmission and unlimited mileage. This does not include tax on car rentals, which is 20%. The busiest months are June through August, when rates may go up 30%. During this time, book at least two to four weeks in advance. Online booking is fine.

Companies frequently restrict rentals to people over age 23 and under age 75. If you are over 70, some companies require you to have your own insurance. If you are under 25, a surcharge of £23 per day plus V.A.T. will apply.

Child car seats usually cost about £10–£25 extra; you must ask for a car seat when you book, at least 48 hours in advance. The same is true for GPS. Adding one extra driver is usually included in the original rental price.

Local Agencies Arnold Clark. ☎ 0141/237–4374 ⊕ www.arnoldclarkrental.com.

Major Rental Agencies Avis. ☎ 0808/284–0014 ⊕ www.avis.co.uk. **Budget.** ☎ 0808/284–4444 ⊕ www.budget.co.uk. **Hertz.** ☎ 0843/309–3099 ⊕ www.hertz.co.uk. **National Car Rental.** ☎ 0800/121–8303 ⊕ www.nationalcar.co.uk.

Wholesalers Auto Europe. ☎ 0800/358–1229 ⊕ www.auto-europe.co.uk. **Europe by Car.** ☎ 800/223–1516 in U.S. ⊕ www.ebctravel.com. **Eurovacations.** ☎ 877/471–3876 in U.S. ⊕ www.eurovacations.com. **Kemwel.** ☎ 877/820–0668 in U.S. ⊕ www.kemwel.com.

▌ TAXI TRAVEL

In Edinburgh, Glasgow, and the larger cities, black hackney taxis—similar to those in London—with their "taxi" sign illuminated can be hailed on the street, or booked by phone (expect to pay an extra 80p charge for this service in Edinburgh). If you call a private-hire taxi from the phone book, expect a regular-looking car to pick you up. The only distinctions are that they have a taxi license and a meter stuck on the dashboard, along with an ID card for the driver. Private-hire taxis are cheaper than black hackney taxis and will pick you up only from a specific location, not off the street.

Scottish taxis are reliable, safe, and metered. In Edinburgh, meters begin at £2.10 weekdays and increase in 25p intervals. Beyond the larger cities, most communities of any size have a taxi service; your hotel will be able to supply telephone numbers.

▌ TRAIN TRAVEL

Train service within Scotland is generally run by ScotRail, one of the most efficient of Britain's service providers. Trains are modern, clean, and comfortable. Long-distance services carry buffet and refreshment cars. Scotland's rail network extends all the way to Thurso and Wick, the most northerly stations in the British Isles. Lowland services, most of which originate in Glasgow or Edinburgh, are generally fast and reliable. A shuttle makes the 50-minute trip between Glasgow and Edinburgh every 15 minutes. It's a scenic trip with plenty of rolling fields, livestock, and traditional houses along the way. Rail service throughout the country, especially the Highlands, is limited on Sunday.

CLASSES

Most trains have first-class and standard-class coaches. First-class coaches are always less crowded; they have wider seats and are often cleaner and newer than standard-class cars, and they're a lot more expensive. However, on weekends you can often upgrade from standard to first class for a fee (often £10 to £20)—ask when you book.

FARES AND SCHEDULES

The best way to find out which train to take, which station to catch it at, and what times trains travel to your destination is to call National Rail Enquiries. It's a helpful, comprehensive service that covers all Britain's rail lines. National Rail will help you choose the best train to take, and then connects you with the ticket office for that train company so that you can buy tickets. You can also check schedules and purchase tickets on its website.

Train fares vary according to class of ticket purchased, time (off-peak travel will be much cheaper), and distance traveled. Before you buy your ticket, stop at the Information Office/Travel Centre and request the lowest fare to your destination and information about any special offers. There's sometimes little difference between the cost of a one-way and round-trip ticket, and returns are valid for one month. So if you're planning on departing from and returning to the same destination, buy a round-trip fare upon your departure, rather than purchasing two separate one-way tickets.

It's often much cheaper to buy a ticket in advance than on the day of your trip (except for commuter services); the closer to the date of travel, the more expensive the ticket will be. Try to purchase tickets at least eight weeks in advance during peak-season summer travel to save money and reserve good seats. You must stick to the train you have booked (penalties can be the full price), and you need to keep

the seat reservation ticket, which is part of the valid ticket.

Check train websites, especially ScotRail, for deals. You can also check the Trainline, which sells discounted advance-purchase tickets from all train companies to all destinations in Britain.

Information National Rail Enquiries.
☎ *03457/484950* ⊕ *www.nationalrail.co.uk.* **ScotRail.** ☎ *0344/811–0141* ⊕ *www.scotrail. co.uk.* **The Trainline.** ☎ *0333/202–2222* ⊕ *www.thetrainline.com.*

PAYING

All major credit cards are accepted for train fares paid in person, online, and by phone.

RESERVATIONS

Reserving your ticket in advance is always recommended.

Tickets and rail passes do not guarantee seats on the trains. For that you need a seat reservation (essential for peak travel trains to and from Edinburgh during the summer festivals), which if made at the time of ticket purchase is usually included in the ticket price, or, if booked separately, must be paid for at a cost of £1 *per train* on your itinerary. You also need a reservation for the overnight sleeper trains.

TRAIN PASSES

Rail passes may save you money, especially if you're going to log a lot of miles. If you plan to travel by train in Scotland, consider purchasing a BritRail Pass, which also allows travel in England and Wales. All BritRail passes must be purchased in your home country; they're sold by travel agents as well as ACP, The Trainline, or Rail Europe. Rail passes do not guarantee seats on the trains, so be sure to reserve ahead. Remember that Eurail Passes aren't honored in Great Britain.

The cost of an unlimited BritRail adult pass for 4 days is $214/$323 (standard/first class); for 8 days, $384/$572; for 15 days, $572/$845; for 22 days, $715/$1,074; and for a month, $845/$1,271. The Youth Pass, for ages 16 to 25, costs $221/$325 for 4 days; $308/$458 for 8 days; $458/$676 for 15 days; $572/$859 for 22 days; and $676/$1,017 for one month. The Senior Pass, for those over 60, costs $265/$341 for 4 days; $384/$486 for 8 days; $572/$718 for 15 days; $715/$913 for 22 days; and $845/$1,081 for one month. The Scottish Freedom Pass allows transportation on all Caledonian Mac-Brayne and Strathclyde ferries in addition to major bus links and the Glasgow underground. You can travel any 4 days in an 8-day period for $229 or any 8 days in a 15-day period for $308.

Information ACP Rail International.
☎ 866/938–7245 ⊕ www.acprail.com. **BritRail Travel.** ⊕ www.britrail.com. **Rail Europe.** ☎ 0844/848–4078, 800/622–8600 in U.S. ⊕ www.raileurope.com.

FROM ENGLAND

There are two main rail routes to Scotland from the south of England. The first, the west-coast main line, runs from London Euston to Glasgow Central; it takes 5½ hours to make the 400-mile trip to central Scotland, and service is frequent and reliable. Useful for daytime travel to the Scottish Highlands is the direct train to Stirling and Aviemore, terminating at Inverness. For a restful route to the Scottish Highlands, take the overnight sleeper service, with sleeping carriages. It runs from London Euston, departing in late evening, to Perth, Stirling, Aviemore, and Inverness, where it arrives the following morning. The new *Caledonian Sleeper* operator as of 2015, Serco Abellio, has introduced some marginal improvements to the long-established service, although new trains, carriages and berths are not due until 2018.

The east-coast main line from London King's Cross to Edinburgh provides the quickest trip to the Scottish capital. Between 8 am and 6 pm there are 16 trains to Edinburgh, 3 of them through to Aberdeen. Limited-stop expresses like the *Flying Scotsman* make the 393-mile London–to–Edinburgh journey in around four hours. Connecting services to most parts of Scotland—particularly the Western Highlands—are often better from Edinburgh than from Glasgow.

Trains from elsewhere in England are good: regular service connects Birmingham, Manchester, Liverpool, and Bristol with Glasgow and Edinburgh. From Harwich (the port of call for ships from Holland, Germany, and Denmark), you can travel to Glasgow via Manchester. But it's faster to change at Peterborough for the east-coast main line to Edinburgh.

SCENIC ROUTES

Although many routes in Scotland run through extremely attractive countryside, several stand out: from Glasgow to Oban via Loch Lomond; to Fort William and Mallaig via Rannoch (ferry connection to Skye); from Edinburgh to Inverness via the Forth Bridge and Perth; from Inverness to Kyle of Lochalsh and to Wick; and from Inverness to Aberdeen.

A private train, the *Royal Scotsman,* does all-inclusive scenic tours, with banquets en route. This is a luxury experience: you choose itineraries from two nights (£2,420) to seven nights (£9,200) per person.

Special Trains Caledonian Sleeper.
☎ 0330/060–0500, 141/ 555–0888 ⊕ www. sleeper.scot. **The Royal Scotsman.** ☎ 0845/077–2222 in the U.K., 800/524–2420 in the U.S. ⊕ www.royalscotsman.com.

ESSENTIALS

▌ ACCOMMODATIONS

Your choices in Scotland range from small, local B&Bs to large, elegant hotels—some of the chain variety. Bed-and-breakfasts tend to be less expensive than large hotels because many are spare rooms in spacious homes. Proprietors keep costs down and guests get a more personal, Scottish touch. Accommodation can seem expensive because the pound has been strong against the dollar, but ongoing economic stagnation means there are special deals if you look. For example, some lodgings offer discounted rates for stays of two nights or longer.

If you haven't booked ahead, you're not likely to be stranded. Even in the height of the season—July and August—hotel occupancy runs at about 80%. However, your choice of accommodations will be extremely limited if you show up somewhere during a festival or golf tournament. Your best bet will be to try for a room in a nearby village.

To secure your first choice, reserve in advance. One option is to reserve through local tourist information centers, making use of their "book-a-bed-ahead" services. Telephone bookings made from home should be confirmed by email or fax. Country hotels expect you to check in by about 6 pm.

Be sure you understand the hotel's cancellation policy. Some places allow you to cancel without any kind of penalty; others, particularly B&Bs, require you to cancel a week in advance or penalize you.

Smoking is banned in all indoor public spaces in Scotland, and this includes hotel rooms. Most hotels allow children under a certain age to stay in their parents' room at no extra charge, but others charge for them as extra adults; find out the cutoff age for discounts.

VisitScotland classifies and grades accommodations using a simple star system. The greater the number of stars, the greater the number of facilities and the more luxurious they are.

The lodgings we list are the cream of the crop in each price category. Unless otherwise noted, all lodgings listed have a private bathroom, a room phone, and a television. When pricing accommodations, always ask what's included. Many hotels and most guesthouses and B&Bs include a breakfast with the basic room rate. Meal-plan information appears at the end of a review. *Prices in the reviews are the lowest cost of a standard double room in high season, including 20% V.A.T. Hotel reviews have been shortened. For full reviews, visit Fodors.com*

APARTMENT AND HOUSE RENTALS

Rental houses and flats (apartments) are becoming more popular lodging choices for travelers visiting Scotland, particularly for those staying in one place for more than a few days. Some places may rent only by the week. Prices can be cheaper than a hotel (though perhaps not less than a bed-and-breakfast), and the space and comfort are much better than what you'd find in a typical hotel.

In the country your chances of finding a small house to rent are good; in the city you're more likely to find a flat (apartment) to let (rent). Either way, your best bet for finding these rentals is online. Individuals and large consortiums can own these properties, so it just depends on what you're looking for. Citybase Apartments is a handy resource for finding an apartment, from single studios to large apartments suitable for families and groups. Dreamhouse Apartments has swanky, serviced flats in Edinburgh, Glasgow, and Aberdeen. The National Trust for Scotland has many unique properties, from island cottages to castles, for rent.

LOCAL DO'S AND TABOOS

GREETINGS
Although many Scots are fantastic talkers, they're less enthusiastic with greetings on the physical front. If you're in less familiar company, a handshake is more appreciated than a kiss or hug.

SIGHTSEEING
When you are visiting houses of worship, modest attire is appreciated, though you will see shorts and even bared midriffs. Photographs are welcome in churches, outside of services. Shorts and other close-fitting attire are allowed just about anywhere else at any time, weather permitting; these days locals tend not to cover up as much as they used to.

It's the same with food; Scots eat and drink just about anywhere, and much of the time they do it standing up or even walking.

ETIQUETTE
In Scotland it's rude to walk away from conversation, even if it's with someone you don't know. If you're at a pub, keep in mind that it's very important to buy a round of drinks if you're socializing with a group of people. You don't simply buy your own drink; you buy a drink for all of the people you're there with, and those people do the same. It can make for a very foggy evening and public drunkenness, especially on Friday and Saturday nights. Conversational topics that are considered taboo are money matters; the Scots are private about their finances. You should give up your seats for elderly people or pregnant women without a second thought. Hold the door open for someone who is leaving or entering the same building as you. Say please and thank you.

Driving etiquette is carefully observed, too; be courteous and allow people to pass. Jaywalking isn't rude or illegal, but it's much safer to cross with the lights, especially if traffic is coming from a direction you might not be used to.

As for waiting in lines and moving through crowds, put your best foot forward. The Scots are very polite and you'll be noticed (and not in a good way) if you're not.

OUT ON THE TOWN
People may dress up for a special restaurant or for clubbing, but other people will be casual. Some restaurants and clubs frown on jeans and sneakers.

If you're visiting a family home, a simple bouquet of flowers is a welcome gift. If you're invited for a meal, bringing a bottle of wine is appropriate, as is some candy for the children. To thank a host for hospitality, either a phone call or thank-you card is always appreciated.

DOING BUSINESS
Punctuality is of prime importance, so call ahead if you anticipate a late arrival. Spouses do not generally attend business dinners, unless specifically invited. If you ask someone to dine, it's usually assumed that you'll pick up the tab. However, if you're the visitor, your host may insist on paying. Nonetheless, it's always polite to offer to pay.

LANGUAGE
The Scots language, which borrows from Scandinavian, Dutch, French, and Gaelic, survives in various forms, with each region having its own dialect. In the northeast they speak Doric, while the Shetland and Orkney "tongue" is influenced by the now-extinct Norn. The Gaelic language, the indigenous language of those from the Western Isles and Highlands, has been given a new lease of life. Many primary schools in the region are teaching a new generation of Gaelic speakers. The language has its own TV channel, BBC Alba, and is being promoted in a huge signage campaign. Otherwise, Scots speak English often with a strong accent (which may be hard for nonnative Brits and Americans to understand), but your ear will soon come to terms with it.

International Agencies Barclay International Group. ☎ 800/845-6636 ⊕ www.barclayweb.com. **Citybase Apartments.** ☎ 0203/701-4966 ⊕ www.citybaseapartments.com. **Dreamhouse Apartments.** ✉ 4 Woodside Pl., Glasgow ☎ 0845/226-0232 ⊕ www.dreamhouseapartments.com. **Forgetaway.** ⊕ www.forgetaway.com. **Home Away.** ⊕ www.homeaway.com. **Interhome.** ☎ 800/882-6864 in the U.S. ⊕ www.interhome.us. **Knight Residence.** ✉ 12 Lauriston St., Edinburgh ☎ 0131/622-8120 ⊕ www.theknightresidence.co.uk. **Villas & Apartments Abroad.** ☎ 212/213-6435 ⊕ www.vaanyc.com.

Local Contacts National Trust for Scotland. ☎ 0131/458-0303, 866/211-7573 in U.S. ⊕ www.nts.org.uk.

BED-AND-BREAKFASTS

Common throughout Scotland, B&Bs are a special British tradition and the backbone of budget travel. Prices average about £50 to £110 per night, depending on the region and the time of year. They're usually in a family home, occasionally don't have private bathrooms, and usually offer only breakfast. More upscale B&Bs, along the line of American B&Bs or small inns, can be found in Edinburgh and Glasgow especially, but in other parts of Scotland as well. Guest houses are a slightly larger, somewhat more luxurious version. All provide a glimpse of everyday life. Note that local tourist offices can book a B&B for you; there may be a small charge for this service.

Reservation Services BedandBreakfast.com. ☎ 512/322-2710, 844/271-6829 ⊕ www.bedandbreakfast.com. **Sawdays.** ☎ 01172 /047810 ⊕ www.sawdays.co.uk. **UK Bed and Breakfast Accommodation.** ⊕ www.bedandbreakfasts.co.uk.

FARMHOUSE AND CROFTING HOLIDAYS

A popular option for families with children is a farmhouse holiday, combining the freedom of B&B accommodations with the hospitality of Scottish family life. You'll need a car if you're staying deep in the country, though. Information

is available from VisitBritain or VisitScotland, from Scottish Farmhouse Holidays, and from the Farm Stay UK.

Contacts Farmstay UK. ☎ 024/7669-6909 ⊕ www.farmstayuk.co.uk. **Scottish Farmhouse Holidays.** ☎ 01334/476370 ⊕ www.scottishfarmhouseholidays.co.uk.

HOME EXCHANGES

With a direct home exchange you stay in someone else's home while they stay in yours. Some outfits also deal with vacation homes, so you're not actually staying in someone's full-time residence, just their vacant weekend place. There can be yearly fees for exchange services of around $100 a year, so check.

Exchange Clubs HomeExchange.com. ☎ 800/877-8723 ⊕ www.homeexchange.com. **HomeLink International.** ☎ 800/638-3841 in U.S. ⊕ www.homelink.org.

HOTELS

Large hotels vary in style and price. Many lean toward Scottish themes when it comes to decoration, but you can expect the same quality and service from a chain hotel wherever you are in the world. Keep in mind that hotel rooms in Scotland are smaller than what you'd find in the United States. Today hotels of all sizes are trying to be greener, and many newer chains are striving for government environmental awards. Discounted rooms are another trend, as are discounts for room upgrades.

In the countryside some older hotels are former castles or converted country homes. These types of hotels are full of character and charm but can be very expensive, and they may not have elevators. Normally they have all the amenities, if not more, of their urban counterparts. Their locations may be so remote that you must eat on the premises, which may be costly.

Some small regional chains operate in Scotland that are not internationally known. Apex (in Edinburgh, Glasgow, Dundee, and London) is modish and has Scandinavian-inspired bedrooms; Malmaison (in Aberdeen, Dundee, Edinburgh, and Glasgow) is luxury on a budget; Hotel du Vin (Glasgow, St. Andrews and Edinburgh), with its chic bistros, sumptuous bedding, and original art, may blow the budget.

Hotel Contacts

Apex Hotels. ⊕ *www.apexhotels.co.uk.*
Hotel du Vin. ⊕ *www.hotelduvin.com.*
Malmaison. ⊕ *www.malmaison.com.*

▌ COMMUNICATIONS

INTERNET

All newer laptops operate equally well on 110 and 220 volts and so require only an adapter. Never plug your computer into any socket without first asking about surge protection: although Scotland is computer-friendly, few hotels and B&Bs outside the major cities have built-in current stabilizers. It's worthwhile to purchase a surge protector in the United Kingdom that plugs into the socket.

All hotels and many B&Bs have facilities for computer users, such as dedicated computer rooms and wired or wireless connections for Internet access. Most cafés offer free Wi-Fi access.

PHONES

The good news is that you can now make a direct-dial telephone call from virtually any point on Earth. The bad news? You can't always do so cheaply. Calling from a hotel is almost always the most expensive option; hotels usually add huge surcharges to all calls, particularly international ones.

When you're calling anywhere in Great Britain from the United States, the country code is 44. When dialing a Scottish or British number from abroad, drop the initial 0 from the local area code. For instance, if you're calling Edinburgh Castle from New York City, dial 011 (the international code), 44 (the Great Britain country code), 131 (the Edinburgh city code without the initial 0), and then 225–9846 (the number proper).

CALLING WITHIN SCOTLAND

There are three types of public pay phones: those that accept only coins, those that accept only phone cards, and those that take British Telecom (BT) phone cards and credit cards. For coin-only phones, insert coins *before* dialing (minimum charge is 60p). Sometimes phones have a "press on answer" (POA) button, which you press when the caller answers.

Calls from residential phones are charged according to the time of day: evenings, nighttime, and weekend rates are cheaper. Daytime rates—weekdays 7 am–7 pm—are 4p per minute for a local call and 8p for a national call. A minimum fee of 60p (including a 40p connection charge) applies to calls from BT public payphones, which will purchase two 10p units of time. Thereafter call time is purchased in 10p units. This excludes calls to free phone services. A daytime call to the United States will cost 24p a minute on a regular phone (evenings 7 pm–7 am, and weekends are a few pence cheaper), and £2 a minute on a pay phone.

To call a number with the same area code as the number from which you are dialing, omit the area-code digits when you dial. For long-distance calls within Britain, dial the area code (which usually begins with 01), followed by the telephone number. In provincial areas the dialing codes for nearby towns are often posted in phone booths.

To call the operator, dial 100; directory inquiries (information), 118–500; international directory inquiries, 118–505.

In Scotland cell phone numbers, the 0800 toll-free code, and local-rate 0345 numbers do not have a 1 after the initial 0, nor do many premium-rate numbers, for example 0891, and special-rate numbers, for example 08705.

Numbers that start with 0800, 0808, or national information numbers that start with 0345 and 0845 are free when called from a U.K. BT landline: other telephone line providers like Virgin charge other rates, and they cost anywhere from 15p to £1 a minute when called from a cellular phone. Additionally, 0870 numbers are *not* toll-free numbers; in fact, numbers beginning with 0871 or the 0900 prefix are premium-rate numbers, and it costs extra to call them. The amount varies and is usually relatively small when dialed from within the country but can be excessive when dialed from outside the United Kingdom. Many businesses, especially those offering low-cost services (such as Ryanair or Megabus) communicate with customers via their websites. If they do have a customer services phone number, it's costly to use it. There are some handy cellphone Android/iPhone Apps (including ⊕ *weq4u.co.uk*) that help you save money on premium rate number calls.

CALLING OUTSIDE SCOTLAND
The country code for the United States is 1.

To make international calls *from* Scotland, dial 00 for international access, then the country code, area code, and number. For the international operator, credit card, or collect calls, dial 155.

Access Codes AT&T Direct. ☏ *0800/331–0500* ⊕ *www.att.com.* **MCI WorldPhone.** ☏ *0800/955–0925* ⊕ *consumer.mci.com.* **Sprint International Access.** ☏ *0808/234–6616* ⊕ *www.sprint.com.*

CALLING CARDS
You can purchase BT (British Telecom) phone cards for use on public phones from shops, post offices, and newsstands. They're ideal for longer calls and come in values of £10 and £20. An indicator panel on the phone shows the number of units you've used; at the end of your call the card is returned. Where credit cards are taken, slide the card through, as indicated. Beware of buying cards that require you to dial a free phone number; some of these are not legitimate. It's better to get a BT card.

MOBILE PHONES
If you have a multiband phone (some countries use different frequencies than what's used in the United States) and your service provider uses the world-standard GSM network (as do T-Mobile, Cingular, and Verizon), you can probably use your phone abroad. Roaming fees can be steep, however: 99¢ a minute is considered reasonable. And overseas you normally pay the toll charges for incoming calls. It's almost always cheaper to send a text message than to make a call, since text messages have a very low set fee (often less than 5¢).

If you just want to make local calls, consider buying a new SIM card (note that your provider may have to unlock your phone for you to use a different SIM card) and a prepaid-service plan in the destination. You'll then have a local number and can make local calls at local rates.

Cell phones are getting less and less expensive to purchase. Rather than renting one, it may be cheaper to buy one to use while you're abroad. Rates run from as low as £20 a month for unlimited calls with a pay-as-you-go card.

Contacts Cellular Abroad. ☏ *800/287–5072* ⊕ *www.cellularabroad.com.* **Mobal.** ☏ *888/888–9162* ⊕ *www.mobalrental.com.*

∎ CUSTOMS AND DUTIES

You're always allowed to bring goods of a certain value back home without having to pay any duty or import tax. But there's a limit on the amount of tobacco and liquor you can bring back duty-free, and some countries have separate limits for perfumes; for exact figures, check with your customs department. The values of so-called duty-free goods are included in these amounts. When you shop abroad, save all your receipts, as customs inspectors may ask to see them as well as the items you purchased. If the total value of your goods is more than the duty-free limit, you'll have to pay a tax (most often a flat percentage) on the value of everything beyond that limit.

Check ahead with the Department for Environment, Food and Rural Affairs if you want to bring a pet into Scotland.

Information in Scotland Department for Environment, Food and Rural Affairs. ☎ *03459/335577* ⊕ *www.defra.gov.uk.* **HM Revenue & Customs.** ⊕ *www.gov.uk.*

U.S. Information U.S. Customs and Border Protection. ⊕ *www.cbp.gov.*

▌ EATING OUT

Today the traditional Scottish restaurant offers more than fish-and-chips, fried sausage, and black pudding. Instead you'll find the freshest of scallops, organic salmon, wild duck, and Aberdeen Angus beef, as well as locally grown vegetables and fruits. There's also a wide array of international restaurants: Chinese, French, Greek, Indian, Italian, Japanese, and Mexican (to name but a few) can be truly exceptional.

Places like Glasgow, Edinburgh, and Aberdeen have sophisticated restaurants at various price levels; of these, the more notable tend to open only in the evening. But fabulous restaurants are popping up in the smaller villages as well. Dining in Scotland can be an experience for all the senses. These meals are rarely cheap, so don't forget your credit card.

Note that most pubs do not have a table service, so go to the bar and order your meal. You're not expected to tip the bartender, but you are expected to tip

restaurant waitstaff by leaving 10% to 15% of the tab on the table.

There are a couple of vegetarian options on every menu, and most restaurants, particularly pubs that serve food, welcome families with young children. Smoking is banned from pubs, clubs, and restaurants throughout Britain.

The restaurants we review in this book are the cream of the crop in each price category. Properties are assigned price categories based on dinner prices. *Prices in the reviews are the average cost of a main course at dinner or, if dinner is not served, at lunch.*

DISCOUNTS AND DEALS

Many city restaurants have good pretheater meals from 5 to 7 pm. Lunch deals can also save you money; some main courses can be nearly half the price of dinner entrées. All supermarkets sell a large variety of high-quality sandwiches, wraps, and salads at reasonable prices. If the weather's dry, opt for a midday picnic.

MEALS AND MEALTIMES

To start the day with a full stomach, try a traditional Scottish breakfast of bacon and eggs served with sausage, fried mushrooms, and tomatoes, and usually fried bread or potato scones. Most places also serve kippers (smoked herring). All this is in addition to juice, porridge, cereal, toast, and other bread products.

"All-day" meal places are becoming prevalent. Lunch is usually served 12:30 to 2:30. A few places serve high tea—masses of cakes, bread and butter, and jam—around 2:30 to 4:30. Dinner is fairly early, around 5 to 8.

Familiar fast-food chains are often more expensive than home-cooked meals in local establishments, where large servings of British comfort food—fish-and-chips, stuffed baked potatoes, and sandwiches—are served. In upscale restaurants cutting costs can be as simple as requesting *tap* water; "water" means a bottle of mineral water that could cost up to £5.

Unless otherwise noted, the restaurants listed in this guide are open daily for lunch and dinner.

PAYING

Credit cards are widely accepted at most types of restaurants. Some restaurants exclude service charges from the printed menu (which the law obliges them to display outside), then add 10% to 15% to the check, or else stamp "service not included" along the bottom, in which case you should add the 10% to 15% yourself. Just don't pay twice for service—unscrupulous restaurateurs add a service charge but leave the total on the credit-card slip blank.

For guidelines on tipping, see Tipping below.

PUBS

A common misconception among visitors to Scotland is that pubs are cozy bars. But they are also gathering places, conversation zones, even restaurants. Pubs are, generally speaking, where people go to have a drink, meet their friends, and catch up on one another's lives. Traditionally, pub hours are open until midnight, with last orders called about 20 minutes before closing time. In the bigger cities pubs can stay open until 1 am or later.

Some pubs are child-friendly, but others have restricted hours for children. If a pub serves food, it will generally allow children in during the day. Some are stricter than others, though, and will not admit anyone younger than 18. If in doubt, ask the bartender. Family-friendly pubs tend to be packed with kids, parents, and all of their accoutrements.

RESERVATIONS AND DRESS

It's a good idea to make a reservation if you can. We mention them specifically only when reservations are essential (there's no other way you'll ever get a table) or when they are not accepted. For popular restaurants, book as far ahead as you can (often 30 days), and reconfirm as soon as you arrive. Large parties should always call ahead to check the reservations policy. We mention dress only when men are required to wear a jacket or a jacket and tie.

Online reservation services make it easy to book a table before you even leave home. Open Table has listings in many Scottish cities.

Contact OpenTable. ⊕ *www.opentable.co.uk.*

WINES, BEER, AND SPIRITS

Bars and pubs typically sell two kinds of beer: lager is light in color, very carbonated, and served cold, while ale is dark, less fizzy, and served just below room temperature. You may also come across a pub serving "real ales," which are handdrawn, very flavorful beers from smaller breweries. These traditionally produced real ales have a fervent following; check out the Campaign for Real Ale's website, ⊕ *www.camra.org.uk.*

You can order Scotland's most famous beverage—whisky (most definitely spelled without an *e*)—at any local pub. All pubs serve single-malt and blended whiskies. It's also possible to tour numerous distilleries, where you can sample a dram and purchase a bottle for the trip home. Most distilleries are concentrated in Speyside and Islay, but there are notable ones on Orkney and Skye.

The legal drinking age in Scotland is 18.

▌ ECOTOURISM

Ecotourism is an emerging trend in the United Kingdom. The Shetland Environmental Agency Ltd. runs the Green Tourism Business Scheme (GTBS), a program that evaluates sites and lodgings in England, Scotland, and Wales and gives them a gold, silver, or bronze rating according to their sustainability. You can find a list of green hotels, B&Bs, apartments, and other properties on the GTBS website. Also check out the VisitBritain and VisitScotland websites, which have information and tips about green travel in Britain.

Contact Green Tourism Business Scheme. ☎ *01738/632162* ⊕ *www.green-business.co.uk.*

ELECTRICITY

The electrical current in Scotland, as in the rest of Great Britain, is 220–240 volts (in line with the rest of Europe), 50 cycles alternating current (AC); wall outlets take three-pin plugs, and shaver sockets take two round, oversize prongs.

Consider making a small investment in a universal adapter, which has several types of plugs in one lightweight, compact unit. Most laptops and mobile-phone chargers are dual voltage (i.e., they operate equally well on 110 and 220 volts), so require only an adapter. These days the same is true of small appliances such as hair dryers. Don't use 110-volt outlets marked "for shavers only" for high-wattage appliances such as hair dryers.

EMERGENCIES

If you need to report an emergency, dial 999 for police, fire, or ambulance. Be prepared to give the telephone number you're calling from. You can get 24-hour medical treatment at British hospitals, but as in U.S. hospitals you should expect to wait for treatment. Treatment from the National Health Service is free to British citizens; as a foreigner, you will be billed after the fact for your care. (Prices are nowhere near what they are in the United States.)

General Emergency Contact Ambulance, fire, police. ☎ 999.

U.S. Embassies American Consulate General. ✉ 3 Regent Terr., Calton ☎ 0131/556–8315 ⊕ edinburgh.usconsulate. gov. **U.S. Embassy.** ✉ 24 Grosvenor Sq., London ☎ 020/7499–9000 ⊕ london. usembassy.gov.

HEALTH

SPECIFIC ISSUES IN SCOTLAND

If you take prescription drugs, keep a supply in your carry-on luggage and make a list of all your prescriptions to keep on file at home while you are abroad. You will not be able to renew a U.S. prescription

at a pharmacy in Britain. Prescriptions are accepted only if issued by a U.K.-registered physician.

If you're traveling in the Highlands and islands in summer, pack some midge repellent and antihistamine cream to reduce swelling: the Highland midge is a force to be reckoned with. Check ⊕ www. midgeforecast.co.uk for updates on these biting pests.

OVER-THE-COUNTER REMEDIES

Over-the-counter medications in Scotland are similar to those in the United States, with a few significant differences. Medications are sold in boxes rather than bottles, and are sold in very small amounts—usually no more than 12 pills per package. There are also fewer brands than you're likely to be used to—you can, for example, find aspirin, but usually only one kind in a store. You can buy generic ibuprofen or a popular European brand of ibuprofen, Nurofen, which is sold everywhere. Tylenol is not sold in the United Kingdom, but its main ingredient, acetaminophen, is—although, confusingly, it's called paracetamol.

Drugstores are generally called pharmacies, but sometimes referred to as chemists. The biggest drugstore chain in the country is Boots, which has outlets in all but the smallest towns. If you're in a rural area, look for shops marked with a sign of a green cross.

Supermarkets and newsagents all usually have a small supply of cold and headache medicines, often behind the cash register. As in the United States, large supermarkets will have a bigger supply.

MEDICAL INSURANCE AND ASSISTANCE

Consider buying trip insurance with medical-only coverage. Neither Medicare nor some private insurers cover medical expenses anywhere outside of the United States. Medical-only policies typically reimburse you for medical care (excluding that related to preexisting conditions) and hospitalization abroad, and provide for evacuation. You still have to pay the bills and await reimbursement from the insurer, though.

Another option is to sign up with a medical-evacuation assistance company. A membership in one of these companies gets you doctor referrals, emergency evacuation or repatriation, 24-hour hotlines for medical consultation, and other assistance. International SOS Assistance Emergency and AirMed International provide evacuation services and medical referrals. MedjetAssist offers medical evacuation.

Medical Assistance Companies
AirMed International. ⊕ *www.airmed.com.*
International SOS. ⊕ *www.internationalsos. com.* **MedjetAssist.** ⊕ *www.medjetassist.com.*

Medical-Only Insurers International Medical Group. ⊕ *www.imglobal.com.*
Wallach & Company. ☎ *800/237–6615, 540/687–3166* ⊕ *www.wallach.com.*

SHOTS AND MEDICATIONS

No particular shots are necessary for visiting Scotland from the United States.

Health Warnings National Centers for Disease Control & Prevention (*CDC*). ☎ *800/232–4636 international travelers' health line* ⊕ *wwwnc.cdc.gov/travel.* **World Health Organization** (*WHO*). ⊕ *www.who.int.*

▌ HOURS OF OPERATION

Banks are open weekdays 9 to 5. Some banks have extended hours on Thursday evening, and a few are open on Saturday morning. The major airports operate 24-hour banking services all week.

Service stations are at regular intervals on motorways and are usually open 24 hours a day, though stations elsewhere are open 7 am to 9 pm; in rural areas many close at 6 pm and on Sunday.

Pharmacies are usually open Monday through Saturday from 9 to 5 or 5:30. At other times, most larger communities will have a supermarket with extended hours that has a pharmacy on the premises, or a rotation system for pharmacists on call (check any pharmacy window for the number to call). In rural areas doctors often dispense medicines themselves. In an emergency the police should be able to locate a pharmacist.

Most museums in cities and larger towns are open daily, although some may be closed on Sunday and Monday. In smaller villages museums are often open when there are visitors around—even late on summer evenings—but closed in poor weather, when visitors are unlikely; there's often a contact phone number on the door.

Usual business hours are Monday through Saturday 9 to 5 or 5:30. In small villages many shops close for lunch. Department stores in large cities and many supermarkets even in smaller towns stay open for late-night shopping (usually until 7:30 or 8) one or more days a week. Apart from some newsstands and small food stores, many shops close Sunday except in larger towns and cities, where main shopping malls remain open. Big supermarkets like Asda and Tesco are open around the clock.

HOLIDAYS

The following days are public holidays in Scotland; note that the dates for England and Wales are slightly different. Ne'er Day and a day to recover (January 1–2), Good Friday, May Day (first Monday in May), Spring Bank Holiday (last Monday in May), Summer Bank Holiday (first Monday in August), and Christmas (December 25–26).

▌ MAIL

Stamps may be bought from post offices (open weekdays 9 to 5:30, Saturday 9 to noon), from stamp machines outside post offices, and from newsstands. Mailboxes—known as post- or letter boxes—are painted bright red; large tubular ones are set on the edge of sidewalks, and smaller boxes are set into post-office walls. Allow at least four days for a letter or postcard to reach the United States by airmail. Surface mail service can take up to four or five weeks.

Airmail letters and postcards to the United States cost £1 (under 10 grams) or £1.33 (under 20 grams). Within the United Kingdom first-class letters cost 63p, second-class letters and postcards 54p. The Royal Mail website is ⊕ *www. royalmail.com.*

If you're uncertain where you'll be staying, you can arrange to have your mail sent to the nearest American Express. The service is free to cardholders; all others pay a small fee. You can also collect letters at any post office by addressing them to *poste restante* at the post office you nominate. In Edinburgh a convenient central office is St. James Centre Post Office, St. James Centre, Edinburgh, EH1 3SR, Scotland.

SHIPPING PACKAGES

Most department stores and retail outlets can arrange to ship your goods home. You should check your insurance for coverage of possible damage. If you want to ship goods yourself, use one of the overnight postal services, such as Federal Express, DHL, or TNT.

To find the nearest branch providing overnight mail services, contact the following agencies.

Express Services
DHL. ☎ *0844/248–0844* ⊕ *www.dhl.co.uk.*
FedEx. ☎ *08456/070809* ⊕ *www.fedex.com.*
TNT. ☎ *0800/100600* ⊕ *www.tnt.com.*

▌ MONEY

Prices can seem high in Scotland largely because of the exchange rate, though this has improved because of the economic downturn. However, travelers do get some breaks: national museums are free, and staying in a B&B or renting a city apartment brings down lodging costs. *The chart below gives some ideas of the kinds of prices you can pay for day-to-day life.*

ITEM	AVERAGE COST
Cup of Coffee	£2.75
Glass of Wine	£4
Pint of Beer	£3.60
Sandwich	£3.50
One-Mile Taxi Ride Edinburgh	£3.55
Newspaper	60p–£3

Prices throughout this guide are given for adults. Substantially reduced fees are almost always available for children, students, and senior citizens.

■ TIP➔ Banks never have every foreign currency on hand, and it may take as long as a week to order. If you're planning to exchange funds before leaving home, don't wait until the last minute.

ATMS AND BANKS

ATMs are available throughout Scotland at banks and numerous other locations such as railway stations, gas stations, and department stores. Three banks with many branches are Lloyds, Halifax, and the Royal Bank of Scotland.

Your own bank will probably charge a fee for using ATMs abroad; the foreign bank you use may also charge a fee. Nevertheless, you'll usually get a better rate of exchange at an ATM than you will at a currency-exchange office or even when changing money in a bank. And extracting funds as you need them is a safer option than carrying around a large amount of cash.

■ TIP➜ **PINs with more than four digits are not recognized at ATMs. If yours has five or more, remember to change it before you leave.**

ATM Locations **MasterCard.** ☏ *0800/964767* ⊕ *www.mastercard.com.* **Visa Plus.** ☏ *0800/891725* ⊕ *www.visadps.com.*

CREDIT CARDS

Credit cards are accepted almost everywhere and for everything (except for bus and taxi fares), as are debit cards. Most cards issued in Europe are now chip-and-PIN credit cards that store user information on a computer chip embedded in the card. In the United States, all credit cards were required to switch to "chip-and-signature" cards in 2015. While European cardholders are expected to know and use their PIN number for all transactions rather than signing a charge slip, U.S. chip-and-signature cards usually still require users to sign the charge slip. (Very few U.S. issuers offer a PIN along with their cards, except for cash withdrawals at an ATM, though this is expected to change in the future.) The good news: unlike the old magnetic-strip cards that gave American travelers in Europe trouble at times, the new chip-and-signature cards are accepted at many more locations, including in many cases at machines that sell train tickets, machines that process automated motorway tolls at unmanned booths, and automated gas stations—even without a signature or PIN. The bad news: not all European locations will accept the chip-and-signature cards, and you won't know until you try, so it's a good idea to carry enough cash to cover small purchases.

Visa and MasterCard are more widely accepted than American Express and Diners Club; it is a good idea to travel with a picture ID in case you're asked for it.

CURRENCY AND EXCHANGE

Britain's currency is the pound sterling, which is divided into 100 pence (100p). Bills (called notes) are issued in the values of £50, £20, £10, and £5. Coins are issued in the values of £2, £1, 50p, 20p, 10p, 5p, 2p, and 1p. Scottish coins are the same as English ones, but have a thistle on them. Scottish notes have the same face values as English notes, and English notes are interchangeable with them in Scotland.

At this writing, the exchange rate was U.S. $1.55 to the pound.

Google does currency conversion. Just type in the amount you want to convert and an explanation of how you want it converted (e.g., "14 Swiss francs in dollars"). Oanda.com also allows you to print out a handy table with the current day's conversion rates. XE.com is another good currency conversion website.

Conversion Sites **Google.** ⊕ *www.google. com.* **Oanda.com.** ⊕ *www.oanda.com.* **XE.com.** ⊕ *www.xe.com.*

▌ PACKING

Travel light. Porters are more or less extinct these days (and very expensive where you can find them). Also, if you're traveling around the country by car, train, or bus, large, heavy luggage is more of a burden than anything else. Save a little packing space for things you might buy while traveling.

In Scotland casual clothes are the norm, and very few hotels or restaurants insist on jackets and ties for men in the evening. It is, however, handy to have something semi-dressy for going out to dinner or the theater. For summer, lightweight clothing is usually adequate, except in the evening, when you'll need a jacket or sweater. A waterproof coat or parka and an umbrella are essential at any time of year. You can't go wrong with comfortable walking shoes, especially when you're climbing Edinburgh's steep urban hills or visiting Glasgow's massive museums. Drip-dry and wrinkle-resistant fabrics are a good bet because only the most prestigious hotels have speedy laundering or dry-cleaning service. Bring insect repellent if you plan to hike.

Some visitors to Scotland appear to think it necessary to adopt Scottish dress. It's not unless you've been invited to a wedding, and even then it's optional. Scots themselves do not wear tartan ties or Balmoral "bunnets" (caps), and only an enthusiastic minority prefers the kilt for everyday wear.

▌PASSPORTS AND VISAS

U.S. citizens need only a valid passport to enter Great Britain for stays of up to six months. Travelers should be prepared to show sufficient funds to support and accommodate themselves while in Britain (credit cards will usually suffice for this) and to show a return or onward ticket. If you're within six months of your passport's expiration date, renew it before you leave—nearly extinct passports are not strictly banned, but they make immigration officials anxious, and may cause you problems. Health certificates are not required for travel in Scotland.

If only one parent is traveling with a child under 17 and his or her last name differs from the child's, then he or she will need a signed and notarized letter from the parent with the same last name as the child authorizing permission to travel. Airlines, ferries, and trains have different policies for children traveling alone, so if your child must travel alone, make sure to check with the carrier prior to purchasing your child's ticket.

U.S. Passport Information U.S. Department of State. ☎ 877/487–2778 ⊕ www.travel.state. gov/passport.

▌RESTROOMS

Most cities, towns, and villages have public restrooms, indicated by signposts to the "WC," "toilets," or "public conveniences." They vary hugely in cleanliness. You'll often have to pay a small amount (usually 30p) to enter; a request for payment usually indicates a high standard of cleanliness. Gas stations, called petrol stations, usually have restrooms (to which the above comments also apply). In towns and cities, department stores, hotels, restaurants, and pubs are usually your best bets for reasonable standards of hygiene.

▌SAFETY

Overall, Scotland is a very safe country to travel in, but be a cautious traveler and keep your cash, passport, credit cards, and tickets close to you or in a hotel safe. Don't agree to carry anything for strangers. It's a good idea to distribute your cash, credit cards, IDs, and other valuables between a deep front pocket, an inside jacket or vest pocket, and a hidden money pouch. Don't reach for the money pouch once you're in public. Use common sense as your guide.

General Information and Warnings U.K. Foreign & Commonwealth Office. ⊕ www. gov.uk/government/organisations/foreign-commonwealth-office. **U.S. Department of State Travel Information.** ⊕ www.travel.state.gov.

▌SHOPPING

Tartans, tweeds, and woolens may be a Scottish cliché, but nevertheless the selection and quality of these goods make them a must-have for many visitors, whether a made-to-measure traditional kilt outfit or a designer sweater from Skye. Particular bargains can be found in Scottish cashmere sweaters; look for Johnstons of Elgin. Glasgow is great for designer wear, although prices may seem high.

Food items are another popular purchase: whether shortbread, smoked salmon, boiled sweets, *tablet* (a type of hard fudge), marmalade and raspberry jams, Dundee cake, or black bun, it's far too easy to eat your way around Scotland.

Unique jewelry is available all over Scotland, but especially in some of the remote regions where get-away-from-it-all craftspeople have set up shop amid the idyllic scenery.

Scottish antique pottery and table silver make unusual, if sometimes pricey, souvenirs: a Wemyss-ware pig for the mantelpiece, perhaps, or Edinburgh silver candelabra for the dining table. Antique pebble jewelry is a unique style of jewelry popular in Scotland; several specialized antique jewelry shops can be found in Edinburgh and Glasgow. Antiques shops and one- or two-day antiques fairs held in hotels abound all over Scotland. In general, goods are reasonably priced. Most dealers will drop the price a little if asked "What's your best price?"

▌ SIGHTSEEING PASSES

Discounted sightseeing passes are a great way to save money on visits to castles, gardens, and historic houses. Just check what the pass offers against your itinerary to be sure it's worthwhile.

The Scottish Explorer Ticket, available from any staffed Historic Scotland (HS) property and from many tourist information centers, allows visits to HS properties for 3 days in a 5-day period (£30) or 7 days in a 14-day period (£40). The Discover Scotland pass is available for 3 days (£27), 7 days (£32), or 14 days (£37) and allows access to all National Trust for Scotland properties. It's available to overseas visitors only and can be purchased online and by phone, or at properties and some of the main tourist information centers.

Discount Passes Historic Scotland.
☎ *0131/668–8081* ⊕ *www.historic-scotland. gov.uk/explorer.* **National Trust for Scotland.**
☎ *0131/458–0303* ⊕ *www.nts.org.uk.*

▌ TAXES

An airport departure tax of £73 (£13 for within U.K. and EU countries) per person is included in the price of your ticket.

The British sales tax, V.A.T. (Value-Added Tax), is 20%. It's almost always included in quoted prices in shops, hotels, and restaurants. The most common exception is at high-end hotels, where prices often

exclude V.A.T. Further details on how to get a V.A.T. refund and a list of stores offering tax-free shopping are available from VisitBritain.

When making a purchase, ask for a V.A.T.-refund form and find out whether the merchant gives refunds—not all stores do, nor are they required to. Have the form stamped by customs officials when you leave the country or, if you're visiting several European Union countries, when you leave the EU. After you're through passport control, take the form to a refund-service counter for an on-the-spot refund or mail it to the address on the form after you arrive home.

▌ TIME

Great Britain sets its clocks by Greenwich Mean Time, five hours ahead of the U.S. East Coast. British summer time (GMT plus one hour) requires an additional adjustment from about the end of March to the end of October. Timeanddate.com can help you figure out the correct time anywhere.

Time Zones Timeanddate.com. ⊕ *www. timeanddate.com/worldclock.*

▌ TIPPING

Tipping is done in Scotland as in the United States, but at a lower level. Some restaurants include a service charge on the bill; if not, add about 10% to 15%. Taxi drivers, hairdressers, and barbers should also get 10% to 15%.

Bartender	£1–£5 depending on the size of the round (in the more modern bars). It's common in traditional pubs to buy the bartender a drink as a tip
Bellhop	£1–£3 per bag
Hotel Concierge	£10 or more, if he or she performs a service for you
Hotel Doorman	£2–£5 if he helps you get a cab
Hotel Maid	£2–£3 a day (either daily or at the end of your stay, in cash)
Hotel Room-Service Waiter	£1–£2 per delivery, even if a service charge has been added
Porter at Airport or Train Station	£1 per bag
Skycap at Airport	£1–£2 per bag checked
Taxi Driver	10%–15%, but round up the fare to the next pound amount
Tour Guide	10% of the cost of the tour, but optional
Valet Parking Attendant	£2–£3, but only when you get your car
Waiter	10%–15%, with 15% being the norm at high-end restaurants; nothing additional if a service charge is added to the bill
Other	Restroom attendants in more expensive restaurants expect some small change or £1. Tip coat-check personnel at least £1–£2 per item checked unless there's a fee.

▌ TOURS

GENERAL-INTEREST TOURS

Many companies offer fully guided tours in Scotland, from basic to luxury. Most of these are full packages including hotels, all food, and transportation costs in one flat fee. Because each tour company has different specialties, do a bit of research—either on your own or through a travel agent—before booking. You'll want to know about the hotels you'll be staying in, how big your group is likely to be, precisely how your days will be structured, and who the other people are likely to be.

CIE Tours. They offer all-inclusive tours of Scotland with various themes from distillery tours, to cruises to Home of Golf and St. Andrews packages. ☎ *0800/680–0611* ⊕ *www.cietours.com* ✉ *From £550 for a 5-day Taste of Scotland tour.*

Globus. Covering Scotland and Great Britain, Globus offers many packages including a 7-day Bonnie Scotland tour from Glasgow to Edinburgh, and a 14-day one that also delves into the Highlands and Islands. ☎ *866/755–8581* ⊕ *www.globusjourneys. com* ✉ *From $1828 excluding airfare for 7-day Bonnie Scotland.*

Heart of Scotland Tours. Offered here are small-group (16 maximum) minibus tours that aim to take you off the beaten track. ☎ *0131/228–2888* ⊕ *www. heartofscotlandtours.co.uk* ✉ *From £45 for a Best of Scotland in a Day excursion.*

Rabbie's Trail Burners. These minibus guided tours include handy day trips for small groups (16 maximum) and depart from Edinburgh and Glasgow. The company has won numerous awards including the Scottish Thistle award for sustainable tourism. ☎ *0131/226–3133* ⊕ *www. rabbies.com* ✉ *From £31 for day trips (Rosslyn Chapel & Scots Borders); 2-day Loch Ness & Inverness trip starts at £71.*

SPECIAL-INTEREST TOURS

You can find tours for many special interests from whisky and vegetarian-friendly to cultural, historic, and wildlife-themed packages.

Celtic Dream Tours. This outfit specializes in extended Celtic-inspired luxury excursions and custom tours, as well as vegetarian-/vegan-friendly and Burns literary adventures. ☎ *813/317–6039* ⊕ *www. celticdreamtours.com* ✉ *From $4295* *(double occupancy) for the Hebridean Journey and Burns & Beyond.*

The Wayfarers. Enjoy walking tours through the countryside and scenic towns, exploring natural and historic sights. ☎ *800/249–4620* ⊕ *www.thewayfarers. com* ✉ *From $4295 per person (double occupancy) for Edinburgh & Central Highlands 6-night tour.*

GOLF TOURS

Scotland has fabulous golf courses; a tour can help enthusiasts make the most of their time. VisitScotland has a dedicated golf website with a list of tour companies.

Golf Scotland. This company has provided luxury golf tours, including tournament specials and the Gleneagles Experience tour, since 1988. ☎ *866/875–4653* ⊕ *www.golfscotland.com* ✉ *From $1350 per person for the Gleneagles Experience.*

Scotland for Golf. Established by St. Andrews pros in 1999, this is the company to consider for those seeking to tour Fife's finest fairways, including the Old Course. ☎ *01334/611466* ⊕ *www. scotlandforgolf.co.uk* ✉ *From $500 per person for His & Her 1-night break playing on the Old Course.*

Thistle Golf. Tailored tours taking in a selection of Scotland's Championship courses are offered here, including an eight-day package that takes in Royal Dornoch, Carnoustie, the Old Course, Royal Troon, plus historic sights on the way. ☎ *0141/942–4043* ⊕ *www. thistlegolf.co.uk.*

PRIVATE GUIDES

Scottish Tourist Guides Association. The association has members throughout Scotland who are fully qualified professional guides able to conduct walking tours in the major cities, half- or full-day tours or extended tours throughout Scotland, driving tours, and special study tours. Fees are negotiable. ☎ *01786/447784* ⊕ *www.stga.co.uk.*

▌ TRIP INSURANCE

Comprehensive trip insurance is valuable if you're booking a very expensive or complicated trip (particularly to an isolated region) or if you're booking far in advance. Comprehensive policies typically cover trip-cancellation and interruption, letting you cancel or cut your trip short because of illness, or, in some cases, acts of terrorism in your destination. Such policies might also cover evacuation and medical care. (For trips abroad you should have at least medical-only coverage. *See Medical Insurance and Assistance under Health.*) Some also cover trip delays because of bad weather or mechanical problems and lost or delayed luggage.

Another type of coverage to consider is financial default—that is, when your trip is disrupted because a tour operator, airline, or cruise line goes out of business. Generally you must buy this when you book your trip or shortly thereafter, and it's available to you only if your operator isn't on a list of excluded companies.

Always read the fine print of your policy to make sure that you're covered for the risks that most concern you. Compare several policies to be sure you're getting the best price and range of coverage available.

Comprehensive Insurers
Allianz. ☎ *866/884–3556* ⊕ *www. allianztravelinsurance.com.* **CSA Travel Protection.** ☎ *800/711–1197* ⊕ *www. csatravelprotection.com.* **Travel Guard.** ☎ *800/826–4919* ⊕ *www.travelguard.com.* **Travel Insured International.** ☎ *800/243–3174* ⊕ *www.travelinsured.com.* **Travelex Insurance.** ☎ *888/228–9792* ⊕ *www. travelexinsurance.com.*

Insurance Comparison Information
InsureMyTrip.com. ☎ *800/487–4722* ⊕ *www. insuremytrip.com.* **Squaremouth.com.** ☎ *800/240–0369* ⊕ *www.squaremouth.com.*

▮ VISITOR INFORMATION

See the Orientation and Planning section at the start of each chapter for regional tourist information offices; look for Essentials sections in towns for local offices.

Contacts in Britain VisitScotland. ✉ *Princes Mall, 3 Princes St., Edinburgh* ☎ *8452/255121* ⊕ *www.visitscotland.com.*

ONLINE RESOURCES

VisitScotland is Scotland's official website and includes a number of special-interest sites on topics from golf to genealogy. VisitBritain, Great Britain's official site, has ample information on Scotland's sights, accommodations, and more.

Historic Scotland (which is being renamed Historic Environment Scotland) cares for the more than 300 historic properties described on its site. The National Trust for Scotland has information about stately homes, gardens, and castles. Both offer sightseeing passes *(see Sightseeing Passes above).*

All About Scotland VisitBritain. ⊕ *www. visitbritain.com.*

Historic Sites Historic Scotland. ⊕ *www. historic-scotland.gov.uk.* **National Trust for Scotland.** ⊕ *www.nts.org.uk.*

INDEX

PHOTO CREDITS

Front cover: Jam World Images / Alamy [Description: Floors Castle, Kelso, Scotland, United Kingdom]. 1, Elxeneize I Dreamstime.com. 2, Chris Morrison I Dreamstime.com. 4, Bill McKelvie/Shutterstock. 5 (top), David Lyons / age fotostock. 5 (bottom), Tomas Rebro/Shutterstock. 6 (top left), John A Cameron/Shutterstock. 6 (top right), Jaime Pharr/Shutterstock. 6 (bottom left), kawhia/Shutterstock. 6 (bottom right), Brendan Howard/Shutterstock. 7 (top), Findlay Rankin / age fotostock. 7 (bottom), Heartland/Shutterstock. 8 (top left), Monkey Business Images/Shutterstock. 8 (top right), Heartland/Shutterstock. 8 (bottom left), Serjio74/Shutterstock. 8 (bottom right), Mitch Gunn/Shutterstock. Chapter 1: Experience Scotland: 13, vichie81/Shutterstock. 22, Doug Houghton/viestiphoto.com. 23, Richard Wareham Fotografie/Alamy. Chapter 2: Edinburgh and the Lothians: 37, Shaiith/Shutterstock. Chapter 3: Glasgow: 115, Grant Glendinning/Shutterstock. Chapter 4: The Borders and the Southwest: 185, Jule_Berlin/Shutterstock. Chapter 5: Fife and Angus: 227, Grant Glendinning/Shutterstock. Chapter 6: The Central Highlands: 261, Tim Stirling/Shutterstock. Chapter 7: Aberdeen and the Northeast: 299, Trgowanlock I Dreamstime.com. Chapter 8: Argyll and the Isles: 347, Valeria Cantone I Dreamstime.com. Chapter 9: Around the Great Glen: 383, Lance Bellers/Shutterstock. Chapter 10: The Northern Highlands and the Western Isles: 419, stocker1970/Shutterstock. Chapter 11: Orkney and Shetland Islands: 461, Ivonne Wierink/Shutterstock. Back cover, from left to right: Björn Kindler/iStockphoto; Merlindo / Shutterstock; Iain Sarjeant/iStockphoto. Spine: Bacek I Dreamstime.com. About Our Writers: All photos are courtesy of the writers.

Fodor's SCOTLAND

Publisher: Amanda D'Acierno, *Senior Vice President*

Editorial: Arabella Bowen, *Editor in Chief*; Linda Cabasin, *Editorial Director*

Design: Tina Malaney, *Associate Art Director*; Chie Ushio, *Senior Designer*; Erica Cuoco, *Production Designer*

Photography: Jennifer Arnow, *Senior Photo Editor*; Mary Robnett, *Photo Researcher*

Production: Linda Schmidt, *Managing Editor*; Evangelos Vasilakis, *Associate Managing Editor*; Angela L. McLean, *Senior Production Manager*

Maps: Rebecca Baer, *Senior Map Editor*; Mark Stroud (Moon Street Cartography), *Cartographer*

Sales: Jacqueline Lebow, *Sales Director*

Marketing & Publicity: Heather Dalton, *Marketing Director*; Katherine Punia, *Publicity Director*

Business & Operations: Susan Livingston, *Vice President, Strategic Business Planning*; Sue Daulton, *Vice President, Operations*

Fodors.com: Megan Bell, *Executive Director, Revenue & Business Development*; Yasmin Marinaro, *Senior Director, Marketing & Partnerships*

Copyright © 2016 by Fodor's Travel, a division of Penguin Random House LLC

Writers: Nick Bruno, Mike Gonzalez, Jack Jewers, Shona Main

Editors: Linda Cabasin (lead project editor), Bethany Beckerlegge, Denise M. Leto

Production Editor: Evangelos Vasilakis

25th Edition

ISBN 978-1-101-87964-1

ISSN 0743-0973

All details in this book are based on information supplied to us at press time. Always confirm information when it matters, especially if you're making a detour to visit a specific place. Fodor's expressly disclaims any liability, loss, or risk, personal or otherwise, that is incurred as a consequence of the use of any of the contents of this book.

SPECIAL SALES

This book is available at special discounts for bulk purchases for sales promotions or premiums. For more information, e-mail specialmarkets@penguinrandomhouse.com.

PRINTED IN THE UNITED STATES OF AMERICA

10 9 8 7 6 5 4 3 2 1

ABOUT OUR WRITERS

Based in Dundee, **Nick Bruno** peddled breathable base layers, led jinxed coach tours across Europe, and translated Italian legalese before taking up travel writing and journalism. He has written for Fodor's for a decade and has authored a half-dozen books about Italy. In recent years, feature writing, photography, sound recording, and work for the BBC have helped Nick avoid a return to a proper job. For this edition, he updated Experience Scotland and Travel Smart Scotland.

Mike Gonzalez is emeritus professor of Latin American Studies at Glasgow University and also writes regularly for the *Herald* and other publications on politics and culture. Mike's assignment for Fodor's was the Glasgow, Borders and the Southwest, Central Highlands, Argyll and the Isles, and the Northern Highlands and the Western Isles chapters. His travels took him to places familiar and less familiar, and included exploring a tiny island on Islay whose houses were once an imperial center and walking in a hidden sculpture park in the hills near Dumfries.

A regular contributor to Fodor's guides, **Jack Jewers** revised the Edinburgh chapter as well as Inverness and Around the Great Glen. An ancestor of his, Thomas Urquhart (1611–60), was a notoriously eccentric Scottish writer. History records that he died laughing after hearing that King Charles II had been restored to the throne.

Shona Main grew up in Shetland; after moving to the mainland, she spent some informative years working on magazines for teenagers. She had a brief career in law and politics before she returned to writing. Now living in Dundee, Shona is working on her first novel, which is inspired by the island she grew up on, and has also moved into filmmaking. Her debut documentary, *Clavel*, follows a Shetland crofter through the seasons. She updated Fife and Angus, Aberdeen and the Northeast, and Orkney and Shetland for this edition.